Advances in Economics and Econometrics

Volume 1

Every 5 years, the World Congress of the Econometric Society brings together scholars from around the world. Leading scholars present state-of-the-art overviews of their areas of research, offering newcomers access to key research in economics. *Advances in Economics and Econometrics: Twelfth World Congress* consists of papers and commentaries presented at the Twelfth World Congress of the Econometric Society. This two-volume set includes surveys and interpretations of key developments in economics and econometrics, and discussions of future directions for a variety of topics, covering both theory and application. The first volume addresses such topics as contract theory, industrial organization, health and human capital, as well as racial justice, while the second volume includes theoretical and applied papers on climate change, time-series econometrics, and causal inference. These papers are invaluable for experienced economists seeking to broaden their knowledge or young economists new to the field.

Victor Chernozhukov is the International Ford Professor in the Department of Economics at MIT and the Center for Statistics and Data Science at MIT. He is a Fellow of the Econometric Society and a recipient of the Alfred P. Sloan Research Fellowship, the Arnold Zellner Award, the Bessel Award, and the G. A. Gamov Award. He was elected to the American Academy of Arts and Sciences in April 2016. In 2019 he was elected a Fellow of the Institute of Mathematical Statistics with the citation "for pathbreaking contributions to high-dimensional inference."

Johannes Hörner is the Alfred Cowles Professor of Economics at Yale University and directeur de recherche at CNRS and the Toulouse School of Economics. He is a Fellow of the Econometric Society and served as Co-Editor of *Theoretical Economics* and *Economic Theory* and Editor of *American Economic Journal: Microeconomics*. His research is in economic theory, with emphasis on game theory.

Eliana La Ferrara is a Professor of Public Policy at Harvard Kennedy School. She is the 2023 President of the Econometric Society and Foreign Honorary

Member of the American Economic Association and of the American Academy of Arts and Sciences. Her research is in Development and Political Economics, particularly on the role of social factors in economic development.

Iván Werning is the Robert M. Solow Professor of Economics at the Massachusetts Institute of Technology, where he has been since earning his PhD from the University of Chicago in 2002. He is an Argentine economist with research interests in macroeconomics, international economics, and public finance. He is a member of the American Academy of Arts and Sciences, a Fellow of the Econometric Society, and a Research Fellow at the National Bureau of Economic Research.

In Memoriam: Emmanuel Fahri. Shortly before the Congress took place, Emmanuel Fahri, one of the scientific organizers of the Congress, and one of the anticipated editors of these volumes, tragically passed away. Iván Werning kindly agreed to take over the important duties that Emmanuel was already fulfilling in this regard. We were privileged to interact with him, and all immensely miss him.

Econometric Society Monograph Series

Editors

Serena Ng, Columbia University
Alessandro Pavan, Northwestern University

The Econometric Society is an international society for the advancement of economic theory in relation to statistics and mathematics. The Econometric Society Monograph Series is designed to promote the publication of original research contributions of high quality in mathematical economics and theoretical and applied econometrics.

Books in the Series

V. Chernozhukov, J. Hörner, E. La Ferrara, & I. Werning, *Advances in Economics and Econometrics: Twelfth World Congress, Vols. I & II*, 2025
T. Strzalecki, *Stochastic Choice Theory*, 2024
C. Hsiao, *Analysis of Panel Data: 4th ed.*, 2022
D. M. Kreps, *The Black–Scholes–Merton Model as an Idealization of Discrete-Time Economies*, 2019
W. Thomson, *How to Divide When There Isn't Enough: From Aristotle, the Talmud, and Maimonides to the Axiomatics of Resource Allocation*, 2019
O. Compte & A. Postlewaite, *Ignorance and Uncertainty*, 2018
I. Molchanov & F. Molinari, *Random Sets in Econometrics*, 2018
B. Honoré, A. Pakes, M. Piazzesi, & L. Samuelson (eds.), *Advances in Economics and Econometrics: Eleventh World Congress, Vols. I & II*, 2017
S. Maurer, *On the Shoulders of Giants: Colleagues Remember Suzanne Scotchmer's Contributions to Economics*, 2017
C. P. Chambers & F. Echenique, *Revealed Preference Theory*, 2016
J.-F. Mertens, S. Sorins, & S. Samir, *Repeated Games*, 2015
C. Hsiao, *Analysis of Panel Data: 3rd ed.*, 2014
C. Cameron & P. Trivedi, *Regression Analysis of Count Data: 2nd ed.*, 2013
A. Harvey, *Dynamic Models for Volatility and Heavy Tails, with Applications to Financial and Economic Time Series*, 2013
D. Acemoglu, M. Arellano, & E. Dekel (eds.), *Advances in Economics and Econometrics: Theory and Applications, Tenth World Congress, Vols. I, II, & III*, 2013
M. Fleurbaey & F. Maniquet, *A Theory of Fairness and Social Justice*, 2011
R. Vohra, *Mechanism Design: A Linear Programming Approach*, 2011
K. Samphantharak & R. Townsend, *Households as Corporate Firms: An Analysis of Household Finance Using Integrated Household Surveys and Corporate Financial Accounting*, 2009
I. Gilboa, *Theory of Decision under Uncertainty*, 2009
F. Vega-Redondo, *Complex Networks*, 2007

Continued on page following the index

Advances in Economics and Econometrics

Twelfth World Congress

Volume 1

Edited by

Victor Chernozhukov
Massachusetts Institute of Technology

Johannes Hörner
Yale University, Connecticut and Toulouse School of Economics

Eliana La Ferrara
Harvard University, Massachusetts

Iván Werning
Massachusetts Institute of Technology

CAMBRIDGE
UNIVERSITY PRESS

CAMBRIDGE
UNIVERSITY PRESS

Shaftesbury Road, Cambridge CB2 8EA, United Kingdom

One Liberty Plaza, 20th Floor, New York, NY 10006, USA

477 Williamstown Road, Port Melbourne, VIC 3207, Australia

314–321, 3rd Floor, Plot 3, Splendor Forum, Jasola District Centre, New Delhi – 110025, India

103 Penang Road, #05–06/07, Visioncrest Commercial, Singapore 238467

Cambridge University Press is part of Cambridge University Press & Assessment, a department of the University of Cambridge.

We share the University's mission to contribute to society through the pursuit of education, learning and research at the highest international levels of excellence.

www.cambridge.org
Information on this title: www.cambridge.org/9781009531320

DOI: 10.1017/9781009589888

When citing this work, please include a reference to the DOI 10.1017/9781009589888

First published 2025

A catalogue record for this publication is available from the British Library.

A Cataloging-in-Publication data record for this book is available from the Library of Congress

ISBN 978-1-009-53129-0 Set of 2 hardback volumes
ISBN 978-1-009-53132-0 Volume 1 Hardback
ISBN 978-1-009-53141-2 Volume 2 Hardback

Contents

Contributors

Arun Advani, *University of Warwick*
Elliott Ash, *ETH Zurich*
Andrea Attar, *Toulouse School of Economics, CNRS, University of Toulouse Capitole, and Università degli Studi di Roma "Tor Vergata"*
David Cai, *London School of Economics*
Kerwin Charles, *Yale University*
Lisa Cook, *Michigan State University*
Janet Currie, *Princeton University*
Matthew O. Jackson, *Stanford University*
Philippe Jehiel, *Paris School of Economics and University College London*
Marlène Koffi, *University of Toronto*
Eliana La Ferrara, *Harvard Kennedy School*
Simon Loertscher, *University of Melbourne*
Thomas Mariotti, *Toulouse School of Economics, CNRS, University of Toulouse Capitole*
Leslie M. Marx, *Duke University*
Volker Nocke, *University of Mannheim, University of Surrey and CEPR*
Nicholas W. Papageorge, *Johns Hopkins University*
Imran Rasul, *University College London*
François Salanié, *Toulouse School of Economics, INRAE, University of Toulouse Capitole*
Juuso Välimäki, *Aalto University Helsinki*
Leonard Wantchekon, *Princeton University*
Alexander Wolitzky, *Massachusetts Institute of Technology*

Contributors

PART I

CONTESTS AND CONTRACTS

CHAPTER 1

Competitive Nonlinear Pricing under Adverse Selection

Andrea Attar, Thomas Mariotti, and François Salanié

This chapter surveys recent attempts at characterizing competitive allocations under adverse selection when each informed agent can privately trade with several uninformed parties: that is, trade is nonexclusive. We first show that requiring market outcomes to be robust to entry selects a unique candidate allocation, which involves cross-subsidies. We then study how to implement this allocation as the equilibrium outcome of a game in which the uninformed parties, acting as principals, compete by making offers to the informed agents. We show that equilibria typically fail to exist in competitive-screening games, in which these offers are simultaneous. We finally explore alternative extensive forms, and show that the candidate allocation can be implemented through a discriminatory ascending auction. These results yield sharp predictions for competitive nonexclusive markets.

1.1 INTRODUCTION

On the vast majority of markets, nonexclusivity is the rule: agents can privately trade with different parties, without having to inform each of them of these multiple relationships. Fortunately, detailed knowledge of individual trades is generally useless for the involved parties. Nor is it usually needed, moreover, to predict market outcomes: instead, by solely relying on the aggregate equality of supply and demand, general-equilibrium theory elegantly sidesteps the lack of such information to focus on the determination of equilibrium prices. These prices in turn convey all the information agents need to know in order to formulate their supplies and demands.

However, there are important cases in which information about the characteristics of the goods for trade is not symmetrically distributed, though it matters directly to the parties involved. The chief example is that of goods whose quality is privately known to a party but unknown to their trading partners, including, for instance, the sale of shares by firms with different returns,

This chapter was presented as a paper at the semi-plenary session "Contests and Contracts" of the 2020 World Congress of the Econometric Society (Università Bocconi, Milano, Italy). This research has benefited from financial support of the ANR (Programme d'Investissement d'Avenir ANR-17-EURE-0010), the MIUR (PRIN 2015), and the research foundation TSE-Partnership.

the supply of labor services by workers with different productivities, or the design of insurance contracts for consumers with different riskiness.

Such common-value situations raise important difficulties for the performance of markets. They also question the relevance of general-equilibrium theory, because, for instance, a buyer may now try to infer the missing information from the seller's behavior and not only from prices. This gives rise to new phenomena such as adverse selection, reflecting that agents who are more eager to trade are often endowed with goods of lower quality; moreover, these inferences are made even more difficult when trade is nonexclusive. Game-theoretical tools then become useful to precisely describe who trades with whom and how the distribution of information impacts behaviors and outcomes.

This chapter surveys recent developments in the theory of competitive markets under adverse selection and nonexclusivity. We are particularly interested in how price competition and the threat of entry lead to sharp predictions for equilibrium outcomes, in spite of the complexities associated with nonexclusive trading. We will show how different approaches often lead to the same prediction, though we also emphasize difficulties for the existence of an equilibrium, depending on the game studied and the solution concept adopted. These results may be of interest for many financial and insurance markets, including over-the-counter, life-insurance, and annuity markets; for labor markets, such as the markets for professionals or freelance workers; and, more generally, for many markets in goods or services, whose quality is the private information of agents on one side of the market.

Because this combination of adverse selection and nonexclusivity is the hallmark of the literature reviewed in this chapter, it may be helpful to briefly recall how these two topics have been addressed in now classical works.

On the one hand, adverse selection has so far typically been studied under exclusive competition. This is by design in Akerlof's (1970) example of a market for an indivisible good. Subsequent works focusing on markets for perfectly divisible goods assume that exclusive contracts are enforceable. In Rothschild and Stiglitz (1976), this allows insurance companies to screen their customers by making low-risk consumers self-select into contracts with higher deductibles. In Leland and Pyle (1977), this allows an entrepreneur to signal the profitability of her project by retaining a greater or lesser equity share. In both cases, the observability of agents' aggregate trades is required to support equilibrium outcomes. Extensions by Prescott and Townsend (1984), Kehoe et al. (2002), Bisin and Gottardi (2006), and Rustichini and Siconolfi (2008) of the standard existence and welfare theorems of general-equilibrium theory to private-information economies similarly restrict feasible allocations to those satisfying incentive compatibility of individual trades on each market, which again requires strong observability assumptions.

On the other hand, nonexclusive competition has so far been mostly studied in private-value environments. As noted above, in such cases, the functioning of Walrasian markets is unaffected by private information. The side-trading literature, from the early works of Hammond (1979, 1987), Allen (1985), and Jacklin (1987) to the more recent contributions of Cole and Kocherlakota (2001), Golosov and Tsyvinski (2007), and Farhi et al. (2009), has accordingly investigated the limits that side trading on Walrasian markets, outside of the central planner's control, imposes on the set of allocations that can be achieved in standard Mirrlees (1971) or Diamond and Dybvig (1983) economies, which feature private information but not adverse selection.

By contrast, in common-value environments, assuming a priori that a Walrasian market exists and perfectly balances supply and demand is too much to ask for; in fact, we shall see in Section 1.2.2 that sellers on such a market, anticipating adverse selection, would like to reduce their competitive supply and thus choose to ration demand. In addition, nonexclusivity means that trades cannot be monitored, so that even a centralized market authority would not be able to ensure that all agents trade at the same price. Instead, the recent literature on nonexclusive markets under adverse selection assumes that contracting is bilateral, and allows for general contracts.

We now present the main findings of this literature. In line with Riley (2001), we adopt in this chapter a strategic approach to the determination of market outcomes; in contrast with him, however, we exclusively focus on screening models.[1] A market is, therefore, described by a set of uninformed sellers competing through menus of contracts, or nonlinear tariffs, to serve the demand emanating from privately informed buyers. Nonexclusivity is captured by the assumption that, while each seller can monitor the trades each buyer conducts with him – which is what makes nonlinear pricing possible – he can monitor none of the trades this buyer makes with his competitors.

A useful entry point into the literature is to first abstract from the determination of individual tariffs and, in a reduced-form way, to directly impose properties on the market tariff that is obtained from them by aggregation. In line with Rothschild and Stiglitz (1976), who characterize the set of exclusive contracts preventing an entrant from making a profit, a desirable property of the market tariff is that it be entry-proof. Under nonexclusivity, this property means that no entrant can make a profit by offering a menu of contracts, given that each buyer is free to combine a contract offered by the entrant with a trade along the market tariff. Restricting attention to entry-proof market tariffs allows us to identify robust predictions for nonexclusive markets under adverse selection, which do not depend on the details of a specific extensive-form game. Section 1.3 of this chapter is devoted to the characterization of such tariffs.

The following insights emerge from the analysis (AMS, 2020, 2021).[2] First, neither the Rothschild and Stiglitz (1976) allocation, nor any of the second-best allocations characterized by Prescott and Townsend (1984) and Crocker

[1] Extending the theory of signaling or, more generally, the informed-principal paradigm of Myerson (1983) to nonexclusive markets is a fascinating task for future research.

[2] To avoid repetitions, AMS hereafter stands for Attar, Mariotti, and Salanié.

and Snow (1985), can be implemented by an entry-proof market tariff. Second, entry-proofness, along with budget-feasibility, singles out a unique market tariff, which generally turns out to be nonlinear. The defining features of this tariff are that each marginal quantity is priced at the expected cost of serving the buyer types who optimally choose to trade it, and that gains from trade are exhausted subject to this constraint. For instance, in the two-type case, the low-cost type purchases her demand at a price equal to the expected cost, while the high-cost type in addition trades the quantity she prefers at a price that equals her own cost. The corresponding allocation, first described by Jaynes (1978), Hellwig (1988), and Glosten (1994) – and henceforth referred to as the JHG allocation – can thus be interpreted as a marginal version of the Akerlof (1970) competitive-equilibrium allocation, and stands out as a focal prediction for nonexclusive competitive markets under adverse selection. The entry-proofness criterion can also be seen as an external constraint imposed on the decisions of a central planner. AMS (2020) emphasize that this constraint is so strong as to limit the planner's feasible policies to a unique policy, which is not second best. The social costs of side trading thus appear to be particularly severe under common values.

In line with the program outlined by Wilson (1989), a natural question is whether the JHG allocation can be implemented as an – ideally, unique – equilibrium outcome of a decentralized trading protocol. The contributions reviewed in Section 1.4 focus on competitive-screening games in which offers are simultaneously made by the uninformed sellers; they thus bring to bear insights and methods from the common-agency literature, in which several uninformed principals compete by posting menus of contracts to deal with a privately informed agent. While, as surveyed by Martimort (2006), common-agency games have mainly been used to tackle issues in industrial organization, public economics, and the theory of organizations – from vertical contracting and the internal structure of the firm to lobbying and the relationships between governments and regulatory agencies – they have also provided, following the seminal contribution of Biais et al. (2000), a powerful tool for modeling competition under common values.

The results of this approach, however, are mixed. The only case in which the JHG allocation can be robustly implemented through a competitive-screening game is when the buyer's preferences are linear, subject to a capacity constraint. The JHG allocation then coincides with the Akerlof (1970) competitive-equilibrium allocation that maximizes the gains from trade, and it is the unique candidate-equilibrium allocation; moreover, there always exists an equilibrium in which sellers post linear tariffs (AMS, 2011). These positive results thus extend the conclusions of Akerlof (1970) to the case of a divisible good. However, when the buyer has strictly convex preferences, the results crucially depend on fine modeling details such as the cardinality of the set of types. When the distribution of types is continuous, Biais et al. (2000) construct an equilibrium in which sellers post strictly convex tariffs, and such that the resulting aggregate equilibrium allocation converges to the JHG allocation as the number of sellers grows large; however, as we show in Section 1.4.4, their existence result requires that some types be excluded from trade. When the distribution of types is discrete, exclusion is even more extreme, as an equilibrium exists only in the degenerate case where all types (except possibly the highest-cost one) do not trade in the JHG allocation (AMS, 2014, 2019).

Section 1.5 provides more positive results, by exploring alternative extensive forms whereby uninformed sellers sequentially receive information about previously signed contracts or previously made offers. The bottom line is that transparency makes it easier for sellers to directly punish deviators, in contrast with competitive-screening games in which the burden of punishments falls entirely on the buyer. In this spirit, Beaudry and Poitevin (1995) and AMS (2021) implement the JHG allocation in a repeated game of signaling and in an ascending discriminatory auction with frequent offers, respectively. We also survey contributions by Jaynes (1978, 2011), Hellwig (1988), and Kosenko et al. (2023) that allow for endogenous information disclosure.

Section 1.6 concludes on the empirical perspectives, in particular about tests for the presence of private information.

1.2 THE ECONOMY

We study a simple economy in which a single buyer (she) trades a divisible good with multiple, identical sellers (he). The buyer is endowed with private information about, for instance, the quality of the traded good. As usual, the buyer/sellers convention can be inverted thanks to a change of variables, so as to encompass a broad variety of situations:

- Insurance companies sell coverage to a consumer: Rothschild and Stiglitz (1976), Prescott and Townsend (1984), Crocker and Snow (1985), Hendren (2013).
- Market-makers provide liquidity to an insider: Glosten (1989, 1994), Biais et al. (2000), Back and Baruch (2013).
- Investors purchase securities issued by a firm: Leland and Pyle (1977), Myers and Majluf (1984), DeMarzo and Duffie (1999), Biais and Mariotti (2005).
- Firms hire the services of a worker: Spence (1973), Miyazaki (1977).

In these situations, the private information of the buyer is directly relevant to the sellers, because it determines their production costs or their opportunity costs of selling. It is this common-value component that may generate adverse selection, as we now discuss in more formal terms.

1.2.1 The Model

Unless stated otherwise, the following assumptions are maintained throughout this chapter.

The Buyer. The buyer's private information is represented by a type $i = 1,\ldots,I$ that takes a finite number of values with strictly positive probabilities m_i. Type i's preferences are represented by a utility function $u_i(Q,T)$ that is continuous and weakly quasiconcave in (Q,T) and strictly decreasing in T, with the interpretation that Q is the nonnegative quantity of the good she purchases and T is the payment she makes in return. To define marginal rates of substitution without assuming differentiability, we let $\tau_i(Q,T)$ be the supremum of the set of prices p such that

$$u_i(Q,T) < \max\{u_i(Q+q,T+pq) : q \geq 0\}.$$

Thus, $\tau_i(Q,T)$ is the slope of type i's indifference curve at the right of (Q,T). Quasiconcavity ensures that $\tau_i(Q,T)$ is finite, except possibly at $Q = 0$, and that it is nonincreasing along any indifference curve of type i. For all i and $p > 0$, we also define the demand $D_i(p)$ of type i as the set of quantities Q that maximize $u_i(Q,pQ)$. These demands are well-defined under the following Inada condition:

$$\text{For all } i,\ (Q,T), \text{ and } p>0,\ \arg\max\{u_i(Q+q,T+pq) : q \geq 0\} < \infty, \tag{1.1}$$

or if the domain of admissible quantities is compact. Types are ordered according to the weak single-crossing condition (Milgrom and Shannon, 1994), which states that higher types are at least as willing to increase their purchases as lower types are:

$$\text{For all } i < j, Q < Q', T, \text{ and } T',$$
$$u_i(Q,T) \leq (<)\, u_i(Q',T') \text{ implies } u_j(Q,T) \leq (<)\, u_j(Q',T').$$

Weak single crossing implies that $\tau_i(Q,T)$ and $D_i(p)$ are weakly increasing in i. For future reference, we also state the slightly stronger, strict single-crossing condition:

$$\text{For all } i < j, Q < Q', T, \text{ and } T',$$
$$u_i(Q,T) \leq u_i(Q',T') \text{ implies } u_j(Q,T) < u_j(Q',T').$$

We shall occasionally make additional assumptions. Theorems 1.1 and 1.3, for instance, require that higher endowments of the good reduce the buyer's marginal rate of substitution:

Assumption 1.1 *For all i and T, $\tau_i(Q,T)$ is nonincreasing in Q.*

Our assumptions on the buyer's preferences hold, for instance, in a Rothschild and Stiglitz (1976) insurance economy in which the loss L is the same for all types: then i indexes the buyer's riskiness, Q is the amount of coverage she purchases, and T is the premium she pays in return. AMS (2021, online appendix C) show that these assumptions also hold in more general insurance economies, allowing for multiple loss levels or various forms of nonexpected utility. But our framework is relevant beyond insurance; in particular, first-best quantities may differ across types.

The Sellers. On the supply side, sellers are identical, risk-neutral, and use the same linear technology. We denote by $c_i > 0$ the unit cost of serving type i, and by $\overline{c}_i$ the corresponding upper-tail conditional expectation of unit costs:

$$\overline{c}_i \equiv \mathbf{E}\left[c_j \,|\, j \geq i\right] = \frac{\sum_{j \geq i} m_j c_j}{\sum_{j \geq i} m_j}.$$

Adverse selection occurs if the unit cost c_i is nondecreasing in i. This case is the least conducive to trade, as types who are more willing to trade are also more costly to serve. In this chapter, we only rely on a slightly weaker assumption, namely, that $\overline{c}_i$ be nondecreasing in i. This weak adverse-selection condition is exactly equivalent to

$$\text{For all } j \leq i,\ c_j \leq \overline{c}_i. \tag{1.2}$$

Contracts. A *contract* (q,t) between a seller and the buyer specifies a nonnegative quantity to be delivered by the seller and a transfer to be made in return by the buyer. Under nonexclusivity, two contracts (q,t) and (q',t') offered by different sellers can be added to form a trade $(q+q',t+t')$. In this chapter, we consider two different settings in turn.

- We first study when a nonexclusive market is entry-proof. We then only rely on the existence of a *market tariff* T, where $T(Q)$ is defined as the minimum transfer that allows the buyer to obtain a quantity Q. If an entrant proposes additional contracts, then the buyer can pick one of them, say, (q,t), together with a trade $(Q,T(Q))$ along the market tariff, ending up with utility $u_i(Q+q,T(Q)+t)$.
- We next study competition in menus of nonexclusive contracts among $K \geq 2$ sellers. We then have to precisely specify the menus that are offered by the sellers $k = 1,\ldots,K$. We impose that each seller must always propose at least the null contract $(0,0)$, so that the buyer may be seen as trading one contract (q^k,t^k) with every seller k, ending up with aggregate trade $(Q,T) \equiv (\sum_k q^k, \sum_k t^k)$ and utility $u_i(Q,T)$.

Let us emphasize that we focus on situations in which trade is not anonymous. Our view of nonexclusivity is thus that a seller can monitor the trades the buyer makes with him, though he cannot monitor the trades the buyer makes with the other sellers. This is a natural assumption to make in insurance markets, because an insurance contract must name a beneficiary. Preventing the buyer from making concealed repeat purchases from the same seller enables each seller to price the quantities he sells in a nonlinear way, charging different prices for different marginal units.

Our analysis and results extend to the case of multiple buyers, provided contracting is bilateral and the buyers' types are independent and identically distributed. Contracting is bilateral if trade between a seller and a buyer is only contingent on the information reported by the buyer to the seller, and not on the information this seller may obtain from other buyers.[3] Together with the linearity of costs, the independence of types across buyers then implies that the interactions between a seller and each of his potential customers can be studied separately. Finally, if the buyers' types are identically distributed, then we can assume, using a symmetry argument, that each seller offers the same contracts to each buyer and that each type of each buyer facing the same choices behaves in the same way. In this way, the analysis of the multiple-buyer case can be reduced to that of the single-buyer case.

1.2.2 Benchmarks

The general question addressed in this chapter is how to define a notion of competitive allocation for the above-described economy. This section discusses a few benchmarks, with the purpose of introducing the main effects and difficulties.

The complete-information benchmark assumes that the buyer's type is made public before sellers make their supply decisions, so that information is symmetric about this collective risk (Malinvaud, 1972). The interpretation is that the good for trade comes in I observable varieties, each representing a different quality. When this quality i is revealed, the sellers learn their cost c_i; competition then implies that type i purchases her demand $D_i(c_i)$ at price c_i and that sellers make zero profits. Therefore, equilibria exist and are efficient.

When information becomes asymmetric, the now privately informed buyer optimally channels her demand to the market with the lowest price $p \equiv \min_i c_i$. But then aggregate profits $\mathbf{E}[(p - c_i)D_i(p)]$ are typically negative, except when unit costs are independent of the buyer's type, that is, $c_i \equiv c$ for all i. In this private-value case, sellers know their costs, while the tastes of the buyer are her private information. Nevertheless, a competitive market still plays its allocative role: in equilibrium, every type i purchases her demand $D_i(c)$ at price c, and sellers make zero profits. Once more, equilibria exist and are efficient.

We allow for private values as a limiting case, but our main focus is on the common-value case where the sellers' unit costs depend on the buyer's type. Proceeding as in Akerlof (1970), Pauly (1974) studies the case where linear pricing is imposed, independently of the quantity traded; that is, sellers stand ready to supply any quantity at the going price. Then an equilibrium exists as soon as demand functions are continuous. Because equilibrium profits must be zero under constant returns to scale, the equilibrium price satisfies the equality

[3] Under multilateral contracting, we enter the realm of multi-principal multi-agents models, in which unrestricted communication can be exploited to support many equilibrium allocations; see, for instance, Yamashita (2010).

$$p = \mathbf{E}\left[c_i \frac{D_i(p)}{\mathbf{E}[D_j(p)]}\right]. \tag{1.3}$$

This formula is widely used in the annuity literature (Sheshinski, 2008; Hosseini, 2015; Rothschild, 2015). When the good is indivisible, each demand term in (1.3) is either zero or one, and we are back to the classical Akerlof (1970) formula which states that the price is equal to the expected unit cost of active types. With a divisible good, the formula in addition weighs the unit cost of serving each type by her demand. Because higher types have higher demands, it generally follows that the equilibrium price must lie above the expected unit cost of active types. Accordingly, the active types with the lowest costs subsidize the higher types, who are more costly to serve.

However, there exists a simple way to reduce the risk of having to sell too much to a high type at the going price: to this end, a seller need only post a *limit order* $(p, \overline{q})$ specifying the maximum quantity $\overline{q}$ he is ready to sell at price p. Such limit orders are commonly used on financial markets, and this may indeed be because they allow sellers to hedge against the risk of a high demand.[4] A well-chosen limit order, with a price just below p, is profitable because it reduces the loss-making sales to high types while preserving the profits from selling to low-cost types.[5] This, incidentally, shows that the Pauly (1974) outcome is not a competitive equilibrium: anticipating adverse selection, sellers would like to reduce their competitive supply, thereby collectively rationing demand.

We conclude that the linear-pricing construction is rather fragile under adverse selection. A natural step forward is to consider a competitive game in which sellers are allowed to post limit orders.[6] Notice that a collection of limit orders gives rise to a convex market tariff and, conversely, that any convex market tariff can be decomposed into a (possibly infinite) collection of (possibly infinitesimal) limit orders. In what follows, we sometimes impose that tariffs be convex, but we also explore cases where tariffs can be arbitrary.

1.3 ENTRY-PROOFNESS

The idea of using entry-proofness as a solution concept first originates in an attempt at simplicity, because this avoids the need to precisely describe the

[4] We follow the literature in using the term "limit order," although the maximum quantity $\overline{q}$ is here understood to apply to a single buyer, whereas a limit order on a financial market specifies the maximum aggregate quantity one is ready to sell to a set of traders.

[5] AMS (2019, lemma 4) formalize this intuition and show that, under adverse selection, such a limit order allows a seller to approximate the maximum profit he can earn when competing with a linear tariff.

[6] The game in which sellers compete by posting a single limit order implements the efficient competitive equilibria when information is symmetric and cost functions are weakly convex. In the present model with asymmetric information and linear cost functions, AMS (2018, pp. 1013–1014) show that this game has a pure-strategy equilibrium only in limiting cases where costs or demands do not depend on the buyer's type.

supply side of the economy or to fully specify the details of an extensive form. Moreover, entry-proof allocations, when they exist, are widely considered as capturing the idea of perfect competition.[7] We begin by studying when inactive markets are entry-proof. We then turn to active markets, for which the distinction between exclusive and nonexclusive competition becomes relevant, and we formulate a definition of entry-proofness consistent with nonexclusivity. We show in particular that entry-proofness selects a unique budget-balanced allocation, which exists under very general conditions. This requirement is thus more fruitful under nonexclusivity than under exclusivity.

1.3.1 Entry-Proofness in Inactive Markets

In this section, we describe the circumstances under which private information impedes trade altogether. We say that a market is *inactive* if the market tariff reduces to a single point, given by $T(0) = 0$, or, equivalently, if only the null contract $(0,0)$ is available. Our goal is to find conditions ensuring that no entrant can make an offer leading to profitable trades. Accordingly, we say that an inactive market is *entry-proof* if, *for any menu of contracts offered by an entrant, the buyer has a best response such that the entrant earns at most zero expected profit.*

To characterize the inactive markets that are entry-proof, we first study the simplest case where the entrant offers a single contract. The key argument here is that, if this contract strictly attracts a type i, then it must also attract all types $j > i$: this is a simple consequence of weak single crossing. Hence, from the entrant's viewpoint, the relevant unit cost is not the individual cost c_i of serving type i, but, rather, the expected cost $\overline{c}_i$ of serving types $j \geq i$. Notice that some other types $j < i$ may also be attracted by the entrant's offer, but the weak adverse-selection condition (1.2) ensures that this can only reduce the entrant's expected unit cost. This shows that the following condition is necessary for entry to be unprofitable.

Condition EP *For each* i, $\tau_i(0,0) \leq \overline{c}_i$.

Notice that Condition EP does not rule out gains from trade, in the usual first-best sense of the term; that is, it may well be that $\tau_i(0,0) > c_i$ for some i. AMS (2021, theorem 1.1) show that this necessary condition for entry-proofness is sufficient even when menus of contracts are allowed:

Theorem 1.1 *Under Assumption 1.1, an inactive market is entry-proof if and only if Condition EP is satisfied.*

The intuition is as follows. If the entrant offers an arbitrary menu of contracts, then, by weak single crossing, the buyer has a best response with nondecreasing quantities, which we denote by $(q_i,t_i)_{i=1}^{I}$. Suppose that $q_i > q_{i-1}$

[7] As argued by Rothschild and Stiglitz (1976, p. 642): "The basic idea underlying competitive markets involves free entry and noncollusive behavior among the participants in the market."

for some type i, and let us first locate the contract (q_{i-1}, t_{i-1}). We can safely assume that t_{i-1} is positive, as the entrant's profit can only be reduced by giving away costly production. We also know that type $i-1$ weakly prefers this contract to the null contract; by weak single crossing again, so does type i. Therefore, the point (q_{i-1}, t_{i-1}) must lie in the north-east quadrant in Figure 1.1, at the right of the indifference curve of type i that goes through the origin.

Now, to be willing to trade the contract (q_i, t_i), it must be that type i, having already traded the contract (q_{i-1}, t_{i-1}), is willing to trade the additional *layer* $(q_i - q_{i-1}, t_i - t_{i-1})$. To evaluate her marginal rate of substitution at (q_{i-1}, t_{i-1}), we can use, in turn, the concavity of the indifference curve of type i, then Assumption 1.1, and finally Condition EP to obtain the following inequalities:

$$\tau_i(q_{i-1}, t_{i-1}) \leq \tau_i(\underline{q}_i, 0) \leq \tau_i(0,0) \leq \overline{c}_i. \tag{1.4}$$

This implies that type i is not ready to pay more than $\overline{c}_i(q_i - q_{i-1})$ for the additional quantity $q_i - q_{i-1}$. Therefore,

$$t_i - t_{i-1} \leq \overline{c}_i(q_i - q_{i-1}).$$

Summing these inequalities over i with appropriate weights yields

$$\sum_i \left(\sum_{j \geq i} m_j \right) [t_i - t_{i-1} - \overline{c}_i(q_i - q_{i-1})] \leq 0.$$

Finally, rearranging terms in the spirit of Wilson (1993), we obtain

$$\sum_i m_i(t_i - c_i q_i) \leq 0,$$

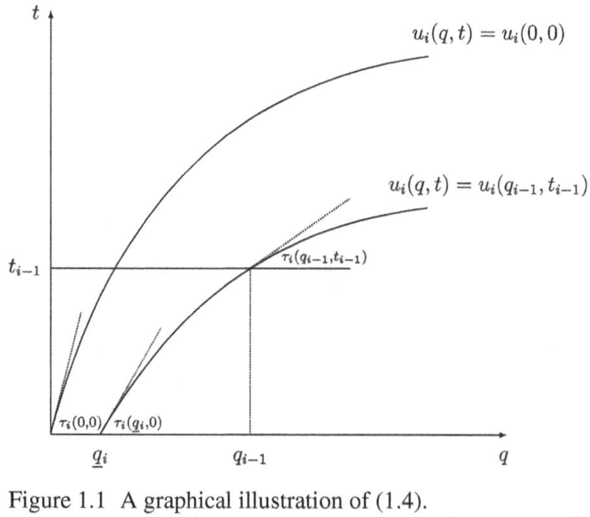

Figure 1.1 A graphical illustration of (1.4).
Source: Copyright American Economic Association, reproduced with permissions of the *American Economic Review*.

which shows that entry cannot be profitable.

A noticeable feature of this proof is that it does not consider every contract (q_i, t_i) in isolation. Instead, the key role is played by layers of the form $(q_i - q_{i-1}, t_i - t_{i-1})$. Under weak single crossing, optimal quantities can be assumed to be nondecreasing in the buyer's type, so that the ith layer can be thought of as traded by all types $j \geq i$, and thus has expected unit cost $\overline{c}_i$. Condition EP implies that, at this price, type i is not strictly willing to trade, so that each layer must yield a nonpositive expected profit. By contrast, some of the *contracts* proposed in a menu may yield positive profits. For instance, although the condition $t_1 \leq \overline{c}_1 q_1$ ensures that the expected profit on the first layer (q_1, t_1) is nonpositive, it may well be that $t_1 > c_1 q_1$.

AMS (2021) show that the assumptions of Theorem 1.1 can be weakened in several ways; however, the weak single-crossing condition and the seemingly innocuous Assumption 1.1 are tight. They also provide a result characterizing *market breakdown*, defined as a situation in which *any menu of contracts that strictly attracts at least some type yields a strictly negative expected profit, even if the buyer's best response is most favorable to the entrant.* Condition EP clearly remains necessary for this stronger concept, and it also remains sufficient under slightly stronger conditions on preferences. Earlier results were obtained by Mailath and Nöldeke (2008) for an economy in which the buyer has quadratic quasilinear preferences, and by Hendren (2013) for a Rothschild and Stiglitz (1976) insurance economy.

1.3.2 Entry-Proofness in Active Markets: The Two-Type Case

We now turn to *active* markets, on which nonnull contracts are available. In line with Rothschild and Stiglitz (1976), our goal is to characterize when entry on such a market is unprofitable, given the contracts available; in contrast with them, we suppose that the buyer can trade with several sellers. To this end, the proper object of study is the *market tariff*, which describes the frontier of the set of aggregate trades that can be achieved by trading on the market.

A market tariff specifies the minimum aggregate transfer $T(Q)$ required to purchase an aggregate quantity Q, with $T(Q) \equiv \infty$ if this is impossible; notice that we obviously have $T(0) = 0$. By assuming that T is lower semicontinuous, with a compact domain, we ensure that, for every type i, the problem of maximizing $u_i(Q, T(Q))$ admits a solution Q_i. We then say that the allocation $(Q_i, T(Q_i))_{i=1}^{I}$ is *implemented* by the tariff T. We assume that types are ordered according to the strict single-crossing condition, so that the optimal quantities Q_i are nondecreasing in i. Moreover, this allocation is *budget-feasible* if

$$\sum_i m_i [T(Q_i) - c_i Q_i] \geq 0. \tag{1.5}$$

Now, suppose an entrant can propose additional trades to the buyer, in the form of a menu of contracts that complement the market tariff. We say that the tariff T is *entry-proof* if, *for any menu of contracts offered by an entrant, the buyer* *has a best response such that the entrant earns at most zero expected profit, given that the buyer is free to combine any contract offered by the entrant with a trade along the tariff T.* The last clause of this definition is crucial, and captures the nonexclusivity of trade.

Our goal is to characterize the set of budget-feasible allocations that are implemented by entry-proof market tariffs. In this section, we focus on the two-type case $I = 2$, which is simple enough to allow for a precise discussion of the proof to the main result; the weak adverse-selection condition (1.2) then amounts to $c_1 \leq c_2$.

Thus, consider an allocation $(Q_i, T_i)_{i=1}^2$ that is implemented by some market tariff T. Because this allocation is incentive-compatible, it satisfies $Q_2 \geq Q_1$ by strict single crossing. Moreover, if T is entry-proof, then we must have

$$u_1(Q_1, T_1) \geq \max\{u_1(q, \bar{c}_1 q) : q \geq 0\}. \tag{1.6}$$

Otherwise, an entrant can offer a contract with unit price slightly above $\bar{c}_1$ that profitably attracts type 1, and remains profitable even if type 2 is attracted – recall that, by definition, $\bar{c}_1 = m_1 c_1 + m_2 c_2$. Similarly, we must have

$$u_2(Q_2, T_2) \geq \max\{u_2(Q_1 + q, T_1 + c_2 q) : q \geq 0\}. \tag{1.7}$$

Otherwise, an entrant can offer a contract with unit price slightly above c_2 that profitably attracts type 2 along with the contract (Q_1, T_1), and is even more profitable if type 1 is also attracted; notice that this second type of entry is specific to the nonexclusive case.[8] It follows from (1.6) that

$$T_1 \leq \bar{c}_1 Q_1. \tag{1.8}$$

Similarly, it follows from (1.7) that

$$T_2 \leq T_1 + c_2(Q_2 - Q_1). \tag{1.9}$$

However, rearranging terms in the spirit of Wilson (1993), the budget-feasibility constraint (1.5) can be rewritten as

$$T_1 - \bar{c}_1 Q_1 + m_2[T_2 - T_1 - c_2(Q_2 - Q_1)] \geq 0. \tag{1.10}$$

Thus, in light of (1.10), (1.8) and (1.9) are in fact equalities. That is, profits are zero on the first layer (Q_1, T_1), which is traded by both types; similarly, profits are zero on the second layer $(Q_2 - Q_1, T_2 - T_1)$, which is traded by type 2 only. This, in turn, implies that the inequalities (1.6) and (1.7) are also equalities. Overall, the four resulting equalities pin down the set of candidates for a budget-feasible allocation that is implemented by an entry-proof tariff. AMS (2020, theorem 1.2) show that these necessary conditions for entry-proofness are sufficient even when menus of contracts are allowed:

[8] In a Rothschild and Stiglitz (1976) insurance economy, Kosenko et al. (2023, definition 1) base their analysis on the assumption that additional coverage is available without limits at price c_2, which implies an inequality similar to (1.7). They do not, however, state the first inequality (1.6).

Theorem 1.2 *Any budget-feasible allocation* $(Q_i^*, T_i^*)_{i=1}^2$ *that is implemented by an entry-proof market tariff satisfies*

$$Q_1^* \in \arg\max\{u_1(Q, \bar{c}_1 Q) : Q \geq 0\}, \tag{1.11}$$

$$T_1^* = \bar{c}_1 Q_1^*, \tag{1.12}$$

$$Q_2^* - Q_1^* \in \arg\max\{u_2(Q_1^* + q, T_1^* + c_2 q) : q \geq 0\}, \tag{1.13}$$

$$T_2^* - T_1^* = c_2(Q_2^* - Q_1^*). \tag{1.14}$$

Conversely, any allocation that satisfies (1.11)–(1.14) *can be implemented by the piecewise-linear convex market tariff*

$$T^*(Q) \equiv 1_{\{Q \leq Q_1^*\}} \bar{c}_1 Q + 1_{\{Q_1^* < Q \leq Q_2^*\}} [\bar{c}_1 Q_1^* + c_2(Q - Q_1^*)], \tag{1.15}$$

and this tariff is entry-proof.

When u_1 and u_2 are strictly quasiconcave – and also, generically, when they are only weakly quasiconcave – conditions (1.11)–(1.14) characterize a unique allocation. Notice that, because the low-cost type 1 obtains her demand at a price equal to the average cost $\bar{c}_1$, she subsidizes the high-cost type 2, though to a lesser degree than in the linear-pricing candidate with price (1.3) discussed in Section 1.2.2.

Concerning the second part of Theorem 1.2, it should be noted that the natural two-point tariff obtained by restricting the market tariff (1.15) to the quantities Q_1^* and Q_2^* does not generally resist entry, as an entrant may cream-skim type 1 and make a profit. To deter entry, we have to ensure that any such offer would also attract type 2. This is exactly what the convex tariff (1.15) achieves, by enabling type 2 to purchase any fraction of the first layer at price $\bar{c}_1$ and any additional quantity at price c_2. This ensures that any entrant's contract that would attract type 1, such as D in Figure 1.2, would also attract type 2, because type 2 can complement this contract by latent contracts made available by the market tariff and thereby reach aggregate trades that she strictly prefers to (Q_2^*, T_2^*). The need for latent contracts to block attempts at cream-skimming contrasts with the exclusive-competition case, where the revelation principle ensures that there is no need to distinguish a market tariff from the allocation it implements.

In summary, in the two-type case, entry-proofness singles out a generically unique budget-balanced allocation; moreover, the existence problem emphasized by Rothschild and Stiglitz (1976) under exclusive competition no longer arises, whatever the distribution of types. The generality of this conclusion is striking: single crossing is only used to ensure that the inequality $Q_2 \geq Q_1$ holds, Assumption 1.1 is not needed, and preferences and candidate tariffs can be arbitrary as long as the maximization problems in (1.6) and (1.7) admit a solution.

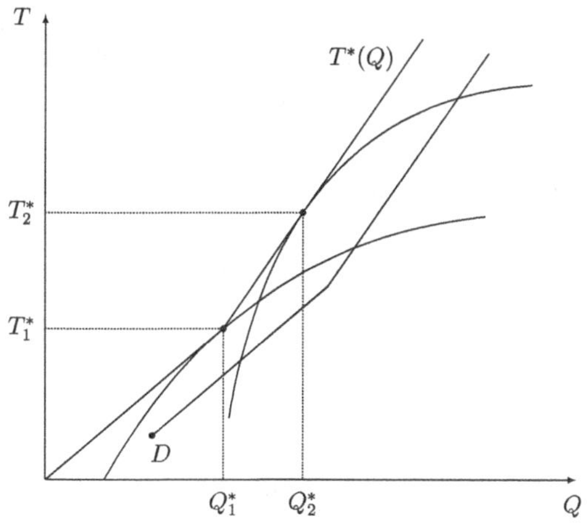

Figure 1.2 Blocking cream-skimming deviations.

1.3.3 Entry-Proofness in Active Markets: The Convex-Tariff Case

We now extend these results to the case of an arbitrary number of types. We will see that this raises a subtle new difficulty; to deal with it, the key restriction we impose in this section is that the market tariff be *convex*. A case in point is when every seller k posts a convex tariff t^k such that $t^k(0) = 0$. An intuitive rationale is that this allows sellers to hedge against the risk of attracting high-cost types buying large quantities; for instance, in the market-microstructure literature, convex tariffs are often used to model collections of limit orders placed by strategic market-makers and executed in order of price priority by an informed insider.[9] Then the market tariff $T(Q) \equiv \min\{\sum_k t^k(q^k) : \sum_k q^k = Q\}$, which incorporates the possibility of trading with several sellers on the market, is indeed a convex function of the aggregate quantity Q.[10]

For a seller contemplating entering on a market where existing trading opportunities are summarized by the market tariff T, everything is as if the market were inactive and every type i's preferences were represented by the indirect utility function

$$u_i^T(q,t) \equiv \max\{u_i(Q+q, T(Q)+t) : Q \geq 0\}. \quad (1.16)$$

Convexity of the market tariff ensures that, if the primitive utility functions $(u_i)_{i=1}^I$ satisfy the strict single-crossing property, then the indirect utility functions $(u_i^T)_{i=1}^I$ satisfy the weak single-crossing property. This allows AMS (2021, theorem 1.2) to rely on Theorem 1.1, which deals with inactive markets, to tackle the case of an active market:

[9] See, for instance, Biais et al. (2000, 2013), Back and Baruch (2013), AMS (2019), and Baruch and Glosten (2019).

[10] This is because T is the *infimal convolution* of the convex tariffs t^k (Rockafellar, 1970, theorem 5.4).

Theorem 1.3 *Under Assumption 1.1, an allocation* $(Q_i^*, T^*(Q_i^*))_{i=1}^I$ *is budget-feasible and is implemented by an entry-proof convex market tariff* T^* *with domain* $[0, Q_I^*]$ *if and only if they jointly satisfy the following recursive system:*

(i) $(Q_0^*, T^*(Q_0^*)) \equiv (0,0)$;

(ii) for each i, $Q_i^* - Q_{i-1}^* \in \arg\max\{u_i(Q_{i-1}^* + q, T^*(Q_{i-1}^*) + \bar{c}_i q) : q \geq 0\}$;

(iii) for each i, *if* $Q_{i-1}^* < Q_i^*$, *then* T^* *is affine with slope* $\bar{c}_i$ *over the interval* $[Q_{i-1}^*, Q_i^*]$.

In particular, any such allocation is budget-balanced.

This result generalizes Theorem 1.2 to more than two types. While item (i) is merely a convention, (ii) and (iii) are substantial, and indicate how to recursively build a complete family of quantities, as well as the corresponding market tariff; by construction, this tariff is convex, because the upper-tail conditional expectation of unit costs is nondecreasing in the buyer's type. The proof parallels the argument provided in Section 1.3.2 for the two-type case: at each step, the entrant must be deterred from supplying a well-chosen quantity at a price slightly above $\bar{c}_i$. By single crossing, if such an offer attracts type i, then it must also attract all types $j \geq i$, so that the offer is profitable as soon as type i is attracted. Therefore, entry-proofness implies the following inequalities:

$$\text{For each } i,\ u_i(Q_i^*, T^*(Q_i^*)) \geq \max\{u_i(Q_{i-1}^* + q, T^*(Q_{i-1}^*) + \bar{c}_i q) : q \geq 0\}. \tag{1.17}$$

It follows that no layer can be profitable:

$$\text{For each } i,\ T^*(Q_i^*) - T^*(Q_{i-1}^*) \leq \bar{c}_i(Q_i^* - Q_{i-1}^*). \tag{1.18}$$

Summing these inequalities as in Section 1.3.2, we obtain that the allocation $(Q_i^*, T^*(Q_i^*))_{i=1}^I$ is budget-balanced, so that the inequalities (1.18) are in fact equalities. Notice that these equalities can be interpreted as a marginal version of Akerlof (1970) pricing: each layer is priced at the expected cost of serving the types who trade it. As a result, the constraints (1.17) must all be binding, and the result follows.

Theorem 1.3 generalizes a similar but weaker entry-proofness result due to Glosten (1994, proposition 1.7). His analysis of limit-order markets requires that the buyer's preferences be quasilinear, and that the entrant's tariff satisfy a property he dubs *single crossing* and that captures a convexity requirement. By allowing for general preferences, Theorem 1.3 makes the result relevant for insurance markets, in which wealth effects may be significant.

Existence of an entry-proof convex market tariff obtains because each maximization problem in (ii) admits a solution under the Inada condition (1.1).[11] Thus, budget-feasibility and entry-proofness are not conflicting requirements

[11] Or, when the buyer's preferences are linear, because of the imposition of a capacity constraint.

under nonexclusivity, in contrast with the pervasive nonexistence problems arising under exclusivity (Rothschild and Stiglitz, 1976). The difference is that, when competition is exclusive, the buyer's indirect utility functions no longer satisfy single crossing: by offering a cream-skimming contract, the entrant can attract a type i without attracting types $j > i$, which allows him to target type i without worrying about adverse selection. The nonexistence of an entry-proof tariff is then arguably not due to private information or entry-proofness per se, but rather to this violation of single crossing – or, to put it more provocatively, to the fact that the exclusive model does not capture the full extent of adverse selection.

Uniqueness of an entry-proof convex market tariff also follows if the solution to each maximization problem in (ii) is unique. This is the case if the buyer's preferences are strictly convex. If they are only weakly convex, then multiple solutions may appear if the marginal rate of substitution of some type i is equal to $\overline{c}_i$ over a whole interval of quantities, but this is clearly a nongeneric phenomenon.

Theorem 1.3 thus characterizes an essentially unique allocation. Following AMS (2014, 2019, 2021), we label this allocation, which was originally introduced in different contexts by Jaynes (1978), Hellwig (1988), and Glosten (1994), the *JHG allocation.*[12] Similarly, the *JHG tariff* T^* consists of a sequence of layers with unit prices $\overline{c}_i$, and features an upward kink at any quantity $Q_i^* \in (0, Q_I^*)$ such that $Q_{i+1}^* > Q_i^*$ and $\overline{c}_{i+1} > \overline{c}_i$. This sequence of layers can be interpreted as a family of limit orders with maximum quantities $Q_i^* - Q_{i-1}^*$ and unit prices $\overline{c}_i$. The JHG allocation and the JHG tariff are illustrated in Figure 1.3 in the case of three types with strictly convex preferences.

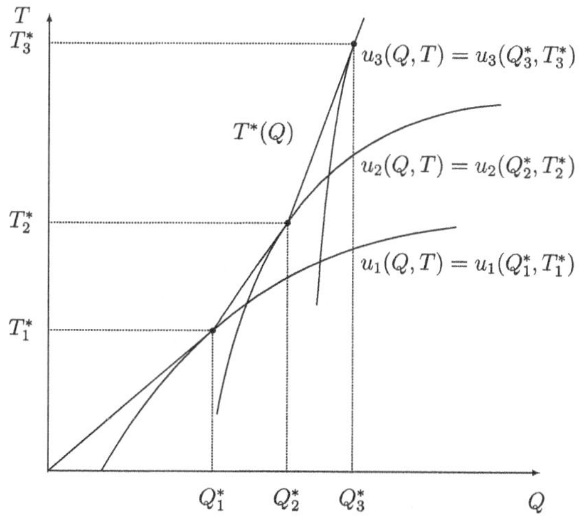

Figure 1.3 The JHG allocation and the JHG tariff for $I = 3$.
Source: Copyright American Economic Association, reproduced with permissions of the *American Economic Review.*

[12] The contributions of Jaynes (1978) and Hellwig (1988) are discussed in Section 1.5.3.

As an application, consider linear utility functions $u_i(Q,T) \equiv v_i Q - T$, subject to a capacity constraint $Q \in [0,1]$. Such linear preferences generalize those in Akerlof (1970) to the case of a divisible good; strict single crossing requires that v_i be strictly increasing in i. Each problem in (ii) admits a unique solution if $v_i \neq \overline{c}_i$ for all i, which we will assume for simplicity. To determine the JHG allocation and the JHG tariff, we apply (ii) in Theorem 1.3 recursively. By convention, $Q_0^* = 0$; then, beginning with type 1, Q_i^* remains zero as long as $v_i < \overline{c}_i$. If this inequality holds for all types, then the market is inactive; in that case, according to (iii), the essentially unique entry-proof convex market tariff is only defined at zero, with $T^*(0) = 0$. Otherwise, let i^* be the lowest type such that $v_i > \overline{c}_i$. Applying (ii) at i^* implies that type i^* trades up to capacity at unit price $\overline{c}_{i^*}$; moreover, types $i > i^*$ must also trade $Q_i^* = 1$, as the capacity constraint is binding in (ii). Finally, according to (iii), the unique entry-proof convex market tariff is linear, with $T^*(Q) = \overline{c}_{i^*} Q$ for all $Q \in [0,1]$. The upshot from this discussion is that, when the buyer's preferences are linear, the JHG allocation generically features a single layer, and corresponds to the competitive-equilibrium allocation in Akerlof (1970) that maximizes the gains from trade.

The property that the indirect utility functions $(u_i^{T^*})_{i=1}^I$ be ordered according to the weak single-crossing condition plays a key role in the above analysis. This property itself results from the two assumptions that the primitive utility functions $(u_i)_{i=1}^I$ be ordered according to the strict single-crossing condition, and that the market tariff T^* be convex. Because this second assumption effectively constrains market outcomes, it is natural to ask whether it can be dispensed with. The answer is positive in the following three settings. In the two-type case, the proof of Theorem 1.2 follows from a direct argument that does not require that the market tariff be convex. When the buyer has linear preferences, as above, AMS (2011, p. 1888) also offers a direct proof. Finally, AMS (2021, online appendix F) show that the JHG allocation turns out to be the only budget-feasible allocation implemented by an entry-proof market tariff that is first convex and then concave. The general case raises, however, a difficult issue: in the absence of single crossing, we do not know for sure whether a contract that attracts type i also attracts all types $j \geq i$, or only a subset of those with a more or less favorable expected cost; as a result, the entry-proofness constraint (1.17) need not hold. While entry-proofness per se selects a convex tariff in a large class of admissible tariffs allowing for quantity discounts, the general problem thus remains open.

1.3.4 Discussion

A noticeable feature of the JHG allocation is the relationship between demand and supply on each layer. On the first layer, the price is the expected cost of serving all types, and the quantity supplied is exactly the demand of the first type at this price. Indeed, supplying less would inefficiently ration demand, while supplying more would entail losses on the excess quantity. On the second layer, the first type is no longer active, and the same reasoning applies: the price is the expected cost of serving all types except the first, and the quantity supplied is exactly the residual demand of the second type at this price – and so on. Overall, the quantity supplied on each layer matches the residual demand of the marginal type, at a price equal to expected cost. On each layer but the last one, relatively low-cost types thus subsidize relatively high-cost ones, in contrast with the absence of cross-subsidies that characterize candidate entry-proof allocations under exclusive competition.

It should also be noted that the JHG allocation typically allows for marginal rates of substitution to differ across types. For instance, in the two-type case under adverse selection, we have $\tau_1(Q_1^*, T_1^*) = \overline{c}_1 < c_2 = \tau_2(Q_2^*, T_2^*)$ when this allocation is interior and separating. This contrasts with private-value models where side trades take place on Walrasian markets, which calls for an equalization of marginal rates of substitution (Hammond, 1979, 1987). Yet, this difference does not create any opportunities for side trading, because the goods under consideration are not the same: for instance, in a Rothschild and Stiglitz (1976) insurance economy, insurance for a low-risk consumer is not the same good as insurance for a high-risk consumer. Indeed, supposing that consumers have access to the same constant-returns-to-scale technology as firms, the opportunity cost for type 1 of selling additional coverage to type 2 is c_2, and at this price type 2 is not willing to buy. Similarly, the opportunity cost of selling coverage to type 1 is only c_1, but at this price all types would be attracted; hence, the relevant unit cost is $\overline{c}_1$, and at this price type 1 is not willing to buy. The JHG allocation thus exhausts the incentive-compatible gains from trade. Together with entry-proofness, these features support the idea that the JHG allocation is a natural candidate for a competitive allocation.

Alternatively, AMS (2020) propose to reconsider this economy from the viewpoint of a social planner endowed with the same linear technology as the buyers and acting under asymmetric information. As in the classical setting of Harris and Townsend (1981), the planner is able to control all communication among the buyers, and in fact he optimally chooses to prohibit all forms of communication apart from a report each agent privately sends to him. Then the only constraints he faces are the incentive-compatibility constraints

$$\text{For all } i \text{ and } j,\ u_i(Q_i, T_i) \geq u_i(Q_j, T_j) \tag{1.19}$$

and the budget constraint (1.5). This leads to the classical definition of second-best allocations as Pareto optima in the set of budget-feasible and incentive-compatible allocations. In general, such allocations form a nondegenerate continuum, according to the weight put on each type; moreover, under single crossing, either the downward or the upward local incentive-compatibility constraints must be binding, apart from special cases.[13]

[13] See, for instance, Prescott and Townsend (1984) and Crocker and Snow (1985) for characterizations of second-best allocations in Rothschild and Stiglitz (1976) insurance economies.

Let us now assume that the planner cannot monitor side trades between different buyers nor prevent the entry of a seller with the same technology. For simplicity, consider the two-type case, and suppose that preferences are strictly convex and satisfy strict single crossing. Two consequences then follow for the set of allocations that the planner can implement. First, according to Theorem 1.2, this set collapses to a single allocation, namely, the JHG allocation. It is thus impossible for the planner to redistribute between types: both quantities and transfers are uniquely defined. Second, in general, this allocation is not second-best efficient, in the sense given above. Indeed, the incentive-compatibility constraints (1.19) are superseded by the entry-proofness constraints (1.17), which turn out to be necessary and sufficient to characterize the JHG allocation. When $Q_2^* > Q_1^*$, (1.17) implies that the local incentive-compatibility constraints do not bind, so that the JHG allocation is not second best.

Overall, the uniqueness of the budget-balanced allocation robust to side trading contrasts with the multiplicity of second-best allocations, which form a nondegenerate frontier. The planner is thus severely constrained by his inability to monitor trades. As discussed in AMS (2020), this result has consequences for actual policies, because the possibility of side trading may undo their effects. For instance, the only possibility for public health insurance is to propose a single basic coverage, sold at average cost, and chosen so as to maximize the utility of low-risk consumers at that price. Private insurers can then compete to provide complementary coverage at price c_2. Another example is provided by bailout policies on financial markets. Under exclusivity, they aim at attracting only the least profitable borrowers, either through direct lending (Philippon and Skreta, 2012), or through the repurchasing of low-quality assets (Tirole, 2012). By contrast, when the borrower can complement a public program with private funds, the only possibility is to provide the same loan Q_1^* to all projects at expected cost, while the riskiest borrowers in addition turn to a competitive market for additional funding at price c_2.

1.4 COMPETITIVE SCREENING

Entry-proofness provides a parsimonious and tractable way of modeling perfect competition, which is relatively insensitive to the details of market interactions; for that reason, the JHG allocation characterized in Section 1.3 is arguably a natural and robust candidate for a competitive-equilibrium allocation of a nonexclusive market subject to adverse selection. Yet, by design, this approach does not shed light on how this allocation may be decentralized; a valuable complement to this approach would thus be to implement the JHG allocation as the unique equilibrium outcome of an extensive-form game in which strategic sellers compete to serve privately informed buyers.

To start with, and by way of comparison, we should observe that decentralization is easy to achieve in the standard case of exclusive competition. Indeed, in this context, the unique entry-proof allocation characterized in the insurance setting of Rothschild and Stiglitz (1976), or in the more general setting of Riley (1979), can be easily supported – as long as it exists – in a pure-strategy equilibrium of a competitive-screening game in which sellers first simultaneously post menus of contracts, from which the buyer then chooses a single contract according to her type; specifically, there exists an equilibrium of this game in which two sellers offer a menu consisting of the trades comprised in this allocation. Therefore, the existence problem under exclusivity is not tied to decentralization per se, but to the fact that an entry-proof allocation may robustly fail to exist.[14]

By contrast, under nonexclusivity, we know that an entry-proof tariff exists, but its decentralization is much more delicate, because the buyer is now free to combine contracts issued by different sellers. As we shall now see, this generates novel strategic effects, which make it more difficult – indeed, in general, impossible – to implement the JHG allocation via competitive-screening games.

1.4.1 The Competitive-Screening Game

To clarify this issue, let us consider a general setting in which a finite number K of sellers simultaneously contract with a single buyer. We throughout assume that types are ordered according to the strict single-crossing condition and, when types are continuously distributed, that the mapping $(i,q,t) \mapsto u_i(q,t)$ is continuous. As discussed in Section 1.2.1, trade is nonanonymous and contracting is bilateral, in the sense that trade between a seller and a buyer can only be made contingent on the information reported by the buyer to this seller. In these situations, the menu theorems of Peters (2001), Martimort and Stole (2002), and Page and Monteiro (2003) allow us to restrict, with no loss of generality, to competition in menus or nonlinear tariffs. The corresponding extensive-form game, which we denote by G^{CS}, unfolds in two stages:

1. Every seller k offers a compact menu of contracts $C^k \subset \mathbb{R}_+ \times \mathbb{R}$ that contains at least the null trade $(0,0)$.
2. After privately learning her type, the buyer selects a contract from each of the menus C^k offered by the sellers.

A pure strategy for type i is a function that maps every menu profile $(C^1,\ldots,C^K)$ into a contract profile $((q^1,t^1),\ldots,(q^K,t^K)) \in C^1 \times \cdots \times C^K$.

[14] While the existence issue has been addressed by considering mixed-strategy equilibria (Rosenthal and Weiss, 1984; Dasgupta and Maskin, 1986; Farinha Luz, 2017) or by considering alternative extensive forms (Miyazaki, 1977; Wilson, 1977; Spence, 1978; Riley, 1979; Engers and Fernandez, 1987; Netzer and Scheuer, 2014; Mimra and Wambach, 2019), the corresponding equilibrium allocations typically do not coincide with the Rothschild and Stiglitz (1976) allocation; see Mimra and Wambach (2014) for a survey.

The compactness of the sellers' menus ensures that every type i's utility-maximization problem

$$\max\left\{u_i\left(\sum_k q^k,\sum_k t^k\right):(q^k,t^k)\in C^k \text{ for each } k\right\}$$

always has a solution. The solution concept for G^{CS} is pure-strategy subgame-perfect Nash equilibrium. For future reference, we let

$$T(Q)\equiv\min\left\{\sum_k t^k:(q^k,t^k)\in C^k \text{ for each } k \text{ and } \sum_k q^k=Q\right\}$$

be the market tariff associated with the equilibrium menus C^k, and we let, for each i,

$$U_i\equiv\max\{u_i(Q,T(Q)):Q\geq 0\}$$

be the equilibrium utility of type i.

It should be noted that the set of strategies for the sellers in G^{CS} is the same as in a standard competitive-screening game under exclusivity. Yet the assumption that the buyer can simultaneously trade with several sellers has two implications for the set of potentially profitable contracts any seller may offer. On the one hand, it tends to expand this set, as this seller may choose to complement his competitors' offers by proposing additional trades to the buyer. On the other hand, it also gives his competitors more instruments to block his deviations, compared to when competition is exclusive; indeed, contracts that are not traded on the equilibrium path may become relevant in case a seller deviates, and in fact equilibria often require the presence of such latent contracts, as we shall now see.

1.4.2 Linear Preferences

Let us first assume that the buyer has linear preferences, subject to a capacity constraint. In this scenario, which extends Akerlof (1970) to the case of a divisible good, the JHG allocation features a single layer, and corresponds to the competitive-equilibrium allocation that maximizes the gains from trade. The following result, due to AMS (2011), shows that this allocation is uniquely supported in any equilibrium of G^{CS}:

Theorem 1.4 *Let $u_i(Q,T)\equiv v_iQ-T$ for $Q\in[0,1]$ and suppose that $v_i\geq c_i$ for all i. Then, generically, any equilibrium of G^{CS} implements the JHG allocation, and there exists a linear-pricing equilibrium with price $\overline{c}_{i^*}$, where i^* is the first type i such that $v_i>\overline{c}_i$.*

In equilibrium, all the buyer types with valuations $v_i>\overline{c}_{i^*}$ trade up to capacity, while all the buyer types with valuations $v_i<\overline{c}_{i^*}$ do not trade at all. Sellers thus earn zero expected profits, and none of them is indispensable to serve any buyer type. Finally, all trades take place at the same price in equilibrium, despite the fact that sellers can propose arbitrary nonlinear tariffs. Thus, Theorem 1.4 provides a game-theoretic foundation for Akerlof's (1970) predictions in a setting where the traded good is divisible and, besides nonexclusivity, few restrictions on feasible trades or instruments are imposed. In particular, low-valuation types such that $c_i < v_i < \overline{c}_{i^*}$ are excluded from trade in equilibrium, unlike what would happen under exclusive competition. The existence and uniqueness of the equilibrium allocation described in Theorem 1.4 paves the way for many applications – notably in finance, where the divisibility assumption is natural.[15]

The driving intuition for these results is that the unobservability of the buyer's aggregate purchases limits the sellers' ability to screen types and thereby the effectiveness of cream-skimming deviations. Suppose, for instance, that the equilibrium price is high, so that low-valuation, and hence on average low-cost types, are not served. A cream-skimming deviation targeted at these types must involve trading a relatively small quantity q at a relatively low price. However, this contract also becomes attractive to high-valuation, and hence on average high-cost types if, along with it, they can trade the additional quantity $1-q$ at the equilibrium price; this is exactly what the linear tariff allows for.

This reasoning illustrates the fact that deviations are blocked by latent contracts, that is, contracts that are not traded on the equilibrium path, but which the buyer may want to trade at the deviation stage.[16] In general, many such contracts are needed to support the equilibrium allocation. This is particularly striking when the distribution of types is discrete, because then only finitely many contracts are effectively traded, while infinitely many latent contracts must be issued. In particular, no equilibrium can in this case be sustained through direct mechanisms, which provides a concrete example of a failure of the revelation principle in common-agency games (Peters, 2001; Martimort and Stole, 2002).

1.4.3 Cournot Convergence under Strictly Convex Preferences

Although Theorem 1.4 holds for general distributions of types,[17] it does not generally extend to the case of strictly convex preferences for the buyer. In a seminal article, Biais et al. (2000) consider a situation in which strategic market-makers (sellers) compete to serve a risk-averse insider (buyer) who has private but imperfect information about the value of an asset, and thus has both informational and hedging motives for trade. Assuming that the buyer

[15] A case in point is the security-design model of DeMarzo and Duffie (1999), to which Theorem 1.4 directly applies; see Biais and Mariotti (2005) for an early result along these lines.

[16] The role of latent contracts has originally been stressed in moral-hazard environments; see, for instance, Hellwig (1983), Arnott and Stiglitz (1991), Bisin and Guaitoli (2004), and Attar and Chassagnon (2009).

[17] Specifically, it holds for any distribution for which $v_i \geq c_i$ at any atom.

has constant absolute risk-aversion α and faces residual Gaussian risk with variance σ^2, they show the following result:

Theorem 1.5 *Let $u_i(Q,T) \equiv v_i Q - \frac{\alpha\sigma^2}{2} Q^2 - T$ and let the buyer's type be continuously distributed. Then, under regularity conditions, G^{CS} admits a symmetric equilibrium in which sellers post the same strictly convex tariff and earn strictly positive expected profits. The equilibrium market tariff converges to the JHG tariff as the number K of sellers grows large.*

This equilibrium exhibits the Cournot-like feature that each seller is indispensable to serve any buyer type who trades a nonzero quantity in equilibrium. Specifically, the strict convexity and symmetry of the equilibrium tariffs implies that any such type has a unique best response that consists in evenly splitting her total purchases between the sellers. This contrasts with the equilibria that obtain in the linear case, in which no seller is indispensable and thus any buyer type who trades up to capacity has multiple best responses that involve trading with different sellers. Because sellers earn strictly positive expected profits in equilibrium, the aggregate equilibrium allocation does not coincide with the JHG allocation; yet, in analogy with classical Cournot-convergence theorems, it converges to the competitive JHG allocation as the number of sellers grows large.

The assumption in Theorem 1.5 that the buyer's type be continuously distributed is key to ensure that, despite being indispensable, a single seller cannot profitably raise his tariff. To illustrate this point, suppose that a seller deviates by replacing a portion of his strictly convex equilibrium tariff by the corresponding chord. This would increase his expected profit if the buyer's behavior remained the same. But such a change raises (lowers) the marginal price for relatively low-cost (high-cost) types who would choose trades in this portion of the tariff. As a result, under adverse selection, trades change in an unfavorable way for the deviating market-maker. This effect is reinforced by the fact that the buyer simultaneously trades with several sellers, as any increase in the quantity she purchases from a seller is compensated by a reduction in the quantity she purchases from his competitors.

1.4.4 Exclusion

We now argue that, in any game G^{CS}, exclusion is a robust feature of any equilibrium that shares two key properties of the Biais et al. (2000) equilibrium. To formulate these properties, we let, for each k:

$$T^{-k}(Q) \equiv \min \left\{ \sum_{l \neq k} t^l : (q^l, t^l) \in C^l \text{ for each } l \neq k \text{ and } \sum_{l \neq k} q^l = Q \right\}$$

be the submarket tariff associated with the equilibrium menus C^l, $l \neq k$, and we let, for all i and k:

$$z_i^{-k}(q,t) \equiv \max \left\{ u_i(q+Q^{-k}, t+T^{-k}(Q^{-k})) : \right.$$

$$\left. Q^{-k} = \sum_{l \neq k} q^l \text{ for some } (q^l, t^l) \in C^l, l \neq k \right\}$$

be type i's indirect utility from trading (q,t) with seller k. The two properties we wish to emphasize can now be stated as follows.

P1 For each k, there exists i such that $U_i = z_i^{-k}(0,0)$.

An equilibrium satisfies P1 if, for each seller, there exists at least one type for whom trading with this seller is not indispensable for her to obtain her equilibrium utility; this reflects the relatively weak requirement that, in equilibrium, the buyer's individual-rationality constraint in her dealings with each seller must bind for at least one type.

P2 For all k and $Q > 0$, $T(Q) < T^{-k}(Q)$.

An equilibrium satisfies P2 if trading with each seller is indispensable for each type who purchases a nonzero aggregate quantity.

The symmetric equilibrium characterized by Biais et al. (2000) satisfies both P1 and P2 because all sellers offer the same strictly convex tariff. Indeed, this implies that each seller is indispensable to minimize the cost of purchasing any strictly positive aggregate quantity, whence P2. This also implies that the indirect utility functions z_i^{-k} satisfy the strict single-crossing condition for all k, so that any seller k for whom the individual-rationality constraint were not binding could raise his tariff without affecting the buyer's incentives, whence P1.

The following theorem, a formal proof of which is provided in the appendix to this chapter, abstracts from the parametric assumptions of Biais et al. (2000) to show that exclusion must more generally take place in any equilibrium of any game G^{CS} that satisfies P1 and P2:

Theorem 1.6 *Consider an equilibrium of a game G^{CS} that satisfies P1 and P2. Then there exists some type i_1 such that, in equilibrium, every type $i \leq i_1$ trades $q_i^k = 0$ with every seller k and obtains utility $U_i = u_i(0,0)$.*

In light of this result, it is worth noticing that Biais et al. (2000) assume that the continuous support of the buyer's type distribution includes an interior type i_0 such that $\tau_{i_0}(0,0) = c_{i_0}$ and thus for which there are no gains from trade.[18] This in turn ensures that there exists an interval of types at the bottom of the type distribution who are excluded from trade in equilibrium, as requested by Theorem 1.6. However, this assumption is fairly restrictive: it does not hold,

[18] Specifically, the insider can trade on both sides of the market, so that types $i > i_0$ ($i < i_0$) are willing to buy (sell) at price c_i. As in Back and Baruch (2013) and Biais et al. (2013), we focus on the ask side of the market.

for instance, in standard Rothschild and Stiglitz (1976) insurance economies, because a risk-averse consumer is always willing to purchase full coverage at the fair price, equal to her riskiness. As we shall now see, the existence of equilibria of G^{CS} games then becomes problematic.

1.4.5 The Existence Conundrum

As a starting point, let us consider the two-type case with $c_2 > c_1$ and strictly convex preferences for the buyer, and let us examine a candidate equilibrium of G^{CS} in which both types 1 and 2 purchase strictly positive quantities. AMS (2014) show that the aggregate equilibrium allocation then has the same structure as the JHG allocation. First, sellers earn zero expected profits. Second, the quantity Q_1 purchased by type 1 is priced at the average cost $\overline{c}_1$, while the additional quantity $Q_2 - Q_1$ purchased by type 2 is priced at the marginal cost c_2. Third, the quantity Q_1 purchased by type 1 is equal to her demand $D_1(\overline{c}_1)$.

This sounds promising but, because type 1 is not excluded from trade, Theorem 1.6 implies that P1 or P2 has to give way. It is intuitive that the weak requirement P1 should be maintained, and thus that P2 should be dropped. Specifically, it can be shown that P1 holds for type 1 and that $T(Q_1) = T^{-k}(Q_1) = \overline{c}_1 Q_1$ for all k, so that no seller is indispensable to provide type 1 with her equilibrium aggregate trade. Because any seller k who trades with both types 1 and 2 on the equilibrium path makes a profit with type 1 and a loss with type 2, this opens the way to a *lemon-dropping* deviation that essentially consists for seller k in convincing type 2 to trade the layer $(Q_1, \overline{c}_1 Q_1)$ with his competitors and the complementary layer $(Q_2 - Q_1, c_2(Q_2 - Q_1))$ with him, thus neutralizing his loss with type 2.

Specifically, the deviation involves two contracts. When $Q_2 > Q_1 > 0$, the first one is essentially that traded by type 1 with seller k on the equilibrium path, while the second one makes the quantity $Q_2 - Q_1$ available at a unit price slightly lower than c_2. Thus, type 2 can strictly increase her utility by trading the second contract on top of the layer $(Q_1, \overline{c}_1 Q_1)$ made available by the sellers other than k; besides, seller k can break ties to make sure that type 2 strictly prefers this contract to the first one. As a result, seller k can make his loss with type 2 arbitrarily small while securing, as $\overline{c}_1 > c_1$, a strictly positive profit with type 1; hence the deviation is profitable. A similar but slightly more involved argument shows that seller k has a profitable deviation also when $Q_2 = Q_1 > 0$.

As a consequence, trade can take place in equilibrium only if type 1 is excluded from trade: in short, the possibility of cross-subsidizing between contracts at the deviation stage makes it impossible to support cross-subsidies between types on the equilibrium path. Specifically, the following result holds (AMS, 2014, theorems 1.1 and 1.2):

Theorem 1.7 *Suppose there are two buyer types with strictly convex preferences, and that $c_2 > c_1$. Then any equilibrium of G^{CS} implements the JHG allocation, but an equilibrium exists if and only if $Q_1^* = 0$ in that* *allocation, that is, if and only if* $\tau_1(0,0) \leq \bar{c}_1$. *If an equilibrium exists, then it can be sustained by each seller posting the JHG tariff, which consists of a single layer with unit price* c_2.

To allow for a finer comparison with the continuous-type model of Biais et al. (2000), let us now suppose as in Section 1.2.1 that there is an arbitrary but finite number I of types, each assumed to have strictly convex preferences. The same difficulty arises as for the characterization of entry-proof tariffs, however: when $I > 2$, the game G^{CS} with no restrictions on admissible menus is hardly tractable. As in Section 1.3.3, a convenient assumption is that sellers are restricted to post convex tariffs, which ensures that the indirect utility functions $(z_i^{-k})_{i=1}^{I}$ are quasiconcave and satisfy the weak single-crossing property for all k. The resulting convex-tariff game G^{CT} can be interpreted as a discriminatory auction in which sellers simultaneously bid quantities at each marginal price. In line with Back and Baruch (2013), this captures oligopolistic competition on a limit-order market where market-makers post collections of limit orders that are executed by an informed insider in order of price priority.

It should be noted that the set of deviations for the sellers is much smaller in G^{CT} than in G^{CS}; in particular, the deviation that led to Theorem 1.7 is no longer feasible. However, the following result, due to AMS (2019, theorems 1.2 and 1.3), shows that, in spite of this, the equilibrium-existence problem only becomes more acute when the number of types increases:

Theorem 1.8 *Suppose there are* I *buyer types with strictly convex quasilinear preferences, and that* c_i *is strictly increasing in* i. *Then any equilibrium of* G^{CT} *implements the JHG allocation, but an equilibrium exists if and only if* $Q_i^* = 0$ *for all* $i < I$ *in that allocation, that is, if* $\tau_i(0,0) \leq \bar{c}_i$ *for all* $i < I$. *If an equilibrium exists, then it can be sustained by each seller posting the JHG tariff, which consists of a single layer with unit price* c_I.

The proof proceeds by showing that, in any candidate equilibrium, the market tariff T is piecewise linear and has a structure similar to that of the JHG tariff. That is, the quantity supplied on each layer but the last one matches the residual demand of the marginal type, at a price equal to the expected cost of serving the buyer types who trade along this layer. This implies that sellers earn zero expected profits, and also that the marginal type on any such layer exhausts the supply at the corresponding marginal price. As a result, each seller offering trades at this marginal price is indispensable for the marginal type and all higher types to reach their equilibrium utility. But one can hardly be indispensable and yet earn zero expected profit: hence any such seller could raise his tariff in a profitable way, a contradiction. This shows that the market tariff T must consist of a single layer and be such that no seller is indispensable to serve the buyer types who trade along it. However, each seller will then want to issue a limit order to hedge against the risk of large purchases emanating from the most costly types. This implies that all types except perhaps the last one must be excluded from trade.

The upshot from Theorems 1.5, 1.7, and 1.8 is twofold. First, the structure of equilibria of discrete-type models, when they exist, is very different from that of the equilibria of continuous-type models that have been emphasized in the literature: namely, pricing is linear and only the last type can trade in equilibrium. Second, necessary and sufficient conditions for the existence of an equilibrium become increasingly stringent as the number of types increases: equilibria fail to exist when there are sufficiently many types with similar preferences, as when we approximate the continuous sets of types postulated by Biais et al. (2000) or Back and Baruch (2013). The pure-strategy-equilibrium correspondence thus fails to be lower hemicontinuous when we move from discrete-type models to continuous-type models. Overall, the predictions of competitive-screening models are very sensitive to fine modeling details, which makes them somewhat fragile.

1.4.6 Ways Out

A natural way to address the equilibrium-existence problem in discrete-type models is to weaken the equilibrium concept. This can be done in two ways.

First, we may consider mixed-strategy equilibria of G^{CS}, the existence of which follows from Carmona and Fajardo (2009). Preliminary investigations of the two-type case have led to a robust example of a mixed-strategy equilibrium that exists when the necessary and sufficient conditions for the existence of a pure-strategy equilibrium are not satisfied (Attar et al., 2021). The key point is that the strategic uncertainty faced by each seller regarding the tariffs offered by his competitors makes it now impossible for him to target specific types, unlike in the deviations used to derive Theorems 1.7 and 1.8. However, this equilibrium bears no obvious relationship with existing equilibrium candidates; the JHG allocation, in particular, does not emerge even when the number of sellers grows large. The systematic characterization of mixed-strategy equilibria nevertheless remains a fascinating – though hard – topic for future research.

Next, we may consider ε-equilibria of G^{CS}. AMS (2019) show that, if every type i has quasilinear utility $u_i(Q,T) \equiv v_i(Q) - T$, then, as the number K of sellers grows large, G^{CS} admits an ε-equilibrium, with ε of the order of $1/K^2$, that supports the JHG allocation. The intuition is that, if $K-1$ sellers contribute to providing a fraction $1/K$ of the JHG tariff, then the residual gains from trade for the remaining seller vanish when K grows large because the resulting market tariff is almost entry-proof. The reason why convergence takes place at rate $1/K^2$ is that these gains from trade are, for every type i, bounded above by

$$v_i(Q_i^*) - v_i\left(\frac{K-1}{K} Q_i^*\right) - \frac{1}{K}\overline{c}_i Q_i^*,$$

which is at most of the order of $1/K^2$ as $v_i'(Q_i^*) \leq \overline{c}_i$ at the JHG allocation. Thus we retrieve the convergence result of Theorem 1.5 for the competitive limit, albeit at the cost of relying on a notion of approximate equilibrium. Glosten

(1994, proposition 2) provides a similar result, assuming from the outset that there is an infinite number of sellers.

1.4.7 Regulation

An alternative route to decentralize the JHG allocation consists in explicitly introducing a market regulation. In this spirit, AMS (2022) study a nonexclusive insurance market in which it is prohibited for sellers to cross-subsidize between contracts. The regulation thus bears on the total profit a seller earns on each contract, and is targeted at dumping practices; it can alternatively be interpreted as banning profits on basic-coverage contracts.[19] Specifically, let G^{CSR} be the regulated game that is obtained from G^{CS} by adding one final stage in which a seller's profit is confiscated whenever he makes a loss on any of the contracts he is trading. The following result then holds (AMS, 2022, theorem 1.2):

Theorem 1.9 *Suppose there are two buyer types with strictly convex preferences, and that $c_2 > c_1$. Then the JHG allocation is the unique candidate-equilibrium allocation of G^{CSR}. Moreover, under regularity conditions on the buyer's preferences, G^{CSR} has an equilibrium as long as there are sufficiently many sellers.*

There are two parts in this result. The necessity part states that the regulation has no anti-competitive implications. The intuition is that each seller aims at increasing his profit by complementing the aggregate coverage provided by its competitors, which gives rise to a form of Bertrand competition over each layer; as a result, the JHG allocation is the unique candidate-equilibrium outcome. The sufficiency part reflects that the regulation, by blocking the cross-subsidies between contracts that were at the root of Theorem 1.7, helps restore existence of an equilibrium even if both types trade in the JHG allocation.

A necessary feature of equilibrium is that sellers must issue latent contracts to discipline their competitors. As in AMS (2011), these contracts are not traded in equilibrium but are meant to block cream-skimming deviations. In the context of insurance, these contracts provide additional coverage that high-risk consumers are willing to combine with the coverage provided by any such deviation. This makes it impossible for a seller to profitably deviate by separating low-risk from high-risk consumers.

[19] Several insurance markets are actually regulated along analogous lines. For instance, in health insurance, Germany and Switzerland rely on a central fund to redistribute costs among firms according to a risk-equalization scheme. These cost-sharing mechanisms, by pooling and redistributing costs among sellers of a standardized basic-coverage contract, prevent firms from earning abnormal profits on such coverage by dropping lemons on their competitors.

1.5 ALTERNATIVE EXTENSIVE FORMS

The main takeaway from the literature surveyed in Section 1.4 is that competitive-screening games generally fail to implement the JHG allocation. This failure can be traced back to a common source, namely, the paucity of instruments allowing us to punish a deviating seller. Indeed, if sellers make their offers simultaneously, then the only device available to block deviations consists in letting the buyer select latent contracts in the nondeviating sellers' menus. However, this device is effective only when the buyer has linear preferences, reflecting the very special property that, if latent contracts are issued at the equilibrium price, then all the types who are willing to trade at this price have the same indirect utility function z_i^{-k}: they are willing to trade a contract issued by a deviating seller if and only if its unit price is less than the equilibrium price. This no longer holds when the buyer has strictly convex preferences and different types trade at different marginal prices.

The generic failure of latent contracts at sustaining equilibria in competitive-screening games – let alone at implementing the JHG allocation – suggests that we look for alternative extensive forms whereby the sellers sequentially receive information over the course of the game. Three kinds of extensive forms have been studied in the literature. The first one allows the buyer to signal her type by recontracting, which requires that all previously signed contracts be publicly observable. The second one lets the sellers bid through an ascending discriminatory auction, in which the offers made at previously quoted prices are publicly observable. The third one enables the sellers – and, possibly, the buyer as well – to voluntarily disclose information about the contracts selected by the buyer; which information eventually becomes available, and to whom, then depends on the agents' disclosure strategies.

1.5.1 Recontracting

Beaudry and Poitevin (1995) study a sequential game in which a risk-averse entrepreneur whose project can be of low or high riskiness can repeatedly solicit financing from successive cohorts of uninformed lenders before the realization of the project's return. An important feature of this game is that there is a potentially infinite number of recontracting rounds. Hence there is no last stage of the game in which the entrepreneur could commit to reject further offers: a lender can never be sure that she will not try to further diversify her risk by selling new claims on her project.[20] That is, nonexclusivity is distinctively linked to the absence of commitment and the sequential nature of contracting.

At each round of recontracting, the entrepreneur can solicit further offers from a new cohort of lenders; if she does so, then she has to provide a summary

[20] This feature is similar to Kahn and Mookherjee's (1998) moral-hazard model of nonexclusive contracting.

of all the contracts she has signed in previous rounds, though not of the contracts she has rejected. This observability assumption stands in contrast to the competitive-screening models surveyed in Section 1.4, in which, by design, no seller has information about existing contractual relationships. Another difference is that, at each round of recontracting, competition is exclusive, in the sense that the entrepreneur can accept at most one offer from one lender. The assumption that lenders are short-lived and cannot observe previously rejected contracts is meant to limit the lenders' ability to sustain collusive outcomes.

In this setup, Beaudry and Poitevin (1995) show that, when the high-risk project has positive net present value and each project can be financed by riskless claims using the entrepreneur's collateralizable wealth, there exists a perfect Bayesian equilibrium that supports the JHG allocation: an entrepreneur with a low-risk project obtains the net claims corresponding to her preferred financial position among the contracts with nonnegative pooling profits, while an entrepreneur with a high-risk project manages to completely diversify her risk without pledging any of her wealth in the project.

This outcome can be supported without recontracting on the equilibrium path, with each lender posting in the first round a menu consisting of the trades comprised in the JHG allocation. If the entrepreneur solicits additional offers, then she is believed to have a high-risk project; for instance, she is offered $Q_2^* - Q_1^*$ at price c_2 if she initially accepted (Q_1^*, T_1^*), and she is offered $(0,0)$ if she initially accepted (Q_2^*, T_2^*). No lender, therefore, can profit by deviating, for any offer that would be accepted by an entrepreneur with a low-risk project would also be accepted by an entrepreneur with a high-risk project in anticipation of future rounds of recontracting. Notice that it is essential for this reasoning that the entrepreneur can only select a single contract at each round, that previously signed contracts be observable, and that there always be further opportunities of recontracting. It is fair to ask whether the first two assumptions are consistent with the intuitive notion of a nonexclusive market; in particular, a prediction of the model is that each entrepreneur trades with a single lender.

1.5.2 A Discriminatory Ascending Auction

An alternative approach consists in sticking more closely to competitive-screening games, while allowing punishments to be carried out by the sellers themselves. This requires, of course, that deviations be observable by the nondeviating sellers, in the spirit of the reactive-equilibrium literature cited in footnote 14. In this respect, the recursive structure of the JHG allocation suggests that it be implemented sequentially, layer by layer, from the bottom up. To validate this intuition, AMS (2021) propose to model the strategic interactions between sellers as a discriminatory ascending auction.

In their model, the auctioneer quotes price sequentially, in increasing order, and according to a discrete price grid with a minimum tick size. Each time he quotes a new price, each seller publicly announces the maximum quantity he stands ready to trade with the buyer at this price; in other terms, he offers a limit order at the current price. Once this auctioning phase is completed, the buyer selects which quantities to purchase from which sellers at each price, according to her type. We denote by G^{DA} the corresponding extensive-form game. The solution concept for G^{DA} is pure-strategy subgame-perfect Nash equilibrium.

It should be noted that G^{DA} can be interpreted as a sequential version of the convex-tariff game G^{CT}. Indeed, as it is optimal for the buyer to take up the best price offers first, she in the end faces a collection of convex tariffs that aggregate into a convex market tariff T. From her perspective, the fact that T was built up sequentially is irrelevant.

For the sellers, by contrast, the fact that bids are made sequentially and publicly during the auctioning phase is crucial, as it allows them to react, at any price, to a deviation at a lower price; indeed, the key advantage of a sequential auction lies in its transparency, a point emphasized in other contexts by Milgrom (2000) and Ausubel (2004). Importantly, such reactions – which can take place almost immediately when the tick size is small – can only take the form of quantity increases or decreases at future prices, while the quantities supplied at lower prices cannot be withdrawn nor augmented. This commitment assumption makes G^{DA} quite different from the Walrasian *tâtonnement* process.

From our implementation perspective, two questions immediately arise. First, does G^{DA} admit an equilibrium? Second, how do equilibrium allocations relate to the JHG allocation? The second question is especially pressing, because the dynamic nature of G^{DA} may perhaps allow us to sustain equilibria with collusive outcomes.

The first result established by AMS (2021) is that G^{DA} admits a very simple Markov perfect equilibrium. The relevant state variables are the current price p and the aggregate quantity Q^- supplied at prices lower than p. Assuming for simplicity that every type i has quasilinear preferences, with demand function D_i, the residual demand of type i in state (p, Q^-) is $\max\{D_i(p) - Q^-, 0\}$; observe that maximizing aggregate expected profits in any state (p, Q^-) asks for serving the residual demand of type i such that $\overline{c}_i < p \leq \overline{c}_{i+1}$, which we shall call the *profitable residual demand* in state (p, Q^-). The following result then holds (AMS, 2021, theorem 1.3):

Theorem 1.10 *Suppose there are I buyer types with strictly convex quasilinear preferences, and that $\overline{c}_i$ is strictly increasing in i. Then there exists a Markov perfect equilibrium of G^{DA} in which, in any state (p, Q^-):*

(i) if $p \leq \overline{c}_1$, then each seller supplies a zero quantity;
(ii) if $\overline{c}_1 < p \leq \overline{c}_I$, then each seller supplies a share $1/K$ of the profitable residual demand;
(iii) if $p > \overline{c}_I$, then each seller supplies an infinite quantity.

Moreover, the resulting aggregate equilibrium allocation converges to the JHG allocation as the tick size goes to zero.

The mechanics of the equilibrium are very simple. First, at any price $p \leq \overline{c}_I$, no unilateral increase in supply is profitable if the profitable types at price p, that is, all types j such that $p > \overline{c}_j$, rationally choose to ignore this deviation and carry on trading the same quantity with each seller; indeed, the deviation can then only lead to losses with unprofitable types at price p and reduce their residual demand at higher prices. Second, at any price $p \leq \overline{c}_I$, no unilateral decrease in supply is profitable, because the corresponding increase in the profitable residual demand at the next price will be shared with the other sellers in the continuation equilibrium. As a result, although each seller is indispensable to serve a strictly positive profitable residual demand, no seller has an incentive to wait for a higher price to be quoted. This stands in stark contrast to the convex-tariff game G^{CT}, in which a seller indispensable at price p can always secretly deviate by bidding a lower quantity at price p and a higher quantity at a slightly higher price.

Given a tick size Δ, the following equilibrium outcome obtains. As soon as the price reaches $\overline{c}_1 + \Delta$, the sellers serve the demand $D_1(\overline{c}_1 + \Delta)$ of type 1; this quantity will also be purchased by types $i > 1$. Then, as soon as the price reaches $\overline{c}_2 + \Delta$, the sellers serve the residual demand $\max\{D_2(\overline{c}_2 + \Delta) - D_1(\overline{c}_1 + \Delta), 0\}$ of type 2; this quantity will also be purchased by types $i > 2$ – and so on, until the price reaches $\overline{c}_I + \Delta$, at which point the sellers flood the market. By construction, the resulting aggregate equilibrium allocation converges to the JHG allocation as Δ goes to zero.

The second result established by AMS (2021) is that every sequence of equilibria of G^{DA} satisfies this convergence property, modulo an intuitive refinement that can be described as follows. In any play of the game, every type i accepts all offers up to some price p_i. However, the sellers' aggregate supply at price p_i may well exceed type i's residual demand at this price; she can then break ties in many different ways, and her choice typically matters to the sellers. An equilibrium of G^{DA} is *robust to irrelevant offers* if every type i's trades at price p_i do not depend on offers made at prices $p > p_i$. Intuitively, the buyer never punishes a seller for deviating at a price at which she is not willing to trade.[21] The following result then holds (AMS, 2021, theorem 1.4):

Theorem 1.11 *In any sequence of equilibria robust to irrelevant offers of G^{DA} associated with a sequence of tick sizes going to zero, the aggregate equilibrium allocations converge to the JHG allocation, and the equilibrium market tariffs converge to the JHG tariff.*

Leaving technical details aside, Theorem 1.11 results from a simple Bertrand undercutting argument. To see this, suppose, by way of contradiction, that, given the limit market tariff, strictly positive expected profits can be earned at some price p. Because the highest price at which trade takes place can be shown to be bounded along any sequence of equilibria when the tick size Δ goes to zero, we can focus on the highest such p. Continuation profits at higher

[21] The tie-breaking rules used in the proof of Theorem 1.10 are consistent with this refinement.

prices must be zero: indeed, the robustness refinement ensures that, if they were strictly negative, then, for Δ small enough, some seller could profitably withdraw all his offers at such prices without affecting his expected profits up to price p. Now, the convergence of aggregate supply functions as Δ goes to zero implies that, for Δ small enough, aggregate supply in a left-neighborhood of p becomes negligible. Hence each seller can, almost without losing priority, undercut his competitors at a price arbitrarily close to p, and supply nothing afterwards; by doing so, he can appropriate almost all expected profits at price p, and the robustness refinement again ensures that his expected profits at lower prices remain the same. But then this deviation would be profitable for at least one seller, a contradiction. Overall, this argument shows that, given the limit tariff, strictly positive expected profits cannot be earned at any price p; given budget-balance, this exhaustion of gains from trade characterizes the JHG tariff, from which Theorem 1.11 follows.

Taken together, Theorems 1.10 and 1.11 provide an implementation of the JHG allocation as the essentially unique equilibrium outcome of competition when each seller can quickly react to his competitors' offers; an attractive feature of this implementation is that, in the spirit of Bertrand competition, it only requires that there be two competing sellers. From a market-design perspective, these positive results invite us to reconsider the role of continuous bidding for financial and insurance markets, and offer a useful complement to studies that advocate a transformation of continuous markets into batch auctions, so as to avoid possible inefficiencies linked to high-frequency trading (Budish et al., 2015).

1.5.3 Information Disclosure

A common feature of the recontracting game of Beaudry and Poitevin (1995) and of the ascending discriminatory auction of AMS (2021) is that the release of information to sellers about previously signed contracts or previously made offers is exogenous. By contrast, following the seminal contribution of Jaynes (1978), several authors have studied what happens when agents can voluntarily disclose information about the contracts they are engaged in, so that the information available to each seller is endogenously determined in equilibrium. Although the buyer can still in principle subscribe to multiple contracts issued by different sellers, each seller can then enforce exclusivity clauses contingent on the information disclosed by his competitors.[22]

Jaynes (1978) considers the following timing. First, each seller offers a menu of contracts, possibly specifying exclusivity clauses; besides, he commits to disclose to a subset of his competitors the contract selected by the buyer from his own menu. Next, the buyer selects a contract from each seller's menu,

[22] In exclusive insurance markets, information sharing enables the construction of joint databases collecting information on each loss so as to ensure that the same loss is not indemnified twice.

information is disclosed, and exclusivity clauses are enforced, which determines the contracts that are eventually executed. The JHG allocation turns out to be the only candidate-equilibrium allocation. In the two-type case, Jaynes' (1978) proposed equilibrium can be described as follows. First, two sellers offer a limit order at price $\overline{c}_1$ with maximum quantity Q_1^*; these sellers share their information and enforce exclusivity clauses, which ensures that they do not make losses by overselling to type 2. Second, two sellers offer a limit order at price c_2 with maximum quantity $Q_2^* - Q_1^*$; these sellers do not share their information.

As pointed out by Hellwig (1988), however, this candidate equilibrium is not robust to a cream-skimming deviation, whereby one of the sellers supposed to offer trades at price $\overline{c}_1$ secretly deviates by offering a contract at a price slightly less than $\overline{c}_1$ that, per se, attracts type 1, but would attract type 2 only in combination with contracts issued by the nondeviating sellers at price $\overline{c}_1$. Thanks to the information disclosed by the nondeviating sellers, the deviating seller is still able to enforce exclusivity on this contract; as a result, he is assured to only attract type 1, and the deviation is profitable. Intuitively, the idea is that sellers by themselves have no basis for treating deviating and nondeviating firms asymmetrically in their disclosure decisions.

In that respect, it should be noted that the above deviation is effective only if the nondeviating sellers are not aware of it. Otherwise, they could punish the deviating seller by concealing from him the contracts selected by the buyer from their menus. In that case, a seller attempting to cream-skim type 1 would no longer be able to enforce exclusivity; as a result, his contract would also become attractive for type 2, along with contracts issued by nondeviating sellers at price $\overline{c}_1$ and, possibly, c_2. Hence, cream-skimming is impossible if the sellers' offers are public. This intuition is formalized by Hellwig (1988), who studies a multi-stage extensive-form game in which each seller can make his disclosure decisions contingent on his competitors' contract offers.

Jaynes (2011) and Kosenko et al. (2023) have more recently argued that information sharing may allow support of the JHG allocation in equilibrium even if sellers cannot change their disclosure decisions in reaction to the offers of their competitors. The idea is that they can instead rely on information revealed by the buyer. In equilibrium, the firms' disclosure strategies induce the buyer to truthfully reveal her information to them, which in turn enables them to treat deviating and nondeviating firms asymmetrically.

1.6 CONCLUDING REMARKS: EMPIRICAL PERSPECTIVES

To conclude, we briefly examine the implications of the theoretical results surveyed in this chapter for empirical work. The discussion will focus on insurance markets, prominent examples of which – life-insurance, annuity, long-term-care, and, to some extent, health-insurance markets – are nonexclusive.

1.6.1 The Positive-Correlation Property

A standard way to test for the presence of adverse selection on insurance markets is to exploit the positive-correlation property, which states that, under adverse selection, the aggregate coverage purchased by a consumer and her riskiness should be positively correlated conditionally on observables (Chiappori and Salanié, 2000). This property is typically satisfied when a consumer's preferences over aggregate coverage–premia pairs (Q,T) only depend on her riskiness; indeed, it is then equivalent to the single-crossing condition, which precisely expresses the fact that riskier consumers are more eager to purchase more coverage. In our notation, this is the case if the riskiness c_i and the willingness-to-pay $\tau_i(Q,T)$ are both increasing in the consumer's type i, so that the demand Q_i for coverage is increasing in c_i.[23] Chiappori and Salanié (2000, 2003) have developed several econometric methods to test this prediction.

Under single crossing, the positive-correlation property is a characteristic of consumer demand; as such, it is independent of whether competition on the market is exclusive or nonexclusive.[24] Yet the empiricist should care about the difference. Indeed, under exclusivity, it does not matter whether his data originate from firms or from consumers, as each consumer's aggregate coverage is provided by a single contract issued by a single firm. This explains the usual reliance on within-firm data, which are easier to obtain. However, under nonexclusivity, such data can be misleading, as low-coverage contracts may disproportionately attract high-risk consumers in combination with other contracts.[25] Thus, the positive-correlation property may still hold at the consumer level, taking into account all sources of coverage; but the contracts sold by a firm may feature a negative correlation between the riskiness of its customers and the coverage it sells to them.

The validity of the positive-correlation property has been at the center stage of empirical studies of nonexclusive insurance markets (Cawley and Philipson, 1999; Finkelstein and Poterba, 2004; Finkelstein and McGarry, 2006). However, because these studies typically use as a benchmark the exclusive-competition model, the above distinction between demand- and supply-side approaches is often overlooked. Rejecting adverse selection on these markets on the basis of the failure of the positive-correlation property is a decision that

[23] This is the case, for instance, if consumer preferences have an expected-utility representation and face a binary loss (Rothschild and Stiglitz, 1976), as well as for many other specifications of consumer preferences and more than two loss levels (AMS, 2021, online appendix C).

[24] In a more general setting, Chiappori et al. (2006) show that the positive-correlation property can alternatively be derived from a simple inequality on equilibrium profits, even if the single-crossing property is not satisfied.

[25] This is actually a prediction of the regulated game G^{CSR} under free entry (AMS, 2022, theorem 1.3): in equilibrium, basic contracts, traded by both low- and high-risk consumers, offer more coverage than complementary contracts, traded by high-risk consumers only. Thus, with data originating from a single firm, we could well observe a negative correlation between risk and coverage.

should, therefore, be taken with some care: in principle, we would need to collect comprehensive data at the consumer level about all sources of coverage. As pointed out by Salanié (2017), this is likely to be a demanding, though worthwhile, task.

1.6.2 Exploiting Price and Cost Data

The analysis of entry-proof tariffs in Section 1.4 leads to a very sharp prediction for the competitive outcomes of nonexclusive insurance markets: each marginal unit of coverage available along the market tariff should be priced at the expected cost of serving the consumer types who choose to purchase it. This suggests an alternative empirical strategy exploiting price and cost data to compare the price of each layer of insurance to its average cost, as measured by the empirical loss frequency of the consumers who trade this layer.

To illustrate this approach, suppose that the loss is binary and that we have data on observationally equivalent consumers $n = 1,\dots,N$, providing information about individual aggregate coverage–premia pairs (Q^n, T^n) and loss realizations $L^n \in \{0,1\}$. Given this data, a natural two-step empirical procedure may run as follows.

The first step would be to construct an estimate of the market tariff T or, more precisely, of the marginal price schedule T'.[26] Although data on firms' offers are typically not available, we could, to this end, use the data on individual aggregate coverage and premia, assuming that each consumer strives to minimize the price she pays for her aggregate coverage. For instance, we could perform a nonparametric regression

$$T^n = T(Q^n) + \varepsilon^n,$$

with one-sided error terms ε^n capturing the idea that consumers may fail to combine the firms' offers optimally.

The second step would be to test whether the estimator $\hat{T}'$ of T' satisfies the property that each marginal quantity is priced at the expected cost of serving the consumers who purchase it. This would involve comparing, for every aggregate coverage level Q, the estimated marginal price $\hat{T}'(Q)$ with the empirical loss frequency

$$\hat{c}(Q) \equiv \frac{\sum_n 1_{\{Q^n \geq Q, L^n = 1\}}}{\sum_n 1_{\{Q^n \geq Q\}}}$$

of the consumers whose aggregate coverage is at least Q.

Estimates of prices and costs play a crucial role in this procedure. This contrasts with tests of the positive-correlation property, which only rely on aggregate coverage amounts and loss realizations. The procedure is thus closer to that proposed by Einav et al. (2010) in a setting where consumers have a zero–one demand for coverage: evidence of adverse selection is obtained if

26 This is in line with the classical problem of estimating a firm's production frontier.

the average cost of serving the consumers choosing to buy an additional layer of insurance is affected by the price of that layer. Our analysis suggests that the upper-tail conditional expectation function is the generalization of the firms' cost function in Einav et al. (2010) to richer environments where firms offer nonexclusive insurance contracts and consumers can choose different levels of coverage. An attractive feature of this approach is that it is fully nonparametric: there is no need to make assumptions about consumers' underlying utility functions nor about the distribution of their private information.

APPENDIX

Proof of Theorem 1.6. The proof consists of three steps.

Step 1. For each i in the support of the distribution of types, let $Q_i^{-k}(0,0)$ be a solution to the maximization problem that defines $z_i^{-k}(0,0)$. Then

$$\begin{aligned} z_i^{-k}(0,0) &= u_i(Q_i^{-k}(0,0), T^{-k}(Q_i^{-k}(0,0))) \\ &\leq u_i(Q_i^{-k}(0,0), T(Q_i^{-k}(0,0))) \leq U_i, \end{aligned} \tag{A1.1}$$

where the first inequality follows from $T \leq T^{-k}$, and the second inequality follows from the fact that U_i is type i's equilibrium utility. Now, if $U_i = z_i^{-k}(0,0)$ for some type i and some seller k, then all the inequalities in (A1.1) are in fact equalities. This has two fundamental consequences. First, we have

$$u_i(Q_i^{-k}(0,0), T^{-k}(Q_i^{-k}(0,0))) = u_i(Q_i^{-k}(0,0), T(Q_i^{-k}(0,0))),$$

which implies

$$T^{-k}(Q_i^{-k}(0,0)) = T(Q_i^{-k}(0,0))$$

and, hence, by P2,

$$Q_i^{-k}(0,0) = 0. \tag{A1.2}$$

Second, we have

$$U_i = u_i(Q_i^{-k}(0,0), T^{-k}(Q_i^{-k}(0,0)))$$

and, hence, by (A1.2),

$$U_i = u_i(0,0). \tag{A1.3}$$

Because $U_i \geq z_i^{-l}(0,0) \geq u_i(0,0)$ for all $l \neq k$, the upshot from this reasoning is that, if $U_i = z_i^{-k}(0,0)$ for some type i and some seller k, then, for this type i, $U_i = z_i^{-k}(0,0)$ for any seller k, and hence (A1.2) must hold for all k. In other terms, the indispensability property P2 implies that, if, for some type, the individual-rationality constraint binds for some seller, then it must bind for all sellers.

Step 2. By P1 and Step 1, there exists some i such that $U_i = z_i^{-k}(0,0)$ for all k. Let (q_i^k, t_i^k) be the contract traded by such a type i with seller k in equilibrium, and let $Q_i^{-k} = \sum_{l \neq k} q_i^l$ be the quantity purchased by type i from the sellers other than k, so that

$$U_i = u_i(q_i^k + Q_i^{-k}, t_i^k + T^{-k}(Q_i^{-k})). \tag{A1.4}$$

We claim that $Q_i^{-k} = 0$. Indeed, suppose, by way of contradiction, that $Q_i^{-k} > 0$. Because type i could abstain from trading with the sellers other than k, it must be that

$$u_i(q_i^k + Q_i^{-k}, t_i^k + T^{-k}(Q_i^{-k})) \geq u_i(q_i^k, t_i^k). \tag{A1.5}$$

Similarly, consider the maximization problem that defines $z_i^{-k}(0,0)$, and whose unique solution, by (A1.2), is $Q_i^{-k}(0,0) = 0$. As type i could instead purchase Q_i^{-k} from the sellers other than k, it must be that

$$u_i(0,0) > u_i(Q_i^{-k}, T^{-k}(Q_i^{-k})). \tag{A1.6}$$

We know from (A1.3) and (A1.4) that the left-hand sides of (A1.5) and (A1.6) are both equal to U_i. Hence

$$u_i(0,0) \geq u_i(q_i^k, t_i^k). \tag{A1.7}$$

Representing by $T = \phi(Q)$ the equilibrium indifference curve of type i, (A1.6) and (A1.7) amount to

$$T^{-k}(Q_i^{-k}) > \phi(Q_i^{-k}) \tag{A1.8}$$

and

$$t_i^k \geq \phi(q_i^k). \tag{A1.9}$$

Because ϕ is concave and $\phi(0) = 0$, ϕ is subadditive. Thus, by (A1.8) and (A1.9),

$$t_i^k + T^{-k}(Q_i^{-k}) > \phi(q_i^k + Q_i^{-k}),$$

which amounts to

$$u_i(0,0) > u_i(q_i^k + Q_i^{-k}, t_i^k + T^{-k}(Q_i^{-k})),$$

in contradiction to (A1.3) and (A1.4). Hence $Q_i^{-k} = 0$, as claimed. Because this is true for all k, we obtain that

$$\sum_k q_i^k = \frac{1}{K-1} \sum_k Q_i^{-k} = 0,$$

and thus that $q_i^k = 0$ for all k.

Step 3. We now verify that there exists some type i_1 such that $Q_i \equiv \sum_k q_i^k$ vanishes if and only if $i \leq i_1$, which concludes the proof. By P1 and Steps 1 and 2, we know that there exists at least one type i for which $Q_i = 0$. This implies in particular that

$$\text{For each } Q > 0,\ u_i(0,0) \geq u_i(Q, T(Q)),$$

and, hence, by strict single crossing, that

$$\text{For all } j < i \text{ and } Q > 0,\ u_j(0,0) > u_j(Q, T(Q)),$$

so that $Q_j = 0$ for all $j < i$. Thus, the set of types who are excluded from trade is an interval $\mathcal{I}^0$ at the bottom of the type distribution. We just need to check that $\mathcal{I}^0$, if it is not reduced to a single type, contains its least upper bound i_1. (This is obvious if the distribution of types is discrete.) By assumption, the mapping $i \mapsto u_i(0,0)$ is continuous, and so is the mapping $i \mapsto U_i$ by Berge's maximum theorem. Because $U_j = u_j(0,0)$ for all $j \in \mathcal{I}_0$, it follows that $U_{i_1} = u_{i_1}(0,0)$ as well, and hence that $U_{i_1} = z_{i_1}^{-k}(0,0)$ for all k. Proceeding as in Step 2 then shows that $Q_{i_1} = 0$, as desired. Hence the result. ■

REFERENCES

Akerlof, G. A. (1970). "The market for 'lemons': Quality uncertainty and the market mechanism," *Quarterly Journal of Economics*, 84(3), 488–500.

Allen, F. (1985). "Repeated principal–agent relationships with lending and borrowing," *Economics Letters*, 17(1–2), 27–31.

Arnott, R. J., and J. E. Stiglitz (1991). "Equilibrium in competitive insurance markets with moral hazard." NBER Working Paper No. 3588.

Attar, A., and A. Chassagnon (2009). "On moral hazard and nonexclusive contracts," *Journal of Mathematical Economics*, 45(9–10), 511–525.

Attar, A., V. Farinha Luz, T. Mariotti, and F. Salanié (2021). "Mixed-strategy equilibria in limit-order markets." Mimeo, Toulouse School of Economics.

Attar, A., T. Mariotti, and F. Salanié (2011). "Nonexclusive competition in the market for lemons," *Econometrica*, 79(6), 1869–1918.

Attar, A., T. Mariotti, and F. Salanié (2014). "Nonexclusive competition under adverse selection," *Theoretical Economics*, 9(1), 1–40.

Attar, A., T. Mariotti, and F. Salanié (2018). "Concurrence non exclusive et sélection adverse," *Revue Economique*, 69(6), 1009–1023.

Attar, A., T. Mariotti, and F. Salanié (2019). "On competitive nonlinear pricing," *Theoretical Economics*, 14(1), 297–343.

Attar, A., T. Mariotti, and F. Salanié (2020). "The social costs of side trading," *Economic Journal*, 130(630), 1608–1622.

Attar, A., T. Mariotti, and F. Salanié (2021). "Entry-proofness and discriminatory pricing under adverse selection," *American Economic Review*, 111(8), 2623–2659.

Attar, A., T. Mariotti, and F. Salanié (2022). "Regulating insurance markets: Multiple contracting and adverse selection," *International Economic Review*, 63(3), 981–1020.

Ausubel, L. M. (2004). "An efficient ascending-bid auction for multiple objects," *American Economic Review*, 94(5), 1452–1475.

Back, K., and S. Baruch (2013). "Strategic liquidity provision in limit order markets," *Econometrica*, 81(1), 363–392.

Baruch, S., and L. R. Glosten (2019). "Tail expectation and imperfect competition in limit order book markets," *Journal of Economic Theory*, 183, 661–697.

Beaudry, P., and M. Poitevin (1995). "Competitive screening in financial markets when borrowers can recontract," *Review of Economic Studies*, 62(3), 401–423.

Biais, B., and T. Mariotti (2005). "Strategic liquidity supply and security design," *Review of Economic Studies*, 72(3), 615–649.

Biais, B., D. Martimort, and J.-C. Rochet (2000). "Competing mechanisms in a common value environment," *Econometrica*, 68(4), 799–837.

Biais, B., D. Martimort, and J.-C. Rochet (2013). "Corrigendum to 'Competing mechanisms in a common value environment'," *Econometrica*, 81(1), 393–406.

Bisin, A., and P. Gottardi (2006). "Efficient competitive equilibria with adverse selection," *Journal of Political Economy*, 114(3), 485–516.

Bisin, A., and D. Guaitoli (2004). "Moral hazard and nonexclusive contracts," *RAND Journal of Economics*, 35(2), 306–328.

Budish, E., P. Cramton, and J. Shim (2015). "The high-frequency trading arms race: Frequent batch auctions as a market design response," *Quarterly Journal of Economics*, 130(4), 1547–1621.

Carmona, G., and J. Fajardo (2009). "Existence of equilibrium in common agency games with adverse selection," *Games and Economic Behavior*, 66(2), 749–760.

Cawley, J., and T. Philipson (1999). "An empirical examination of information barriers to trade in insurance," *American Economic Review*, 89(4), 827–846.

Chiappori, P.-A., B. Jullien, B. Salanié, and F. Salanié (2006). "Asymmetric information in insurance: Some testable implications," *RAND Journal of Economics*, 37(4), 783–798.

Chiappori, P.-A., and B. Salanié (2000). "Testing for asymmetric information in insurance markets," *Journal of Political Economy*, 108(1), 56–78.

Chiappori, P.-A., and B. Salanié (2003). "Testing contract theory: A survey of some recent work." In M. Dewatripont, L. P. Hansen, and S. J. Turnovsky (eds.), *Advances in Economics and Econometrics: Theory and Applications, Eighth World Congress*, vol. 1. Cambridge: Cambridge University Press, pp. 115–149.

Cole, H. L., and N. R. Kocherlakota (2001). "Efficient allocations with hidden income and hidden storage," *Review of Economic Studies*, 68(3), 523–542.

Crocker, K. J., and A. Snow (1985). "The efficiency of competitive equilibria in insurance markets with asymmetric information," *Journal of Public Economics*, 26(2), 207–219.

Dasgupta, P., and E. Maskin (1986). "The existence of equilibrium in discontinuous economic games, II: Applications," *Review of Economic Studies*, 53(1), 27–41.

DeMarzo, P., and D. Duffie (1999). "A liquidity-based model of security design," *Econometrica*, 67(1), 65–99.

Diamond, D. W., and P. H. Dybvig (1983). "Bank runs, deposit insurance, and liquidity," *Journal of Political Economy*, 91(3), 401–419.

Einav, L., A. Finkelstein, and M. R. Cullen (2010). "Estimating welfare in insurance markets using variation in prices," *Quarterly Journal of Economics*, 125(2), 877–921.

Engers, M., and L. Fernandez (1987). "Market equilibrium with hidden knowledge and self-selection," *Econometrica*, 55(2), 425–439.

Farhi, E., M. Golosov, and A. Tsyvinski (2009). "A theory of liquidity and regulation of financial intermediation," *Review of Economic Studies*, 76(3), 973–992.

Farinha Luz, V. (2017). "Characterization and uniqueness of equilibrium in competitive insurance," *Theoretical Economics*, 12(3), 1349–1391.

Finkelstein, A., and K. McGarry (2006). "Multiple dimensions of private information: Evidence from the long-term care insurance market," *American Economic Review*, 96(4), 938–958.

Finkelstein, A., and J. Poterba (2004). "Adverse selection in insurance markets: Policyholder evidence from the U.K. annuity market," *Journal of Political Economy*, 112(1), 183–208.

Glosten, L. R. (1989). "Insider trading, liquidity, and the role of the monopolist specialist," *Journal of Business*, 62(2), 211–235.

Glosten, L. R. (1994). "Is the electronic open limit order book inevitable?," *Journal of Finance*, 49(4), 1127–1161.

Golosov, M., and A. Tsyvinski (2007). "Optimal taxation with endogenous insurance markets," *Quarterly Journal of Economics*, 122(2), 487–534.

Hammond, P. J. (1979). "Straightforward individual incentive compatibility in large economies," *Review of Economic Studies*, 46(2), 263–282.

Hammond, P. J. (1987). "Markets as constraints: Multilateral incentive compatibility in continuum economies," *Review of Economic Studies*, 54(3), 399–412.

Harris, M., and R. M. Townsend (1981). "Resource allocation under asymmetric information," *Econometrica*, 49(1), 33–64.

Hellwig, M. F. (1983). "On moral hazard and non-price equilibria in competitive insurance markets." Discussion Paper No. 109, Sonderforschungsbereich 21, Universität Bonn.

Hellwig, M. F. (1988). "A note on the specification of interfirm communication in insurance markets with adverse selection," *Journal of Economic Theory*, 46(1), 154–163.

Hendren, N. (2013). "Private information and insurance rejections," *Econometrica*, 81(5), 1713–1762.

Hosseini, R. (2015). "Adverse selection in the annuity market and the role for social security," *Journal of Political Economy*, 123(4), 941–984.

Jacklin, C. J. (1987). "Demand deposits, trading restrictions, and risk sharing." In E. C. Prescott and N. Wallace (eds.), *Contractual Arrangements for Intertemporal Trade*. Minneapolis, MN: University of Minnesota Press, pp. 26–47.

Jaynes, G. D. (1978). "Equilibria in monopolistically competitive insurance markets," *Journal of Economic Theory*, 19(2), 394–422.

Jaynes, G. D. (2011). "Equilibrium and strategic communication in the adverse selection insurance model." Economics Department Working Paper No. 91, Yale University.

Kahn, C. M., and D. Mookherjee (1998). "Competition and incentives with nonexclusive contracts," *RAND Journal of Economics*, 29(3), 443–465.

Kehoe, T. J., D. K. Levine, and E. C. Prescott (2002). "Lotteries, sunspots, and incentive constraints," *Journal of Economic Theory*, 107(1), 39–69.

Kosenko, A., J. Stiglitz, and J. Yun (2023). "Bilateral information disclosure in adverse selection markets with nonexclusive competition," *Journal of Economic Behavior & Organization*, 205(Jan), 144–168.

Leland, H. E., and D. H. Pyle (1977). "Informational asymmetries, financial structure, and financial intermediation," *Journal of Finance*, 32(2), 371–387.

Mailath, G., and G. Nöldeke (2008). "Does competitive pricing cause market breakdown under extreme adverse selection?," *Journal of Economic Theory*, 140(1), 97–125.

Malinvaud, E. (1972). "The allocation of individual risks in large markets," *Journal of Economic Theory*, 4(2), 312–328.

Martimort, D. (2006). "Multi-contracting mechanism design." In R. Blundell, W. K. Newey, and T. Persson (eds.), *Advances in Economics and Econometrics: Theory and Applications, Ninth World Congress*, vol. 1. Cambridge: Cambridge University Press, pp. 57–101.

Martimort, D., and L. Stole (2002). "The revelation and delegation principles in common agency games," *Econometrica*, 70(4), 1659–1673.

Milgrom, P. (2000). "Putting auction theory to work: The simultaneous ascending auction," *Journal of Political Economy*, 108(2), 245–272.

Milgrom, P., and C. Shannon (1994). "Monotone comparative statics," *Econometrica*, 62(1), 157–180.

Mimra, W., and A. Wambach (2014). "New developments in the theory of adverse selection in competitive insurance," *Geneva Risk and Insurance Review*, 39(2), 136–152.

Mimra, W., and A. Wambach (2019). "Contract withdrawals and equilibrium in competitive markets with adverse selection," *Economic Theory*, 67(4), 875–907.

Mirrlees, J. A. (1971). "An exploration in the theory of optimum income taxation," *Review of Economic Studies*, 38(2), 175–208.

Miyazaki, H. (1977). "The rat race and internal labor markets," *Bell Journal of Economics*, 8(2), 394–418.

Myers, S. C., and N. S. Majluf (1984). "Corporate financing and investment decisions when firms have information that investors do not have," *Journal of Financial Economics*, 13(2), 187–221.

Myerson, R. B. (1983). "Mechanism design by an informed principal," *Econometrica*, 51(6), 1767–1797.

Netzer, N., and F. Scheuer (2014). "A game theoretic foundation of competitive equilibria with adverse selection," *International Economic Review*, 55(2), 399–422.

Page, F. H. Jr., and P. K. Monteiro (2003). "Three principles of competitive nonlinear pricing," *Journal of Mathematical Economics*, 39(1–2), 63–109.

Pauly, M. V. (1974). "Overinsurance and public provision of insurance: The roles of moral hazard and adverse selection," *Quarterly Journal of Economics*, 88(1), 44–62.

Peters, M. (2001). "Common agency and the revelation principle," *Econometrica*, 69(5), 1349–1372.

Philippon, T., and V. Skreta (2012). "Optimal interventions in markets with adverse selection," *American Economic Review*, 102(1), 1–28.

Prescott, E. C., and R. M. Townsend (1984). "Pareto optima and competitive equilibria with adverse selection and moral hazard," *Econometrica*, 52(1), 21–45.

Riley, J. G. (1979). "Informational equilibrium," *Econometrica*, 47(2), 331–359.

Riley, J. G. (2001). "Silver signals: Twenty-five years of screening and signaling," *Journal of Economic Literature*, 39(2), 432–478.

Rockafellar, R. T. (1970). *Convex Analysis*. Princeton, NJ: Princeton University Press.

Rosenthal, R. W., and A. Weiss (1984). "Mixed-strategy equilibrium in a market with asymmetric information," *Review of Economic Studies*, 51(2), 333–342.

Rothschild, C. (2015). "Nonexclusivity, linear pricing, and annuity market screening," *Journal of Risk and Insurance*, 82(1), 1–32.

Rothschild, M., and J. E. Stiglitz (1976). "Equilibrium in competitive insurance markets: An essay on the economics of imperfect information," *Quarterly Journal of Economics*, 90(4), 629–649.

Rustichini, A., and P. Siconolfi (2008). "General equilibrium in economies with adverse selection," *Economic Theory*, 37(1), 1–29.

Salanié, B. (2017). "Equilibrium in insurance markets: An empiricist's view," *Geneva Risk and Insurance Review*, 42(1), 1–14.

Sheshinski, E. (2008). *The Economic Theory of Annuities*. Princeton, NJ: Princeton University Press.

Spence, M. (1973). "Job market signaling," *Quarterly Journal of Economics*, 87(3), 355–374.

Spence, M. (1978). "Product differentiation and performance in insurance markets," *Journal of Public Economics*, 10(3), 427–447.

Tirole, J. (2012). "Overcoming adverse selection: How public intervention can restore market functioning," *American Economic Review*, 102(1), 29–59.

Wilson, C. (1977). "A model of insurance markets with incomplete information," *Journal of Economic Theory*, 16(2), 167–207.

Wilson, R. B. (1989). "Game-theoretic analyses of trading processes." In T. F. Bewley (ed.), *Advances in Economic Theory, Fifth World Congress*. Cambridge: Cambridge University Press, pp. 33–70.

Wilson, R. B. (1993). *Nonlinear Pricing*. Oxford: Oxford University Press.

Yamashita, T. (2010). "Mechanism games with multiple principals and three or more agents," *Econometrica*, 78(2), 791–801.

CHAPTER 2

Information in Contests

Juuso Välimäki

In this chapter, I review the recent literature that incorporates private information and incomplete information into contest models. Connections to the substance and techniques of auction theory and assignment models are emphasized throughout. Contests with finite numbers of contestants as well as large contests with non-atomic contestants are discussed.

2.1 INTRODUCTION

A contest is a game where the players, also called contestants, exert costly effort in order to win one or more of the available prizes. In contrast to other allocation mechanisms such as markets or standard auctions, the effort cost is sunk and not conditional on the prize won. Examples of contests range from organized sports competitions and political campaigns with detailed rules for determining the winner to more informal contests ranging from conflicts between countries to competitive recruitment.

While the role of incomplete information has been central to recent developments in auction theory and more generally for the area of mechanism design, much of the literature on contests has focused on the case of complete information. From an economic standpoint, it seems reasonable to assume that the contestants have dispersed private information on their valuations of the prizes and their ability to succeed in the contest. In this chapter, I review the part of the literature that emphasizes the role of private information.

At its simplest, a contest is modeled as a simultaneous move game where the players, called contestants, choose how much privately costly effort to exert. The vector of effort choices results in a possibly probabilistic assignment of prizes to the contestants. A key element in contests is that the winner is not known in advance. In dynamic versions of the game, effort is chosen over time and the winner or winners depend on the profile of dynamic effort paths.

Since the allocation of prizes depends on the realized vector of efforts in the static case, optimal effort decisions must be based on the contestants'

This chapter was prepared for the Econometric Society World Congress 2020 at Bocconi University, Milan. My co-authors Chang-Koo Chi and Pauli Murto have taught me a lot about contests and all-pay auctions and I have benefited from numerous discussions with them on these topics. Any errors are, of course, mine.

expectations on others' effort choices. It is quite likely that contestants with a higher effort cost exert less effort. If these costs are private information, then the (Bayesian) equilibrium analysis of contests with a single prize bears a strong resemblance to the theory of auctions. Higher effort wins the prize with a higher probability, but since the effort cost is sunk, it must be paid even when not winning. In fact, contests are intimately linked to non-standard auctions called all-pay auctions, where all potential buyers pay their bid. More generally, ideas and techniques from mechanism design have proved very useful in the analysis of contests also in the case of contests with multiple prizes.

Prime examples of dynamic contests are wars of attrition where contestants decide over time whether to continue exerting effort or whether to drop out from the contest and patent races where contestants invest in R&D in order to achieve a research breakthrough. It is easy to imagine how private information might play a role in both cases. The cost of remaining in the contest could be private information or the participants in a patent race might have incomplete information on the probability with which patentable innovations are made.

It is not possible to cover all recent developments in contest theory that have a connection to economics of information within the scope of this chapter. My focus on static models with incomplete information should not be interpreted as implying that they are the most relevant for economic theory. The aim is rather to take advantage of the earlier developments in auction theory and assignment models to gain a more detailed understanding of some contest situations. I discuss the role of private information in dynamic races in the last section of the chapter.

2.2 CONTESTS AS GAMES

2.2.1 Players and Actions

Each player i (also called contestant i) in a set of players $\mathcal{N} := \{1,...,N\}$ chooses a strategy called an effort $e_i \in E_i$ with the aim of winning one of the available prizes $k \in \mathcal{K} := \{1,...,K\}$. The prizes are allocated amongst the contestants based on the vector $e = (e_i)_{i \in \mathcal{N}}$ of chosen efforts. In static contests, effort is chosen simultaneously, and in most cases, $E_i = \mathbb{R}_+$.[1] In dynamic contests, one can distinguish between sequential contests where the contestants choose their efforts in a predetermined order and contests, often called races, where each player chooses her effort in multiple periods and the game ends when some contestant succeeds in winning the prize.

[1] A notable exception is the Blotto game introduced by Borel (1921), where two contestants partition a fixed total effort between multiple subcontests.

2.2.2 Outcomes and Payoffs

Contests are characterized by different allocation rules for the prizes, also called contest success functions. The contest success function determines the individual probabilities $p_{ik}(e)$ of contestant i winning prize k as a function of the profile of efforts e.

Contestant i values prize k at v_{ik}. If she chooses effort e_i, she incurs a private cost $c_i(e_i)$. In most of the literature, her payoff is assumed to take the linearly separable (and risk-neutral) form

$$u_i(e) = \sum_k v_{ik} p_{ik}(e) - c_i(e_i). \tag{2.1}$$

2.2.3 Private Information

The parameters of the model may be uncertain and the contestants may have private information on them. In this case, static contests are modeled as Bayesian games where each contestant observes her type $\theta_i \in \Theta_i$ drawn from a commonly known prior distribution $F(\theta)$ on type vectors $\theta = (\theta_1, ..., \theta_N) \in \Theta := \times_i \Theta_i$. A strategy is a rule assigning a possibly mixed effort choice to each type. In dynamic contests, additional private information may arise endogenously during the contest if effort choices are not publicly observable. Behavioral strategies are possibly mixed-effort choices conditional on types and private histories.

2.2.4 Solution Concept

The standard solution concept for static contests with complete information is the Nash equilibrium. The Bayesian Nash equilibrium is used for static contests with incomplete information. The focus in this chapter is on symmetric models and on symmetric equilibria of the contests. In dynamic contests, typical solution concepts are sequential equilibrium and Markov perfect equilibrium, depending on the focus of the model.

2.2.5 Contest Success Function

In his seminal paper on rent-seeking static contests for a single prize, Tullock (1980) introduced the following contest success function:

$$p_i(e) = \frac{(e_i)^r}{\sum_{j \in \mathcal{N}} (e_j)^r}. \tag{2.2}$$

With this specification, contestant i's probability of winning the contest $p_i(e)$ is strictly increasing in e_i when $r > 0$. Different choices of $r \geq 0$ result in qualitatively different allocation rules.[2] If $r = 0$, the allocation is uniform across the players, regardless of their efforts. For $r = 1$, i's winning probability equals her share of the contribution to the total effort.[3] If $r \to \infty$, the (joint) winning probability of contestant(s) exerting the highest effort converges to 1. Contests with this rule are called all-pay contests. For small r and convex effort cost, the payoff functions in (2.1) are concave in own effort, and the game has a pure-strategy Nash equilibrium. For all-pay contests, and more generally contests with a high r, the game does not have pure-strategy equilibria.

All-pay contests can easily be generalized to the case of multiple prizes: the contestant with the kth highest effort gets to select a prize after all the contestants with a higher effort have made their choice. In most cases analyzed thus far in the literature, all contestants have the same ranking for the prizes but the prizes may be vertically differentiated. Unfortunately, the Tullock-type contest success functions with $r < \infty$ do not generalize in a unique way to many prizes.

An alternative formulation, called the rank-order tournament for determining the winners, assumes that individual effort e_i determines a random performance y_i for each contestant. In this case, each y_i is drawn from a probability distribution $F_i(\cdot; e_i)$ parametrized by e_i. The prizes are allocated in the rank order of realized performances, that is:

$$p_i(e) = \Pr\{Y_i > Y_j \text{ for all } j \neq i\}. \tag{2.3}$$

This formulation dates back to Lazear and Rosen (1981) on contests for promotions within a firm.[4] The game admits a pure-strategy equilibrium if the performance measure is sufficiently noisy. If y_i measures e_i too accurately, then the payoffs are well approximated by the payoffs in the all-pay contest and the game admits only equilibria in mixed strategies.

2.2.6 Economics of Contests

When evaluating the performance of a contest, at least two dimensions should be kept in mind. If the contestants value the prizes differently, then ex-post efficiency of the allocation demands that the prizes be won by the contestants with the highest valuations.

A second key consideration involves the effort expenditure in the contest. Tullock (1980) views effort as wasteful means of trying to influence the division of surplus and hence a successful contest is one that induces little wasteful effort. Lazear and Rosen (1981) take the opposite view and consider contests as a means to incentivize workers to exert productive effort. From this point of

[2] More general types of contest success functions have been considered in contests with complete information. They are surveyed in Corchón and Serena (2018).

[3] This is sometimes called a lottery-form success function, since additional effort can be thought as purchasing more lottery tickets in a raffle.

[4] Typical specifications for the measurement include the additive case: $y_i = e_i + \varepsilon_i$ and multiplicative case: $y_i = e_i\varepsilon_i$, where ε is an idiosyncratic random term.

view, a successful contest is one that maximizes equilibrium effort provision. In some cases, such as contests for architectural designs, a good goal may be to maximize the equilibrium effort of the winner of the contest.

The game form of contests is much more restricted than in general mechanism design problems. This means that the possibilities for designing contests are also similarly limited, and the main parameters to be considered are the set of prizes, the contest success function, and the number of contestants. This approach leaves open the question of why contests have been selected as the means of inducing effort.[5] In dynamic contests, the designer may also control the information flow from early stages to later stages.

2.3 STATIC CONTESTS WITH PRIVATE VALUES

Contests are conceptually easy to describe and have general economic appeal, but in the case of complete information, their solution often requires techniques that are quite specific to the details of the model. Any asymmetries between the contestants further complicate the analysis. Often it makes sense to assume that the contestants are aware of their own ability (or their valuation for the prize) but uncertain about their opponents' incentives.

In auction theory, ex-ante symmetric models with independent private values, where any asymmetries are realized at the interim stage, have provided a useful benchmark model, and the same is true for closely related contest models. In this section, I concentrate on the case where the players are uncertain about other contestants' effort costs. As long as the cost type is drawn independently for all contestants from a commonly known distribution on an interval, the tools from mechanism design can be used in the analysis to obtain clear-cut results.

2.3.1 Contest Design with All-Pay Success Function

Weber (1985) observed that the analysis of symmetric contests with all-pay auction rules has strong similarities to the analysis of optimal auctions when the contestants have independent private values for the prize. When discussing optimal prize designs, it is more convenient to use the isomorphic payoff structure where the contestants have private information on a multiplicative parameter on their effort cost but the prize is equally valuable to all contestants.

The analysis is simplified by the assumption that private information is summarized in one-dimensional cost types $\theta_i \in \Theta_i = \Theta = [\underline{\theta}, \overline{\theta}] \in \mathbb{R}_+$ drawn independently from a common distribution $F(\cdot)$ with a well-defined density function $f(\cdot)$. In contrast to all-pay contests with complete information where equilibria are in mixed strategies, this contest with incomplete information has

[5] An interesting approach to this based on delegated monitoring of performance is proposed by Letina et al. (2020).

a pure-strategy Bayesian Nash equilibrium that can be analyzed with the usual envelope arguments.

Moldovanu and Sela (2001) analyze the optimal prize design for all-pay contests with independently distributed privately known multiplicative cost parameters θ_i. The designer's objective is to maximize the total expected equilibrium effort by dividing a total prize sum V into $K < N$ individual prizes $v_1 \geq v_2 \geq \cdots \geq v_K$. The expected payoff to contestant i with cost parameter θ_i at effort profile e is

$$u(\theta_i, e) = \sum_{k=1}^{K} v_k p_{ik}(e) - \theta_i c(e_i). \tag{2.4}$$

In any symmetric equilibrium in strictly decreasing strategies $e(\theta)$, the winners are determined by looking at the order statistics in a sample of N independent draws from F. The contestant with the kth lowest θ_i chooses the kth highest effort in equilibrium and wins the kth prize. Let $\pi_k(\theta_i) = \Pr\{\theta_i \text{ wins prize } k\}$ be the equilibrium probability of winning prize k at type θ_i and let $c(\theta_i) = c(e(\theta_i))$ denote the equilibrium effort cost of type θ_i.

Let $U(\theta_i)$ denote the equilibrium expected payoff to a contestant with cost type θ_i. Since the payoff function has a bounded partial derivative in θ_i in the range where effort cost is below the value of the highest prize, we can use the envelope theorem to get

$$U(\theta_i) = U(\overline{\theta}) - \int_{\theta_i}^{\overline{\theta}} U'(\theta) d\theta = \int_{\theta_i}^{\overline{\theta}} c(\theta) d\theta, \tag{2.5}$$

where $U(\overline{\theta}) = 0$ since with strictly decreasing symmetric strategies, the highest type never wins. Equilibrium expected payoff can also be expressed as in equation (2.4), and combining these two expressions, we have

$$\int_{\theta_i}^{\overline{\theta}} c(\theta) d\theta = \sum_{k=1}^{K} v_k \pi_k(\theta_i) - \theta_i c(\theta_i).$$

Since this equality holds for all θ_i, we get by differentiating w.r.t. θ_i:

$$\theta_i c'(\theta_i) = \sum_{k=1}^{K} v_k \pi_k'(\theta_i).$$

The fundamental theorem of calculus then gives

$$c(e(\theta_i)) = \sum_{k=1}^{K} v_k \int_{\theta_i}^{\overline{\theta}} -\frac{1}{y} \pi_k'(y) dy. \tag{2.6}$$

It is worth observing that since the probability of having the kth lowest type is not monotonic in θ for intermediate k, the probability of winning the kth prize is not monotonic in effort either. Moldovanu and Sela (2001) show that this candidate equilibrium profile is nevertheless strictly decreasing for all allowed

$(v_1, \ldots, v_K)$ and all $F(\cdot)$.[6] To see that the local optimality of the equilibrium strategy $e(\theta)$ as expressed in (2.6) is sufficient for global optimality, observe that the payoff difference relative to the (candidate) equilibrium choice for type θ from choosing $e(\hat{\theta})$ can be written using equation (2.5) as

$$\sum_{k=1}^{K} v_k \pi_k(\theta) - \theta c(\theta) - \left(\sum_{k=1}^{K} v_k \pi_k(\hat{\theta}) - \theta c(\hat{\theta}) \right)$$
$$= \int_{\hat{\theta}}^{\theta} \left(c(\hat{\theta}) - c(y)\right) dy \geq 0,$$

where the last inequality follows since $c(\cdot)$ is decreasing.

Departing from the winner-takes-all prize structure where $v_1 = V$ induces different incentives for contestants with different costs. The contestants with the lowest effort costs may choose a lower effort since the marginal gain from being at the top is smaller. Contestants with higher effort costs, on the other hand, have a better chance of winning a positive prize and may exert more effort. The designer balances these two effects by choosing the competitiveness of the contest through the optimal selection of prizes.

If effort cost is linear, that is, $c(e_i) = e_i$, individual equilibrium effort is also linear in the prize amounts, and as a result, optimal prize structures are extremal points in $\{(v_1, \ldots, v_K) \in \mathbb{R}_+ | v_i \geq v_{i+1} \sum_k v_k = V\}$. Moldovanu and Sela (2001) show that for this case, winner-takes-all contests where $v_1 = V$ are optimal.[7] If effort cost is convex, then it is optimal to award multiple strictly positive prizes for some F.

Equation (2.6) can be used in the analysis of other objective functions as well. Chawla et al. (2019) show that when effort costs are linear, the expected effort of the winning contestant is also maximized in a winner-takes-all contest as long as the private cost parameters are drawn from a distribution with a monotone hazard rate. In contrast to standard auctions where only the winner pays, the expected equilibrium effort of the winning contestant need not be increasing in the number of contestants. Chawla et al. (2019) show that specifying a minimum effort level in addition to the winner-takes-all prize structure yields the optimal contest. Moldovanu and Sela (2006) show that this non-monotonicity in the number of contestants can rationalize multistage elimination contests where the first-stage winners proceed to a second stage final where the prize is allocated.

Moldovanu et al. (2007) consider a total effort-maximizing contest for status based on rank classes. A typical example would be one where students are assigned letter grades based on their performance (effort here). The design question is how many top performers should be given As, how many should

[6] Recall that the v_k are ordered in decreasing order and the probability that θ is amongst the k lowest draws from F is decreasing in θ. By letting $\Delta v_k = (v_k - v_{k+1}) \geq 0$, we can write $\sum_{k=1}^{K} v_k \pi_k(\theta_i) = \sum_{k=1}^{K-1} \Delta_k \Pi_k(\theta_i)$, where $\Pi_k(\theta_i)$ is the probability that θ_i is amongst the k highest-order statistics in $(\theta_1, \ldots, \theta_N)$.

[7] This result also holds for concave $c(\cdot)$.

be given Bs, and so on. Moldovanu et al. (2007) postulate that the payoff to the contestants takes the zero-sum form where each competitor in a class below one's own class adds to the payoff and each competitor in a higher class deducts from the payoff. As long as the contestants' ability (i.e., the inverse of their effort cost parameter) is drawn from a distribution with increasing hazard rate, it is optimal to have perfectly discriminating rank classes, that is, to report individual ranks in the contest. With sufficiently concave distributions, coarse status classes can be optimal.

Liu et al. (2018) show that it may be optimal to use negative prizes to induce high equilibrium expected effort. This is true even when requiring that the contestants' interim participation constraints are satisfied. All contestants split the original budget equally if no contestant exerts effort above an optimally set threshold. If the highest effort exceeds the threshold, then all other contestants make a fixed-size payment in addition to the original prize money to the winner.

Fullerton and McAfee (1999) consider a two-stage design where contestants have statistically independent initial private information about their constant marginal effort costs. An all-pay auction is conducted in the first stage to select K participants for a second-stage research contest with a Tullock-type contest success function where the effort costs are made public. Since the second-period efforts depend on the realized cost profile of the participants, the first-stage all-pay auction is one with interdependent values. Fullerton and McAfee show that a first-stage all-pay contest has a monotonic equilibrium that results in the choice of the K lowest-cost contestants being selected for the second stage. With fixed costs in the effort cost function in the second period, the optimal K is often 2.

The two-stage designs in Fullerton and McAfee (1999) and Moldovanu and Sela (2006) make specific assumptions on the information flows across stages. Fullerton and McAfee (1999) assume public revelation of private information before second-stage play, but Moldovanu and Sela (2006) assume that only the fact that second-stage players won their first-stage contest is public information.[8] While these assumptions may be reasonable for specific contexts, the larger question of optimal information design for two-stage contests might yield new insights into the optimal design of dynamic contests.[9]

Symmetric equilibria of symmetric models give important insights into the role of independent private information in contests. Unfortunately, much less is known about asymmetric models and even asymmetric equilibria in symmetric models. For the two-player case, Amann and Leininger (1996) prove the existence and uniqueness of equilibria for asymmetric models with

[8] Zhang and Wang (2009) observe that strictly monotonic equilibrium effort in both stages is not compatible with public revelation of first-stage efforts. Münster (2009) and Catepillan et al. (2022) analyze signaling the effort cost in repeated contests.

[9] Dworczak (2020) analyzes the optimal release of information across different stages in the context of auctions.

independent private values. Without clear equilibrium characterizations, the potential benefits of asymmetric designs are hard to measure.

2.3.2 Static Contests with Stochastic Success

There is less work on incomplete-information versions of Tullock-type contests and rank-order tournaments. Perhaps because the rules for selecting the winners for multiple prizes are not unambiguously determined for Tullock-type contests, the main design focus has been on the comparison of expected equilibrium efforts in complete versus incomplete-information versions of the contest rather than for different prize structures.

Wärneryd (2003) analyzes a two-player Tullock-type contest with common values where one contestant is fully informed and the other is completely uninformed of the value of the single prize. He shows that the expected sum of equilibrium efforts in the asymmetric model is always smaller than either the expected effort in the completely uninformed contest (where both contestants are uninformed of the true value) or the expected effort in the contest with complete information. Wasser (2013) covers the case of independent private values and shows that with symmetric contestants, the expected equilibrium effort under ignorance is lower than the expected effort with private values and the expected effort with complete information.[10] Myerson and Wärneryd (2006) show that adding uncertainty about the number of contestants reduces the expected equilibrium aggregate effort in Tullock-type contests for $r \leq 1$ in 2.2 (i.e., when success in the contest is sufficiently noisy).

Rank-order tournaments with private information have not been systematically analyzed thus far. An interesting special case of this is presented in Fang and Noe (2019), where two types of candidates compete for selection into a higher status class. For each candidate type, each strategy has the same type-dependent expected performance score, but the strategies differ in their riskiness. Fang and Noe assume that the objective in the contest is to classify strong candidates in a top status class. For this objective, relatively lax standards (many seats in the top category) often outperform stricter standards by inducing a better equilibrium correlation between high performance and high candidate type.

2.3.3 Correlated All-Pay Contests

Correlated private information brings new challenges to the equilibrium analysis of contests. With independent private information, contestant i's posterior probability on other contestants is independent of own type. This implies that any best response is monotonic in own type and therefore all Bayes Nash equilibria are also monotone in type. With correlated types, this is no longer

[10] Zhang and Zhou (2016) investigate optimal information design where the private value of one contestant can be revealed to her competitor.

true and monotone equilibria may fail to exist altogether. In this case, searching for equilibria (in non-monotonic strategies) becomes much harder.

In this section, I consider mainly the case of affiliated valuations for the prize and common linear effort costs. This allows for an easier interpretation of the affiliated common values case and also for an easier comparison with the literature on auctions.

We say that a single-prize all-pay contest is affiliated if the prior density f on the $\Theta := \times_i \Theta_i$ is log-supermodular in θ and the value $v_i(\theta_1, ..., \theta_N)$ of the prize is (weakly) increasing in all θ_j for all i, j. With affiliated types, the type of contestant i is affiliated with the type of every other contestant and therefore also with the highest type amongst the other contestants. If the effort choice of all contestants j is strictly increasing in θ_j, then the highest-order statistic amongst the effort choices from other contestants $e_{-i}^{(1)}(\theta_{-i})$ is also affiliated with θ_i. In other words, contestants with higher types face higher competition in the sense that the distribution of $e_{-i}^{(1)}$ is first-order stochastically increasing in θ_i.

This divergence of beliefs is present also in other games with affiliated values, and in particular, in auctions. The seminal analysis of auctions with affiliated values in Milgrom and Weber (1982) shows that many standard auction formats nevertheless have monotone pure-strategy equilibria when the types are drawn from atomless affiliated distributions. In standard auctions, the cost of submitting a high bid is limited by the fact that payment is conditional: only the winner pays her bid. Any bidder can guarantee a nonnegative payoff by placing a bid below her expected value of the object conditional on winning. In contests, effort is sunk and losing a contest is more costly than losing in a standard auction. When types are strongly affiliated, the higher level of competition that strong contestants expect may in fact discourage them from higher effort choices.

Krishna and Morgan (1997) consider the symmetric model with a single prize and a symmetric type distribution. They observe that when types are highly correlated, symmetric equilibria in monotone strategies do not necessarily exist for all pay auctions in this model.

Denote the expected value of the prize for a contestant with type θ when the highest type amongst the other contestants is y by[11]

$$v(\theta, y) := \mathrm{E}\left[v(\theta) | \theta_i = \theta, \theta_{-i}^{(1)} = y\right].$$

Let $f_{\theta_{-i}^{(1)}}(y|\theta)$ denote the conditional density of the highest type amongst i's competitors when $\theta_i = \theta$. Krishna and Morgan show that a symmetric monotone pure-strategy equilibrium exists if $v(\theta, y) f_{\theta_{-i}^{(1)}}(y|\theta)$ is increasing in θ for all values of y.

[11] If the contest has an equilibrium in strictly increasing strategies, then winning the prize gives information on the highest-order statistic amongst the other contestants. The expectation is taken over the other contestants' types.

To see why this is the case, assume that $e(\theta)$ is a symmetric strictly increasing equilibrium strategy. The expected payoff for a contestant with type θ from choosing the candidate equilibrium effort of type $\hat{\theta}$ is

$$\Pi(\hat{\theta},\theta) := \int_{\underline{\theta}}^{\hat{\theta}} v(\theta,y) f_{\theta_{-i}^{(1)}}(y|\theta) dy - e(\hat{\theta}).$$

Differentiating with respect to $\hat{\theta}$ and requiring the first-order condition for the optimality of the candidate equilibrium strategy (i.e., derivative of the payoff must be zero at $\hat{\theta} = \theta$) gives, after integrating and observing that $e(\underline{\theta}) = 0$:

$$e(\theta) = \int_{\underline{\theta}}^{\theta} v(y,y) f_{\theta_{-i}^{(1)}}(y|y) dy. \tag{2.7}$$

Substituting into the expression for the expected equilibrium payoff gives

$$\Pi(\hat{\theta},\theta) := \int_{\underline{\theta}}^{\hat{\theta}} \left[v(\theta,y) f_{\theta_{-i}^{(1)}}(y|\theta) - v(y,y) f_{\theta_{-i}^{(1)}}(y|y) \right] dy. \tag{2.8}$$

If $v(\theta,y) f_{\theta_{-i}^{(1)}}(y|\theta)$ is increasing in θ, the integrand is positive (negative) whenever $\hat{\theta} < (>)\ \theta$, yielding the optimality of $\hat{\theta} = \theta$.[12]

This argument shows that in order to rule out profitable global deviations, more structure must be imposed on the model even in this simplest case of an affiliated all-pay contest for a single prize. The condition guaranteeing the existence of monotone equilibria is not easily satisfied in many natural cases. It fails, for example, in the mineral rights model with a large number of contestants where the common value of the prize depends on a state of the world and the types of the contestants are conditionally i.i.d. Whenever local first-order conditions are not sufficient for optimality, equilibrium characterization becomes hard.[13]

When monotone equilibria exist, Krishna and Morgan compare the expected equilibrium effort in the all-pay contest to the revenues in standard auctions and wars of attrition.[14] From this perspective, the all-pay contest performs better than a standard first-price auction and sometimes better than a standard second-price auction, while the war of attrition dominates the three other formats.

[12] Lizzeri and Persico (2000) show the existence and uniqueness of monotone pure-strategy equilibria in asymmetric affiliated all-pay contests with two players under the assumption that $v_i(\theta_i, \theta_{-i}) f(\theta_{-i}|\theta_i)$ be increasing in θ_i for both i.

[13] For a particular example of how to construct a non-monotonic equilibrium with a continuum of types, see appendix B of Lu and Parreiras (2017).

[14] A war of attrition is related to a dynamic contest where the contestants decide in continuous time whether to stay in the contest and pay a cost or drop out (to stop the payments). When only a single contestant remains, she wins the prize. In order for this game to have a symmetric equilibrium, the remaining players are only told that the game continues but not the number of remaining contestants. This silent form of the war of attrition is sometimes also referred to as a second-price all-pay auction. See Klemperer and Bulow (1999) for an exposition of the existence issues that arise if all exits are immediately reported.

Siegel (2014) considers all-pay contests with general correlated information and asymmetric contestants. He assumes a finite set of possible types and shows the existence and uniqueness of equilibria for the two-contestant case whenever a discrete analogue of the monotonicity condition in Krishna and Morgan (1997) is satisfied. With discrete types, equilibria will necessarily be in mixed strategies as in all-pay contests with complete information.

Rentschler and Turocy (2016) consider a symmetric two-contestant setting with discrete types, but they drop the monotonicity assumption. They show the existence of symmetric equilibria and provide an algorithm for finding them. The procedure for finding equilibria relies on the simplified indifference conditions that follow from having a single opponent in the contest. Nevertheless, the task of finding equilibria is hard and the possibilities for qualitatively different non-monotonic equilibria are numerous, since no other restrictions beyond symmetry are put on the type distributions and payoffs.

Chi et al. (2019) extend the analysis of Krishna and Morgan (1997) to cover non-monotonic equilibria. They consider an affiliated binary-type model where the distribution of contestant types is conditionally i.i.d. given an aggregate state variable.[15] Modeling correlation through aggregate uncertainty on the type distributions allows for comparative statics in the number of contestants and a flexible interpretation of both common values and affiliated private values in the same framework. With common values, the value of the prize depends only on the (unknown) state. With affiliated private values, the value depends only on the contestant's own type.

Chi et al. show that whenever the equivalent of the monotonicity condition in Krishna and Morgan fails, all rent is dissipated in the symmetric equilibrium of the model. Monotonicity fails in these equilibria in the sense that contestants with a low type win over contestants with a high type with a positive probability. With models of affiliated private values, this implies a welfare loss, and the inefficiency caused by this non-monotonicity does not vanish even as $N \to \infty$.[16] This inefficiency has consequences for revenue comparisons between different contests and different auction formats. An all-pay contest reduces the equilibrium rent of the contestants relative to standard auctions, but standard auctions are efficient. As a result, the comparison between the formats depends on the number of contestants, in contrast to Krishna and Morgan (1997), where only monotone (and hence efficient) equilibria are considered.[17]

Similar problems for finding monotone equilibria arise in other correlated games, such as auctions with endogenous participation decisions. Murto and Välimäki (2020) show that with sufficiently affiliated signals, monotone equilibria may fail to exist if the bidders must sink a cost to participate

[15] This means that the probability that contestant i is of high type is larger in a higher state than in a lower state.

[16] This inefficiency result extends to multiple types and multiple states of the world.

[17] Chi et al. (2019) also compare expected revenues in contests and auctions to the war of attrition.

in an auction. Since auctions with participation costs combine a sunk and a conditional payment, this shows that correlation causes problems for the existence of monotone Bayes Nash equilibria in settings well beyond contest models.[18]

2.4 LARGE CONTESTS

The inherent endogenous uncertainty in the allocation of prizes complicates the analysis of contests. One might hope that this uncertainty would be reduced in contests with large numbers of contestants and prizes. Recent literature following Olszewski and Siegel (2016) has started to explore equilibria in contests that are large in the sense that $N \to \infty$ and $K \to \infty$.

Consider as a starting point the finite matching model of Bulow and Levin (2006), where firms of productivity θ_i with $\theta_i > \theta_{i+1} > 0$ for $i \in \{1,...,N-1\}$ compete for $K = N$ workers with productivity v_k with $v_k > v_{k+1} > 0$ for $k \in \{1,...,K\}$ by offering wages e_i. After observing the profile of wages $(e_1,...,e_N)$, the workers choose the highest wage offer available in the order of their productivity.

The payoff to firm i for hiring worker k at wage e_i takes the multiplicative form

$$u_i(e) = \theta_i v_k - e_i, \tag{2.9}$$

and the game can be analyzed as an all-pay contest with multiple prizes and complete information.

The equilibrium of the game is shown to be unique and in atomless mixed strategies. Constructing the equilibrium is quite intricate and, for example, determining the firms that randomize on any given interval is far from trivial. Bulow and Levin also show that when $N \to \infty$, any inefficiencies in the model disappear in the sense that the equilibrium matching between firms and workers converges to the competitive perfectly assortative matching. They also show that the equilibrium wages converge to their competitive counterparts (though at a lower rate).

2.4.1 The Limit Contest

Given that the competitive allocation and the competitive prices supporting that allocation are relatively easy to compute, the general convergence result derived by Olszewski and Siegel (2016) establishes a useful benchmark for matching games and many other models. They postulate a symmetric formulation where a contestant's payoff from receiving prize $v \in [0,1]$ is

[18] Landsberger (2007) discusses the problems with monotone equilibria in more general Bayesian games.

given by $\theta v - e$, if her type is $\theta \in [0,1]$ and she chooses effort e.[19] The empirical distribution of contestants' types is denoted $F^N(\cdot)$ and the empirical distribution of prizes by $G^N(\cdot)$ in contests with N contestants and prizes.

Suppose that a continuous and strictly increasing distribution function F and some distribution function G exist such that

$$F^N(\theta) \to F(\theta) \text{ and } G^N(v) \to G(v),$$

in distribution as $N \to \infty$. In this case, the model with a continuum of contestants and prizes distributed according to F, G is said to be the large contest limit of the finite contests.

An assortative matching in the limit model assigns prizes to contestants in the same rank order, that is, type θ contestant is assigned the prize $v(\theta) = G^{-1}(F(\theta))$, where $G^{-1}(y) = \inf\{z | G(z) \geq y\}$ is the generalized inverse of G.

In order to analyze the limit model, we can consider the mechanism design problem of implementing the assortative matching using the effort choices as transfers. The direct mechanism $(v(\theta), e(\theta))$ is incentive-compatible if no type θ benefits by misreporting her type as $\hat{\theta} \neq \theta$. Since the payoff function is strictly supermodular in (v, θ) and since $v(\theta)$ is increasing in θ, the mechanism is incentive-compatible if $e(\theta)$ is computed using the envelope theorem:

$$e(\theta) = \theta v(\theta) - \int_0^\theta v(z)dz. \tag{2.10}$$

The main theorem in Olszewski and Siegel (2016) shows that for any $\varepsilon > 0$, there is an $\bar{N}$ such that for all $N \geq \bar{N}$, at least at fraction $1 - \varepsilon$ of players of type θ obtain with probability at least $1 - \varepsilon$ a prize $v^N(\theta) \in (v(\theta) - \varepsilon, v(\theta) - \varepsilon)$ and choose effort $e^N(\theta) \in (e(\theta) - \varepsilon, e(\theta) - \varepsilon)$ with probability at least $1 - \varepsilon$. The rates at which the outcomes in the finite contests converge to the large contest limit are also computed.

In comparison to the cumbersome equilibrium analysis of the finite contests, it is remarkably easy to compute the associated effort profile for the limit game. To appreciate the generality of the result, notice that the limit game can be viewed both as the limit of asymmetric contests with complete information (as in Bulow and Levin, 2006) and also as the limit of a multi-prize contest where the types of N contestants are drawn independently from F. A typical example of a large contest is the game where 10% of the candidates drawn from a talent distribution F are selected for college admissions based on their chosen effort in high school.

Of course, one could start directly with the continuum model and investigate the competitive allocations one might expect in that model. This has been the traditional approach in the literature on matching and assignment with

[19] The main theorem is valid also for a more general payoff function $u(\theta, v, e)$ as long as it satisfies strict single crossing and the regularity conditions needed for the Milgrom and Segal (2002) envelope theorem.

transfers. The limit result of Olszewski and Siegel shows that the competitive model serves as a useful benchmark also for contest models when the number of contestants becomes large. Because of this connection between the two classes of models, questions that arose in contest models have recently been posed in typical assignment settings.

2.4.2 Designing Large Contests

Olszewski and Siegel (2020) revisit the design problem for maximizing aggregate effort in a contest when a contestant with type θ derives utility $\theta u(v)$ from prize v.[20] Similar to Moldovanu and Sela (2001), they allow for non-linear effort costs $c(e)$ and find that for the large contest

$$e^{v}(\theta) = c^{-1}\left(\theta u(v(\theta)) - \int_0^{\theta} u(\theta)(z, v(z))dz\right).$$

Notice that $e^{v}(\theta)$ depends on the prize distribution G through function v as explained in the previous section. If the designer of the contest has access to total resources V, then the maximization problem can be written as

$$\max_{G \in \mathcal{G}} \int_0^1 e^{v}(\theta) f(\theta) d\theta \tag{2.11}$$

$$\text{subject to} \int_0^1 v(\theta) f(\theta) d\theta \leq V, \tag{2.12}$$

where $\mathcal{G}$ is the set of probability distributions on the positive real line.

Olszewski and Siegel (2020) show, for the case of linear cost functions, that whenever the budget V is sufficiently large, then the optimal prize structure is to award a positive mass of homogenous prizes. For small budgets, the optimal shape of the prize distribution depends on the curvature of u. For strictly convex cost functions and $u(v) = v$ (or more generally, for weakly concave $u(v)$), prizes are distributed on an interval in the optimal prize design.

Olszewski and Siegel (2019) ask a related design question with essentially the same model specification, but under a different objective function for the contest designer. Motivated by a rather grim view of standardized tests (such as SATs) as not having any intrinsic value, they look for contests that induce Pareto improvements on the ex-post equilibrium welfare of contestants. The prizes in the contest are interpreted as college seats, and the preferences of colleges are not taken into account in this analysis. The main insight in the paper is that lumping performances together (so that each contestant in the same

[20] Olszewski and Siegel assume that the contestants have private information on their valuation for the prize, whereas Moldovanu and Sela (2001) assume privately known effort costs. The two models are strategically equivalent when the type enters the payoffs multiplicatively. The non-linear valuation function $u(v)$ for the prizes makes the models different.

performance category is treated the same) results in a Pareto improvement if and only if the highest type in the interval benefits from the change.[21]

Bodoh-Creed and Hickman (2018) also look at the large contest approximation of the competition for college seats between prospective students. The main question in their paper is the selection of minority vs. majority students. To analyze the effects of different policies on admissions, they extend the model to have students' effort costs drawn from separate distributions, F_M for minority students and F_N for majority students. College seats are again viewed as prizes in the contest that grants admission to students based on their effort in the contest.

Admission rules can be modified using two instruments. A quota rule sets aside seats at different colleges for minority students. A rule with admission preferences maps the effort of each minority student to a modified effort $\tilde{e}_m = \phi(e_m)$, where ϕ is an increasing function with $0 < \underline{\lambda} < \phi'(e_m) < \overline{\lambda}$ for all e_m. The students are selected to colleges in the rank order of these modified effort scores (where the effort choices e_n of non-minority students are not modified).

Bodoh-Creed and Hickman analyze three versions of the admission contest, one with color-blind rules (the large contest with contestants drawn from $\mu F_M + (1-\mu)F_N$, where μ is the fraction of minority students in the population), and contests with a quota system or an admissions preference. The main results are that an equilibrium for the large limit game exists, is unique, and has a symmetric (within student groups) equilibrium effort strategy for all three systems. Second, for each quota system, there exists an equivalent admissions preference mapping that produces the same equilibrium outcome (and vice versa) and hence these two instruments implement the same set of effort strategies and college admissions.

In large contests, equilibrium effort choice pins down the prize that the contestant receives. Hence the distinction between contests and markets based on the conditional versus unconditional transfers vanishes. The equilibrium effort needed to obtain prize v coincides with the competitive equilibrium price for that prize.

2.4.3 Large Rank-Order Tournaments

If the contest success function is determined by the rank-order tournament success function, the randomness in the performance of each contestant means that their own success remains uncertain even in large contests. The analysis remains very complicated for the case of general prize distributions. Morgan et al. (2018) analyze the equilibrium effort decision $e_i(\theta_i)$ in an additive model where a unit mass of contestants compete for a mass $x \in [0,1]$ of identical prizes as a building block of their more general model where the contestants choose between available contests.

21 Kleiner et al. (2021) develop new techniques based on majorization that allow for sharper results on the shape of the optimal schemes for the contestants and for the effort maximizing designer based on the monotonicity of the failure rate of F.

Individual performance y_i is determined from

$$y_i = e_i + \varepsilon_i,$$

where ε_i is idiosyncratic noise in performance, and the effort cost is given by $c(e_i, \theta_i)$. Morgan et al. demonstrate the existence of an equilibrium for this case and derive some comparative statics in the competitiveness of the contest (modeled as the mass of prizes).

As of now, optimal designs to elicit maximal aggregate effort from all contestants, or to achieve other objectives, have not been systematically explored within the context of rank-order tournaments.

2.4.4 Correlated Large Contests

If the contestants have correlated types, the allocations remain stochastic even in the large game limit of the all-pay contest. A natural way to model correlation for large contests while maintaining the symmetry of the model (symmetric payoffs and types of contestants modeled as exchangeable random variables) is to assume that the contestants are drawn independently from a distribution indexed by a state of the world as in Chi et al. (2019).

Consider for simplicity the case where the state of the world is binary, $\omega \in \{H, L\}$. Even with an increasing effort strategy $e(\theta)$ and assortative matching of types to prizes, the assignment function $v^{\omega} = G^{-1}(F^{\omega}(\theta))$ depends on the state. This means that the prize allocation for each effort level e is state-dependent. The example below shows that we should not expect monotone equilibria for the limit large game in general.

For concreteness, assume that contestants in the highest decile of effort choices are awarded a homogenous prize worth θ_i for a contestant i. Suppose that the two states are equally likely, and in state $\omega = H$, $\frac{4}{5}$ of the contestants have their type drawn uniformly from $[0.5, 1]$ and $\frac{1}{5}$ of the contestants are drawn uniformly from $[0, 0.5)$. In state $\omega = L$, the fractions are reversed and $\frac{1}{5}$ of the contestants are drawn uniformly from $[0.5, 1]$ while $\frac{4}{5}$ of the contestants are drawn uniformly from $[0, 0.5)$.

Bayes' rule implies that each contestant in $[0.5, 1]$ assigns posterior probability $\frac{4}{5}$ to $\{\omega = H\}$, and each contestant in $[0, 0.5)$ assigns posterior probability $\frac{1}{5}$ on the high state.

The equilibrium effort in the symmetric competitive equilibrium of this large contest with correlated values takes the following form:

$$e(\theta) = \begin{cases} \frac{15}{16} \text{ if } \theta \geq \frac{15}{16}, \\ 0 \text{ if } \frac{1}{2} < \theta < \frac{15}{16}, \\ \frac{29}{80} \text{ if } \frac{29}{64} \leq \theta < \frac{1}{2}, \\ 0 \text{ if } \theta < \frac{29}{64}. \end{cases} \tag{2.13}$$

This non-monotonic effort profile allocates a prize to contestants with high types $\theta \geq \frac{15}{16}$ in both states. This requires an effort level that leaves the marginal type at $v = \frac{15}{16}$ indifferent between winning the prize and not. Higher types earn positive rents at this effort level. Any lower effort wins a prize only in the low state L, where fewer high-type bidders are present for this affiliated-type distribution. All types with $\theta \geq \frac{1}{2}$ assign only probability 0.2 to the event $\{\omega = L\}$, and hence any effort above 0.2 results in a negative payoff.

Contestants with types $\theta < \frac{1}{2}$ consider state L relatively likely. In that state, mass $0.1 - \frac{1}{16} \cdot \frac{2}{5} = \frac{3}{40}$ of prizes remain available at effort levels below $\frac{15}{16}$. In state L, there are $\frac{3}{40}$ contestants in the interval $\left[\frac{29}{64}, \frac{1}{2}\right]$. The marginal type breaks even if $e\left(\frac{29}{64}\right) = \frac{29}{64} \cdot \frac{4}{5} = \frac{29}{80}$. All types in $\frac{29}{64} < \theta < \frac{1}{2}$ earn a positive rent at this effort while all other types earn a negative payoff at this effort.

This simple example demonstrates why the monotonicity of equilibria with conditionally i.i.d. types often fails. In large contests, equilibrium effort levels result in allocations that are deterministic conditional on the state. Since the state is uncertain and the contestants have different probability assessments on their relative likelihoods, contestants with lower types may be willing to pay more for a lottery ticket that wins the prize only in the low state. The value of such a lottery is given by $q^L(\theta)v(\theta)$, where $q^L(\theta)$ denotes the posterior of type θ contestant on the event that the state is L. In affiliated models, this posterior is decreasing in type, and as a result, the product $q^L(\theta)v(\theta)$ may easily be non-monotonic in θ.

Notice that in the example above, the equilibrium is inefficient since the matching in state L is not positively assortative. If the relatively low-type bidders with $\theta < \frac{1}{2}$ were removed altogether from the model, the only uncertainty would be about the number of contestants. For this modification, types $\theta \in \left[\frac{3}{4}, \frac{15}{16}\right)$ would choose effort $e = \frac{3}{4} \cdot \frac{1}{5} = \frac{3}{20}$ and the equilibrium would be efficient. Hence we see that adding new contestants with different beliefs on the state may harm the performance of correlated large contests.[22]

Even in the case where the number of prizes is fixed, large numbers of contestants facilitate the analysis. In contrast to large contests in the sense as described above, rent vanishes in equilibrium as the number of contestants grows in contests with finitely many prizes. This allows for simpler computations in the IPV case as well as in the correlated private values case.[23]

With large numbers of contestants, it is not possible to start with the limit model since even the simplest all-pay contest with complete information does not have well-defined symmetric equilibria when a continuum of agents compete for a single prize. Nevertheless, finite contests have symmetric equilibria, and one can switch attention away from the characterization of individual strategies to the characterization of equilibrium outcomes: determine along

[22] Based on the large limit versions of the model in Chi et al. (2019), we are currently investigating equilibrium efficiency and rent extraction in such models.

[23] It may seem unappealing to consider large numbers of contestants competing for a few prizes, but by setting a minimum effort level $\underline{e}$, the model has a symmetric equilibrium with a (Poisson) random number of active contestants.

a sequence of symmetric equilibria $e^N(\theta)$ of contests with N contestants the probability of winning, $\pi^N(e)$, when choosing effort e.[24]

Murto and Välimäki (2017) show that in the case where the types are i.i.d. draws from a distribution on the unit interval (with a strictly positive density $f(1)$ at the top of the distribution), the limiting probability for winning a single prize $\pi^N(e)$ with effort e must satisfy $\lim_N \pi^N(e) = e$. Based on a similar argument for the kth asymptotic order statistics, they compute the distributions for the k highest efforts in the contest. With linear effort costs, this model says little about optimal design of contests. Since the contestants do not earn any rents, equilibrium expected effort coincides with the total value of the prizes. The analysis can be generalized to obtain less trivial results in the case with convex effort costs and other objectives (maximizing the expected highest effort).

This limiting approach also gives a useful benchmark in the analysis of contests with a finite number of prizes where the types of contestants are drawn from a distribution that depends on an aggregate state. The relevant equilibrium outcome is then the probability of winning at effort e in state ω.

2.5 DISCUSSION: PATENT RACES WITH INCOMPLETE INFORMATION

Contestants in dynamic games may have private information regarding many dimensions of the game. They may be privately informed about the feasibility of a research project aiming, for example, to obtain a vaccination against a disease, or they may have private information on their effort cost. Analyzing dynamic games with private information is unfortunately very hard, and making any progress has required quite strong modeling assumptions.

The simplest model of patent races assumes that N contestants are competing in an infinite-horizon model with discounting to be the first to obtain a patentable innovation. Staying in the race for an additional time increment dt costs $c_i dt$ to contestant i until she quits the race and receives a payoff 0. If she stays in the race, she receives the innovation with probability $\lambda_i dt$. The first contestant to get the innovation receives a patent (the prize) worth v_i and simultaneous innovations happen with probability 0. In the typical winner-takes-all race, the remaining contestants receive no prize. This contest does not have very interesting dynamic properties if it is played under complete information since the contestants that decide to stay in the game for any positive amount of time stay until an innovation arrives.

If the λ_i depend on an unknown parameter θ, the game features learning about θ on the equilibrium path as noticed by Choi (1991). If the event $\{\lambda_i(\theta) = 0 \text{ for all } i\}$ has positive prior probability, then not observing an innovation during any time interval where some contestant is still in the game leads,

[24] In the IPV case, this would just be the probability with which the highest-order statistic amongst $N-1$ other bidders falls below $(e^N)^{-1}(\theta)$.

via Bayesian updating, to a higher posterior on this event.[25] This gives rise to non-trivial dynamics in the game. The contestants become more and more pessimistic as they do not observe an innovation, and at some point, they are no longer willing to pay the cost for staying in the game. As a result, the race is transformed into a game of optimal stopping.

Moscarini and Squintani (2010) analyze a somewhat more general model of this game where two contestants receive private information θ_i on θ prior to the start of the race. They assume that only the decision to quit is observable to the other contestants once the contest has started. This allows them to sidestep difficulties that would arise if the contestants could signal their type through, for example, their effort choices. They show that the decisions to quit the race are more closely paced in this case relative to the case where the θ_i are publicly observed.

Halac et al. (2017) ask a research contest design question related to the symmetric incomplete-information version of the model where $c_i = c$, $\lambda_i(\theta) = \lambda\theta$ for all i and $\theta \in \{0,1\}$. The designer has a total purse of V to be allocated as prizes. She wants to maximize the probability of eventual success in a contest where the contestants pay privately their cost of staying in the race. Halac et al. show that if the arrival of innovations is public and cannot be hidden, then a winner-takes-all contest where V is given to the first contestant to get the innovation is optimal. Somewhat surprisingly, it may be optimal to commit to not disclosing all innovations (if this is feasible) and sharing V between multiple contestants.[26]

There are many other dimensions on which one could model the uncertainty. For example, the number of contestants may be uncertain at the start of the game. If no innovations arrive, this could be a signal about either a lower than expected success probability or a lower than expected number of contestants in the game.

2.6 CONCLUSION

I have concentrated in this chapter on the relatively recent literature on static contests with private information. While the tools from mechanism design and using the large contest limit have allowed for a better understanding of some particular types of contests, it should be clear that many interesting questions remain open. Optimal design of rank-order tournaments with privately known abilities or effort costs, and the trade-off between rent accruing to the contestants and efficiency in correlated contests are examples of such questions.

[25] See the survey by Hörner and Skrzypacz (2017) for a discussion of experimentation and learning in similar models.

[26] Bimpikis et al. (2019) also demonstrate the benefits from hiding prior successes for contest design.

REFERENCES

Amann, E., and W. Leininger (1996). "Asymmetric all-pay auctions with incomplete information: The two-player case," *Games and Economic Behavior*, 14(1), 1–18.

Bimpikis, K., S. Ehsani, and M. Mostagir (2019). "Designing dynamic contests," *Operations Research*, 67(2), 339–356.

Bodoh-Creed, A. L., and B. R. Hickman (2018). "College assignment as a large contest," *Journal of Economic Theory*, 175, 88–126.

Borel, E. (1921). "La théorie du jeu et les équations intégrales à noyau symétrique," *Comptes Rendus de l'Académie*, 173(13041308), 97–100.

Bulow, J., and J. Levin (2006). "Matching and price competition," *American Economic Review*, 96(3), 652–668.

Catepillan, J., N. Figueroa, and J. Lemus (2022). "Signaling in dynamic contests with heterogenous rivals." Discussion Paper.

Chawla, S., J. D. Hartline, and B. Sivan (2019). "Optimal crowdsourcing contests," *Games and Economic Behavior*, 113, 80–96.

Chi, C. K., P. Murto, and J. Välimäki (2019). "All-pay auctions with affiliated binary signals," *Journal of Economic Theory*, 179, 99–130.

Choi, J. P. (1991). "Dynamic R&D competition under 'hazard rate' uncertainty," *The RAND Journal of Economics*, 22, 596–610.

Corchón, L., and M. Serena (2018). "Contest theory." In L. Corchón and M. Marini (eds.), *Handbook of Game Theory and Industrial Organization*, vol. II. Cheltenham: Edward Elgar, pp. 97–112.

Dworczak, P. (2020). "Mechanism design with aftermarkets: Cutoff mechanisms," *Econometrica*, 88(6), 2629–2661.

Fang, D., and T. Noe (2019). "Less competition, more meritocracy." Working Paper.

Fullerton, R. L., and R. P. McAfee (1999). "Auctioning entry into tournaments," *Journal of Political Economy*, 107(3), 573–605.

Halac, M., N. Kartik, and Q. Liu (2017). "Contests for experimentation," *Journal of Political Economy*, 125(5), 1523–1569.

Hörner, J., and A. Skrzypacz (2017). "Learning, experimentation, and information design." In B. Honoré, A. Pakes, M. Piazzesi, and L. Samuelson (eds.), *Advances in Economics and Econometrics: Eleventh World Congress*, vol. 1. Cambridge: Cambridge University Press, pp. 63–98.

Kleiner, A., B. Moldovanu, and P. Strack (2021). "Extreme points and majorization: Economic applications," *Econometrica*, 89(4), 1557–1593.

Klemperer, P., and J. Bulow (1999). "The generalized war of attrition," *American Economic Review*, 89(1), 175–189.

Krishna, V., and J. Morgan (1997). "An analysis of the war of attrition and the all-pay auction," *Journal of Economic Theory*, 72(2), 343–362.

Landsberger, M. (2007). "Non-existence of monotone equilibria in games with correlated signals," *Journal of Economic Theory*, 132(1), 119–136.

Lazear, E. P., and S. Rosen (1981). "Rank-order tournaments as optimum labor contracts," *Journal of Political Economy*, 89(5), 841–864.

Letina, I., S. Liu, and N. Netzer (2020). "Delegating performance evaluation," *Theoretical Economics*, 15(2), 477–509.

Liu, B., J. Lu, R. Wang, and J. Zhang (2018). "Optimal prize allocation in contests: The role of negative prizes," *Journal of Economic Theory*, 175, 291–317.

Lizzeri, A., and N. Persico (2000). "Uniqueness and existence of equilibrium in auctions with a reserve price," *Games and Economic Behavior*, 30(1), 83–114.

Lu, J., and S. O. Parreiras (2017). "Monotone equilibrium of two-bidder all-pay auctions Redux," *Games and Economic Behavior*, 104(C), 78–91.

Milgrom, P., and I. Segal (2002). "Envelope theorems for arbitrary choice sets," *Econometrica*, 70(2), 583–601.

Milgrom, P. R., and R. J. Weber (1982). "A theory of auctions and competitive bidding," *Econometrica*, 50(5), 1089–1122.

Moldovanu, B., and A. Sela (2001). "The optimal allocation of prizes in contests," *American Economic Review*, 91(3), 542–558.

Moldovanu, B., and A. Sela (2006). "Contest architecture," *Journal of Economic Theory*, 126(1), 70–96.

Moldovanu, B., A. Sela, and X. Shi (2007). "Contests for status," *Journal of Political Economy*, 115, 338-363.

Morgan, J., D. Sisak, and F. Várdy (2018). "The ponds dilemma," *The Economic Journal*, 128(611), 1634–1682.

Moscarini, G., and F. Squintani (2010). "Competitive experimentation with private information: The survivor's curse," *Journal of Economic Theory*, 145(2), 639–660.

Münster, J. (2009). "Repeated contests with asymmetric information," *Journal of Public Economic Theory*, 11(1), 89–118.

Murto, P., and J. Välimäki (2017). "Common value auctions with costly entry." Discussion Paper, Aalto University School of Business and HECER.

Murto, P., and J. Välimäki (2020). "Informal affiliated auctions with costly entry." Working Paper.

Myerson, R., and K. Wärneryd (2006). "Population uncertainty in contests," *Economic Theory*, 27, 469–474.

Olszewski, W., and R. Siegel (2016). "Large contests," *Econometrica*, 84, 835–854.

Olszewski, W., and R. Siegel (2019). "Pareto improvements in the contest for college admissions." Working Paper.

Olszewski, W., and R. Siegel (2020). "Performance-maximizing large contests," *Theoretical Economics*, 15(1), 57–88.

Rentschler, L., and T. L. Turocy (2016). "Two-bidder all-pay auctions with interdependent valuations, including the highly competitive case," *Journal of Economic Theory*, 163(C), 435–466.

Siegel, R. (2014). "Asymmetric all-pay auctions with interdependent valuations," *Journal of Economic Theory*, 153(C), 684–702.

Tullock, G. (1980). "Efficient rent seeking." In J. Buchanan, R. Tollison, and G. Tullock (eds.), *Toward a Theory of Rent Seeking Society*. College Station, TX: Texas A&M University Press, pp. 97–112.

Wärneryd, K. (2003). "Information in conflicts," *Journal of Economic Theory*, 110(1), 121–136.

Wasser, C. (2013). "Incomplete information in rent-seeking contests," *Economic Theory*, 53, 239–268.

Weber, R. J. (1985). "Auctions and competitive bidding." In H. P. Young (ed.), *Fair Allocation*. Ann Arbor, MI: American Mathematical Society, pp. 143–170.

Zhang, J., and R. Wang (2009). "The role of information revelation in elimination contests," *The Economic Journal*, 119(536), 613–641.

Zhang, J., and J. Zhou (2016). "Information disclosure in contests: A Bayesian persuasion approach," *The Economic Journal*, 126(597), 2197–2217.

PART II

TOPICS IN INDUSTRIAL ORGANIZATION

CHAPTER 3

Incomplete-Information Models for Industrial Organization

Simon Loertscher and Leslie M. Marx

Recent advances have demonstrated that pertinent issues in industrial organization and antitrust, such as the profit-surplus tradeoff and countervailing power, arise naturally in incomplete-information models. These models also explain, coherently, a host of issues such as why first-degree price discrimination is not possible, why uniform pricing is optimal when revenue is concave, and why opaque pricing and rationing (which may induce resale) is optimal otherwise. This chapter provides an overview of the relevant literature, explains the key mechanics of the framework, discusses applications to horizontal mergers, vertical integration, and buyer and countervailing power, and lays out a roadmap for the work ahead.

3.1 INTRODUCTION

Industrial organization (IO) covers imperfectly competitive markets and incentives within firms and organizations. It derives particular real-world relevance through its application to regulation, consumer protection, antitrust, and competition policy, as well as related court cases. Naturally, it aims to analyze the effects of alternative arrangements, such as horizontal and vertical integration, workers' right to unionize, and firms' ability to price discriminate, on consumer and social surplus, and the inevitable tradeoffs between them.

This applicability and real-world exposure simultaneously constrain the field and give it direction and purpose. As anyone privy to policy debates or courtroom arguments will readily attest, it is not the fanciest and theoretically most advanced arguments ("Shouldn't you be doing dynamic mechanism design here?") that win the day, partly because of the need for evidence-based decision-making and the inevitable limitations of data and empirical methods, and partly because of the need for those arguments to be comprehended by intelligent, non-economist policymakers and judges.[1] At the same time,

We thank the audience at the Econometric Society & Bocconi University Virtual World Congress and the 6th World Congress of the Game Theory Society for valuable comments. Financial support from the Samuel and June Hordern Endowment and Australian Research Council Discovery Project Grant DP200103574 is gratefully acknowledged.

[1] Baye and Wright (2011) state: "We find that decisions involving the evaluation of complex economic evidence are significantly more likely to be appealed, and decisions of judges trained in

the fundamental need for conceptual frameworks to contemplate and communicate genuine counterfactuals – changes in the economic environment from the known into the unknown – is painstakingly clear. In an ever-changing world, there are simply never going to be enough takeovers of Instagram by Facebook or Time Warner by AT&T for any empiricist to make conclusive inferences, one way or another, without relying on assumptions. In other words, the field inevitably requires a combination of theory and empirics within a framework that generates a tradeoff between profits and social and consumer surplus, allows for social surplus effects of varying bargaining power, and accommodates incentives for investment and innovation.

In this chapter, we provide an introduction to what we call the *Incomplete-Information Industrial Organization* framework – or *Triple-IO*. The aims of this chapter are, on the one hand, to demonstrate to readers not familiar with it the framework's tractability, discipline, and flexibility, and, on the other hand, to illustrate and discuss its internal consistency and external validity. The chapter first discusses the background and backdrop for Triple-IO. Then we review progress to date. The chapter concludes with an overview of outstanding questions and the path ahead.

3.2 MOTIVATION

In this section, we provide background for antitrust economics and an overview of recent developments in industrial organization and antitrust, taking these as motivation for incomplete-information models.

3.2.1 Background

Monopoly behavior is a longstanding and ongoing focus of interest in industrial organization and antitrust, and thus serves well as a lead-in to discussion of alternative models. Traditional approaches – by which we mean approaches that are not based on incomplete-information models – to monopoly pricing typically assume that a monopoly is, for reasons that are outside the model (e.g., resale among buyers), restricted to setting a uniform price to consumers. The deeper, although not necessarily widely publicized, reason for imposing this assumption is that it prevents the monopoly from perfectly price discriminating among the consumers, in which case there would be no social surplus rationale for regulating monopolies or preventing monopolies from forming. The goal of a monopoly that captures all of the social surplus that it creates is perfectly aligned with the social planner's objective since it grabs all surplus. As we will see, incomplete information immediately implies a tradeoff

basic economics are significantly less likely to be appealed than are decisions by their untrained counterparts. Our analysis supports the hypothesis that some antitrust cases are too complicated for generalist judges."

between social surplus and profit because eliciting information about agents' values has an incentive cost.

While the dependence of the predictions and prescriptions on these assumptions has long been recognized, the modeling device of assuming uniform pricing remains influential in undergraduate teaching, research, and practical applications. As a case in point, successive uniform pricing monopolies give rise to double marginalization (Spengler, 1950), whose elimination continues to be an influential and widely accepted efficiency-based argument in favor of vertical integration (see, e.g., the 2020 US vertical merger guidelines; U.S. Department of Justice and the Federal Trade Commission, 2020).

The basic tenet in the monopoly model that one side of the market sets the price for the other carries over to oligopoly models à la Cournot or Bertrand, which are used to model imperfectly competitive markets. The main effect of competition in these models is that it renders each firm's residual demand function more price elastic and, therefore, makes it behave more aggressively. Competition does not alter the fact that one side of the market (in consumer markets, typically the supply side) sets the terms of trade. These models are therefore incapable of capturing notions like shifts in bargaining power, buyer power, or countervailing power. This creates a disconnect between the reliance on these notions in practice[2] and the models being used to analyze and quantify associated effects, which remain largely grounded in oligopoly models à la Cournot or Bertrand.[3]

Antitrust concerns and thinking in their current form emerged in an era of steel and rail. The regulation of *natural monopolies* that arise because of nonconvex cost functions was a central concern, and took on the form, for example, of Ramsey pricing (see, e.g., Ramsey, 1927; Wilson, 1993), which involves a convex combination of perfectly competitive prices and monopoly prices. Such approaches recognize that, because of the cost structure and network organization of the problems at hand, perfectly competitive pricing would not allow the operators to break even (and would provide poor incentives for maintaining and improving infrastructure), and that the monopoly price would have undesirable effects for consumer and social surplus. Even

[2] The 2010 US horizontal merger guidelines (U.S. Department of Justice and the Federal Trade Commission, 2010), which both guide and reflect antitrust practice in the United States, note in section 6.2 on "Bargaining and Auctions" that "Buyers commonly negotiate with more than one seller, and may play sellers off against one another," and in section 8 on "Powerful Buyers" that "Powerful buyers are often able to negotiate favorable terms with their suppliers." Further, the guidelines allow that agencies could identify a *price discrimination market* defined by a single powerful buyer.

[3] For example, the reliance of competition authorities around the globe on merger screens based on the Herfindahl–Hirschman Index (HHI) has foundations in the Cournot oligopoly model (see, e.g., Werden, 2008; Werden and Froeb, 2008). A variety of well-accepted merger review tools and simulation techniques are grounded in the differentiated products Bertrand oligopoly model (see, e.g., Epstein and Rubinfeld, 2004). Much of the analysis surrounding collusive conduct has as its conceptual framework a model of repeated Cournot competition along the lines of Green and Porter (1984) (see, e.g., Ivaldi et al., 2007).

though it may not have been achievable, marginal cost pricing was a clear and sensible benchmark against which one could evaluate firms' behavior. As the discussion below will make clear, this is a luxury that concurrent issues in antitrust are no longer necessarily afforded because notions of competitive pricing are often vague or vacuous.

3.2.2 Recent Developments in Antitrust

The two salient developments in antitrust in recent times are, on the one hand, an upsurge of concern with big tech companies and, on the other hand, a recognition of the need to account for bargaining and negotiation procedures that are not captured by standard oligopoly models.

The last few years have seen an upsurge of interest in and concern with competition issues in the digital age. In 2019 alone, the Australian Competition and Consumer Commission, the European Commission, the Digital Competition Expert Panel in the United Kingdom, and the Stigler Center for Study of the Economy and the State produced four substantive reports devoted to that.[4] In the United States and Europe, 2020 saw investigations and antitrust cases launched against Google, Facebook, and Apple, and combinations thereof. The ongoing nature of the concerns is also evident in the creation in 2019 by the U.S. Federal Trade Commission of a permanent "Technology Enforcement Division," which is tasked with monitoring competition and investigating potential anticompetitive conduct in US technology markets. Further, officials at the U.S. Department of Justice have said that: "We plan to *continue* our review of competitive practices by market-leading online platforms, and where necessary address those as well."[5]

Over the last decade or so, there have been a large number of substantial merger cases in which bargaining – understood as a process to determine the terms of trade that is not adequately captured by off-the-shelf oligopoly models – played an important role. Recent cases include the AT&T–Time Warner merger, where a key concern was the merger's effect on negotiations between the merged entity and video content distributors, as well as numerous other media mergers.[6] There is a similarly long list of healthcare mergers, including, for example, the merger of Hackensack Meridian Health and Englewood Healthcare, which raise issues related to negotiations between hospitals

[4] See Australian Competition and Consumer Commission (2019), Cémer et al. (2019), Furman et al. (2019), and Stigler Center (2019).

[5] "Introductory remarks of Deputy Attorney General at announcement of civil antitrust lawsuit filed against Google," October 20, 2020, https://url.uk.m.mimecastprotect.com/s/8_0sCOyllcB7n2BskVUsv?domain=justice.gov (emphasis in the original).

[6] For example, the Nexstar–Tribune merger raised issues related to negotiations between broadcasters and advertisers. For additional examples, see the list on the U.S. Department of Justice's "Antitrust Case Filings" website, https://url.uk.m.mimecastprotect.com/s/QLw5CPZmmuLjW5LIjmVGh?domain=justice.gov

and insurers,[7] as well as other mergers where the relevant market is most appropriately viewed as a bilateral oligopoly, such as the proposed merger of Halliburton-Baker Hughes in oilfield services. Antitrust matters related to the licensing of intellectual property, particularly among pharmaceutical and high-tech firms,[8] are reflected in recently issued antitrust guidelines for the licensing of intellectual property and require an evaluation of the relative bargaining power of the licensor and licensee for the calculation of damages.[9]

Consistent with the cases just mentioned, the 2010 guidelines emphasize the importance and relevance of bargaining and auctions, stating: "In many industries, especially those involving intermediate goods and services, buyers and sellers negotiate to determine prices and other terms of trade. In that process, buyers commonly negotiate with more than one seller, and may play sellers off against one another. Some highly structured forms of such competition are known as auctions. Negotiations often combine aspects of an auction with aspects of one-on-one negotiation, although pure auctions are sometimes used in government procurement and elsewhere" (U.S. Department of Justice and the Federal Trade Commission, 2010, section 6.2).

3.2.3 Recent Developments in Industrial Organization

There has been an upsurge of interest in bargaining in the empirical IO literature, driven both by the advent of big datasets and the need to accommodate negotiated outcomes in counterfactual analyses.

For example, issues of market power and the possibility of countervailing market power are prominent in recent debates surrounding Internet giants such as Google. For example, Decarolis and Rovigatti (2020) show that consolidation among online advertising intermediaries has increased their buyer power, countervailing Google's significant market power in online search, and is consistent with the theoretical result that consolidation that equalizes bargaining power between the buyer and seller sides of the market can increase welfare. Related to online negotiations through eBay's Best Offer bargaining platform, Backus et al. (2020, p. 2) find that "the observation that bargaining very frequently ends in disagreement is consistent with the presence of incomplete information and bargaining costs," and Backus et al. (2019) find that agents take steps to credibly communicate the strength of their bargaining positions.

[7] U.S. Federal Trade Commission, "Merger Review" website, https://url.uk.m.mimecastprotect.com/s/XFeSCQ0JJcw2ONwHrYUm-?domain=ftc.gov

[8] For example, *VirnetX, Inc. v. Cisco Systems* (2014) related to technology used in the FaceTime and VPN features in iOS devices and Mac computers, and *FTC v. Actavis, Inc.* (2013) related to negotiated payments by a drug patentee to a generic drug manufacturer known as "pay-for-delay."

[9] U.S. Department of Justice and Federal Trade Commission, "Antitrust guidelines for the licensing of intellectual property," 2017, https://url.uk.m.mimecastprotect.com/s/xwvaCRoYYF3MEg3fododi?domain=justice.gov. See, e.g., Sidak (2015) on the role of bargaining power in the *Georgia–Pacific* framework for damages calculations and courts' rejection of Nash bargaining for the quantification of damages.

Outside the realm of big Internet firms, Larsen (2020) estimates a model of incomplete-information bargaining in the context of negotiations in the wholesale used-car industry, documenting, empirically, the efficiency effects of private information. Byrne et al. (2022) find evidence of bargaining power effects in negotiations between simulated customers and call centers for providers of retail electricity, where customers demonstrating a greater willingness and ability to search and bargain obtained better prices. Sweeting et al. (2018) examine data on US beer sales and show that signaling effects that arise with incomplete information can cause merger simulations that assume complete information to significantly underpredict post-merger price rises. Related to the licensing of intellectual property, Caves et al. (1983) find evidence that patent owners cannot fully appropriate a licensee's maximum rent due, in part, to incomplete information, and Kankanhalli and Kwan (2019) provide empirical evidence that royalty rates in intellectual property licensing agreements are affected by bargaining power.

In contrast to the research just mentioned, to date, the more standard approach to the empirical analysis of markets with negotiated prices has been to use the complete-information models of Nash bargaining and Nash-in-Nash bargaining.[10] The Nash bargaining solution has the feature that parties divide a fixed pie, with no tradeoff between the division of the pie and its overall size. For example, one way that greater bargaining power might express itself is through more aggressive offers, with the result that bargaining is more likely to break down. But because bargaining breakdown does not occur in Nash bargaining on the equilibrium path, that model is a poor fit for settings where there is systematic bargaining breakdown on the equilibrium path. For example, Backus et al. (2020) find a breakdown probability of roughly 55% in data covering 25 million observations of bilateral negotiations on eBay.[11]

The Nash-in-Nash model, introduced by Horn and Wolinsky (1988), extends Nash bargaining to accommodate multiple simultaneous Nash bargains.[12] In that model, the bargaining equilibrium is the Nash equilibrium of a game in which players participate in potentially many Nash bargains, but with each player essentially sending separate representatives to each Nash bargain, with no coordination across the representatives of a player. As noted by Crawford and Yurukoglu (2012, p. 659): "This setup does not allow for advantages due to informational asymmetries... We view this absence of informational asymmetries as a weakness of the bargaining model. In return, however, we gain tractability in determining how the threat of unilateral disagreement

[10] The remarks of Nevo (2014) describe the important role that the theory of Nash bargaining plays in antitrust practice, and Shapiro (2018) uses the Nash bargaining model to analyze and quantify competitive harms associated with the AT&T–Time Warner merger.

[11] As described by Crawford (2014), there are regular blackouts of broadcast television stations on cable and satellite distribution platforms due to the breakdown of negotiations over the terms for retransmission of the broadcast signal.

[12] Collard-Wexler et al. (2019) and Rey and Vergé (2019) provide theoretical foundations for the Nash-in-Nash model.

determines input costs in a bilaterally oligopolistic setting." Thus, although the Nash-in-Nash model constrains the market interaction in a way that raises concerns, it is viewed as offering a benefit in terms of tractability.

The large literature making use of Nash-based models is testament to the relevance of negotiated outcomes, bargaining power, and countervailing power in industrial organization. On the effects of hospital mergers on bargaining power and negotiated outcomes, see, for example, Capps et al. (2003), Sorensen (2003), Capps and Dranove (2004), Dafny (2009), Gaynor and Town (2012), Cutler and Scott Morton (2013), Gowrisankaran et al. (2015), Ho and Lee (2017, 2019), Craig et al. (2020), and Prager and Schmitt (2021).[13] For example, Ho and Lee (2017) apply the Nash-in-Nash framework to the question of countervailing power by insurers when negotiating with hospitals and find evidence that consolidation among insurers improves their bargaining position vis-à-vis hospitals. Craig et al. (2020) find evidence that following mergers, hospitals are able to negotiate somewhat lower prices for medical supplies, consistent with mergers involving countervailing effects of improved buyer power and managerial disruption.[14] For media mergers, where negotiations play a role in determining what content is distributed where and at what prices and what rates are paid by advertisers, see, for example, Gal-Or and Dukes (2003, 2006) and Crawford et al. (2018). Related to bundling and vertical integration, see Crawford and Yurukoglu (2012) and Crawford et al. (2018). Related to intellectual property, for Nash bargaining-based models of patent hold-up and litigation, see, for example, Katz and Shapiro (1985), Bessen and Meurer (2006), Shapiro (2010), Ganglmair et al. (2012), Lemus and Temnyalov (2017), and Choi and Gerlach (2017).

3.2.4 The Case for Incomplete-Information IO Models

As mentioned, in models of complete-information bargaining, the only thing to be bargained over is the distribution of the pie; whether or not there is a pie to share and, if so, its size is common knowledge before bargaining even starts. This not only makes it difficult for complete-information bargaining models to account for the salient real-world phenomenon of bargaining breakdown, but also deprives bargaining of some of its most important features.[15] While complete-information bargaining models have been criticized by some

[13] On bargaining between hospitals and suppliers of medical devices, see Grennan (2013, 2014) and Grennan and Swanson (2020). In work on insurer–hospital bargaining, Lewis and Pflum (2015) find that bargaining power (the share of generated surplus captured by an agent) is a greater determinant of post-merger markups than bargaining positions (the agent's threat point).

[14] They conclude that price savings seem "modest relative to the cross-sectional price variation across hospitals and claims of potential savings via increased 'buyer power'" (Craig et al., 2020, p. 41). Related to buyer power more generally, see, for example, Snyder (1996) and Caprice and Rey (2015).

[15] Or, as Fudenberg and Tirole (1991, p. 399) put it: "bargaining derives much of its interest from incomplete information."

economists[16] (and, of course, been embraced by many others), some skepticism vis-à-vis complete-information bargaining has also been uttered by practitioners, perhaps most vocally by Judge Leon in the AT&T–Time Warner merger case. Upon hearing the government's Nash bargaining model, he wrote: "I wondered on the record whether its complexity made it seem like a Rube Goldberg contraption... But in fairness to Mr. Goldberg, at least his contraptions would normally move a pea from one side of a room to another. By contrast, the evidence at trial showed that [the] model lacks both 'reliability and factual credibility,' and thus fails to generate probative predictions of future harm associated with the Government's increased-leverage theory" (Leon, 2018, p. 32).

3.2.4.1 Incomplete-Information Bargaining

The modeling backbone for incomplete-information bargaining that we work with is the bilateral trade model of Myerson and Satterthwaite (1983), which we revisit in the next section, and its generalizations such as Williams (1987), who extended it to allow the traders to have different bargaining weights, and Gresik and Satterthwaite (1989), who generalized it to multiple traders on each side of the market. As observed by Ausubel et al. (2002, p. 1934), in light of the results of Myerson and Satterthwaite (1983), insisting on efficiency in incomplete-information bargaining is "fruitless." The methodology we employ is mechanism design, and empowered and encouraged by the revelation principle (see below), our focus is on direct mechanisms. It is our view, and our aim to convince readers, that the time is ripe to do so.[17]

Earlier literature on incomplete-information bargaining has paid considerable attention to the extensive-form game in which bargaining takes place. Part of the reason for this was theoretical. Ausubel et al. (2002, p. 1908) note that, despite its virtues, the mechanism-design approach has the weaknesses of relying on common knowledge of agents' beliefs and utility functions and of assuming too much commitment. They write: "In practice bargainers use simple trading rules – such as a sequence of offers and counteroffers – that do not depend on beliefs or utility functions. And bargainers may be unable to walk away from known gains from trade." As will become clear from the analysis below, it is precisely by varying an agent's ability to walk away from known gains from trade that the mechanism-design approach is

[16] For example, Holmström and Myerson (1983, p. 1809) note: "Some economists, following Coase have ... argued that we should expect to observe efficient allocations in any economy where there is complete information and bargaining costs are small. However, this positive aspect of efficiency does not extend to economies with incomplete information." For a similar view, see Samuelson (1985).

[17] Fifteen to 20 years ago, there was something of a breakthrough of auction theory into "mainstream" economics, with Paul Klemperer explaining "why every economist should learn some auction theory" (Klemperer, 2002); see also Krishna (2002), Klemperer (2004), and Milgrom (2004). With that in mind, the view and belief expressed here is that now is the time to move to another level of abstraction and to embrace the mechanism-design approach.

able to capture notions like bargaining and buyer power, which have social surplus effects. So we view the ability of the mechanism-design approach to endow agents with such commitment power as a merit rather than as a shortcoming. Of course, we maintain the assumption of common knowledge of type distributions and payoff functions throughout. In defense of this assumption, we merely note that every model has to start somewhere and stipulating that agents share a common prior has proved a productive assumption in economics. Further, the assumption is not specific to incomplete-information models, although it is almost exclusively raised in the context of incomplete-information models, perhaps because it is, somewhat ironically, more glaring there. With complete information, agents do not only have common knowledge of distributions and utility functions, but they also happen to know that every agent's distribution is degenerate with the lower bound of support equal to its upper bound. Put differently, progress toward models that dispense with the common-knowledge assumption would add value, but lack thereof is nothing that sets incomplete-information models at any disadvantage relative to complete-information models because, whatever criticism applies to the former, *a fortiori* applies to the latter.

Another part of the motivation for extensive-form representations of bargaining seems to have been empirical. For example, the structural estimation approach in auctions makes use of knowledge of the auction format – for example, first-price auction in Guerre et al. (2000) – and assumptions about type distributions and equilibrium – in this case, identical distributions and Bayes Nash equilibrium – to estimate the distributions of types based on bidding data. From a practical modeling perspective, the problem of relying on extensive forms is that they permit tractability only in special cases. For example, the first-price auction is tractable with identical distributions but rarely otherwise.[18] Likewise, the k-double-auction of Chatterjee and Samuelson (1983) is tractable for two bidders and uniform distributions, but not otherwise. This severely impedes the use of these models for, say, merger review because the distributions cannot sensibly be stipulated to be the same across all bidders before and after two agents merge. These problems are compounded in an empirical context, where it is arguably more often than not the case that the outside observers cannot be sure that they observe the precise bargaining game that is being played.[19]

[18] Of course, the first-price auction is detail-free in the sense of Wilson (1987), which makes it appealing for practical use. But that does not make it a suitable theoretical device to model price formation any more than the great theoretical properties of the second-price (or Vickrey) auction make it appealing for practical use.

[19] As Fudenberg and Tirole (1991, pp. 398–399) note: "Even with complete information, any split of the pie can be obtained by changing the extensive form for bargaining. This is worrisome because we, as outside observers of a bargaining process, usually have little information about which extensive form is being played, and furthermore the extensive form is likely to vary from one situation to the next. Of course, in any application of game theory the conclusions can vary

Fortunately, reliance on knowledge of the extensive form is not required empirically either. As Larsen and Zhang (2018) show, incentive compatibility and the revelation principle can be used, together with the hypothesis that agents' actions constitute a Bayes Nash equilibrium, to infer type distributions from limited observations of agents' actions, payments, and allocations. We illustrate their approach in Section 3.4.5 below.

3.2.4.2 From Extensive Forms to Direct Mechanisms

Real-world bargaining can take a variety of forms. Its description might be relatively straightforward, such as when a seller posts a take-it-or-leave-it price, which a buyer can then either accept or reject. Or, the price-determination process might involve significant back and forth, with the buyer and seller engaging in a set of unstructured offers and counteroffers and other communication over time, eventually settling on terms of trade. The process might be partially structured, with an initial auction phase in which suppliers submit bids to an online platform, but then the buyer might continue to negotiate with one or more of the auction participants, perhaps asking for additional concessions or asking for quantity discounts, after the auction phase is over. The specification of the details of a bargaining process is referred to as its *extensive form*. Extensive forms have in common that they take as inputs the characteristics and private information of the parties, particularly as related to the good being traded, and, through the application of agents' optimal strategies given their private information, produce as outputs a specification of what trades occur and what payments are made. These inputs and outputs are also the information required to evaluate the contribution of the bargaining process to consumer, producer, and social surplus. This raises the question: To understand how a particular set of inputs (agent characteristics and private information) affect outcomes such as consumer, producer, and social surplus, do we need to allow for all the possible extensive-form bargaining games that could be played and how they might be played? Happily, the answer to this is no. The *revelation principle* implies that any extensive-form game that agents with independent private information might play can be reformulated as a *direct mechanism* that maps agents' reports of their private information to allocations and transfers. Somewhat more precisely, given an extensive-form game and optimal strategies for all the players as a function of their independent private information, there exists a direct mechanism such that it is optimal for each agent to truthfully report its private information to the mechanism and such that the direct mechanism replicates the outcome associated with the agents' optimal strategies in the extensive-form game (see, e.g., Myerson, 1981, lemma 1; Börgers, 2015, proposition 2.1). This powerful result simplifies our task greatly because it implies that without loss of generality, we can focus on direct mechanisms.

with the extensive form chosen, but the issue seems more serious here than in other contexts, in which we may be able to limit attention to a smaller set of extensive forms."

3.2.5 Of Maps and Models

Models, like maps, are abstractions. As such, they deliberately violate certain facts and data in order to shed light on others. Just as the usefulness of a map depends on its purpose, so does the value of a specific model. In industrial organization and antitrust, the purpose of a model is to serve as a conceptual framework for problems that involve tradeoffs between social surplus and profit and to permit the conceptualization of policy counterfactuals. Using a flat map does not make a traveler a flat-worlder, nor does adhering to a model with rational, risk-neutral agents with a common prior mean that the economists who do so believe that these assumptions are factual descriptions. No user of a flat map would ever be accused of holding the erroneous and demonstrably wrong belief that buildings are two-dimensional. Those who use these kinds of maps and models find them useful because they serve the purpose of guiding them from here to there.

It is also worth remembering that new scientific theories often precede the arrival of data substantiating them. This was true for Copernicus and Galilei, who stipulated – without evidence (for centuries to come) – that the Sun rather than the Earth is the center of our solar system, for Darwin's theory of evolution, and Einstein's theory of relativity (and, if you like, the independent private values model). It was not notions of plausibility and realism of the assumptions that won the day for these new approaches.[20] Indeed, it is difficult to argue that the idea that we and everything on Earth move at all times at speeds faster than bullets fly is more plausible or realistic than stipulating that Earth stands still. This seems worth bearing in mind when discussing and evaluating the pros and cons of the incomplete information approach to IO.

3.3 METHODOLOGY

In this section, we first describe the setup, and then explore implications of incentive compatibility and individual rationality. Then we examine optimal and efficient mechanisms. We conclude with a discussion of the uniqueness of the properties of the independent private values setting.

3.3.1 Setup

We consider a setup with multiple buyers and sellers, although in some cases we specialize to the case of bilateral trade, where there is just one buyer and just one seller, or even to the case of a single agent interacting with a mechanism designer. In the baseline setup, there are n buyers and m sellers.

We assume that agents have independent private types. Each buyer i has private value v_i for one unit of a good, where v_i is drawn independently from the distribution F with support $[\underline{v}, \overline{v}]$. Each seller j can produce one unit of the

[20] See, for example, Kuhn (1970).

good at private cost c_j drawn independently from distribution G with support $[\underline{c},\overline{c}]$. We assume that $\underline{c} < \overline{v}$ so that gains from trade are possible.

We assume that agents are risk-neutral, implying that the expected payoff of buyer i with value v_i that trades expected quantity q and makes an expected payment to the mechanism of m is $qv_i - m$, and the expected payoff of seller j with cost c_j that trades expected quantity q and receives expected payment from the mechanism of m is $m - qc_j$.

3.3.2 Incentive Compatibility, Individual Rationality, and their Implications

To explore the powerful implications of incentive compatibility, focus temporarily on a single agent, which could be either a buyer or a seller. To embrace both possibilities, we denote the agent's type by $x \in [\underline{x},\overline{x}]$, which would be $v \in [\underline{v},\overline{v}]$ for a buyer and $c \in [\underline{c},\overline{c}]$ for a seller. Take as given a direct mechanism $\langle q,m\rangle$, where $q : [\underline{x},\overline{x}] \to [0,1]$ for a buyer and $q : [\underline{x},\overline{x}] \to [-1,0]$ for a seller, and where $m : [\underline{x},\overline{x}] \to \mathbb{R}$. The mechanism maps the agent's reported type $z \in [\underline{x},\overline{x}]$ onto an expected quantity traded $q(z)$ and expected payment to the mechanism $m(z)$.[21] As mentioned above, by the *revelation principle* (see, e.g., Myerson, 1981, lemma 1; Börgers, 2015, proposition 2.1), a focus on direct mechanisms is without loss of generality.

The payoff of an agent with type x that reports z is

$$U(x,z) \equiv q(x)x - m(z),$$

and the payoff of an agent with type x under truthful reporting is

$$U(x) \equiv q(x)x - m(x). \tag{3.1}$$

The mechanism is *incentive-compatible* if an agent's payoff from truthful reporting is greater than or equal to its payoff from reporting any other type.[22] That is, for all $x,z \in [\underline{x},\overline{x}]$,

$$U(x) \geq q(z)x - m(z) = U(z) + q(z)(x-z). \tag{3.2}$$

Individual rationality is satisfied if, for all $x \in [\underline{x},\overline{x}]$, $U(x) \geq 0$.

For example, if $q(z) > 0$ and $m(z) > 0$, then the agent is a buyer that receives $q(z)$ units of a good for which it has a per-unit value of x in exchange for a

[21] With multiple agents, define $q(z)$ and $m(z)$ to be the agent's expected allocation and transfer when its report is z, with the expectation taken over the other agents' types.

[22] With multiple agents, one can distinguish between incentive compatibility as we have defined it, that is, evaluated at the interim stage when an agent knows its own type, but not the types of the other agents, and ex-post, also known as dominant strategy, incentive compatibility, which requires that an agent's payoff is maximized by truthful reporting for all possible reports of the other agents' types. In our independent private values setting, the outcome of any interim (Bayesian) incentive-compatible and interim individually rational mechanism can be implemented with a mechanism that satisfies dominant strategy incentive compatibility and ex-post individual rationality (Gershkov et al., 2013).

payment of $m(z)$. If instead $q(z) < 0$ and $m(z) < 0$, then the agent is a seller that produces $|q(z)|$ units of a good at a per-unit cost of x and receives a payment of $m(z)$ from the mechanism.

Following standard arguments (see, e.g., Börgers, 2015, chapter 2), we can write the definition of incentive compatibility in (3.2) as: for all $x \in [\underline{x}, \overline{x}]$,

$$U(x) = \max_{z \in [\underline{x}, \overline{x}]} q(z)x - m(z).$$

This implies that U is a maximum of a family of affine functions, which implies that U is convex and so absolutely continuous and differentiable almost everywhere in the interior of its domain.[23]

Further, the definition of incentive compatibility in (3.2) is equivalent to: for all $x, z \in [\underline{x}, \overline{x}]$,

$$U(x) - U(z) \geq q(z)(x - z).$$

Dividing both sides by $x - z$, one obtains, for $x > z$, $\frac{U(x)-U(z)}{x-z} \geq q(z)$ and, for $x < z$, $\frac{U(x)-U(z)}{x-z} \leq q(z)$. Letting $z \to x$ thus yields $U'(x) \geq q(x) \geq U'(x)$ at every point at which U is differentiable, forcing the conclusion that at every such point, $U'(x) = q(x)$. In other words, for all x, $q(x)$ is the slope of a line that supports the function U at the point x. This is illustrated in Figure 3.1.

Because U is convex, it follows that q is nondecreasing. Further, because every absolutely continuous function is the definite integral of its derivative, for any $x, z \in [\underline{x}, \overline{x}]$, we have

$$U(x) = U(z) + \int_z^x q(t)dt. \tag{3.3}$$

Equation (3.3) is often referred to as the *payoff equivalence theorem* (Börgers, 2015, lemma 2.3) because it implies that, up to the constant $U(z)$, the agent's

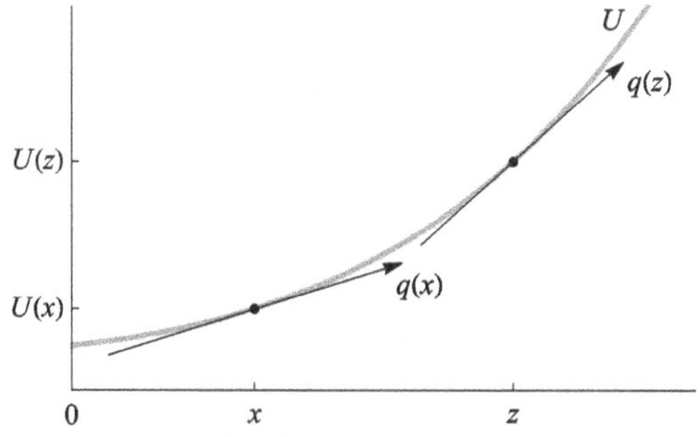

Figure 3.1 Illustration of the convexity of U (Krishna, 2010, figure 5.2).

[23] A function $h : [\underline{x}, \overline{x}] \to \mathbb{R}$ is absolutely continuous if for all $\varepsilon > 0$ there exists $\delta > 0$ such that whenever a finite sequence of pairwise disjoint sub-intervals (x_k, x_k') of $[\underline{x}, \overline{x}]$ satisfies $\sum_k (x_k' - x_k) < \delta$, then $\sum_k |h(x_k') - h(x_k)| < \varepsilon$. One can show that absolute continuity on the compact interval $[a, b]$ implies that h has a derivative h' almost everywhere, the derivative is Lebesgue integrable, and $h(x) = h(a) + \int_a^x h'(t)dt$ for all $x \in [a, b]$ (see, e.g., theorem 18 in chapter 6 of Royden and Fitzpatrick, 2010).

payoff when its type is x is pinned down by the allocation rule q.[24] That is, all incentive-compatible mechanisms with the same allocation rule give the agent the same payoff up to an additive constant. The payoff equivalence theorem provides the important insight that the allocation rule is the key component. For example, if one is interested in efficient allocation, an agent's payoff is, up to an additive constant, pinned down. In addition, the payoff equivalence theorem has the important implication for IO applications that perfect price discrimination is ruled out. If two different types of the same agent get the same allocation, they must get or make the same payment. Hence, holding the allocation fixed, the price cannot vary.

Using the payoff equivalence theorem, it follows from (3.3) with $z = \underline{v}$ that for a buyer, $U'(v) = q(v) \geq 0$, and so the buyer with type $\underline{v}$ is the worst-off type of buyer. Using (3.3) with $z = \overline{c}$, we have $U(c) = U(\overline{c}) + \int_{\overline{c}}^{c} q(t)dt = U(\overline{c}) - \int_{c}^{\overline{c}} q(t)dt$, so for a seller, who has $q(c) \leq 0$, $U'(c) = q(c) \leq 0$, implying that the seller with type $\overline{c}$ is the worst-off type of seller. It is then necessary and sufficient for individual rationality that for a buyer $U(\underline{v}) \geq 0$ and for a seller $U(\overline{c}) \geq 0$.

Equating the expressions for $U(x)$ from (3.1) and (3.3) yields the following implication of the payoff equivalence theorem:

$$m(x) = q(x)x - \int_{z}^{x} q(t)dt - U(z). \tag{3.4}$$

This is sometimes referred to as the *revenue equivalence theorem* (Börgers, 2015, lemma 2.4) because it states that the (expected) payment to or from an agent of type x is pinned down, up to a constant, by the allocation rule. Riley and Samuelson (1981) noticed an instance of this principle in their analysis of revenue equivalence among "standard auctions" with identically distributed types, where a standard auction is defined as an auction that always allocates the good to the highest bidder and gives a payoff of zero to the lowest possible type, that is, is characterized by $U(\underline{x}) = 0$.

While the analysis above shows that incentive compatibility implies that q is nondecreasing, one can also show that if q is nondecreasing, then the mechanism with allocation rule q and payment rule given by (3.4) is incentive-compatible. To see this, note that given the payment rule in (3.4), the payoff of an agent with type x that reports $\hat{x}$ is

$$U(x,\hat{x}) \equiv (x-\hat{x})q(\hat{x}) + \int_{z}^{\hat{x}} q(t)dt + U(z),$$

which means that the incremental payoff of an agent with type x that reports truthfully versus reporting $\hat{x}$ is

[24] An early instance of this theorem, under the assumption that the ex-post allocation rule is efficient, was established by Holmström (1979).

$$
\begin{aligned}
U(x) - U(x,\hat{x}) &= \int_z^x q(t)dt - (x-\hat{x})q(\hat{x}) - \int_z^{\hat{x}} q(t)dt \\
&= \int_{\hat{x}}^x q(t)dt - (x-\hat{x})q(\hat{x}) \\
&= \int_{\hat{x}}^x (q(t)-q(\hat{x}))dt,
\end{aligned}
$$

which is nonnegative if q is nondecreasing, establishing incentive compatibility. Thus, the mechanism $\langle q,m \rangle$ is incentive-compatible if and only if q is nondecreasing and m satisfies (3.4) (Börgers, 2015, proposition 2.2).

If we now make use of information on the distribution of the agent's type, we can derive an expression for the agent's expected payment. For this purpose, assume that the agent's type is distributed according to distribution H with support $[\underline{x},\overline{x}]$ and continuous, positive density h. Define the agent's *virtual value* function Φ_H and *virtual cost* function Γ_H by

$$
\Phi_H(x) \equiv x - \frac{1-H(x)}{h(x)} \quad \text{and} \quad \Gamma_H(x) \equiv x + \frac{H(x)}{h(x)}.
$$

For the case of a buyer, we have $H = F$, $h = f$, and $[\underline{x},\overline{x}] = [\underline{v},\overline{v}]$. In this case, the relevant virtual value function is $\Phi_F \equiv \Phi$, where we drop the distribution subscript. For the case of a seller, we have $H = G$, $h = g$, and $[\underline{x},\overline{x}] = [\underline{c},\overline{c}]$, and the relevant virtual cost function is $\Gamma_G \equiv \Gamma$. We assume that Φ and Γ are increasing. We discuss the role of this assumption below – it is analogous to the assumption of decreasing marginal revenue and increasing marginal cost.

Given $z \in [\underline{x},\overline{x}]$, we can write the agent's expected payment as follows (for details on how one obtains this expression, see Appendix A3.1):

$$
\begin{aligned}
\mathbb{E}_x[m(x)] &= \int_{\underline{x}}^{\overline{x}} m(t)h(t)dt \\
&= \int_{\underline{x}}^{z} \Gamma_H(t)q(t)h(t)dt + \int_z^{\overline{x}} \Phi_H(t)q(t)h(t)dt - U(z) \\
&= \mathbb{E}_x[\Gamma_H(x)q(x) \mid x \le z]\Pr(x \le z) \\
&\quad + \mathbb{E}_x[\Phi_H(x)q(x) \mid x \ge z]\Pr(x \ge z) - U(z).
\end{aligned}
$$

Thus, we have the result that in any incentive-compatible direct mechanism $\langle q,m \rangle$, the agent's expected payment to the mechanism (and, symmetrically, the expected revenue to the mechanism) is pinned down by the allocation rule, virtual type functions, and type distribution, up to an additive constant.

For example, if the agent is a buyer, then its worst-off type is $\underline{v}$. Letting $z = \underline{v}$ in the expression above, the buyer's expected payment to the mechanism is

$$
\mathbb{E}_v[m(v)] = \mathbb{E}_v[\Phi(v)q(v)] - U(\underline{v}).
$$

If the agent is a seller, then its worst-off type is $\overline{c}$. Letting $z = \overline{c}$ implies that the seller's expected payment *from* the mechanism is

$$-\mathbb{E}_c[m(c)] = \mathbb{E}_c[\Gamma(c)|q(c)|] + U(\overline{c}).$$

Of course, by combining these expressions for the expected payment to the mechanism by buyers and the expected payment from the mechanism to sellers, we can obtain expressions for the expected budget surplus of the mechanism itself, which, as this shows, depends critically on the allocation rule. This leads us to the following discussion of optimal and efficient mechanisms.

3.3.3 Optimal and Efficient Mechanisms

Given the mechanism-design setup just discussed, we can consider key questions of what is the optimal mechanism and whether efficient mechanisms exist that satisfy incentive compatibility and individual rationality and do not run a deficit.

We begin by considering optimal mechanisms. We revisit Myerson's (1981) derivation of the optimal auction of an object for which the auctioneer has commonly known cost $c < \overline{v}$ to a buyer with private value v defined as above to be drawn from distribution F on $[\underline{v}, \overline{v}]$. We seek the mechanism $\langle q, m \rangle$ that maximizes the auctioneer's expected payoff subject to incentive compatibility and individual rationality. We know from the analysis above that we can write the auctioneer's expected payoff from any incentive-compatible mechanism $\langle q, m \rangle$ as

$$\mathbb{E}_v[m(v) - cq(v)] = \mathbb{E}_v[(\Phi(v) - c)q(v)] - U(\underline{v}).$$

If Φ is increasing, which Myerson (1981) refers to as the *regular* case, then the auctioneer optimally sets $q(v) = 1$ if $\Phi(v) \geq c$ and $q(v) = 0$ otherwise, and sets $U(\underline{v}) = 0$, which is the lowest amount such that the buyer's individual-rationality constraint is satisfied. This amounts to a take-it-or-leave-it offer by the auctioneer of $\Phi^{-1}(c)$ (or an ascending-bid auction with a reserve of $\Phi^{-1}(c)$).[25] Analogously, assuming that Γ is increasing, the optimal mechanism for the purchase of one unit for which the auctioneer has commonly known value $v > \underline{c}$ from a seller with private cost c drawn from distribution G on $[\underline{c}, \overline{c}]$ is a take-it-or-leave-it offer of $\Gamma^{-1}(v)$.[26]

As observed by Mussa and Rosen (1978), virtual value functions can be interpreted as marginal revenue functions and, analogously, virtual cost functions can be interpreted as marginal cost functions. To see this, drawing on Bulow and Roberts (1989), note that the demand at price p by a buyer whose value is drawn from distribution F is $D(p) = 1 - F(p)$, and so the revenue associated with quantity Q is $R(Q) \equiv QF^{-1}(1-Q)$. Noting that $R'(Q) = F^{-1}(1-Q) - \frac{1-F(F^{-1}(1-Q))}{f(F^{-1}(1-Q))} = \Phi(F^{-1}(1-Q))|_{p=F^{-1}(1-Q)} = \Phi(p)$, the

[25] For $c < \Phi(\underline{v})$, define $\Phi^{-1}(c) \equiv \underline{v}$, implying that the seller's take-it-or-leave-it offer is $\underline{v}$.
[26] For $v > \Gamma(\overline{c})$, define $\Gamma^{-1}(v) \equiv \overline{c}$, implying that the buyer's take-it-or-leave-it offer is $\overline{c}$.

assumption of decreasing marginal revenue is then equivalent to the assumption that the virtual value function Φ is increasing. Thus, Myersonian regularity, that is, the assumption of an increasing virtual value function, corresponds to decreasing marginal revenue, or equivalently, concave revenue, and, analogously, the assumption of an increasing virtual cost function corresponds to increasing marginal cost.[27] Further, because a monopoly seller with a constant or increasing marginal cost function and concave revenue function optimally sets a uniform price, uniform pricing follows as a conclusion, not an assumption, from our mechanism-design setup with regularity.[28]

To consider the existence of efficient mechanisms, let us now move to a bilateral trade setting with one buyer with private value v and one seller with private cost c. In that case, the direct mechanism $\langle Q, M_B, M_S \rangle$ maps the type vector (v,c) to a quantity traded, $Q(v,c) \in \{0,1\}$, a payment from the buyer, $M_B(v,c)$, and a payment to the seller $M_S(v,c)$. Of course, the mechanism is required to be incentive-compatible and individually rational. As mentioned above, incentive compatibility and individual rationality are defined in terms of the agent's interim expected allocation and payment. For the buyer, those are $q_B(v) \equiv \mathbb{E}_c[Q(v,c)]$ and $m_B(v) \equiv \mathbb{E}_c[M_B(v,c)]$, and for the seller, they are $q_S(c) \equiv \mathbb{E}_v[Q(v,c)]$ and $m_S(c) \equiv \mathbb{E}_v[M_S(v,c)]$. We say that a mechanism satisfies the *no-deficit* condition if the mechanism does not run a deficit in expectation, that is, if $\mathbb{E}_{v,c}[m_B(v) - m_S(c)] \geq 0$. Under the view that a mechanism represents a market outcome, it makes sense to restrict attention to mechanisms that satisfy the no-deficit condition so that no resources have to be injected into the system, and a risk-neutral intermediary would be willing to facilitate the mechanism.

Consider the question of whether efficient trade can be achieved in the bilateral trade setup. That is, does there exist an incentive-compatible, individually rational, no-deficit mechanism that has the efficient allocation rule $Q^E(v,c) = 1$ if $v \geq c$ and $Q^E(v,c) = 0$ otherwise? Myerson and Satterthwaite (1983) provide an answer to this question: it depends on whether the supports of the distributions of v and c overlap. Economically, overlapping supports mean that trade is sometimes but not always ex-post efficient. Myerson and Satterthwaite (1983) show that if $\underline{v} < \overline{c}$, that is, the type spaces overlap, then there is no such mechanism. This is their famous *impossibility* result.

We can now see how the power of incentive compatibility comes into play to prove the Myerson–Satterthwaite impossibility result. We first prove the impossibility result for the special case in which the buyer's and seller's

[27] If the virtual type functions are not increasing, then more care is required to ensure that incentive compatibility holds, that is, that the allocation rule is nondecreasing. This is where Myerson's (1981) "ironing" techniques come into play. While the expected payment $\mathbb{E}_v[m(v)]$ is characterized by the "unironed" virtual types, regardless of whether the virtual type functions are increasing, the allocation rule for the optimal mechanism must be defined in terms of "ironed" virtual types in the absence of regularity. See Section 3.4.4 for further discussion.

[28] In contrast, if the monopoly has increasing marginal costs and the revenue function that it faces is not concave, then setting non-market-clearing prices may be optimal; see the discussion in Section 3.4.4.

support are identical and, without further loss of generality, equal $[0,1]$, and then we generalize. Define $q_B^E(v) \equiv \mathbb{E}_c[Q^E(v,c)] = G(v)$ and $q_S^E(c) \equiv \mathbb{E}_v[Q^E(v,c)] = 1-F(c)$. It follows that the expected payment from the buyer is $\mathbb{E}_v[\Phi(v)G(v)]$ and the expected payment to the seller is $\mathbb{E}_c[\Gamma(c)(1-F(c))]$ up to constants which must be nonnegative by individual rationality. If any such mechanism satisfies the no-deficit constraint, then it includes the one with the constants equal to zero, so we proceed with that mechanism. Hence, expected revenue to the mechanism is

$$\begin{aligned}\mathbb{E}_v[\Phi(v)G(v)] - \mathbb{E}_c[\Gamma(c)(1-F(c))] &= \int_0^1 \Phi(v)G(v)f(v)dv \\ &\quad - \int_0^1 \Gamma(c)(1-F(c))g(c)dc \\ &= -\int_0^1 (1-F(x))G(x)dx \\ &< 0,\end{aligned}$$

where the second equality follows from substituting the expression for Φ and Γ, noting that $G(x)f(x)-(1-F(x))g(x) = -\frac{d}{dx}[(1-F(x))G(x)]$, and integrating by parts. The inequality is a consequence of the integrand being positive for all $x \in (0,1)$ and nonnegative at the bounds. Notice that the mechanism's deficit $\int_0^1 (1-F(x))G(x)dx$ is equal to the expected social surplus, which is $\int_0^1 \int_0^v (v-c)g(c)f(v)dcdv$. For example, for F and G uniform, the expected social surplus and the deficit are $1/6$.

To generalize this argument, and to see how the deficit result depends on $\underline{v} < \overline{c}$, consider the dominant-strategy implementation of the efficient allocation rule whose payment rule is given by $\hat{M}_B(v,c) \equiv \max\{c,\underline{v}\}$ if $v \geq c$ and $\hat{M}_B(v,c) \equiv 0$ otherwise, and $\hat{M}_S(v,c) \equiv \min\{v,\overline{c}\}$ if $v \geq c$ and $\hat{M}_S(v,c) \equiv 0$ otherwise.[29] The mechanism $\langle Q^E, \hat{M}_B, \hat{M}_S\rangle$ is incentive-compatible by the usual second-price auction logic, and the mechanism satisfies individual rationality since $U(\underline{v}) = 0 = U(\overline{c})$. If $\underline{v} < \overline{c}$, then

$$\hat{M}_B(v,c) - \hat{M}_S(v,c) \leq 0,$$

with strict inequality with positive probability given that the distributions of v and c are continuous.[30] Because the dominant-strategy implementation runs a deficit, it follows that *any* incentive-compatible, individually rational bilateral trade mechanism with the efficient allocation rule runs a deficit. (For a more

[29] This argument follows closely Krishna (2010, section 5.3.3).

[30] To see this, notice first that if $v \leq \overline{c}$ and $c \geq \underline{v}$, we have $\hat{M}_B(v,c) - \hat{M}_S(v,c) = c - v$, which is negative given that trade is efficient. If $v > \overline{c}$ and $c \geq \underline{v}$, then $\hat{M}_B(v,c) - \hat{M}_S(v,c) = c - \overline{c}$, which is negative (unless $c = \overline{c}$), and if $v > \overline{c}$ and $c < \underline{v}$, then $\hat{M}_B(v,c) - \hat{M}_S(v,c) = \underline{v} - \overline{c}$, which is negative by assumption. Finally, if $c < \underline{v}$ and $v \leq \overline{c}$, then $\hat{M}_B(v,c) - \hat{M}_S(v,c) = \underline{v} - v$, which is negative unless $v = \underline{v}$.

formal demonstration, see Appendix A3.2.) In other words, efficient bilateral trade is not possible without running a deficit.

Intuitively, the deficit for $\underline{v} < \overline{c}$ arises because the buyer and seller are complementary inputs into social surplus. By the usual Vickrey–Clarke–Groves logic (Vickrey, 1961; Clarke, 1971; Groves, 1973), each agent obtains as its payoff its social marginal product, which because of complementarity is larger with the other agent present. Hence, the sum of marginal products exceeds the total product, which is social surplus. This is maybe easiest to see with identical support, that is, if $\underline{v} = \underline{c}$ and $\overline{v} = \overline{c}$. Then each agent's marginal product is simply social surplus. Consequently, the mechanism has to pay two times social surplus and generates it only once, hence incurring a deficit equal to social surplus, which explains the observation made above that with identical supports the expected deficit is equal to expected social surplus.[31] Notice also that if $\underline{v} \geq \overline{c}$, then trade is always efficient and $\hat{M}_B(v,c) - \hat{M}_S(v,c) = \underline{v} - \overline{c} \geq 0$. That is, ex-post efficient trade is possible.[32]

The Myerson–Satterthwaite impossibility result raises the question of what is the maximum expected social surplus that can be achieved in a bilateral trade setting when $\underline{v} < \overline{c}$. Chatterjee and Samuelson (1983) analyze the k-double auction mechanism, in which the buyer submits bid p_B and the seller submits bid p_S and trade occurs if and only if $p_B \geq p_S$, in which case the buyer pays $kp_B + (1-k)p_S$ to the seller. The mechanism satisfies the no-deficit condition by construction. For the case of agents whose types are drawn from the same uniform distribution and who play according to their linear Bayes Nash equilibrium bidding strategies, the k-double auction with $k = 1/2$ is a second-best mechanism (Myerson and Satterthwaite, 1983). Any movement in k away from $1/2$ not only shifts surplus between the two agents, but also reduces the total expected surplus, highlighting the centrality of the payoff–surplus tradeoff. Agents' bargaining power affects not only the division of surplus in bilateral bargaining, but also the total surplus created.

[31] Generalizing Loertscher et al. (2015), Delacrétaz et al. (2019) explore this intuition systematically and show that it extends to a large range of environments with multi-unit traders. The complementarity between agents is also at the source of the deficit in public goods problems, of which, as noted by Mailath and Postlewaite (1990), the bilateral trade problem is a special case.

[32] Another observation is worth making. Under the dominant strategy implementation of the efficient allocation rule, every agent is the residual claimant to the social surplus it creates. Because the implementation does not depend on the distribution from which the agent draws its type, keeping its support fixed, it thus provides the agent with incentives to invest to improve this distribution that align with those of the social planner (see, e.g., Milgrom, 2004). As explored in more detail in Loertscher and Marx (2021a), efficient bargaining under incomplete information thus implies efficient investments. In other words, under efficient incomplete-information bargaining there is no hold-up of the form that is central to the inefficient investments results with complete information bargaining (see, e.g., Grossman and Hart, 1986; Hart and Moore, 1990).

3.3.4 Uniqueness of the Properties of the Independent Private Values Setting

As we have seen, the mechanism-design setup with independent private types and risk-neutral agents allows for the powerful payoff equivalence and revenue equivalence theorems. One might wonder whether even greater applicability could be obtained by venturing outside of these bounds. However, as we now discuss, the literature identifies significant challenges when one relaxes any of the core assumptions.

We have assumed a setup with single-dimensional, independent, private types drawn from continuous distributions, which implies that for a given objective, the mechanism that maximizes this objective, subject to incentive compatibility, individual rationality, and no deficit, is well defined and pinned down (up to a constant in the payments) by the allocation rule, which is unique. As discussed above, it also has the feature that, quite generally, there is a tradeoff between allocating efficiently and extracting payments, which is of particular interest for IO. If one relaxes the assumption of private types, then agents become subject to hold up in a way that they are not when types are private, and the privacy of types means that first-degree price discrimination is not possible.

Dropping the assumption of risk-neutrality, Maskin and Riley (1984) and Matthews (1984) show that optimal mechanisms depend on the nature of risk aversion, are not easily characterized, and may require payments to and/or from losers. Without independence, as foreshadowed by Myerson (1981), Crémer and McLean (1985, 1988) show that there is no tradeoff between profit and social surplus. Without private values, additional, and, therefore, in some sense arbitrary, restrictions may be required to maintain tractability and/or the tradeoff between profit and social surplus (Mezzetti, 2004, 2007). Notwithstanding recent progress, with multi-dimensional private information and multiple agents, the optimal mechanism is not known (see, e.g., Daskalakis et al., 2017). With discrete types, there is no payoff equivalence theorem. In other words, the mechanism is not pinned down by the allocation rule.

Thus, our focus on the setup with single-dimensional, independent, private types drawn from continuous distributions and risk-neutral agents is motivated not only by the power and applicability of that setup, but also by the conclusion that these are essentially the *only* assumptions that permit a tractable approach and that maintain the core tradeoff between profit and social surplus.

3.4 PROGRESS TO DATE

In this section, we review progress in analyzing agents' power in incomplete-information IO models. We start with the definition and analysis of buyer power in Section 3.4.1. Then, in Section 3.4.2, we examine the implications of bargaining power for efficiency. In Section 3.4.3, we illustrate these ideas and others in the context of a k-double auction. In Section 3.4.4, we revisit standard monopoly pricing through the lens of mechanism design. Finally, in Section 3.4.5, we discuss and illustrate estimation in the context of incomplete-information bargaining.

3.4.1 Buyer Power

Notions of buyer power and countervailing power figure prominently in antitrust debates – indeed, there's a long history, with Galbraith referring to the mitigation or regulation of economic power as the oldest of economic problems. Both buyer power and countervailing power are discussed in the context of merger review. Agencies' merger guidelines in the United States state that "The Agencies consider the possibility that powerful buyers may constrain the ability of the merging parties to raise prices" (U.S. Department of Justice and the Federal Trade Commission, 2010), while the European Commission recognizes that it is possible that "buyer power would act as a countervailing factor to an increase in market power resulting from the merger" (European Commission, 2004). Further, the notion has traction in a litigation context: "Although the strong-buyer defense may be valid in a variety of circumstances, I believe that the courts have sometimes embraced it as if it had talismanic power that cured all doubts about a merger" (Steptoe, 1993). As an example, the buyer power of the large oil companies Shell, BP, and ExxonMobil in the purchase of oilfield services was recognized by competition authorities in their evaluation of the proposed merger of Halliburton and Baker Hughes. Let us consider what these seemingly power buyers do when they purchase inputs. The large oil companies hold auctions plus follow-on negotiations for the oilfield services that they purchase. Computer manufacturers such as Dell and HP hold online auctions plus face-to-face negotiations with suppliers of computer components. And governments often hold competitive procurements. This suggests that a natural model of buyer power involves a buyer that uses a procurement mechanism, where buyer power is the ability to use an optimal procurement.

Contributions in the theoretical literature related to buyer power include Galbraith (1952), Stigler (1954), Snyder (1996, 2008), Nocke and Thanassoulis (2014), Caprice and Rey (2015), Loertscher and Marx (2019a), and Decarolis and Rovigatti (2020). Here we focus on the definition of buyer power provided in Loertscher and Marx (2019a), which, similar to Bulow and Klemperer (1996), views buyer power as a buyer's ability to use the optimal mechanism rather than an efficient mechanism. Under this definition, one can analyze buyer power in a mechanism-design setup with one-sided private information where, pre-merger, m sellers have costs drawn from distribution G and one buyer has a commonly known value v. We model a merger of sellers as creating a merged entity whose cost is drawn from the distribution of the minimum of two independent draws from G, which is the distribution $\hat{G}(c) \equiv 1-(1-G(c))^2$.[33]

[33] As discussed in Loertscher and Marx (2019a), most results extend to sellers who are asymmetric pre-merger.

Having no buyer power means that the buyer holds an efficient procurement, thereby ensuring, as suggested by the quote from Ausubel et al. (2002), that no gains from trade remain unrealized. Specifically, one can think of the buyer with no power as using a second-price auction with a reserve r equal to the minimum of the buyer's value and the upper bound of support of the sellers' cost distribution, $r = \min\{v, \overline{c}\}$. This says that a buyer with power can commit not to purchase even if the lowest cost is less than v, but a buyer without power cannot.

As shown in Loertscher and Marx (2019a) and as discussed below, mergers always harm the buyer, regardless of whether the buyer is powerful.[34] Essentially, a merger eliminates a bidder, and that is bad for the buyer. Without buyer power, mergers are always profitable and neutral for rivals because, regardless of the merger, the low-cost seller always trades with the buyer whenever their cost is below the buyer's value. The only change caused by the merger is that the buyer has to pay more if the bid that was eliminated by the merger was the second-lowest cost. In contrast, with buyer power, mergers are not always profitable and, with pre-merger symmetry, benefit rivals and entrants. This occurs because, with buyer power, the buyer discriminates against the merged entity because of its stronger productive power, which tips the scale towards the rivals and potential entrants.

Digging in a bit more on what the optimal procurement looks like in this setup, in the pre-merger market with pre-merger symmetry, one can think of the optimal procurement as selecting the bidder with the lowest cost and then allowing the buyer to make a take-it-or-leave-it offer to that bidder. In the post-merger market, there is no symmetry because the merged entity now draws its cost from the distribution $\hat{G}$. In that case, the optimal procurement selects the bidder with the lowest virtual cost – this has the effect of handicapping the merged entity, so that it has to submit a distinctly lower bid to win – and then allows the buyer to make a take-it-or-leave-it offer to that bidder, where the buyer's optimal take-it-or-leave-it offer is lower for the merged entity than for the other sellers.

As above, denote the virtual cost function for the pre-merger sellers by Γ, and denote the virtual cost function for the merged entity by $\hat{\Gamma}$. Then the optimal take-it-or-leave-it offers are the prices p and $\hat{p}$ that equate the buyer's value with the corresponding virtual cost. Notice that for all $c \in (\underline{c}, \overline{c})$,

$$\Gamma(c) = c + \frac{G(c)}{g(c)} < c + \frac{2 - G(c)}{2 - 2G(c)} \frac{G(c)}{g(c)} = c + \frac{\hat{G}(c)}{\hat{g}(c)} = \hat{\Gamma}(c),$$

which means that the take-it-or-leave-it offer to the merged entity, $\hat{p} = \hat{\Gamma}^{-1}(v)$, is less than the take-it-or-leave-it offer to the other sellers, $p = \Gamma^{-1}(v)$. That

[34] While here we focus on the so-called unilateral effects of a merger, an incomplete-information approach to analyzing additional merger harms due to coordinated effects can be found in Loertscher and Marx (2021b).

is, the buyer negotiates more aggressively with the merged entity than with the pre-merger sellers.

This illustrates a distinction between productive power and bargaining power. A buyer without power is harmed by a merger – buyer surplus decreases because the buyer receives one fewer bid. But, interestingly, a buyer with power is also harmed by the merger. To see this, note that a buyer with power could replicate the post-merger mechanism in the pre-merger market, but because it chooses not to, by revealed preference, the buyer is better off in the pre-merger market than in the post-merger market, and so is harmed by the merger.[35] But as long as the merging sellers are symmetric, buyer power does act as a countervailing force in the sense that a buyer with power is harmed less by a merger than a buyer without power. Intuitively, a buyer with power is able to use discrimination in the post-merger market, which has asymmetric sellers, which reduces the harm experienced by a buyer with power relative to that experienced by a buyer without power, but at the same time introduces distortions in the allocation rule that reduce expected social surplus.

A limitation of the analysis in Loertscher and Marx (2019a) is that sellers have no power and whether the buyer is powerful or not is, largely, treated as exogeneously given.[36] Consequently, there can be no possibility of a merger of sellers causing the bargaining power of those sellers to increase, possibly countervailing the buyer's power. And, the buyer's power is defined to be all or nothing and not to change with a merger. This is the motivation for recent work that relaxes these assumptions, including Loertscher and Marx (2019b, 2021a), which we discuss next. We first review the key results from the prior literature on which this work builds.

3.4.2 Bargaining Power and Social Surplus

Given Myerson and Satterthwaite's impossibility theorem, the efficient allocation rule is "off the table" in bilateral bargaining with overlapping supports, which means that any incentive-compatible, individually rational mechanism that avoids a deficit will be inefficient. Given this, Williams (1987) notes that there can be many allocation rules such that the expected payoffs to the buyer and seller are not Pareto-dominated by the expected payoffs under any other allocation rule. And, there will be an allocation rule that is best for the buyer and others that are best for the seller. Thus, Williams (1987) brings the notion of bargaining power into the incomplete-information bargaining setup. Williams (1987) derives the Pareto frontier of payoff vectors that are possible in incentive-compatible, individually rational, no-deficit, bilateral-trade

35 To be more precise, as there is one more bidder pre-merger, the mechanisms necessarily differ. However, one can implement the post-merger optimal allocation rule pre-merger by having the two merging suppliers compete for the right to produce whenever this allocation induces production by the merged entity; see Loertscher and Marx (2019a) for more details.

36 The exception pertains to a discussion showing that a merger makes a buyer more inclined to *acquire* buyer power.

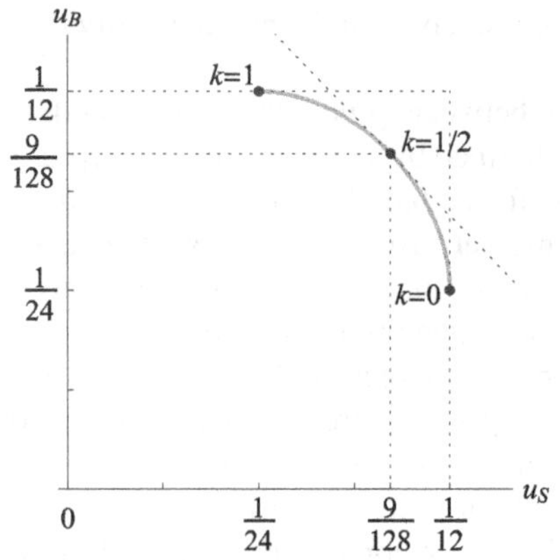

Figure 3.2 Expected payoffs of the buyer, u_B, and the seller, u_S, in the k-double auction for $k \in [0,1]$. Assumes that the buyer's value and the seller's cost are uniformly distributed on $[0,1]$.

mechanisms, which we refer to as the *Williams frontier*. Figure 3.2 illustrates the Williams frontier for the case where the agents' types are drawn from the uniform distribution on $[0,1]$. As the figure shows, the farther from equal division of surplus one moves, the greater is the loss of social surplus. For general distributions, Williams shows that the outcomes of the k-double auction with $k = 1$ ("buyer's bid mechanism") and with $k = 0$ ("seller's price mechanism") are on the Pareto frontier. These points correspond, respectively, to the buyer-optimal and the seller-optimal mechanism.

Keeping bargaining weights the same across all agents, Gresik and Satterthwaite (1989) show that as the number of traders increases, the inefficiency is reduced. They characterize the rate at which a bound on the expected inefficiency of the mechanism's allocations relative to ex-post efficient allocations diminishes as the number of traders increases. Of course, this has implications for how we evaluate the effects of mergers, which reduce the number of traders, in addition to potentially affecting agents' type distributions and bargaining power. In what follows, we illustrate the combination of these effects in the context of a k-double auction.

3.4.3 Illustration Based on the k-Double Auction

We now use the k-double auction of Chatterjee and Samuelson (1983), to illustrate key attributes of the incomplete-information framework. As we show, the model embodies the key payoff-versus-social-surplus tradeoff, allows one to parameterize separately firms' productive power and their bargaining power, and offers scope for analyzing countervailing power. Further, it allows an illustration of the link between investment incentives and the efficiency of the bargaining process.

As mentioned above, in the k-double auction model there is one buyer with a value drawn from distribution F and one seller with a cost drawn from distribution G. Given $k \in [0,1]$, the buyer and seller in a k-double auction simultaneously submit bids p_B and p_S, and trade occurs at the price $kp_B + (1-k)p_S$ if and only if $p_B \geq p_S$. By construction, the k-double auction never incurs a deficit. For $k \in \{0,1\}$, the k-double auction reduces to take-it-or-leave-it offers – by the buyer if $k = 1$ and by the seller if $k = 0$.

3.4.3.1 *Payoff versus Social Surplus Tradeoff*

If the agents' types are uniformly distributed on $[0,1]$, then in the linear Bayes Nash equilibrium of the k-double auction, a buyer of type v bids $p_B(v) \equiv (1-k)k/(2(1+k)) + v/(1+k)$, and a seller with cost c bids $p_S(c) \equiv (1-k)/2 + c/(2-k)$. Thus, the linear Bayes Nash equilibrium of the k-double auction results in trade if and only if $v \geq c\frac{1+k}{2-k} + \frac{1-k}{2}$. The associated expected payoffs of the buyer and seller are illustrated in Figure 3.2.

As illustrated in Figure 3.2, bargaining in the incomplete-information framework entails a payoff-surplus tradeoff. As k increases, the buyer's (seller's) expected payoff increases (decreases) but the sum of expected payoffs is maximized at $k = 1/2$. Indeed, as first noted by Myerson and Satterthwaite (1983), for $k = 1/2$ and uniformly distributed types, the k-double auction yields the second-best outcome. Williams (1987) noted that this insight generalizes insofar as, for uniformly distributed types and any $k \in [0,1]$, the k-double auction implements the outcomes of incomplete-information bargaining for some bargaining weights.

3.4.3.2 *Bargaining Power versus Productive Power and Scope for Countervailing Power*

It is straightforward to extend the uniform–uniform k-double auction model by parameterizing the distributions so that for some $a \in [0,1/2]$, the buyer draws its value from the uniform distribution on $[a,1]$ and the seller draws its cost from the uniform distribution on $[0,1-a]$. Then, as a increases from 0 to 1/2, the productive power of both the buyer and the seller increases, and, separately, the k of the k-double auction parameterizes the agents' relative bargaining powers.

In this setup,[37] there is a linear Bayes Nash equilibrium in which a buyer of type v bids

$$p_B(v) \equiv \begin{cases} \frac{v}{1+k} + \frac{k(1-k)}{2(1+k)} & \text{if } v \leq \frac{1+k}{2-k}(1-a) + \frac{1-k}{2}, \\ \frac{1-a}{2-k} + \frac{1-k}{2} & \text{otherwise,} \end{cases}$$

and a seller of type c bids

$$p_S(c) \equiv \begin{cases} \frac{a}{1+k} + \frac{k(1-k)}{2(1+k)} & \text{if } c < \frac{2-k}{1+k}a - \frac{(1-k)(2-k)}{2(1+k)}, \\ \frac{c}{2-k} + \frac{1-k}{2} & \text{otherwise.} \end{cases}$$

[37] Example 2 of Chatterjee and Samuelson (1983) encompasses this setup (note: typos in the bid functions as stated in the 1983 paper).

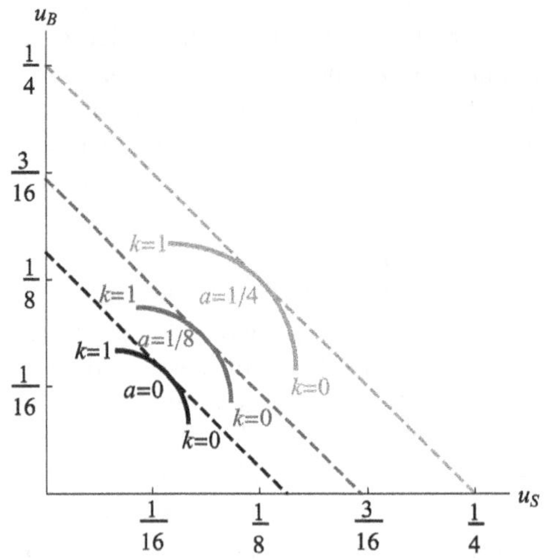

Figure 3.3 Expected payoffs of the buyer, u_B, and the seller, u_S, in the k-double auction for $k \in [0,1]$. Assumes that the buyer's value is uniformly distributed on $[a,1]$ and that the seller's cost is uniformly distributed on $[0,1-a]$. The dashed lines show the second-best frontiers for different values of a.

Expected payoffs of the buyer and seller are illustrated in Figure 3.3.

As suggested by these results, the k of the k-double auction can be viewed as a *bargaining power* parameter, with $k = 1/2$ corresponding to equal bargaining power between the buyer and the seller. In contrast, the *productive power* of the agents is captured by their distributions. We illustrate this in Figure 3.3, which shows how productive power and bargaining power separately affect the agents' payoffs and the efficiency of bargaining.[38]

As this shows, the incomplete-information framework allows one to capture the notion of countervailing power – an equalization of bargaining power has the potential to outweigh productive power effects. In a market with extreme bargaining power, a change in agents' productive power, for example due to a merger, that reduces social surplus might be counterbalanced by an equalization of bargaining power.

3.4.3.3 Investment Incentives

To consider investment incentives, we adapt the prior k-double auction setup so that the buyer's value is drawn from the uniform distribution on $[a_B,1]$, denoted

[38] Using the Nash-in-Nash model, Crawford and Yurukoglu (2012) document that differences in bargaining power explain pricing differentials in multichannel television markets, finding that small cable operators and satellite providers have slightly less bargaining power than large cable operators. They rely on bargaining power differences to explain price differences, without allowing differences in the productive power of, for example, small and large cable operators and satellite providers. Incomplete-information models have the potential to differentiate between the two sources of price differentials.

F_{a_B}, and the seller's cost is drawn from the uniform distribution on $[0, 1 - a_S]$, denoted G_{a_S}. Suppose a_B is determined by the buyer's investment, with $a_B \in [0, 1)$ having cost $I_B(a_B)$, and that a_S is determined by the seller's investment, with $a_S \in [0, 1)$ having cost $I_S(a_S)$. Assume that investment occurs prior to type realizations and that the buyer and seller do not observe the investment of the other agent. For our purposes here, we assume that all optima are defined by first-order conditions.

Suppose that there is a symmetric Nash equilibrium investment a^*; that is, in equilibrium, $a_B = a_S = a^*$. Denote by p_B^* and p_S^* the bid functions defined above but with $a = a^*$. Let $u_B^*(a_B, a_S)$ be the expected payoff of a buyer, not including investment costs, when its type is drawn from F_{a_B}, the seller's type is drawn from G_{a_S}, the seller bids according to p_S^*, and the buyer bids optimally given that it believes that the seller bids according to p_S^* and has type drawn from G_{a^*}. Analogously, let $u_S(a_B, a_S)$ be the expected payoff of a seller, not including investment costs, when its type is drawn from G_{a_S}, the buyer's type is drawn from F_{a_B}, the buyer bids according to p_B^*, and the seller bids optimally given that it believes that the buyer bids according to p_B^* and has type drawn from F_{a^*}.

By the assumptions that investments $a_B = a_S = a^*$ are a Nash equilibrium and that the rival's investment is not observed, each agent's investment maximizes its expected payoff given that the other agent bids according to its equilibrium bid function and has a type drawn from its equilibrium distribution, that is,

$$\left.\frac{\partial u_B(a_B, a^*)}{\partial a_B}\right|_{a_B=a^*} = I_B'(a^*) \quad \text{and} \quad \left.\frac{\partial u_S(a^*, a_S)}{\partial a_S}\right|_{a_S=a^*} = I_S'(a^*).$$

In contrast, investments $a_B = a_S = a^*$ are optimal for the planner if and only if

$$\left.\frac{\partial u_B(a_B, a^*)}{\partial a_B}\right|_{a_B=a^*} + \left.\frac{\partial u_S(a_B, a^*)}{\partial a_B}\right|_{a_B=a^*} = I_B'(a^*)$$

and

$$\left.\frac{\partial u_B(a^*, a_S)}{\partial a_S}\right|_{a_S=a^*} + \left.\frac{\partial u_S(a^*, a_S)}{\partial a_S}\right|_{a_S=a^*} = I_S'(a^*).$$

It follows that Nash equilibrium investments are optimal for the planner if and only if the allocation and payment are not affected by the investments. If the solution to the planner's problem has $a_B = a_S = a^* < 1/2$, so that the buyer's and seller's type distributions overlap, then the agents' Nash equilibrium investments are not socially optimal. However, if $a^* \geq 1/2$ and if trade occurs at the fixed price of, say, 1/2, then each agent is the residual claimant to its investment, and Nash equilibrium investments are socially optimal. Loertscher and Marx (2021a) show, in a more general incomplete-information bargaining setup, that first-best investments are a Nash equilibrium outcome if (and under additional conditions only if) incomplete-information bargaining is efficient.

3.4.3.4 *Illustration that Mergers Harm the Buyer*

Let us now focus on the case of $k = 1$ and $a = 0$, that is, assume that the buyer has all the bargaining power and types are drawn from the uniform distribution on $[0,1]$. When the buyer faces two or more sellers, it holds an optimal procurement. This is consistent with the k-double auction in that when $k = 1$ and there is only one seller, the equilibrium of the k-double auction is equivalent to the buyer making a take-it-or-leave-it offer to the seller, which is the optimal procurement in that case.

As above, we assume that when the two sellers merge, the merged entity's cost is drawn from the distribution of the minimum of two independent draws from G. Supposing that the sellers draw their costs from the distribution $G(c) = 1 - \sqrt{1-c}$ on $[0,1]$, then the merged entity's cost distribution, $\hat{G}(c) \equiv 1-(1-G(c))^2 = c$, is the uniform distribution on $[0,1]$.

Before the merger, the optimal reserve of a buyer with value $v \leq 1$ is p_B satisfying $\Gamma(p_B) = v$.[39] Thus, $p_B(v) = \frac{1}{9}\left(4+3v-2\sqrt{4-3v}\right)$. However, after the merger, the buyer's optimal reserve is $\hat{p}_B(v) = v/2$, which is lower for all $v \in (0,1]$. This illustrates the point discussed above that the buyer negotiates more aggressively when facing the merged entity than when facing the two competing sellers.

Nevertheless, the buyer is harmed by the merger of sellers. Before the merger, a buyer with value 1 has an optimal reserve of 5/9 and an expected payoff of

$$\mathbb{E}_{c_1,c_2}[(1-\min\{\max\{c_1,c_2\},\Gamma^{-1}(1)\})\cdot \mathbf{1}_{\min\{c_1,c_2\}<\Gamma^{-1}(1)}] = 0.41.$$

After the merger, its optimal reserve is 1/2, and its expected payoff is 1/4.

As another illustration, consider a buyer with a value of greater than or equal to $\max_{c\in[\underline{c},\overline{c}]}\Gamma(c)$. Prior to the merger, the buyer benefits from competition between the sellers, paying the maximum of the two sellers' costs, which is less than $\overline{c}$ with probability one. But after the merger, the transaction price is just $\overline{c}$, implying that the buyer is harmed by the merger.

3.4.3.5 *Countervailing Power*

In pre-merger markets in which sellers sell their product to powerful buyers, a merger among sellers has the potential to have countervailing effects (Galbraith, 1952). In particular, consolidation may increase expected social surplus if the enhanced market power of the combined seller serves to counterbalance the power of the buyers. This thinking is laid out in the Australian government's 1999 (now superseded) guidelines, which state: "If pre-merger prices are distorted from competitive levels by market power on the opposite side of the market, a merger may actually move prices closer to competitive levels and increase market efficiency. For example, a merger of buyers in a market may create countervailing power which can push prices down closer

[39] For $v \in [0,1]$, $\Gamma^{-1}(v)$ is well defined.

to competitive levels" (Australian Competition and Consumer Commission, 1999, para. 5.131).

As an illustration, reconsider the setup above with one buyer and two pre-merger sellers, where the buyer's value is uniformly distributed on $[0,1]$ and the pre-merger sellers' costs are drawn from $G(c) = 1 - \sqrt{1-c}$. If the buyer has all the bargaining power in the pre-merger market, then the pre-merger expected social surplus is

$$\mathbb{E}_{v,c_1,c_2}\left[(v - \min\{c_1,c_2\}) \cdot \mathbf{1}_{\min\{c_1,c_2\} \leq p_B(v)}\right] = \frac{953}{7290} \approx 0.13,$$

where, as above, $p_B(v) = \frac{1}{9}(4 + 3v - 2\sqrt{4-3v})$.

In contrast, if one assumes that after the merger between the two sellers, k changes, then social surplus can be larger after merger, as shown in Figure 3.3 (for the case of $a = 0$). In particular, given a post-merger value of k denoted $\hat{k}$, the post-merger expected social surplus is $\frac{1}{16}(2-\hat{k})(1+\hat{k})$, which is concave in $\hat{k}$ and achieves its maximum value of $\frac{9}{64} \approx 0.14$ when $\hat{k} = 1/2$. The expected social surplus increases as a result of the merger combined with the reduction in k to $\hat{k}$ for all $\hat{k} \in (0.102, 0.898)$.[40] In particular, the bargaining power of the buyer must be reduced from the pre-merger level of $k = 1$, but the buyer must retain some bargaining power in the post-merger market, so that we do not simply trade an all-powerful buyer for an all-powerful seller. This gives rise to the countervailing power result that if, as a result of the merger, the bargaining power of the buyer and seller are sufficiently equalized, then the merger-plus-reduction-in-buyer-power results in an increase in expected social surplus (and is profitable for sellers and harms the buyer). While here we focus on the k-double auction, Loertscher and Marx (2021a) analyze the scope for social-surplus-increasing countervailing power in a general incomplete-information bargaining setup.

3.4.4 Monopoly Pricing Revisited

3.4.4.1 Optimal Rationing and Randomization

It is commonly perceived as puzzling that sellers would set below-market clearing prices, randomly ration consumers, and then either try to prevent the resale that ensues from the inefficient initial allocation or at least complain about the emergence of resale.[41] Would the seller not be better off setting a market clearing price, whereby it would pre-empt resale and *make* more revenue, thereby killing two birds with one stone? Following Loertscher and

[40] With one buyer and one seller drawing their types from the uniform distribution, $k = 1$ and $k = 0$ are equivalent for social surplus. It may seem natural to expect that for any $k \in (0,1)$, social surplus increases. However, this is not the case because pre-merger there are two sellers, and the competition between them mitigates the detrimental effects of the buyer's bargaining power.

[41] See, for example, Becker (1991).

Muir (2022), we now briefly revisit monopoly pricing problems and show that rationing is optimal for a monopoly only if the revenue function is not concave and, using their insights, connect this to opaque pricing of vertically differentiated products. Heuristically, this exercise also illustrates why market clearing pricing is optimal when revenue is concave.

Consider a monopoly who, for now, has K units of a homogeneous good for sale, facing a continuum of consumers with single-unit demand described by the downward-sloping inverse demand function $P(Q)$ that, under market clearing pricing, gives rise to the revenue $R(Q) \equiv P(Q)Q$. As an alternative to selling K units at the market clearing price $P(K)$, suppose the seller uses a two-price mechanism with prices $p_1 > p_2$. These prices are such that in equilibrium all $Q_1 < K$ consumers with values no less than $P(Q_1)$ buy at price p_1 and are served for sure, while $Q_2 - Q_1$ with $Q_2 > K$ consumers participate in a lottery where they are served with probability $\alpha \equiv \frac{K-Q_1}{Q_2-Q_2} < 1$. (While for notational ease we keep the dependence of α on K, Q_1, and Q_2 implicit, we emphasize this dependence as it matters below.) Making the participation for the marginal consumers bind yields $p_2 = P(Q_2)$. The incentive-compatibility constraint for the consumers with value $P(Q_1)$ is $P(Q_1) - p_1 = \alpha(P(Q_1) - p_2)$, which, using $p_2 = P(Q_2)$, is equivalent to $p_1 = (1-\alpha)P(Q_1) + \alpha P(Q_2)$. In other words, p_1 is a convex combination of $P(Q_1)$ and $P(Q_2)$. Multiplying p_1 by Q_1 and p_2 by the quantity sold at that price, which is $K - Q_1$, yields the revenue

$$(1-\alpha)R(Q_1) + \alpha R(Q_2), \tag{3.5}$$

which is larger than the revenue $R(K)$ from market-clearing pricing if and only if R is not concave at K. Maximizing $(1-\alpha)R(Q_1) + \alpha R(Q_2)$ over Q_1 and Q_2 yields the convex hull (or concavification) of R, denoted $\bar{R}(K)$, that is,

$$\bar{R}(K) \equiv \max_{Q_1, Q_2} (1-\alpha)R(Q_1) + \alpha R(Q_2),$$

which is the smallest concave function such that $\bar{R}(K) \geq R(K)$ for all K in the domain of R. See Figure 3.4 for an illustration.

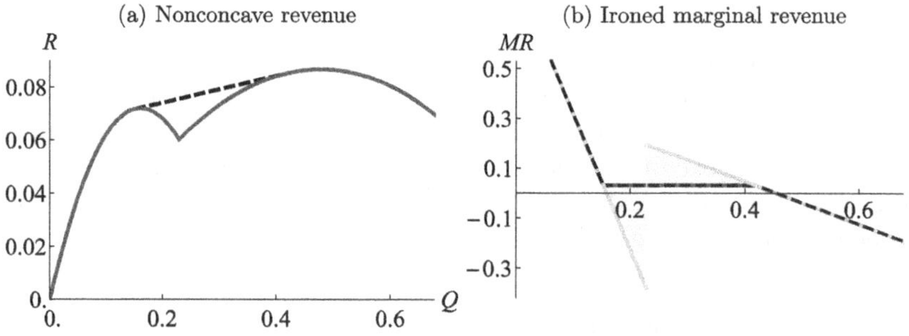

Figure 3.4 Illustration of nonconcave revenue and the construction of ironed marginal revenue. (a) The dashed line concavifies the revenue function. (b) The two shaded areas are equal, and the dashed line indicates the ironed marginal revenue function.

Denoting by F the distribution of consumers' values, we have $P(Q) = F^{-1}(1-Q)$, and taking the derivative of $\bar{R}(K)$ yields what Myerson (1981) termed the *ironed virtual valuation*, which we denote $\bar{\Phi}(v)$, that is, $\bar{R}'(K) \equiv \bar{\Phi}(F^{-1}(1-K))|_{v=F^{-1}(1-K)} = \bar{\Phi}(v)$. Using Myerson's arguments, one can show that the optimal mechanism for the monopoly involves rationing (see, e.g., Bulow and Roberts, 1989).[42] Intuitively, rationing when revenue is not concave – or equivalently, marginal revenue is not monotone – is better than market clearing prices because it allows the monopoly to serve the highest marginal revenue consumers (who are not necessarily the consumers with the largest values) subject to not violating the incentive-compatibility constraint that $q(v)$ must be nondecreasing. The best the monopoly can do, subject to incentive compatibility, is to serve consumers with lower values and higher marginal revenue with the same probability as it serves higher-value consumers with lower marginal revenue. Thus, uniform (or random) rationing is optimal.

Note that consumers pay the price p_2 if and only if they are successful in the lottery. As Loertscher and Muir (2022) observe, the monopoly can alternatively achieve the revenue $\bar{R}(K)$ by creating a vertically differentiated, inferior good that consists of $K - Q_1$ high-quality units (of quality 1) and $Q_2 - K$ lower-quality units (of quality 0), whose expected quality is thus α. The market clearing price for this *opaquely priced* good is $\tilde{p}_2 = \alpha P(Q_2)$, and incentive compatibility for the consumers with value $P(Q_1)$ implies that the price $\tilde{p}_1$ for the high-quality good is $\tilde{p}_1 = (1-\alpha)P(Q_1) + \tilde{p}_2$ because the consumers can only be charged the incremental quality improvement $1-\alpha$. Multiplying $\tilde{p}_1$ by Q_1 and $\tilde{p}_2$ by $Q_2 - Q_1$ yields the expression in (3.5), whose maximum is $\bar{R}(K)$. Of course, the conflated good consisting of $Q_2 - K$ units of quality 0 is, in a sense, degenerately conflated. Loertscher and Muir (2022) show that the argument extends to any quality $\theta \in [0,1)$ and to an arbitrary number of vertically differentiated goods that are available in given capacities.

Loertscher and Muir (2022) also analyze the effects of resale that ensues from randomization and show that, while it harms the seller, it does not offset all the benefits from randomization. In other words, they show that once one accounts for incomplete information (and allows for nonconcave revenue), there is no puzzle. The seller dislikes resale much in the same way that an incumbent in a game with an entrant dislikes entry, yet accommodates it because it is more profitable than deterring entry. They also show that randomization – in the form of rationing and conflation – can have positive effects on the quantity that the monopoly sells in equilibrium, and that if this effect is strong enough, then randomization increases consumer surplus. By a similar logic, allowing for highly efficient resale can have an adverse quantity effect,

[42] Without relating to mechanism-design arguments or to Myerson (1981), Wilson (1988) and Ferguson (1994) establish, respectively, the optimality of two-price mechanisms and their relation to rationing. Optimal monopoly pricing with nonconcave revenue was first analyzed by Hotelling (1931) and Mussa and Rosen (1978).

and if this effect is strong enough, then consumers may be harmed by too efficient resale. This suggests the possibility of a consumer surplus rationale for the Better Online Tickets Sales (BOTS) Act of 2016 in the United States, which reduced the efficiency of resale without banning it. The reason for why there can be large quantity effects of randomization is that randomization renders the optimized revenue function of the seller concave. Hence, the optimal quantity sold varies smoothly in the parameters of the problem. In contrast, when the optimized revenue is not concave (either because randomization is prohibited or made less effective, which is the typical effect of resale), the revenue-maximizing quantity can vary discontinuously.

Of course, the practical relevance of these insights hinges on whether or not revenue is concave. Empirically, when concavity of revenue is not imposed, the hypothesis that revenue is concave (or equivalently, that virtual values are monotone) is regularly rejected; see, for example, Celis et al. (2014), Larsen and Zhang (2018, appendix D), and Larsen et al. (2020, section 5).[43] Loertscher and Muir (2022) provide theoretical reasons – such as the integration of markets – as to why revenue may not be concave. Maybe more fundamentally, even though it is standard to assume that revenue is concave, this does not make it so, and there are simply no theoretical reasons for revenue to be concave.

3.4.4.2 Digital Monopolies

As noted for example by Loertscher and Marx (2020b), larger markets are better, all else equal, because they can execute the same trades as smaller, standalone markets, and sometimes execute more or more valuable trades. This feature of increasing returns to scale in market-making is inherent in the independent private values model, in which the market-maker's payoff function (be it social surplus, profit, a weighted average of the two, or social surplus under the second-best mechanism) increases more than linearly in market size. More precisely, denote by $W(\mathcal{N})$ the expected value of the market-maker's objective when there is a set $\mathcal{N}$ of buyers and sellers, each drawing their values and costs independently from some distributions F and G with overlapping supports. Then for two disjoint and finite sets $\mathcal{N}$ and $\mathcal{N}'$, we have

$$W(\mathcal{N})+W(\mathcal{N}')<W(\mathcal{N}\cup\mathcal{N}'),$$

because, reflecting Williamson's (1985) notion of selective intervention, the market-maker can always replicate what it would do in the standalone markets and sometimes do better.[44] This basic insight is of relevance for the ongoing

[43] Celis et al. (2014) analyze advertising bidding data from Microsoft Advertising Exchange and find that, to a large extent because, empirically, virtual values are not monotone, one can do better in terms of revenue and consumer surplus with mechanisms other than a second-price auction with an optimal reserve.

[44] The insight that larger markets perform better has been prominently explored by Gresik and Satterthwaite (1989), who show that the performance of the second-best mechanism relative to first-best improves as market size increases, and in the subsequent double-auctions literature. However, the insight is not restricted to this class of mechanisms or to a specific objective.

antitrust debates concerning big tech mentioned in Section 3.2 because it provides a simple and coherent rationale for why, in principle, gigantic market-makers can emerge without engaging in anticompetitive conduct. Indeed, when firms are primarily market-makers, or otherwise subject to increasing returns to scale (e.g., because of the value of aggregating data), efficiency may dictate that there is a single active firm. Borrowing from the notion of natural monopolies, Loertscher and Marx (2020b) refer to firms in such environments as *digital monopolies*.

The analogy is also useful because it suggests that seemingly "old-school," brick-and-mortar approaches that proved useful in dealing with natural monopolies may also be productive in the digital age. In particular, when increasing returns to scale loom large, breaking up large firms may deprive society of these benefits of increased market thickness, and price regulation may be an effective instrument to distribute these gains more evenly across society. It is not clear, a priori, why it should not be possible to regulate, say, the fee Apple charges for selling products via its App Store or to restrict the algorithms that Amazon and others use to price (and target) the goods that they sell.

To illustrate the problems that may arise in the starkest and simplest terms, consider a platform in the presence of two users that generates a value of $V > 0$ if both users join (and, say, forego their privacy) and has zero value otherwise. V could be the social value of the platform or the profit it generates to the platform. The cost of joining the platform for each user i with $i \in \{1,2\}$ is c_i, which is net of the private benefit that the platform generates for the user. So, if V is the social value of the platform, it is efficient for the platform to operate if and only if $\sum_{i=1}^{2} c_i < V$.

To see that a competitive (or Walrasian) price p that induces the efficient allocation may fail to exist, notice that for the platform to be willing to acquire both inputs/attract both users (assuming for simplicity that it appropriates the entire social value V if it operates), it must be that $V - 2p > 0$, assuming that the outside option of the platform is 0. For user i to be willing to sell at price p, it must be that $p - c_i > 0$, where 0 is the value of the outside option of the user. Taken together, this means that a market clearing price that supports the efficient allocation exists if and only if $V - 2\max\{c_1, c_2\} > 0$, while efficiency dictates that the platform should operate whenever $V - (c_1 + c_2) > 0$. Thus, whenever

$$2\max\{c_1, c_2\} > V > c_1 + c_2,$$

the platform should operate, but there is no competitive price that supports that outcome.

Not surprisingly, once one has to account for the agents' private information about their costs, the obstacles do not necessarily become smaller. To see this, suppose the two agents are privately informed about their costs c_i of joining the platform and consider first the dominant-strategy implementation of the efficient allocation rule. As above, let the value of their outside option be 0. To make the problem interesting, let $\overline{c}$ be the largest possible cost for each agent and assume that $V < 2\overline{c}$, so that it is not always efficient to operate the platform. Let $p_i(\mathbf{c})$ be the price offered to i when the costs are $\mathbf{c} = (c_1, c_2)$. If $\sum_{i=1}^{2} c_i \geq V$, then it is efficient not to operate the platform, and so the smallest price that can be offered to the agents, without violating their individual rationality constraints, is 0. If $\sum_{i=1}^{2} c_i < V$, then it is efficient to operate the platform, and each agent i is offered a price equal to the highest cost it could report without changing the allocation, that is, $p_i(\mathbf{c}) = \min\{V - c_j, \overline{c}\}$, where $j \neq i$. It is straightforward to establish that whenever the platform operates under efficiency, the payments to the agents exceed the value of the platform, that is, $\sum_{i=1}^{2} p_i(\mathbf{c}) > V$.[45] Thus, this efficient mechanism that satisfies dominant strategies and agents' (ex-post) individual rationality constraints always runs a deficit when it is efficient to operate the platform.[46] If we assume that the agents' costs are independently distributed on the interval $[\underline{c}, \overline{c}]$ according to some distributions G_1 and G_2 with positive densities, then it follows that *any* efficient, incentive-compatible and individually rational mechanism runs a deficit.[47] Admittedly, the assumption that the agents are perfect complements (and that there are only two agents) is strong.[48] However, it is useful as it makes the point that the competitive benchmark cannot be taken for granted for pricing when there are strong complementarities among agents, which is, for example, the case in data-driven industries where one consumer's data are primarily valuable in conjunction with data from other consumers.

Of course, the main activity of many platforms and big-tech companies is not necessarily that they match literally buyers and sellers and gain from the trades they execute. This is certainly the case for companies such as Google, Facebook, and Twitter (now known as X), which create value for their users by facilitating certain flows of information. Accordingly, a major policy concern in regard to companies like these is how these platforms steer information flows, to what extent they create "echo chambers," facilitate the spread of conspiracy theories, what (if anything) are the limits to freedom of speech, and the like. Our discussion sheds little light on these important aspects of the problem other than perhaps suggesting that the old-school approach of subjecting social media to qualitatively similar rules and restrictions to those that were imposed when radio and TV broadcasting emerged in the first half of the twentieth century may be preferable to dismantling social media networks, in particular if

45 To see this, assume first that $V - c_i < \overline{c}$ for $i \in \{1,2\}$. In this case, $\sum_{i=1}^{2} p_i(\mathbf{c}) > V$ is equivalent to $2V - (c_1 + c_2) > V$, which is equivalent to $V > c_1 + c_2$, which is the case because it is efficient to operate the platform. Next, assume that $V - c_i \geq \overline{c}$ for $i \in \{1,2\}$, in which case $\sum_{i=1}^{2} p_i(\mathbf{c}) > V$ is equivalent to $2\overline{c} > V$, which is true by assumption. Last, assume that $V - c_i < \overline{c} \leq V - c_j$ for $i \neq j$, in which case $\sum_{i=1}^{2} p_i(\mathbf{c}) > V$ is equivalent to $\overline{c} > c_i$, which is the case.

46 Individual rationality constraints are said to be satisfied ex post if agents are better off participating even after the payments have been made and the allocation is determined. It contrasts with interim individual rationality, which only stipulates that agents are better off participating at the time they report their types.

47 This is, of course, reflective of the public goods problem and, more generally, the issues arising from complementarities mentioned in and around footnote 31.

48 One can show that the deficit problem remains with an arbitrary number of agents n, provided $n\overline{c} > V$ and provided the agents are perfect complements.

the returns to scale that are the driving force behind them are so strong that as soon as one network is dismantled another one pops up.

3.4.5 Empirical Work

3.4.5.1 Estimation in the Context of Incomplete-Information Bargaining

We now turn to empirical estimation of incomplete-information bargaining and illustrate the recent work by Larsen and Zhang (2018) mentioned in Section 3.2. They make use of the power of the revelation principle and the implications of incentive compatibility to develop estimation methods tailored to a general incomplete-information bargaining setup.

To illustrate the estimation approach of Larsen and Zhang (2018), consider the case of a bilateral bargaining. Suppose that you have repeated observations on bargaining outcomes between a buyer and a seller (not necessarily the same buyer and seller over time, but all buyers and all sellers are assumed to draw their types from the same distributions F and G over time). You do not observe the exact mechanism through which bargaining occurs, but you do observe reports by agents (think of these as the agents' initial offers), and you observe bargaining outcomes. Specifically, for each bargain j, you observe actions a_j^B and a_j^S, an indicator x_j that is 1 if there is trade and 0 otherwise, and transfer t_j from the buyer to the seller.

For example, if the underlying mechanism is a k-double auction with $k = 3/4$ and the underlying type distributions are the uniform distribution on $[0, 1]$, then one might observe the following dataset:

j	a_j^B	a_j^S	x_j	t_j
1	0.30	0.20	1	0.28
2	0.43	0.49	0	0
3	0.59	0.52	1	0.57
4	0.28	0.57	0	0
5	0.34	0.16	1	0.30

Note that one should not expect to observe buyer bids less than $\frac{1-k}{2} = \frac{1}{8}$ or seller bids greater than $\frac{2-k}{2} = \frac{5}{8}$ because such bids have zero probability of resulting in trade in equilibrium.

Letting $p_B(v)$ be the (unobserved) mapping from buyer types to actions and $p_S(c)$ be the (unobserved) mapping from seller types to actions, one can use this data to estimate the inverses p_B^{-1} and p_S^{-1} using the methodology of Larsen and Zhang (2018). Specifically, for $a \in \mathbb{R}$, let

$$\hat{\beta}^B(a) \equiv (\hat{\beta}_0^B(a), \hat{\beta}_1^B(a), \hat{\beta}_2^B(a))$$
$$\equiv \arg\min_{\beta} \sum_j \left(\left(t_j - \sum_{\ell=0}^{2} \beta_\ell (a_j^B - a)^\ell \right)^2 \kappa_{h'}(a_j^B - a) \right)$$

and

$$\hat{\gamma}^B(a) \equiv (\hat{\gamma}_0^B(a), \hat{\gamma}_1^B(a), \hat{\gamma}_2^B(a))$$
$$\equiv \arg\min_{\gamma} \sum_j \left(\left(x_j - \sum_{\ell=0}^{2} \gamma_\ell (a_j^B - a)^\ell \right)^2 \kappa_{h^x}(a_j^B - a) \right),$$

where κ_h is a kernel function with bandwidth h (see Larsen and Zhang, 2018 for a discussion of appropriate kernel and bandwidth choices). Then $\hat{\beta}^B(a)$ and $\hat{\gamma}^B(a)$ are defined for any a not included as a buyer action in the dataset, and, as shown by Larsen and Zhang (2018), for any such a, a consistent estimator of $p_B^{-1}(a)$ is given by

$$\hat{p}_B^{-1}(a) \equiv \frac{\hat{\beta}_1^B(a)}{\hat{\gamma}_1^B(a)}.$$

One can then extend the definition of $\hat{p}_B^{-1}(a)$ to all buyer actions using linear interpolation. Defining things analogously for sellers, and using $-t_j$ instead of t_j and $-x_j$ instead of x_j,

$$\hat{p}_S^{-1}(a) \equiv \frac{\hat{\beta}_1^S(a)}{\hat{\gamma}_1^S(a)}$$

provides a consistent estimate of $p_S^{-1}(a)$ for any a not included as a seller action in the dataset. Similarly, this can be extended to all seller actions using linear interpolation.

Given these estimates of the inverse strategy mappings, one can estimate the underlying types and construct the empirical distributions of those types using $\hat{v}_j \equiv \hat{p}_B^{-1}(a_j^B)$ and $\hat{c}_j \equiv \hat{p}_S^{-1}(a_j^S)$. We illustrate the results of such estimation in Figure 3.5, with the details contained in Appendix A3.3.

Because this approach allows one to estimate the underlying type distributions, one can then use those types to estimate the agents' expected payoffs by using the average payoffs in the data. That is, given J total observations, we have

$$\hat{u}_B \equiv \frac{1}{t} \sum_{j=1}^{J} (\hat{v}_j x_j - t_j) \quad \text{and} \quad \hat{u}_S \equiv \frac{1}{t} \sum_{j=1}^{J} (t_j - \hat{c}_j x_j),$$

where it is important to note that the theoretical expected payoffs would also "average in" some zeros because we only observe agents with types sufficiently "efficient" that they trade with positive probability. In the simulation underlying Figure 3.5, we get $\hat{u}_B = 0.1430$ as compared with the relevant theoretical benchmark of $u_B = 0.1458$, which is the expected payoff of a buyer in a k-double auction with $k = 3/4$ and uniformly distributed values on $[\frac{1}{8}, 1]$ and uniformly distributed costs on $[0, \frac{5}{8}]$. For the sellers, we get $\hat{u}_S = 0.0995$ as compared with the theoretical value of $u_S = 0.1041$.

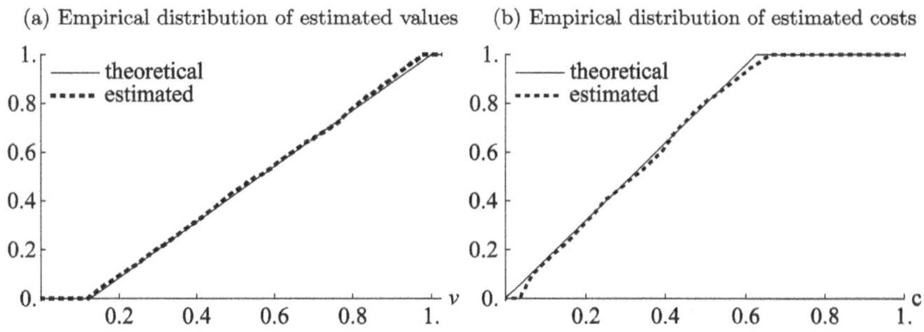

Figure 3.5 Empirical distributions of estimated type compared with the theoretical distributions. Estimates are based on the observation of 4000 randomly drawn outcomes of a k-double auction with $k = 3/4$ and actual types drawn from the uniform distribution on $[0, 1]$, assuming agents use their linear Bayes Nash equilibrium strategies. In this case, buyers with values less than 1/8 and sellers with costs greater than 5/8 do not participate, and so the relevant theoretical distributions are the uniform distributions truncated at those types, as shown.

One can further use the methods of Loertscher and Marx (2020a) to estimate the virtual types. Specifically, letting $\hat{v}_{(j)}$ denote the jth highest estimated value and, letting $\hat{c}_{[j]}$ denote the jth lowest estimated cost, uniformly consistent estimators for $\frac{1-F(v_{(j)})}{f(v_{(j)})}$, where F is the theoretical value distribution, and $\frac{G(c_{[j]})}{g(c_{[j]})}$, where G is the theoretical cost distribution, respectively, are given by

$$\hat{h}_j^B \equiv j\sigma_j^B \text{ and } \hat{h}_j^S \equiv j\sigma_j^S,$$

where σ_j^B and σ_j^S are the average spacing between nearby types:

$$\sigma_j^B \equiv \frac{\hat{v}_{(j-\min\{r,j-1\})} - \hat{v}_{(j+\min\{r,J-j\})}}{\min\{r, j-1\} + \min\{r, J-j\}} \quad \text{and}$$
$$\sigma_j^S \equiv \frac{\hat{c}_{[j+\min\{r,J-j\}]} - \hat{c}_{[j-\min\{r,j-1\}]}}{\min\{r, J-j\} + \min\{r, j-1\}},$$

where r is the number of spacings on each side of a type that are included in the spacing estimate, defined to be $J^{4/5}$, rounded to the nearest integer.[49]

One can then use $(\hat{v}_{(j)}, \hat{h}_j^B)_{j=1}^J$ to define the estimate $\hat{h}^B(v)$ of $\frac{1-F(v)}{f(v)}$ for all v in the relevant range using linear interpolation.[50] Similarly, one can use $(\hat{c}_{(j)}, \hat{h}_j^S)_{j=1}^J$ to define the estimate $\hat{h}^S(c)$ of $\frac{G(c)}{g(c)}$ for all c in the relevant range using linear interpolation.[51] We illustrate in Figure 3.6.

[49] See Loertscher and Marx (2020a) for a discussion of the choice of the number of spacings to include in the estimator.

[50] Interpolation is only used for the purposes of creating figures – in our estimates we only evaluate $\hat{h}^B$ and $\hat{h}^S$ at estimated types.

[51] One might be able to improve estimates by constraining $\hat{h}^B$ and $\hat{h}^S$ to be positive. We have not done this for the purposes of our illustration.

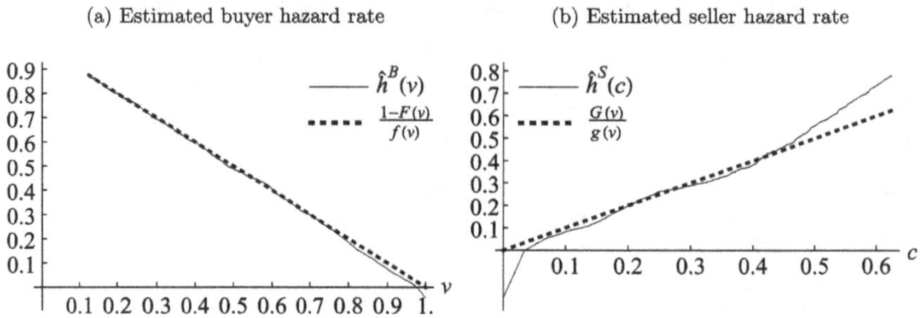

Figure 3.6 Estimated hazard rates based on the observation of 4000 randomly drawn outcomes of a k-double auction with $k = 3/4$ and actual types drawn from the uniform distribution on $[0, 1]$, assuming agents use their linear Bayes Nash equilibrium strategies. In this case, buyers with values less than 1/8 and sellers with costs greater than 5/8 do not participate, and so the relevant theoretical distributions are the uniform distributions truncated at those types.

Given these estimates, for any bargaining weights $(w_B, w_S) \in [0,1]^2$, with at least one weight being positive, and any $\rho \geq 1$, we can define the allocation rule $Q^{\mathbf{w},\rho}$ as follows:

$$Q^{\mathbf{w},\rho}(v,c) \equiv \begin{cases} 1 & \text{if } v - (1 - \frac{w_B}{\rho})\hat{h}^B(v) \geq c + (1 - \frac{w_S}{\rho})\hat{h}^S(c), \\ 0 & \text{otherwise.} \end{cases}$$

Given $\mathbf{w}$, define the empirical budget surplus by

$$\hat{\pi}^{\mathbf{w},\rho} \equiv \frac{1}{J}\sum_{j=1}^{J}\left[(\hat{v}_j - \hat{h}^B(\hat{v}_j)) - (\hat{c}_j + \hat{h}^S(\hat{c}_j))\right] Q^{\mathbf{w},\rho}(\hat{v}_j, \hat{c}_j)$$

and define $\rho^{\mathbf{w}}$ to be the smallest $\rho \geq 1$ such that $\hat{\pi}^{\mathbf{w},\rho} \geq 0$.

Then, letting $\eta_B^{\mathbf{w}} \equiv 1$ if $w_B > w_S$, $\eta_B^{\mathbf{w}} \equiv 0$ if $w_B < w_S$, and $\eta_B^{\mathbf{w}} \equiv 1/2$ if $w_B = w_S$, and analogously for $\eta_S^{\mathbf{w}}$ (i.e., $\eta_S^{\mathbf{w}} \equiv 1 - \eta_B^{\mathbf{w}}$), estimated payoffs in the incomplete-information bargaining mechanism with bargaining weights $\mathbf{w}$ are

$$\hat{u}_B(\mathbf{w}) \equiv \eta_B^{\mathbf{w}}\hat{\pi}^{\mathbf{w},\rho^{\mathbf{w}}} + \frac{1}{J}\sum_{j=1}^{J}\hat{h}^B(\hat{v}_j)Q^{\mathbf{w},\rho^{\mathbf{w}}}(\hat{v}_j, \hat{c}_j)$$

and

$$\hat{u}_S(\mathbf{w}) \equiv \eta_S^{\mathbf{w}}\hat{\pi}^{\mathbf{w},\rho^{\mathbf{w}}} + \frac{1}{J}\sum_{j=1}^{J}\hat{h}^S(\hat{c}_j)Q^{\mathbf{w},\rho^{\mathbf{w}}}(\hat{v}_j, \hat{c}_j).$$

As before, these estimates do not account for payoffs of zero associated with types that have no probability of trading, which are missing from our dataset.

One can then find the $\mathbf{w}$ that minimize the distance between $(\hat{u}_S(\mathbf{w}), \hat{u}_B(\mathbf{w}))$ and $(\hat{u}_S, \hat{u}_B)$, giving us an estimate $\hat{\mathbf{w}}$ of the agents' bargaining weights. We illustrate this in Figure 3.7(a). As shown there, we find $(\hat{w}_B, \hat{w}_S) = (1, 0.5)$, consistent with the data being simulated based on a k-double auction with $k = 3/4$. To explore the precision of the estimation procedure and the effects of sample size, we calculate bootstrap confidence intervals for the

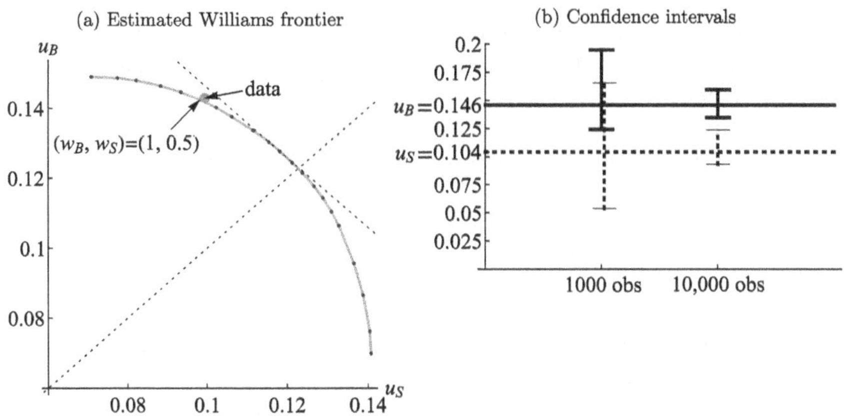

Figure 3.7 Estimated Williams frontier and bootstrap confidence intervals for agents' expected payoffs compared with theoretical values. (a) The point labeled "data" is $(\hat{u}_S, \hat{u}_B)$. The small points along the frontier are $(\hat{u}_S(\mathbf{w}), \hat{u}_B(\mathbf{w}))$ for a grid of values for $\mathbf{w}$ with one bargaining weight equal to 1 and the other an element of $\{0, 0.1, \ldots, 1\}$. The point labeled with bargaining weights is the grid point that is closest to the "data" point. Estimated types and hazard rates are based on the observation of 4000 randomly drawn outcomes (Larsen and Zhang, 2018 also perform estimates for a sample size of 4000) of a k-double auction with $k = 3/4$ and actual types drawn from the uniform distribution on $[0, 1]$, assuming agents use their linear Bayes Nash equilibrium strategies. (b) 95% confidence intervals based on estimates of buyer and seller expected surplus for 100 independently drawn simulated datasets of 1000 observations each and, separately, for 100 independently drawn simulated datasets of 10,000 observations each for a k-double auction with $k = 3/4$ and actual types drawn from the uniform distribution on $[0, 1]$, assuming agents use their linear Bayes Nash equilibrium strategies; u_B and u_S are the associated theoretical values.

agents' expected payoffs for sample sizes of 1000 and 10,000, as shown in Figure 3.7(b). The figure compares the bootstrap 95% confidence intervals to the theoretical values for the agents' expected payoffs.

Thus, as we have just illustrated, data on bids and outcomes are sufficient to allow the identification of agents' type distributions and bargaining weights associated with incomplete-information bargaining. Although the k-double auction setup is special and results in that setup depending on specific distributions, this illustration shows that the incomplete-information framework provides a tractable, intuitive approach to the payoff-surplus tradeoff, the separation of bargaining and productive power, countervailing power, and merger harms.

3.4.5.2 Bargaining Breakdown on the Equilibrium Path

As mentioned above, standard complete-information bargaining models focus on the division of a fixed surplus, not the size of the surplus. In those models, when there are gains from trade, trade always occurs. In contrast, in incomplete-information bargaining with overlapping type distributions, negotiations break down on the equilibrium path with positive probability. This occurs for two reasons. First, it may be that the buyer's value is below the seller's cost, but because of private information, the two parties do not know this before they sit down at the negotiating table. Second, by the Myerson–Satterthwaite impossibility result, even if the buyer's value exceeds the seller's cost, the constraints imposed by incentive compatibility, individual rationality, and no deficit may prevent ex-post efficient trade from taking place.

The possibility of bargaining breakdown that arises in incomplete-information bargaining captures features of reality that complete-information models cannot accommodate. Casual empiricism suggests that bargaining breakdown is common – we observe strikes and blackouts and government shutdowns. More systematically, Backus et al. (2020) examine millions of eBay transactions involving bilateral bargaining and document the prevalence of bargaining breakdown. Data suggest that approximately half of negotiations that are initiated end without a transaction. This, of course, is not a stylized fact that can be accommodated by complete-information bargaining models such as Nash bargaining. However, in an incomplete-information context, as we have seen, bargaining breakdown arises naturally. Indeed, the observation of bargaining breakdown in data can be used to calibrate distributions in an incomplete-information setup.

For example, under the assumption that incomplete-information bargaining maximizes expected social surplus subject to incentive compatibility, individual rationality, and no deficit, and that the buyer and seller are treated symmetrically, one can use the observed frequencies of negotiation breakdowns to back out the parameters of the distributions from which the buyer and the seller draw their types. To illustrate, assume that the buyer's value v is drawn from the distribution $F(v) = 1 - (1-v)^{1/\kappa}$ and the seller's cost c is drawn from the distribution $G(c) = c^{1/\kappa}$, whose supports are $[0, 1]$, where $\kappa \in (0, \infty)$ has the interpretation of a "capacity." Figure 3.8 plots the probability that negotiations break down as a function of κ under the assumptions stated. For example, if, as in the dataset of Backus et al. (2020), 55% of all negotiations break down, eyeballing the figure indicates that κ must be around 1.5.[52] Rather than treating negotiation breakdowns as measurement error as in the case with complete information, with incomplete information the frequency of those breakdowns is valuable information that can be used for estimation.

The suitability of our approach for applied work is reinforced by the ability to calibrate straightforward parameterizations of the agents' type distributions based on data such as the observed probability with which negotiations break

[52] More precisely, for the case considered, a breakdown probability of 55% corresponds to $\kappa = 1.60904$.

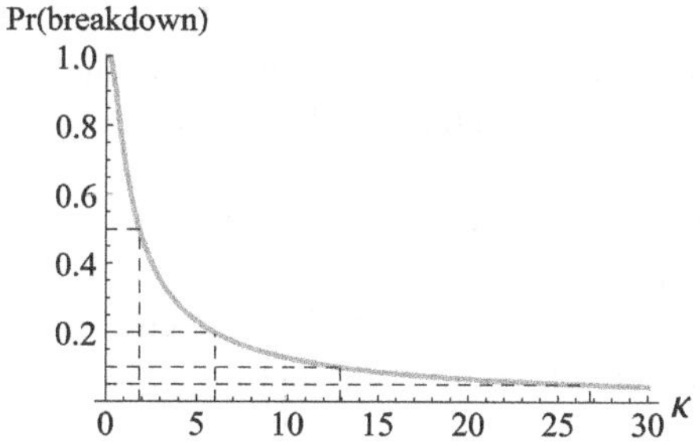

Figure 3.8 Probability of the breakdown of negotiations in incomplete-information bargaining as a function of κ assuming $F(v) = 1 - (1-v)^{1/\kappa}$ and $G(c) = c^{1/\kappa}$ on $[0,1]$.

down.[53] Given the calibrated distributions, the bargaining solution is easily computed. For example, with one buyer and one seller, each drawing their types from the uniform distribution on $[0,1]$,[54] incomplete-information bargaining modeled as a k-double auction with $k = 1/2$ gives each agent an expected surplus of $9/128 \approx 0.07$, which is slightly less than the expected surplus under Nash bargaining of $1/12 \approx 0.08$. One can also accommodate general distributions, asymmetries, and one-to-many bargaining (Loertscher and Marx, 2021a).

Of course, it may be that in many instances empirical analysts do not have the luxury of observing bargaining breakdown. But this does not necessarily mean that what is not observed does not matter (just like it would be hard to argue that nuclear weapons played no role during the cold war on the grounds that nuclear war did not occur). Methods to account for unobserved bargaining breakdown might advance progress here.

3.5 OPEN ISSUES AND THE ROAD FORWARD

Of course, there are many open issues, and a lot of work remains to be done. In this section, we highlight a few of these issues and the possible avenues for future work.

3.5.1 Determinants of Bargaining Power

As discussed above, the mechanism-design-based approach to incomplete-information bargaining allows one to incorporate differential bargaining power for agents and, given data, to estimate the relative bargaining power of agents. Questions remain, however, regarding what determines this bargaining power

[53] For one-to-many bargaining, the market shares of the competing agents can also be used for calibration.

[54] A buyer and seller each drawing its type from the uniform distribution on $[0,1]$ corresponds to a breakdown probability of approximately 72%, which is greater than the 50% breakdown probability in an efficient bargaining setup with the same type distributions.

in the first place. This is particularly pertinent given the recent upsurge in interest in bargaining. Avenues for future work include the analysis of how bargaining power varies with market structure and how it depends on firm size, as well as other things.

A possible avenue to pursue this more systematically is touched upon in Loertscher and Marx (2019a), who discuss the incentives of the buyer to acquire, at some cost, buyer power and show that these incentives are stronger after the merger of two suppliers. This suggests that one could more generally ask whether merging parties have stronger incentives to increase their bargaining weight before or after the merger.

3.5.2 Mergers that Create Multi-unit Traders

As discussed above, the incomplete-information IO framework loses its tractability if agents' types are not single dimensional. One can easily work within those bounds for a fixed market structure. In particular, the setup accommodates multiple buyers with multi-unit demands, if a buyer's marginal value for each unit is a linear function of the agent's single-dimensional type; and there can be multiple sellers with multi-unit capacities, if a seller's marginal cost for each unit is a linear function of the agent's single-dimensional type.

Modeling mergers is then straightforward in some cases. For example, if the total quantity demanded by the buyers in the market is D, and if sellers i and j each have constant marginal cost (equal to their types) up to a capacity of D, then a merger of sellers i and j can be modeled as creating a merged entity that has capacity D and a constant marginal cost equal to the minimum of two independent cost draws, one from seller i's type distribution and one from seller j's type distribution. This scenario applies in the case of one buyer with single-unit demand purchasing from some number of sellers analyzed above, or more generally when multiple agents on one side of the market trade with a single agent with single-unit demand or capacity on the other side of the market.

Modeling challenges arise when the merged entity might trade more units than either of the pre-merger agents can produce or consume. For example, suppose that there is one buyer with two-unit demand and there are two sellers, each with one-unit capacity. Let G_1 and G_2 be the cost distributions of the two pre-merger sellers. The merged entity might be expected to supply two units for some type realizations, but how should one model the merged entity's costs for those two units? A way to transform G_1 and G_2 into a one-dimensional distribution is required to maintain the features of the Myersonian mechanism-design approach. A number of possibilities suggest themselves. Noting that the joint supply by the two pre-merger sellers at price p is

$$S(p) = G_1(p) + G_2(p) = 2\frac{G_1(p) + G_2(p)}{2},$$

one could model the merged entity as having two-unit supply at a constant marginal cost drawn from the distribution $\tilde{G}(c) \equiv \frac{G_1(c)+G_2(c)}{2}$. Or, one could view the merged entity as having type $\hat{c}$ drawn from the distribution of the minimum of c_1 and c_2, given by $\hat{G}(c) \equiv 1-(1-G_1(c))(1-G_2(c))$, and then viewing that type $\hat{c}$ as the merged entity's marginal cost for its first unit and letting $a\hat{c}$ be the merged entity's marginal cost for its second unit for some commonly known $a \geq 1$ (see, e.g., Loertscher and Marx, 2023a). For example, one could choose a to be the ratio of the expected value of $\max\{c_1, c_2\}$ to the expected value of $\min\{c_1, c_2\}$.

As we now discuss, additional, related challenges present themselves for the case of vertical mergers.

3.5.3 Vertical Integration

As in the case of horizontal mergers discussed above, one can easily accommodate vertical integration within the incomplete-information setup for some market structures, assuming that after integration, the integrated firm can efficiently solve its internal agency problem, which is a standard assumption.[55] For example, suppose that the pre-integration market has one buyer with single-unit demand and value drawn from distribution F and multiple sellers with costs drawn from distribution G. The integration of the buyer with seller 1 creates an entity that has demand for one unit, which can either be sourced internally or externally. The integrated firm never acts as a seller because there are no external buyers. Thus, the integrated firm's type that is relevant for trade with the external sellers is the integrated firm's willingness to pay for an external unit. Viewing the downstream component of the integrated firm as having a willingness to pay of v and the upstream component as having a cost to supply of c_1, the willingness to pay of the integrated firm for an external unit is then $\min\{v, c_1\}$. So one can naturally view the integrated firm as drawing a single-dimensional willingness to pay for an external unit from the distribution of the minimum of v and c_1. Things are similarly straightforward if the pre-integration market has only one seller with single-unit supply. In that case the willingness of the integrated firm to sell in the external market is the maximum of the types of the integrated buyer and integrated seller.

Interestingly, as shown in Loertscher and Marx (2021a), this immediately gives us the result that vertical integration can, under general conditions, cause an efficient market to no longer be efficient. To see this, consider the case of non-overlapping supports with $\overline{c} \leq \underline{v}$ and suppose that there are two suppliers and one buyer in the pre-integration market. That is, efficient trade is possible prior to integration – for example, a second-price auction would suffice – but following integration, the vertically integrated firm's willingness to pay for an external unit is $\min\{v_1, c_1\} = c_1$, which has overlapping support with the cost of the external supplier, so the Myerson–Satterthwaite impossibility result applies. Efficient trade is possible prior to integration, but following

[55] This assumption can be rationalized, for example, on the grounds that integration slackens the individual rationality constraints within the integrated firm.

integration, there is no incentive-compatible, individually rational, no-deficit mechanism that implements the efficient allocation.

Turning to the case of a pre-integration market with multiple buyers and multiple suppliers, challenges arise because the integrated firm might act as either a buyer or a seller in the external market, depending on type realizations. Vertical integration creates a market in which at least one agent, the vertically integrated firm, cannot be categorized ex ante as either a buyer or a seller. Following Loertscher and Marx (2020c), we refer to such a market as an *asset market*.[56] While many models presume that markets have two sides – agents are either buyers or sellers with ex-ante determined trading positions – in asset markets some agents' trading positions – buy, sell, do not trade – are determined endogeneously; see, for example, Lu and Robert (2001), Chen and Li (2018), Johnson (2019), and Loertscher and Marx (2020c, 2023b). In practice, the gig economy has resulted in formerly two-sided markets becoming asset markets, with examples such as eBay, Uber, and Airbnb.

Interest in accommodating asset markets adds to the appeal of the incomplete-information approach because it offers scope for productively modeling asset markets. In contrast, for standard oligopoly models with price-taking consumers on one side of the market, it is not clear how one would even shift bargaining power between the buyer side and seller side of the market, much less how one would adapt such models to handle ex-ante non-identified traders.

Extending the incomplete-information framework to accommodate flexibly asset markets would allow analysis of mergers between intermediaries who take positions and, depending on circumstances, either buy or sell. This would pave the way for the analysis of settings that have "three sides" in the sense that there are buyers, sellers, and integrated firms that can be either buyers or sellers.

3.6 CONCLUSIONS

We show that the incomplete-information model is tractable for capturing central issues in industrial organization and antitrust, such as the tradeoff between social surplus and profit and the effects of buyer power, bargaining power, and countervailing power. Moreover, the model predicts bargaining breakdown on the equilibrium path; implies that perfect price discrimination is not possible because, holding fixed the quantity a buyer is allocated, the price cannot vary with the buyer's willingness to pay; provides conditions on the primitives that imply that uniform pricing by a monopoly is optimal; and gives rise, without any additional assumptions, to increasing return to scale in market-making. This chapter provides an overview of the relevant literature, explains the key mechanics, and lays out a roadmap for the work ahead.

[56] Lu and Robert (2001), and Chen and Li (2018) following them, refer to these markets as markets with "ex ante unidentified traders." More recently, Johnson (2019) uses the term "one-sided" to refer to these problems.

APPENDIX

A3.1 Expected Payment Details

Given $z \in [\underline{v}, \overline{v}]$, we have

$$\begin{aligned}
\mathbb{E}_v[m(v)] &= \int_{\underline{v}}^{\overline{v}} m(v) f(v) dv \\
&= \int_{\underline{v}}^{\overline{v}} \left(q(v)v - \int_z^v q(x)dx \right) f(v)dv - U(z) \\
&= \int_{\underline{v}}^{z} \left(q(v)v + \int_v^z q(x)dx \right) f(v)dv \\
&\quad + \int_{z}^{\overline{v}} \left(q(v)v - \int_z^v q(x)dx \right) f(v)dv - U(z) \\
&= \int_{\underline{v}}^{z} q(v)vf(v)dv + \int_{\underline{v}}^{z} \int_{\underline{v}}^{x} q(x)f(v)dvdx + \int_{z}^{\overline{v}} q(v)vf(v)dv \\
&\quad - \int_{z}^{\overline{v}} \int_{x}^{\overline{v}} q(x)f(v)dvdx - U(z) \\
&= \int_{\underline{v}}^{z} q(v)vf(v)dv + \int_{\underline{v}}^{z} q(x)F(x)dx + \int_{z}^{\overline{v}} q(v)vf(v)dv \\
&\quad - \int_{z}^{\overline{v}} q(x)(1-F(x))dx - U(z) \\
&= \int_{\underline{v}}^{z} \left(x + \frac{F(x)}{f(x)} \right) q(x)f(x)dx \\
&\quad + \int_{z}^{\overline{v}} \left(x - \frac{1-F(x)}{f(x)} \right) q(x)f(x)dx - U(z) \\
&= \int_{\underline{v}}^{z} \Gamma(x)q(x)f(x)dx + \int_{z}^{\overline{v}} \Phi(x)q(x)f(x)dx - U(z) \\
&= \mathbb{E}_v[\Gamma(v)q(v) \mid v \leq z] \Pr(v \leq z) \\
&\quad + \mathbb{E}_v[\Phi(v)q(v) \mid v \geq z] \Pr(v \geq z) - U(z),
\end{aligned}$$

where the first equality uses the definition of the expectation, the second uses (3.4), the third through sixth rearrange, including switching the order of integration, the seventh uses the definition of the virtual cost and virtual value functions Γ and Φ, and the last equality uses the definition of the expectation.

A3.2 Details of the Demonstration of the Myerson–Satterthwaite Impossibility Result

Suppose that $\underline{v} < \overline{c}$ and define $\hat{M}_B(v,c) \equiv \max\{c, \underline{v}\}$ if $v \geq c$ and $\hat{M}_B(v,c) \equiv 0$ otherwise, and $\hat{M}_S(v,c) \equiv \min\{v, \overline{c}\}$ if $v \geq c$ and $\hat{M}_S(v,c) \equiv 0$ otherwise. The mechanism $\langle Q^E, \hat{M}_B, \hat{M}_S \rangle$ is incentive-compatible by the usual second-price auction logic: an agent's report affects only whether it trades, not its payment if it does trade, and trade is only an agent's interest when it is efficient, so agents cannot profit from misreporting their types. In addition, the mechanism satisfies individual rationality with equality: a buyer with value $\underline{v}$ is the worst-off type of buyer and has an expected payoff of zero, and similarly for a seller with cost $\overline{c}$.

We can now apply the revenue equivalence theorem. Suppose that there exists a payment rule $(\tilde{M}_B, \tilde{M}_S)$ such that mechanism $\langle Q^E, \tilde{M}_B, \tilde{M}_S\rangle$, with interim expected payoff function for the buyer of $\tilde{U}_B$ and for the seller of $\tilde{U}_S$, is incentive-compatible and individually rational. Then we have

$$\begin{aligned}
\mathbb{E}_{v,c}\left[\tilde{m}_B(v) - \tilde{m}_S(c)\right] &= \mathbb{E}_{v,c}\left[(\Phi(v) - \Gamma(c))\, Q^E(v,c)\right] - \tilde{U}_B(\underline{v}) - \tilde{U}_S(\overline{c}) \\
&\leq \mathbb{E}_{v,c}\left[(\Phi(v) - \Gamma(c))\, Q^E(v,c)\right] \\
&= \mathbb{E}_{v,c}\left[\hat{m}_B(v) - \hat{m}_S(c)\right] \\
&< 0,
\end{aligned}$$

where the first equality uses the revenue equivalence theorem applied to $\langle Q^E, \tilde{M}_B, \tilde{M}_S\rangle$, the first inequality uses the implication of individual rationality that $\tilde{U}_B(\underline{v}) \geq 0$ and $\tilde{U}_S(\overline{c}) \geq 0$, the second equality uses the revenue equivalence theorem applied to $\langle Q^E, \hat{M}_B, \hat{M}_S\rangle$ and the fact that the interim expected payoffs of the worst-off types are zero in that mechanism, and the final inequality follows because under mechanism $\langle Q^E, \hat{M}_B, \hat{M}_S\rangle$, the payment by the buyer, $\max\{c, \underline{v}\}$, is less than or equal to the payment to the seller, $\min\{v, \overline{c}\}$, and strictly so for an open interval of types when $\underline{v} < \overline{c}$. Thus, when the set of possible buyer values overlaps with the set of possible seller costs, $\underline{v} < \overline{c}$, *any* incentive-compatible, individually rational bilateral trade mechanism with the efficient allocation rule runs a deficit. In other words, efficient bilateral trade is not possible without running a deficit.

A3.3 Details of the Estimation Illustration

We begin by considering the theoretical application of the k-double auction, assuming that agents' types are uniformly distributed on $[0,1]$ and that agents use their linear Bayes Nash equilibrium strategies, where a buyer of type v bids $p_B(v) \equiv (1-k)k/(2(1+k)) + v/(1+k)$, and a seller with cost c bids $p_S(c) \equiv (1-k)/2 + c/(2-k)$.

Let (P_B, T_B) be the menu faced by the buyer, where $P_B(b)$ is the probability that the buyer trades given a bid b and $T_B(b)$ is the expected payment by the buyer to the mechanism given a bid b. Then we have

$$P_B(b) = p_S^{-1}(b)$$

and

$$T_B(b) = \int_0^{p_S^{-1}(b)} (kb + (1-k)p_S(c))dc.$$

As required by incentive compatibility, the menu defines a convex frontier as shown in Figure A3.1(a).

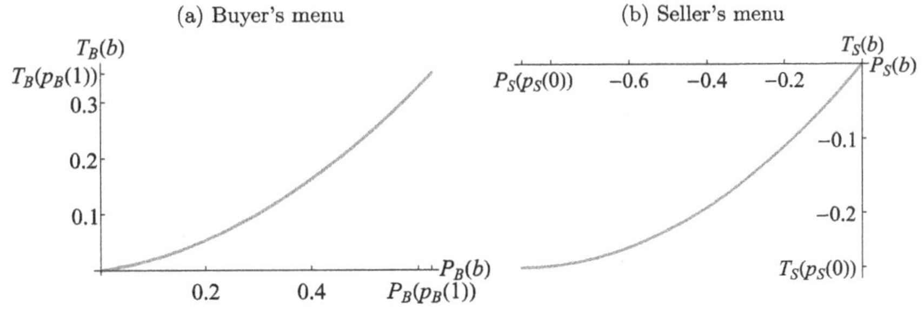

Figure A3.1 Menu of expected allocations and transfers as a function of bids for a k-double auction with $k = 3/4$ and types drawn from the uniform distribution on $[0,1]$, assuming agents use their linear Bayes Nash equilibrium strategies.

Analogously, let (P_S, T_S) be the menu faced by the buyer, where $-P_S(b)$ is the probability that the seller trades given a bid b and $-T_S(b)$ is the expected payment to the seller from the mechanism given a bid b. Then we have

$$P_S(b) = -(1 - p_B^{-1}(b))$$

and

$$T_S(b) = -\int_{p_B^{-1}(b)}^{1} (kp_B(v) + (1-k)b)dv.$$

Again, as required by incentive compatibility, the menu defines a convex frontier as shown in Figure A3.1(b).

A3.3.1 Simulated Data

We generate a large number of pairs of uniform [0, 1] values and costs, discarding those where the value is less than $\frac{1}{8}$ or the seller cost is greater than $\frac{5}{8}$, so that we ultimately have 4000 type vectors. From these, we calculate the bids of the buyer and seller according to p_B and p_S with $k = \frac{3}{4}$ and calculate the associated allocation and transfers.

A3.3.2 Bandwidth Estimation

We use the data to calculate the bandwidth for use in the kernel estimation procedure.[57] Following this procedure, we find bandwidths between 0.05 and 0.06.

[57] To do this, regress the vector of 4000 transfers on a quintic polynomial of the observed buyer bids and calculate the variance of the residuals σ_T^2. Let $\widehat{T}'''$ denote the third derivative of the fitted equation. Define bandwidth

$$h_T \equiv C\left(\frac{\sigma_T^2}{\Sigma_{j=1}^{4000}\left(\widehat{T}'''(a_j^B)\right)^2}\right)^{1/7},$$

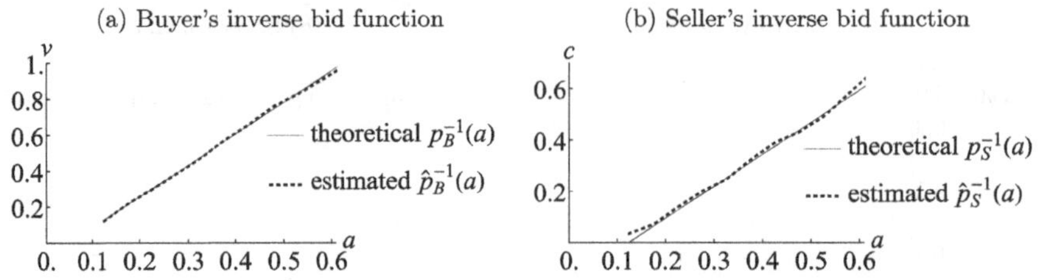

Figure A3.2 Estimated and theoretical inverse bid functions for a k-double auction with $k = 3/4$ and types drawn from the uniform distribution on $[0,1]$, assuming agents use their linear Bayes Nash equilibrium strategies.

A3.3.3 Estimation of Inverse Strategy for the Buyer

We now estimate the first derivative of T_B using the local polynomial regression estimator for $T_B(a)$ at a given bid a with degree 2, bandwidth h_T, and the Gaussian kernel. We use the value of $\hat{\beta}_1(a)$ derived from

$$(\hat{\beta}_0^B(a), \hat{\beta}_1^B(a), \hat{\beta}_2^B(a))$$
$$\equiv \arg\min_{\beta} \sum_{j=1}^{4000} \left(\left(t_j - \sum_{\ell=0}^{2} \beta_\ell (a_j^B - a)^\ell \right)^2 \kappa_{h_T}(a_j^B - a) \right).$$

Similarly, we estimate the first derivative of P_B using the value of $\hat{\gamma}_1(a)$ derived from

$$(\hat{\gamma}_0^B(a), \hat{\gamma}_1^B(a), \hat{\gamma}_2^B(a))$$
$$\equiv \arg\min_{\gamma} \sum_{j=1}^{4000} \left(\left(x_j - \sum_{\ell=0}^{2} \gamma_\ell (a_j^B - a)^\ell \right)^2 \kappa_{h_P}(a_j^B - a) \right).$$

Then we estimate $\hat{p}_B^{-1}(b)$ using $\frac{\hat{\beta}_1^B(a)}{\hat{\gamma}_1^B(a)}$, and similarly for $\hat{p}_S^{-1}(b)$.

Further, $\hat{\beta}_1^B(a)$ and $\hat{\gamma}_1^B(a)$ are estimates of the first derivatives of T_B and P_B, respectively, so we can use those to reconstruct T_B and P_B and calculate the (P_B, T_B) frontier, which we confirm is convex (see Figure A3.2).

where $C = 0.884$ is a constant for the Gaussian kernel. Analogously, define the bandwidth for the allocation rule by

$$h_P \equiv C \left(\frac{\sigma_P^2}{\sum_{j=1}^{4000} \left(\hat{P}'''(a_j^B) \right)^2} \right)^{1/7}.$$

REFERENCES

Australian Competition and Consumer Commission (1999). *Merger Guidelines*. https://www.accc.gov.au/.

Australian Competition and Consumer Commission (2019). *Digital Platforms Inquiry: Final Report*. https://www.accc.gov.au/focus-areas/inquiries-ongoing/digital-platforms-inquiry.

Ausubel, L. M., P. Cramton, and R. J. Deneckere (2002). "Bargaining with incomplete information." In R. Aumann and S. Hart (eds.), *Handbook of Game Theory*, vol. 3. Amsterdam: Elsevier, pp. 1897–1945.

Backus, M., T. Blake, B. Larsen, and S. Tadelis (2020). "Sequential bargaining in the field: Evidence from millions of online bargaining interactions," *Quarterly Journal of Economics*, 135, 1319–1361.

Backus, M., T. Blake, and S. Tadelis (2019). "On the empirical content of cheap-talk signaling: An application to bargaining," *Journal of Political Economy*, 127, 1599–1628.

Baye, M. R., and J. D. Wright (2011). "Is antitrust too complicated for generalist judges? The impact of economic complexity and judicial training on appeals," *Journal of Law and Economics*, 54, 1–24.

Becker, G. S. (1991). "A note on restaurant pricing and other examples of social influences on price," *Journal of Political Economy*, 99, 1109–1116.

Bessen, J. E., and M. J. Meurer (2006). "Patent litigation with endogenous disputes," *American Economic Review*, 96, 77–81.

Börgers, T. (2015). *An Introduction to the Theory of Mechanism Design*. Oxford: Oxford University Press.

Bulow, J., and P. Klemperer (1996). "Auctions versus negotiations," *American Economic Review*, 86, 180–194.

Bulow, J., and J. Roberts (1989). "The simple economics of optimal auctions," *Journal of Political Economics*, 97, 1060–1090.

Byrne, D. P., L. A. Martin, and J. S. Nah (2022). "Price discrimination, search, and negotiation in an oligopoly: A field experiment in retail electricity," *Quarterly Journal of Economics*, 137(4), 2499–2537.

Capps, C., and D. Dranove (2004). "Hospital consolidation and negotiated PPO prices," *Health Affairs*, 23, 87–109.

Capps, C., D. Dranove, and M. Satterthwaite (2003). "Competition and market power in option demand markets," *RAND Journal of Economics*, 34, 737–763.

Caprice, S., and P. Rey (2015). "Buyer power from joint listing decision," *Economic Journal*, 125, 1677–1704.

Caves, R. E., H. Crookell, and J. P. Killing (1983). "The imperfect market for technology licenses," *Oxford Bulletin of Economics and Statistics*, 45, 249–267.

Celis, L. E., G. Lewis, M. Mobius, and H. Nazerzadeh (2014). "Buy-it-now or take-a-chance: Price discrimination through randomized auctions," *Management Science*, 60, 2927–2948.

Cémer, J., Y.-A. de Montjoye, and H. Schweitzer (2019). *Competition Policy for the Digital Era, Final Report*. Brussels: European Commission.

Chatterjee, K., and W. Samuelson (1983). "Bargaining under incomplete information," *Operations Research*, 31, 835–851.

Chen, Y.-C., and J. Li (2018). "Revisiting the foundations of dominant-strategy mechanisms," *Journal of Economic Theory*, 178, 294–317.

Choi, J. P., and H. Gerlach (2017). "A theory of patent portfolios," *American Economic Journal: Microeconomics*, 9, 315–351.

Clarke, E. (1971). "Multipart pricing of public goods," *Public Choice*, 11, 17–33.

Collard-Wexler, A., G. Gowrisankaran, and R. S. Lee (2019). "Nash-in-Nash: A microfoundation for applied work," *Journal of Political Economy*, 127, 163–195.

Craig, S., M. Grennan, and A. Swanson (2020). "Mergers and marginal costs: New evidence on hospital buyer power." Working Paper, University of Pennsylvania.

Crawford, G., R. Lee, M. Whinston, and A. Yurukoglu (2018). "The welfare effects of vertical integration in multichannel television markets," *Econometrica*, 86, 891–954.

Crawford, G., and A. Yurukoglu (2012). "The welfare effects of bundling in multichannel television markets," *American Economic Review*, 102, 643–685.

Crawford, G. S. (2014). "Cable regulation in the internet era." In N. L. Rose (ed.), *Economic Regulation and Its Reform: What Have We Learned?* Chicago, IL: University of Chicago Press, pp. 137–193.

Crémer, J., and R. McLean (1985). "Optimal selling strategies under uncertainty for a discriminating monopolist when demands are interdependent," *Econometrica*, 53, 345–361.

Crémer, J., and R. McLean (1988). "Extraction of the surplus in Bayesian and dominant strategy auctions," *Econometrica*, 56, 1247–1257.

Cutler, D. M., and F. Scott Morton (2013). "Hospitals, market share, and consolidation," *JAMA*, 310, 1964–1970.

Dafny, L. (2009). "Estimation and identification of merger effects: An application to hospital mergers," *Journal of Law and Economics*, 52, 523–550.

Daskalakis, C., A. Deckelbaum, and C. Tzamos (2017). "Strong duality for a multiple-good monopolist," *Econometrica*, 85, 735–767.

Decarolis, F., and G. Rovigatti (2020). "From mad men to maths men: Concentration and buyer power in online advertising." Working Paper, Bocconi University.

Delacrétaz, D., S. Loertscher, L. Marx, and T. Wilkening (2019). "Two-sided allocation problems, decomposability, and the impossibility of efficient trade," *Journal of Economic Theory*, 179, 416–454.

Epstein, R. J., and D. L. Rubinfeld (2004). *Effects of Mergers Involving Differentiated Products*. Technical Report, COMP/B1/2003/07.

European Commission (2004). "Guidelines on the assessment of horizontal mergers under the council regulation on the control of concentrations between undertakings," *Official Journal of the European Union* 2004/C 31/03.

Ferguson, D. G. (1994). "Shortages, segmentation, and self-selection," *The Canadian Journal of Economics*, 27, 183–197.

Fudenberg, D., and J. Tirole (1991). *Game Theory*. Cambridge, MA: MIT Press.

Furman, J., A. Fletcher, D. Coyle, and D. M. P. Marsden (2019). *Unlocking Digital Competition*. Report of the Digital Competition Expert Panel.

Gal-Or, E., and A. Dukes (2003). "Mimimum differentiation in commercial media markets," *Journal of Economics & Management and Strategy*, 12, 291–325.

Gal-Or, E., and A. Dukes (2006). "On the Profitability of Media Mergers," *Journal of Business*, 79, 489–525.

Galbraith, J. K. (1952). *American Capitalism: The Concept of Countervailing Power*. Boston, MA: Houghton Mifflin.

Ganglmair, B., L. M. Froeb, and G. J. Werden (2012). "Patent hold-up and antitrust: How a well-intentioned rule could retard innovation," *Journal of Industrial Economics*, 60, 249–273.

Gaynor, M., and R. J. Town (2012). "Competition in health care markets." In T. G. McGuire, M. V. Pauly, and P. Barros (eds.), *Handbook of Health Economics*, vol. 2. Amsterdam: Elsevier, pp. 449–637.

Gershkov, A., J. K. Goeree, A. Kushnir, B. Moldovanu, and X. Shi (2013). "On the equivalence of Bayesian and dominant strategy implementation," *Econometrica*, 81, 197–220.

Gowrisankaran, G., A. Nevo, and R. Town (2015). "Mergers when prices are negotiated: Evidence from the hospital industry," *American Economic Review*, 105, 172–203.

Green, E. J., and R. H. Porter (1984). "Noncooperative collusion under imperfect price information," *Econometrica*, 52, 87–100.

Grennan, M. (2013). "Price discrimination and bargaining: Empirical evidence from medical devices," *American Economic Review*, 103, 145–177.

Grennan, M. (2014). "Bargaining ability and competitive advantage: Empirical evidence from medical devices," *Management Science*, 60, 3011–3025.

Grennan, M., and A. Swanson (2020). "Transparency and negotiated prices: The value of information in hospital–supplier bargaining," *Journal of Political Economy*, 128, 1234–1268.

Gresik, T., and M. Satterthwaite (1989). "The rate at which a simple market converges to efficiency as the number of traders increases: An asymptotic result for optimal trading mechanisms," *Journal of Economic Theory*, 48, 304–332.

Grossman, S. J., and O. D. Hart (1986). "The costs and benefits of ownership: A theory of vertical and lateral integration," *Journal of Political Economy*, 94, 691–719.

Groves, T. (1973). "Incentives in teams," *Econometrica*, 41, 617–631.

Guerre, E., I. Perrigne, and Q. Vuong (2000). "Optimal nonparametric estimation of first-price auctions," *Econometrica*, 68, 525–574.

Hart, O., and J. Moore (1990). "Property rights and the nature of the firm," *Journal of Political Economy*, 98, 1119–1158.

Ho, K., and R. Lee (2017). "Insurer competition in health care markets," *Econometrica*, 85, 379–417.

Ho, K., and R. Lee (2019). "Equilibrium provider networks: Bargaining and exclusion in health care markets," *American Economic Review*, 109, 473–522.

Holmström, B. (1979). "Groves' scheme on restricted domains," *Econometrica*, 47, 1137–1144.

Holmström, B., and R. B. Myerson (1983). "Efficient and durable decision rules with incomplete information," *Econometrica*, 51, 1799–1819.

Horn, H., and A. Wolinsky (1988). "Bilateral monopolies and incentives for merger," *RAND Journal of Economics*, 19, 408–419.

Hotelling, H. (1931). "The economics of exhaustible resources," *Journal of Political Economy*, 39, 137–175.

Ivaldi, M., B. Jullien, P. Rey, P. Seabright, and J. Tirole (2007). "The economics of tacit collusion: Implications for merger control." In V. Ghosal and J. Stennek (eds.), *The Political Economy of Antitrust*. Amsterdam: Elsevier, pp. 217–239.

Johnson, T. R. (2019). "One-sided markets." Working Paper, University of Notre Dame.

Kankanhalli, G., and A. Kwan (2019). "Bargaining power in the market for intellectual property: Evidence from licensing contract terms." Working Paper, Cornell University.

Katz, M. L., and C. Shapiro (1985). "On the licensing of innovations," *RAND Journal of Economics*, 16, 504–520.

Klemperer, P. (2002). "What really matters in auction design," *Journal of Economic Perspectives*, 16, 169–189.

Klemperer, P. (2004). "Using and abusing auction theory." In P. Klemperer (ed.), *Auctions: Theory and Practice*. Princeton, NJ: Princeton University Press, pp. 123–148.

Krishna, V. (2002). *Auction Theory*. San Diego, CA: Academic Press.

Krishna, V. (2010). *Auction Theory* (2nd ed.). Amsterdam: Elsevier.

Kuhn, T. S. (1970). *The Structure of Scientific Revolutions*. Chicago, IL: University of Chicago Press.

Larsen, B. J. (2020). "The efficiency of real-world bargaining: Evidence from wholesale used-auto auctions," *Review of Economic Studies*, 88, 851–882.

Larsen, B. J., C. H. Lu, and A. L. Zhang (2020). "Mediation in bargaining: Evidence from large-scale field data on business-to-business negotiations." Working Paper, Stanford University.

Larsen, B. J., and A. Zhang (2018). "A mechanism design approach to identification and estimation." NBER Working Paper No. 24837.

Lemus, J., and E. Temnyalov (2017). "Patent privateering, litigation, and R&D incentives," *RAND Journal of Economics*, 48, 1004–1026.

Leon, R. (2018). *U.S. v. AT&T Inc.* Civil Case No. 17-2511 (RJL), Memorandum Opinion, June 12.

Lewis, M. S. and K. E. Pflum (2015). "Diagnosing hospital system bargaining power in managed care networks," *American Economic Journal: Economic Policy*, 7, 243–274.

Loertscher, S., and L. M. Marx (2019a). "Merger review for markets with buyer power," *Journal of Political Economy*, 127, 2967–3017.

Loertscher, S., and L. M. Marx (2019b). "Merger review with intermediate buyer power," *International Journal of Industrial Organization*, 67, 1–16.

Loertscher, S., and L. M. Marx (2020a). "Asymptotically optimal prior-free clock auctions," *Journal of Economic Theory*, 187, 105030.

Loertscher, S., and L. M. Marx (2020b). "Digital monopolies: Privacy protection or price regulation?," *International Journal of Industrial Organization*, 71, 102623.

Loertscher, S., and L. M. Marx (2020c). "A dominant-strategy asset market mechanism," *Games and Economic Behavior*, 120, 1–15.

Loertscher, S., and L. M. Marx (2021a). "Incomplete information bargaining with applications to mergers, investment, and vertical integration." Working Paper, University of Melbourne.

Loertscher, S., and L. M. Marx (2021b). "Coordinated effects in merger review." Working Paper, University of Melbourne.

Loertscher, S., and L. M. Marx (2023a). "Bilateral trade with multi-unit demand and supply," *Management Science*, 69(2), 1146–1165.

Loertscher, S. and L. M. Marx (2023b). "Asymptotically optimal prior-free asset market mechanisms," *Games and Economic Behavior*, 137, 68–90.

Loertscher, S., L. Marx, and T. Wilkening (2015). "A long way coming: Designing centralized markets with privately informed buyers and sellers," *Journal of Economic Literature*, 53, 857–897.

Loertscher, S., and E. V. Muir (2022). "Monopoly pricing, optimal randomization, and resale," *Journal of Political Economy*, 130(3), 566–635.

Lu, H., and J. Robert (2001). "Optimal trading mechanisms with ex ante unidentified traders," *Journal of Economic Theory*, 97, 50–80.

Mailath, G. J., and A. Postlewaite (1990). "Asymmetric information bargaining problems with many agents," *Review of Economic Studies*, 57, 351–367.
Maskin, E., and J. Riley (1984). "Optimal auctions with risk averse buyers," *Econometrica*, 52, 1473–1518.
Matthews, S. (1984). "On the implementability of reduced form auctions," *Econometrica*, 52, 1519–1522.
Mezzetti, C. (2004). "Mechanism design with interdependent valuations: Efficiency," *Econometrica*, 72, 1617–1626.
Mezzetti, C. (2007). "Mechanism design with interdependent valuations: Surplus extraction," *Economic Theory*, 31, 473–488.
Milgrom, P. (2004). *Putting Auction Theory to Work*. Cambridge: Cambridge University Press.
Mussa, M., and S. Rosen (1978). "Monopoly and product quality," *Journal of Economic Theory*, 18, 301–317.
Myerson, R., and M. Satterthwaite (1983). "Efficient mechanisms for bilateral trading," *Journal of Economic Theory*, 29, 265–281.
Myerson, R. B. (1981). "Optimal auction design," *Mathematics of Operations Research*, 6, 58–73.
Nevo, A. (2014). "Mergers that increase bargaining leverage." Remarks at the Stanford Institute for Economic Policy Research, January 22. https://www.justice.gov/atr/file/517781/download.
Nocke, V., and J. Thanassoulis (2014). "Vertical relations under credit constraints," *Journal of the European Economic Association*, 12, 337–367.
Prager, E., and M. Schmitt (2021). "Employer consolidation and wages: Evidence from hospitals," *American Economic Review*, 111, 397–427.
Ramsey, F. P. (1927). "A contribution to the theory of taxation," *The Economic Journal*, 37, 47–61.
Rey, P., and T. Vergé (2019). "Secret contracting in multilateral relations." TSE Working Paper.
Riley, J. G., and W. F. Samuelson (1981). "Optimal auctions," *American Economic Review*, 71, 381–392.
Royden, H., and P. Fitzpatrick (2010). *Real Analysis* (4th ed.). Englewood Cliffs, NJ: Prentice Hall.
Samuelson, W. (1985). "A comment on the Coase Theorem." In A. E. Roth (ed.), *Game-Theoretic Models of Bargaining*. New York: Cambridge University Press, pp. 321–339.
Shapiro, C. (2010). "Injunctions, hold-up, and patent royalties," *American Law and Economics Review*, 12, 280–318.
Shapiro, C. (2018). Expert Report of Carl Shapiro. *U.S. v. AT&T Inc., DirecTV Group Holdings, LLC, and Time Warner Inc.* Case No. 1:17-cv-02511 (RJL). https://www.justice.gov/atr/case-document/file/1081336/download.
Sidak, J. G. (2015). "Bargaining power and patent damages," *Stanford Technology Law Review*, 19, 1–31.
Snyder, C. M. (1996). "A dynamic theory of countervailing power," *RAND Journal of Economics*, 27, 747–769.
Snyder, C. M. (2008). "Countervailing power." In S. N. Durlauf and L. E. Blume (eds.), *The New Palgrave Dictionary of Economics*. London: Palgrave Macmillan, pp. 1188–1189.

Sorensen, A. (2003). "Insurer–hospital bargaining: Negotiated discounts in post-deregulation Connecticut," *Journal of Industrial Economics*, 51, 469–490.

Spengler, J. J. (1950). "Vertical integration and antitrust policy," *Journal of Political Economy*, 58, 347–352.

Steptoe, M. L. (1993). "The power-buyer defense in merger cases," *Antitrust Law Journal*, 61, 493–504.

Stigler, G. J. (1954). "The economist plays with blocs," *American Economic Review (Papers and Proceedings)*, 44, 7–14.

Stigler Center (2019). *Stigler Committee on Digital Platforms*. Final Report.

Sweeting, A., X. Tao, and X. Yao (2018). "Dynamic oligopoly pricing with asymmetric information: Implications for mergers." Working Paper, University of Maryland.

U.S. Department of Justice and the Federal Trade Commission (2010). *Horizontal Merger Guidelines*. https://www.justice.gov/atr/horizontal-merger-guidelines-08192010.

U.S. Department of Justice and the Federal Trade Commission (2020). *Vertical Merger Guidelines*. https://www.ftc.gov/system/files/documents/reports/us-department-justice-federal-trade-commission-vertical-merger-guidelines/vertical_merger_guidelines_6-30-20.pdf.

Vickrey, W. (1961). "Counterspeculation, auction, and competitive sealed tenders," *Journal of Finance*, 16, 8–37.

Werden, G. J. (2008). "Unilateral competitive effects of horizontal mergers I: Basic concepts and models." In *Issues in Competition Law and Policy*, ABA Section of Antitrust Law, vol. II, pp. 1319–1341.

Werden, G. J., and M. L. Froeb (2008). "Unilateral competitive effects of horizontal mergers." In P. Buccirossi (ed.), *Handbook of Antitrust Economics*. Cambridge, MA: MIT Press, pp. 43–104.

Williams, S. R. (1987). "Efficient performance in two agent bargaining," *Journal of Economic Theory*, 41, 154–172.

Williamson, O. E. (1985). *The Economic Institutions of Capitalism*. New York: Free Press.

Wilson, C. A. (1988). "On the optimal pricing policy of a monopolist," *Journal of Political Economy*, 96, 164–176.

Wilson, R. (1987). "Game theoretic analysis of trading processes." In T. Bewley (ed.), *Advances in Economic Theory*. Cambridge: Cambridge University Press, pp. 33–70.

Wilson, R. (1993). *Nonlinear Pricing*. Oxford: Oxford University Press.

CHAPTER 4

Advances in Horizontal Merger Analysis

Volker Nocke

4.1 INTRODUCTION

Mergers play an important allocative role in the global economy. By exploiting potential synergies between tangible and intangible assets of the merging firms, they may improve the efficiency of production. At the same time, mergers may create or enhance market power at the expense of consumers and society. This concern is particularly important for horizontal mergers – combinations of firms competing in the same market. Horizontal merger control is therefore one of the central pillars of antitrust policy.

In this chapter, I provide a survey of recent advances in the academic literature on horizontal merger policy. Throughout, I focus on mergers' *unilateral effects*, ignoring potential *coordinated effects*. That is, I abstract from the impact that mergers may have when attempting to collude. This focus reflects antitrust practice in the last two decades or more: nowadays, most merger investigations revolve around unilateral effects, perhaps also because coordinated effects are much less well understood. This chapter provides a rather idiosyncratic reading of the recent literature in that I focus almost exclusively on my own work on the topic, developed in collaboration with my co-authors Michael Whinston, Nicolas Schutz, and others.

In Section 4.2, I begin by reviewing the seminal contributions on the static (Williamson) trade-off between the market power and efficiency effects of horizontal mergers: Williamson (1968) and Farrell and Shapiro (1990). I then turn to recent advances in the analysis of this trade-off: mergers in multiproduct-firm oligopoly (Nocke and Schutz, 2018), concentration screens for horizontal mergers (Nocke and Whinston, 2022), and mergers in open economies (Breinlich et al., 2020).

In Section 4.3, I survey recent contributions that derive the optimal merger approval policy in environments with endogenous merger proposals: merger policy in a dynamic model with endogenous but disjoint mergers (Nocke and Whinston, 2010), merger policy in a static model in which firms can choose which merger to propose (Nocke and Whinston, 2013), and merger policy in

I thank Nicolas Schutz for very helpful comments on an earlier draft. Financial support from the German Research Foundation (DFG) through CRC TR 224 (Project B03) is gratefully acknowledged.

a dynamic model with endogenous investment and entry (Mermelstein et al., 2020).

In Section 4.4, I conclude by briefly discussing a few promising avenues for future research.

4.2 THE WILLIAMSON TRADE-OFF

At the heart of any unilateral effects analysis of mergers is the trade-off between the *market power effect* and the possible *efficiency effect*. The former arises from the internalization of competitive externalities post-merger, while the latter may arise from merger-induced synergies in procurement, production, or distribution. This trade-off was first identified by Williamson (1968) in a diagrammatic analysis of a merger of a perfectly competitive industry to monopoly.

4.2.1 Merger of a Perfectly Competitive Industry to Monopoly

Consider an industry with market demand $Q(\cdot)$ and inverse demand $P(\cdot)$, satisfying the standard assumptions, notably $P'(Q) < 0$ and $P'(Q) + QP''(Q) < 0$ for all Q such that $P(Q) > 0$, and $\lim_{Q\to\infty} P(Q) = 0$. Suppose that there are n identical firms, each with constant marginal cost c, that behave as price-takers. The equilibrium price is thus $p^* = c$ and the equilibrium industry-level output $Q^* = Q(c)$. Suppose now that these n firms merge to monopoly and that the post-merger marginal cost is $\overline{c}$. The resulting post-merger quantity, $\overline{Q}^*$, satisfies the first-order condition $P(\overline{Q}^*) - \overline{c} + \overline{Q}^* P'(\overline{Q}^*) = 0$.

While Williamson (1968) focuses on the merger's impact on aggregate surplus, it is instructive to consider first the impact on consumer surplus. (In most jurisdictions, antitrust authorities have adopted something close to a consumer surplus standard.[1]) From the first-order condition of profit maximization, the merger is *CS-nondecreasing* (i.e., it either raises consumer surplus or leaves it unchanged) if

$$\underbrace{c - \overline{c}}_{\text{efficiency effect}} \geq \underbrace{-Q(c)P'(Q(c))}_{\text{market power effect}}; \tag{4.1}$$

it is *CS-decreasing* if the l.h.s. is strictly smaller than the r.h.s.; and it is *CS-neutral* if the equation holds with equality. The l.h.s. of equation (4.1) represents the merger's efficiency effect – the change in profit from the marginal unit of output. The r.h.s. represents the market power effect – the reduction in infra-marginal revenue from raising output slightly above its pre-merger level.

[1] The perceived wisdom on merger authorities' objective function is summarized by Whinston (2007) as follows: "[...] enforcement practice in most countries (including the U.S. and the E.U.) is closest to a consumer surplus standard."

Rewriting equation (4.1), we can see that the merger is CS-nondecreasing if and only if the post-merger marginal cost $\overline{c}$ is below some cutoff $\hat{c}$, defined as

$$\hat{c} \equiv c + Q(c)P'(Q(c)) < c. \quad (4.2)$$

The sign of the aggregate surplus effect can be derived in a similar fashion. The merger is *AS-nondecreasing* (i.e., does not decrease aggregate surplus) if and only if

$$c - \overline{c} \geq \frac{\int_{\overline{Q}^*}^{Q^*} [P(Q) - c] dQ}{\overline{Q}^*}. \quad (4.3)$$

It is straightforward to show that there exists a unique cutoff such that the merger is AS-nondecreasing if and only if the post-merger marginal cost is below that cutoff.

The Williamson (1968) analysis focuses on a setting that is very special, in at least three dimensions. First, it considers a merger to monopoly. However, if there are nonmerging outsiders (as there almost always are in practice), then the overall welfare impact of the merger will crucially depend on how these outsiders respond to the merger partners' changed incentive to produce output. Second, Williamson (1968) assumes that the market is perfectly competitive prior to the merger. This implies that the integrand on the r.h.s. of condition (4.3) is no longer zero, but strictly positive, when evaluated at the pre-merger equilibrium output level. Hence, reducing aggregate output below its pre-merger level has only a second-order effect on the r.h.s. of equation (4.3) – whereas it would have a first-order effect if the pre-merger profit margin were positive. Third, Williamson (1968) assumes that all firms produce at the same marginal cost prior to the merger. However, if firms have heterogeneous marginal costs, then the merger has the potential to increase productive efficiency by shifting output across its partners. In their seminal paper, Farrell and Shapiro (1990) address these issues by analyzing the Williamson trade-off in the homogeneous-goods Cournot model.

4.2.2 Mergers in the Homogeneous-Goods Cournot Model

Consider a homogeneous-goods industry in which a set $\mathcal{F}$ of firms compete in a Cournot fashion. Using a constant returns-to-scale technology, let c_f and q_f denote the marginal cost and output of firm $f \in \mathcal{F}$, respectively.[2] Inverse demand is given by $P(Q)$, where $Q = \sum_{f \in \mathcal{F}} q_f$ is aggregate output, and assumed to satisfy the standard assumptions made above. Given a profile of output choices $(q_g)_{g \in \mathcal{F}}$, firm f's profit is given by $\pi_f = [P(Q) - c_f]q_f$. Note that this expression depends on the output choices of rivals only through the "aggregator" Q; the homogeneous-goods Cournot model is thus an *aggregative game*.

[2] While Farrell and Shapiro (1990) allow for nonconstant marginal costs, for expositional simplicity, I will focus here on the case of constant returns to scale.

Before analyzing mergers, it is useful to review the aggregative games approach to studying equilibrium in the Cournot model.[3] This approach requires that first-order conditions are sufficient for individual optimality, which they are in the Cournot model under the standard assumptions on demand (made above). The aggregative games approach proceeds in two steps. First, for any given level of aggregate output, derive each firm's profit-maximizing output. Second, find the level of aggregate output that is consistent with firms' individual output choices.

Fix aggregate output Q, and consider firm f. If $P(Q) \leq c_f$, firm f's optimal output level is zero; if instead $P(Q) > c_f$, it is uniquely determined by the familiar first-order condition

$$P(Q) - c_f + q_f P'(Q) = 0.$$

The firm's profit-maximizing quantity can thus be written as

$$q_f = r(Q;c_f) \equiv \max\left(\frac{P(Q) - c_f}{-P'(Q)}, 0\right).$$

The *fitting-in function* $r(Q;c)$ gives the optimal output level of a firm with marginal cost c when aggregate output is Q. If $r(Q;c) > 0$, the fitting-in function is locally strictly decreasing in both Q and c: the larger is the aggregate output or the higher is its marginal cost, the less does a firm optimally produce.

In equilibrium, the sum of firms' individual output levels must be equal to aggregate output:

$$R(Q) \equiv \sum_{f \in \mathcal{F}} r(Q;c_f) - Q = 0.$$

As $R(Q)$ is strictly decreasing in Q, $R(0) \geq 0$ (with strict inequality if $P(0) > \min_{f \in \mathcal{F}} c_f$), and $R(Q) < 0$ for Q sufficiently large, there exists a unique Q^* such that $R(Q^*) = 0$. That is, there exists a unique equilibrium in the Cournot model: aggregate output is Q^* and firm f's output is $q_f^* = r(Q^*;c_f)$.

Comparative statics are well behaved. Consider an increase in firm f's marginal cost c_f, assuming that the firm is initially active in that $q_f^* = r(Q^*;c_f) > 0$. As this change in c_f does not affect the fitting-in function of any firm other than f, and decreases $r(Q;c_f)$ for any Q at which $r(Q;c_f) > 0$, it immediately follows that equilibrium aggregate output Q^* decreases. Moreover, since $r(Q;c_g)$ is decreasing in Q, this in turn implies that the equilibrium output and profit of any firm $g \neq f$, $q_g^* = r(Q^*;c_g)$ and $\pi_g^* = [P(Q^*) - c_g]r(Q^*;c_g)$ increases (and strictly so if firm g was initially active). By contrast, the equilibrium profit of firm f, π_f^*, decreases due to the increase in own marginal cost c_f and the induced increase of rivals' outputs.

Consider now a merger M between the firms in set $M \subset \mathcal{F}$, and let $\overline{c}_M$ denote the post-merger marginal cost. For expositional simplicity, suppose that

[3] In the context of the Cournot model, this approach was pioneered by McManus (1962, 1964) and Selten (1970) and applied by Szidarovszky and Yakowitz (1977) and Novshek (1985).

all merger partners are active before the merger: $r(Q^*, c_f) > 0$ for all $f \in M$, where Q^* denotes the equilibrium aggregate output prior to the merger.

As the merger does not affect the fitting-in functions of the nonmerging outsiders, it is CS-neutral if and only if

$$r(Q^*; \overline{c}_M) = \sum_{f \in M} r(Q^*; c_f)$$

or, equivalently,

$$P(Q^*) - \overline{c}_M = \sum_{f \in M} [P(Q^*) - c_f]. \tag{4.4}$$

Rewriting, the merger is CS-neutral if and only if

$$\overline{c}_M = P(Q^*) - \sum_{f \in M} [P(Q^*) - c_f] \equiv \hat{c}_M. \tag{4.5}$$

Since equilibrium aggregate output (and thus consumer surplus) is strictly decreasing in the post-merger marginal cost $\overline{c}_M$, the merger is CS-decreasing if $\overline{c}_M > \hat{c}_M$ and CS-increasing if $\overline{c}_M < \hat{c}_M$. A key insight of Farrell and Shapiro (1990) is that a merger among active firms has to involve (sufficiently large) synergies for it to be CS-nondecreasing: equation (4.5) implies that $\hat{c}_M < \min_{f \in M} c_f$.

By contrast, aggregate surplus does not necessarily increase with the merger-induced efficiencies.[4] Farrell and Shapiro (1990) therefore focus on the merger's *external effect*, defined as the induced change in the sum of consumer surplus and the nonmerging outsiders' joint profit. To the extent that a merger is proposed only if it is in the merger partners' interest, a positive external effect would thus be a sufficient condition for the merger to increase aggregate surplus.

Formally, let $\mathcal{O} \equiv \mathcal{F} \setminus M$ denote the set of nonmerging outsiders, and

$$W(Q) \equiv \int_0^Q [P(z) - P(Q)]dz + \sum_{f \in \mathcal{O}} [P(Q) - c_f] r(Q; c_f)$$

the sum of consumer surplus and the profit of the nonmerging outsiders when (equilibrium) aggregate output is Q. The external effect of merger M is thus given by $W(\overline{Q}^*) - W(Q^*)$. A useful "trick" used by Farrell and Shapiro (1990) consists in rewriting the external effect as

$$W(\overline{Q}^*) - W(Q^*) = \int_{Q^*}^{\overline{Q}^*} W'(Q) dQ,$$

where $W'(Q)dQ$ can be thought of as the external effect of an "infinitesimal" merger that changes equilibrium aggregate output by dQ. Differentiating $W(Q)$ yields

[4] In fact, if the merged firm is sufficiently inefficient, so that $P(Q^*) - \overline{c}_M$ is sufficiently close to zero, a small reduction in the post-merger marginal cost $\overline{c}_M$ necessarily decreases aggregate surplus by shifting output from more efficient outsiders to the merged firm; see Lahiri and Ono (1988) and Zhao (2001).

$$W'(Q) = -QP'(Q) + P'(Q) \sum_{f \in \mathcal{O}} r(Q;c_f) + \sum_{f \in \mathcal{O}} [P(Q) - c_f] \frac{\partial r(Q;c_f)}{\partial Q}. \tag{4.6}$$

Let $s_f(Q) \equiv r(Q;c_f)/Q$ denote the market share of firm f and $\sigma(Q) \equiv -QP''/P'(Q) < 1$ the curvature of inverse demand. As

$$\frac{\partial r(Q;c_f)}{\partial Q} = -1 + \sigma(Q) s_f(Q), \tag{4.7}$$

equation (4.6) can be rewritten as

$$W'(Q) = -QP'(Q) \left\{ 1 - \sum_{f \in \mathcal{O}} s_f(Q) - \sum_{f \in \mathcal{O}} s_f(Q) \left[1 - \sigma(Q) s_f(Q) \right] \right\}.$$

Hence, evaluated at Q, an infinitesimal CS-decreasing (i.e., output-decreasing) merger has a nonnegative external effect if and only if

$$1 - \sum_{f \in \mathcal{O}} s_f(Q) \leq \frac{1}{2} \left[1 - \sigma(Q) \sum_{f \in \mathcal{O}} s_f^2(Q) \right]. \tag{4.8}$$

It is straightforward to verify that this condition is "more likely" to hold if any outsider $f \in \mathcal{O}$ commands a larger market share $s_f(Q)$.[5] The intuition is simple. While the decrease in aggregate output decreases consumer surplus, there are two countervailing effects on the profits of nonmerging outsiders, both of which depend on market structure. First, the induced increase in price raises the outsiders' profits – and the size of this effect is proportional to outsiders' market shares.[6] Second, the outsiders optimally respond by increasing their outputs; the corresponding increase in outsiders' profits is also proportional to their market shares if demand curvature is zero.[7] The magnitude of this output response, however, is heterogeneous across outsiders in case of nonzero demand curvature: as can be seen from equation (4.7), it is larger for larger firms if $\sigma(Q) < 0$, and larger for smaller firms if $\sigma(Q) > 0$. Since larger firms command a larger markup, this means that condition (4.8) is easier to satisfy after a sum-preserving spread (resp., contraction) of the market shares of the outsiders if $\sigma(Q) < 0$ (resp., $\sigma(Q) > 0$).

Consider a CS-decreasing merger that reduces equilibrium aggregate output from Q^* to $\overline{Q}^* < Q^*$. If demand curvature is nondecreasing (i.e., $\sigma'(Q) \geq 0$ for all $Q \in [\overline{Q}^*, Q^*]$), then for this merger to have a nonnegative external effect, it

[5] To see this, let $\Psi \equiv 1 - \sum_{f \in \mathcal{O}} s_f - \frac{1}{2} \left[1 - \sigma \sum_{f \in \mathcal{O}} s_f^2 \right]$. The assertion follows from $\partial \Psi / \partial s_f = -1 + \sigma s_f < 0$.

[6] For an infinitesimal merger, this effect corresponds to the second term on the r.h.s. of equation (4.6).

[7] For an infinitesimal merger, this effect corresponds to the third term on the r.h.s. of equation (4.6). Noting that the markup $[P(Q) - c_f]$ is equal to $-r(Q;c_f)P'(Q)$, this third term is equal to the second term if $\sigma(Q) = 0$.

suffices that condition (4.8) is satisfied at the pre-merger equilibrium aggregate output level Q^*:[8]

$$s_M(Q^*) \le \frac{1}{2}\left[1-\sigma(Q^*)\sum_{f\in\mathcal{O}}\mathrm{HHI}^{\mathcal{O}}(Q^*)\right],$$

where $s_M(Q^*) \equiv \sum_{f\in M} s_f(Q^*)$ is the sum of the pre-merger market shares of the merger partners and $\mathrm{HHI}^{\mathcal{O}}(Q^*) \equiv \sum_{f\in\mathcal{O}} s_f^2(Q^*)$ is the pre-merger Herfindahl index among non-merging outsiders. This is a remarkable result, as the condition requires knowledge only of pre-merger market shares and pre-merger demand curvature. In the special case of linear demand ($\sigma(Q)=0$), the condition takes a particularly simple form: a CS-decreasing merger has a nonnegative external effect if and only if the joint market share of the merger partners does not exceed 50%. More generally, the external effect of a CS-decreasing merger is nonnegative as long as the sum of the pre-merger market shares of the merger partners is sufficiently small.

4.2.3 Mergers in Multiproduct-Firm Oligopoly

Most firms offer multiple products. However, because of technical difficulties in dealing with multiproduct-firm oligopoly, the literature has long been lacking an equilibrium model of horizontal mergers in such a setting. Building on the aggregative games approach to multiproduct-firm oligopoly developed in Nocke and Schutz (2018), Nocke and Schutz (2018) provide an extensive analysis of the unilateral effects of horizontal mergers under price competition with (nested) CES and MNL demands.

Let $\mathcal{N}$ denote the set of products. Abstracting from the nested demand structure for expositional simplicity, consumer surplus is given by

$$V(p) = \log H(p),$$

where $p = (p^k)_{k\in\mathcal{N}}$ is the price vector and

$$H(p) \equiv \sum_{k\in\mathcal{N}} h^k(p^k) + H_0.$$

Here, H_0 represents the value of the outside option, $h^k(p^k) = a^k(p^k)^{1-\sigma}$ in the case of CES demand and $h^k(p^k) = \exp((a^k - p^k)/\lambda)$ in the case of MNL demand, with $a^k > 0$ a measure of product quality, and $\sigma > 1$ and $\lambda > 0$ measures of price sensitivity.

The set of firms, $\mathcal{F}$, is a partition of $\mathcal{N}$. Assuming a constant returns-to-scale technology, the profit of firm $f \in \mathcal{F}$ can be written as

[8] To see this, let $\Psi(Q) \equiv 1 - \sum_{f\in\mathcal{O}} s_f(Q) - \frac{1}{2}[1-\sigma(Q)\sum_{f\in\mathcal{O}} s_f^2(Q)]$. Differentiating yields $\Psi'(Q) = -[1-\sigma(Q)]\sum_{f\in\mathcal{O}} s'_f(Q) + \frac{1}{2}\sigma'(Q)\sum_{f\in\mathcal{O}} s_f^2(Q) \ge 0$, where the inequality follows from $\sigma(Q) < 1$, $\sigma'(Q) \ge 0$, and $s'_f(Q) \le 0$.

$$\pi_f(p) = \sum_{k \in f} (p^k - c^k) \frac{-h^{k\prime}(p^k)}{H(p)}.$$

Note that firm f's profit depends on the prices set by other firms only through the value of the unidimensional aggregator $H(p)$. The associated multiproduct-firm pricing game is therefore aggregative. As in Section 4.2.2, this allows solving for the equilibrium in two steps. First, holding fixed the value of the aggregator H, derive each firm's optimal price vector using first-order conditions. Second, solve for the value of H that is consistent with firms' optimal pricing decisions.

From the first-order conditions of profit maximization,

$$\frac{p^k - c^k}{p^k} \iota^k(p^k) = \frac{p^l - c^l}{p^l} \iota^l(p^l) \equiv \mu_f \quad \forall k, l \in f, \tag{4.9}$$

where $\iota^k(p^k) \equiv -p^k h^{k\prime\prime}(p^k)/h^{k\prime}(p^k)$ is the price elasticity of demand for product k as perceived under monopolistic competition (where firms would take the value of the aggregator as given). Nocke and Schutz (2018) dub this the *common ι-markup property*: there exists a scalar μ_f such that firm f optimally sets its percentage markup for each product k equal to that scalar, divided by that product's perceived price elasticity ι^k. As $\iota^k(p^k) = \sigma$ under CES demand, and $\iota^k(p^k) = p^k/\lambda$ under MNL demand, this means that firm f optimally sets the same relative markup on all its products under CES demand, and the same absolute markup on all its products under MNL demand. The common ι-markup property implies a reduction in the dimensionality of the problem: it suffices to solve for each firm's optimal ι-markup μ_f, as the firm's prices for the various products can then be backed out from equation (4.9).

Under CES/MNL demands, an additional aggregation property applies: *type aggregation*. That is, all relevant information about firm f – the vector of firm f's products with its associated qualities and marginal costs – can be summarized in a single-dimensional sufficient statistic, its type T_f. Firm f's type is defined as $T_f \equiv \sum_{k \in f} h^k(c^k)$, and is equal to the firm's contribution to the aggregator (and thus to consumer surplus) if it were to price all its products at marginal cost.

From the demand function, firm f's market share, s_f, measured in value under CES demand and in volume under MNL demand, can be written as

$$s_f = \frac{T_f}{H}\left(1 - \frac{\mu_f}{\sigma}\right)^{\sigma - 1}$$

in the CES case, and

$$s_f = \frac{T^f}{H} e^{-\mu^f}$$

in the MNL case. From the first-order condition, we get another relationship between firm f's market share and its optimal ι-markup μ_f:

$$\mu_f(1 - \alpha s_f) = 1,$$

where $\alpha = (\sigma - 1)/\sigma$ in the CES case and $\alpha = 1$ in the MNL case. In each case, the system of two equations has a unique solution in μ_f and s_f: the *markup fitting-in function* $m(T_f/H)$ and the *market share fitting-in function* $S(T_f/H)$. Both fitting-in functions are strictly increasing: the higher is the firm's type (i.e., the larger is T_f) or the less intense is competition (i.e., the lower is H), the larger is the firm's optimal markup and market share.

The equilibrium value of the aggregator, H^*, is the unique solution in H of the condition

$$\sum_{f \in \mathcal{F}} S\left(\frac{T_f}{H}\right) + \frac{H_0}{H} = 1,$$

which simply says that market shares (including the share of the outside option) have to add up to one.

Nocke and Schutz (2018) show that the type aggregation property is very useful for merger analysis: while a merger may affect the merger partners' product portfolio in different ways (through the number of products, product qualities, and marginal costs), all that is required for the analysis is the firm's post-merger type $\overline{T}_M$. Note that in the case of no synergies – in which the merged firm produces exactly the same number of products, with the same qualities and at the same marginal costs, as the merger partners did jointly before the merger – we would have $\overline{T}_M = \sum_{f \in M} T_f$. For the merger to be CS-nondecreasing, however, requires that

$$S\left(\frac{\overline{T}_M}{H^*}\right) \geq \sum_{f \in M} S\left(\frac{T_f}{H^*}\right), \tag{4.10}$$

or

$$\overline{T}_M \geq S^{-1}\left(\sum_{f \in M} S\left(\frac{T_f}{H^*}\right)\right) \equiv \hat{T}_M,$$

and for it to be CS-neutral requires that these equations hold with equality. From the sub-additivity of the market share fitting-in function, it follows that $\hat{T}_M > \sum_{f \in M} T_f$. In short, a CS-nondecreasing merger must induce sufficiently large synergies.

Nocke and Schutz (2018) show that aggregate surplus is strictly increasing in the post-merger type $\overline{T}_M$. Hence, there exists a threshold type $\tilde{T}_M$ such that the merger is AS-nondecreasing if and only if $\overline{T}_M \geq \tilde{T}_M$. (Recall from our discussion above that no analog of this result is available in the homogeneous-goods Cournot model.) Moreover, as a CS-neutral merger is profitable for the merger partners (and does not affect the profit of the nonmerging outsiders), $\tilde{T}_M < \hat{T}_M$.

Following Farrell and Shapiro (1990), Nocke and Schutz (2018) also analyze a merger's external effect. They show that the external effect of an infinitesimal merger that changes the value of the aggregator by dH can be written as $-\eta(H)dH/H$, where

$$\eta(H) \equiv -1 + \sum_{f \in \mathcal{O}} \frac{T_f}{H} m'\left(\frac{T_f}{H}\right) = -1 + \sum_{f \in \mathcal{O}} \frac{\alpha s_f(1 - s_f)}{(1 - \alpha s_f)(1 - s_f + \alpha s_f^2)},$$

with $\mathcal{O}$ denoting again the set of nonmerging outsiders. The external effect of a CS-decreasing merger is necessarily negative if $\alpha \leq \overline{\alpha} \equiv 3(\sqrt{57} - 7)/2 \approx 0.82$. If, however, $\alpha > \overline{\alpha}$ – which always holds under MNL demand and holds under CES demand for σ large – then there exist CS-decreasing mergers with a positive external effect; this effect is "more likely" to be positive when the nonmerging outsiders have higher or more concentrated market shares.

Johnson and Rhodes (2021) analyze horizontal mergers in the Johnson and Myatt (2006) Cournot model with pure vertical product differentiation. There are two quality levels, a low quality and a high quality. Each firm may produce either quality, or both, using a constant-returns-to-scale technology. Denoting the aggregate quantity of both qualities by Q_1 and that of high quality only by $Q_2 \leq Q_1$, the resulting prices for the good's low-quality and high-quality version are given by $P_1(Q_1)$ and $P_1(Q_1) + P_2(Q_2)$, respectively.[9] Each firm's profit therefore depends on the actions of its rivals through *two* aggregators, Q_1 and Q_2. Compared to the homogeneous-goods Cournot model, this additional flexibility implies that some of the conclusions of Farrell and Shapiro (1990) do not hold in their setting.

Most importantly, mergers without synergies may sometimes benefit consumers. To see this, consider a merger between two firms that produce only the low-quality version of the good. Suppose also that there is a nonmerging outsider that offers only high quality. Absent synergies, the merged firm has an incentive to restrict the output of low quality. The best response of the nonmerging outsider consists in increasing its own high-quality output. It is possible to construct examples in which the latter effect may be so strong that the consumer benefit from the increase in high-quality output outweighs the consumer harm from the decrease in low-quality output.

4.2.4 Welfare Impact and Concentration Measures

Concentration measures play an important role in merger control, both at the screening stage (at which antitrust authorities have to decide whether to investigate further a proposed merger) as well as in court proceedings. In the United States, the horizontal merger guidelines state safe-harbor presumptions as well as presumption of anticompetitive effects based on the (post-merger) Herfindahl index and the merger-induced change in that index, both naively computed (i.e., assuming that the market shares of the nonmerging outsiders do not change). Nocke and Whinston (2022) argue that the basis for these presumptions, both in form and level, is unclear.

[9] That is, $P_1(\cdot)$ is the inverse demand function for the low-quality version and $P_2(\cdot)$ the inverse demand function for the "upgrade" to high quality.

One possible approach to shed light on this issue involves relating the possible welfare impact of a merger to concentration measures. This is the route taken in Nocke and Schutz (2018), for the benchmark case in which the merger does not induce any synergies. Considering price competition with (nested) CES and MNL demands with an outside option $H_0 > 0$, they provide a second-order approximation of the consumer surplus and aggregate surplus effects of a merger, with the approximation being taken around small market shares.[10]

The approximation proceeds in several steps. First, fix a pre-merger vector of market shares, $s = (s_f)_{f \in \mathcal{F}}$, assuming the market share of the outside good is strictly positive. Second, use this vector to recover the pre-merger type vector and the pre-merger values of consumer surplus, $\mathrm{CS}(s) = \log H_0 + \log(1 - \sum_{f \in \mathcal{F}} s_f)$, and aggregate surplus, $\mathrm{AS}(s) = \mathrm{CS}(s) + \sum_{f \in \mathcal{F}} \alpha s_f/(1 - \alpha s_f)$, where $\alpha = (\sigma - 1)/\sigma$ for CES demand and $\alpha = 1$ for MNL demand. Third, use the post-merger type vector, assuming no merger-induced synergies, to obtain the post-merger vector of marginal costs, $\overline{s}(s) = (\overline{s}_f(s))_{f \in \mathcal{F}}$, and the post-merger values of the welfare measures, $\mathrm{CS}(\overline{s}(s))$ and $\mathrm{AS}(\overline{s}(s))$. Finally, apply Taylor's theorem to obtain

$$\mathrm{CS}(\overline{s}(s)) - \mathrm{CS}(s) = -\alpha \Delta \mathrm{HHI}(s) + o(||s||^2)$$

and

$$\mathrm{AS}(\overline{s}(s)) - \mathrm{AS}(s) = -\alpha \Delta \mathrm{HHI}(s) + o(||s||^2),$$

where $\Delta\mathrm{HHI}(s)$ is the naively computed change in the Herfindahl index. That is, both the consumer surplus and the aggregate surplus loss induced by a merger without synergies is approximately proportional to the merger-induced change in the naively computed index.

An alternative approach involves relating the synergy level required to make the merger CS-neutral to concentration measures. This is the route taken, both theoretically and empirically, in Nocke and Whinston (2022). In the theoretical part of their paper, Nocke and Whinston derive the required synergy level in the homogeneous-goods Cournot model and in the (multiproduct-firm) pricing games with CES and MNL demands. For the merger to be CS-neutral, the efficiency must be such that, when evaluated at the pre-merger level of the aggregator, the merged firm's (market share) fitting-in function is equal to the sum of the merger partners' pre-merger fitting-in functions.[11] Whether this condition is satisfied depends only on the pre-merger level of the aggregator and the pre-merger types of the merger partners. Hence, the required synergy level is related to the market shares of the merger partners, but not to those of the nonmerging outsiders.

Importantly, this required synergy level is the higher, the larger are the market shares of the merger partners. Moreover, a sum-preserving contraction of

[10] They also provide an approximation around monopolistic competition "conduct."

[11] In the case of CES/MNL demands, this amounts to equation (4.10) holding with equality.

the merger partners' market shares also increases the required synergies. These results suggest that the likelihood of a merger harming consumers is positively related to the induced *change* in the Herfindahl index but unrelated to the *level* of the index when controlling for the change.[12]

In the empirical part of their paper, Nocke and Whinston (2022) examine the required synergies in the context of 390 potential (local) mergers in the US brewing industry, using the (random-coefficient MNL) demand and marginal cost estimates of Miller and Weinberg (2017).[13] They find that the required synergy is strongly increasing in the merger-induced change in the Herfindahl index and largely unrelated to the level. Nocke and Whinston (2022) also argue that the presumptions in the 2010 horizontal merger guidelines are likely too lax, at least unless one is crediting efficiencies of 5% or larger to the typical mergers, or is presuming that other factors such as entry or product-repositioning would prevent any anti-competitive effects.

4.2.5 Mergers in Open Economies

In a globalized world, many firms not only sell in their domestic markets but also abroad. Yet, trade frictions imply that markets are not perfectly integrated internationally. As a result, a merger may raise consumer surplus in one market but reduce it in another.

Breinlich et al. (2020) analyze this issue in a model of international trade with oligopolistic competition.[14] In their baseline, firms compete in a Cournot fashion and markets are segmented; $P^i(\cdot)$ denotes the inverse demand function in country i. Firms incur iceberg-type trade costs when selling in the foreign country. Specifically, for one unit of the output to arrive in country j, a firm located in country i has to ship τ^{ij} units, where $\tau^{ii} = 1$.

Consider a merger M among active firms located in country i, and consider its effect on consumers in country j (which may or may not be equal to i). Adjusting condition (4.4) to account for trade costs, the merger is CS-neutral in country j if and only if

$$P^j(Q^{j*}) - \tau^{ij}\overline{c}_M = \sum_{f\in M} \left[P^j(Q^{j*}) - \tau^{ij}c_f\right] \tag{4.11}$$

or, equivalently,

$$\overline{c}_M = \left(\sum_{f\in M} c_f\right) - (|M|-1)\frac{P^j(Q^{j*})}{\tau^{ij}} \equiv \hat{c}_M^{ij},$$

[12] Nocke and Whinston (2022) exclusively focus on the unilateral price effects of mergers, abstracting from potential coordinated effects. The level of the Herfindahl index would matter for the likelihood of consumer harm if the level of the merger-induced efficiencies, or the probability of merger-induced entry or product-repositioning, depended on industry concentration.

[13] In the Miller and Weinberg (2017) dataset, there are 39 local markets and five firms, amounting to 10 potential mergers in each of the 39 markets.

[14] See Breinlich et al. (2017) for a survey of the literature on horizontal merger policy in open economies.

where $|M|$ denotes the number of merger partners. Hence,

$$\hat{c}_M^{ij} - \hat{c}_M^{ii} = (|M| - 1)\left(P^i(Q^{i*}) - \frac{P^j(Q^{j*})}{\tau^{ij}}\right).$$

Because markets are segmented (implying that consumer prices in the two countries may differ from each other) and because of trade costs, the post-merger cost threshold below which the merger benefits consumers in the foreign country $j \neq i$, $\hat{c}_M^{ij}$, is likely to differ from that in the home country i. If so, the two countries have potentially conflicting interests: while the merger is CS-nondecreasing in both countries if $\overline{c}_M \leq \min\left(\hat{c}_M^{ij}, \hat{c}_M^{ii}\right)$ and CS-decreasing in both countries if $\overline{c}_M > \max\left(\hat{c}_M^{ij}, \hat{c}_M^{ii}\right)$, it is CS-decreasing in one but CS-increasing in the other if $\min\left(\hat{c}_M^{ij}, \hat{c}_M^{ii}\right) < \overline{c}_M < \max\left(\hat{c}_M^{ij}, \hat{c}_M^{ii}\right)$.

Breinlich et al. (2020) define the "conflict statistic"

$$\rho^{ij} \equiv \tau^{ij}\frac{P^i(Q^{i*})}{P^j(Q^{j*})}$$

as the price ratio between the domestic market i and the foreign market j, adjusted for trade costs that firms from country i face when exporting to country j. If $\rho^{ij} \geq 1$, then a merger M that is CS-nondecreasing in its home market i is necessarily also CS-nondecreasing in the foreign market j, since $\hat{c}_M^{ii} \leq \hat{c}_M^{ij}$ in that case. By contrast, if $\rho^{ij} < 1$ or, equivalently, $\hat{c}_M^{ii} > \hat{c}_M^{ij}$, then merger M may be CS-nondecreasing in market i and CS-decreasing in market j (whereas if it is CS-nondecreasing in market j, it must also be CS-nondecreasing in market i).[15]

That is, if antitrust authorities maximize consumer surplus in their own country, then foreign authorities want to block mergers that have been approved by their domestic authorities only if the value of the conflict statistic is less than one. Importantly, the value of that statistic is market-specific but not merger-specific. Calibrating the model to industry-level data from Canada and the United States, Breinlich et al. (2020) find that, at the current level of trade costs, the conflict statistic exceeds one in the vast majority of markets, so that any potential conflict is of the "too-tough-for-thy-neighbor" type.

4.3 ENDOGENOUS MERGERS AND DYNAMICS

A static analysis of the Williamson trade-off ignores that mergers are endogenous and not one-time events. If merger opportunities arise over time and mergers are proposed only if it is in the merger partners' interest, then a merger approval policy based only on whether a merger is anti-competitive given current market structure may not be appropriate. This is for at least two reasons, both due to competitive externalities. First, the approval decision on

[15] Breinlich et al. (2020) show that the same conflict statistic – with the equilibrium price in each country being replaced by the CES price index in that country – obtains under multiproduct-firm price competition with CES demand.

a merger proposed today will generally affect the profitability of a potential future merger, and therefore the likelihood of the future merger being proposed. Second, the approval decision on a merger proposed today will affect the welfare consequences of a future merger, and therefore the likelihood of the future merger being approved.

4.3.1 Optimal Dynamic Merger Approval Policy

Analyzing the optimal dynamic approval policy in a model in which merger opportunities arise stochastically over time and, in every period, the partners in a feasible merger have to decide whether to propose it, and the antitrust authority has to decide which (if any) of the currently proposed mergers to approve, appears to be a hopelessly complicated problem. Nocke and Whinston (2010) show that, under some conditions, this problem has a surprisingly simple solution: An antitrust authority that aims at maximizing (discounted) consumer surplus can achieve its goal by adopting a completely *myopic* merger approval policy, whereby it approves in every period the subset of proposed mergers that maximizes current consumer surplus, completely ignoring the possibility of future mergers. Remarkably, the outcome induced by such a myopic policy is dynamically optimal in a very strong sense: The antitrust authority could not improve upon it even if it had perfect foresight about future merger possibilities (which it does not) nor if it could undo previously approved mergers (which it cannot).

Nocke and Whinston (2010) prove this result in the context of a homogeneous-goods Cournot model with constant returns to scale. There is a set of potential mergers, $M_1, ..., M_N$, that may become available over T periods. The probability that merger M_k becomes feasible in period $1 \leq t \leq T$ is p_{kt}, with $\sum_{t=1}^{T} p_{kt} \leq 1$. Once a merger M_k has become feasible in period t, the merger partners draw their post-merger marginal cost $\overline{c}_{M_k}$ from some set C_{kt}. Firms involved in a feasible but not-yet-approved merger then decide whether or not to propose their merger for approval to the antitrust authority.[16]

Nocke and Whinston (2010) make two conceptually important assumptions. First, mergers that have been rejected in the past can be proposed again. Second, potential mergers are *disjoint* in that every firm is party to at most one potential merger. As we will see, the first assumption implies that the antitrust authority will not regret blocking a merger that would harm consumers at the time of approval, whereas the second implies *inter alia* that mergers are not mutually exclusive.

The dynamic optimality of a myopic appoval policy derives from a series of three key results. The first and most immediate one is:

[16] Bargaining between merger partners is efficient so that the merger will be proposed if and only if it is in their joint interest to do so.

Result 4.1 (Nocke and Whinston, 2010) *Suppose that merger M_k is CS-nondecreasing given current market structure. Then, merger M_k is profitable in that it raises the joint profit of the merger partners.*

To see this result, recall from equation (4.4) that, following a CS-neutral merger, the profit margin of the merged firm is equal to the sum of the pre-merger profit margins of the merger partners and, moreover, the merged firm produces the same quantity of output as the merger partners did jointly before the merger. It follows that a CS-neutral merger is profitable. As reducing the marginal cost of a firm raises that firm's equilibrium profit, it also follows that a CS-increasing merger is profitable as well.

The next result uses the following important observation: the threshold post-merger marginal cost level that makes merger M just CS-neutral, $\hat{c}_M$, is strictly increasing in pre-merger aggregate output Q^*. This observation follows from equation (4.5) and implies a fundamental sign-preserving complementarity of mergers that share the same sign in terms of their consumer surplus effect:

Result 4.2 (Nocke and Whinston, 2010) *Consider two disjoint mergers, M_1 and M_2. If both mergers are CS-nondecreasing (and therefore profitable) in isolation, then each remains CS-nondecreasing (and therefore profitable) once the other merger has been implemented. Conversely, if both M_1 and M_2 are CS-decreasing in isolation, then each remains CS-decreasing once the other one has taken place.*

To see the assertion on the sign-preserving complementarity of CS-nondecreasing mergers, note that merger M_k $(k = 1,2)$ being CS-nondecreasing means that $\overline{c}_{M_k} \leq \hat{c}_{M_k}$. If the other merger is implemented, aggregate output and thus $\hat{c}_{M_k}$ must weakly increase, implying that the post-merger marginal cost $\overline{c}_{M_k}$ still lies below the (now weakly higher) threshold $\hat{c}_{M_k}$, that is, M_k must remain CS-nondecreasing given the new market structure. A similar argument implies the sign-preserving complementarity of CS-decreasing mergers.

The observation that $\hat{c}_M$ is strictly increasing in pre-merger aggregate output also means that, by changing aggregate output, a CS-nondecreasing merger can induce a merger that otherwise would have been CS-decreasing to become CS-nondecreasing (and the reverse):

Result 4.3 (Nocke and Whinston, 2010) *Suppose that merger M_1 is CS-nondecreasing in isolation and merger M_2 is CS-decreasing in isolation but CS-nondecreasing once M_1 has been implemented. Then, merger M_1 remains CS-nondecreasing (and therefore profitable) once M_2 has taken place. Moreover, the joint profit of the partners to M_1 is strictly higher if both M_1 and M_2 take place than if neither does.*

Before providing a sketch of the proof, note that the last part of the result is quite remarkable: after all, once M_1 has been implemented, merger M_2 (by virtue of being CS-nondecreasing) imposes a (weakly) negative externality on the merged M_1. (Moreover, this result extends to any number of mergers: If one merger induces, directly or indirectly, n other mergers to become CS-nondecreasing, the firms involved in the first are still better off if their merger and all of the others take place than if none does, no matter how large is n and even though all of these n other mergers hurt the firms involved in the first.)

To see why Result 4.3 holds, note that if the mergers are implemented in the order M_1 first and M_2 second, then – at each step – consumer surplus (weakly) increases by assumption. Consider now the thought experiment of implementing the two mergers in the reverse order. Then, by assumption, consumer surplus falls strictly at the first step (when M_2 is implemented) and rises strictly at the second (when M_1 is implemented). That is, once M_2 has taken place, M_1 is CS-increasing (and therefore profitable). Moreover, when M_2 is implemented at the first step, the profit of all the (active) nonmerging outsiders (including the firms involved in M_1) strictly increases as M_2 is CS-decreasing when implemented in isolation. Hence, the joint profit of the merger partners in M_1 increases at each step and is therefore higher when both mergers take place than when neither does.

While Nocke and Whinston (2010) derive Results 4.1 to 4.3 for the homogeneous-goods Cournot model, Nocke and Schutz (2018) show that these results, and therefore the conclusion on the dynamic optimality of a myopic merger policy, extend to models of multiproduct-firm price competition with (nested) CES and MNL demands.

Suppose the antitrust authority adopts a myopic merger approval policy. To see the intuition for the dynamic optimality of that policy, consider the special case in which there are only two possible mergers, M_1 and M_2, and only two periods, $T = 2$.

Let us ignore for the moment the moral hazard problem, which arises because the antitrust authority can approve only mergers that are proposed. To this end, suppose that in each period every feasible and not-yet-approved merger is indeed proposed. In the special case with only two possible mergers and two periods, for the outcome of the myopic policy not to be dynamically optimal the following must happen: in period 1, only one merger, say M_1, becomes feasible (and is proposed) and, in period 2, the other merger (M_2) becomes feasible (and is proposed) – and the arrival of this second merger makes the authority regret its decision on M_1.

To see that such an outcome cannot arise, consider first the case in which M_1 is CS-nondecreasing in isolation. Adopting a myopic policy, the antitrust authority would thus approve the merger in period 1, thereby (weakly) raising consumer surplus in period 1. Obviously, implementing M_1 is still the optimal decision from the viewpoint of maximizing consumer surplus in period 2 if merger M_2 does not become feasible in period 2. The same is true if M_2 becomes feasible (and is proposed) but is CS-decreasing given that M_1 has already been implemented, implying that the authority blocks it in period 2; from Result 4.2 this means that M_2 must be CS-decreasing in isolation, and so period-2 consumer surplus is maximized by implementing M_1 but not M_2. If, on the other hand, M_2 becomes feasible, is proposed and approved in period 2 because it is CS-nondecreasing given that M_1 has already been implemented, then period-2 consumer surplus is maximized by implementing both M_1 and M_2. M_2 must be either CS-nondecreasing in isolation (i.e., even without implementing M_1) or CS-decreasing in isolation but CS-nondecreasing once M_1 has taken place; Results 4.2 and 4.3 imply that M_1 remains CS-nondecreasing given that M_2 takes place. In short, no matter what the characteristics are of M_2 in period 2, the antitrust authority will not have ex-post regret about having approved a merger in period 1 that was CS-nondecreasing at the time of approval.

Consider next the case in which M_1 is CS-decreasing in isolation, so that the antitrust authority – following a myopic policy – blocks it in period 1. But this is optimal not only from the viewpoint of period-1 consumer surplus but also from that in period 2: as the blocked merger can and will be proposed again in period 2, the authority is free to implement in period 2 the set of mergers that maximizes period-2 consumer surplus. In short, no matter what the characteristics are of M_2 in period 2, the antitrust authority will not have ex-post regret about having blocked a merger in period 1 that was CS-decreasing at the time of the decision.

Let us now turn to firms' merger proposal incentives when the antitrust authority adopts a myopic approval policy. Note first that any merger that is approved must be CS-nondecreasing given the market structure at the time of approval – and by Result 4.1 raise the joint profit of the merger partners – given the market structure at the time of approval. Moreover, as discussed above, a merger that was approved in period 1 must also be CS-nondecreasing (and therefore profitable) in period 2, given period-2 market structure. Market structure is, however, endogenous: by proposing a merger that is approved, firms may affect whether another merger is implemented. But if merger M_k is approved, it must be CS-nondecreasing at the time of approval, and therefore raise the post-merger marginal cost threshold $\hat{c}_{M_l}$ below which the other merger M_l is CS-nondecreasing. Hence, proposing a merger can only increase the likelihood that another merger is implemented. If proposing merger M_k does indeed induce the approval of merger M_l, then – from Result 4.3 – the firms involved in M_k are still better off if both mergers take place than if neither does. In short, firms' proposal incentives are fully aligned with the interests of a consumer-surplus-oriented antitrust authority.

As mentioned above, a key assumption for the conclusion on the dynamic optimality of a myopic approval policy is that mergers are disjoint in that no firm can be party to more than one potential merger. This assumption may appear reasonable in environments where firms have natural merger partners. In other environments, however, firms may have a choice between alternative merger partners.

4.3.2 Optimal Merger Policy with Merger Choice

Nocke and Whinston (2013) study the optimal merger policy in a static setting in which firms can choose *which* merger to propose. They show that there is a systematic misalignment of firms' proposal incentives with the interests of consumers. To mitigate those, the antitrust authority optimally commits to discriminate against mergers involving larger firms.[17]

In Nocke and Whinston's (2013) baseline model, firms compete in a Cournot fashion in a homogeneous-goods industry. There is a single acquirer, firm 0, that can make a public take-it-or-leave-it offer to one possible target $k = 1,...,K$ of its choosing. If the offer is accepted, the merger is proposed for approval to the antitrust authority. Otherwise, or if the proposed merger is blocked, no merger takes place.[18]

The possible targets can be ordered according to their pre-merger marginal cost, with $c_1 > \cdots > c_K$, so that firm 1 is the smallest possible merger partner and firm K the largest. The feasibility and post-merger marginal cost are stochastic and drawn independently across mergers. The post-merger marginal cost of merger $M_k = \{0,k\}$ is denoted $\overline{c}_{M_k}$, continuously distributed on some interval $[l, h_k]$.

Before the feasibility of mergers, and their associated marginal costs, are realized, the antitrust authority commits to an approval set $\mathcal{A} \equiv \{M_k : \overline{c}_{M_k} \in \mathcal{A}_k\}$, where $\mathcal{A}_k \subseteq [l, h_k]$ for $k \in \{1,...,K\}$ gives the post-merger marginal cost levels that would lead to approval of merger M_k. If no merger is proposed, the status quo ("null merger") M_0 remains in place.

Let $\Delta CS(M_k)$ and $\Delta\Pi(M_k)$ denote, respectively, the change in consumer surplus and the change in the bilateral profit of firms 0 and k induced by merger M_k.[19] Given an approval policy $\mathcal{A}$ and a realized set of feasible mergers $\mathcal{M}$, firm 0 is going to propose the "most profitable," feasible, and allowable merger $M^*(\mathcal{F}, \mathcal{A})$, where

$$M^*(\mathcal{M},\mathcal{A}) = \begin{cases} \arg\max_{M_k \in (\mathcal{M}\cap\mathcal{A})} \Delta\Pi(M_k) & \text{if } \max_{M_k \in (\mathcal{M}\cap\mathcal{A})} \Delta\Pi(M_k) > 0, \\ M_0 & \text{otherwise.} \end{cases}$$

(To see that this is indeed the proposed merger, note that if firm 0 wants to propose merger M_k, it will make an offer to firm k that gives firm k exactly the same profit it would obtain in the absence of a merger. That is, firm 0 extracts all of the bilateral surplus $\Delta\Pi(M_k)$ from merger M_k.) The antitrust authority in turn chooses the approval set $\mathcal{A}$ that maximizes the expected change

17 Lyons (2003) also noted a misalignment of interests when firms can choose between alternative mergers, making commitment to a merger approval policy valuable.

18 That is, the bargaining process takes the form of Segal's (1999) "offer game." Nocke and Whinston (2013) also consider a more general "scoring-rule" bargaining process, which encompasses efficient Coasian bargaining as a special case.

19 $\Delta\Pi(M_k)$ is thus equal to the profit of the merged M_k minus the sum of the pre-merger profits of merger partners 0 and k.

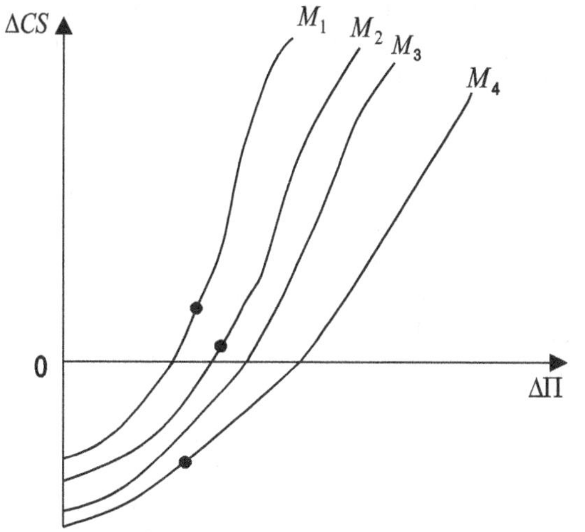

Figure 4.1 Each curve labeled M_k depicts the relationship between the change in consumer surplus and the change in bilateral profit for a merger between firms 0 and k, with each point on the curve corresponding to a different realization of merger M_k's post-merger marginal cost. The heavy dots illustrate one possible realization (with no feasible merger M_3).

in consumer surplus, where the expectation is taken with respect to the set of feasible mergers, $\mathcal{M}$. That is, the antitrust authority's problem can be written as

$$\max_{\mathcal{A}} E_{\mathcal{M}}\left[\Delta CS(M^*(\mathcal{M},\mathcal{A}))\right].$$

Figure 4.1 illustrates the support of merger realizations in outcome space $(\Delta\Pi, \Delta CS)$ for the case of four potential mergers ($K = 4$). It is important to highlight three properties illustrated in this figure. First, for each potential merger M_k, the support of possible realizations is an upward-sloping curve in $(\Delta\Pi, \Delta CS)$-space. This *monotonicity property* obtains since a decrease in post-merger marginal cost $\overline{c}_{M_k}$ is associated both with an increase in consumer surplus $\Delta CS(M_k)$ as well as with an increase in the merged firm's profit and thus in $\Delta\Pi(M_k)$. Second, for each M_k, the merger curve intersects the horizontal axis to the right of the origin. This *willingness-to-propose property* follows from the fact that a CS-neutral merger is bilaterally profitable (recall Result 4.1): if $\Delta CS(M_k) = 0$, then $\Delta\Pi(M_k) > 0$. Third, in the positive orthant of the $(\Delta\Pi, \Delta CS)$-space, the merger curves are ordered in that those corresponding to larger mergers lie to the right of those for smaller mergers. This *ordered bias property* follows from a systematic misalignment of incentives:

Result 4.4 (Nocke and Whinston, 2013) *Suppose two mergers, M_i and M_j, with $j > i$, induce the same nonnegative change in consumer surplus, $\Delta CS(M_i) = \Delta CS(M_j) \geq 0$. Then, the larger merger M_j induces a larger increase in the bilateral profit of the merger partners:* $0 < \Delta\Pi(M_i) < \Delta\Pi(M_j)$.

To get some intuition, suppose first that both mergers M_i and M_j are CS-neutral, $\Delta CS(M_i) = \Delta CS(M_j) = 0$. The increase in the bilateral profit of a CS-neutral merger M_k can be written as[20]

$$\Delta\Pi(M_k) = [P(Q^*) - c_0]\, q_k^* + [P(Q^*) - c_k]\, q_0^*,$$

where Q^* and q_k^* denote pre-merger aggregate and firm-k output, respectively. Noting that $c_i > c_j$ and $q_i^* < q_j^*$, we obtain $0 < \Delta\Pi(M_i) < \Delta\Pi(M_j)$. The result can be shown to extend to CS-increasing mergers by proving that $\Delta\Pi(M_j) - \Delta\Pi(M_i)$ increases with an increase in the post-merger aggregate output.

Returning to Figure 4.1, the dots represent one possible realization of feasible mergers, namely CS-increasing mergers M_1 and M_2, no feasible merger M_3 (illustrated by the absence of a dot), and a CS-decreasing merger M_4. If all three feasible mergers were allowable (i.e., if all were in set $\mathcal{A}$), then merger M_2 would be proposed (and approved), as it is the feasible merger with the largest increase in the merging firms' bilateral profit $\Delta\Pi$. However, from the viewpoint of the antitrust authority, the best merger is M_1 as it is the feasible merger with the largest increase in consumer surplus ΔCS.

The problem faced by the antitrust authority is that it has to choose an approval set before knowing the realization of feasible mergers. In choosing whether to include a particular merger M_k (or, rather, a small interval of mergers around a particular point on the merger curve), the antitrust authority has to condition on the event that this is the most profitable allowable merger as the choice matters only in that event.

A "naive" approval policy would allow all CS-nondecreasing mergers. This is indeed optimal for the approval set $\mathcal{A}_1$ pertaining to the smallest merger M_1: any CS-nondecreasing merger M_1 that is the most profitable allowable merger would, by Result 4.4, necessarily also be the best for consumers. However, this does not hold for any larger merger M_k, $k > 1$. For example, including the realized merger M_2 in Figure 4.1 in the approval set may not be optimal: the merger raises consumer surplus by not much; if the authority commits to blocking it, the expected increase in consumer surplus – conditional on that merger otherwise (i.e., if it were included in $\mathcal{A}$) being the most profitable one – may well be larger as, with some probability, a less profitable but better-for-consumers merger M_1 may be feasible.

Let $\underline{\Delta CS}_k$ denote the change in consumer surplus induced by the merger M_k with the highest allowable post-merger cost level $\overline{c}_{M_k}$. That is, $\underline{\Delta CS}_k$ gives the minimum consumer surplus increase necessary for merger M_k to be included in the approval set. Nocke and Whinston (2013) show that the optimal merger approval policy blocks some mergers that would increase consumer surplus,

[20] To see this, note first that the joint pre-merger profit of the two merger partners is $[P(Q^*) - c_0]q_0^* + [P(Q^*) - c_k]q_k^*$. Recall from Section 4.2.2 that a CS-neutral merger does not change the merger partners' joint equilibrium output nor aggregate equilibrium output. The merged firm's profit is therefore given by $[P(Q^*) - \overline{c}_{M_k}](q_0^* + q_k^*) = [P(Q^*) - c_0 + P(Q^*) - c_k](q_0^* + q_k^*)$, where the equality follows from equation (4.4).

requires a higher minimum standard for larger mergers, and may always block the largest possible merger(s):[21]

Result 4.5 (Nocke and Whinston, 2013) *Any optimal approval policy $\mathcal{A}$ has the following properties:*

1. *it approves the smallest merger M_1 if and only if it is CS-nondecreasing;*
2. *only mergers $M_1, ..., M_{\hat{K}}$, where $\hat{K} \leq K$, are approved with positive probability;*
3. *the minimum increase in consumer surplus necessary for a merger to be included in the approval set is higher for larger mergers: $0 = \underline{\Delta CS}_1 < \underline{\Delta CS}_2 < \cdots < \underline{\Delta CS}_{\hat{K}}$.*

Nocke and Whinston (2013) show that the conclusion continues to hold for alternative merger bargaining processes (notably, industry-wide Coasian bargaining), alternative welfare standards (notably, a weighted average of consumer surplus and aggregate surplus), and differentiated-products price competition (with CES or MNL demands).

4.3.3 Dynamic Merger Policy with Endogenous Investment

Reflecting both the academic literature and antitrust practice, the discussion so far has focused on the short-run price (or quantity) effects of mergers. However, mergers also affect firms' incentives to invest, to innovate, or to shape product characteristics. Such long-run effects are much less well understood, and harder to quantify, than the short-run price effects though – explaining why such effects have for a long time been ignored. In recent years, however, mergers' investment effects have played an important role in a number of merger investigations, not least in a series of mobile telephony mergers in the European Union and the United States as well as in the European Commission's investigation of the DowChemical/DuPont merger.

In recent work, Motta and Tarantino (2021) and Bourreau et al. (2019) analyze the investment effects of mergers in static models of price (or quantity) competition, enriched by investment in cost reduction or quality improvement. While such static models have the advantage of tractability, they may appear less appropriate when analyzing the effect of policy on long-run decisions such as investments. What is taken as given in a static model – the initial state of the industry (e.g., the initial vector of marginal costs) – is affected by policy in a dynamic model.

Mermelstein et al. (2020) analyze merger policy in a dynamic computational model in which firms can reduce their marginal costs by investing in

[21] The optimal approval policy does not necessarily have a cutoff structure in that it may be optimal to commit to approving merger M_k when it would raise consumer surplus by $\Delta CS \geq \underline{\Delta CS}_k$ but block it when it would raise it by $\Delta CS' > \Delta CS$. However, Nocke and Whinston (2013) provide a condition under which the optimal policy does have a cutoff structure.

capital or by combining capital through mergers. Firms compete in quantities in a homogeneous-goods industry, using an increasing returns-to-scale technology that combines labor and capital. The model builds on the computational literature on industry dynamics pioneered by Pakes and McGuire (1994) and Ericson and Pakes (1995) but amends the investment and depreciation technologies to make the model more appropriate for merger analysis.

In particular, Mermelstein et al. (2020) assume the following. First, each unit of capital that a firm owns depreciates with some probability (the realization of which is independent across capital units). Second, for each unit of capital that a firm owns, it receives an independent random cost draw at which the firm can choose to augment that unit of capital by adding a second. In conjunction, these two assumptions imply that investment and depreciation are "merger-neutral" in that mergers do not change the investment opportunities that are available in the market. Moreover, compared to the literature building on Pakes and McGuire (1994) and Ericson and Pakes (1995), the investment technology allows for much richer investment dynamics.[22]

Firms can add to their capital (and reduce their marginal cost) not only by investing ("internal growth") but also by merging and combining their capital stocks ("external growth"). The decision to propose a merger is endogenous and determined by a bargaining process. While a commitment policy is also considered, the analysis focuses on the case in which the antitrust authority is a strategic player, endowed with an objective function (discounted consumer surplus or discounted aggregate surplus) but without the power to commit to its future policy. Whenever a merger is proposed and approved, a new potential entrant appears; while such an entrant has no initial capital, it can engage in "greenfield investment."[23] In short, the model endogenizes entry, investment, and mergers, and captures the idea that entry and investment are costly and time-consuming, with uncertain outcomes.

Mermelstein et al. (2020) show that the desirability of approving a proposed merger crucially depends on the impact that this decision has on future investment behavior, not only of the merger partners but also of nonmerging outsiders. In their model, approving a merger often leads to higher investments by new entrants or small firms, a form of "entry for buyout" (Rasmusen, 1988), and such behavior can come at a significant welfare cost if investment costs of small entrants are higher than those of large incumbents. Conversely, investment behaviors can be greatly impacted by firms' beliefs about future merger policy. In particular, if the antitrust authority adopts a more permissive merger policy, this will spur entry-for-buyout behavior by firms seeking to be acquired.

22 In that literature, firms can add at most one unit of capital in each period, so that a merger reduces the investment opportunities not only for the merging firms but also for the market.

23 Such greenfield investment is, however, associated with higher costs than incumbents' capital augmentation technology.

Mermelstein et al. also show that the optimal merger approval policy under commitment may be very different from the policy that an antitrust authority adopts if it cannot commit. In particular, in their baseline specification, a more permissive merger policy improves firms' investment incentives in almost all industry states. Despite this, such a policy reduces average investments by changing the equilibrium distribution over states: under such a policy, the industry spends a significantly larger fraction of time in states with high industry concentration in which firms invest less. In the absence of commitment power, it may therefore be optimal to endow the authority with a tougher welfare standard. This may help explain why, in many jurisdictions, authorities have adopted a consumer-surplus rather than an aggregate-surplus standard.

4.4 AVENUES FOR FUTURE RESEARCH

The above discussion of recent advances in the analysis of horizontal merger policy has left out some important issues.

Merger control involves not only the binary choice between blocking and approving a proposed merger. Rather, the antitrust authority has a much richer tool kit: it can make its approval decision subject to behavioral remedies (e.g., the licensing of intellectual property) or structural remedies (e.g., the divestiture of tangible assets). Indeed, antitrust authorities are much more likely to impose such remedies than to block a merger: Affeldt et al. (2018) report that, between 1990 and 2014, the European Commission approved 15 times more mergers subject to remedies than it prohibited.

Despite this, surprisingly little is known about the optimal design of such remedies (and their empirical effects).[24] Some researchers have tried to understand the conditions under which divestitures can eliminate any harm that a merger would otherwise inflict on consumers. Notably, Vergé (2010) analyzes an interesting benchmark case.

Nocke and Rhodes (2025) develop a framework to analyze structural remedies, both when mergers impact a single market only and when they "cross" different markets. They impose mild assumptions on how asset divestitures affect the marginal costs of the merger partners and those of the asset-receiving outsiders. In the single-market analysis, they show that remedies can partially but not fully compensate for a lack of merger-induced efficiencies. Moreover, as the market becomes less competitive, it is more likely that to prevent consumer harm a remedy must involve the creation of a new competitor. In the multi-market analysis, Nocke and Rhodes (2025) introduce the concept of the remedies exchange rate – which gives the amount of profit that the merger partners would have to give up via remedies to achieve an extra dollar of consumer surplus. The authors show that the remedies exchange becomes more

[24] A notable exception, Friberg and Romahn (2015) empirically study the effect of a merger among brewing companies that involved the required divestiture of 18 products to a small rival firm. They also perform a structural simulation, both with and without divestitures.

favorable as more assets are divested. As a result, the optimal multi-market merger proposal is "bang-bang": the merger partners propose large divestitures in a (small) number of markets and no divestitures in all other markets.

As touched upon in the introduction, the coordinated effects of mergers are much less well understood, both theoretically and empirically, than the unilateral effects of mergers. Much of the common intuition for the coordinated effects of horizontal mergers stems from the textbook model of an infinitely repeated, homogeneous-goods Bertrand game: in that model, the critical discount factor is strictly increasing in the number of (symmetric) firms – suggesting that a merger that reduces the number of players facilitates collusion. As Compte et al. (2002) show, however, this intuition may be incorrect once firms are (differentially) capacity constrained and a merger allows firms to combine their capacities. In their model, a merger may increase or reduce the critical discount factor, depending on merger and market characteristics. More work along these lines in richer models of competition would be most welcome.

Two objections against such an approach may be raised though. First, the standard repeated-game framework provides an embarrassment of riches in the form of a huge multiplicity of equilibria. Applied researchers have responded to this by focusing on the "best" (or "most collusive") equilibrium, albeit without much in terms of empirical support. Second, in the industrial organization literature, a merger (or some other change in market structure) is typically said to facilitate collusion if it raises the critical discount factor above which the monopoly outcome can be supported. But what does such a reduction in the critical discount factor mean if the true discount factor is well above that level? To address that second objection, it would seem desirable to turn the focus to richer models with imperfect monitoring.

Finally, much more (empirical) work is needed on merger-induced synergies and on understanding the extent to which entry, product repositioning, and other factors tend to ameliorate the unilateral anti-competitive effects of mergers.

REFERENCES

Affeldt, P., T. Duso, and F. Szücs (2018). "EU merger control database: 1990–2014." Deutsches Institut für Wirtschaftsforschung, Data Documentation 95.

Bourreau, M., B. Jullien, and Y. Lefouili (2019). "Mergers and demand-enhancing innovation." Mimeo.

Breinlich, H., V. Nocke, and N. Schutz (2017). "International aspects of merger policy: A survey," *International Journal of Industrial Organization*, 50, 415–429.

Breinlich, H., V. Nocke, and N. Schutz (2020). "Merger policy in a quantitative model of international trade," *Economic Journal*, 130, 393–421.

Compte, O., F. Jenny, and P. Rey (2002). "Capacity constraints, mergers and collusion," *European Economic Review*, 46(1), 1–29.

Ericson, R., and A. Pakes (1995). "Markov-perfect industry dynamics: A framework for empirical work," *Review of Economic Studies*, 62(1), 53–82.

Farrell, J., and C. Shapiro (1990). "Horizontal mergers: An equilibrium analysis," *American Economic Review*, 80(1), 107–126.

Friberg, R., and A. Romahn (2015). "Divestiture requirements as a tool for competition policy: A case from the Swedish beer market," *International Journal of Industrial Organization*, 42, 1–18.

Johnson, J. P., and D. P. Myatt (2006). "Multiproduct Cournot oligopoly," *RAND Journal of Economics*, 37(3), 583–601.

Johnson, J. P., and A. Rhodes (2021). "Multiproduct mergers and quality competition," *RAND Journal of Economics*, 52(3), 633–661.

Lahiri, S., and Y. Ono (1988). "Helping minor firms reduces welfare," *Economic Journal*, 98(393), 1199–1202.

Lyons, B. R. (2003). "Could politicians be more right than economists? A theory of merger standards." European University Institute Working Paper 2003/14.

McManus, M. (1962). "Numbers and size in Cournot oligopoly," *Yorkshire Bulletin of Social and Economic Research*, 14(1), 14–22.

McManus, M. (1964). "Equilibrium, numbers and size in Cournot oligopoly," *Yorkshire Bulletin of Social and Economic Research*, 16(2), 68–75.

Mermelstein, B., V. Nocke, M. A. Satterthwaite, and M. D. Whinston (2020). "Internal versus external growth in industries with scale economies: A computational model of optimal merger policy," *Journal of Political Economy*, 128(1), 301–341.

Miller, N. H., and M. C. Weinberg (2017). "Understanding the price effects of the Miller–Coors joint venture," *Econometrica*, 85(6), 1763–1791.

Motta, M., and E. Tarantino (2021). "The effect of horizontal mergers, when firms compete in prices and investments," *International Journal of Industrial Organization*, 78, 102774.

Nocke, V., and A. Rhodes (2025). "Optimal merger remedies." Mimeo.

Nocke, V., and N. Schutz (2018). "Multiproduct-firm oligopoly: An aggregative games approach," *Econometrica*, 86(2), 523–557.

Nocke, V., and N. Schutz (2018). "An aggregative games approach to merger analysis in multiproduct-firm oligopoly." CEPR Discussion Paper 12905.

Nocke, V., and M. D. Whinston (2010). "Dynamic merger review," *Journal of Political Economy*, 118(6), 1200–1251.

Nocke, V., and M. D. Whinston (2013). "Merger policy with merger choice," *American Economic Review*, 103(2), 1006–1033.

Nocke, V., and M. D. Whinston (2022). "Concentration thresholds for horizontal mergers," *American Economic Review*, 112(6), 1915–1948.

Novshek, W. (1985). "On the existence of Cournot equilibrium," *Review of Economic Studies*, 52(1), 85–98.

Pakes, A., and P. McGuire (1994). "Computing Markov-perfect Nash equilibria: Numerical implications of a dynamic differentiated product model," *RAND Journal of Economics*, 25(4), 555–589.

Rasmusen, E. (1988). "Entry for buyout," *Journal of Industrial Economics*, 36(3), 281–300.

Segal, I. (1999). "Contracting with externalities," *Quarterly Journal of Economics*, 114(2), 337–388.

Selten, R. (1970). *Preispolitik der Mehrproduktenunternehmung in der Statischen Theorie*. Berlin: Springer.

Szidarovszky, F., and S. Yakowitz (1977). "A new proof of the existence and uniqueness of the Cournot equilibrium," *International Economic Review*, 18(3), 787–789.

Vergé, T. (2010). "Horizontal mergers, structural remedies, and consumer welfare in a Cournot oligopoly with assets," *Journal of Industrial Economics*, 58(4), 723–741.

Whinston, M. D. (2007). "Chapter 36: Antitrust policy toward horizontal mergers." In M. Armstrong and R. H. Porter (eds.), *Handbook of Industrial Organization*, vol. 3. Amsterdam: Elsevier, pp. 2369–2440.

Williamson, O. (1968). "Economies as an antitrust defense: The welfare tradeoffs," *American Economic Review*, 58(1), 18–36.

Zhao, J. (2001). "A characterization for the negative welfare effects of cost reduction in Cournot oligopoly," *International Journal of Industrial Organization*, 19(3–4), 455–469.

PART III

HEALTH AS HUMAN CAPITAL

CHAPTER 5

Child Mental Health as Human Capital

Janet Currie

The concept of human capital is one of the most powerful in economics. It succinctly captures two key ideas: That much of society's wealth is embedded in people, and that investments in human capital have concrete returns. Following the lead of Gary Becker and Jacob Mincer, economic research on human capital formation initially focused on investments in education and training. Grossman (1972) pointed out that investments in health were also important and could have returns in the form of reductions in sick days and increased education and earnings. Over the past 20 years, there has been increasing attention to *child* health as a form of human capital that can have especially high returns (Almond and Currie, 2011a; Almond et al., 2018).

This chapter makes the case that child mental health is particularly important from the perspective of human capital development. The chapter begins with an overview of the conceptual framework underlying studies of child health as a form of human capital. The discussion then turns to the evidence connecting child mental health to economically important future outcomes such as education, disability, and earnings. I also discuss the relationship between the importance of noncognitive skills, which is the subject of a large body of literature, and mental health. Section 5.4 provides an overview of the literature showing that exogenous events can harm child mental health, while Section 5.5 covers the emerging literature about ways that social programs can improve child mental health. Section 5.6 delves into a nascent branch of literature about the effectiveness of child mental health treatment, suggesting that there is much work to be done. Section 5.7 discusses some of the challenges particular to researching child mental health. Section 5.8 draws some conclusions and provides suggestions for future research.

I thank my co-authors, especially Anna Chorniy, Emily Cuddy, Bentley MacLeod, and Mark Stabile, for their contributions to our joint work. Nicholas Papageorge, participants at the August 2020 Econometric Society meetings, and seminar participants at Tufts, Simon Fraser, and Georgetown universities deserve thanks for their helpful feedback. I would also like to thank the NOMIS foundation for their financial support.

5.1 CONCEPTUAL FRAMEWORK

It is useful to allow investments to differ with a child's age and to be impacted by random events or "shocks" at different ages. Accordingly, suppose that health, h, is produced via the following two-period constant elasticity of substitution production function:

$$h2 = A[g(\bar{I}_1 + m_1)^f + (1-g)(I_2 + m_2)^f]^{1/f}, \tag{5.1}$$

where m_t denotes exogenous shocks and I_t denotes investments. A bar over I_1 indicates that first-period investments have already taken place. Equation (5.1) could, of course, be amended to allow for investments and shocks at multiple time periods rather than only two periods.

Parents choose investments to maximize their own utility subject to budget constraint

$$\max U = U(C,h) \text{ s.t. } Y = p_c C + p_I I_1 + [p_I I_2/(1+r)], \tag{5.2}$$

where C indicates parental consumption, Y is income, prices p_c and p_I are given, and r is the rate of interest. Parents are assumed to care about both child health production and their own consumption.

One of the key issues involved in making investment decisions is whether investments in different periods are substitutes or complements (Heckman, 2007). Suppose there is perfect substitutability of investments so that $f = 1$. If parental utility is additively separable in C and h, then

$$U = (1-a)\log C + a \log h \tag{5.3}$$

and

$$dI_2^*/dm_1 = -(1-a)g/(1-a) < 0. \tag{5.4}$$

In this case, a positive shock in period 1 will be compensated for by a reduction in parental investments in period 2. Conversely, judicious investments in period 2 could make up for a negative shock in period 1.

Alternatively, if investments are perfect complements, then

$$dI_2^*/dm_1 = g/(1-g) > 0, \tag{5.5}$$

and a positive shock in period 1 will lead to more parental investment in period 2. In this case the impact of an initial negative shock (or even a negative draw in terms of endowments) will be magnified over time, and early childhood may be a particularly critical period for child development.

Families can differ in terms of parameters A, a, g, f and also in terms of the prices they face: p_I. Social programs may affect these parameters (e.g., by lowering prices for health inputs) and they may change production functions, utility functions, or budget constraints. The same investment may also have different effects depending on one's position on the production function (i.e., location on a flatter or steeper portion of the curve). Hence, one takeaway is that one should expect significant heterogeneity in the effects of shocks (e.g., by parental education and income). A key question is to what extent social programs actually change these parameters in a way that promotes child development.

A second insight is that the effects of early life events, both shocks and investments, may not "depreciate" and fade away over time, but could grow. This insight may be especially important for mental health, since although many mental health conditions are believed to originate in early childhood or even in utero, symptoms may not appear until adolescence or young adulthood. At this point it remains unknown how this de facto latency of mental illness is affected or whether it can be interrupted by events between an initial precipitating shock (such as high levels of maternal stress during pregnancy) and the diagnosable appearance of a mental illness in adolescence. Moreover, it remains unknown how treatment of mental illness when it emerges impacts lifetime economic outcomes, although some new research on this question is discussed below.

5.2 THE RELATIONSHIP BETWEEN CHILD MENTAL HEALTH AND FUTURE OUTCOMES

One reason to believe that child mental health is important is because it so often predicts poor adult mental health. It has long been known that mental health problems are a leading cause of lost work days among adult workers, as well as an important reason that many adults are unable to participate in the labor market.[1] For example, the UK's Health and Safety Executive reports that in 2017–2018, 57 percent of worker days lost in the United Kingdom were due to stress, depression, and anxiety, compared to 25 percent lost because of musculoskeletal issues such as back pain (Health and Safety Executive, 2020). Many US workers indicate that they have a significant number of bad mental health days. For example, since 2002, the U.S. General Social Survey has asked employed individuals about the number of days in the past month that their mental health was "not good."[2] Figure 5.1 shows the responses to this question over time: about 40 percent consistently report that they had some bad mental health days in the past month, while over 10 percent report that they had 10 or more such days. Interestingly, these proportions seem to be insensitive to aggregate economic conditions, as evidenced by the fact that these profiles were quite flat throughout the "Great Recession" of 2008–2009.

Childhood mental health conditions are predictive of poorer future outcomes in longitudinal studies. Currie and Stabile (2006) examine young US and Canadian children with symptoms of attention deficit hyperactivity

[1] Currie and Madrian (1999) provide a summary of the literature up to that date.

[2] The specific question is: "Now thinking about your mental health, which includes stress, depression, and problems with emotions, for how many days during the past 30 days was your mental health not good?"

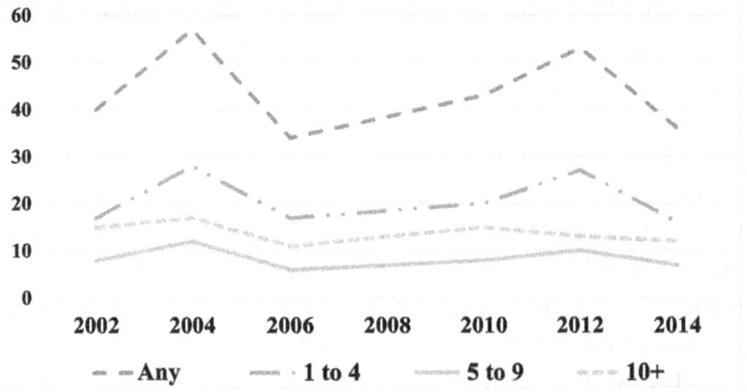

Figure 5.1 The number of days in the past 30 when mental health was not good as a percentage of employed U.S. General Social Survey respondents.
Note: The question was "Now thinking about your mental health, which includes stress, depression, and problems with emotions, for how many days during the past 30 days was your mental health not good?"

disorder (ADHD) using large nationally representative surveys that asked screening questions to all children, thereby avoiding biases due to selection into diagnosis. In models with sibling fixed effects to control for family background, they find that having ADHD predicts a higher probability of delinquency, grade repetition, and special education, as well as reduced test scores. The estimated effects were remarkably similar in the two countries. Currie and Stabile (2009) extend these results by including a broader range of mental health conditions, including mood disorders. Fletcher (2010) extends them by specifically examining adolescent depression. He finds that relative to their siblings, teens with a one standard deviation increase in depressive symptoms are 25 to 30 percent more likely to drop out of school.

Currie et al. (2010) use registry data from the Canadian province of Manitoba to go beyond educational outcomes. They find that children with ADHD and conduct disorders in childhood are much more likely (30–100 percent more likely depending on the child's age) to be on welfare after age 18. These effects were much larger than those found for common physical health conditions such as asthma and major injuries. Similarly, Smith and Smith (2010) use retrospective survey data from the U.S. Panel Study of Income Dynamics – and a sibling fixed effects model – to find that in addition to lower educational attainment, adults who suffered from mental health problems before the age of 16 have family incomes 20 percent less than their own siblings, with a lifetime difference of $300,000. Some of this negative impact may come from a lower probability of being married; another important mechanism is a reduction in weeks worked. Goodman et al. (2011) use data from the National Child Development Study, which followed 17,634 children born in Great Britain during a single week in March 1958. They find that children with psychological problems in childhood had 28 percent lower family incomes by age 50. As in the United States, these effects reflect reductions in labor supply and in marriage.

These studies generally find that mental health problems are more predictive of negative educational and labor market outcomes than poor childhood physical health.

Biasi et al. (2020) use Danish registry data to document that people with specific diagnoses of depression, bipolar disorder, or schizophrenia have earnings 31, 36, and 73 percent less than their siblings. Much of the earnings penalty comes from being less likely to have any earnings at all. People with these diagnoses are also more likely to receive government disability payments.

5.3 RELATIONSHIP TO NONCOGNITIVE SKILLS DISCUSSED IN THE ECONOMICS LITERATURE

Until recently, few economists explicitly studied childhood mental health; concepts related to mental health have frequently been subsumed in the broader category of "noncognitive skills." Heckman and Rubinstein (2001) emphasize that people with similar levels of cognitive skill as measured by standardized test scores often have vastly different outcomes. Clearly something other than cognitive skills must be important. This idea was further developed by Heckman et al. (2006), who show that measures of noncognitive skills are strongly predictive of education and earnings as well as of risky behaviors. Over time, a large body of literature has developed concerning the importance of noncognitive skills, with the term embracing concepts as diverse as the "Big Five" personality traits (extroversion, agreeableness, openness, conscientiousness, and neuroticism), "grit" or perseverance, and things that might be thought of as actual skills that can be taught, such as self-control and social skills (Zhou, 2016).

Attanasio et al. (2020) compare cohorts of British children born in 1970 and 2000 and divide noncognitive skills in young children into "internalizing" and "externalizing" behaviors: anxiety and depression fall into the former category, while ADHD and conduct disorders fall into the latter. They find that these skills at age five are important predictors of adult outcomes, and that inequalities stemming from these two kinds of skills increased between the two cohorts, especially among boys. They decompose the increase in inequality into two parts: the increase due to changes in the characteristics of mothers and the increase due to "returns" to those characteristics. They do this for different points in the skill distribution using recentered influence function (RIF) regressions. They show that while about half of the increase in inequality in externalizing behaviors can be explained by changes in maternal characteristics (e.g., maternal smoking and employment), most of the increase in inequality in internalizing behaviors is due to changes in returns to maternal characteristics.

More generally, mental health can be thought of as strongly impacting a subset of noncognitive skills. For example, Goodman et al. (2011) find that childhood mental illness is negatively associated with the "Big Five" traits of conscientiousness and agreeableness. Moreover, specific mental health conditions are associated with certain deficits in noncognitive skills. For example, Edin et al. (2022) use Swedish registry data to follow military recruits and measure changes in the returns to noncognitive skills over time. Recruits were assessed in terms of their skills in four specific areas: social maturity, focus, internal motivation, and stress tolerance. Significant deficits in each of these areas correspond to specific mental health conditions: children with autism spectrum disorder often struggle with social skills, children with ADHD have difficulty with focus, those with depression can lack internal motivation, and those who struggle with anxiety lack stress tolerance. Hence, the literature on the importance of noncognitive skills can be interpreted as further evidence supporting the long-term impacts of childhood mental health conditions.

5.4 CHILD MENTAL HEALTH CAN BE HARMED BY EXOGENOUS FACTORS

Many economists no longer consider longitudinal observational studies or sibling fixed effects estimates to be sufficient to establish evidence of "causal" effects. Despite the large magnitudes of the estimated associations and their consistency across studies, it is possible that other factors could be associated with an individual child within a household that predict both childhood mental illness and future adult outcomes. Some of the strongest evidence in favor of causal effects of events and conditions on future mental health comes from studies of the fetal period. Since the period in utero is short and well-defined, it is possible to identify children who were affected by specific exogenous events while they were in utero. These cohorts can then be followed and compared to either siblings or cohorts born shortly before or after the index cohort.

This "fetal origins" literature is now well developed (see surveys in Almond and Currie, 2011a, 2011b; Almond et al., 2018). From the beginning, the research has found evidence that events in utero affect adult mental health, although most studies do not focus on this outcome. For example, some of the earliest studies concern the Dutch "Hunger Winter" during World War II. This famine resulted from a Nazi blockade of the cities of the western Netherlands. In some cases, the inhabitants were reduced to eating tulip bulbs. The famine resulted in an estimated 20,000 to 30,000 deaths. Brown et al. (1995) found that the cohort of surviving children who were affected by starvation in utero was more likely to suffer affective disorders (such as depression) in adulthood. This finding was followed by research showing that in utero famine exposure doubled the incidence of schizophrenia as well as increasing schizoid and antisocial personality disorders (see Lumey et al., 2011 for an excellent review of this literature). More recent literature in economics focuses on relatively mild nutritional deprivation occasioned by Ramadan fasting and finds consistent effects on mental disability across a range of settings (Almond and Mazumder, 2011; Almond et al., 2015; Hoffmann, 2014; Shultz-Nielsen et al., 2016).

Economists have moved beyond investigating the effects of maternal nutrition during pregnancy to examine the impacts of many other types of shocks. Some of this literature shows that maternal mental health, and especially high levels of maternal stress during pregnancy, has negative impacts on outcomes including the IQ and education of adult offspring. For example, Aizer et al. (2016) study data that includes direct measures of maternal stress (cortisol levels) rather than measures of exposure to stressful events. They show that mothers of lower socioeconomic status experience more prenatal stress than other mothers, and that this stress has harmful effects on their infants. These findings demonstrate that maternal mental health is a possible mechanism for the intergenerational transmission of inequality.

But most of these studies of the impact of maternal stress have not explicitly examined the effects of in utero conditions on offspring mental health. An important exception is Persson and Rossin-Slater (2018), who compare mothers who lost a family member while they were expecting to those who lost family members in the year after the birth. This design is cleaner than comparing mothers with a death in the family to mothers without a death, because families of lower socioeconomic status are more likely to lose family members. Using Swedish registry data to follow affected individuals up to age 30, they find that children of mothers who lost a family member while they were expecting were 23 percent more likely to have children who used ADHD medication, and that their children were 9 percent more likely to use antidepressants as adults.

5.5 CHILD MENTAL HEALTH CAN BE IMPROVED THROUGH A RANGE OF INTERVENTIONS

The fact that an individual's mental health can be harmed by events early in life does not necessarily mean that there is anything society can do to mitigate these harms. Yet, now that researchers have begun to think about mental health as an important outcome, evidence about the potential impacts of policy on children's mental health is starting to accumulate.

The US Medicaid expansions are a case in point. As of the late 1980s, only low-income mothers on welfare and their children were eligible for public health insurance. Beginning in the late 1980s and continuing throughout the 1990s, eligibility for public health insurance under the Medicaid program was greatly expanded. The rollout occurred in a staggered manner across states and over time. Several recent papers look at the long-term effects of these expansions (Brown et al., 2020; Cohodes et al., 2016; Currie et al., 2008; Miller and Wherry, 2019; Wherry and Meyer, 2016; Wherry et al., 2018). These studies follow cohorts of children who received Medicaid coverage in utero or in early childhood. The staggered implementation of the expansions offers an opportunity to identify the effect of eligibility for public health insurance in these groups. These studies show positive effects on a range of outcomes including educational attainment, employment, earnings, and absence of disability.

Intriguingly, Miller and Wherry (2019) also demonstrate that young adults who benefitted from Medicaid coverage in early life because of the expansions had lower scores on the Kessler Psychological Distress Scale. Specifically, mean scores were 2.2 points lower, where the scale's cutoff for mental illness is 13. As mental illness is one of the leading causes of disability among young adults, it is possible that reductions in disability also reflect improvements in mental health in these cohorts, although this has not yet been demonstrated.

There is also evidence that Medicaid expansions have improved the mental health of adults, which may indirectly benefit children. For example, Baicker et al. (2013) find that people who won a Medicaid "lottery" in Oregon showed improved mental health as measured via a depression screener. Using a difference-in-difference design with states that did and did not expand Medicaid, Courtemanche et al. (2018) and Winkelman and Chang (2018) find that Medicaid expansion is associated with a reduction in the number of poor mental health days in low-income adults with chronic conditions.

In a finding that echoes the earlier literature connecting prenatal nutrition and mental health, Chorniy et al. (2020) study the Supplemental Nutrition Program for Women, Infants, and Children (WIC) and find that children whose mothers participated in WIC during pregnancy were 5.3 percent less likely to have been diagnosed with ADHD at ages 6 to 11 than siblings who did not benefit from WIC in utero (on a baseline of 16.6 percent). They were also 6.4 percent less likely to have been diagnosed with other mental health conditions commonly diagnosed in early childhood, such as anxiety and adjustment disorders (on a baseline of 18.6 percent). The benefits were largest for African-American children, who saw a 9.5 percent reduction in ADHD (on a baseline of 15.1 percent) and a 9 percent reduction in other mental health conditions (on a baseline of 17.8 percent). Although WIC emphasizes nutrition, women on WIC are automatically eligible for Medicaid and more likely to access health benefits than other Medicaid-eligible women. This may be because maternal and child health clinics often host WIC centers. Hence, the benefits of WIC may stem in part from better access to prenatal care or reduced maternal stress levels in addition to improved nutrition.

Studies that examine the effect of income on mental health may be among the most interesting from an economic point of view. Several studies have shown that receiving more money improves adult mental health. For example, Gardner and Oswald (2007) study lottery winners and show that two years later, winners of medium-sized lottery prizes are significantly happier than non-winners and people who won smaller amounts.[3] More relevant to children, Evans and Garthwaite (2014) show that increases in the US Earned Income Tax Credit improved the mental health of eligible mothers. Adhvaryu et al. (2019) examine the effects of economic circumstances in early life on adult

[3] See also Haushofer and Shapiro (2016), who show in an experimental context in Kenya that cash transfers improved psychological wellbeing.

mental health using variation induced by fluctuations in cocoa prices in cocoa-producing regions of Ghana. They find that a one standard deviation increase in prices in the first years of life reduces the probability of severe adult mental distress by 3 percentage points, which is half of the mean prevalence. Baird et al. (2013) report the results of an experiment in Malawi in which adolescent girls in the treatment group were given money. They find that these income supplements reduced measures of psychological distress, although the effect lasted only as long as the supplements.

In-kind transfers have also been shown to have positive effects. For example, Kling et al. (2007) found that the Moving to Opportunity Experiment in the United States had positive impacts on youth mental health. This large-scale randomized experiment for public housing residents was conducted in several US cities. Families in the treatment group were offered vouchers that could be used only in lower-poverty neighborhoods and they also received assistance in locating suitable housing. Families in the control group received conventional public housing services. In a seven-year follow-up, youths in the treatment group showed significantly less mental distress, fewer symptoms of generalized anxiety, and less depression than youths in the control group.[4]

5.6 THE EFFECTIVENESS OF MENTAL HEALTH TREATMENT FOR CHILDREN

One would think that mental health treatment would be one of the most important potential interventions to improve outcomes for children and adolescents suffering from mental illness. One might also assume that clinical studies had already established the efficacy of treatment for many common conditions. But the evidence about the effects of treatment on economic outcomes, such as completed education, disability status, and labor force participation, is surprisingly weak, in part because so few studies follow children for any length of time, include a reasonable control group in the study, and account for selection into treatment.[5]

Some of the best evidence regarding the effectiveness of treatment comes from studies of ADHD. The number of American children whose parents

[4] On a somewhat similar note, Stillman et al. (2009) find that adult Tongans who were chosen by lottery to migrate to Australia also showed significantly improved mental health.

[5] Shapiro (2022) points out that the evidence regarding the effects of psychiatric drugs on the labor market outcomes of adults is also somewhat inconclusive. He uses data on direct-to-consumer advertising in different television markets combined with administrative data from the Truven Health MarketScan Health and Productivity Management (HPM) database for approximately 500,000 individuals employed at participating firms from 2007 to 2010. He finds that a 10 percent increase in advertising led to a 0.3 percent increase in antidepressant use and a reduction in absenteeism. Butikofer et al. (2019) use Norwegian registry data and find that the addition of "black box" warning labels to antidepressant packaging in 2007 reduced antidepressant prescriptions and labor supply among women aged 35–49. However, they found no effects among men or younger women. However, drugs that work well in adults may not be suitable for children and many are not approved for use in children.

reported that they had ever been diagnosed with ADHD increased by two million between the 2003 and 2011 waves of the National Survey of Children's Health, rising to 11 percent of all school-aged children (Visser et al., 2014). Children suffering from ADHD face behavioral, learning, developmental, and emotional problems that extend into adulthood. Currie and Stabile (2006) use a screener for ADHD that was administered to all children in their sample and find a large negative effect of ADHD on children's academic test scores and schooling attainment relative to siblings. Fletcher and Wolfe (2009) and Fletcher (2014) report a higher probability of engaging in criminal behavior as well as lower employment probabilities, lower wages, and higher accident probabilities among children with ADHD.

Medication is the first-line treatment for ADHD and the vast majority of children diagnosed with ADHD are prescribed medication, with a smaller number also receiving behavioral therapies. Many studies have shown short-term improvements in attention and decreases in disruptive behavior in medicated children, although the longer-term effects of medication for ADHD are more controversial (Scheffler et al., 2009; Visser et al., 2014).

Economists have contributed to this literature by focusing on longer-term, economically relevant outcomes and by seeking causal identification strategies. For example, Currie et al. (2014) consider a policy change in the Canadian province of Quebec that extended prescription drug coverage to large numbers of previously uncovered children. They find that the policy change increased the number of children taking ADHD medication but did not improve their educational outcomes.

Dalsgaard et al. (2014), Chorniy and Kitashima (2016), and Chorniy (2018) all use an instrumental variables framework in which the probability of a child's being prescribed ADHD medication is determined by the prescription propensities of the providers in their local areas. Dalsgaard et al. (2014) use Danish registry data, while Chorniy and Kitashima (2016) and Chorniy (2018) use similar data for South Carolina constructed by linking Medicaid claims, educational, and criminal justice records. The first two papers find that ADHD medication has positive effects on health outcomes. Specifically, children are less likely to seek medical care for injuries or for the consequences of risky behaviors (e.g., there is less teen pregnancy and drug taking). However, like Currie et al. (2014), Chorniy (2018) finds little effect of prescription ADHD medication on educational outcomes, although the study confirms the previous positive effects on health outcomes. It appears that ADHD medication affects behavior in a way that improves safety and health outcomes but it does not address academic difficulties that may be due, for example, to differences in how children with ADHD learn and process information.

As noted above, Biasi et al. (2020) use Danish registry data to track the impact of bipolar disorder (BD) on cohorts born between 1946 and 1976. BD is typically diagnosed in the late teens or early 20s. The study shows that while bipolar disorder has a substantial negative effect on outcomes, the negative impact has decreased over time. They attribute this improvement to the advent of lithium, which was approved as a treatment for BD in Denmark in 1976. Hence, people born after 1956 would have had access to an effective treatment in their early 20s, while people in earlier cohorts would not have had access to this treatment until later in life, after they might already have suffered substantial negative impacts of BD on their educational and career prospects.

However, they find that even for the cohorts born after 1956, all of whom had access to lithium in their early 20s, the negative effects of BD declined over time. This result suggests that other factors, such as the de-institutionalization of the mentally ill, the advent of community care, a new emphasis on helping people to maintain employment, and laws establishing the rights of the mentally ill, may also have played a large role in reducing the negative labor market impacts of mental health disorders over time. Moreover, only 55 percent of individuals with BD ever fill a prescription for lithium, suggesting that many patients are not accessing this treatment, perhaps due to side effects.

A few studies focus specifically on the prescription of antidepressants and suicide. Ludwig et al. (2009) use country-year-level panel data to examine the relationship between suicide and the rise in the use of selective serotonin reuptake inhibitors (SSRIs) during the 1990s and beyond. To explain variation in SSRI use, they relied on institutional differences when each country approved SSRIs and general growth in drug sales. They find that an increase in the prescribing of one SSRI pill per capita (a 12 percent increase over sales in 2000) reduced suicide by 5 percent. They find even larger reductions among youth aged 15–24, although they could not observe sales of SSRIs by age group. One reason they rely on cross-country comparisons is that youth suicide is a sufficiently rare outcome so that within-country studies tend to have low power. Yet cross-country comparisons may be contaminated by other factors changing differentially across countries.

Currie and MacLeod (2019) suggest using an alternative measure of mental health that is much more frequently observed: emergency room (ER) visits and in-patient hospitalizations for mental health. In the United States, patients having a mental health crisis are universally advised to go to the nearest ER for assessment. If necessary, hospitals without psychiatric units will arrange for the patient to be safely transported to an appropriate facility. Currie and MacLeod (2019) report that in six large US states, 13.4 percent of ER visits in 2014 involved a mental health diagnosis (although there may also be other diagnoses on the ER record). Of these visits, the majority are for depression and anxiety. ER visits have a significant impact on healthcare costs. Using this outcome measure allows the analyst to take advantage of the huge variation in the probability of receiving an antidepressant prescription across areas within countries, as shown using county-level data for the United States in Figure 5.2.

Cuddy and Currie (2020a, 2020b) exploit this variation to examine patterns in mental health prescribing and the subsequent utilization of medical care in US adolescents. They use health insurance claims data from a large national private health insurer. They focus on treatment of a child's first mental health episode, which is defined with reference to both diagnoses and treatments.

Figure 5.2 30-day prescriptions of antidepressant drugs per 1000 persons 10–19 years old in 2014, by county.
Note: The source is the author's calculations from data provided by IQVIA.

Of the children eligible for sample inclusion, 9.2 percent have a first mental health episode. Most of the children in this sample suffer from depression, anxiety, an adjustment disorder, or some combination.

One advantage of focusing on first episodes is that treatment guidelines are relatively clear and clinicians will not be constrained by choices made by previous clinicians (e.g., if the child is already taking one medication, a clinician might not want to change it even if they would have initially prescribed something else). It seems reasonable to suppose that when faced with a young adolescent with a first episode of mental illness (the mean age of onset is 12), a clinician would first try therapy, would stick to drugs that are approved for use in children, and would avoid drugs that are addictive, dangerous in overdose, or that have dangerous side effects.

Yet, as Figures 5.3(a) and (b) show, much of the treatment received falls short of this standard. Almost one-third of sample children have not received any follow-up care after three months, even though they are all well insured. Another fifth are treated only with drugs, with no trial of therapy. Of those children receiving drug treatment, 45 percent receive a drug that raises a "red flag" given that the child is being treated for the first time. These red-flag drugs include older-generation tricyclic antidepressants, which have not been shown to be effective in children and which may cause serious side effects; benzodiazepines, which are prescribed to adults for anxiety, but which have not been shown to be effective in children and are also addictive; and drugs that have not been approved for use in a child of the specific age of the index child for any indication.

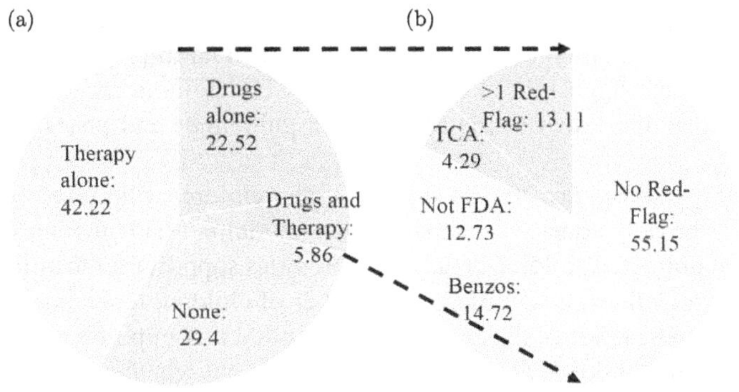

Figure 5.3 (a) Type of treatment, first three months. (b) Red-flag drug treatment, first three months.
Note: This figure is based on data from Cuddy and Currie (2020a) which looks at treatment of adolescents with an initial mental health episode. Panel 3a shows the types of treatments received within 3 months of the initial episode. Panel 3b shows the type of drug treatment if any drug treatment was received. A "red-flag" drug treatment includes tricyclic antidepressants, benzodiazepines, and drugs that are not FDA approved for a child of the child's age for any indication. The original figure is Figure 1 in https://www.pnas.org/doi/10.1073/pnas.2007484117.

Some of the variation in care is due to differences in the supply of clinicians. For example, Cuddy and Currie (2020a) show that in areas with relatively more therapists, children are more likely to get therapy and less likely to only get drugs. In areas with relatively more child psychiatrists, children are more likely to get drugs alone. Areas with more child psychiatrists are also more likely (rather than less likely) to see prescriptions of red-flag drugs.

However, Currie and Cuddy (2020b) show that much of the variation in prescribing patterns is within areas so it cannot be explained by the supplies of therapists and psychiatrists. This variation is associated with individual provider practice styles rather than with counts of provider types. Currie and Cuddy use measures of the practice styles of the clinicians serving children in each zipcode tabulation area to predict the treatment each child receives. Given the many potential weak instruments and the large sample size, their choice of instruments is guided by the post-Lasso procedure proposed by Belloni et al. (2012).

They find that receiving follow-up mental health treatment in the first three months after an initial claim increases total health care costs over the next 24 months. These higher costs are entirely accounted for by children who receive treatment that is not consistent with practice guidelines, and especially by those who receive "red-flag" drugs including benzodiazepines, tricyclic anti-depressants, and other drugs not approved for use in children of the index child's age. Their estimates imply that over the following two years, children who initially received a red-flag drug had total medical costs 205 percent higher than those of the average treated child and were 131 percent more likely to have used an emergency room or experienced an in-patient hospitalization. These results suggest that large numbers of US children are receiving mental health care that falls outside of accepted guidelines and poses risks to their health.

Cuddy and Currie (2020a) also show that children who received treatment that was broadly consistent with treatment guidelines had outcomes better than those of untreated children. This result provides support for the utility of adherence to guidelines. Given the large number of children receiving questionable psychiatric treatments, these results suggest that it is important to consider not only whether children are receiving treatment, but whether they are receiving appropriate treatment.

Cowan and Zhuang (2020) examine increases in access to psychiatric treatment that followed the 2014 Affordable Care Act (ACA) in the United States. Many states expanded Medicaid coverage after passage of the ACA, which increased the fraction of low-income individuals with health insurance. The ACA also strengthened protections for people with pre-existing conditions and mandated coverage of mental health conditions. Using data from the annual "Healthy Minds" web-based survey of college students' mental health, they focus on first-generation college students who reported that their financial situation was stressful while they were growing up. This group was more likely to have public insurance in expansion states compared to non-expansion states after 2014. There was no similar change in insurance coverage among students with college-graduate parents or among students who reported that their families suffered little or no financial stress when they were growing up. The expansion of insurance coverage was accompanied by an increase in both the diagnosis and treatment of common mental health conditions. This increase eliminated the gap between the more and less-advantaged students.[6] Before the expansions, 24 percent of the more-advantaged students had been diagnosed with a mental health condition, and 16 percent were taking psychotropic medications. The comparable figures for the less-advantaged students were 18 percent and 12 percent, respectively.

However, surprisingly, they did not find that closing the gap in diagnosis and treatment led to any improvement in student grade point averages, hours spent on schoolwork, substance abuse, or self-assessed negative impacts of mental health on academic outcomes. Given the findings in Cuddy and Currie (2020a, 2020b), one possible explanation for the disconnect between treatment and outcomes may be that many students received inappropriate or ineffective treatment. Alternatively, the study may lack the statistical power to detect small effects on some outcomes.

[6] The increases experienced by college-aged students are similar to those reported more generally. Using state-level data, Maclean et al. (2018) find that in expansion states, Medicaid-reimbursed prescriptions for antidepressants increase by 34 percent. Prescriptions for anti-anxiety drugs increased by 23 percent, and prescriptions for the stimulant drugs used for ADHD went up by 16 percent.

Despite being sparse, the evidence regarding the effects of treatment of maternal depression is more encouraging. Cuijpers et al. (2015) performed a meta-analysis that included seven small-scale experimental studies and concluded that while most studies showed positive effects of treatment on maternal depression and parenting practices, weaknesses in their designs indicated that more research was necessary. Baranov et al. (2020) conducted a large, cluster-randomized, controlled trial of 903 women who were depressed prior to giving birth in rural Pakistan, and found that therapy was very effective in reducing postpartum depression. In a follow-up seven years after the end of treatment, they found that the improvements in mental health persisted and that depression had been reduced by 17 percent. The intervention also improved women's financial autonomy and increased the children's attendance in private schools and the number of learning materials available in the home by 0.2 to 0.3 standard deviations. These findings suggest that treating maternal depression could have positive effects on children more generally, but that more research into the question is necessary.

5.7 CHALLENGES FACING RESEARCH INTO CHILD MENTAL HEALTH

One of the biggest problems faced by researchers who are interested in studying the effects of child mental health on human capital development is finding data that reliably measure mental health and being able to link them to child outcomes of interest. Several of the studies discussed above use data from countries with comprehensive "registries" linking various administrative databases. While these registries are incredibly rich and make new analyses possible, they are not without their own limitations. Typically, data is much more complete for later years than for earlier years, and data on mental health diagnoses and treatments, as well as data on pharmaceutical prescriptions, may have only been collected in these later years. In some cases (like Canada) visits to clinicians who are not medical doctors (i.e., psychologists and other therapists) fall outside the scope of provincial health insurance plans and therefore are not captured in administrative databases.

However, the most vexing data problem has to do with diagnosis of mental illness. A pervasive problem in health economics is that people who do not see a clinician for their health problems will not have a diagnosis. Hence, one is often dealing with a selected sample of diagnosed individuals. In the Cowan and Zhuang (2020) paper discussed above, the base level of diagnosis and treatment was lower in disadvantaged students, even though their self-reported mental health symptoms were higher.

It is common to observe people being treated for mental illness (i.e., with therapy or psychotropic drugs) even though there is no mental health diagnosis associated with the treatment (Druss et al., 2007). It is possible that in some cases this absence of diagnostic information reflects a clinician's uncertainty about the appropriate diagnosis. For instance, a doctor who is uncertain about a diagnosis of bipolar disorder might prescribe mood stabilizers and then conclude that a patient who responded did in fact have bipolar disorder rather than a different condition.

Diagnosis of mental illness is objectively difficult and doctors make many mistakes; for example, it often takes more than eight years for patients with bipolar disorder to be correctly diagnosed and treated (Fritz et al., 2017). These considerations suggest researchers should consider measures of mental illness that include both diagnoses and treatments and should allow for the fact that diagnoses may change over time (i.e., search backward and forward in the patient's record for indications of mental illness rather than relying only on point-in-time measures).

Missing diagnoses may also reflect the extreme stigma that still surrounds mental illness. Some conditions (e.g., personality disorders) are so stigmatized that some providers will refuse to treat patients with these diagnoses; consequently, providers are reluctant to diagnose patients less than 18 years old with this disorder at all (Aviram et al., 2006). On the patient side, Bharadwaj et al. (2017) compare patient self-reports to administrative records on diagnosis and prescription drug use for mental illness. They find that survey respondents underreported mental health diagnoses 36 percent of the time and underreported prescription drug use 20 percent of the time. In contrast, there was little underreporting of diabetes or hypertension. Diabetes and hypertension are interesting comparison conditions because they are arguably more amenable to improvement through behavioral change than mental illness, so one might expect them to be more, rather than less, subject to stigma.[7] Another factor is that until the ACA in 2010, private US health insurance plans were allowed to exclude pre-existing conditions. Hence, many US doctors began to practice in an era when a childhood diagnosis of mental illness might mean that a person was ineligible for future mental health coverage. In such circumstances, treating a person without giving them a diagnosis might be the most humane option. This all means that diagnoses may often be missing as well as being measured with considerable error.

Measurement error that is stable over time is less problematic than measurement error that shifts temporally. Yet some diagnoses have shown growth over time that is unlikely to reflect only changes in the underlying prevalence of the condition.[8] For example, according to the U.S. Centers for Disease Control, the incidence of autism increased from about one in 150 children in 2000

[7] Cronin et al. (2020) report that many adult patients opt out of therapy, perhaps because of stigma, but also potentially because therapy is time-consuming and it may be difficult to see evidence of effectiveness. Patient noncompliance with prescribed therapeutic regimes could be considered an additional form of measurement error.

[8] Attanasio et al. (2020) run into a similar problem in their discussion of childhood noncognitive skills. They find that although they can compare the inequality in skills across the two cohorts, they cannot tell whether the levels of the underlying skills are higher or lower in the two cohorts because the meaning that mothers attach to certain child behaviors seems to have changed over time.

to one in 54 children in 2016. But much of this increase is due to an expanding definition of autism. The process of revising the definition culminated in the creation of a new "autism spectrum disorder" umbrella in the 2013 fifth edition of the *Diagnostic and Statistical Manual of Mental Disorders*. This new category encompasses four previous categories: "autism," "Asperger's," "pervasive developmental disorder," and "childhood disintegrative disorder." In a study using autism registry data from California that included all known cases, King and Bearman (2011) found that children living in different communities were at significantly different risk of diagnosis for autism. Community characteristics, such as the resources available for diagnosis and community awareness of the disorder, were strongly predictive of the prevalence of diagnosis. Because resources are more abundant in high-socioeconomic-status neighborhoods, these neighborhoods also saw faster growth in autism diagnoses. In some cases, new treatments may increase the benefits of receiving a diagnosis. Conti et al. (2011) argue that the availability of SSRIs as a treatment for depression resulted in many more new diagnoses: once a treatment was available, it became worthwhile for people to endure the stigma of being diagnosed with a mental illness. Likewise, Biasi et al. (2020) find that diagnoses of depression in Denmark increased over time, although diagnoses of bipolar disorder and schizophrenia were flat. To date, no one has studied these dynamics: it is possible that increasing the number of people diagnosed with a condition might reduce the stigma associated with diagnosis and cause even more people to seek diagnosis and treatment over time.

A related issue is that incentives built into the medical system may cause providers to be more or less likely to diagnose a mental illness. Chorniy et al. (2018) study children in South Carolina who were enrolled in Medicaid. The state mandated that children be switched from a fee-for-service version of the program to managed care in the mid-2000s, and different counties switched at different times. Their study follows about 210,000 children less than age 17 who appeared in the Medicaid records before and after the switch. As Figure 5.4 shows, the switch to managed care resulted in increases in the number of children being diagnosed with depression and ADHD in the next 12 months.

However, these increases in mental health diagnoses are similar in magnitude to increases in the diagnoses of physical health conditions such as asthma. In part, these increases in mental health diagnoses corresponded with increases in the number of children receiving well-child visits and developmental screenings. To be clear, all Medicaid children were supposed to be receiving these services all along, but the switch to managed care made it more likely that they would actually receive them. The state achieved increased well-child visits and developmental screenings with a combination of carrots and sticks. First, insurers participating in the managed-care program received higher capitated payments for children with chronic conditions, so they worked hard to encourage providers in their networks to screen more aggressively. This incentive effect does not explain all of the results in Figure 5.4, however, because insurers did

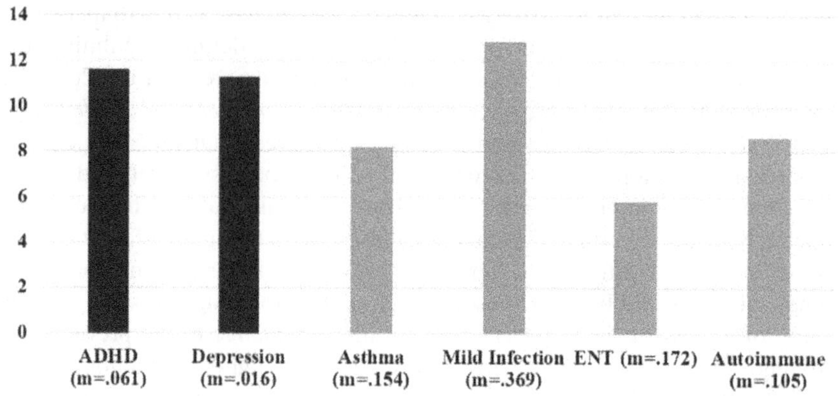

Figure 5.4 Estimated percentage increase in diagnoses in the 12 months after a switch to Medicaid-managed care in South Carolina, child fixed effects models.

Note: These figures come from table 3 of Chorniy et al. (2018). They are estimated using the rollout of a change from fee-for-service Medicaid to Medicaid-managed care in South Carolina that affected about 210,000 children. The same child was followed using Medicaid records before and after the change.

not receive higher payments for conditions such as mild infections – yet diagnoses of infections still rose. Second, managed-care plans were penalized for falling behind their peers in terms of performing screenings. As a practical matter, it was more feasible for the state to monitor the compliance of a few managed-care plans than to monitor the compliance of the individual clinicians who had been participating in the fee-for-service version of the program.

These measurement issues suggest that analysts should be wary of overinterpreting large changes in diagnosed cases and should pay close attention to underlying trends in diagnoses, changes in definitions, and changes in the incentives of both patients and providers. Whenever possible, it is helpful to verify trends obtained from diagnostic data with data from screeners administered to a less selected set of individuals. For example, depression screeners such as the CES-D (Center for Epidemiologic Studies, Depression) are now included in several survey-based datasets.

5.8 CONCLUSIONS AND FUTURE DIRECTIONS

The last few years have seen an explosion of economics papers examining child mental health. This rapid growth reflects the increasing realization that mental health is one of the most important aspects of children's human capital development. Mental health often has larger effects on important economic outcomes, such as completed education, disability, employment, and family formation, than common physical health problems.

Some of the most important directions for future research include examining the relationship between family economic status and policies that affect economic status and child mental health, examining spillovers between family members, examining the determinants and cost effectiveness of treatment, and understanding the interactions and dynamics between child mental health conditions and parental investments.

Answering these questions has become all the more pressing given the reported impacts of the COVID-19 pandemic on the mental health of parents and children. Fear and loss, as well as social isolation and unprecedented interruptions to people's daily routines, may induce or exacerbate mental illnesses including anxiety, depression, obsessive compulsive disorder, and post-traumatic stress syndrome. Racine et al. (2020) surveyed some of the initial published studies about the pandemic and mental illness in children and adolescents. They concluded that the findings pointed to increases in depression and anxiety in this group, but they cautioned that these studies generally lacked a pre-COVID-19 baseline comparison group and didn't look at whether the increases in symptoms were clinically significant. Youth suicides, self-harm, and suicidal ideation also rose during the pandemic, though attempts to examine the impact of the pandemic on suicides are complicated by the rising trend in youth suicides over the past decade – Curtin (2020) reports that in the United States, suicides among those aged 10–24 rose 56 percent between 2007 and 2018. Clearly it is important to understand the factors underlying this alarming trend.

Currie et al. (2021a) find that drug overdose deaths in Ohio spiked in the first two months of the pandemic, particularly among the young, but then returned to levels consistent with past trends. Currie et al. (2021b) find that in the United States as a whole, existing substance abuse patients were able to maintain access to treatment, but that new patients' entry into treatment fell. To the extent that this was true for other types of mental health treatment, it might indicate that new patients were especially at risk.

It is too soon to tell whether increases in symptoms of mental illness will be sustained over time. However, the research reviewed above suggests that pandemic-related stress among pregnant women could well have negative effects on unborn children, and that children and adolescents who developed clinically significant mental illnesses during the pandemic are at risk of long-term negative outcomes such as disability, school dropout, and detachment from the labor market. Because children's mental health is such an important determinant of future outcomes, the subject merits the increasing research attention it has been receiving from economists.

REFERENCES

Adhvaryu, A., J. Fenske, and A. Nyshadham (2019). "Early life circumstance and adult mental health," *Journal of Political Economy*, 127(4), 1516–1549.

Aizer, A., L. Stroud, and S. Buka (2016). "Maternal stress and child outcomes: Evidence from siblings," *Journal of Human Resources*, 51(3), 523–555.

Almond, D., and J. Currie (2011a). "Human capital development before five." In D. Card and O. Ashenfelter (eds.), *Handbook of Labor Economics*, vol. 4(Part B). Amsterdam: Elsevier, pp. 1315–1486.

Almond, D., and J. Currie (2011b). "Killing me softly: The fetal origins hypothesis," *Journal of Economic Perspectives*, 25(3), 153–172.

Almond, D., J. Currie, and V. Duque (2018). "Childhood circumstances and adult outcomes: Act II," *Journal of Economic Literature*, 56(4), 1360–1446.

Almond, D., and B. Mazumder (2011). "Health capital and the prenatal environment: The effect of Ramadan observance during pregnancy," *AEJ Applied*, 3(4), 56.

Almond, D., B. Mazumder, and R. Van Ewijk (2015). "In utero Ramadan exposure and children's academic performance," *The Economic Journal*, 125(589), 1501–1533.

Attanasio, O., R. Blundell, G. Conti, and G. Mason (2020). "Inequality in socio-emotional skills: A cross-cohort comparison," *Journal of Public Economics*, 191, 104171.

Aviram, R. B., B. S. Brodsky, and B. Stanley (2006). "Borderline personality disorder, stigma, and treatment implications," *Harvard Review of Psychiatry*, 14(5), 249–256.

Baicker, K., S. Taubman, H. Allen, M. Bernstein, J. Gruber, J. Newhouse, et al. (2013). "The Oregon experiment—effects of Medicaid on clinical outcomes," *New England Journal of Medicine*, 368(18), 1713–1722.

Baird, S., J. de Hoop, and B. Özler (2013). "Income shocks and adolescent mental health," *Journal of Human Resources*, 48(2), 370–403.

Baranov, V., S. Bhalotra, P. Biroli, and J. Maselko (2020). "Maternal depression, women's empowerment, and parental investment: Evidence from a randomized controlled trial," *American Economic Review*, 110(3), 824–859.

Belloni, A., D. Chen, V. Chernozhukov, and C. Hansen (2012). "Sparse models and methods for optimal instruments with an application to eminent domain," *Econometrica*, 80, 2369–2429.

Bharadwaj, P., M. Pai, and A. Suziedelyte (2017). "Mental health stigma," *Economics Letters*, 159, 57–60.

Biasi, B., M. Dahl, and P. Moser (2020). "Career effects of mental health." Available at SSRN: 2544251.

Brown, A. S., E. S. Susser, S. P. Lin, R. Neugebauer, and J. Gorman (1995). "Increased risk of affective disorders in males after second trimester prenatal exposure to the Dutch hunger winter of 1944–45," *British Journal of Psychiatry*, 166(5), 601–606.

Brown, D., A. Kowalski, and I. Lurie (2020). "Long-term impacts of childhood Medicaid expansions on outcomes in adulthood," *The Review of Economic Studies*, 87(2), 792–821.

Butikofer, A., C. Cronin, and M. Skira (2019). "Employment effects of healthcare policy: Evidence from the 2007 FDA black box warning on antidepressants." NHH Department of Economics Discussion Paper (1).

Chorniy, A. V. (2018). "AddItAll: The effects of ADHD treatment on children's wellbeing." Northwestern Feinberg School of Medicine Working Paper.

Chorniy, A. V., and L. Kitashima (2016). "Sex, drugs, and ADHD: The effects of ADHD pharmacological treatment on teens' risky behaviors," *Labour Economics*, 43, 87–105.

Chorniy, A., J. Currie, and L. Sonchak (2018). "Exploding asthma and ADHD caseloads: The role of Medicaid managed care," *Journal of Health Economics*, 60, 1–15.

Chorniy, A., J. Currie, and L. Sonchak (2020). "Does prenatal WIC participation improve child outcomes?," *American Journal of Health Economics*, 6(2), 169–198.

Cohodes, S. R., D. S. Grossman, S. A. Kleiner, and M. F. Lovenheim (2016). "The effect of child health insurance access on schooling: Evidence from public insurance expansions," *Journal of Human Resources*, 51(3), 727–759.

Conti, R., A. B. Busch, and D. M. Cutler (2011). "Overuse of antidepressants in a nationally representative adult patient population in 2005," *Psychiatric Services*, 62(7), 720–726.

Courtemanche, C., J. Marton, B. Ukert, A. Yelowitz, and D. Zapata (2018). "Early effects of the Affordable Care Act on health care access, risky health behaviors, and self-assessed health," *Southern Economic Journal*, 84(3), 660–691.

Cowan, B., and H. Zhuang (2020). "Medicaid expansion and the mental health of college students." NBER Working Paper No. 27306.

Cronin, C., M. Forsstrom, and N. Papageorge (2020). "What good are treatment effects without treatment? Mental health and the reluctance to use talk therapy." NBER Working Paper No. 27711.

Cuddy, E., and J. Currie (2020a). "Treatment of mental illness in American adolescents varies widely within and across areas," *Proceedings of the National Academy of Sciences*, 117(39), 24039–24046.

Cuddy, E., and J. Currie (2020b). "Rules vs. discretion: Treatment of mental illness in U.S. adolescents." NBER Working Paper No. 27890.

Cuijpers, P., E. Weitz, E. Karyotaki, J. Garber, and G. Andersson (2015). "The effects of psychological treatment of maternal depression on children and parental functioning: A meta-analysis," *European Journal of Child and Adolescent Psychiatry*, 24(2), 237–245.

Curtin, S. (2020). "State suicide rates among adolescents and young adults aged 10–24: United States, 2000–2018," *National Vital Statistics Reports*, 69(11).

Currie, J., S. Decker, and W. Lin (2008). "Has public health insurance for older children reduced disparities in access to care and health outcomes?," *Journal of Health Economics*, 27(6), 1407–1652.

Currie, J., and W. B. MacLeod (2019). "Understanding doctor decision making: The case of depression treatment," *Econometrica*, 88(3), 847–878.

Currie, J., and B. Madrian (1999). "Health, health insurance and the labor market." In D. Card and O. Ashenfelter (eds.), *The Handbook of Labor Economics*, vol. 3c. Amsterdam: North-Holland, pp. 3309–3407.

Currie, J., M. Schnell, H. Schwandt, and J. Zhang (2021a). "Trends in drug overdose mortality in Ohio during the first seven months of the COVID-19 pandemic," *JAMA Network Open*, 4(4), e217112.

Currie, J., M. Schnell, H. Schwandt, and J. Zhang (2021b). "Prescribing of opioid analgesics and buprenorphine for opioid-use disorder during the pandemic," *JAMA Network Open*, 4(4), e216147.

Currie, J., and M. Stabile (2006). "Child mental health and human capital accumulation: The case of ADHD," *Journal of Health Economics*, 25(6), 1094–1118.

Currie, J., and M. Stabile (2009). "Mental health in childhood and human capital." In J. Gruber (ed.), *An Economic Perspective on the Problems of Disadvantaged Youth*. Chicago, IL: University of Chicago Press for NBER.

Currie, J., M. Stabile, and L. Jones (2014). "Do stimulant medications improve educational and behavioral outcomes for children with ADHD?," *Journal of Health Economics*, 37, 58–69.

Currie, J., M. Stabile, P. Manivong, and L. Roos (2010). "Child health and young adult outcomes," *Journal of Human Resources*, 45(3), 517–548.

Dalsgaard, S., H. S. Nielsen, and M. Simonsen (2014). "Consequences of ADHD medication use for children's outcomes," *Journal of Health Economics*, 37, 137–151.

Druss, B. F., P. S. Wang, N. A. Sampson, M. Olfson, H. A. Pincus, K. B. Wells, and R. C. Kessler (2007). "Understanding mental health treatment in persons without mental diagnoses: Results from the National Comorbidity Survey Replication," *Archives of General Psychiatry*, 64, 1196–1203.

Edin, P. A., P. Fredriksson, M. Nybom, and B. Ockert (2022). "The rising return to noncognitive skill," *AEJ Applied*, 14, 78–100.

Evans, W. N., and C. L. Garthwaite (2014). "Giving mom a break: The impact of higher EITC payments on maternal health," *American Economic Journal: Economic Policy*, 6(2), 258–290.

Fletcher, J. M. (2010). "Adolescent depression and educational attainment: Results using sibling fixed effects," *Health Economics*, 19(7), 855–871.

Fletcher, J. M. (2014). "The effects of childhood ADHD on adult labor market outcomes," *Health Economics*, 23(2), 159–181.

Fletcher, J., and B. Wolfe (2009). "Long-term consequences of childhood ADHD on criminal activities," *The Journal of Mental Health Policy and Economics*, 12(3), 119–138.

Fritz, K., A. M. Russell, C. Allwang, S. Kuiper, L. Lampe, and G. S. Malhi (2017). "Is a delay in the diagnosis of bipolar disorder inevitable?," *Bipolar Disorder*, 19, 396–400.

Gardner, J., and A. J. Oswald (2007). "Money and mental wellbeing: A longitudinal study of medium-sized lottery wins," *Journal of Health Economics*, 26(1), 49–60.

Goodman, A., R. Joyce, and J. P. Smith (2011). "The long shadow cast by childhood physical and mental problems on adult life," *Proceedings of the National Academy of Sciences*, 108(15), 6032–6037.

Grossman, M. (1972). "On the concept of health capital and the demand for health," *Journal of Political Economy*, 80(2), 223–255.

Haushofer, J., and J. Shapiro (2016). "The short-term impact of unconditional cash transfers to the poor: Experimental evidence from Kenya," *Quarterly Journal of Economics*, 131(4), 1973–2042.

Health and Safety Executive (2020). *Health and Safety at Work: Summary Statistics for Great Britain 2018*. https://www.hse.gov.uk/statistics/overall/hssh1718.pdf.

Heckman, J. (2007). "The economics, technology, and neuroscience of human capability formation," *Proceedings of the National Academy of Sciences*, 104(33), 13250–13255.

Heckman, J., and Y. Rubinstein (2001). "The importance of noncognitive skills: Lessons from the GED testing program," *American Economic Review*, 91(2), 145–149.

Heckman, J., J. Stixrud, and S. Urzua (2006). "The effects of cognitive and noncognitive abilities on labor market outcomes and social behavior," *Journal of Labor Economics*, 24(3), 411–482.

Hoffmann, A. B. (2014). "Adverse in utero experiences and distortions of the sex ratio: Evidence from prenatal fasting," Department of Economics, University of Copenhagen Working Paper.

King, M., and P. Bearman (2011). "Socioeconomic status and the increased prevalence of autism in California," *American Sociological Review*, 76(2), 320–346.

Kling, J. R., J. B. Liebman, and L. F. Katz (2007). "Experimental analysis of neighborhood effects," *Econometrica*, 75(1), 83–119.

Ludwig, J., D. E. Marcotte, and K. Norberg (2009). "Anti-depressants and suicide," *Journal of Health Economics*, 28(3), 659–676.

Lumey, L. H., A. D. Stein, and E. Susser (2011). "Prenatal famine and adult health," *Annual Review of Public Health*, 32, 237–262.

Maclean, J. C., B. Cook, N. Carson, and M. F. Pesko (2018). "Public health insurance and prescription medications for mental illness," *The B.E. Journal of Economic Analysis and Policy*, 19(1).

Miller, S., and L. Wherry (2019). "The long-term effects of early life Medicaid coverage," *Journal of Human Resources*, 54(3), 785–824.

Persson, P., and M. Rossin-Slater (2018). "Family ruptures and intergenerational transmission of stress," *American Economic Review*, 108(4), 1214–1252.

Racine, N., J. E. Cooke, R. Eirich, D. J. Korczak, B. McArthur, and S. Madigan (2020). "Child and adolescent mental illness during COVID-19: A rapid review," *Psychiatry Research*, 292, 113307.

Scheffler, R. M., T. T. Brown, B. D. Fulton, S. P. Hinshaw, P. Levine, and S. Stone (2009). "Positive association between attention-deficit/hyperactivity disorder medication use and academic achievement during elementary school," *Pediatrics*, 123(5), 1273–1279.

Schultz-Nielsen, M. L., E. Tekin, and J. Greve (2016). "Labor market effects of intrauterine exposure to nutritional deficiency: Evidence from administrative data on Muslim immigrants in Denmark," *Economics and Human Biology*, 21, 196–209.

Shapiro, B. (2022). "Promoting wellness or waste? Evidence from antidepressant advertising," *AEJ: Applied*, 14, 439–477.

Smith, J. P., and G. C. Smith (2010). "Long-term economic costs of psychological problems during childhood," *Social Science and Medicine*, 71, 110–115.

Stillman, S., D. McKenzie, and J. Gibson (2009). "Migration and mental health: Evidence from a natural experiment," *Journal of Health Economics*, 28(3), 677–687.

Visser, S. N., M. L. Danielson, R. H. Bitsko, J. R. Holbrook, M. D. Kogan, R. M. Ghandour, et al. (2014). "Trends in the parent-report of health care provider-diagnosed and medicated attention-deficit/hyperactivity disorder: United States, 2003–2011," *Journal of the American Academy of Child and Adolescent Psychiatry*, 53(1), 34–46.

Wherry, L., and B. Meyer (2016). "Saving teens: Using a policy discontinuity to estimate the effect of Medicaid eligibility," *Journal of Human Resources*, 51(3), 556–588.

Wherry, L., S. Miller, R. Kaestner, and B. Meyer (2018). "Childhood Medicaid coverage and later life health care utilization," *Review of Economics and Statistics*, 100(2), 287–302.

Winkelman, T. N., and V. W. Chang (2018). "Medicaid expansion, mental health, and access to care among childless adults with and without chronic conditions," *Journal of General Internal Medicine*, 33(3), 376–383.

Zhou, K. (2016). "Non-cognitive skills: Definitions, measurement and malleability." Paper commissioned as background for the UNESCO 2016 Global Education Monitoring Report *Education for People and Planet: Creating Sustainable Futures for All*. https://unesdoc.unesco.org/ark:/48223/pf0000245576.

CHAPTER 6

Modeling Behavior During a Pandemic Using HIV as an Historical Analogy

Nicholas W. Papageorge

Many models from epidemiology are not designed to capture tradeoffs between health and economic well-being and few are equipped to predict how these tradeoffs interact with individuals' preferences to influence behavior.[1] Policies based on such models may not reflect societal preferences or capture how preferences affect behavior and disease spread. Models with epidemiological processes that do incorporate behavior change or health–wealth tradeoffs (mostly from economics) drastically limit individual-level heterogeneity to remain tractable. This makes it difficult to understand variation in behavioral responses and distributional consequences of the pandemic, which should be central to any evaluation of pandemic-related policy. Without the proper tools, we are unable to fully address even basic policy questions, such as whether the long-run effects of social distancing justify the costs – and if so, for whom and under what circumstances. After reviewing modeling approaches from epidemiology and economics (among other fields), I propose a framework adapted from earlier work on the HIV/AIDS epidemic. Analysis of individual behavior is based on the idea that health is a form of human capital in which individuals invest through their choices. The model integrates individual-level variation that other frameworks omit, but does so at the cost of drastically limiting aggregate economic and epidemiological processes. I conclude that what is needed is a multi-disciplinary effort that helps to bridge gaps across disciplines, which would amount to constructing models that capture key features of different approaches. To be useful in evaluating pandemic-related policy, such a model should have rich heterogeneity and capture how individual choices are linked to the broad contours of disease spread and aggregate economic output. Whether such an effort would be feasible and fruitful remains to be seen.

This chapter was prepared for the Econometric Society Monograph Series based on a 2020 World Congress talk entitled "Behavior and policy during a pandemic: HIV as an historical analogy." I am grateful for helpful comments from Jérôme Adda, David Dowdy, Barton Hamilton, Emma Kalish, Eliana La Ferrara, Daniel Polsky, and Matthew Zahn, along with participants in the 2020 World Congress of the Econometric Society. I also acknowledge excellent research assistance from Emma Kalish and Matthew Zahn. The usual caveats apply.

[1] Between the time of writing this chapter and the time of publication in 2025, there have been substantial developments to improve economic epidemiological modeling. The closest effort to the type of model discussed in this chapter is a paper I have coauthored (Hongru et al., 2024) based on an effort outlined in Darden et al. (2022).

6.1 INTRODUCTION

The Covid-19 pandemic has affected virtually everyone on the planet, many through illness and death and far more through massive changes in how we live our lives. Many shifts in behavior have stemmed from government policies designed to slow the spread of illness. Others have amounted to individuals' choices to avoid infection. The long-run effects of these behavior changes are difficult to predict. As the pandemic wears on (and current predictions suggest the coronavirus may become endemic), we are only just beginning to understand the full set of social, cultural, and economic consequences of school and business closures, stay-at-home orders, self-quarantine, social distancing, and so on. Yet, private efforts to avoid infection and population-wide efforts to slow the pandemic have largely depended on these shifts in behavior. Understanding people's behavior is thus critical for understanding the spread of illness.

Complicating matters, the Covid-19 pandemic, and policies to combat it, have placed uneven burdens on people from different socio-demographic groups.[2] This has led to stark variation in behavior, depending on a host of factors that go beyond health risks and government policy to include work arrangements, housing quality, and economic resources (Ashraf, 2020; Chiou and Tucker, 2020; Papageorge et al., 2021; Wright et al., 2020). For example, individuals who have been able to comfortably telework or who have had access to outside space at home have been more likely to socially distance during the height of the pandemic. Younger and poorer individuals facing lower risk of severe illness, but with little savings, have faced stronger incentives to carry on with their lives, including working in high-risk environments (Berube and Bateman, 2020; Gould and Kassa, 2020). Among other issues, this gives rise to an externality, which absent policy can lead to sub-optimal behavior.

To evaluate potential pandemic-related policies, we need models that can capture variation in individual behavior and its interactions with disease spread and economic well-being. The proximate motivation for developing such tools is the Covid-19 pandemic, but the goal is to consider pandemics more generally. Designing better policy responses to existing and future pandemics requires the development of better models. Models from several disciplines capture some critical features of a pandemic, but do so at the cost of omitting others. Many models from epidemiology are not designed to capture tradeoffs between health and economic well-being and few are equipped to predict how these tradeoffs interact with individuals' preferences to affect behavior. Policies based on these models are unlikely to reflect societal preferences or to capture how preferences influence behavior and, thus, disease spread. Models with epidemiological processes that do incorporate behavior change or health–wealth tradeoffs (most from economics) drastically limit individual-level heterogeneity to remain tractable. This makes it difficult to

[2] See DeLuca et al. (2020) for early speculation on the uneven burden of the pandemic and measures to control it.

understand variation in behavioral responses and distributional consequences of the pandemic, which should be central to any evaluation of pandemic-related policy.

Given the available set of models, it is difficult to fully address relevant policy questions, such as whether the long-run effects of social distancing justify the costs – and if so, for whom and under what circumstances. We are in no position to evaluate more complex dynamic tradeoffs, such as whether the short-run benefits of school closures justify the long-run (indeed, intergenerational) costs. Bear in mind that school closures will have outsize effects on the educational trajectories of poor students and, moreover, that low educational attainment is causally linked not only to lower income and employment (Card, 1999), but also to criminal activity (Machin et al., 2011), incarceration (Lochner and Moretti, 2004), lack of political engagement (Dee, 2004), and, indeed, poor health and mortality (Grossman, 2006). Avoiding the latter two is the goal of closing schools in the first place. This example highlights a general challenge of health policy: while it is true that health undergirds economic well-being, poverty is also deadly.

This chapter explores modeling behavior during a pandemic, relying on two key ideas.

1. Envisioning health as a form of human capital (à la Grossman, 1972) is a useful starting point for understanding what drives variation in individual health decisions. According to the basic framework, individuals invest in their health until the long-run marginal benefits of doing so no longer exceed the upfront costs. Health investments include taking medication, exercising, eating healthy foods, or avoiding risky health behaviors, such as drinking excess alcohol or smoking. In the case of a pandemic, avoiding behaviors that raise the probability of infection can be envisioned as a costly investment in health. The framework also links health to employment: health can affect productivity and health investments could interfere with work.
2. While the magnitude of the current crisis seems unprecedented, there are important historical antecedents, most having occurred on a more limited scale, but which nonetheless offer clues concerning behavior change during a pandemic. The HIV/AIDS (Human Immunodeficiency Virus/Acquired Immunodeficiency Syndrome) epidemic in the United States serves as a useful – if imperfect – historical analogy to the current crisis. Lessons learned from this earlier health crisis can increase our understanding of the current one and guide preparations for future pandemics, though with some caveats, which I will discuss below.[3]

[3] I am not the only person to draw a link between these pandemics. If you are reading this, please also read Marcus (2020) and other work by the author. She argues convincingly that shaming people into avoiding risky behavior (both at the height of the AIDS epidemic and during the

I begin with a partial review of research on modeling pandemics, focusing on purposes and limitations of different approaches. First, I describe epidemiological models, highlighting how they differ from economic models. While epidemiological models predict disease spread, often taking individual behavior as an input, they are not built to study endogenous behavioral responses to policy or the tradeoffs between public health and the economy. A small subfield of economics known as *economic epidemiology* attempts to bridge this gap, though a drawback is that models severely limit individual-level heterogeneity. Second, I discuss research specifically related to Covid-19. The aim is not to cover a massive set of papers from numerous fields, but to consider how "reduced form" correlational or descriptive empirical studies that evidence rich heterogeneity in behavior are misaligned with models in the economic epidemiological tradition with limited heterogeneity. Third, I detail earlier research estimating structural microeconomic models of individual health decision-making, based on the Grossman framework and applied to an earlier pandemic: HIV/AIDS. These models incorporate many dimensions of heterogeneity that other models miss. However, given that the AIDS epidemic was far less widespread than Covid-19, the models are limited in how they capture aggregate disease spread and do not look at aggregate output at all, suggesting limitations to the HIV analogy.

Next, I introduce a model of behavior during a pandemic adapted from the earlier work on the AIDS epidemic in the United States. The model takes into account limitations to the HIV analogy for the Covid-19 context by specifying aggregate processes for economic output and spread of the virus. The aim is to clarify what a rich microeconomic framework might capture that other models do not. In contrast to epidemiological frameworks, behavior change is endogenous. The Grossman framework is operationalized as a dynamic choice model of risky health behaviors and work choices, which captures a tradeoff between work and health, taking into account that some individuals cannot work while engaging in protective behaviors, such as social distancing. The model also emphasizes rich individual-level heterogeneity (e.g., age, gender, race, socioeconomic status, work arrangements, and housing quality) in contrast to economic epidemiological models that only allow for some heterogeneity (e.g., young vs. old). Finally, in contrast to existing reduced-form work, the model is structural, intended for use in conducting counterfactual policy simulations.

While these features are no doubt desirable, the cost of integrating them is to drastically reduce attention on general equilibrium effects and to exclude many dimensions of heterogeneity used in epidemiological models. Even from a microeconomic perspective, the model leaves out many desirable features relevant to policy-making, such as indirect effects of Covid on addiction, mental health, and schooling. Moreover, the model would be difficult to estimate

Covid-19 pandemic) is unlikely to be effective and can backfire, since we miss an opportunity to inform people about how to mitigate risk.

given currently available data and thus can help to highlight the kinds of information we ought to collect during future pandemics. In sum, I view the model I present as an initial suggestion of a type of model that has not yet been put forth but should be a part of the discussion on future modeling priorities.

Where does this leave us? We have several classes of models that can be used to develop and evaluate policy related to pandemics. Each captures some features of the pandemic, but omits others. Perhaps that is the best we can do, though it means it is difficult to evaluate the full impacts of pandemic-related policies, such as mask wearing, restrictions on gatherings, and more complex and controversial mandates, such as school closures. To appropriately evaluate the resulting tradeoffs, we need better models. A multi-disciplinary effort involving epidemiologists, different flavors of economists, and other experts could try to construct a "consensus model," one that incorporates sufficient heterogeneity in individual socio-demographic characteristics and behavior along with the broad contours of the macroeconomy and of disease spread so that policies can be evaluated in light of their short-run and long-run costs and benefits and distributional consequences across socio-demographic groups.[4] Should such an effort prove to be futile, a more achievable goal may simply be to write models in each tradition, which means omitting factors deemed important by other fields, but to do so as part of a multi-disciplinary group so that omissions and their consequences for model implications are better understood or more thoughtfully implemented. Any such effort would require serious collaboration, openness to other fields, and an earnest willingness to compromise where possible.

The remainder of this chapter is organized as follows. Section 6.2 reviews the literature. Section 6.3 introduces the model. Section 6.4 concludes.

6.2 LITERATURE

This section provides a broad review of literatures that relate to pandemics. Hopefully, this section makes clear that missing from extant work are models that focus on individual heterogeneity, but that also capture dynamic and aggregate processes of disease spread and economic output, which could be used to study the full impacts of pandemic-related policy.

6.2.1 Epidemiology and Economic Epidemiology

Since the beginning of the Covid-19 pandemic, many researchers from outside epidemiology have become acquainted with the susceptible, infected, and

[4] In this sense, I wholeheartedly agree with suggestions to work together across disciplines, as discussed in Murray (2020). Moreover, there are certainly potential cases where policy can improve health and wealth (e.g., loosening mask restrictions as a way to incentivize vaccination). However, given the emphasis I place on recognizing health–wealth tradeoffs, I worry that the author's conclusion, "[W]e need not choose between a healthy public and a healthy economy," downplays the central importance of recognizing such tradeoffs when developing policy.

removed (SIR) model. This is a classic framework for modeling infectious diseases first introduced by Kermack and McKendrick (1927). It essentially uses infection rates and the fraction of the population that is susceptible to infection (against those who are already infected or immune) to predict total infection rates at different points in time. While the model is conceptually straightforward and still underlies more modern methods, it is extremely outdated.

Current models incorporate far more features than the simple SIR model. These include spatial heterogeneity, age structures, and complex networks, among others (Li et al., 2020; Martcheva, 2015). These developments reflect increased understanding of how diseases are transmitted and the different ways that susceptible populations increase their risk of infection. As a result of these innovations, models have become increasingly better at predicting disease spread. For example, over the last few years the Centers for Disease Control and Prevention (CDC) have run the "Predict the Influenza Season Challenge" to foster innovation in modeling and predicting the spread of the flu each year.[5] One winning team used data assimilation methods commonly employed in numerical weather prediction to train and optimize a forecasting model for real-time influenza outcomes.[6] Researchers have produced other forecasting models for diseases such as Ebola, Zika, and Covid-19, among many others (Asher, 2018; Chowell et al., 2016; Funk et al., 2018; Roosa et al., 2020).

However, models from epidemiology often share a common assumption. Either explicitly or implicitly, human behavior is seen as fixed, including under counterfactual pandemic circumstances, policies, or disease scenarios. In reality, the spread of a disease and policies to combat it affect choices made by individuals and vice versa. Funk et al. (2015) address the lack of dynamic behavior in epidemiological models. They identify at least two drawbacks. First, endogenous behavioral change may mean forecasts are unreliable. Second, pandemic mitigation policies often target individual behavior and not the macro-scale dynamics that inform forecasting models. This is a critical disconnect since models are not equipped to evaluate whether individual behavior should be expected to match assumptions about aggregate behavior. Without capturing the endogenous behavioral responses of individuals as the pandemic progresses, epidemiological models omit an important component that ought to inform public health policy. As the authors note, incorporating individual behavior into these epidemiological models is quite challenging and a research frontier that will require cross-discipline dialogues. I wholeheartedly agree with their assessment. However, I add that models that omit economic behavior suffer from an additional drawback: they cannot be used to explore tradeoffs between economic and public health consequences of policies to answer questions, such as whether the public health benefits of business closures outweigh the economic costs.

[5] Centers for Disease Control and Prevention (2020).

[6] Centers for Disease Control and Prevention (2014); Shaman Group (2014).

I highlight four sets of papers that incorporate individual behavior into epidemiology. A subfield known as *economic epidemiology* has made progress in this direction. Gersovitz and Hammer (2004) apply the canonical SIR framework to a representative agent model to examine the externalities of disease prevention and therapy. Fenichel et al. (2011) build a similar framework with agents of varying latent types that make different choices based on their type. Simulations of their model indicate that shifts in individual behavior have meaningful implications for the course of epidemics. Aadland et al. (2013) capture a similar effect in their study of syphilis cycles. The role of group interactions in spreading a disease is studied by Galeotti and Rogers (2013) in the context of strategic immunizations.[7] Finally, Greenwood et al. (2019) present a model of HIV transmission in Africa to evaluate the effectiveness of public health measures to fight the disease. In contrast to HIV in the United States, HIV in Africa requires more careful incorporation of aggregate effects given that infection rates are much higher. Agents in this model search for different types of sexual relationships, which carry different risks of contracting HIV. Aggregated choices affect how the disease spreads among the population, which in turn affects the expectations of agents when making relationship choices.[8] In general, the models discussed here facilitate analysis of health–wealth tradeoffs, but the style of model means that heterogeneity remains very limited to maintain tractability. For example, there is often a representative agent, a small number of latent types or two to three dimensions of heterogeneity. In contrast, structural micro-economic models, such as those discussed in Section 6.2.3, allow tens of thousands of ways that individuals can differ.

A second set of papers incorporating behavior into epidemiology appeals to game-theoretic concepts.[9] These models are noteworthy because they allow for policies or changes to the course of the pandemic to affect incentives and thus behavior. Moreover, they allow researchers to formalize and incorporate the idea that individual behavior is not necessarily socially optimal and that society can get stuck in a bad equilibrium given a prisoner's dilemma type of setup (Jentsch et al., 2020; McAdams, 2020). These models have been used to study vaccination, in particular the idea that an individual's incentives to become vaccinated decline as vaccination rates rise (Bauch, 2005; Yang et al., 2016). While incorporating game theory is clearly a crucial step in the right direction, once again, individual-level heterogeneity remains severely limited in these models and so it is difficult to understand the multiple ways that individuals may react to one another and to policy. Also, to my knowledge, health–wealth tradeoffs remain largely unaddressed in these models.

[7] Manfredi and D'Onofrio (2013) provide additional citations of other epidemiological models that incorporate some elements of human behavior to model disease spread. Typically, endogenous behavior responses are not directly modeled and heterogeneity is limited.

[8] Similar frameworks are used for Covid-19, which will be discussed in more detail later.

[9] Game-theoretic concepts were initially introduced into biological models by Smith and Price (1973) and Taylor and Jonker (1978) as evolutionary stable strategies that described the steady state of a dynamic game.

Third, Adda (2016) builds up a unique epidemiological model of disease transmission that is a function of economic activity. The approach is noteworthy because it incorporates many types of activity (e.g., school closure and transport networks). The model can be used to relate curtailment of economic activity to disease spread, but also calculates the long-run economic costs. The author finds that reducing interactions effectively controls the spread of a disease but is not cost-effective when looking at the lost economic activity. The framework is applied to influenza, but could be extended to other pandemics and could lead to different policy recommendations. It is possible that a similar model would suggest that policies slowing economic activity are worth the costs in the Covid-19 context. A difference between the framework in Adda (2016) and the framework I present below is that endogenous individual decision-making is not taken into account. Regardless of whether this is a defensible omission in the case of influenza, as earlier literature has shown, it is a crucial factor in understanding the spread of Covid-19.

The final set of papers emphasize the importance of heterogeneity as it pertains to health behavior and health policy. Adda (2007) studies how individuals reacted to the "mad cow" crisis in the United Kingdom during the late 1990s. Among the questions explored in this paper, the author seeks to understand how new information about susceptibility to this disease affected health-related behaviors and whether there was variation across individuals with differential health risks. The author's analysis finds meaningful heterogeneity in health behavior responses to the risk posed by the "mad cow" crisis. Individuals with low and high susceptibility to the disease did not alter their behaviors. However, those with medium susceptibility curbed risky behaviors that exposed them to the disease but did not completely abandon them. This heterogeneity complicates the government's policy response to addressing health inequalities. Adhvaryu (2014) explores similar challenges in the case of a new malaria treatment in Tanzania. Misdiagnosis of this disease is common and can introduce short and long-run consequences for health and economic well-being. The author documents how malaria misdiagnoses interact with latent health heterogeneity (i.e., those with malaria and those without it), leading to slower adoption of new disease treatments that would reap higher returns from adoption. These studies demonstrate the important role of heterogeneity in models of health behavior and policy. Models that omit this feature run the risk of missing important elements driving agent behavior and can imply sub-optimal policy recommendations. Thus, the framework I present below stresses individual heterogeneity.

6.2.2 Covid-19 Literature

Given the rapid proliferation of studies related to Covid-19, it is hard to know where to begin.[10] Many academic communities have turned their attention

[10] Given the nearly constant addition of studies, it is impossible to claim that this review is current. To be specific, this review was current in May 2021 and does not include studies released after that date.

to the pandemic and it is impossible to do them all justice. First, there is a massive medical, public health, and epidemiological literature trying to understand the disease. Medical researchers are focusing on how to treat the disease (Beigel et al., 2020; Felsenstein et al., 2020; Wu et al., 2020b; Zhu et al., 2020); public health scholars are investigating how people are responding to the disease, differences in risk factors, and health disparities brought on by the disease (Bhatraju et al., 2020; Labgold et al., 2021; Lighter et al., 2020; Poulson et al., 2021; Ravi, 2020; Rozenfeld et al., 2020; Smith et al., 2020; Wu et al., 2020a); and epidemiologists are focusing on how the disease will spread (Brooks et al., 2020; Dowd et al., 2020; Ray et al., 2020; Zhang et al., 2020).[11] There is also a large literature related to vaccines. Part of this work focuses on how to distribute vaccine resources, which is a question related to medical ethics and efficiently combating the disease (Gayle et al., 2020). Others have studied how to optimally develop vaccines for future pandemics. Ahuja et al. (2021) find that if the policy objective is to accelerate vaccine delivery, buyers should directly fund manufacturing capacity and thus shoulder most of the risk of failure, while preserving some direct incentives for speed. Goodkin-Gold et al. (2020) solve for the optimal vaccine subsidy by integrating a vaccine market with rational agents into a standard epidemiological model. They find that the optimal subsidy is nonmonotonic in disease infectiousness, peaking for diseases that spread quickly but not so quickly to drive universal vaccination.

Social scientists have also contributed to our understanding of Covid-19. Many have sought to evaluate the effectiveness of measures such as shelter-in-place orders. Examples include Friedson et al. (2020), Gupta et al. (2020), Hsiang et al. (2020), McLaren and Wang (2020), Chernozhukov et al. (2021), and Dave et al. (2021), which use causal inference methods to assess the impact of government interventions, generally showing that a host of measures have been successful at decreasing infection rates and deaths. Others have looked into factors less directly associated with health. Studies such as Allcott et al. (2020), Barrios and Hochberg (2020), and Simonov et al. (2020) have documented a relationship between political affiliations and self-protective behaviors, generally finding conservatives are less likely to adopt these behaviors. While Allcott et al. (2020) incorporate the cost of social distancing into their model, most of these studies do not directly evaluate costs (though they do discuss them when motivating the research).

In general, descriptive and correlational studies of the pandemic have found evidence to suggest there is substantial heterogeneity in behavioral responses across individuals. Papageorge et al. (2021) document socioeconomic behavior gradients for self-protective behaviors such as social distancing. Respondents with higher incomes, flexible work arrangements such as

[11] Professor Ben Bolker of the Mathematics & Statistics and Biology Departments at McMaster University has compiled a list of over 30 open source epidemiological models of the Covid-19 pandemic available here.

telework, and access to open air at home were more likely to adopt these self-protective behaviors. The authors argue that respondents without these characteristics face a higher cost of adopting these actions, which explains the observed lower levels of take-up. Ashraf (2020) explores the relationship between socioeconomic factors, government policy, and Covid-19 health outcomes using a rich panel dataset covering 80 countries. The author finds a strong negative association between Covid-19 cases and socioeconomic conditions, which can be alleviated by government policy. Other papers, such as Andersen (2020), Chiou and Tucker (2020), and Wright et al. (2020), rely on cellphone data to track individual behavior during the pandemic. These papers have documented that the adoption of social distancing measures varies across observable characteristics, such as average neighborhood income. Ilin et al. (2020) demonstrate how mobility data can be used to provide real-time feedback to local policymakers on the effectiveness of nonpharmaceutical policy interventions to control the spread of Covid-19 and improve forecast accuracy. The methods proposed by the authors are simple and allow policymakers to recognize heterogeneous responses to policy actions within their communities.

Attempts have also been made by researchers to extend the economic epidemiology models to the Covid-19 pandemic. In addition to describing some of these efforts by other researchers, Atkeson et al. (2020, 2021) demonstrate how the SIR framework with endogenous behavior can be used to fit key features of data on Covid-19 deaths in a variety of different geographies. Chang et al. (2021) develop a dynamic model of individual location choices in the context of a pandemic by embedding a SIR model of disease spread. In their model, a subset of individuals decide how to distribute time in or out of their homes. These choices influence their incomes (taken as exogenous given their choices) and the probability of becoming infected with the disease. The authors calibrate their model and use it to simulate the effects of income transfers (like those from the CARES Act). They find that the cash transfers generate multiple waves of infection as the transfer only temporarily increases the incentive to remain indoors. Farboodi et al. (2020) develop a similar model of dynamic choices with an epidemiological component where forward-looking agents choose their level of social interaction. Unlike the models described in the next paragraph, these models include no individual heterogeneity or macroeconomic processes.

Other studies add additional economic features to epidemiological models.[12] For example, Acemoglu et al. (2020), Brotherhood et al. (2020), Aguirregabiria et al. (2021), and Eichenbaum et al. (2021a) present full-blown macroeconomic models that incorporate epidemiological processes of disease

[12] For another perspective on the usefulness of these integrated approaches, see Boppart et al. (2020). This report also includes references to many other economic epidemiological models specifically focused on Covid-19.

spread.[13] Eichenbaum et al. (2021a) was one of the first models to incorporate the SIR framework into an economic model to study Covid-19. In their model, an economy is populated by identical agents who make choices about how much to consume and work. These choices interact with the SIR features of the model, influencing how the disease spreads and infects others. The model also captures the roles of firms as they produce consumable goods using labor supplied by the agents and the government, which can attempt to contain the disease through simple policy measures to limit interactions. Because individuals do not internalize the impact their choices have on the spread of the disease, the competitive equilibrium does not align with the socially optimal outcome.[14] The authors simulate the effects of simple policies to contain the spread of the disease, finding that the best containment policy increases the severity of the economic recession but saves a substantial amount of lives.[15] While this model captures many desirable elements (e.g., individual choices, economic production, a host of government policy tools, and disease spread) there is no individual-level heterogeneity among the agents.

Determining the optimal pandemic policy is the focus of Acemoglu et al. (2020). The authors extend the classic SIR framework to consider three different age groups of individuals with varying rates of infection, hospitalization, and fatality. In addition, members of each group produce some measure of economic output which is affected by the lockdown policy in place. The authors are particularly interested in the policy tradeoff between saving lives and improving economic outcomes. They find that age-targeted policies are welfare-enhancing by reducing the amount of deaths and/or economic damage due to the pandemic. Similar to epidemiological models, in the framework, individuals' responses to policies are fixed rather than endogenous. Moreover, heterogeneity is limited to age groups.

Another example is Brotherhood et al. (2020), who present a framework with endogenous behavior choices and disease spread. Their model features old and young agents with varying levels of risk from Covid-19. Agents are able to choose between work and nonwork social distancing. These choices influence the probability the agent becomes infected with the disease. Finally, the labor supply decisions and wages of individuals are used to construct a measure of economic output. The authors find that young and old agents make different optimal choices in equilibrium, with older people engaging in substantially more social distancing than the young. Relative to epidemiological

[13] Other examples of macro models that incorporate epidemiological processes include Alvarez et al. (2020) and Hall et al. (2020).

[14] This type of externality is not unique to Covid-19. Hamilton et al. (2018) find that HIV-infected men who do not use new or experimental medications slow the process of HIV treatment innovation, which negatively affects other patients. As they do not take account of public health impacts of their private choices, there is a negative externality and sub-optimally slow innovation.

[15] Eichenbaum et al. (2021b) incorporate testing into a similar framework.

models that do not account for endogenous behavior changes, the increase in protective behaviors halves the death rate from the disease. They consider the effects of various policies to fight the pandemic, finding that age-specific quarantines and testing schemes may be especially effective at decreasing deaths and increasing individual utility.

Finally, Aguirregabiria et al. (2021) present a model that captures production and social networks in the context of an infectious disease outbreak. In their framework, individuals choose to work and consume outside or remotely from home. The tradeoff is that work outside is more productive and generates complementarities. On top of these choices, there is a SIR-inspired model of disease spread which depends upon (and influences) the network choices of the agents. Work choices are mapped to a production function that not only determines the earnings of individuals, but also the aggregate output of the economy. The authors calibrate this model and perform several policy simulations, including ones related to work-from-home subsidies and testing access. Their analysis finds work-from-home subsidies are successful in getting individuals to remain at home and control disease spread, while only modestly increasing the impact of the pandemic recession due to reduced productivity. Increasing testing allows for individuals to confine earlier and exit the in-person labor force. These actions simultaneously lower infections and limit the depths of the recession as it is safer for people to work in person at a higher level of productivity.

This summary merely scratches the surface of the depth and breadth of the research into Covid-19. In varying ways, several of the aforementioned papers represent Herculean efforts to merge economics with the epidemiology of Covid-19. Each paper captures economy-wide factors. Yet, each does so at the cost of limiting individual heterogeneity. The first (Eichenbaum et al., 2021a) assumes a representative agent, while the second and third (Acemoglu et al., 2020; Brotherhood et al., 2020) allow different age groups. The fourth (Aguirregabiria et al., 2021) captures individual heterogeneity in terms of their work and consumption networks but not along any socio-demographic dimensions. While age is a crucial distinction in Covid-19, there are many more differences that other literature has shown to be potentially important. Specifically, we are missing a model that captures the tradeoff individuals make between health and economic well-being that also takes into account the well-documented individual heterogeneity in behavioral responses. For example, prolonged policies of social distancing may appear desirable at a high level but may be incredibly costly for certain groups of people, such as those facing relatively low risk of serious illness, but who cannot work from home or who live in uncomfortable housing. Policies based on models that assume that levels of compliance do not vary other than by age group are unlikely to be realistic or sustainable. The importance of socioeconomic gradients in understanding behavior differences, including responses to pandemic-related policy, is evident from research in the context of HIV/AIDS, which I discuss next.

6.2.3 Grossman and Models of the HIV/AIDS Epidemic

This section focuses on models that apply the Grossman (1972) framework to behavior during the HIV/AIDS epidemic. I present these models in slightly more detail as they serve as a basis for the model of behavior during Covid-19, presented in Section 6.3. The implicit argument is that HIV provides a useful historical analogy for our understanding of Covid-19 and pandemics in general.[16]

HIV is a virus that reduces the ability of the immune system to fight off routine infections (a condition known as AIDS). It reached epidemic proportions in several countries, including the United States, starting in 1984. It is transmitted through bodily fluids, most notably through sexual contact. It has disproportionately affected men who have sex with men (MSM) due to relatively high rates of riskier sex behaviors (e.g., multiple partners or not using protection).[17] Worldwide, it has killed over 32 million people, and in the United States it has killed more than 700,000.[18] Absent treatment, an individual newly infected with HIV lives an average of 11 years and the advent of the AIDS epidemic brought drastic shifts in risky sexual behavior. The early years of the epidemic were quite bleak, as treatments were not very effective. A medical breakthrough in 1996 dramatically shifted the prognosis. Known as HAART (highly active anti-retroviral treatment), it reduced mortality rates dramatically. It also made HIV-infected (henceforth, HIV-positive or HIV+) people less infectious, which means it also reduced the risk of infection from the perspective of uninfected (henceforth, HIV-negative or HIV−) people.[19]

Applying Grossman (1972) to HIV, behaviors that improve health (or avoidance of risky behavior that diminish health) are viewed as investments. In the models I present, this insight is operationalized as a structural model of dynamic choices that affect people's health, including risky sex behavior and use of medication with side effects.[20] In specifying these models and

[16] I discuss the limitations of the analogy when motivating the model in Section 6.3.

[17] Another factor is engagement in anal sex, which has higher rates of infection.

[18] Kaiser Family Foundation (2019); Joint United Nations Programme on HIV and AIDS (2020).

[19] The next three papers use data from the Multi-Center AIDS Cohort Study (MACS). MACS is an ongoing longitudinal investigation that has followed a periodically refreshed sample of MSM in four US cities. Descriptive statistics from the dataset are shown in Table 6.1 for the full sample and then separately for HIV− and HIV+ men in both the pre-HAART and post-HAART eras. Further details on the dataset are found in the papers described in this section.

[20] The original framework is theoretical and its insights have often been used in reduced-form analyses in a variety of settings, for example, to examine parental investments in children's health (Currie, 2009). Others have used this insight to study risky health behaviors. Cawley and Ruhm (2011) provide an excellent summary of this literature. Another group of studies, closer to the models presented here, uses the Grossman (1972) framework to build up structural models of health decision-making, which can then be used to evaluate counterfactual policies. This approach has been used to study the timing of medical care decisions, the decision to consume alcohol or cigarettes, and use of mental health treatments, among others (Arcidiacono et al., 2007; Chan and Hamilton, 2006; Crawford and Shum, 2005; Cronin et al., 2020; Darden, 2017; Gilleskie, 1998).

Table 6.1 *Summary statistics: MACS dataset*

	(1)	(2)	(3)	(4)	(5)
	Total	HIV-negative		HIV-positive	
		pre-HAART	post-HAART	pre-HAART	post-HAART
HIV-positive	0.41	0.00	0.00	1.00	1.00
Age	44	42	49	40	46
College+	0.63	0.67	0.68	0.55	0.58
CD4 count	725	1066	971	406	483
Death	0.02	0.002	0.003	0.05	0.01
Seroconversion	0.003	0.00	0.00	0.01	0.004
Moderate & risky	0.56	0.54	0.60	0.55	0.56
Moderate	0.51	0.50	0.55	0.51	0.50
Risky	0.04	0.03	0.05	0.04	0.06
Any medication	0.28	0.00	0.00	0.55	0.79
HAART	0.11	0.00	0.00	0.00	0.59
Ailments	0.28	0.17	0.20	0.41	0.42
Full-time work	0.74	0.81	0.76	0.70	0.61
Income (6 months)	18,465	18,347	21,031	16,605	18,464

Notes: Summary statistics are based on 47,763 biannual person-visit observations from 3999 men between 1990 and 2003. The post-HAART period starts in mid-1995. Death is defined as the probability that an individual leaves the sample due to death between the current period and the next. Seroconversion is defined as the probability that an HIV− individual in the current period is HIV+ in the following visit. High-risk sex means individuals engage in anal sex with multiple partners without consistent condom usage. Moderate-risk sex means limiting anal sex to one partner or using condoms consistently. Ailments include sweats, fever, diarrhea, fatigue, and headache. Public data available at https://statepi.jhsph.edu/macs/pdt.html.

matching them to data, the goal is to estimate parameters that capture individual preferences governing tradeoffs related to health. Parameters are "structural" in that they are assumed invariant to policy changes, which means estimated models can be used to investigate how behavior would change under counterfactual policy simulations.

6.2.3.1 *Health, Risky Behavior, and the Value of Medical Innovation for Infectious Disease*

In the first paper I discuss applying Grossman (1972) to HIV/AIDS (Chan et al., 2016), the aim is to examine the value of a medical innovation, HAART, from the perspective of HIV− MSM at risk of becoming infected through their sex decisions. The value of HAART accrues to these individuals in expectation since they only need it if they become positive. Each sexual activity has a corresponding utility and probability of future infection. If infected, agents continue to make decisions based on their own preferences and their health. Medical innovation shifts incentives by lowering mortality and improving health of

HIV+ individuals, and also by lowering infection rates, all of which lower the implicit price of risky sex. The model also imposes equilibrium constraints. Infection rates that HIV− men face are in part a function of the optimal behavior of HIV+ men. Thus, when they make risky sex decisions, HIV− men must form expectations over infection, which includes the likelihood that their partner is HIV+ given their endogenous sexual behavior. HIV− men also respond to whether or not HIV+ men are using HAART, which lowers infection. Ultimately, the estimated model is used to calculate the lifetime value of HAART and of a counterfactual vaccine. Two key findings emerge. While the value of HAART for HIV− men is far lower than it is for HIV+ men, it is substantial (roughly six years of life). Given that the vast majority of MSM are HIV−, roughly half of the total value of HAART accrues, in expectation, to uninfected men who are unlikely to ever need it. Moreover, the model shows that the marginal value of a fully functional vaccine is relatively small since HAART already lowered infection rates and lowered the lifetime utility costs of HIV infection.

6.2.3.2 How Medical Innovation Creates Value: Health, Human Capital, and the Labor Market

In a second paper (Papageorge, 2016), the focus is on another health behavior: use of medication with side effects. The model envisions HIV+ individuals as choosing whether or not to work and whether or not to take potentially life-saving medications, which may lead to side effects. The model is dynamic because current-period medication choices affect future health and mortality. Moreover, work not only provides income and consumption today, but also leads to higher future earnings through experience. Finally, health and labor interact. Health can affect productivity and thus income, while side effects can influence the disutility of work. The model reveals that side effects play a major role in decision-making because they lower utility directly and make work difficult. Because of how side effects interfere with work, an interesting pattern emerges, which is deemed "optimal treatment cycling." When HIV+ men are sick with AIDS, they face a high probability of illness and death, which incentivizes using HAART despite side effects. However, when they recover, the returns to using HAART are lower and so some stop using HAART and return to work. The estimated model is used to examine employment and income assuming HAART was invented as observed and then under a counterfactual innovation: a version of HAART without side effects. A key finding is that lowering side effects not only increases uptake of HAART, but also substantially raises labor supply and income. Broadly, this means that treatment side effects can affect not only health, but also labor market behaviors.

6.2.3.3 Innovation and Health Disparities During a Pandemic: The Case of HIV

In a third paper (Hamilton et al., 2020a), the model focuses on behavior differences across socio-demographic groups. As in the earlier paper, HIV+ men in the model make medication and work decisions while facing side effects, though the focus is on variation in behavior by education group (college or more vs. less than college). The estimated model reveals that both education groups take risks by not always using medication with side effects and that both groups respond to incentives (e.g., the uptake of HAART is very high for sick people in both groups). A key difference, however, is that the tradeoff between side effects and health is different across education groups, especially when it comes to work. In particular, individuals in the lower education group are more willing to forgo health to reduce side effects in comparison to their higher-education counterparts. This could be for a number of reasons, including some evidence that the sorts of occupations low-education people sort into are less flexible and more physical, which would suggest jobs that are less able to be done with side effects. In other words, people with less education face higher costs of making health investments. A counterfactual non-labor income subsidy decreases employment for all groups. For lower-education groups, for whom the health–work tradeoff is starker, it also increases use of HAART and improves health. Broadly, this captures a dynamic that is applicable to Covid-19, a pandemic during which lower-income groups were less likely to engage in self-protecting behaviors in part due to the incompatibility of doing so while remaining employed (Papageorge et al., 2021).

6.3 A GROSSMAN MODEL OF BEHAVIOR DURING A PANDEMIC

6.3.1 Motivation

In this section, I introduce a discrete-choice dynamic model of individual behavior during the Covid-19 pandemic, adapted from the models from the previous section used to study behavior during the AIDS epidemic.[21] As with those models, the goal is to identify deep structural parameters governing behavior, in particular, how different individuals face tradeoffs between health and other factors affecting well-being, such as work and income. Armed with credible estimates, the model could then be used to examine the impact of counterfactual policies on behavior and the spread of illness.

Before introducing the model, I briefly discuss HIV as an analogy for Covid, including limitations. This helps to motivate key model features that make it more applicable to the Covid-19 pandemic, but also to clarify where the model falls short. During both the HIV/AIDS epidemic and the Covid-19 pandemic: (i) we face a widespread, viral pathogen that causes grave illness and death; (ii) costly health investments lower infection risk and also affect how quickly and widely the pathogen spreads; (iii) there is heterogeneity in how people respond to the pandemic and policies to curb it imply different burdens across socio-demographic groups. Thus, as in the HIV/AIDS context,

[21] A more elaborate version of the model is found in Hamilton et al. (2020b).

a central feature of a model capturing behavior is a dynamic tradeoff: costly health-related behaviors in the current period can improve future health.

The US AIDS epidemic as an analogy to the current crisis breaks down, however, because HIV affected far fewer individuals and did not cause widespread cessation of economic activity. A model for Covid-19 would need to account for these types of aggregate economic effects. In presenting the framework, I make an initial attempt to incorporate two aggregate processes: disease spread and economic output. These factors are critical components since the aim is to link behavior to the spread of illness and the macroeconomy, where the latter two interact.

It bears mentioning upfront that, while the type of model I present here has several key strengths that should be part of discussions about future modeling priorities, it also sheds light on the work that lies ahead – including data collection – required to build a truly credible and estimable consensus model of a worldwide pandemic. I return to this discussion, which includes specific drawbacks of this model, once I have presented it.

6.3.2 Basic Framework

6.3.2.1 Timing

Prior to period t, agent i observes their state variables, which include the state of the pandemic. The agent forms expectations over the aggregate infection rate and their income shocks. Based on these expectations, the agent makes a joint health and labor supply decision, where the health decision is a costly protective action.[22] The choice is individually optimal given individual i's beliefs about how these decisions will impact whether they contract the disease (and subsequent consequences). However, aggregate protective actions may affect the course of the pandemic and thus affect other people's utility. Individual i does not take this latter impact into account, which leads to an externality (i.e., choices that are individually optimal may not be socially optimal). After making their choice, the individual realizes their income shocks and consumes. At this point, current-period payoffs accrue. At the end of period t, state variables update according to transition processes. By the start of period $t+1$, the agent observes the updated state variables and the process repeats.

6.3.2.2 Choices

At time t, agent i makes a joint decision regarding protective behaviors and labor supply, $d_{it} \in \mathcal{D} \equiv \{1, \ldots, D\}$:

$$d_{it} = \begin{cases} 0 & \text{no action taken; does not work} \\ 1 & \text{no action taken; works} \\ 2 & \text{action taken; does not work} \\ 3 & \text{action taken; works} \end{cases}.$$

[22] In the case of HIV, these actions included avoidance of risky sex or use of medications.

I assume that there are two different types of agents: low skill and high skill (and these are assumed fixed over time). Agents with different skills face different choice sets. Namely, low-skill workers are not able to choose to take a protective action, such as social distancing, and work. This assumption is intended to reflect the reality that low-skill workers may only have access to jobs that are not amenable to social distancing, such as retail or gig work. To simplify the model, consumption is treated as an outcome and not a choice, as explained below.

6.3.2.3 States and Outcomes

States. The vector of state variables for agent i at time t is denoted Z_{it}. The set of observed state variables contained in Z_{it} includes:

$$\begin{aligned} h_{it} &\in \{0,1,2,3,4\} : \text{health status at } t \\ X_{it} &\in \{X^1,...,X^M\} : \text{non-health state variables at } t \\ \delta_{it} &\in \{0,1\} : \text{death before } t \\ a_{it} &: \text{assets at the start of } t \\ \hat{d}_{it} &: \text{history of optimal choices before } t \\ \bar{\lambda}_{t-1} &: \text{aggregate infection rate last period.} \end{aligned}$$

During any period t, an agent can belong to one of five possible health states:

$$h_{it} = \begin{cases} 0 & \text{healthy and not immune} \\ 1 & \text{infected, asymptomatic, and unaware} \\ 2 & \text{infected, asymptomatic, and aware} \\ 3 & \text{infected and symptomatic} \\ 4 & \text{healthy and immune} \end{cases}.$$

Additional observable state variables are grouped in X_{it}. The M notation reflects the total possible combinations of non-health state variables. Examples of non-health state variables included in X_{it} are:

1. Agent type $w_i \in \{\texttt{low}, \texttt{high}\}$.
2. Age indicator A_{it}, where:

$$A_{it} = \begin{cases} 0 & \text{if } i \text{ is not in an at-risk age group at } t \\ 1 & \text{if } i \text{ is in an at-risk age group at } t \end{cases}.$$

3. Pre-existing condition indicator B_{it}, where:

$$B_{it} = \begin{cases} 0 & \text{if } i \text{ does not have a pre-existing condition at } t \\ 1 & \text{if } i \text{ does have a pre-existing condition at } t \end{cases}.$$

4. Government transfer payment G_{it}, where:

$$G_{it} = \begin{cases} 0 & \text{if } i \text{ does not receive a government transfer at } t \\ 1 & \text{if } i \text{ receives a government transfer at } t \end{cases}.$$

5. A vector of socioeconomic characteristics S_{it}. This object captures individual characteristics such as race, education, home characteristics, and living arrangements among others. Reduced-form studies of the pandemic, such as Papageorge et al. (2021), have documented substantial heterogeneity in behaviors during the pandemic along these characteristics. This framework seeks to capture that same heterogeneity in a structural setting.

The state variable δ_{it} measures whether individual i has died from the disease before the beginning of period t. The state variable a_{it} is an indicator for whether individual i has three months' worth of saved assets or not. The remaining variable in the vector Z_{it} is $\hat{d}_t$, which counts the number of continuous periods in which the agent has adopted protective behaviors up to period t.[23] This is meant to capture either fatigue or growing accustomed to protective actions.

In this model there are aggregate processes that impact an agent's optimal choices. These are the aggregate amount of social distancing across all agents in period t ($\bar{d}_t$) and the aggregate infection rate in period t ($\bar{\lambda}_t$). These processes are endogenous to the model and will be discussed in Section 6.3.4. The agent is able to observe last period's aggregate infection rate $\bar{\lambda}_{t-1}$ as a state variable. Among other factors, the agent uses this information to form expectations over this period's aggregate infection rate when making their optimal choice for period t, as will be explained below when we discuss the aggregate processes.

The final component of agent i's state variables is a vector of choice-specific i.i.d. utility shocks known to the agent, denoted ε_{it}. As these are choice-specific shocks, the size of this vector is D.

Income Process.[24] In period t, if individual i chooses to work, they earn labor income y_{it}. They also have non-labor income b_{it}, which includes savings and government transfers:

$$y_{it} = f(X_{it}) + v_{wt}^{y} \quad v_{wt}^{y} \sim \mathcal{N}(0, \sigma_{vw}^{2}),$$
$$b_{it} = g(X_{it}) + v_{it}^{b} \quad v_{it}^{b} \sim \mathcal{N}(0, \sigma_{vb}^{2}),$$

where $f(X_{it})$ and $g(X_{it})$ are estimated from earnings data. The amount that the agent then consumes, c_{it}, is a function of these income sources:

23 To be clear, if an agent started protective actions at $t = 3$ and has continued to do so until $t = 5$, then $\hat{d}_5 = 2$. Once an agent stops choosing protective behaviors, this variable will reset to zero until they begin to adopt protective behaviors again.

24 As mentioned previously, this model is not directly modeling individual consumption and saving decisions. That said, I want to capture elements of these decisions as part of the individual's dynamic problem in this model.

$$c_{it} = h(y_{it}, b_{it}).$$

This relationship can also be estimated from data. Within the model, the amount an agent consumes depends on their choices, which will impact their total income in period t. This is a simple way to incorporate consumption as part of the model without imposing the computational burdens of fully modeling consumption and savings in addition to the protective action and labor supply decisions. The limitations brought on by this simplification are perhaps justifiable given that my focus is on the effects that individual protective actions play on aggregate disease spread throughout the population.

6.3.2.4 Current-Period Payoffs

Taking measures against an infectious disease requires agents to make sacrifices during the outbreak to prevent getting infected and possible death. The cost of taking these measures will vary by agent based on their observable characteristics and health status. The cost that agent i pays for choice $d = j$ given their health condition h and non-health characteristics X is

$$U_{jt}(c_t, W_t, h_t, X_t, \hat{d}_t) + \varepsilon_{jt} = \log(c_t) + W_t \times \theta_W + \theta_h + A_t \times \theta_{A,j} + B_t \times \theta_{B,j} + S_t \times \theta_{S,j} + \hat{d}_t \times \theta_{\hat{d}} + \varepsilon_{jt},$$

where the log operator on c_t captures diminishing marginal returns to consumption and W_t indicates whether or not the agent chooses to work in period t. This setup reflects several points about the costs agents incur during an infectious disease outbreak. First, there is a standalone disutility from supplying labor. Second, their utility parameters are choice-specific, and also interact with the agent's observable characteristics. Third, the cost of taking these measures can change if the agent engages in them over multiple periods.

6.3.3 Individual Processes and State-to-State Transitions

State transitions are especially important in this model. As discussed in Section 6.3.2, the agent's behaviors are a function of how likely they are to contract the disease according to the prevailing infection rate. These infection rates are also a function of aggregate optimal behavior. I will return to this idea in Section 6.3.4. In this section, I describe the transition processes for the state variables in the model.

In this model there are two sets of transitions to track.

1. **Health status**. There are five types of health transitions:
   - *Healthy to infected.* Health state transitions for healthy people are given by $P_t(h_{t+1} = 1 | h_t = 0, X_t, d_t, \hat{d}_t)$. This formulation represents this transition probability as a function of the agent's characteristics and their protective action decision. However, this does not capture the influence that aggregate social distancing actions ($\bar{d}_t$) and infection rates ($\bar{\lambda}_t$) have on the probability

that a healthy agent becomes infected. This probability can be reformulated to capture these two effects:

$$P_t(h_{t+1} = 1 | h_t = 0, X_t, d_t, \hat{d}_t) = \sum_{\bar{h}_t=1}^{3}$$
$$P_t(h_{t+1} = 1 | h_t = 0, X_t, d_t, \bar{d}_t, \bar{\lambda}_t) \times P_t(\bar{d}_t | \bar{h}_t) P_t(\bar{\lambda}_t).$$

This specification captures how an individual's health transition depends on their protective action choice, the protective action choice of other people, and the aggregate infection rate. These aggregate processes will be described more in the following section. The first probability on the right-hand side could be taken from data, reduced-form estimates, or estimated as part of the model. I place an equilibrium constraint on $P_t(\bar{d}_t | \bar{h}_t)$ (i.e., the aggregate choices of other agents in the model) which requires the optimal choices of individuals to be consistent with those predicted by the model. Intuitively, this transition captures the probability that a healthy person not taking protective action will interact with a sick person who is also not taking protective action and become infected themselves. Finally, I make the normalization that the probability a healthy agent who engages in social distancing will transition into the unhealthy state is small and denoted ω.

- *Infected, asymptomatic, and unaware to aware.* An infected asymptomatic agent becomes aware of their infection status through testing. The probability that an agent receives a test depends on their non-health observable characteristics and is denoted $\tau(X_{it})$.
- *Infected, asymptomatic to symptomatic.* The probability that an infected asymptomatic agent (aware or unaware) becomes symptomatic depends on their non-health observable characteristics and is denoted $\zeta(X_{it})$.
- *Infected to healthy without immunity.* This basic framework does not currently incorporate treatment. Absent this effect, an agent will recover from the disease with some fixed probability. The rate at which an agent recovers from the disease without immunity is denoted ψ. To simplify this transition, ψ will be normalized to 0 if the agent does not choose to take protective actions. This means a sick agent can only recover if they choose to protect themselves.
- *Infected to healthy with immunity.* The rate at which an agent recovers from the disease with immunity is denoted ρ. For my current purposes, I will assume agents are unable to develop immunity from the disease (i.e., $\rho = 0$).

2. **Death.** In this initial model, the probability of death for an infected person is a function of an agent's infection status and non-health characteristics and is denoted $P(\delta_{it}|X_{it})$. Death is realized at the end of a period. For now, I assume non-infected agents do not die.

6.3.4 Aggregate Processes

The spread of disease plays important roles in this model. First, individuals respond to disease spread. In the near term, it impacts their current behavior choices. Social distancing may be necessary when the illness is spreading rapidly and the risk of infection is high. As agents look forward, they form expectations for how the disease will continue to spread in the future, which also weighs on their current-period behavior choices. Second, individual behavior affects aggregate disease spread. When choosing whether to adopt social distancing, an individual does not internalize the impact of their decision on the overall infection rate, leading to an externality. I have previously addressed the first point. In this section, I discuss the second point about how individual behaviors influence aggregate disease spread.

6.3.4.1 Aggregate Self-Protective Behaviors

Aggregate social distancing is summarized by $\bar{d}_t$, which is a $5 \times D$ matrix where element (h, j) is the proportion of agents with health status h making choice j. This element is denoted $d^j(h, \bar{\lambda}_t, \hat{d}_t)$ and written

$$d^j(h, \bar{\lambda}_t, \hat{d}_t) = \sum_{X_{it}} P_t(X_{it}|h) \times d^j(X_{it}, h, \bar{\lambda}_t, \hat{d}_t),$$

where $P(X_{it}|h)$ is the health-state conditional distribution of observed state variables at time t. This expression also depends on the aggregate infection rate $\bar{\lambda}_t$, which will be discussed in the next section. The term $d^j(X_{it}, h, \bar{\lambda}_t, \hat{d}_t)$ is the probability that an agent will make choice j given the values of the state variables Z_{it}.

6.3.4.2 Aggregate Infection Rate

As mentioned previously, the aggregate infection rate in the model is denoted $\bar{\lambda}_t$. To be clear, my goal is to build a model of individually optimal behavior that incorporates features of an epidemiological model, not an epidemiological model that forecasts the spread of an infectious disease. Thus, our method of modeling the aggregate infection rate will be naive relative to the more sophisticated methods used by epidemiologists. I will start by describing the theory behind the aggregate infection rate, followed by an empirical specification that will be included in the dynamic choice model.

Theory. Consistent with the literature, our model will present a specification for the aggregate infection rate consistent with the classical SIR model. For convenience, I will provide a brief summary of the SIR framework as presented in Gersovitz and Hammer (2004). Start by defining the population within a geographic region g as

$$\mathbf{S}+\mathbf{I}+\mathbf{R}=\mathbf{N},$$

where $\mathbf{S}$ denotes the total number of people in g that are susceptible to the disease, $\mathbf{I}$ is the number of people immune to the disease, and $\mathbf{R}$ is the total number of people that have recovered or died from the disease. These collectively sum to $\mathbf{N}$, the total population. The proportions of these groups in the population are denoted by non-bold versions of the variables: $S, I,$ and R, where $S+I+R=1$. The continuous time flows for each of these variables are expressed as

$$\begin{aligned}
\dot{\mathbf{N}} &= \kappa\mathbf{N}-\delta\mathbf{I},\\
\dot{\mathbf{S}} &= \kappa\mathbf{N}-\alpha\mathbf{S}I+\psi\mathbf{I},\\
\dot{\mathbf{I}} &= \alpha\mathbf{S}I-\mathbf{I}(\psi+\delta+\rho),\\
\dot{\mathbf{R}} &= \rho\mathbf{I}.
\end{aligned}$$

The change in the population rate depends on the birth rate κ and the death rate δ of those infected with the disease. Changes in the susceptible population depend on the inflow of new people, the outflow of susceptible people that have contracted the disease, and the inflow of people that have recovered from the disease that are not immune. Here, α captures the rate of infection and ψ represents the recovery rate without immunity. Under a random contact assumption, $\mathbf{S}I$ represents the number of susceptible people that were in contact with an infected person. Next, the change in the number of infected people depends on the inflows from the susceptible population, outflows from those that recover but remain susceptible, those that recover from the disease and become immune at a rate γ, and those that die from the disease. These equations expressed in terms of the population proportions are

$$\begin{aligned}
\dot{S} &= (1-S)\kappa+(\delta-\alpha)SI+\psi I,\\
\dot{I} &= \alpha SI+\delta I^2-I(\kappa+\delta+\psi+\rho),\\
\dot{R} &= \delta IR+\rho I-\kappa R.
\end{aligned}$$

This theoretical framework allows us to specify a process for the aggregate infection rate $\dot{I}$. The key parameter that determines the amount of new cases is α. It also directly relates to the choices facing agents in our dynamic discrete-choice model. The value of α also likely depends on characteristics of the geographic area such as the population size and density. Similar to Adda (2016), this framework could be extended to decompose α by geography, to capture new cases developed by within-geography exposure or cross-geography exposure. This will be deferred for now.

Empirical Model. In our empirical model, the aggregate infection rate in region g is denoted $\bar{\lambda}_{gt}$. The aggregate infection rate represents the number of new cases of the disease, normalized by the size of the population in region g. For now, I assume there is only a single geographic region. This simplification means that the growth in infections will only depend on characteristics from within geography g. This, of course, could be expanded to consider multiple geographies and how cross-geographic features may influence the spread of the disease. Drawing from the theoretical model and suppressing region notation, we have

$$\bar{\lambda}_{t+1} = \alpha S_t I_t + \delta I_t^2 + \gamma G_{t+1} + \xi_{t+1},$$

where $S_t I_t$ is the product of the proportion of the susceptible population and the proportion of the infected population in period t.[25] These proportions are assumed to be analogous to the corresponding elements of $\bar{d}_t$, which are denoted $\tilde{d}(h_t, j_t)$. As discussed previously, agents in this model jointly choose protective actions and labor supply. Choices where the agent does not take protective action are denoted $j_t(0)$ and choices where the agent does take protective action are denoted $j_t(1)$. The term G_{t+1} is a vector of geographic characteristics such as population density or geographic fixed effects. Finally, ξ_{t+1} represents the shock, which may be serially correlated during a disease outbreak. In order to address this bias I can introduce an AR(1) component into the specification. Substituting for S_t and I_t along with the AR(1), we have

$$\begin{aligned}\bar{\lambda}_{t+1} = {} & (1-\phi)\bar{\lambda}_t + \alpha_1 \tilde{d}(0, j_t(0)) \sum_{\bar{h}_t=1}^{3} \tilde{d}(\bar{h}_t, j_t(0)) \\ & + \alpha_2 \tilde{d}(0, j_t(1)) \sum_{\bar{h}_t=1}^{3} \tilde{d}(\bar{h}_t, j_t(0)) \\ & + \delta \left(\sum_{\bar{h}_t=1}^{3} \tilde{d}(\bar{h}_t, j_t) \right)^2 + \gamma G_{t+1} + \xi_{t+1}.\end{aligned}$$

There are several features to note about this specification. First, the susceptible population is broken down into two categories. The first is the aggregate proportion of healthy people not taking protective actions $\tilde{d}(0, j_t(0))$ and the second is the aggregate proportion of healthy people that are taking protective actions $\tilde{d}(0, j_t(1))$. This formulation allows the infection to spread at different rates across these two susceptible groups (hence the two different α coefficients). The susceptible population can become exposed to the disease by interacting with the infected population who are not taking protective actions, denoted $\sum_{\bar{h}_t=1}^{3} \tilde{d}(\bar{h}_t, j_t(0))$. Second, the parameter δ in this specification is associated with the death rate from the disease, which impacts anybody infected regardless of their self-protective behavior choice. This value is observable and could be incorporated into the estimation of this process as a constraint. This

[25] An implicit assumption in this specification is that the disease incubates for a single period, but this could be altered as needed.

formulation highlights how the optimal choices of individuals within the model can impact the aggregate infection rate and subsequent decisions the agents will make. Finally, this specification is flexible enough to allow for the infection rate to vary across the observable characteristics of the agents. This is similar to the approach used by Adda (2016), which estimated different infection rates for various age groups. This procedure would yield infection rates as a function of individual characteristics that could be used in the associated transition probabilities.

As noted above, this specification gets us the spread of the disease as a function of individual behavior through the elements of $\bar{d_t}$. By extension, this allows us to understand how the spread of the disease depends on the distribution of observable characteristics. In practice, estimates of this process will come from a sample and not the entire population. One can assume as a constraint that I can re-weight as needed so that, conditional on the observable characteristics, our sample is random.

6.3.4.3 Macroeconomic Processes

The Covid-19 pandemic has highlighted how protective behaviors adopted by individuals and governments to promote public health can have severe effects on the macroeconomy. From our model, it is possible to construct measures of employment and output. For example, following the approach used in Brotherhood et al. (2020), GDP in period t could be calculated by summing the wage rate multiplied by the amount of time the individual spent working:

$$Y_t = \sum_w \sum_i W_{it} y_{it}^w .$$

A similar approach could be used to calculate the unemployment rate of individuals in the model. These methods are straightforward but other approaches could be adopted. A further extension would be to allow these macroeconomic processes to influence other elements of the model. For instance, if the economy enters a recession, the amount of jobs or wages available to the individuals could be impacted. These effects would influence the optimal work and consumption choices agents make within the dynamic model but substantially increase the complexity of the model. Eichenbaum et al. (2021a) is an example of a model that endogenizes wages. In the model, wages are not only impacted by the choice of firms but also the spread of the disease. However, as discussed previously, this model includes no individual-level heterogeneity apart from the agent's infection status.

6.3.5 The Value Function and Choice Probabilities

For an agent that has not died before period t, their value function for choice $j \in \mathcal{D}$ is

$$V_{jt}(Z_t) = U_{jt}(c_t, W_t, h_t, X_t, \hat{d}_t) + \varepsilon_{jt} + \sum_{Z_{t+1}} f_{jt}(Z_{t+1}|Z_t, \bar{d}_t, \bar{\lambda}_t)$$
$$\times \beta \left[E_\varepsilon \left(\max_k \{ V_{kt+1}(Z_{t+1}) + \varepsilon_{kt+1} \} \right) \times (1 - \delta_{t+1}) + v \times \delta_{t+1} \right],$$

where $U_{jt}(c_t, W_t, h_t, X_t, \hat{d}_t) + \varepsilon_{jt}$ represents the agent's current-period payoffs, $f_{jt}(Z_{t+1}|Z_t, \bar{d}_t, \bar{\lambda}_t)$ represents the probability distribution over future values of the state variables, and β is the discount factor over future choices. The term v represents a "scrap value" of life parameter that could be estimated or normalized to zero.[26] The objects of the model are summarized in Table 6.2.

Table 6.2 *Model objects*

Parameter	Source	Notation
Disutility of work	Estimate	θ_W
Health	Estimate	θ_h
Age	Estimate	$\theta_{A,j}$
Pre-existing condition	Estimate	$\theta_{B,j}$
Socioeconomic characteristics	Estimate	$\theta_{S,j}$
Cost of protection	Estimate	$\theta_{\hat{d}}$
Healthy to infected: not taking action	Data, reduced form, or estimate	$P_t(h_{t+1} = 1 \| h_t = 0, X_t, d_t, \bar{d}_t, \bar{\lambda}_t)$
Healthy to infected: taking action	Data, calibrate	ω
Infected, asymptomatic, and unaware to aware	Data, calibrate	$\tau(X_{it})$
Infected, asymptomatic, to symptomatic	Data, calibrate	$\zeta(X_{it})$
Infected to healthy without immunity	Data	ψ
Infected to healthy with immunity	Data	ρ
Death	Data, calibrate	$P(\delta\|X_{it})$
AR(1) coefficient	Reduced form	ϕ
Susceptible: taking action	Reduced form	α_1
Susceptible: not taking action	Reduced form	α_2
Death rate	Reduced form	δ
Geographic factors	Reduced form	γ
Labor income	Reduced form/match	$f(X_{it})$
Labor income shock variance	Calibrate	σ^y_{vw}
Non-labor income	Reduced form/match	$g(X_{it})$
Non-labor income shock variance	Calibrate	σ^b_{vb}
Consumption	Reduced form/match	$h(y_{it}, b_{it})$

Notes: This table summarizes objects in the structural model that I present that are either estimated or calibrated. The first column describes the parameter. The second column describes whether the parameter is estimated, recovered from data, or calibrated to match an external source. The third column shows the notation used for that parameter from the model write-up.

26 For the remainder of this discussion, I will proceed with the latter approach.

6.3.5.1 Choice Probabilities in Equilibrium

Given the normalizations and assumptions of the model, the net-of-errors value function for choice j for agent i is

$$\bar{V}_{jt}(Z_t) = U_{jt}(c_t, W_t, h_t, X_t, \hat{d}_t) + \sum_{Z_{t+1}} f_j(Z_{t+1}|Z_t, \bar{d}_t, \bar{\lambda}_t)$$
$$\times \beta \left[\left(\varsigma + \log \left[\sum_k^D \exp(\bar{V}_{kt+1}(Z_{t+1})) \right] \right) \times (1 - \delta_{t+1}) \right].$$

Euler's constant is denoted ς. Given the error-term assumptions, the conditional choice probability for choice j is

$$\phi_{jt}(Z_t) = \frac{\exp(\bar{V}_{jt}(Z_t))}{\sum_k^D \exp(\bar{V}_{kt}(Z_t))}.$$

Similar to Chan et al. (2016), there will be an equilibrium constraint incorporated into the health transition from healthy to infected. This transition probability can be expressed as

$$P_t(h_{t+1} = 1 | h_t = 0, X_t, d_t, \hat{d}_t) = P_t(h_{t+1} = 1 | h_t = 0, X_t, d_t, \bar{d}_t, \bar{\lambda}_t)$$
$$\times d^j(h_t, \bar{\lambda}_t, \hat{d}_t)\bar{\lambda}_t,$$

where $P_t(\bar{d}_t | \bar{h}_t) = d^j(h_t, \bar{\lambda}_t, \hat{d}_t)$ and $P_t(\bar{\lambda}_t) = \bar{\lambda}_t$. When defining this expression, I have assumed that the probability of choosing d conditional on health status h comes from the $\bar{d}_t$ matrix, whose (h, j) element is expressed as

$$d^j(h, \bar{\lambda}_t, \hat{d}_t) = \sum_{X_{it}} P_t(X_{it} | h) \times d^j(X_{it}, h, \bar{\lambda}_t, \hat{d}_t).$$

The equilibrium constraint is that the individual choice probabilities in this expression are equal to the optimal choice probabilities implied by the model:

$$d^j(X_{it}, h, \bar{\lambda}_t, \hat{d}_t) = \phi_{jt}(Z_t).$$

Defining the vector of structural parameters in the model as Ξ, the optimal choice probabilities when the market is at equilibrium are

$$\phi_{jt}(Z_t; \Xi) = \frac{\exp(\bar{V}_{jt}(Z_t, \phi_{jt}(Z_t; \Xi)))}{\sum_k^D \exp(\bar{V}_{kt}(Z_t, \phi_{kt}(Z_t; \Xi)))}.$$

As a result of this equilibrium constraint, the structural parameters will not only influence an agent's optimal choice, but also how they respond to the optimal equilibrium behavior of other agents. It is important to note that there may be multiple equilibria in these choice probabilities. For instance, consider the interpretation of protective actions as wearing a mask. If mask wearing throughout the population increases, any given individual is safer from the disease and may find it optimal for them to not engage in this behavior. Alternatively, if mask wearing has become commonplace, a social norm may have developed around this behavior. As such, it may be costlier for an individual to not engage in this action and they continue to wear masks despite facing less risk from the disease. Finally, the appendix to this chapter addresses the estimation procedure and data requirements for the model.

6.3.6 Discussion of the Model

As specified, the model I present is problematic. It is not clear whether it is tractable enough to solve and to estimate. Among other things, there may be multiple equilibria, which makes it difficult to credibly conduct counterfactual policy simulations. It is also not clear if aggregate processes are sufficiently captured to make this model useful for policy analysis in the context of a worldwide pandemic. Moreover, data limitations could thwart efforts to identify key parameters. Even now, over a year into the Covid-19 pandemic at the time of writing, we lack basic figures, such as the number of people who have been infected (vs. the number who have merely tested positive). Finally, while the model provides richer individual-level heterogeneity compared to existing models in the economic epidemiological tradition, it contains far fewer variables related to disease spread compared to standard models from epidemiology. Even by the standards of structural microeconomic models, this model omits many crucial factors that limit its usefulness and could also lead to biased estimates of key parameters capturing tradeoffs. For example, the model is silent on addiction or mental health issues, both of which could influence behavior during the pandemic and would likely be subsumed in the various "cost" parameters. Among other issues, this means such parameters may not be fixed under counterfactual policies. Thus, while this model offers some nice features that other models lack, it falls short on many dimensions. It is best viewed as an initial suggestion of some of the tradeoffs we should be considering more carefully in any discussion of future modeling priorities and attempts to develop more helpful tools.

6.4 CONCLUDING REMARKS: WHAT LIES AHEAD?

To date, we lack models of behavior during a pandemic that incorporate rich heterogeneity in how people approach health–wealth tradeoffs, and which credibly capture aggregate processes such as economic growth and disease spread. It is therefore difficult to answer many relevant policy questions. Consider the following: What is the optimal proportion of the population that should avoid contact with anyone outside their household given a local rate of infection? Messaging and politics aside, the number is very unlikely to be 0 or 100. Even if society decided that public health is our only concern, the optimal number is still not 100 because economic downturns have all sorts of negative consequences that affect health directly (e.g., addiction and intimate partner violence) and indirectly (e.g., job losses and widening educational attainment gaps across socio-demographic groups). Even if economic well-being were the only concern, the number would not be 0 because health affects the economy in many complex ways.

Whether a consensus model (or perhaps a suite of models that communicate with one another) can be developed that reasonably address such policy questions is not clear. The likelihood may not be terribly high, though if no attempt is made to reach across disciplines to discuss modeling priorities, the likelihood is zero. Thus, my first suggestion is deliberate dialogue across disciplines. Even if that does not lead to an agreed-upon consensus model or set of models, it might clarify what each set of models ought and ought not be used to do. It may also highlight what sorts of data need to be collected during a pandemic (e.g., from randomized testing so we have some idea of how many infections have gone undetected) and which modeling features are deemed most or least crucial by different disciplines. That is a place to start.

Absent such an attempt, my fear is that we will continue to develop policy without the right modeling tools, essentially asking models from one field or another to provide guidance in ways they are not designed to, which leads to non-credible policy. Alternatively, we offer conflicting policy suggestions that depend on different modeling approaches. Even worse, policymakers, frustrated with competing advice from different academics, develop policy without science, which opens the door for politics, wishful thinking, moral imperatives, or conspiracies to drive policymaking. Depressingly, the HIV/AIDS context once again provides an historical analogy. Unrealistic "abstinence only" messages ignored the daily reality of serious tradeoffs that people faced. Such messaging also limited opportunities to provide information to mitigate risk (Marcus, 2020). Similarly, "all-or-nothing" approaches have abounded during Covid-19. Recent reporting has suggested that allowing 20% capacity at bars and restaurants could maintain over half of visits and decrease infections by nearly 90%. Sadly, it took until December 2020 for this point to be made in a newspaper.[27] Appropriate scientific modeling of behavior and the virus could have clarified these tradeoffs much earlier.[28]

There are many reasons to continue efforts to build appropriate models for this pandemic. The current pandemic is far from over, despite widespread availability of vaccines in some countries. Models can still help to guide policy during later stages of the current crisis. As this plight eventually subsides, better modeling tools will be able to help us understand which policies during Covid-19 were most helpful and which were unduly costly, harmful, or

[27] Similarly, the likelihood of HIV transmission varies substantially across sexual behaviors (Varghese et al., 2002). Providing this type of information early on and clearly might have allowed people to make more informed choices, lowering the spread of infection while recognizing that intimacy is a fundamental part of people's lives (Godlonton et al., 2016).

[28] See Serkez (2020).

misguided. Such tools can also shed light on the distributional consequences of Covid-19, the repercussions of which will be with us for years to come. This work will likely continue for a while; scholars continue to provide evidence of the economic, social, and cultural shifts from the height of the US AIDS epidemic (Fernández et al., 2019; Godlonton et al., 2016; Papageorge et al., 2019; White, 1991). Moreover, it is only a matter of time before the next pandemic arrives. When it does, we will want to have achieved a better understanding of human behavior during a pandemic, including socio-demographic differences in behavior and the role of health–wealth tradeoffs, along with the distributional consequences of the pandemic and of policies to curb it. Tools developed to analyze the current pandemic could then be tailored to evaluate policies related to the next crisis.

APPENDIX: MODEL ESTIMATION AND DATA REQUIREMENTS

I will briefly describe how the structural parameters of this model can be estimated via maximum likelihood. Some objects within the model that do not vary with the structural parameter estimates are computed or calibrated in a first stage. These objects are the health transition processes (i.e., symptom and immunity development, recovery, and death) and the parameters of the aggregate infection rate.

In the second step, these processes are used to recover the structural parameters iteratively. The algorithm begins with an initial guess for the conditional choice probabilities for each choice j by health status an individual may make and the aggregate infection rate. Given a candidate set of parameters Ξ, compute the current-period payoffs for each choice j and combinations of the state variables. Next, given the choice probabilities for action j by health status and the aggregate infection rate for the current period, generate an estimate for $\bar{\lambda}_{t+1}$. From here, use the estimated $\bar{\lambda}_{t+1}$ and the transition processes to compute the net-of-errors value functions ($\bar{V}_{jt}$) and use them to recover the choice probabilities implied by the model (ϕ_{jt}).

The choice probabilities ϕ_{jt} reflect optimal behavior given the structural parameters and the initial guesses for the choice probabilities conditional on health status. When ϕ_{jt} is aggregated to the market level, these probabilities may differ from the initial guesses used for the expectations in calculating the net-of-errors value functions. As a result, I have calculated optimal behavior with beliefs that are not consistent with the equilibrium behavior implied by ϕ_{jt}. In this case, the choice probabilities ϕ_{jt} are aggregated and used to update the initial conditional choice probabilities. The second step is repeated until the equilibrium constraint is satisfied. In other words, the second step is repeated until the optimal behavior implied by the model ϕ_{jt} is consistent with the agent's expectations about optimal behavior (i.e., the choice probabilities conditional on health status). This process is the calculation for a given set of structural parameters Ξ. The process repeats for different candidate Ξ until the likelihood function is maximized.

To estimate this model, individual-level survey data during an infectious disease outbreak is required. These data ought to include information about the individual's health status, other characteristics, and their behavioral choices, ideally both work and pandemic related. Beliefs and perceptions about the pandemic or infection rate would also be valuable. These data should include geographic details for the respondents so that they can be supplemented with other data sources to provide information about the environment where the respondent lives and works. From these data, one can recover empirical estimates of the conditional choice probabilities as well as the transition processes that will be included in the model. Epidemiological data about the infectious disease in question may also be necessary to estimate this model. For example, the SIR model presented in my framework requires information about the rates of recovery and immunity development, among others. To the extent these transitions are not readily recoverable from survey data, it may be necessary to get this information from medical sources to calibrate them.

REFERENCES

Aadland, D., D. C. Finnoff, and K. X. D. Huang (2013). "Syphilis cycles," *The B.E. Journal of Economic Analysis and Policy*, 14(1), 297–348.

Acemoglu, D., V. Chernozhukov, I. Werning, and M. D. Whinston (2020). "A multi-risk SIR model with optimally targeted lockdown." NBER Working Paper No. 27102.

Adda, J. (2007). "Behavior towards health risks: An empirical study using the 'mad cow' crisis as an experiment," *Journal of Risk and Uncertainty*, 35(3), 285–305.

Adda, J. (2016). "Economic activity and the spread of viral diseases: Evidence from high frequency data," *Quarterly Journal of Economics*, 131(2), 891–941.

Adhvaryu, A. (2014). "Learning, misallocation, and technology adoption: Evidence from new malaria therapy in Tanzania," *The Review of Economic Studies*, 81(4), 1331–1365.

Aguirregabiria, V., J. Gu, Y. Luo, and P. Mira (2021). "Diffusion of Covid-19 in social and production networks: Simulation evidence from a dynamic model," *Annals of Economics and Statistics*, 142, 179–210.

Ahuja, A., S. Athey, A. Baker, E. Budish, J. C. Castillo, R. Glennerster, et al. (2021). "Preparing for a pandemic: Accelerating vaccine availability." NBER Working Paper No. 28492.

Allcott, H., L. Boxell, J. Conway, M. Gentzkow, M. Thaler, and D. Y. Yang (2020). "Polarization and public health: Partisan differences in social distancing during the coronavirus pandemic," *Journal of Public Economics*, 191, 104254.

Alvarez, F. E., D. Argente, and F. Lippi (2020). "A simple planning problem for COVID-19 lockdown." NBER Working Paper No. 26981.

Andersen, M. (2020). "Early evidence on social distancing in response to COVID-19 in the United States." SSRN Working Paper 3569368.

Arcidiacono, P., H. Sieg, and F. Sloan (2007). "Living rationally under the volcano? An empirical analysis of heavy drinking and smoking," *International Economic Review*, 48(1), 37–65.

Asher, J. (2018). "Forecasting Ebola with a regression transmission model," *Epidemics*, 22, 50–55.

Ashraf, B. N. (2020). "Socioeconomic conditions, government interventions and health outcomes during COVID-19," *Covid Economics*, 37, 141–162.

Atkeson, A. G., K. Kopecky, and T. Zha (2020). "Behavior and the transmission of Covid-19." Mimeo, University of California Los Angeles.

Atkeson, A. G., K. Kopecky, and T. Zha (2021). "Behavior and the transmission of Covid-19," *AEA Papers and Proceedings*, 111, 356–360.

Barrios, J. M., and Y. Hochberg (2020). "Risk perception through the lens of politics in the time of the COVID-19 pandemic." NBER Working Paper No. 27008.

Bauch, C. T. (2005). "Imitation dynamics predict vaccinating behaviour," *Proceedings of the Royal Society, Series B*, 272(1573), 1669–1675.

Beigel, J. H., K. M. Tomashek, L. E. Dodd, A. K. Mehta, B. S. Zingman, A. C. Kalil, et al. (2020). "Remdesivir for the treatment of Covid-19 – final report," *New England Journal of Medicine*, 383(19), 1813–1826.

Berube, A., and N. Bateman (2020). "Who are the workers already impacted by the COVID-19 recession?" Metropolitan Policy Program Covid-19 Analysis, Brookings Institute.

Bhatraju, P. K., B. J. Ghassemieh, M. Nichols, R. Kim, K. R. Jerome, A. K. Nalla, et al. (2020). "Covid-19 in critically ill patients in the Seattle region – case series," *New England Journal of Medicine*, 382(21), 2012–2022.

Boppart, T., K. Harmenberg, J. Hassler, P. Krusell, and J. Olsson (2020). *Confronting Epidemics: The Need for Epi-econ IAMs*. Stockholm: Konjunkturinstitutet.

Brooks, L. C., E. L. Ray, J. Bien, J. Bracher, A. Rumack, R. J. Tibshirani, and N. G. Reich (2020). "Comparing ensemble approaches for short-term probabilistic COVID-19 forecasts in the U.S." International Institute of Forecasters.

Brotherhood, L., P. Kircher, C. Santos, and M. Tertilt (2020). "An economic model of the Covid-19 pandemic with young and old agents: Behavior, testing and policies." Discussion Paper 175, Collaborative Research Center Transregio 224.

Card, D. (1999). "The causal effect of education on earnings." In O. C. Ashenfelter and D. Card (eds.), *Handbook of Labor Economics*, vol. 3. Amsterdam: Elsevier, pp. 1801–1863.

Cawley, J., and C. J. Ruhm (2011). "The economics of risky health behaviors." In M. V. Pauly, T. G. McGuire, and P. P. Barros (eds.), *Handbook of Health Economics*, vol. 2. Amsterdam: Elsevier, pp. 95–199.

Centers for Disease Control and Prevention (2014). "CDC announces winner of the 'Predict the Influenza Season Challenge'." https://www.cdc.gov/flu/news/predict-flu-challenge-winner.htm.

Centers for Disease Control and Prevention (2020). "FluSight: Flu forecasting." https://www.cdc.gov/flu/weekly/flusight/index.html.

Chan, T. Y., and B. H. Hamilton (2006). "Learning, private information, and the economic evaluation of randomized experiments," *Journal of Political Economy*, 114(6), 997–1040.

Chan, T. Y., B. H. Hamilton, and N. W. Papageorge (2016). "Health, risky behaviour and the value of medical innovation for infectious disease," *Review of Economic Studies*, 83(4), 1465–1510.

Chang, R., H. Martínez, and A. Velasco (2021). "Pandemics, incentives, and economic policy: A dynamic model." NBER Working Paper No. 28636.

Chernozhukov, V., H. Kasaha, and P. Schrimpf (2021). "Causal impact of masks, policies, behavior on early COVID-19 pandemic in the U.S," *Journal of Econometrics*, 220(1), 23–62.

Chiou, L., and C. Tucker (2020). "Social distancing, internet access and inequality." NBER Working Paper No. 26982.

Chowell, G., D. Hincapie-Palacio, J. Ospina, B. Pell, A. Tariq, S. Dahal, et al. (2016). "Using phenomenological models to characterize transmissibility and forecast patterns and final burden of Zika epidemics," *Public Library of Science Currents*, 8.

Crawford, G. S., and M. Shum (2005). "Uncertainty and learning in pharmaceutical demand," *Econometrica*, 73(4), 1137–1173.

Cronin, C. J., M. P. Forsstrom, and N. W. Papageorge (2020). "What good are treatment effects without treatment? Mental health and the reluctance to use talk therapy." NBER Working Paper No. 27711.

Currie, J. (2009). "Healthy, wealthy, and wise: Socioeconomic status, poor health in childhood, and human capital development," *Journal of Economic Literature*, 47(1), 87–122.

Darden, M. (2017). "Smoking, expectations, and health: A dynamic stochastic model of lifetime smoking behavior," *Journal of Political Economy*, 125(5), 1465–1522.

Darden, M. E., D. Dowdy, L. Gardner, B. H. Hamilton, K. Kopecky, M. Marx, N. W. Papageorge, et al. (2022). "Modeling to inform economy-wide pandemic policy: Bringing epidemiologists and economists together," *Health Economics*, 31(7), 1291–1295.

Dave, D., A. I. Friedson, K. Matsuzawa, and J. J. Sabia (2021). "When do Shelter-in-place orders fight Covid-19 best? Policy heterogeneity across states and adoption time", *Economic Inquiry*, 59(1), 29–52.

Dee, T. S. (2004). "Are there civic returns to education?," *Journal of Public Economics*, 88(9), 1697–1720.

DeLuca, S., N. W. Papageorge, and E. Kalish (2020). "The unequal cost of social distancing." Johns Hopkins University Coronavirus Resource Center. https://coronavirus.jhu.edu/from-our-experts/the-unequal-cost-of-social-distancing.

Dowd, J. B., L. Andriano, D. M. Brazel, V. Rotondi, P. Block, X. Ding, et al. (2020). "Demographic science aids in understanding the spread and fatality rates of COVID-19," *Proceedings of the National Academy of Sciences*, 117(18), 9696–9698.

Eichenbaum, M. S., S. Rebelo, and M. Trabandt (2021a). "The macroeconomics of epidemics." NBER Working Paper No. 26882.

Eichenbaum, M. S., S. Rebelo, and M. Trabandt (2021b). "The macroeconomics of testing and quarantining." NBER Working Paper No. 27104.

Farboodi, M., G. Jarosch, and R. Shimer (2020). "Internal and external effects of social distancing in a pandemic." NBER Working Paper No. 27059.

Felsenstein, S., J. A. Herbert, P. S. McNamara, and C. M. Hedrich (2020). "COVID-19: Immunology and treatment options," *Clinical Immunology*, 215, 108448.

Fenichel, E. P., C. Castillo-Chavez, M. G. Ceddia, G. Chowell, P. A. Gonzalez Parra, G. J. Hickling, et al. (2011). "Adaptive human behavior in epidemiological models," *Proceedings of the National Academy of Sciences*, 108(15), 6306–6311.

Fernández, R., S. Parsa, and M. Viarengo (2019). "Coming out in America: AIDS, politics, and cultural change." NBER Working Paper No. 25697.

Friedson, A. I., D. McNichols, J. J. Sabia, and D. Dave (2020). "Did California's Shelter-in-place order work? Early coronavirus-related public health effects." NBER Working Paper No. 26992.

Funk, S., S. Bansal, C. T. Bauch, K. T. D. Eames, W. J. Edmunds, A. P. Galvani, and P. Klepac (2015). "Nine challenges in incorporating the dynamics of behaviour in infectious diseases models," *Epidemics*, 10, 21–25.

Funk, S., A. Camacho, A. J. Kucharski, R. M. Eggo, and W. J. Edmunds (2018). "Real-time forecasting of infectious disease dynamics with a stochastic semi-mechanistic model," *Epidemics*, 22, 56–61.

Galeotti, A., and B. W. Rogers (2013). "Strategic immunization and group structure," *American Economic Journal: Microeconomics*, 5(2), 1–32.

Gayle, H., W. Foege, L. Brown, and B. Kahn (eds.) (2020). *Framework for Equitable Allocation of COVID-19 Vaccine*. Washington, DC: The National Academies Press.

Gersovitz, M., and J. S. Hammer (2004). "The economical control of infectious diseases," *The Economic Journal*, 114(492), 1–27.

Gilleskie, D. B. (1998). "A dynamic stochastic model of medical care use and work absence," *Econometrica*, 66(1), 1–45.

Godlonton, S., A. Munthali, and R. Thornton (2016). "Responding to risk: Circumcision, information, and HIV prevention," *Review of Economics and Statistics*, 98(2), 333i–349.

Goodkin-Gold, M., M. Kremer, C. M. Snyder, and H. L. Williams (2020). "Optimal vaccine subsidies for endemic and epidemic diseases." NBER Working Paper No. 28085.

Gould, E., and M. Kassa (2020). "Young workers hit hard by the COVID-19 economy." White Paper, Economic Policy Institute.

Greenwood, J., P. Kircher, C. Santos, and M. Tertilt (2019). "An equilibrium model of the African HIV/AIDS epidemic," *Econometrica*, 87(4), 1081–1113.

Grossman, M. (1972). "On the concept of health capital and the demand for health," *Journal of Political Economy*, 80(2), 223–255.

Grossman, M. (2006). "Education and nonmarket outcomes." In E. A. Hanushek and F. Welch (eds.), *Handbook of the Economics of Education*. Amsterdam: Elsevier, pp. 577–633.

Gupta, S., T. D. Nguyen, F. Lozano Rojas, S. Raman, B. Lee, A. Bento, et al. (2020). "Tracking public and private response to the Covid-19 epidemic: Evidence from state and local government actions." NBER Working Paper No. 27027.

Hall, R. E., C. I. Jones, and P. J. Klenow (2020). "Trading off consumption and COVID-19 deaths." NBER Working Paper No. 27340.

Hamilton, B. H., A. Hincapié, R. A. Miller, and N. W. Papageorge (2018). "Innovation and diffusion of medical treatment." NBER Working Paper No. 24577.

Hamilton, B. H., A. Hincapié, E. C. Kalish, and N. W. Papageorge (2020a). "Innovation and health disparities during a pandemic: The case of HIV." Mimeo, Johns Hopkins University.

Hamilton, B. H., N. W. Papageorge, and M. V. Zahn (2020b). "Modeling an infectious disease from an individual dynamic discrete choice perspective." Mimeo, Johns Hopkins University.

Hongru, D., M. Zahn, S. Loo, T. Alleman, S. Truelove, B. Patenaude, et al. (2024). "Modeling dynamic disease-behavior feedbacks for improved epidemic prediction and response." medRxiv 2024-11.

Hsiang, S., D. Allen, S. Annan-Phan, K. Bell, I. Bolliger, T. Chong, et al. (2020). "The effect of large-scale anti-contagion policies on the COVID-19 pandemic," *Nature*, 584(7820), 262–267.

Ilin, C., S. E. Annan-Phan, X. Hui Tai, S. Mehra, S. M. Hsiang, and J. E. Blumenstock (2020). "Public mobility data enables COVID-19 forecasting and management at local and global scales." NBER Working Paper No. 28120.

Jentsch, P., M. Anand, and C. T. Bauch (2020). "Prioritising COVID-19 vaccination in changing social and epidemiological landscapes." Working Paper 2020.09.i25.20201889, medRxiv.

Joint United Nations Programme on HIV and AIDS (2020). "Fact sheet – World AIDS Day 2020." Global HIV and AIDS Statistics.

Kaiser Family Foundation (2019). "The HIV/AIDS epidemic in the United States: The basics." https://www.kff.org/hivaids/fact-sheet/the-hivaids-epidemic-in-the-united-states-the-basics/.

Kermack, W. O., and A. G. McKendrick (1927). "A contribution to the mathematical theory of epidemics," *Proceedings of the Royal Society of London, Series A*, 115(772), 700–721.

Labgold, K., S. Hamid, S. Shah, N. R. Gandhi, A. Chamberlain, F. Khan, et al. (2021). "Estimating the unknown: Greater racial and ethnic disparities in COVID-19 burden after accounting for missing race and ethnicity data," *Epidemiology*, 32(2), 157–161.

Li, X.-Z., J. Yang, and M. Martcheva (2020). *Age Structured Epidemic Modeling*. Berlin: Springer.

Lighter, J., M. Phillips, S. Hochman, S. Sterling, D. Johnson, F. Francois, and A. Stachel (2020). "Obesity in patients younger than 60 years is a risk factor for COVID-19 hospital admission," *Clinical Infectious Diseases*, 71(15), 896–897.

Lochner, L., and E. Moretti (2004). "The effect of education on crime: Evidence from prison inmates, arrests, and self-reports," *American Economic Review*, 94(1), 155–189.

Machin, S., O. Marie, and S. Vujić (2011). "The crime reducing effect of education," *The Economic Journal*, 121(552), 463–484.

Manfredi, P., and A. D'Onofrio (2013). *Modeling the Interplay Between Human Behavior and the Spread of Infectious Diseases*. Cham: Springer Science and Business Media.

Marcus, J. (2020). "Quarantine fatigue is real." *The Atlantic*. https://www.theatlantic.com/ideas/archive/2020/05/quarantine-fatigue-real-and-shaming-people-wont-help/611482/.

Martcheva, M. (2015). *An Introduction to Mathematical Epidemiology*. Berlin: Springer.

McAdams, D. (2020). "Nash SIR: An economic-epidemiological model of strategic behavior during a viral epidemic," *Covid Economics*, 16, 115–134.

McLaren, J., and S. Wang (2020). "Effects of reduced workplace presence on Covid-19 deaths: An instrumental-variables approach." NBER Working Paper No. 28275.

Murray, E. J. (2020). "Epidemiology's time of need: COVID-19 calls for epidemic-related economics," *Journal of Economic Perspectives*, 34(4), 105–120.

Papageorge, N. W. (2016). "Why medical innovation is valuable: Health, human capital, and the labor market," *Quantitative Economics*, 7(3), 671–725.

Papageorge, N. W., G. C. Pauley, M. Cohen, T. E. Wilson, B. H. Hamilton, and R. A. Pollak (2019). "Health, human capital and domestic violence," *Journal of Human Resources*, 56(4), 997–1030.

Papageorge, N. W., M. V. Zahn, M. Belot, E. van den Broek-Altenburg, S. Choi, J. C. Jamison, and E. Tripodi (2021). "Socio-demographic factors associated with self-protecting behavior during the Covid-19 pandemic," *Journal of Population Economics*, 34(2), 691–738.

Poulson, M., A. Geary, C. Annesi, L. Allee, K. Kenzik, S. Sanchez, et al. (2021). "National disparities in COVID-19 outcomes between black and white Americans," *Journal of the National Medical Association*, 113(2), 125–132.

Ravi, K. (2020). "Ethnic disparities in COVID-19 mortality: Are comorbidities to blame?," *The Lancet*, 396(10243), 22.

Ray, E. L., N. Wattanachit, J. Niemi, A. Hannan Kanji, K. House, E. Y. Cramer, et al. (2020). "Ensemble forecasts of coronavirus disease 2019 (COVID-19) in the U.S." Working Paper 2020.08.19.20177493, medRxiv.

Roosa, K., Y. Lee, R. Luo, A. Kirpich, R. Rothenberg, J. M. Hyman, et al. (2020). "Real-time forecasts of the COVID-19 epidemic in China from February 5th to February 24th, 2020," *Infectious Disease Modelling*, 5, 256–263.

Rozenfeld, Y., J. Beam, H. Maier, W. Haggerson, K. Boudreau, J. Carlson, and R. Medows (2020). "A model of disparities: Risk factors associated with COVID-19 infection," *International Journal for Equity in Health*, 19(1), 1–10.

Serkez, Y. (2020). "The magic number for reducing infections and keeping businesses open," *New York Times*. https://www.nytimes.com/interactive/2020/12/16/opinion/coronavirus-shutdown-strategies.html.

Shaman Group (2014). "Influenza forecast." https://blogs.cuit.columbia.edu/jls106/projects/influenza-forecast/.

Simonov, A., S. K. Sacher, J.-P. H. Dubé, and S. Biswas (2020). "The persuasive effect of Fox News: Non-compliance with social distancing during the Covid-19 pandemic." NBER Working Paper No. 27237.

Smith, A. A., J. Fridling, D. Ibhrahim, and P. S. Porter Jr. (2020). "Identifying patients at greatest risk of mortality due to COVID-19: A New England perspective," *Western Journal of Emergency Medicine*, 21(4), 785.

Smith, J. M., and G. R. Price (1973). "The logic of animal conflict," *Nature*, 246(5427), 15–18.

Taylor, P. D., and L. B. Jonker (1978). "Evolutionary stable strategies and game dynamics," *Mathematical Biosciences*, 40(1–2), 145–156.

Varghese, B., J. E. Maher, T. A. Peterman, B. M. Branson, and R. W. Steketee (2002). "Reducing the risk of sexual HIV transmission: Quantifying the per-act risk for HIV on the basis of choice of partner, sex act, and condom use," *Sexually Transmitted Diseases,* 29(1), 38–43.

White, E. (1991). *States of Desire: Travels in Gay America*. New York: Plume Books.

Wright, A. L., K. Sonin, J. Driscoll, and J. Wilson (2020). "Poverty and economic dislocation reduce compliance with COVID-19 shelter-in-place protocols," *Journal of Economic Behavior & Organization*, 180, 544–554.

Wu, C., X. Chen, Y. Cai, J. Xia, X. Zhou, S. Xu, et al. (2020a). "Risk factors associated with acute respiratory distress syndrome and death in patients with coronavirus disease 2019 pneumonia in Wuhan, China," *Journal of the American Medical Association Internal Medicine*, 180(7), 934–943.

Wu, R., L. Wang, H.-C. Dina Kuo, A. Shannar, R. Peter, P. J. Chou, et al. (2020b). "An update on current therapeutic drugs treating COVID-19," *Current Pharmacology Reports*, 6(3), 56–70.

Yang, J., M. Martcheva, and Y. Chen (2016). "Imitation dynamics of vaccine decision-making behaviours based on the game theory," *Journal of Biological Dynamics*, 10(1), 31–58.

Zhang, R., Y. Li, A. L. Zhang, Y. Wang, and M. J. Molina (2020). "Identifying airborne transmission as the dominant route for the spread of COVID-19," *Proceedings of the National Academy of Sciences*, 117(26), 14857–14863.

Zhu, N., D. Zhang, W. Wang, X. Li, B. Yang, J. Song, et al. (2020). "A novel coronavirus from patients with pneumonia in China, 2019," *New England Journal of Medicine*, 382(8), 727–733.

PART IV

SOCIAL INTERACTIONS AND DEVELOPMENT

CHAPTER 7

Inequality's Economic and Social Roots: The Role of Social Networks and Homophily

Matthew O. Jackson

I discuss economic and social sources of inequality and elaborate on the role of social networks in inequality, economic immobility, and economic inefficiencies. The lens of social networks clarifies how the entanglement of people's information, opportunities, and behaviors with those of their friends and family leads to persistent differences across communities, resulting in inequality in education, employment, income, health, and wealth. The key role of homophily in separating groups within the network is highlighted. A network perspective's policy implications differ substantially from a narrower economic perspective that ignores social structure. I discuss the importance of "policy cocktails" that include aspects aimed at both the economic and social forces driving inequality.

> Look over our vast city, and what do we see? On one side a very few men richer by far than it is good for a man to be, and on the other side a great mass of men and women struggling and worrying and wearying to get a most pitiful living.
>
> Henry George, October 5, 1886

7.1 INTRODUCTION

Given how pervasive and persistent inequality is – across places, demographics, and time – we should expect it to be driven by many forces, both independently and in concert.

For example, the economics literature has detailed how several different economic forces lead to inequality: excess returns to capital, monopoly rents, market imperfections that limit people's ability to acquire human capital, as well as various forms of discrimination.[1] Similarly, there are many writings

I gratefully acknowledge financial support under NSF grant SES-2018554, thank Eliana La Ferrara for organizing the session, and thank Raj Chetty, Ben Golub, Mark Granovetter, Nathan Hendren, Willemien Kets, Scott Page, Anirudh Sankar, and Johannes Stroebel for helpful comments and suggestions.

[1] For some background, see Atkinson (1975, 2015), Bourguignon and Morrisson (2002), Bowles and Gintis (2002), Heathcote et al. (2010), Banerjee and Duflo (2011), Benhabib et al. (2011),

on the sociology and psychology of inequality, including factors such as social stratification, institutional and geographic segregation, group competition, racism and sexism, and cultural hegemony.[2] Even altogether, these factors miss an important perspective on inequality and key causes for many people. These causes trace to the interplay between social structures and economic behaviors, such as how homophily in social networks constrains economic behaviors in labor markets, education, and other investments.

The purpose of this chapter is to provide a high-level overview of the many factors – both economic and social – driving inequality and how they fit together; and to highlight the interaction of social structure with economic behaviors. Taking this wider perspective – accounting for the interaction between social structure and economic opportunities and behaviors – provides a richer understanding of how and when inequality can be systematically addressed by policies, and how policies can be better structured to take advantage of that interaction.

Humans are a heavily social species. Social structure has enabled us to specialize and advance far beyond what any one of us can produce (Henrich, 2015), but with that also comes a heavy dependence upon others. We are dependent upon our social networks[3] for information, opportunities, and norms of behavior. These dependencies tie people's fates to the fates of their friends, families, and acquaintances.

Understanding when and why this dependency leads to inequality and immobility involves recognizing that these interdependencies occur in networks that are strongly divided. Such divides reflect the prevalence of homophily: people's tendencies to associate with others of similar demographics and backgrounds. Given that people depend on their networks for information and opportunities, divisions in a network lead information and opportunities to stay concentrated within parts of society and not reach other parts. For example, if none of a person's friends are employed in a given industry and job interviews come via referrals inside that industry, then that person is effectively shut out of the industry. The strong divisions and homophily that characterize social networks imply that different parts of a network can have very different information, access, and cultures. This provides a foundation for persistent inequality, and operates through many channels including employment, but also education and other investments.

Heckman and Mosso (2014), Alvaredo et al. (2018), Benhabib and Bisin (2018), Smith et al. (2019), Chetty and Jackson (2025). Many additional references on specific topics appear below.

2 See McCall (2001), Hurst et al. (2016), Huggins and Thompson (2021), Roberts and Rizzo (2020) for some background and references.

3 Throughout what follows, I use the term "social network" broadly to encompass a person's friends, neighbors, acquaintances, colleagues, and peers, and not to refer to a social media platform.

Here, I first provide an overview of key economic[4] drivers of inequality – concentration of wealth and capital and increasing returns to investments, imperfect competition and rents to monopolies, frictions in borrowing and constraints in development of human capital, other forms of poverty traps, and discrimination. The first two of these help explain some aspects of wealth inequality, while the others provide insights into other forms of inequality, including in education, employment, and wages. Developing a fuller understanding of inequalities, especially in these latter three areas, requires adding social structures to help see how networks drive and sustain differences in education, employment, and wages. Roughly, the economic drivers focus on financial and other resources, how those multiply, and how a lack of them results in lower investments and poorer outcomes. Divides in social networks lead to three additional forces behind inequality: unequal access to jobs and other opportunities, unequal distributions of awareness of opportunities and information about how to take advantage of them, and differences in norms and cultures.[5] The fact that homophily in networks ties younger cohorts of a community to older cohorts leads inequality to reproduce itself across generations, with the same groups being disadvantaged over time. That provides key insights behind the tight relationship between inequality and its persistence: immobility.

This perspective on social networks provides a social capital complement to the usual financial and human capital inheritance stories. Including both is vital since, for instance, in Chetty et al. (2022a) we find that two-thirds of differences in upward economic mobility across communities can be predicted by differences in a measure of social capital that captures how little homophily there is by socioeconomic status. The results are robust to controlling for standard explanatory variables measuring education, income, ethnic composition, and household structure. The structure of social networks plays a starring role in predicting mobility and inequality, and a very different role from financial capital and family.

The importance of distinguishing the variety of forces behind inequality becomes most evident when we turn to the discussion of policies for overcoming inequality. Some economic drivers can be addressed by redistribution, regulation, and subsidies. However, those policies do not eliminate the social drivers and hence can leave long-term inequality and economic immobility

[4] Here I artificially refer to "economic" as drivers that do not include any social structure other than family, inheritance, or broad forms of discrimination; and in which network structures are not considered.

[5] Coleman (1988) discusses three forms of social capital that are important in the development of human capital. There is some parallel between two of the three types of interactions here, and two of Coleman's three types of social capital. Inequality in network positions can be thought of as forms of inequality in social capital. Jackson (2020) offers more background and references on social capital and how networks relate to various forms of it. Here the focus is instead on how homophily in networks affects three types of interactions and how those drive inequality.

largely unaffected. Resources spent in such ways can end up dissipating, with short-term alleviation of symptoms but little long-term impact. Social factors and unequal distribution of social capital require policies that overcome informational frictions and divides in networks, and take advantage of the feedback effects and social multipliers inherent in networks. These include mentorships, internships, affirmative action, and subsidizing education. Lessons from network formation and homophily also suggest important ways in which the structuring of schools and other institutions can be better designed to lower homophily and improve the reach of people's networks.

Key roles of social networks as a driver of inequality are discussed in an excellent antecedent to this paper by DiMaggio and Garip (2012) (see also Small, 2009, DiMaggio and Garip, 2011, as well as the afterward of the second edition of Granovetter, 1995). My focus is broader on some dimensions, including discussion of economic drivers of inequality, and more extensive on other dimensions, including discussion of the relationships between homophily, inequality, immobility, and productive inefficiencies. I also discuss the different policy implications of the variety of forces underlying inequality.

7.2 BACKGROUND

Before proceeding to discuss the drivers of inequality, it is useful to briefly discuss a few key facts about inequality, as well as why we care about it.

7.2.1 Why Inequality Matters

Discussing why we care about inequality helps focus our attention and frame a discussion of which policy interventions can be justified when. The voluminous literature on the philosophy of inequality and welfare would take us on a tangent here, but it is worth mentioning a few key points.

Given how resilient and widespread inequality is, it has been a central subject of many studies in political philosophy, sociology, and economics over the decades. The roots of modern thinking trace to prominent contributions including those by Jean-Jacques Rousseau (1754, 1762), Freidrich Engels (1845), John Stuart Mill (1859a, 1869),[6] Karl Marx (1867), Henry George (1879), Max Weber (1921), John Rawls (1971), James Coleman (1974), Anthony Atkinson (1975), and Amartya Sen (1992).[7]

[6] Ironically, although "The Subjection of Women" was published with John Stuart Mill as sole author, he acknowledged that some of the text was inspired by writings and ideas of his stepdaughter Helen Taylor and that much of his writing on the subject was influenced by extensive discussions with his wife Harriet Taylor Mill. He also stated that his collaboration with his wife was extensive in the writing of "On Liberty."

[7] There are also a variety of influential works on specific forms of oppression and inequality, such as key feminist writings (e.g., Mary Wollstonecraft, 1792), and a long string of prominent abolitionist writings including those by James Ramsay, Harriet Beecher Stowe, and Frederick

At its core, concerns about inequality are often based on some notion of fairness, as well as what we might refer to as social insurance. People can end up in disadvantageous circumstances (for reasons beyond their volition),[8] and should not suffer from those disadvantages. One of the most powerful tools in framing this perspective was articulated by Rawls (1971) and is a hypothetical exercise where one imagines that one could have been born into any position of a human in the world. As Rawls states, "Among the essential features of this situation is that no one knows his place in society, his class position or social status, nor does any one know his fortune in the distribution of natural assets and abilities, his intelligence, strength, and the like... The principles of justice are chosen behind a veil of ignorance."

One way to use the veil of ignorance to address inequality is to ask what policies we would like to implement to make the world the best possible, if we consider that we could have ended up in any position in society. However, while Rawls's hypothetical frames the discussion nicely in terms of endowments of natural characteristics, as well as the economic and social capital that one is born into, it can still lead to a wide variety of views on what fairness means and how one should evaluate various policies. One possibility is to view our position as a chance phenomenon, and say that we could equally likely have been anyone in the world (or even in future generations), and then ask what policies maximize the overall average welfare of society. This is the perspective of utilitarians (e.g., Bentham, 1789; Mill, 1859b; Harsanyi, 1977), who weight the relative utilities or enjoyment of the benefits of different outcomes across a population. Interestingly, instead of looking at the outcomes for all positions as a utilitarian would, Rawls instead argued for concentrating on the welfare of the worst positions. I won't venture into that debate here,[9] but regardless of how one evaluates welfare from thinking behind the veil of ignorance, it provides a justification for comparing the circumstances of different individuals and the consequences of those circumstances.

Most fundamentally, the veil of ignorance gives us a reason for a form of social insurance. If the circumstances of one's birth substantially limit the opportunities and outcomes that an individual can expect, it is too late for the individual to be able to insure against those circumstances. There are many things that can lead to unequal outcomes. For instance, some families have their house burn down and their possessions destroyed, while others do not. This is something that people can privately insure against. In contrast, being born into poverty and ending up with poor childhood health and education is not something that a person has a chance to buy private insurance against. By most any definition of fairness operating behind the veil of ignorance, a society has a moral obligation to address those circumstances that disadvantage an

Douglass; not to mention various discussions of religious and ethnic oppression throughout history.

8 Unpacking the extent to which people are responsible for their outcomes is an important subtheme in this literature, but it is clear that much of immobility is not self-imposed.

9 See Barberà and Jackson (1988) for axioms that characterize Rawls's approach.

individual from birth. The individual cannot insure against the event, but society can. It requires society to do two things: one is to compensate people for the outcomes that are beyond their control, but the other is to ensure opportunities are more evenly available to people regardless of the position into which they are born.[10]

Orthogonal to the moral underpinnings of fairness and social insurance, there are also basic economic reasons for caring about missing opportunities and frictions in a society. Missed opportunities lead to a loss of production, which leads to a smaller overall pie. Society loses when people's talents are under-utilized or mis-matched with their profession and other positions in society. These losses can compound over time, leading to lower growth (Persson and Tabellini, 1994).[11] At a most basic level, inequality can lead to differences in health outcomes and stress (Adler and Newman, 2002). Ill health for an individual, especially when it begins in childhood, compounds itself over time and is costly for society, both in the lost production and the resources used in the care for that individual. Inequality can also manifest itself in things like differences in group participation and social capital (Alesina and La Ferrara, 2000; La Ferrara, 2002), which also have productive consequences. Inequality can also cause political frictions, leading to less effective government, and also cause a society to focus on redistribution instead of investment (e.g., Voorheis et al., 2015).

7.2.2 Inequality and Immobility

As is clear from Henry George's quote above, systemic inequality has been endemic for centuries. In fact, we see it going back millennia and across most societies – for instance, in the contrast between the more than one hundred kilograms of gold that plated King Tutankhamun's innermost coffin and the plain graves of the workers who built his tomb. Lui Jin, a key courtesan during the Ming Dynasty, died with hundreds of thousands of kilograms of gold, while much of his society's booming population had no property or savings at all. Nicolas Fouquet's stunning Château de Vaux-le-Vicomte earned the envy and ire of Louis XIV and inspired the Château de Versailles, at the same time that repeated famines ravaged France. John D. Rockefeller's ruthless monopoly

[10] The details of what this entails are something that I will not delve into here, but of course they are very important. Allowing people to access a highly productive life rather than just one that passes a minimum standard of subsistence can be a difference between changing opportunities and providing some ex-post redistribution. How does one account for things like free will and dignity? Which outcomes and situations are ones that should be the concern of a society? How much should it depend on choices and liberties afforded to the individuals? Various forms of diversity can be at odds with some notions of equality and liberty. These are the subject of important further discussions, such as that of Sen (1992).

[11] For additional discussion see, for instance, Benabou (1996b) and Stiglitz (2012). The relationship between inequality and productivity is challenging to identify (Barro, 2000), but recent data offers increasing evidence for the relationship and potential channels (e.g., Berg et al., 2018; Aiyar and Ebeke, 2020).

amassed more than a billion dollars when the per capita income in the United States was on the order of a hundred dollars a year.

As systematic data have become more available over recent decades, we have increasingly sharp and broad measures of the extent and dynamics of inequality and economic immobility,[12] as well as their prevalence across societies and geography.[13]

Regardless of short and medium-term trends and changes, inequality is a persistent phenomenon, and its spatial and demographic correlation patterns indicate that it is not just a chance phenomenon (Chetty et al., 2014; Corak, 2016). From our perspective, a particularly important piece of the puzzle is that inequality is closely related to economic immobility: we can predict which people from the next generation will be most likely to end up at the bottom of the income distribution. This is particularly problematic when viewed from the perspective of Rawls's veil of ignorance.

The relationship between inequality and economic immobility was crystallized by Alan Krueger in a speech in 2012 in which he depicted the "Great Gatsby Curve," built on the work of Miles Corak.[14] The observed fact is that countries with higher inequality also tend to have higher economic immobility. An updated version of the Great Gatsby Curve appears in Figure 7.1,[15] and it depicts the relationship between inequality – as measured by an income Gini coefficient – versus economic immobility – as measured by intergenerational earnings elasticity (the coefficient of a regression of log child's earnings on log parents' earnings).

The correlation is observational, but growing evidence shows that there are causal aspects to it (e.g., see Section 7.5.2.2). Most importantly from our perspective here, the concepts behind the Great Gatsby Curve help in guiding theory and policy. People born into poor circumstances are disadvantaged in terms of their networks (social capital), as well as the financial and human capital of their families, and this can lead them to end up with worse information and opportunities, which translate into worse outcomes.[16] The perpetuation

[12] For instance, see Bourguignon and Morrisson (2002), Bowles and Gintis (2002), Atkinson et al. (2011), Piketty (2014), Corak (2016), Saez and Zucman (2016), Hubmer et al. (2020). Such measures continue to evolve as reliable data for parts of the world are still difficult to obtain, but there are new methods of inference (e.g., Mirza et al., 2021).

[13] See, for example, Charles and Grusky (2005), Bowles et al. (2010b), Corak (2013), Atkinson and Morelli (2014), Chetty et al. (2014), Alfani (2021).

[14] See Corak (2013, 2016) for more background, and Andrews and Leigh (2009) for related observations.

[15] Some data are from Corak (2016), supplemented with data from the CIA World Factbook, Borisov and Pissarides (2016), and Kim (2017). I have reversed the axes from the original. This reversal conceptualizes immobility as the base force, and (recurrent) inequality as a result of it.

[16] For some measurements of the intergenerational persistence of human capital, see Adermon et al. (2021).

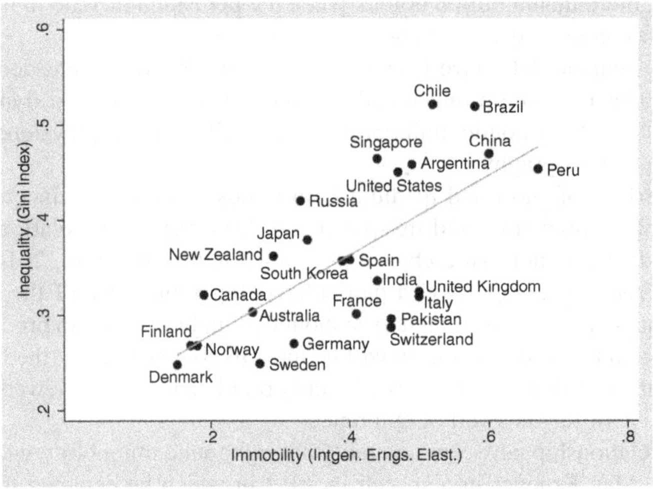

Figure 7.1 The Great Gatsby Curve: Inequality (income Gini coefficient) plotted against economic immobility (intergenerational earnings elasticity).

appears as immobility, and the disparities across communities manifest as inequality, but they are both features of the same phenomenon.[17]

7.2.3 Homophily

As homophily plays a starring role in the discussion of the social shaping of inequality, I give a brief description of the important aspects of it for our inequality discussion and refer the reader to McPherson et al. (2001) and Jackson (2019a) for more detailed background and references.

Homophily is a relatively modern term, coined by Lazarsfeld and Merton (1954), for the long-standing phenomenon of people associating with others who are similar to themselves. To give an idea of its extent, consider an early empirical study by Verbrugge (1977). She found substantial homophily on all the characteristics in her data, including age, years of schooling, profession, religion, marital status, and employment status. In particular, she examined 240 different categories and examined odds ratios of whether people named other people with the same characteristic as their closest friends. As an example, she compared the frequency with which Catholics named a Catholic as their closest friend to the frequency with which non-Catholics named Catholics as their closest friend. A ratio of 1 corresponds to no homophily. She found

[17] This relationship comes out of a variety of forces. For instance, Loury (1981) and Durlauf and Seshadri (2018) discuss how it can come out of investments in education across generations, and Benabou (1993, 1996a) and Chetty and Jackson (2025) show how it can depend on neighborhood choice. Bolte et al. (2025) show how it comes from a model of homophily and job referrals (more on this in Section 7.4). These generally involve some social aspect: family and community effects.

that the odds ratio for the category Catholic was 6.3 in Detroit and 6.8 in Alt Neustadt. All of the 240 categories she examined had odds ratios above 1, and 225 of the 240 odds ratios were statistically significantly above 1 – with odds ratios between 2.2 and 81. Indeed, this study is just one example, and it is difficult to find dimensions on which human networks are not homophilous. Homophily even extends to personality characteristics.[18] Obviously, many dimensions are correlated, but the important fact for understanding the impact of homophily is that it leads to networks in which groups can be relatively isolated from each other socially, even when they are in close proximity.

It is worth emphasizing that homophily exists for many reasons, and these become policy relevant as we discuss in Section 7.5.[19] In order to better understand the reasons for homophily and policies that can help mitigate it and its impact, it is useful to decompose homophily into two parts. One is that homophily is driven by exposure and contact patterns (Allport, 1954). It is easier to form and maintain friendships with people who are physically or virtually close by. For instance, students of the same age are grouped in schools together and sometimes even placed in tracks based on their prior achievements, people with similar education levels work together, and people of the same religion attend services together. Housing prices often vary by the amenities and location of neighborhoods, which can then segregate people by income. Thus, exposure is a primary driver of homophily, given people's heavy tendency to interact with those whom they are around – and given that people are often partitioned in physical and virtual spaces according to their characteristics and interests,[20] this leads to substantial homophily. The other part of homophily is people making choices about whom they interact with, even conditional on exposure. That is, in a room of people with diverse backgrounds, they will often gravitate towards those with shared backgrounds and interests. People find it easier to interact with people with whom they share a common background, as they share history, expectations, and norms of behavior. Sharing a background also correlates the challenges people face and what they can learn from each other.[21] New parents of a certain income and education level share very similar challenges in raising their children. Thus, homophily ends up being driven not only by the ways in which people are separated into communities within a society, but also people's tendencies to choose similarity even when faced with diverse choices.[22] This distinction between exposure and

[18] See Morelli et al. (2017) and Jackson et al. (2022).

[19] See Jackson (2019a) for a more extensive overview and Currarini et al. (2009, 2010) and Chetty et al. (2022a,b) for some empirical background.

[20] There are many reasons for such separations that I won't detail here, but see Jackson (2019a) for more background and discussion.

[21] See Lobel and Sadler (2016) and Aybas and Jackson (2024) for models of the tradeoff between shared preferences versus more diverse information sources.

[22] See Currarini et al. (2009, 2010) and Chetty et al. (2022b) for analyses that examine such decompositions empirically. Both appear to be substantial, although it is not always easy to distinguish the two from observational data, as some aspects of exposure patterns are not observed

choices conditional upon exposure is important not only because informed policy decisions depend on what drove the networks to form the way they did, but also because these different reasons have different consequences, as discussed in Section 7.5.

7.3 ECONOMIC SOURCES OF INEQUALITY

Now I turn to discussing some of the sources of inequality, beginning with some of the most prominent economic ones.

7.3.1 Unequal Returns to the Factors of Production

A basic economic source of inequality is unequal returns to the factors of production. This can come in a variety of forms. As made popular by the studies of Piketty (2014), for instance, a greater return to capital compared to the growth of the rest of the economy ("$r > g$") can lead those holding capital to have their wealth grow more rapidly than the rest of society. The importance of capital and its potential role in inequality has roots in the writings of Marx (1867) and the literature that followed, but is examined from a different perspective by Piketty.

Piketty's approach echoes the theory that Henry George presented in his book *Progress and Poverty* (1879), which was one of the most widely sold books in the world up to the end of the nineteenth century. It also concerns the idea that inequality can be driven by certain factors of production earning higher returns than others. However, instead of capital, George's focus was on rent: the returns to owning land. He noted that people owning land earned much more from its cultivation than the people who worked the land. George works at explaining *why* one should expect a disparity. In particular, he asks (George, 1879, chapter 11), "To say that wages remain low because rent advances is like saying that a steam-boat moves because its wheels turn round. The further question is, what causes rent to advance? What is the force or necessity that, as productive power increases, distributes a greater and greater proportion of the produce as rent?" The answer that George gives stems from imperfect competition. He states (chapter 14), "That as land is necessary to the exertion of labour in the production of wealth, to command the land that is necessary to labour is to command all the fruits of labour save enough to enable labour to exist." And later, "Material progress cannot rid us of our dependence upon land; it can but add to the power of producing wealth from land; and hence, when land is monopolized, it might go on to infinity without increasing wages or improving the condition of those who have but their labour."

and are partly endogenous. People make choices that change the sets of people with whom they interact: for instance, if someone goes to a university that has people who are mostly similar to themselves, is that part of exposure or was that a deliberate choice as they wanted to have that exposure?

A caricature of George's argument is that labor is supplied competitively, earning its subsistence value, while land is monopolized and earns the entire remaining value of the fruits of production.

Piketty's core argument has a similar structure to George's (1879) core argument, substituting returns to capital for the rents earned from land. Piketty (2014) also provides some other scenarios under which returns to capital could exceed returns to labor, as well as a detailed look at the accounting of inequality and a number of perspectives on its incidence, dynamics, and implications for taxation.[23]

Over time, one can see a progression in which forms of capital are most vital and monopolizable. As agriculture became a shrinking part of the economy, more of the returns moved to the financial capital and control of means of industrial production (e.g., the oil and railroad barons of the nineteenth centuries). More recently, growth has moved increasingly to service industries, which rely less on financial capital but can still hold enormous economies of scope and scale.[24] For example, substantial growth in modern monopolies has come from social media, where the more users and content a given site has, the more attractive it becomes. The profits to such monopolies have been enormous and very concentrated. For instance, as Atkeson and Irie (2020) show, one can explain much of the large amount of wealth concentrated at the very top of the distribution, simply by accounting for families that make undiversified investments in businesses that happen to become very large and profitable.[25] Thus, some random chance, coupled with undiversified investments and extreme returns to some enterprises, can also lead to a large concentration of wealth at the top of the distribution, without any special returns to capital on average. More generally, how the fruits of production are shared depends on property rights, regulation, and a variety of cultural norms (e.g., see Borgerhoff-Mulder et al., 2009; Bowles et al., 2010a).

Nonetheless, as Piketty (2014) acknowledges (see also Piketty, 2015), much of the recent growth in inequality is in income. This can partly be tied to increased returns to education. Thus, while excess returns to land, capital, and monopolies can be important drivers of wealth inequality, they leave much unexplained about the large amount of income inequality that still exists even when we completely ignore the wealthiest few percent of the population.

Let us next turn to some economic explanations for the sizeable inequality in employment and earnings that we see across the world and within many countries. This inequality is substantial even when we ignore the highly

[23] For a variety of comments and debate surrounding Piketty's argument, evidence, and conclusions, see Krugman (2014), Acemoglu and Robinson (2015), Jones (2015), Mankiw (2015), and Piketty (2015).

[24] There are also effects of globalization on inequality, as discussed, for instance, by Krugman and Venables (1995).

[25] For more background on churn among the very wealthy, see Gomez (2021). The level of wealth that one has upon inheritance can also affect how wealth accumulates or is depleted across generations, as found in Nekoei and Seim (2019).

wealthy; and includes the gap between outcomes for those with post-secondary education and those without. It is a type of inequality that social factors have the most to say about.

7.3.2 Frictions in Human Capital and Other Poverty Traps

The ratio of the wages of those having a college degree compared to just a high school degree or less has more than doubled in the last half-century.[26] Again, a short caricature is that technological advances are making high-skilled labor more productive, while those same advances are replacing low-skilled labor. That is, technology in the form of improved computing power, communication, and automation has been complementary to high-skilled labor while substituting for low-skilled labor.

This is not just a modern phenomenon: it happened also during the Industrial Revolution when agricultural labor was increasingly displaced and returns to skills in manufacturing grew. It happened again a century later when labor was displaced in manufacturing in many industrialized countries and shifted to services. The natural adjustment of this should be that more people invest in education making them better suited for the new productive opportunities. In the current setting, this would drive up the supply of people with high levels of education and drive down the supply of relatively uneducated labor, bringing wages back into balance (adjusting for the costs of education).[27]

There are many frictions here. Some are geographic, as taking advantage of new opportunities can require uprooting, which is both risky and costly – leading people with fewer resources to stay behind (e.g., see Connor and Storper, 2020). Some reflect the slow growth in availability of the supply of education needed. For instance, access to higher education has been slow and in fact stagnant in many countries.[28] Some reflect the barriers to the necessary investment among poor families, and other related inheritance issues (e.g., see Benhabib et al., 2011; Bowles and Gintis, 2002; Fagereng et al., 2018; Herbst and Hendren, 2021; Sacerdote, 2007). As education is cumulative, differences

[26] See the background and references in Jackson (2019a) and Autor et al. (2020). The wage gap is also mirrored by a growing longevity gap, as found by Case and Deaton (2021).

[27] See Tinbergen (1975) for a classic discussion of this, and Goldin and Katz (2009) for a more detailed discussion of the relative rates of technological change and education advancements. See also the empirical analysis and theory of Kuznets (1955), who posited that growth and changes in production could lead to increased inequality as capitalists profit from expanding industries, while competitive wages and some moving frictions lead to falling wages in areas left behind and slow wage growth in the new industries. He also predicted an eventual decline in inequality once the period of change subsided. Evidence for this Kuznets curve is mixed (e.g., see Alfani, 2021).

[28] For example, see the statistics on investments in education and amount of higher education from the US National Center for Educational Statistics. In contrast, since the 1990s higher education has been growing rapidly in China – although still not at a fast enough rate to compensate for the rapidly increasing demand for qualified graduates.

in parents' resources, opportunity costs, and approaches to educating their children at early ages, as well as available public resources, can be constraining (e.g., Bowles, 1972; Falk et al., 2021; Lareau, 2011).[29]

This can be seen as an example of a more general form of poverty trap (e.g., see Carter and Barrett, 2006), where a lack of resources leads to underinvestment and low returns, which leads to a lack of resources. Effectively there are increasing returns to investment, and without minimal investment, one cannot get out of poverty. Such vicious cycles reflect difficulties in borrowing, especially given the lack of collateral and the moral hazard and adverse selection issues associated with such lending; not to mention the early ages at which such investments are often most effective (e.g., see Loury, 1981). There are related poverty traps in health, as poor nourishment and health leads to lower productivity and prolonged poverty, which then lead to lower nourishment and health. These sorts of poverty traps, and lack of adjustments to shifting technologies and economies, also have important social network/social capital aspects to them: adjusting takes both the knowledge of how to adjust, as well as the opportunities to do so, as discussed more in Section 7.4.

7.3.3 Discrimination and Statistical Discrimination

Another long-standing source of inequality, and one that appears in many forms, is discrimination. An advantaged group favors its own members and discriminates against another group's members, such as according to ethnicity, social class, religion, gender, caste, language, and other characteristics. It has been wide-ranging across millennia and cultures, and has manifested itself in the forms of slavery, caste systems, clan systems, racism, segregation, sexism, stereotyping, and in the many ways in which some groups are favored in access to education, jobs, and political positions. There is extensive evidence of discrimination showing that not only is it widespread, but also that its impact can be large.[30]

Researchers have distinguished between two forms of discrimination: one is a direct culturally driven discrimination in its many sociological forms, and is sometimes referred to as "taste-based" (Becker, 1957; Pager and Shepherd, 2008); the other is often referred to as "statistical discrimination" (Arrow, 1971; Phelps, 1972). A prominent theory for culturally driven discrimination is due to Weber (1921): a group socially closes itself in order to gain or maintain exclusive access to scarce resources. It can use various identifiable characteristics to distinguish itself, and hence to discriminate against outsiders. In

[29] See also Durlauf (1996) who embeds such an education poverty trap within a model in which families choose neighborhoods in which to reside. Wealthier families choose to live in neighborhoods that are not affordable to poorer families, for the greater financing of education as well as the peer dependence on educational attainment.

[30] For example, see Newman (1978), Fix et al. (1993), Fershtman and Gneezy (2001), Bertrand and Duflo (2017), Hangartner et al. (2021), and Huber et al. (2021).

contrast, under statistical discrimination, people distinguish others based on expectations that they will have lower human capital and productivity. That expectation makes it more difficult for the discriminated group to get good employment. Given the worse employment, members of that group then have less of an incentive to invest in becoming productive and so the group ends up being less productive, which confirms the expectation. Statistical discrimination can be seen as another form of poverty trap, and a particularly pernicious one, since the group that is being discriminated against cannot escape even if they are given the resources to invest in developing their human capital, as they are still stereotyped as being less productive. These two forms of discrimination are not necessarily mutually exclusive, since group competition can lead a group to exclude out-group members, which leads them to invest less, which then makes the discrimination statistically self-fulfilling.[31]

7.4 SOCIAL DRIVERS

As mentioned above, inequality has been a central topic of the sociology literature, including major theories of social stratification and class distinctions, discrimination, and collectivism (groups having priority over individuals), among others. Rather than attempt to survey that enormous literature, I take a narrow focus that is more micro-oriented and operational, and examines the interplay between social networks and economic behaviors. Many of these basic sociological forces end up driving inequality through the divisions in social networks that they induce, and thus much of the policy discussion in Section 7.5 still directly, or indirectly, addresses those social forces.

I focus on three main ways that people's friends and acquaintances impact their behaviors and outcomes, and result in inequality and immobility. I take each in turn.

7.4.1 Unequal Job Opportunities via Social Connections

The pervasive use of referrals and connections in obtaining jobs has been extensively documented.[32] The data from such studies show that connections are a primary channel through which people obtain jobs across almost all professions and education levels, and across countries and cultures.

There are several reasons for which jobs are often filled via connections rather than open applications or other means. One is that there is a lot of uncertainty about how an applicant will actually perform in a new job. Are they

[31] For more background and more discussion of the relationship and distinctions between these two forms of discrimination, and what evidence there is for each, see Arrow (1998), Lang and Lehmann (2012), and Bohren et al. (2019).

[32] For example, see Myers and Shultz (1951), Rees (1966), Rees and Shultz (1970), Granovetter (1973, 1995), Montgomery (1991), Ioannides and Datcher-Loury (2004), Topa (2011), Rubineau and Fernandez (2013), and Zeltzer (2020).

sufficiently skilled? Will they work well with others? Will they be responsible and productive? Will they stay for a long time? Interviews and resumés provide very imperfect answers to these questions. References and referrals provide much more insight (e.g., see Bewley, 1999). Most importantly, current employees and people well connected to a company know what a particular job entails, and they are best suited to find good matches for an open job. For example, many applicants may have some background in coding a certain software and be literate enough to pass an interview, but the applicant might still not have the skill to perform a project that the employer has in mind. This is something that someone who is involved in the project or knows it well, and has either worked with this person or overseen that person, would know. Thus, the personal connection becomes very useful. Indeed, there is ample evidence that people hired via referrals are more productive, creative, and stay longer in their positions than people hired without referrals.[33]

A second reason for using referrals is that employers often wish to find people similar to the best of their current employees (e.g., see Fernandez et al., 2000). These employees have the right background for the position, and fit well with the time demands, and have not quit. It can be hard to find similar people from looking at applications, whereas by using the social network an employer can actually take advantage of homophily. The demands of the job might not have anything to do with skill levels, but more basic things like not stealing from the company, being willing to work long hours, or travel extensively, or work strange shifts, or be available for extra work at short notice, and so on. By hiring via the network they are more likely to hire someone who is very similar to their current employees who have these characteristics. This might not diversify their workforce, but often an employer's priority is finding someone who can do the job and will not quit too soon.

A third reason is that friendships with other workers can directly affect the performance of employees as well as their turnover – having friends within an organization can lead a person to perform better and stay longer (e.g., Brown et al., 2012; Fernandez et al., 2000; Fiorillo and Nappo, 2014). On the flip side of this are forms of nepotism and favoritism, which can have negative effects (Bramoullé and Goyal, 2016; Ponzo and Scoppa, 2010), but those depend on the level of homophily (Horváth, 2014).

Regardless of the reason, when coupled with homophily, the reliance on referrals leads to feedback effects and can be a basic force behind inequality in both employment and wages. If one group has higher employment than another group, in some industry or just in general, then due to homophily the first group's members can expect to receive more referrals than the other group's members, on average. Getting more referrals leads to a higher chance of being employed, as well as being matched most productively. The intuition behind

[33] For example, see Fernandez et al. (2000), Brown et al. (2012), Fernandez and Galperin (2014), Burks et al. (2015), Dustmann et al. (2016), Pallais and Sands (2016), Benson et al. (2019), and Bond and Fernandez (2019).

this is straightforward: taking the best option out of a set gets better when that set is larger. Having more options also improves a person's bargaining power, leading to higher expected wages and promotions. For instance, as discussed by Arrow and Borzekowski (2004) and Okafor (2020), relatively small differences in the number of referrals different groups have access to can explain a substantial amount of the differences in wages by race.[34] In addition, there is also a further feedback in that employment helps build more contacts, further enriching a person's network and opportunities (e.g., see Granovetter, 1988).[35]

Referrals via people's networks also end up correlating the employment and wages among friends, as analyzed by Calvo-Armengol and Jackson (2004, 2007). Having more employed friends leads a person to have a greater chance of getting referrals, and multiple referrals.[36] There is substantial (causal) evidence for this correlating effect of referrals in a variety of settings.[37]

Moreover, since higher current employment of the members of some group leads to higher employment for that group's next generation, this also correlates employment and wages across generations, as analyzed by Calvo-Armengol and Jackson (2009), Bolte et al. (2025), and Buhai and van der Leij (2020). Thus, the combination of homophily and heavy use of referrals in employment can lead to immobility and provides an understanding for the strong relationship between inequality and immobility.

In addition, the resulting inequality and immobility also have productivity implications. The fact that people with poor connections have fewer chances to find jobs, and those with more connections can get multiple offers, means that the chances for people to be matched to an employer is unevenly spread around the population (Bolte et al., 2025). In general, if the value of an additional referral to a person in terms of matching that person to the most productive employment is diminishing in the number of referrals that the person already has, then maximizing a society's productivity involves spreading the referrals as evenly as possible throughout the population. Instead, homophily leads referrals to be unevenly spread, and more heavily concentrated among groups that are already well employed. Moreover, this can even further concentrate

[34] People's positions in their networks affect their bargaining power and who they are neighbors with more generally, and can lead to quite unequal outcomes when there are strong asymmetries in position, as discussed by Kets et al. (2011) and Cheng and Xing (2021).

[35] Homophily can also affect the contacts that one has within a firm or other organization, which can affect one's chances for retention and promotion (e.g., see Opper et al., 2015). It can also affect one's cultural fit within an organization (Stephens et al., 2014), which is known to affect hiring (Rivera, 2012) but can also matter afterwards.

[36] Employment over time can also affect the accumulation of friendships, which can have a further feedback effect (e.g., see Avin et al., 2015).

[37] For example, see Sacerdote (2001), Munshi (2003), Beaman (2012), Patacchini and Zenou (2012), Laschever (2013), Clauset et al. (2015), Lalanne and Seabright (2016), and Beaman et al. (2018). The wage effects are more subtle than employment effects, and may depend on details of the setting and the numbers of connections. For instance, the analysis of Arrow and Borzekowski (2004) suggests that wages are concave in the number of connections, which is seen empirically by Berardi et al. (2019).

the referrals, as they end up passed along to the relatively few unemployed among the advantaged group rather than to the relatively larger group of unemployed among the disadvantaged group. Thus, the combination of homophily and referrals not only has inequality and immobility implications, but also average and total productivity implications. Spreading referrals more evenly throughout a population increases both the average level of productivity of those who are employed, and can increase the total amount of employment in the economy.

The combination of homophily and referrals can also distort investment incentives and result in a form of poverty trap. For instance, a person who has, or expects to have, few employed friends has a low incentive to invest in acquiring skills to take advantage of employment opportunities.[38] This is not only a question of being employed or not, but extends to many forms of investments in skills. For instance, someone who never expects to rise to a management position has a low incentive to invest in acquiring the skills to become a manager. This can also affect the expectations of employers, who then do not expect members of some groups to have the backgrounds needed for some positions – which can play back into a form of statistical discrimination.

7.4.2 Unequal Access to Valuable Information

Job opportunities are just one form of information that flows through networks. People also learn about many other things from friends, acquaintances, and various media. This affects a broad set of behaviors, including everything from adoption of a fertilizer or new crop (e.g., Bandiera and Rasul, 2006; Conley and Udry, 2010) to participation in a microfinance program (e.g., Banerjee et al., 2013), a vaccination program (e.g., Banerjee et al., 2019), or a tax-deferred retirement program (e.g., Duflo and Saez, 2003) to teen pregnancy (Kearney and Levine, 2015) and education decisions (e.g., Sacerdote, 2011). Having networks that provide good information can be extremely important in determining people's lifetime health and well-being trajectories and outcomes (e.g., Bourdieu, 1986; Loury, 1977, 2009).

One might imagine that technological advances might overcome unequal access to various forms of information. However, the information that people have and the opinions they form are heavily dependent upon their social networks, even in a social media-rich world. A powerful example of this comes from Bakshy et al. (2015), which shows that exposure of people to cross-cutting political content is lowered not only by the homophily in their networks, but also by what is fed to them via a platform, and additionally by

[38] For example, see Calvo-Armengol and Jackson (2004), Jackson (2007), Bowles et al. (2014), Bolte et al. (2025), and Buhai and van der Leij (2020). It also affects network formation (e.g., Calvó-Armengol, 2004; Galeotti and Merlino, 2014) and career choices (Buhai and van der Leij, 2020), which then further correlate outcomes across groups. In addition, people with fewer employed friends expect longer durations of unemployment over time (Calvo-Armengol and Jackson, 2004), and so the duration of unemployment spells can differ widely across groups (Kaila et al., 2021).

what they pay attention to. When put together, in their data only about a quarter of the content that people end up viewing is from sources with different political views. That study examines news content, which can be shared broadly. Information concerning investing in education, pursuing a career, and other large life choices is often complex and nuanced, and learned from friends over long periods of time. Given the strong levels of homophily among friends, this can lead to even more inequality in access to information about such important investments.

The role of homophily is nuanced. Homophily is a double-edged sword in social learning settings (Aybas and Jackson, 2024; Lobel and Sadler, 2016). For instance, as discussed above, a person can learn more from people who are similar to themselves. A student who is from a low-income family and has limited preparation for university learns more about what attending university requires from others who have similar backgrounds, than from someone from a wealthier background in a special preparatory school. On the other hand, given that far more people from wealthier backgrounds attend university (Chetty et al., 2020), homophily can also disadvantage poorer people in terms of the number of people whom they know with any university experience who show them whether attending college would be beneficial to them. Ultimately one needs not only access to high-quality information from closely matching peers, but across a variety of options. This is the foundation behind some mentorship programs, in which people are connected to others outside of their own friendship circle and who can provide valuable advice, but also whom the mentees can relate to, understand, and emulate (e.g., see Putnam, 2016).

Importantly, homophily means that information about key opportunities and decisions can be distributed unequally across a population. Without awareness of the availability of various choices and the costs and benefits of those choices, and enough information to be confident in a decision, people miss out on valuable opportunities. For instance, if people of one ethnic or social group participate in higher education at a greater rate, then friends and families of those people gain more information about that experience and its benefits. This then feeds back to lead next generations of the group with more experience to invest at greater rates, and the other group to continue to under-invest, so that there is a feedback across cohorts (Aybas and Jackson, 2024).[39] Again, this suggests that divisions in the network not only lead to inequality within a generation, but transmission of that across generations.

This is borne out in strong empirical evidence that networks of connections across economic boundaries predict economic mobility. For instance, we find in Chetty et al. (2022a) that the economic mobility of low socioeconomic status (SES) people in a given community is strongly predicted by

[39] It is worth emphasizing that informational disadvantages can be particularly problematic for the very poor. For them, uncertain outcomes – even with high expected values – can be too risky to take advantage of since the costs of failure can be relatively enormous (e.g., Banerjee and Duflo, 2011).

the extent to which low socioeconomic status people are connected to high SES people. This is what the theory would predict, given that information and opportunities are more often in the hands of the high SES people, and so greater access to those people provides increased chances of having better economic outcomes. In fact, the extent of these cross-income connections within a community (strongly) out-predicts other standard community measures of poverty, segregation, social capital, and human capital, when it comes to explaining economic mobility,[40] and in fact remains a strong predictor when one includes other usual variables on a community's poverty level, ethnic composition, education levels, and so on.[41] Interestingly, we also find evidence that these cross-income connections are at the heart of the Great Gatsby Curve. In particular, once we control for a community's cross-income connections, the relationship between inequality and immobility disappears (see Chetty et al., 2022a, table 2 regressions on the Gini coefficient).

Different types of social capital can have different effects on learning and behavior. Having a tightly knit community on a local level can help that community function in providing incentives for people to cooperate and share with each other.[42] However, that local support and clustering can be insufficient to help in economic mobility, as a very cooperative and supportive group can still be missing vital information and opportunities that it needs to succeed.[43] Gaining that information and those opportunities can require cross-cutting relationships, which is a very different form of social capital, and social network feature, which is what we see in the data of Chetty et al. (2022a). In fact, their support within the community turns out to be more advantageous in settings in which there is integration across socioeconomic lines, so the two appear to have some complementarity. More generally, the connectedness of people to information also depends on the quality of the local institutions that they are a part of, such as child-care centers, and the outside resources and connections that such institutions offer and which vary widely across geography (e.g., see Small, 2006). Thus, one can think of economic connectedness as a feature not only of individual networks, but also of the networks of institutions through which people interact.

It is also worthwhile distinguishing two types of consequences of homophily and learning in networks. One we can call passive. This refers to the fact that homophily can lead different groups to hold different beliefs over

40 For additional evidence on how the geography and long range of people's networks impact many behaviors, see Bailey et al. (2018) and Jahani et al. (2022).

41 It mediates those relationships.

42 See, for instance, Coleman (1988) and Jackson et al. (2012). See also Ambrus et al. (2014) for the importance of expansion properties of a network.

43 In fact, there are reasons for which such tight-knit structures impede mobility, as people may have to leave their groups and their support in order to take advantage of opportunities (e.g., Austen-Smith and Fryer, 2005; Barron et al., 2020; Munshi and Rosenzweig, 2009). However, on the other hand, having tightly knit groups can be effective in improving local public goods provision and collective action (e.g., see Ostrom, 1990).

time, and to be slow or never converge to a consensus (Golub and Jackson, 2012; Lobel and Sadler, 2016). The other we can call active. This refers to the feedback effects in actual decisions, as for instance outlined by Aybas and Jackson (2024). The fact that a group does not take advantage of some opportunity leads that group to learn less about that action and then be less likely to take that decision in the future. The active part involves feedback and a lack of exploration, while the passive part refers to the lack of learning due to having less information to exploit. Both matter, but can have different policy implications, as overcoming active learning consequences (e.g., a group's lack of role models who can illustrate the benefits of education) can require policies like affirmative action or mentorships, while passive issues (e.g., a lack of information about the benefits and risks of some vaccine) can require supplementing information and contacts. Given that many decisions and opportunities carry economic benefits, those benefits can be unevenly distributed across the population due to a lack of learning, leading to inequality and immobility patterns that match the homophily. And, in parallel to the job contact situation, many behaviors can be suboptimal. People miss out on valuable decisions – such as educating themselves – that have consequences not only for themselves but also for the overall productivity of society.

Note that many different forces can all operate at once. Having a productive life requires proper training and development, information on how to put that to its best use, and opportunities to use it. Economic and social hurdles hinder education and development, homophily limits the extent to which information reaches a group and to which that group tries certain options, and then homophily and the roles of networks in referrals and advancement hinder employment and advancement even conditional upon having the right skills and match for a job. All of these complement each other, and that complementarity has implications for how combinations of policies can be more effective than policies in isolation, as discussed more below.

7.4.3 Norms, Culture, and Peer Influence

The clustering of behaviors can occur for reasons beyond information sharing. For instance, children imitate siblings and peers, people adopt fashions and fads, people prefer to see movies and read books that they can talk to their peers about. The many pressures that push people to similar behaviors can shape very consequential decisions, including pursuing education (e.g., see Austen-Smith and Fryer, 2005).

Once again, homophily plays a starring role, as splits in the network can lead to different norms of behavior across homophily divides (e.g., see Golub and Jackson, 2012; Jackson, 2007; Jackson and Storms, 2025). As a simplest example, imagine that people choose to drop out of school if a majority of their friends do, but not if a majority of their friends stay in school. So, they simply prefer to do the same thing as the majority of their friends – the simplest version of a game on a network (see Jackson and Zenou, 2014 for background).

In many networks it is easy to find (many) splits of the network into two groups such that each member of a group has a majority of their friends within that same group. Then it is an equilibrium for everyone in one group to stay in school and everyone in the other group to drop out.

This is a stylized example, but the phenomenon is clear: homophily leads to strong divisions across a network so that different groups have most of their connections within that same group. This can lead groups to have different norms of behavior and cultures, even when they might be in close proximity to each other, and even have social connections with each other. For instance, the friendships in many schools split along ethnic lines, and there can be very different behaviors across groups even within the same school. These effects can be amplified by the fact that people can misperceive behaviors in their own social circles to be more representative of norms overall than they really are (Bursztyn et al., 2020; Frick et al., 2020; Jackson, 2019a,b).

It is also important to remark that peer effects are not only passive, but sometimes can be active. That is, people may deliberately push their friends to act in certain ways: students may bully students who do not conform to a group norm (Austen-Smith and Fryer, 2005), or people may pressure others until they behave in certain ways (e.g., see Calvó-Armengol and Jackson, 2010), or try to lead by example in hopes of getting others to act (e.g., see Acemoglu and Jackson, 2014; Jimenez-Gomez, 2021). This can lead behaviors to become even more governed by network divides.

Note that many behaviors that are influenced by networks are cumulative. Education, health, and aspirations can have cumulative effects, so that as deficiencies become entrenched over time it becomes harder to eliminate them. Moreover, the peer effects and lack of information that can lead to poor study habits, health habits, and low aspirations feed back through the network both within and across generations to amplify these deficiencies.

7.5 POLICIES TO OVERCOME INEQUALITY

The variety of factors that can lead to inequality in outcomes suggest a corresponding variety of policies to deal with that inequality.[44] The policies to overcome the wealth concentrated in the hands of the top percentiles of the population are different from those needed to deal with widespread and persistent differences in health, education, employment, and income by ethnicity, caste, and gender that exist in many countries. Nonetheless, one does not need a different policy for each issue. Although more than one feature of social structure matters and more than one outcome is affected, understanding common sources and patterns can help us focus in on a few policy combinations, and can help us see that a common network driver – homophily – is responsible

[44] See Page (2018) for a discussion of using many models to both understand effect sizes as well as the limitations of focusing on just one framing of an issue, especially inequality.

for many differences in outcomes across groups. Let us consider the logic behind various policies.

7.5.1 Redistribution: Addressing Symptoms or Causes?

A class of policies often associated with combatting inequality is redistribution. Such policies come in many forms: progressive taxes, subsidies, universal basic income, price and wage controls, as well as government-run retirement, health, and welfare programs. Effectively, these are all programs that reallocate resources across the population. Such programs reduce inequality to the extent that net benefits are seen by poorer individuals and net costs are seen by wealthier or higher-income individuals.

It is important to distinguish two different reasons for redistribution.

The first comes from Rawls's veil of ignorance, which justifies redistribution as a form of social insurance. By reallocating resources from those in better circumstances to those in worse circumstances, a society is essentially offering a form of insurance when viewed from behind the veil of ignorance. The question of how much redistribution there should be, and who should benefit and who should pay the costs, is something that elicits a variety of views. What is viewed as optimal traces back to the moral foundations of society's responsibilities to its individuals versus their responsibilities to themselves. This is well illustrated in Sen's (1992) discussion of the "equality of what?"[45]

The second justification for redistribution is to combat poverty traps. For example, if people cannot afford education, and cannot borrow privately to pay for it,[46] then having a government provide it and/or help pay for it can overcome the market imperfection. The same is true of other forms of government-sponsored loans and programs that spur investments in human capital and health.

This is an important distinction, since social insurance is essentially an ex-post remedy to deal with the symptoms of inequality. On the other hand, a justification for redistribution based on overcoming market imperfections in which people are trapped in poverty is aimed at overcoming causes. Policies aimed at the causes also deal more directly with immobility and inefficiencies in production.

Both justifications are important. In treating a disease, one treats symptoms as well as causes – treating inequality is similar. Nonetheless, the distinction is vital, since much attention is focused on remedies for the symptoms and some of those will not eliminate the causes of inequality or its longer-run effects like

[45] Beyond the moral issues, there are also a variety of incentive issues as such programs can distort people's behaviors. For instance, for an illuminating discussion of the incentive issues associated with equal sharing of resources, see Abramitzky (2011, 2018).

[46] There are many impediments to borrowing based on uncertain future values in the absence of having collateral to post, including moral hazard and adverse selection issues, as well as the fixed costs of administering relatively small or highly idiosyncratic loans.

immobility, but instead will only overcome some of its immediate negative impact. Some taxes, especially those aimed at wealth and inheritance, fall into both categories, as do regulations that combat monopolies and other forms of market-driven inequality, as they not only redistribute but also undo some of the sources of inequality (e.g., for a discussion of some of the impacts, see Chetty, 2009; Dworczak et al., 2021).

Policies can also be distinguished in terms of how leveraged they are. For instance, investments in early education – even at preschool level – have generally been found to have large snowball effects. Especially, early gains in non-cognitive skills help children gain further knowledge and skills.[47] Some such policies more than pay for themselves when one estimates the social benefits compared to the cost of the policy (e.g., see Hendren and Sprung-Keyser, 2020). It is worth noting that many aspects of children's education are determined by parents (e.g., see Becker, 2009; Doepke et al., 2019; Lareau, 2002, 2011), and thus educating parents about how to parent can be an important part of an effective policy. Evidence for this point dates at least to some of the findings from the original Coleman Report (*Equality of Educational Opportunity*, 1966) regarding the importance of various peer effects, local culture, and community factors, and has been studied in detail (e.g., see Agostinelli et al., 2020; Almond et al., 2018; Gelber and Isen, 2013; Small et al., 2010). Moreover, peer effects among parents mean that there are network effects that should be addressed and leveraged by such policies.

7.5.2 Addressing the Social Causes of Inequality: Leveraging Network Effects and Overcoming Homophily

Understanding how homophily affects opportunities, information, and behaviors provides specific insights into constructing policies to overcome the resulting inequality, immobility, and production inefficiencies.

There are two different approaches that can each be effective in its own way. One is to change the networks to try to lessen homophily and eliminate some of its perverse effects. The other is to overcome the effects of homophily by providing opportunities, information, and changing damaging norms of behavior. Any form of policy can have unintended consequences, and social engineering can be especially dangerous, so it is important to consider how each of these works, and how the costs and benefits of each type of program work.

[47] For example, see Currie (2001), Garces et al. (2002), Heckman et al. (2010), Huggett et al. (2011), Aizer and Cunha (2012), Heckman (2012), Heckman and Mosso (2014), Felfe and Lalive (2018), Kulic et al. (2019), Bailey et al. (2020), Fryer Jr. et al. (2020), Carneiro et al. (2021), and Garcıa et al. (2021). Note, however, that the research is not uniform in its findings (e.g., see Durkin et al., 2022).

7.5.2.1 Network Effects and Social Multipliers

One aspect of networks that is especially useful in policy design is that they are full of externalities and involve feedback and cascading effects. On the negative side, these are at the heart of the causes of inequality and immobility, but these effects also work in reverse and can make well-designed policies much more effective.

To illustrate the point, consider a policy of affirmative action in overcoming unequal access to job opportunities. As discussed by Bolte et al. (2025) (see also Granovetter, 1995), the placement of people into jobs not only benefits those people directly, but also helps their networks of friends (and their friends, ...). They can then offer referrals to others, as well as information that can help their communities better prepare for particular careers. Thus, such a program should not be evaluated just on its direct effects on the individuals involved, but what it means for others within their communities.[48] Role model effects are often mentioned in such a context, but there are more basic network effects that the individuals involved can provide access and information to their friends, family, and acquaintances, well beyond simply showing that it can be done. Moreover, because networks of relationships expand outwards exponentially, these effects can be substantial, even if the direct bilateral peer effects are small. It also means that a temporary program can have long-lasting impact: giving one person a job that they would not have otherwise had can lead them to help others, who can then help others, and so on.[49,50]

This perspective implies two things. First, it means that one should evaluate network-designed programs based on their full impact. Second, it means that one should take advantage of network structure in optimally targeting a policy.

To see this second point, consider a network policy in the presence of peer effects. The causal evidence for such peer effects is now quite extensive over many domains including, for instance, exercise (e.g., Aral and Nicolaides, 2017), vaccination decisions (e.g., Banerjee et al., 2021), voting (e.g., DellaVigna et al., 2016), and education (e.g., Hasan and Bagde, 2013; Sacerdote, 2001). To understand how network structure matters in the presence of such peer effects, consider a specific application of students in high school and their decisions on whether to continue to post-secondary education. They can pay attention to their peers for many reasons. One is that they simply enjoy behaving similarly, as that provides more commonality in experience

[48] Those indirect effects can be muted if, for instance, people placed into positions via affirmative action do not provide referrals and information to others who are similarly disadvantaged (e.g., see the discussion in Bolte et al., 2025).

[49] Such social multiplier effects are not just present in job markets, but in many other contexts too, such as crime (Glaeser et al., 2003), tax evasion (e.g., Galbiati and Zanella, 2012), and smoking (e.g., Cutler and Glaeser, 2010), to name a few.

[50] There are also many other issues associated with such programs in terms of who bears the cost of short-term implementation and potential loss in productivity, how they affect people's perceptions of different groups, and the difficulties in changing programs over time (e.g., Jehiel and Leduc, 2021).

and makes them feel as if they belong, and it can also be that they learn from their peers, or that they see more benefits from continuing education as more friends do (e.g., from future job market contacts, etc.).

To make things concrete, suppose that students prefer to choose the same behavior as the majority of their friends. Consider some community in which students all choose to stop their education at some point – essentially, stuck in a bad equilibrium. If we have a limited number of scholarships (or other types of help) to give out to encourage students to continue their education, it makes a big difference as to how we place these within the network. If the scholarships are randomly scattered around the network, it can be that we only get the direct effect. Those students go on to secondary education, but none of the other students have a majority of their friends continuing their education. If instead, we carefully seed the scholarships within cliques and subgroups – so that they are concentrated and near each other – then they can lead other students to have a majority of their friends continuing. This then leads those friends to continue, and this can cascade outwards.[51] Indeed, as Jackson and Storms (2025) show, the benefits to carefully targeting such seeds in the presence of peer effects can lead to arbitrarily large advantages compared to random placement.[52]

This is reflective of differences between the diffusion of basic awareness compared to norms and complex behaviors (e.g., see Centola, 2018; Golub and Jackson, 2012; Jackson and Storms, 2025). To be aware of a program subsidizing education might only require hearing from one friend, but to know how to take advantage of that program and actually participate in it might take observing several friends go through it. Thus, how one injects information and opportunities into a network to overcome inequality is not only governed by the shape of the network, but also by how different sorts of behaviors and outcomes are shaped by the network.

7.5.2.2 Changing Networks and the Challenges of Social Engineering

Let us now return to discuss the two approaches to overcoming the effects of homophily, beginning with shaping networks. Even though homophily operates differently through the opportunities, information, and norms that communities have, homophily is a common force that correlates barriers to advancement on many fronts at the same time. This means that there is an advantage to addressing homophily directly.

The impact of changing a person's network can be substantial. Some of the most eye-opening evidence of this comes from the impact of the "Moving to Opportunity" program, in which some families were subsidized to move from poor neighborhoods into wealthier ones. As shown by Chetty et al. (2016),

[51] See Calvo-Armengol and Jackson (2004), Jackson (2007, 2019a), and Gall et al. (2019) for more examples and discussion of this point.

[52] For additional nuances see Jackson and Zenou (2014), Efferson et al. (2020), Galeotti et al. (2020), and Ye (2020).

the long-term effects can be enormous, especially when children are moved at an early age. There were sizeable effects on health, education, and long-term income, and they estimate, for instance, that an eight-year-old child who moved saw an average lifetime earnings increase of $302,000.[53] An interesting aspect of this effect is that it decreased with the age of the child. Older children are more embedded in networks and behaviors, and both are harder to change when they have accumulated to a greater extent.

The formation of networks of friendships and other relationships is heavily driven by whom a person is in contact with (Blau, 1977, 1987; Blau and Schwartz, 1984). If people have substantial contact with others who have access to opportunities and information, then they can take advantage of those connections. By moving a child out of a poor neighborhood and into a wealthy one, all of the things we have been talking about are changed: information flows, opportunities, and norms of expected behaviors.

As Chetty and Jackson (2025) show, homophily can also lead families to segregate by income and educational background, which then leads to differences in children's access to social capital. This affects their networks and has the many consequences discussed above. Such separating forces can be quite powerful and help explain why many families do not move to neighborhoods with improved educational outcomes for their children, even when given the financial resources to make such a move, and even if they are altruistic and fully aware of the children's benefits.

Although experimental programs like "Moving to Opportunity" show what is possible, shifting large groups of people around is not practical, at least in the short run. Moreover, it might not even have the desired effect. Moving a few families into different neighborhoods and seeing them integrate is very different from making large-scale changes. In particular, just putting people in contact does not necessarily alter their networks, unless they are a small minority who have little choice but to integrate. One group having contact with another is necessary for forming cross-group connections, but can be far from sufficient. For example, as found by Currarini et al. (2009, 2010), Mosleh et al. (2021), and Chetty et al. (2022b), both exposure and choices conditional upon exposure matter to a sizeable degree in friendship formation. In fact, some of the largest and most racially balanced high schools in the United States are some of the most fragmented along ethnic lines, while smaller high schools are more integrated (Currarini et al., 2009, 2010).

An example of how a policy designed to help individuals by engineering their communities can lead to unintended consequences comes from Carrell et al. (2013). Entering cadet classes in the US Air Force Academy were carefully structured to match together students who had the lowest predicted grade point averages with students who were expected to perform well. Prior data

[53] For another important example of this sort of effect, see the analysis in Abramitzky et al. (2019) regarding the importance of location in the mobility of immigrants.

had shown that cadets with low-predicted achievement performed above predicted levels when they had greater exposure to higher-ranked peers. What was unexpected is that when the experiment built whole classes of roughly half very low-predicted achievement and half high-scoring cadets, then the cadets would self-segregate. Just as discussed above, when groups have larger critical masses, the friendships are more likely to splinter. So although exposure of low-predicted achievers to higher-predicted achievers was optimized, the choices conditional upon exposure led to high homophily. The idea behind this effect is intuitive. In small communities, people have relatively little choice over whom they are friends with – groups are forced together. When communities become larger, each group reaches a critical mass so that people can sustain a natural number of friendships just within their own community. People's proclivity towards homophily can take over and people have plenty of other people who are very similar to themselves with whom to be friends. What happened in the Air Force Academy experiment was that instead of having small numbers of low-predicted achievement cadets integrating with high-scoring cadets, they provided the low-predicted achievement students with many more opportunities to form friendships among themselves, leading to more segregation and worse outcomes.[54]

Thus, although reshaping networks can be incredibly powerful at lifting people out of poverty, these sorts of nuances mean that social engineering is tricky and can have substantial unintended consequences.[55] Nonetheless, research to date suggests several insights that can be helpful in shaping successful policies.

One is the fact, just mentioned above, that smaller communities with a given composition of groups foster greater integration across groups than larger communities with that same composition. It suggests a new approach to lowering homophily can be to improve the structuring of large organizations and communities by reshaping them into relatively small and well-mixed sub-communities. Many aspects of urban planning, as well as the structuring of universities, companies, and other large institutions, are aimed at trying to create smaller communities within them. This suggests that not only can this be done to create tight community structures within larger organizations, but also to help build bridges across different demographic and socioeconomic groupings. If a high school has huge numbers of students, then putting them into smaller communities who take many of their basic classes together, take meals together, and so on is like putting them in a smaller school where we know that more cross-group connections tend to be built.[56]

[54] It could also be that the high-scoring cadets having a critical mass allowed them to form friendships that excluded the lows, as discussed by Golub and Sadler (2021).

[55] People can be involved in many networks at the same time, and changing one can end up affecting others, as can changing things that interact with them (e.g., see Atkisson et al., 2020; Banerjee et al., 2020).

[56] This also can tell us why some of the initiatives in the United States in the late 1950s through to the end of the last century to build large schools that were well integrated, via busing

Second, the network effects that we mentioned above mean that providing new opportunities to diversify connections across a network has a sizeable impact. In line with this prediction, our analysis in Chetty et al. (2022a) finds a strong relationship between economic mobility and increasing connectedness.[57] The roughly linear relationship that appears in the data may reflect that each marginal bit of connection conveys similar benefits, or it may be that there are underlying threshold effects that are smoothed out when averaged across a community. Further exploration of economic connectedness may help uncover which aspects of the connectedness – information, opportunities, or peer effects – are empirically most relevant. Regardless, it is clear that cross-income connections hold promise as a key to improving economic mobility.

Third, simply increasing exposure can also affect discrimination and racism (Allport, 1954), and recent studies show that contact can causally impact people's views and longer-term prejudice and behaviors (Bursztyn et al., 2021; Rao, 2019; Strother et al., 2021). This can be true independently of the resulting friendship networks. Moreover, contact can result in nonsocial and weak ties that are useful conduits of information and opportunities even if they do not become strong relationships (e.g., see Small, 2009).

Fourth, there are benefits from homophily that can be undone if people's networks are disrupted, and so it can be better to supplement rather than dramatically rewire existing relationships. Tearing communities apart, without ensuring that new ones provide all the support that people need, can have damaging consequences (e.g., Barnhardt et al., 2016).

Fifth, as technology becomes increasingly instrumental in shaping people's networks and their information, the design of the algorithms that steer networks, exposure, and information is becoming increasingly important. Competition between platforms and profit motivations can lead platforms to steer people towards connections and content that most closely mirror their backgrounds. Even though such algorithms can enlarge the size of people's networks, they can also end up increasing homophily rather than decreasing it (Jackson, 2019a). Seemingly small design choices behind the algorithms that people use for communication, connection, and search can have profound consequences. Moreover, the incentives of the designers are not necessarily aligned with the greater social good, especially given the large network externalities at work. Better understanding of the workings and impact of these

and redistricting, failed to lead to well-integrated friendships and interactions, and the desired improvements in achievement. Without structuring the internal workings of the schools to foster tight small-group interactions, students could self-segregate within their new schools just as they were segregated across their old ones. The Air Force Academy experiment is a warning, however, that creating small groups that are too bimodal can still lead to segregation, even in relatively small cohorts.

57 To put the slope in perspective, changing from the 10th to the 90th percentile in economic connectedness predicts a 10 percentile increase in the income rank at age 35 of children from low-income families (which is comparable to the estimated gap in upward mobility between Black and White Americans).

services, as well as the incentives of the designers, is an important input into future policy design.

7.5.2.3 *Overcoming Network Structure*

Next, let us consider overcoming the effects of homophily and network structure without altering the networks, but instead by counteracting their effects.

Some of the policies that help overcome the effects of networks are naturally suggested by the limitations that homophily imposes. In particular, to overcome the lack of information and opportunities that people have due to not being well connected, one can directly provide the missing information and opportunities. This provides a logic for mentorships, role models, and affirmative action policies.[58] As mentioned above, the network effects lead the information and opportunities to diffuse more widely and thus can result in far-reaching and long-lasting effects (Bolte et al., 2025; Holzer and Neumark, 2000; Miller, 2017).

The informational barriers in job markets can also be overcome by helping organizations find good matches without having to rely on referrals. This can come in various forms. One is subsidizing internships for relatively disadvantaged groups, so that firms get to know the workers. Another is to provide better information about people's skills, by programs that allow them to show that they have reached certain skill levels. In this direction, there is some hope that the proliferation of online education and certification will help close some gaps. A less obvious factor in overcoming informational barriers is labor market rigidity. If it is very hard to fire a worker, then the initial hiring decision becomes even more important and referrals become even more valuable. This can lead to increased inequality. Thus, regulations that are intended to provide job security can actually have a side effect of increasing inequality (e.g., see the analysis in Bolte et al., 2025).

Some policies, such as mentorships and affirmative action, can end up counteracting all three of the negative effects of homophily that we discussed above. Not only can these policies end up helping information and opportunities diffuse through the network, but also, as people from a given group end up having successful careers, they can serve as prominent examples for their communities and help reshape the norms, expectations, and culture within the community (e.g., Acemoglu and Jackson, 2014). These effects can also have increasing returns, at least initially. That is, each additional success can make the possibilities more visible and change people's expectations and aspirations even more, which also has further peer effects.[59]

[58] All of these policies can also be thought of as reshaping networks to some extent, but that is often less their direct intention.

[59] Again, this is a place where age can make a difference, and earlier interventions can be even more effective, and role models can have a wide impact on education attainment and trajectories (e.g., Beaman et al., 2012).

7.5.3 Policy Cocktails

As argued by Alfani (2021), "human agency" – with an interpretation of the implementation of deliberate policies to overcome inequality – is a main predictor of the trends of inequality over time; and when economies are left to operate unbridled, resources tend to accumulate highly unequally.[60]

As we have discussed here, there are many forces behind such inequality and immobility, both economic and social, which suggest that a coordinated policy cocktail will be much more effective than any policy in isolation. Moreover, some policies deal with symptoms while others deal with causes, of which there are many, and both causes and symptoms need to be treated.

A policy cocktail to fully address inequality requires at least four ingredients. First up are the basic safety net policies and redistribution that provide social insurance and address the symptoms, or in an analogy to the treatment of a disease, overcome the pain. Second are the long-standing economic policies that address the large wealth imbalances that accumulate from monopoly rents and increasing returns to various forms of capital. These include targeted regulation and taxation to address these issues without damaging economic incentives.[61] Third are subsidies to overcome basic financial poverty traps, including various loans, scholarships, subsidized day care, and early childhood education, among others. Fourth are policies aimed at overcoming homophily and opening up entrenched social networks. These include enriching people's networks through enabling more contact across groups and restructuring organizations, as well as providing people with the information, opportunities, and role models that they are missing in their existing networks – via affirmative action, mentorships, internships, and certification programs. Importantly, network feedbacks and multiplier effects not only lead to large and persistent differences in behaviors and opportunities across groups, but also help leverage well-designed and appropriately concentrated policies to be more effective in overcoming inequality and immobility.

Most all of the necessary policies have been used in various forms before.[62] The most novel policy discussed here is the use of small communities inside larger organizations and institutions to foster more cross-group exposure and interaction. The idea of fostering teamwork and community bonds is part of

60 See also, for instance, Hubmer et al. (2020), who find that changes in tax progressivity explain rises in wealth inequality.

61 There is a large literature on the structuring of various programs, and how they can affect incentives as well as how easy it is for people to access a program (e.g., Chetty, 2008; Currie, 2006; Katz and Meyer, 1990; Krueger and Meyer, 2002; Mirrlees, 1971). I don't address those issues here, but instead focus on the interaction of social and economic factors and the basic insights on policy that are generated from that perspective. This interaction raises its own set of questions of policy side effects, such as how they change social structure, that are also beyond the scope here (e.g., Banerjee et al., 2020) but are important for future research.

62 However, many policies – such as affirmative action – have been used at a small scale relative to what would be needed, for instance, to balance the demographics of those attending higher education with those of the general population (e.g., see Chetty et al., 2020).

many organizations, but this instead leverages what we have seen in our network analysis to use small communities and teams to build fruitful bridges across informational and opportunity barriers.

Importantly, a policy cocktail not only addresses different drivers and symptoms of inequality, but it can also be designed to take advantage of complementarities between policies. For example, enriching people's networks and information can have a greater effect if they have stronger bases from early-childhood education and help in overcoming the investments and opportunity costs needed for higher education. Conversely, offering subsidized loans for education to a disadvantaged group has a greater impact if they have good information about how to best make use of such resources in furthering their education, and also if opportunities to become employed are eventually available. Offering loans without information and opportunities will not have much impact, and similarly improving information without the resources and eventual opportunities will not work, nor would making opportunities available to a population that does not have the resources and information to take advantage of them. All three of these policies are enhanced by the presence of the others. This is a "weakest-link" challenge, where outcomes only change if a number of conditions are met and a failure of any of those conditions leads to an overall failure. Thus, policies that attack one condition at a time will be much less effective than ones that ensure all conditions are met at the same time. Further complementarities come from the fact that improvements in the outcomes for a member of some disadvantaged group put that person in a better position to then offer information, opportunities, and serve as a role model for others within that group. This is part of the network externalities. Combining policies like affirmative action together with mentorships gives an extra boost to the power of each, by both improving the situation of some people in the network and then enhancing the communication through the network.[63] More generally, any policy that improves a person's situation then has network effects, and those can be further enhanced by policies that help those improvements transfer through the network. This applies not only to education and employment, but also to things like health, literacy, and other investments.

Taking this view means, due to their network effects, that policies can have far-reaching and long-lasting impacts, as well as spillovers to other policies. This makes it important to design combinations with a network perspective, and then also to evaluate them by looking beyond the directly treated individuals.[64]

There is much more that we need to understand, especially some of the potential side effects of any social engineering. Networks serve many

[63] Some policies are less costly and scale more easily, which is also an important consideration. The point here is that combined policies, and ones that take into account social forces, can be more effective than policies in isolation or ones that do not account for social structures. Optimizing such policy cocktails to deal with costs is more context dependent.

[64] For an approach to evaluating such policy cocktails, see Banerjee et al. (2021).

productive purposes and disrupting them can have unintended consequences.[65] Network effects can be highly nonlinear, and having a better understanding of how to concentrate policies within a network is an active area of research. More generally, we are involved in many networks of different forms of relationships: family, friends, co-workers, neighbors, and so on, and they all provide different forms of interaction and support. Understanding those distinctions, and the interactions between different forms of networks, is another active area of research.

Finally, the rapid proliferation of technologies that mediate human interactions can have a profound impact on the shape of our networks. The platforms that mediate many human interactions and what information people see are being designed by companies that are profit-motivated, and they are performing social engineering. They provide the feeds and suggestions of connections, and often with deep knowledge of people's preferences and tendencies. While they are increasing the volume and speed at which people interact, they can also be amplifying homophily and its impact.[66] Moreover, platform-mediated interactions enable even greater network inequalities to emerge, as some people amass not only thousands but millions of followers. Understanding how the incentives of platform designers deviate from social welfare, and how to best leverage technology to improve our interactions and welfare, is another important area for further study.

REFERENCES

Abramitzky, R. (2011). "Lessons from the kibbutz on the equality–incentives trade-off," *The Journal of Economic Perspectives*, 25(1), 185–207.

Abramitzky, R. (2018). *The Mystery of the Kibbutz: Egalitarian Principles in a Capitalist World.* Princeton, NJ: Princeton University Press.

Abramitzky, R., L. Platt Boustan, E. Jácome, and S. Pérez (2019). *Intergenerational Mobility of Immigrants in the US over Two Centuries.* NBER Technical Report.

Acemoglu, D., and M. O. Jackson (2014). "History, expectations, and leadership in the evolution of social norms," *The Review of Economic Studies*, 82(2), 423–456.

Acemoglu, D., and J. A. Robinson (2015). "The rise and decline of general laws of capitalism," *The Journal of Economic Perspectives*, 29(1), 3–28.

Adermon, A., M. Lindahl, and M. Palme (2021). "Dynastic human capital, inequality and intergenerational mobility," *American Economic Review*, 111(5), 1523–1548.

Adler, N. E., and K. Newman (2002). "Socioeconomic disparities in health: Pathways and policies," *Health Affairs*, 21(2), 60–76.

Agostinelli, F., M. Doepke, G. Sorrenti, and F. Zilibotti (2020). *It Takes a Village: The Economics of Parenting with Neighborhood and Peer Effects*. NBER Technical Report.

[65] There are other helpful policies that can have unintended consequences. For instance, as we find in Banerjee et al. (2020), access to a microfinance program that can help people with investment and consumption smoothing can lead to the deterioration of social networks even among people not involved in the program.

[66] For a look at some of the countervailing forces affecting assortative matching in the context of online dating sites, see, for example, Skopek et al. (2011) and Thomas (2020).

Aiyar, S., and C. Ebeke (2020). "Inequality of opportunity, inequality of income and economic growth," *World Development*, 136, 105115.

Aizer, A., and F. Cunha (2012). *The Production of Human Capital: Endowments, Investments and Fertility*. NBER Technical Report.

Alesina, A., and E. La Ferrara (2000). "Participation in heterogeneous communities," *Quarterly Journal of Economics*, 115(3), 847–904.

Alfani, G. (2021). "Economic inequality in preindustrial times: Europe and beyond," *Journal of Economic Literature*, 59(1), 3–44.

Allport, G. W. (1954). *The Nature of Prejudice*. Garden City, NJ: Doubleday.

Almond, D., J. Currie, and V. Duque (2018). "Childhood circumstances and adult outcomes: Act II," *Journal of Economic Literature*, 56(4), 1360–1446.

Alvaredo, F., L. Chancel, T. Piketty, E. Saez, and G. Zucman (2018). *World Inequality Report 2018*. Cambridge, MA: Belknap Press.

Ambrus, A., M. Mobius, and A. Szeidl (2014). "Consumption risk-sharing in social networks," *American Economic Review*, 104(1), 149–182.

Andrews, D., and A. Leigh (2009). "More inequality, less social mobility," *Applied Economics Letters*, 16(15), 1489–1492.

Aral, S., and C. Nicolaides (2017). "Exercise contagion in a global social network," *Nature Communications*, 8, 14753.

Arrow, K. J. (1971). *Some Models of Racial Discrimination in the Labor Market*. Technical Report. Rand Corporation.

Arrow, K. J. (1998). "What has economics to say about racial discrimination?," *Journal of Economic Perspectives*, 12(2), 91–100.

Arrow, K. J., and R. Borzekowski (2004). "Limited network connections and the distribution of wages." FEDS Working Paper.

Atkeson, A., and M. Irie (2020). "Understanding 100 years of the evolution of top wealth shares in the US: What is the role of family firms?," NBER Working Paper No. 27465.

Atkinson, A. B. (1975). *The Economics of Inequality*. Oxford: Claredon Press.

Atkinson, A. B. (2015). *Inequality: What Can be Done?* Cambridge, MA: Harvard University Press.

Atkinson, A. B., and S. Morelli (2014). "Chartbook of economic inequality." ECINEQ Working Paper 324.

Atkinson, A. B., T. Piketty, and E. Saez (2011). "Top incomes in the long run of history," *Journal of Economic Literature*, 49(1), 3–71.

Atkisson, C., P. J. Górski, M. O. Jackson, J. A. Hołyst, and R. M. D'Souza (2020). "Why understanding multiplex social network structuring processes will help us better understand the evolution of human behavior," *Evolutionary Anthropology*, 29, 102.

Austen-Smith, D., and R. G. Fryer, Jr. (2005). "An economic analysis of 'acting White'," *Quarterly Journal of Economics*, 120(2), 551–583.

Autor, D., C. Goldin, and L. F. Katz (2020). "The race between education and technology revisited." In *AEA Papers and Proceedings*, vol. 110, pp. 347–351.

Avin, C., B. Keller, Z. Lotker, C. Mathieu, D. Peleg, and Y.-A. Pignolet (2015). "Homophily and the glass ceiling effect in social networks." In *Proceedings of the 2015 Conference on Innovations in Theoretical Computer Science*, pp. 41–50.

Aybas, Y., and M. O. Jackson (2024). "Social learning and the countervailing effects of homophily." Stanford Mimeo.

Bailey, M., R. Cao, T. Kuchler, J. Stroebel, and A. Wong (2018). "Social connectedness: Measurement, determinants, and effects," *Journal of Economic Perspectives*, 32(3), 259–280.

Bailey, M. J., B. D. Timpe, and S. Sun (2020). *Prep School for Poor Kids: The Long-Run Impacts of Head Start on Human Capital and Economic Self-sufficiency*. NBER Technical Report.

Bakshy, E., S. Messing, and L. A. Adamic (2015). "Exposure to ideologically diverse news and opinion on Facebook," *Science*, 348(6239), 1130–1132.

Bandiera, O., and I. Rasul (2006). "Social networks and technology adoption in Northern Mozambique," *The Economic Journal*, 116(514), 869–902.

Banerjee, A. V., and E. Duflo (2011). *Poor Economics: A Radical Rethinking of the Way to Fight Global Poverty*. New York: Public Affairs.

Banerjee, A. V., A. G. Chandrasekhar, E. Duflo, and M. O. Jackson (2013). "Diffusion of microfinance," *Science*, 341(6144), 1236498.

Banerjee, A., A. G. Chandrasekhar, E. Duflo, and M. O. Jackson (2019). "Using gossips to spread information: Theory and evidence from two randomized controlled trials," *The Review of Economic Studies*, 86(6), 2453–2490.

Banerjee, A. V., E. Breza, A. G. Chandrasekhar, E. Duflo, M. O. Jackson, and C. Kinnan (2020). "Changes in social network structure in response to exposure to formal credit markets." SSRN Working Paper 3245656.

Banerjee, A., A. G. Chandrasekhar, E. Duflo, J. Floretta, M. O. Jackson, H. Kannan, et al. (2021). "Selecting the most effective nudge: Evidence from a large scale experiment on immunization." MIT and Stanford, Mimeo.

Barberà, S., and M. Jackson (1988). "Maximin, leximin, and the protective criterion: Characterizations and comparisons," *Journal of Economic Theory*, 46(1), 34–44.

Barnhardt, S., E. Field, and R. Pande (2016). "Moving to opportunity or isolation? Network effects of a randomized housing lottery in urban India," *American Economic Journal: Applied Economics*, 9(1), 1–32.

Barro, R. J. (2000). "Inequality and growth in a panel of countries," *Journal of Economic Growth*, 5(1), 5–32.

Barron, D., Y. Guo, and B. Reich (2020). "Too big for their boots." Mimeo.

Beaman, L., E. Duflo, R. Pande, and P. Topalova (2012). "Female leadership raises aspirations and educational attainment for girls: A policy experiment in India," *Science*, 335(6068), 582–586.

Beaman, L., N. Keleher, and J. Magruder (2018). "Do job networks disadvantage women? Evidence from a recruitment experiment in Malawi," *Journal of Labor Economics*, 36(1), 121–157.

Beaman, L. A. (2012). "Social networks and the dynamics of labour market outcomes: Evidence from refugees resettled in the U.S.," *Review of Economic Studies*, 79(1), 128–161.

Becker, G. S. (1957). *The Economics of Discrimination*. Chicago, IL: University of Chicago Press.

Becker, G. S. (2009). *A Treatise on the Family*. Cambridge, MA: Harvard University Press.

Benabou, R. (1993). "Workings of a city: Location, education, and production," *Quarterly Journal of Economics*, 108(3), 619–652.

Benabou, R. (1996a). "Equity and efficiency in human capital investment: The local connection," *Review of Economic Studies*, 63(2), 237–264.

Benabou, R. (1996b). "Inequality and growth," *NBER Macroeconomics Annual*, 11, 11–74.

Benhabib, J., and A. Bisin (2018). "Skewed wealth distributions: Theory and empirics," *Journal of Economic Literature*, 56(4), 1261–1291.

Benhabib, J., A. Bisin, and S. Zhu (2011). "The distribution of wealth and fiscal policy in economies with finitely lived agents," *Econometrica*, 79(1), 123–157.

Benson, A., S. Board, and M. Meyer-ter Vehn (2019). "Discrimination in hiring: Evidence from retail sales." UCLA Preprint.

Bentham, J. (1789). *An Introduction to the Principles of Morals and Legislation.*

Berardi, N., M. Lalanne, and P. Seabright (2019). "Professional networks and their coevolution with executive careers." Banque de France Working Paper.

Berg, A., J. D. Ostry, C. G. Tsangarides, and Y. Yakhshilikov (2018). "Redistribution, inequality, and growth: New evidence," *Journal of Economic Growth*, 23(3), 259–305.

Bertrand, M., and E. Duflo (2017). "Field experiments on discrimination." In *Handbook of Economic Field Experiments*, vol. 1, pp. 309–393. Amsterdam: Elsevier.

Bewley, T. F. (1999). *Why Wages Don't Fall During a Recession.* Cambridge, MA: Harvard University Press.

Blau, P. M. (1977). "A macrosociological theory of social structure," *American Journal of Sociology*, 83(1), 26–54.

Blau, P. M. (1987). "Contrasting theoretical perspectives." In J. C. Alexander (ed.), *The Micro–Macro Link.* Berkeley, CA: University of California Press, pp. 71–85.

Blau, P. M., and J. E. Schwartz (1984). *Crosscutting Social Circles: Testing a Macrostructural Theory of Intergroup Relations.* New York: Academic Press.

Bohren, J. A., K. Haggag, A. Imas, and D. G. Pope (2019). *Inaccurate Statistical Discrimination.* NBER Technical Report.

Bolte, L., N. Immorlica, and M. O. Jackson (2025). "The role of referrals in inequality, immobility, and inefficiency in labor markets," *Journal of Labor Economics*, doi/10.1086/733048.

Bond, B. M., and R. M. Fernandez (2019). "Networks for the unemployed?" In D. J. Brass and S. P. Borgatti (eds.), *Social Networks at Work.* New York: Routledge.

Borgerhoff-Mulder, M., S. Bowles, T. Hertz, A. Bell, J. Beise, G. Clark, et al. (2009). "Intergenerational wealth transmission and the dynamics of inequality in small-scale societies," *Science*, 326(5953), 682–688.

Borisov, G. V., and C. A. Pissarides (2016). *The Intergenerational Transmission of Human Capital and Earnings in Contemporary Russia.* Technical Report. IZA Discussion Papers.

Bourdieu, P. (1986). "The forms of capital." In *Handbook of Theory and Research for the Sociology of Education.*

Bourguignon, F., and C. Morrisson (2002). "Inequality among world citizens: 1820–1992." *American Economic Review*, 92(4), 727–744.

Bowles, S. (1972). "Schooling and inequality from generation to generation," *Journal of Political Economy*, 80(3, Part 2), S219–S251.

Bowles, S., and H. Gintis (2002). "The inheritance of inequality," *Journal of Economic Perspectives*, 16(3), 3–30.

Bowles, S., G. C. Loury, and R. Sethi (2014). "Group inequality," *Journal of the European Economic Association*, 12(1), 129–152.

Bowles, S., E. A. Smith, and M. Borgerhoff Mulder (2010a). "The emergence and persistence of inequality in premodern societies: Introduction to the special section," *Current Anthropology*, 51(1), 7–17.

Bowles, S., E. A. Smith, and M. Borgerhoff-Mulder (eds.) (2010b). "Intergenerational Wealth Transmission and Inequality in Premodern Societies." *Special Issue of Current Anthropology*, 51(1).

Bramoullé, Y., and S. Goyal (2016). "Favoritism," *Journal of Development Economics*, 122, 16–27.

Brown, M., E. Setren, and G. Topa (2012). *Do Informal Referrals Lead to Better Matches? Evidence from a Firm's Employee Referral System*. FRB of New York Staff Report 568.

Buhai, I. S., and M. J. van der Leij (2020). "A social network analysis of occupational segregation." arXiv:2004.09293.

Burks, S. V., B. Cowgill, M. Hoffman, and M. Housman (2015). "The value of hiring through employee referrals," *Quarterly Journal of Economics*, 130(2), 805–839.

Bursztyn, L., A. L. González, and D. Yanagizawa-Drott (2020). "Misperceived social norms: Women working outside the home in Saudi Arabia," *American Economic Review*, 110(10), 2997–3029.

Bursztyn, L., T. Chaney, T. A. Hassan, and A. Rao (2021). *The Immigrant Next Door: Exposure, Prejudice, and Altruism*. NBER Technical Report.

Calvó-Armengol, A. (2004). "Job contact networks," *Journal of Economic Theory*, 115(1), 191–206.

Calvo-Armengol, A., and M. O. Jackson (2004). "The effects of social networks on employment and inequality," *The American Economic Review*, 94(3), 426–454.

Calvo-Armengol, A., and M. O. Jackson (2007). "Networks in labor markets: Wage and employment dynamics and inequality," *Journal of Economic Theory*, 132(1), 27–46.

Calvo-Armengol, A., and M. O. Jackson (2009). "Like father, like son: Labor market networks and social mobility," *American Economic Journal: Microeconomics*, 1(1), 124–150.

Calvó-Armengol, A., and M. O. Jackson (2010). "Peer pressure," *Journal of the European Economic Association*, 8(1), 62–89.

Carneiro, P., I. Lopez Garcia, Kjell G. Salvanes, and E. Tominey (2021). "Intergenerational mobility and the timing of parental income," *Journal of Political Economy*, 129(3), 712443.

Carrell, S. E., B. I. Sacerdote, and J. E. West (2013). "From natural variation to optimal policy? The importance of endogenous peer group formation," *Econometrica*, 81(3), 855–882.

Carter, M. R., and C. B. Barrett (2006). "The economics of poverty traps and persistent poverty: An asset-based approach," *The Journal of Development Studies*, 42(2), 178–199.

Case, A., and A. Deaton (2021). "Life expectancy in adulthood is falling for those without a BA degree, but as educational gaps have widened, racial gaps have narrowed," *Proceedings of the National Academy of Sciences*, 118(11).

Centola, D. (2018). *How Behavior Spreads: The Science of Complex Contagions*, vol. 3. Princeton, NJ: Princeton University Press.

Charles, M., and D. B. Grusky (2005). *Occupational Ghettos: The Worldwide Segregation of Women and Men*, vol. 200. Stanford, CA: Stanford University Press.

Cheng, C., and Y. Xing (2021). "Which networks permit stable allocations? A theory of network-based comparisons," Johns Hopkins Carey Business School Research Paper (20-01).

Chetty, R. (2008). "Moral hazard versus liquidity and optimal unemployment insurance," *Journal of Political Economy*, 116(2), 173–234.

Chetty, R. (2009). "Sufficient statistics for welfare analysis: A bridge between structural and reduced-form methods," *Annual Review of Economics*, 1(1), 451–488.
Chetty, R., N. Hendren, P. Kline, and E. Saez (2014). "Where is the land of opportunity? The geography of intergenerational mobility in the United States," *Quarterly Journal of Economics*, 129(4), 1553–1623.
Chetty, R., N. Hendren, and L. F. Katz (2016). "The effects of exposure to better neighborhoods on children: New evidence from the Moving to Opportunity experiment," *The American Economic Review*, 106(4), 855–902.
Chetty, R., D. Grusky, M. Hell, N. Hendren, R. Manduca, and J. Narang (2017). "The fading American dream: Trends in absolute income mobility since 1940," *Science*, 356(6336), 398–406.
Chetty, R., J. N. Friedman, E. Saez, N. Turner, and D. Yagan (2020). "Income segregation and intergenerational mobility across colleges in the United States," *Quarterly Journal of Economics*, 135(3), 1567–1633.
Chetty, R., M. O. Jackson, T. Kuchler, J. Stroebel, N. Hendren, R. Fluegge, et al. (2022a). "Social capital in the United States I: Measurement and associations with economic mobility," *Nature*, 608, 108–121.
Chetty, R., M. O. Jackson, T. Kuchler, J. Stroebel, N. Hendren, R. Fluegge, et al. (2022b). "Social capital in the United States II: Determinants of economic connectedness," *Nature*, 608, 122–134.
Chetty, R., and M. O. Jackson (2025). "A theory of social capital formation and economic mobility." Mimeo, Stanford University.
Clauset, A., S. Arbesman, and D. B. Larremore (2015). "Systematic inequality and hierarchy in faculty hiring networks," *Science Advances*, 1(1), e1400005.
Coleman, J. S. (1974). "Inequality, sociology, and moral philosophy," *American Journal of Sociology*, 80(3), 739–764.
Coleman, J. S. (1988). "Social capital in the creation of human capital," *American Journal of Sociology*, 94(1), S95–S120.
Conley, T. G., and C. R. Udry (2010). "Learning about a new technology: Pineapple in Ghana," *The American Economic Review*, 100(1), 35–69.
Connor, D. S., and M. Storper (2020). "The changing geography of social mobility in the United States," *Proceedings of the National Academy of Sciences*, 117(48), 30309–30317.
Corak, M. (2013). "Income inequality, equality of opportunity, and intergenerational mobility," *Journal of Economic Perspectives*, 27(3), 79–102.
Corak, M. (2016). "Inequality from generation to generation: The United States in comparison." IZA DP No. 9929.
Currarini, S., M. O. Jackson, and P. Pin (2009). "An economic model of friendship: Homophily, minorities, and segregation," *Econometrica*, 77(4), 1003–1045.
Currarini, S., M. O. Jackson, and P. Pin (2010). "Identifying the roles of race-based choice and chance in high school friendship network formation," *Proceedings of the National Academy of Sciences*, 107(11), 4857–4861.
Currie, J. (2001). "Early childhood education programs," *Journal of Economic Perspectives*, 15(2), 213–238.
Currie, J. (2006). "The take-up of social benefits." NBER Working Paper 10488.
Cutler, D. M., and E. L. Glaeser (2010). "Social interactions and smoking." In D. A. Wise (ed.), *Research Findings in the Economics of Aging*. Chicago, IL: University of Chicago Press, pp. 123–141.

DellaVigna, S., J. A. List, U. Malmendier, and G. Rao (2016). "Voting to tell others," *The Review of Economic Studies*, 84(1), 143–181.

DiMaggio, P., and F. Garip (2011). "How network externalities can exacerbate intergroup inequality," *American Journal of Sociology*, 116(6), 1887–1933.

DiMaggio, P., and F. Garip (2012). "Network effects and social inequality," *Annual Review of Sociology*, 38, 93–118.

Doepke, M., G. Sorrenti, and F. Zilibotti (2019). "The economics of parenting," *Annual Review of Economics*, 11, 55–84.

Duflo, E., and E. Saez (2003). "The role of information and social interactions in retirement plan decisions: Evidence from a randomized experiment," *Quarterly Journal of Economics*, August, 815–842.

Durkin, K., M. W. Lipsey, D. C. Farran, and S. E. Wiesen (2022). "Effects of a statewide pre-kindergarten program on children's achievement and behavior through sixth grade," *Developmental Psychology*, 58(3), 470–484.

Durlauf, S. N. (1996). "A theory of persistent income inequality," *Journal of Economic Growth*, 1(1), 75–93.

Durlauf, S. N., and A. Seshadri (2018). "Understanding the Great Gatsby Curve," *NBER Macroeconomics Annual*, 32(1), 333–393.

Dustmann, C., A. Glitz, U. Schönberg, and H. Brücker (2016). "Referral-based job search networks," *The Review of Economic Studies*, 83(2), 514–546.

Dworczak, P., S. D. Kominers, and M. Akbarpour (2021). "Redistribution through markets," *Econometrica*, 89(4), 1665–1698.

Efferson, C., S. Vogt, and E. Fehr (2020). "The promise and the peril of using social influence to reverse harmful traditions," *Nature Human Behaviour*, 4(1), 55–68.

Engels, F. (1845). *The Condition of the Working Class in England* [English transl. 1887]. Leipzig: Otto Wigand.

Fagereng, A., M. Mogstad, and M. Ronning (2018). "Why do wealthy parents have wealthy children?" University of Chicago, Becker Friedman Institute for Economics Working Paper (2019-22).

Falk, A., F. Kosse, P. R. Dovern-Pinger, H. Schildberg-Hörisch, and T. Deckers (2021). "Socio-economic status and inequalities in children's IQ and economic preferences," *Journal of Political Economy*, 129(9), 714992.

Felfe, C., and R. Lalive (2018). "Does early child care affect children's development?," *Journal of Public Economics*, 159, 33–53.

Fernandez, R. M., E. J. Castilla, and P. Moore (2000). "Social capital at work: Networks and employment at a phone center," *American Journal of Sociology*, 105(5), 1288–1356.

Fernandez, R. M., and R. V. Galperin (2014). "The causal status of social capital in labor markets," *Contemporary Perspectives on Organizational Social Networks*, 40, 445–462.

Fershtman, C., and U. Gneezy (2001). "Discrimination in a segmented society: An experimental approach," *Quarterly Journal of Economics*, 116(1), 351–377.

Fiorillo, D., and N. Nappo (2014). "Job satisfaction in Italy: Individual characteristics and social relations," *International Journal of Social Economics*, 41(8), 683–704.

Fix, M., G. C. Galster, and R. J. Struyk (1993). "An overview of auditing for discrimination." In M. Fix and R. J. Struyk (eds.), *Clear and Convincing Evidence: Measurement of Discrimination in America*. Washington, DC: Urban Institute Press.

Frick, M., R. Iijima, and Y. Ishii (2020). "Misinterpreting others and the fragility of social learning," *Econometrica*, 88(6), 2281–2328.

Fryer Jr., R. G., S. D. Levitt, J. A. List, and A. Samek (2020). *Introducing CogX: A New Preschool Education Program Combining Parent and Child Interventions*. NBER Technical Report.

Galbiati, R., and G. Zanella (2012). "The tax evasion social multiplier: Evidence from Italy," *Journal of Public Economics*, 96(5–6), 485–494.

Galeotti, A., and L. P. Merlino (2014). "Endogenous job contact networks," *International Economic Review*, 55(4), 1201–1226.

Galeotti, A., B. Golub, and S. Goyal (2020). "Targeting interventions in networks," *Econometrica*, 88(6), 2445–2471.

Gall, T., P. Legros, and A. F. Newman (2019). "College diversity policy and investment incentives." Mimeo.

Garces, E., D. Thomas, and J. Currie (2002). "Longer-term effects of Head Start," *The American Economic Review*, 92(4), 999–1012.

Garcıa, J. L., J. J. Heckman, and V. Ronda (2021). "The lasting effects of early childhood education on promoting the skills and social mobility of disadvantaged African Americans." SSRN Working Paper 3888323.

Gelber, A., and A. Isen (2013). "Children's schooling and parents' behavior: Evidence from the Head Start Impact Study," *Journal of Public Economics*, 101, 25–38.

George, H. (1879). *Progress and Poverty*.

Glaeser, E. L., B. I. Sacerdote, and J. A. Scheinkman (2003). "The social multiplier," *Journal of the European Economic Association*, 1(2–3), 345–353.

Goldin, C. D., and L. F. Katz (2009). *The Race Between Education and Technology*. Cambridge, MA: Harvard University Press.

Golub, B., and M. O. Jackson (2012). "How homophily affects the speed of learning and best-response dynamics," *Quarterly Journal of Economics*, 127(3), 1287–1338.

Golub, B., and E. Sadler (2021). "Games on endogenous networks." arXiv:2102.01587.

Gomez, M. (2021). "Decomposing the rise in top wealth shares." Preprint.

Granovetter, M. (1988). "The sociological and economic approaches to labor market analysis." In G. Farkas and P. England (eds.), *Industries, Firms, and Jobs*, pp. 187–216. Cham: Springer Nature.

Granovetter, M. S. (1973). "The strength of weak ties," *The American Journal of Sociology*, 78(6), 1360–1380.

Granovetter, M. S. (1995). *Getting a Job: A Study of Contacts and Careers* (2nd ed.). Chicago, IL: University of Chicago Press.

Hangartner, D., D. Kopp, and M. Siegenthaler (2021). "Monitoring hiring discrimination through online recruitment platforms," *Nature*, 589, 572–576.

Harsanyi, J. C. (1977). "Rule utilitarianism and decision theory," *Erkenntnis*, 11(1), 25–53.

Hasan, S., and S. Bagde (2013). "The mechanics of social capital and academic performance in an Indian college," *American Sociological Review*, 78(6), 1009–1032.

Heathcote, J., F. Perri, and G. L. Violante (2010). "Unequal we stand: An empirical analysis of economic inequality in the United States, 1967–2006," *Review of Economic Dynamics*, 13(1), 15–51.

Heckman, J. J. (2012). "Invest in early childhood development: Reduce deficits, strengthen the economy," *The Heckman Equation*, 7.

Heckman, J. J., and S. Mosso (2014). "The economics of human development and social mobility," *Annual Review of Economics*, 6(1), 689–733.

Heckman, J. J., S. H. Moon, R. Pinto, P. A. Savelyev, and A. Yavitz (2010). "The rate of return to the HighScope Perry Preschool Program," *Journal of Public Economics*, 94(1), 114–128.

Hendren, N., and B. Sprung-Keyser (2020). "A unified welfare analysis of government policies," *Quarterly Journal of Economics*, 135(3), 1209–1318.

Henrich, J. (2015). *The Secret of Our Success: How Culture is Driving Human Evolution, Domesticating Our Species, and Making Us Smarter*. Princeton, NJ: Princeton University Press.

Herbst, D., and N. Hendren (2021). "Opportunity unraveled: Private information and the missing markets for financing human capital." NBER Working Paper No. 29214.

Holzer, H., and D. Neumark (2000). "Assessing affirmative action," *Journal of Economic Literature*, 38(3), 483–568.

Horváth, G. (2014). "Occupational mismatch and social networks," *Journal of Economic Behavior & Organization*, 106, 442–468.

Huber, K., V. Lindenthal, and F. Waldinger (2021). "Discrimination, managers, and firm performance: Evidence from 'Aryanizations' in Nazi Germany," *Journal of Political Economy*, 129(9), 714994.

Hubmer, J., P. Krusell, and A. A. Smith (2020). "Sources of US wealth inequality: Past, present, and future." In *NBER Macroeconomics Annual 2020*, vol. 35. Chicago, IL: University of Chicago Press.

Huggett, M., G. Ventura, and A. Yaron (2011). "Sources of lifetime inequality," *American Economic Review*, 101(7), 2923–2954.

Huggins, R., and P. Thompson (2021). *A Behavioural Theory of Economic Development: The Uneven Evolution of Cities and Regions*. Oxford: Oxford University Press.

Hurst, C. E., H. M. Fitz Gibbon, and A. M. Nurse (2016). *Social Inequality: Forms, Causes, and Consequences*. Abingdon: Routledge.

Ioannides, Y. M., and L. Datcher-Loury (2004). "Job information networks, neighborhood effects and inequality," *Journal of Economic Literature*, 424, 1056–1093.

Jackson, M. O. (2007). "Social structure, segregation, and economic behavior." Nancy Schwartz Memorial Lecture, April 2007, Northwestern University. Available at SSRN: 1530885.

Jackson, M. O. (2019a). *The Human Network: How Your Social Position Determines Your Power, Beliefs, and Behaviors*. New York: Pantheon Books.

Jackson, M. O. (2019b). "The friendship paradox and systematic biases in perceptions and social norms," *Journal of Political Economy*, 127(2), 777–818.

Jackson, M. O. (2020). "A typology of social capital and associated network measures," *Social Choice and Welfare*, 54, 311–336.

Jackson, M. O., S. M. Nei, E. Snowberg, and L. Yariv (2022). "The evolution of networks and homophily." Mimeo, Stanford University.

Jackson, M. O., T. R. Rodriguez-Barraquer, and X. Tan (2012). "Social capital and social quilts: Network patterns of favor exchange," *American Economic Review*, 102(5), 1857–1897.

Jackson, M. O., and E. C. Storms (2025). "Behavioral communities and the atomic structure of networks," forthcoming in *American Economic Journal: Microeconomics*.

Jackson, M. O., and Y. Zenou (2014). "Games on networks." In H. P. Young and S. Zamir (eds.), *Handbook of Game Theory*, pp. 95–163. Amsterdam: Elsevier.

Jahani, E., S. Fraiberger, M. Bailey, and D. Eckles (2022). "Origins and consequences of long ties in social networks." SocArXiv:10.31235/osf.io/g2nkq.

Jehiel, P., and M. V. Leduc (2021). "On why affirmative action may never end and why it should." Available at SSRN: 3842996.

Jimenez-Gomez, D. (2021). "Social pressure in networks induces public good provision," *Games*, 12(1), 4.

Jones, C. I. (2015). "Pareto and Piketty: The macroeconomics of top income and wealth inequality," *Journal of Economic Perspectives*, 29(1), 29–46.

Kaila, M., E. Nix, and K. Riukula (2021). "Disparate impacts of job loss by parental income and implications for intergenerational mobility." Working Paper.

Katz, L. F., and B. D. Meyer (1990). "The impact of the potential duration of unemployment benefits on the duration of unemployment," *Journal of Public Economics*, 41(1), 45–72.

Kearney, M. S., and P. B. Levine (2015). "Media influences on social outcomes: The impact of MTV's 16 and Pregnant on teen childbearing," *American Economic Review*, 105(12), 3597–3632.

Kets, W., G. Iyengar, R. Sethi, and S. Bowles (2011). "Inequality and network structure," *Games and Economic Behavior*, 73(1), 215–226.

Kim, S. (2017). "Intergenerational mobility in Korea," *IZA Journal of Development and Migration*, 7(1), 1–18.

Krueger, A. B., and B. D. Meyer (2002). "Labor supply effects of social insurance." In A. J. Auerbach and M. Feldstein (eds.), *Handbook of Public Economics*, vol. 4, pp. 2327–2392. Amsterdam: Elsevier.

Krugman, P. (2014). "Why we're in a new gilded age." *The New York Review of Books*, May 8.

Krugman, P., and A. J. Venables (1995). "Globalization and the inequality of nations," *Quarterly Journal of Economics*, 110(4), 857–880.

Kulic, N., J. Skopek, M. Triventi, and H.-P. Blossfeld (2019). "Social background and children's cognitive skills: The role of early childhood education and care in a cross-national perspective," *Annual Review of Sociology*, 45, 557–579.

Kuznets, S. (1955). "Economic growth and income inequality," *The American Economic Review*, 45(1), 1–28.

La Ferrara, E. (2002). "Inequality and group participation: Theory and evidence from rural Tanzania," *Journal of Public Economics*, 85(2), 235–273.

Lalanne, M., and P. Seabright (2016). "The old boy network: The impact of professional networks on remuneration in top executive jobs." SAFE Working Paper No. 123.

Lang, K., and J-Y. K. Lehmann (2012). "Racial discrimination in the labor market: Theory and empirics," *Journal of Economic Literature*, 50(4), 959–1006.

Lareau, A. (2002). "Invisible inequality: Social class and childrearing in black families and white families," *American Sociological Review*, 67(5), 747–776.

Lareau, A. (2011). *Unequal Childhoods: Class, Race, and Family Life*. Berkeley, CA: University of California Press.

Laschever, R. A. (2013). "The doughboys network: Social interactions and labor market outcomes of World War I veterans." SSRN Discussion Paper 1205543.

Lazarsfeld, P. F., and R. K. Merton (1954). "Friendship as a social process: A substantive and methodological analysis." In M. Berger, T. Abel, and H. Charles (eds.), *Freedom and Control in Modern Society*. New York: Van Nostrand.

Lobel, I., and E. Sadler (2016). "Preferences, homophily, and social learning," *Operations Research*, 64(3), 564–584.

Loury, G. (1977). "A dynamic theory of racial income differences," *Women, Minorities, and Employment Discrimination*, 153, 86–153.

Loury, G. C. (1981). "Intergenerational transfers and the distribution of earnings," *Econometrica*, 49(4), 843–867.

Loury, G. C. (2009). *The Anatomy of Racial Inequality*. Cambridge, MA: Harvard University Press.

Mankiw, N. G. (2015). "Yes, $r > g$. So what?," *American Economic Review*, 105(5), 43–47.

Marx, K. (1867). *Das Kapital, Kritik der politischen Ökonomie*. Hamburg: Verlag von Otto Meisner.

McCall, L. (2001). "Sources of racial wage inequality in metropolitan labor markets: Racial, ethnic, and gender differences," *American Sociological Review*, 66(4), 520–541.

McPherson, M., L. Smith-Lovin, and J. M. Cook (2001). "Birds of a feather: Homophily in social networks," *Annual Review of Sociology*, 27, 415–444.

Mill, J. S. (1859a). *On Liberty*. London: J. W. Parker & Son.

Mill, J. S. (1859b). "Utilitarianism." In *Utilitarianism, Liberty, Representative Government*, pp. 7–9.

Mill, J. S. (1869). *The Subjection of Women*, vol. 1. Piscataway, NJ: Transaction Publishers.

Miller, C. (2017). "The persistent effect of temporary affirmative action," *American Economic Journal: Applied Economics*, 9(3), 152–190.

Mirrlees, J. A. (1971). "An exploration in the theory of optimum income taxation," *The Review of Economic Studies*, 38(2), 175–208.

Mirza, M. U., C. Xu, B. van Bavel, E. H. van Nes, and M. Scheffer (2021). "Global inequality remotely sensed," *Proceedings of the National Academy of Sciences*, 118(18).

Montgomery, J. D. (1991). "Social networks and labor-market outcomes: Toward an economic analysis," *The American Economic Review*, 81(5), 1408–1418.

Morelli, S. A., D. C. Ong, R. Makati, M. O. Jackson, and J. Zaki (2017). "Empathy and well-being correlate with centrality in different social networks," *Proceedings of the National Academy of Sciences*, 114(37), 9843–9847.

Mosleh, M., C. Martel, D. Eckles, and D. G. Rand (2021). "Shared partisanship dramatically increases social tie formation in a Twitter field experiment," *Proceedings of the National Academy of Sciences*, 118(7).

Munshi, K. (2003). "Networks in the modern economy: Mexican migrants in the US labor market," *Quarterly Journal of Economics*, 118(2), 549–599.

Munshi, K., and M. Rosenzweig (2009). *Why is Mobility in India So Low? Social Insurance, Inequality, and Growth*. NBER Technical Report.

Myers, C. A., and G. P. Shultz (1951). *The Dynamics of a Labor Market*. Westport, CT: Greenwood Press.

Nekoei, A., and D. Seim (2019). "How do inheritances shape wealth inequality? Theory and evidence from Sweden." Available at SSRN: 3192778.

Newman, J. M. (1978). "Discrimination in recruitment: An empirical analysis." *ILR Review*, 32(1), 15–23.

Okafor, C. O. (2020). "Social networks as a mechanism for discrimination." arXiv:2006.15988.

Opper, S., V. Nee, and S. Brehm (2015). "Homophily in the career mobility of China's political elite," *Social Science Research*, 54, 332–352.

Ostrom, E. (1990). *Governing the Commons: The Evolution of Institutions for Collective Action*. Cambridge: Cambridge University Press.

Page, S. E. (2018). *The Model Thinker: What You Need to Know to Make Data Work for You*. New York: Basic Books.

Pager, D., and H. Shepherd (2008). "The sociology of discrimination: Racial discrimination in employment, housing, credit, and consumer markets," *Annual Review of Sociology*, 34, 181–209.

Pallais, A., and E. Glassberg Sands (2016). "Why the referential treatment? Evidence from field experiments on referrals," *Journal of Political Economy*, 124(6), 1793–1828.

Patacchini, E., and Y. Zenou (2012). "Ethnic networks and employment outcomes," *Regional Science and Urban Economics*, 42(6), 938–949.

Persson, T., and G. Tabellini (1994). "Is inequality harmful for growth?," *The American Economic Review*, 84(3), 600–621.

Phelps, E. S. (1972). "The statistical theory of racism and sexism," *The American Economic Review*, 62(4), 659–661.

Piketty, T. (2014). *Capital in the Twenty-First Century*. Cambridge, MA: Harvard University Press.

Piketty, T. (2015). "About capital in the twenty-first century," *American Economic Review: Papers and Proceedings*, 105(5), 48–53.

Ponzo, M., and V. Scoppa (2010). "The use of informal networks in Italy: Efficiency or favoritism?," *The Journal of Socio-Economics*, 39(1), 89–99.

Putnam, R. D. (2016). *Our Kids: The American Dream in Crisis*. New York: Simon & Schuster.

Rao, G. (2019). "Familiarity does not breed contempt: Generosity, discrimination, and diversity in Delhi schools," *American Economic Review*, 109(3), 774–809.

Rawls, J. (1971). *A Theory of Justice*. Cambridge, MA: Harvard University Press.

Rees, A. (1966). "Information networks in labor markets," *The American Economic Review*, 56(1/2), 559–566.

Rees, A., and G. P. Shultz (1970). *Workers and Wages in an Urban Labor Market*. Chicago, IL: University of Chicago Press.

Rivera, L. A. (2012). "Hiring as cultural matching: The case of elite professional service firms," *American Sociological Review*, 77(6), 999–1022.

Roberts, S. O., and M. Rizzo (2021). "The psychology of American racism," *American Psychologist*, 76(3), 475–487.

Rousseau, J-J. (1754). *Discourse on the Origin and Basis of Inequality Among Men*.

Rousseau, J-J. (1762). "The social contract."

Rubineau, B., and R. M. Fernandez (2013). "Missing links: Referrer behavior and job segregation," *Management Science*, 59(11), 2470–2489.

Sacerdote, B. (2001). "Peer effects with random assignment: Results for Dartmouth roommates," *Quarterly Journal of Economics*, 116(2), 681–704.

Sacerdote, B. (2007). "How large are the effects from changes in family environment? A study of Korean American adoptees," *Quarterly Journal of Economics*, 122(1), 119–157.

Sacerdote, B. (2011). "Peer effects in education: How might they work, how big are they and how much do we know thus far?" In E. A. Hanushek, S. Machin, and L. Woessmann (eds.), *Handbook of the Economics of Education*, vol. 3. Amsterdam: Elsevier, pp. 249–277.

Saez, E., and G. Zucman (2016). "Wealth inequality in the United States since 1913: Evidence from capitalized income tax data," *Quarterly Journal of Economics*, 131(2), 519–578.

Sen, A. (1992). *Inequality Reexamined*. Oxford: Oxford University Press.

Skopek, J., F. Schulz, and H.-P. Blossfeld (2011). "Who contacts whom? Educational homophily in online mate selection," *European Sociological Review*, 27(2), 180–195.

Small, M. L. (2006). "Neighborhood institutions as resource brokers: Childcare centers, interorganizational ties, and resource access among the poor," *Social Problems*, 53(2), 274–292.

Small, M. L. (2009). *Unanticipated Gains: Origins of Network Inequality in Everyday Life*. Oxford: Oxford University Press.

Small, M. L., D. J. Harding, and M. Lamont (2010). "Reconsidering culture and poverty," *The Annals of the American Academy of Political and Social Science*, 629(1), 0002716210362077.

Smith, M., D. Yagan, O. Zidar, and E. Zwick (2019). "Capitalists in the twenty-first century," *Quarterly Journal of Economics*, 134(4), 1675–1745.

Stephens, N. M., H. R. Markus, and L. Taylor Phillips (2014). "Social class culture cycles: How three gateway contexts shape selves and fuel inequality," *Annual Review of Psychology*, 65, 611–634.

Stiglitz, J. E. (2012). *The Price of Inequality: How Today's Divided Society Endangers Our Future*. New York: W. W. Norton & Co.

Strother, L., S. Piston, E. Golberstein, S. E. Gollust, and D. Eisenberg (2021). "College roommates have a modest but significant influence on each other's political ideology," *Proceedings of the National Academy of Sciences*, 118(2).

Thomas, R. J. (2020). "Online exogamy reconsidered: Estimating the Internet's effects on racial, educational, religious, political and age assortative mating," *Social Forces*, 98(3), 1257–1286.

Tinbergen, J. (1975). *Income Distribution: Analysis and Policies*. Amsterdam: North-Holland.

Topa, G. (2011). "Labor markets and referrals." In J. Benhabib, A. Bisin, and M. O. Jackson (eds.), *Handbook of Social Economics*, vol. 1. Amsterdam: North-Holland, pp. 1193–1221.

Verbrugge, L. M. (1977). "The structure of adult friendship choices," *Social Forces*, 56(2), 576–597.

Voorheis, J., N. McCarty, and B. Shor (2015). "Unequal incomes, ideology and gridlock: How rising inequality increases political polarization," *Ideology and Gridlock: How Rising Inequality Increases Political Polarization*, August 21.

Weber, M. (1921). *Wirtschaft und Gesellschaft* [English transl. 1978].

Wollstonecraft, M. (1792). *A Vindication of the Rights of Woman, with Strictures on Political and Moral Subject*. London: J. Johnson.

Ye, K. J. (2020). "Understanding peer effects in educational decisions: Evidence from theory and a field experiment." Mimeo, University of Chicago.

Zeltzer, D. (2020). "Gender homophily in referral networks: Consequences for the Medicare physician earnings gap," *American Economic Journal: Applied Economics*, 12(2), 169–197.

PART V

POLICY SESSION: WHAT CAN ECONOMICS DO FOR RACIAL JUSTICE?

CHAPTER 8

Introduction to the Session "What Can Economics Do For Racial Justice?"

Eliana La Ferrara

Recent events have brought the issue of racial injustice to the forefront of the political debate. While the events may be recent, this is just the tip of the iceberg for a problem that has very deep roots. As the Econometric Society, we felt it was important to take the opportunity of this World Congress to have a discussion on how, as economists, we can contribute to the goal of eliminating racial inequalities.

Four distinguished speakers have accepted to contribute to this panel:

Kerwin Kofi Charles is the Indra Nooyi Dean & Frederic Wolfe Professor of Economics, Policy, and Management at the Yale School of Management. He has done extensive research on race and discrimination, as well as on inequality and intergenerational mobility.

Lisa Cook is Professor of Economics and International Relations at Michigan State University. She does research in macro and finance, and has done fascinating work on lynchings and racial disparities in the United States.

Imran Rasul is Professor of Economics at University College London and Managing Editor of the *Journal of the European Economic Association.* His research is broadly in applied micro, including labor, development, and public economics. While he has done research on migration and race, as you will see, his talk will bring the perspective of his editorial experience.

Leonard Wantchekon is Professor of Politics and International Affairs at Princeton University. His research is in political economy and development, in particular on ethnicity, clientelism, and democratization. He is the Founder and President of the African School of Economics, which opened in Benin in 2014.

When we planned the format of the session with the speakers, we agreed it would have two angles. The first is on economics as a discipline, asking: "Is the research currently done in economics helpful to reduce racial inequalities in our societies? If not, why?" The second angle is on economics as a profession, asking whether we have enough diversity in our faculties, in methodological approaches, and so on. It makes sense to touch on both angles as they are likely to be interconnected.

Finally, while I expect a lot of discussion on where we stand and how we got here, I would be grateful to the panelists and to the audience if we could also discuss ways to improve, including practical suggestions.

CHAPTER 9

Race-Related Research in Economics and Other Social Sciences

Arun Advani, Elliott Ash, David Cai, and Imran Rasul

How does economics compare to other social sciences in its study of issues related to race and ethnicity? We assess this using a corpus of 500,000 academic publications in economics, political science, and sociology. Using an algorithmic approach to classify race-related publications, we document that economics lags far behind the other disciplines in the volume and share of race-related research, despite having higher absolute volumes of research output. Since 1960, there have been 13,000 race-related publications in sociology, 4000 in political science, and 3000 in economics. Since around 1970, the share of economics publications that are race-related has hovered just below 2% (although the share is higher in top-five journals); in political science the share has been around 4% since the mid-1990s, while in sociology it has been above 6% since the 1960s and risen to over 12% in the last decade. Finally, using survey data collected from the *Social Science Prediction Platform*, we find economists tend to overestimate the amount of race-related research in all disciplines, but especially so in economics.

9.1 INTRODUCTION

2020 is a year that will go down in history: not only was this the year of a global pandemic, but it was also the year in which issues of racial justice – driven in part by the Black Lives Matter movement – rose to the top of public debate on both sides of the Atlantic. This has prompted much discussion within the academy and economics. Exemplifying this trend, the August 2020 Econometric Society World Congress organized a special policy panel titled "What Can Economics Do For Racial Justice?" A simple answer to the question would

We gratefully acknowledge financial support from the ESRC through CPP at IFS (ES/H021221/1) and CAGE at Warwick (ES/L011719/1). We thank the authors of Angrist et al. (2020) for sharing their data on journal weights. We thank Andrea Moro, Eva Vivalt, and seminar participants from the Marist School of Management and the University of Warwick for valuable comments. We also thank the team at the Social Science Prediction Platform for their support in setting up the survey. This chapter is based on evidence presented at the Econometric Society World Congress meeting in August 2020, in a policy session titled "What Can Economics Do For Racial Justice?" All errors remain our own.

be for economists to research and publish on the causes and consequences of racial inequality – an issue highlighted by Cook (2021). From a practical perspective, then, it is important to know how many economists are already doing such research, and how that quantity compares to other disciplines.

To that end, this chapter quantifies the volume and share of research in economics on race- and ethnicity-related issues, comparing this volume of research output to two other social sciences: sociology and political science. We make comparisons to these disciplines because they are social sciences where the study of race and ethnicity would a priori also be of central importance.[1]

Of course, the publications process is closely interlinked with (i) incentives individual academics have to conduct such research and (ii) the selection of individuals into economics (see also Charles, 2021). In a more extensive companion paper (Advani et al., 2021), we examine these issues in greater detail. In this volume, Koffi and Wantchekon (2021) also highlight that even where scholars from under-represented backgrounds select into economics – African scholars in their case – the "evidence points to some degree of discrimination" in terms of access to networks such as the National Bureau of Economic Research. In this chapter, our focus is on a simple cross-disciplinary comparison of the production of race-related research.

9.2 METHOD

Corpus. We build a corpus of publications for economics, political science, and sociology. The foundation for this corpus is the *JSTOR* database of academic journals (`jstor.org`). We consider all publications in journals that *JSTOR* classifies under the disciplines of economics, sociology, and political science. Although publication series are available back to the 1880s, our analysis focuses on publications from 1960 through 2020, where for each publication we use information on the journal it is published in, when it is published, the article title, and the full text of the abstract. *JSTOR* has gaps in its publication series (especially in more recent years) and is missing some prominent journals. We fill these gaps using comparable publications data from *Web of Science* (`webofknowledge.org`) and *Scopus* (`scopus.com`). The Data Appendix describes the procedure through which we access these databases, other details on how we classify journals by discipline, and what is recorded for each publication.

Panel A of Figure A9.1 details the time series of journals covered in our corpus. For each discipline this rises steadily over time. Our working sample from 1960 to 2020 covers nearly half a million journal publications:

[1] There are, of course, many normative views on what should constitute economics, including Lionel Robbins' definition: "the science which studies human behavior as a relationship between ends and scarce means which have alternative uses." Our approach takes the practical and positive view of economics as what economists do, whereby the subject matter is defined by what research is actually published.

224, 855 publications from 231 economics journals, 138, 188 publications from 185 sociology journals, and 110, 835 publications from 213 political science journals.

Identifying Race-Related Research. Given the volume of publications considered, it is infeasible to codify race-related research by hand. We thus take an automated approach and use an algorithm to classify race-related publications. We do so using keywords along two dimensions: (i) the racial or ethnic group being studied; and (ii) the issue being studied. Examples of (case-insensitive) keywords along the group dimension are race, african-american, person of color, and ethnicity. Examples of (case-insensitive) issue keywords include discrimination, prejudice, and stereotype.[2]

Our algorithm selects a publication as being race-related if: (i) at least one group keyword is in the title; or (ii) at least one group keyword and at least one issue keyword are mentioned in the title or abstract. For rule (ii) we drop the last sentence of the abstract to avoid false positives from research that only mentions race parenthetically, say because it is part of some robustness check rather than the primary focus of study.

The group and issue keywords are designed to reflect race-related research in the United States and other countries, and to allow for changing groups and issues over time and place. However, we fully recognize that there is no definitive way to classify race-related research, and indeed there might be reasonable normative differences on what such a body of work should constitute. Therefore, we take an approach where we gradually extend our group keywords to cover broader notions of race and ethnicity.

Specifically, we define three bands of group keywords that gradually expand on the racial or ethnic groups being studied. Band 0 consists of only abstract or generic keywords denoting racial and ethnic groups (e.g., race, ethnic, under-represented minority). Band 1 adds group keywords relating to the main minority groups in the United States (African American, Latinos, and Native Americans). Band 2 adds less salient group keywords (e.g., White, South Asian, Indian American, Japanese American) and other minorities based on religious beliefs (e.g., Muslim, Jewish). The full lexicon of group keywords used by band are shown in Appendix Table A9.1.

The lexicon of issue keywords, shown in Appendix Table A9.2, are held constant and not split into bands. These words and phrases are broadly split across five broader topics: discrimination, inequality, diversity, identity, and historical issues. For example, discrimination includes prejudice and stereotypes, while inequality includes disparity and disadvantage.

Our primary results below are based on Band 1 group keywords, but we also show how our main results vary using other bands.

[2] Along each dimension we use wildcard keywords, so the keyword rac* captures race, races, racial, racist, and racism. Similarly, wildcard issue keywords include discriminat*, prejudi*, and stereotyp*. See Tables A9.1 and A9.2 for the full list of group and issue keywords.

Two further points on the selection of keywords are of note. First, the issue keywords are purposefully chosen to be economics-oriented. We are thus likely to under-count race-related research in other disciplines. Second, we do not aim to capture research that is not specifically about race but could potentially be applied to understand racial inequalities.[3] There might also be related theoretical work, say on the formation of social preferences, or papers on discrimination that do not mention any group keywords but instead refer to "blue" and "red" groups. Such work is relevant to study racial gaps, but if those publications do not explicitly mention racial/ethnic groups or issues in their abstract or title, they will not be captured by our algorithm. If such work is more common in economics than other social sciences, this can lead us to overstate gaps between disciplines in race-related research. We return to this point below, and make precise how voluminous such work would have to be in order to close race-related publication gaps between economics and other disciplines.

False Positives and False Negatives. Using an automated approach to classify race-related research leads to misclassification errors in the form of false negatives and false positives. To reduce the rate of false negatives (publications that are truly race-related but missed by our algorithm), we are relatively inclusive in the construction of the lexicon. On false positives, qualitatively we have found that using the combination of group *and* issue keywords removes many instances of non-race-related research that might otherwise match our lexicon patterns. These include, for example, publications about econometric bias, black markets, and so on. Dropping the last sentence of abstracts before applying the algorithm also helps reduce false positives by excluding many papers where race/ethnicity is not the primary focus.

To quantify potential rates of false negatives and false positives, we start with the sample of all publications in top-five (T5) general-interest economics journals: *American Economic Review*, *Econometrica*, *Journal of Political Economy*, *Quarterly Journal of Economics*, and *Review of Economic Studies*. We take all publications in T5 journals that are classified as race-related using our automated classification procedure. We then compute rates of false positives and false negatives in this sample by comparing the machine-coded classifications to a hand-coded classification. Hand-coding was done by manually checking all T5 articles that contain a group *or* issue keyword, whether or not they contain both. As this is obviously a selected sample of all publications in economics, we have to make the following assumptions in order to apply these rates to our full corpus in economics: (i) no race-related research is conducted in T5 publications that exclude both these group and issue keywords;

[3] Cook and Logan (2020) discuss many policies that have unintended impacts on racial inequality, including those with urban biases or those related to tax/benefit exemptions. Minorities might also be more impacted by changes in minimum wages (Derenoncourt and Montialoux, 2021).

and (ii) the resulting hand-coded misclassification rates found in the T5 apply equally to non-T5 journals.

Following this approach, the rate of false positives is given by

$$\frac{\#\text{Non-race-related publications labeled as race-related}}{\#\text{False positive} + \#\text{True negative}} = 3.65\% \tag{9.1}$$

and the rate of false negatives is given by

$$\frac{\#\text{Race-related publications labeled as not race-related}}{\#\text{False negative} + \#\text{True positive}} = 25.4\%. \tag{9.2}$$

Combining both forms of misclassification error, the implied ratio of true race-related research compared to identified race-related research is

$$\frac{\#\text{Race-related publications}}{\#\text{Publications labeled as race-related}} = \frac{\#\text{False negative} + \#\text{True positive}}{\#\text{False positive} + \#\text{True positive}} = 98.8\%. \tag{9.3}$$

In the Appendix, we show what trends in the estimated volume of race-related research are in the worst-case and best-case scenarios based on these rates of misclassification error.

Journal Weights. Our counts of race-related research make no adjustment for the quality of journals that work is published in. It will, however, be useful to consider both the quantity and quality of race-related research. To adjust for journal quality, we adapt the journal weighting scheme employed by Angrist et al. (2020) in their study of the intermural influence of economics on other disciplines. Journal weights are given by the relative frequency with which the journal is cited by the top "trunk" journal in the discipline. For the disciplines we focus on, these trunk journals are: *American Economic Review*, *American Sociological Review*, and *American Political Science Review*. The weight of journal j in year t is given by

$$w_j^t = \frac{\#\text{Citations to journal } j \text{ by trunk journal in year } t}{\#\text{Citations to all journals in the same discipline by trunk journal in year } t}. \tag{9.4}$$

As these weights are time-varying, they capture the rise and fall of the importance of journals within their discipline.

We use these weights to measure the quality of journals in our corpus over time. Panel B of Figure A9.1 shows that from the 1980s onwards, the quality of journals in our sample is relatively stable. It is not the case that progressively higher- or lower-ranked journals over time are selected into the corpus, and this is so for all three disciplines considered.

9.3 RESULTS

9.3.1 Comparing Economics to Other Disciplines

Figure 9.1 presents our main results. Figure 9.1A shows the total number of journal publications over time (covering any issue), by discipline. Following Kleven (2018) and Angrist et al. (2020), we plot five-year moving averages to smooth year-to-year noise but still pick up trends. There has been a steady rise in publications in all three social sciences, with the greatest increase being in economics. Economics has nearly always produced more publications than political science, and economics overtook sociology in the volume of publications in the mid-1980s. By the 2010s, there were around 6000 publications

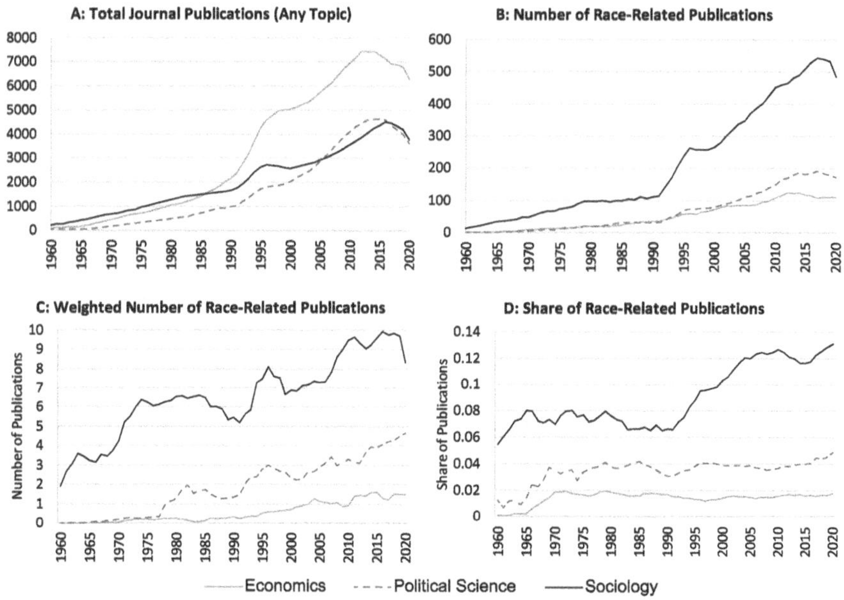

Figure 9.1 Race-related publications, by year and discipline.
Notes: We use data from JSTOR, Scopus, and the Web of Science to construct the number and shares of race-related publications in economics, political science, and sociology. Panel A reports the total number of publications in each discipline. As the publication series starts in the 1880s, the publication numbers do not start exactly at zero in 1960, the first year of our working sample. Panel B reports the number of articles that are determined to be race-related by our algorithm. Panel C reports a journal-weighted version of Panel B using the journal quality weights from Angrist et al. (2020). Panel D reports the share of articles determined to be race-related by our algorithm in each discipline. All series presented are 5-year moving averages.

annually in economics, compared to something closer to 4000 publications annually in sociology and in political science.[4]

Despite this higher volume of total research output, Figure 9.1B shows that economics lags behind sociology and political science in the absolute number of race-related publications (using our Band 1 definition of such research). Indeed, for the most recent years, around five times as many race-related papers were published in sociology than in economics each year, with just under double the number being published annually in political science than economics. Since the start of our study period in 1960, a greater volume of race-related research has always been published in sociology than economics – there never was a golden age where economists published more of such work. Cumulatively, from 1960 to 2020, there have been 13,000 race-related publications in sociology, 4000 in political science, and 3000 in economics. The cumulative number of race-related publications in economics by 2020 is at the level that political science reached in 2014, and where sociology reached in 1996. These differences are all despite our classification lexicon being biased towards economics-related issue keywords (as shown in Table A9.2).

As mentioned earlier, we might under-count the volume of race-related research in economics by not including theoretical work that does not mention any group keywords but instead refers more abstractly to "blue" and "red" groups, say. The publication gaps shown in Figure 9.1B give a sense that such work would have to (implausibly) constitute the vast majority of race-related work in economics in order to close the gap with the other disciplines.

To move beyond the quantity of race-related research but also account for its quality, Figure 9.1C shows journal-weighted time series of race-related publications by discipline. As in the raw count data, each discipline displays a steady upward trend but the ranking across disciplines remains unchanged. By the end of our sample, each year economics produces around half the quality-adjusted volume of race-related research as political science, and a quarter of that in sociology. This suggests that the overall disparity in publication output between economics and the other disciplines is not compensated by publication in relatively higher-quality journals (as measured by the Angrist trunk-journal citation weights).

Finally, Figure 9.1D shows the unweighted *share* of race-related publications by year and discipline. The lower number of race-related publications in economics (Figure 9.1B) is compounded by the higher number of total publications in the discipline (Figure 9.1A), so that the share of race-related publications in economics is far below that in sociology and political science. Moreover, there is no longer an upward trend in the share of race-related publications, in contrast to the (weighted) number of such publications in economics. Since around 1970, the share of publications in economics that are race-related has hovered just below 2%; in political science the share has been

[4] As the publication series starts in the 1880s, the publication numbers do not start exactly at zero in 1960, the first year of our working sample.

around 4% since the mid-1990s, while in sociology it has been above 6% since the 1960s, and risen to over 12% in the last decade. There is no period in our sample where economics produces a higher share of race-related research than the other disciplines.

Robustness. Panel A of Figure A9.2 shows that our measure of the broad level and trends in race-related research in economics is robust to: (i) narrowing the definition of race-related research to only use Band 0 group keywords; (ii) broadening the definition of race-related research to also use Band 2 group keywords; (iii) deriving the upper and lower bounds on our baseline definition using rates of false positives and negatives derived above; and (iv) dropping the rule requirement of not using the last sentence of abstracts to classify race-related research. Panel B shows similar robustness using the journal quality-weighted time series for economics.

9.3.2 Top-Five Economics Journals

We next narrow in on the T5 economics journals. It is useful to consider this top tier separately because it represents what is considered general interest and reflects the views of leading scholars, editors, and referees. In addition, these papers tend to be highly cited (Heckman and Moktan, 2020).

Figure 9.2A shows the total number of race-related publications in T5 journals. There appears to be a structural break in the number of race-related published articles around 2000, with a level shift up since then. Pre-2000, there were fewer than three race-related papers published each year in this top tier, while since 2000 this number has trebled. Still, the top tier economics journals collectively struggle to publish 10 race-related papers per year.

The absolute number of publications reflects the restricted supply of slots in the top-tier journals. Figure 9.2B shows the share of all T5 publications that are race-related, comparing it to the share in non-T5 journals. Here we see a more encouraging picture emerging: since the early 2000s, the share of race-related publications has been higher in T5 journals than other journals. If we view publications in the T5 as important for career incentives, this could be an important indication that the discipline is steadily providing greater incentives to work on such issues. We examine this in greater detail in Advani et al. (2021).

9.4 DO ECONOMISTS RECOGNIZE THIS?

To return to the central theme of the World Congress policy panel, if we view the lower publication rate of race-related research in economics relative to sociology and political science as concerning, then a first step in correcting this is for economists to recognize the problem. To assess the extent to which economists are aware of the facts described above, we used the

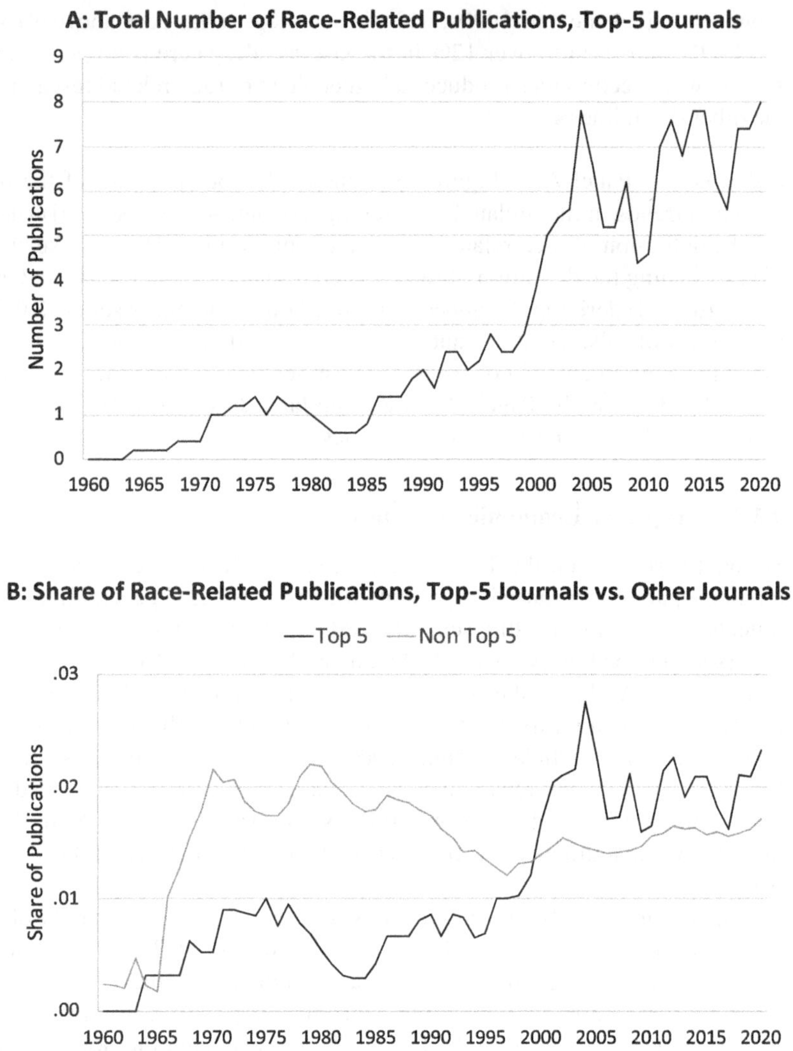

Figure 9.2 Race-related publications, top-five journals.
Notes: We show the presence of race-related research in Top-5 economics journals: the *American Economic Review*, the *Journal of Political Economy*, the *Quarterly Journal of Economics, Econometrica*, and the *Review of Economic Studies*. All series presented are 5-year moving averages.

Social Science Prediction Platform to survey economists on the share of race-related publications in the three disciplines. Academic participants were recruited via direct emails and Twitter advertising of the poll. Public-sector economists were recruited via emails to the UK Government Economics Service and Bank of England internal mailing lists. We gathered a sample of 240 responses from academic and public-sector economists in the 10 days prior to the ESWC in August.[5]

We asked participants to state their beliefs about the share of race-related research produced in economics and other disciplines, over time, and between T5 and other economics journals (see Advani et al., 2020 for the complete survey). Questions were of the form: "What share of articles published in [discipline/journal type] between [dates] do you think were race-related?" These questions were asked after a brief explanation of our definition of a race-related publication (that is close to what is described as Band 1 above).

Comparing Disciplines. Figure 9.3A shows a box-and-whisker plot of the reported estimate of the share of race-related publications by discipline for the 2000–2020 period. We show the 10th, 25th, median, 75th, and 90th percentiles of each prediction. The black line on each plot replicates the statistics from Figure 9.1D on the actual share of race-related research by discipline, as estimated using our algorithm and based on Band 1 group keywords. Economists correctly predict the disciplinary ranking but overestimate the share of race-related research in all three disciplines. Two-thirds of economists overestimate the share of race-related research in sociology, 80% do so for political science, while 90% overestimate it in economics. The ratio of the median estimate to the true rate is 4.04 for economics, 2.47 for political science, and 1.24 for sociology. Hence economists appear least informed and most optimistic about the publication of race-related research in their own discipline.

Comparing Trends and T5 Journals. Figure 9.3B shows predictions for different time periods across all economics journals, and also specifically for the T5 economics journals. As before, economists tend to overestimate the relative share of race-related publications: whether now or in the past, at least 80% of economists are overly optimistic. Economists also overestimate the increase in the share of race-related research since 2000. The median prediction for the period since 2000 is 38% higher than the median prediction for the pre-2000 period. This is in the right direction, although almost four times larger than the true (10%) increase in this publication share.

Moreover, economists incorrectly predict that race-related research is less prevalent in the T5 journals. At an individual level, 78% of economists make this prediction, and among this group the median prediction is a difference of 2pp (or around 40% less likely in relative terms). As seen in Figure 9.2B, while this was true pre-2000, T5 journals are now (slightly) more likely to publish race-related research than non-T5 journals. Despite being pessimistic about the T5 relative to other journals, even here 70% of economists overpredict the share of race-related research.

[5] Of the 240 responses, 48% were from academics and 52% from economists working in the public sector. We had an additional 28 responses from non-economist academics, mainly sociologists and political scientists, and a further 28 from individuals in the private or charity sectors. We do not perform further analysis with these latter groups as they are too small to be considered separately.

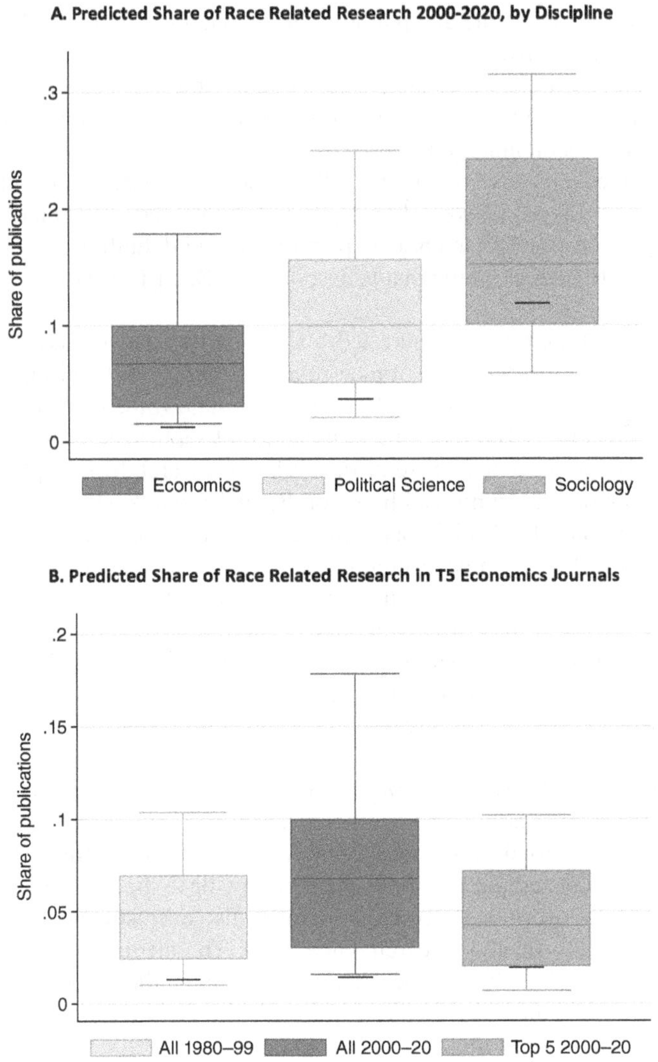

Figure 9.3 Social Science Prediction Platform results ($N = 240$).

Notes: We summarize results from a survey we ran on the Social Science Prediction Platform. Questions were of the form "What share of articles published in [discipline/journal type] between [dates] do you think were race-related?" and were asked after an explanation of our definition of a race-related publication. Panel A compares responses across disciplines, covering all publications 2000–20 in those disciplines. Panel B looks within economics to compare over time and between all journals and Top 5 journals. The box-and-whisker plots show the 10th, 25th, 50th, 75th, and 90th percentiles of responses. The black horizontal lines indicate true values as measured by our algorithm.

Finally, we note that there were no meaningful differences in the median reports between tenured faculty, untenured faculty, and students/postdocs. With the caveat that we have small sample sizes for these breakdowns (between 30 and 43), the pattern suggests that experience or cohort effects are unlikely to lead to improved recognition of the gaps in research priorities. Thus there is scope for information or policies to address incorrect beliefs about the production and publication of race-related research.

9.5 DISCUSSION

So, what can economics do for racial justice? The starting point for any answer is for economists to first study the causes and consequences of racial inequalities (Charles, 2021). In comparison to sociology and political science, economics potentially has a decades-long gap to make up – a gap that would be even wider if our lexicon of keywords extended beyond economics-focused issues, and one that is unlikely to be fully explained by under-counting some kinds of race-related research in economics. If efforts for racial justice can be measured by the volume of publications, economists might have some catching up to do.

Normatively speaking, these differences in research outputs may reflect acceptable differences in subject matter across economics, sociology, and political science. In the companion working paper (Advani et al., 2021), we show that if the topics in economics articles are re-weighted to match those in sociology (using an unsupervised topic model applied to abstract texts), the gap closes somewhat but a large disparity remains. If subject matter can only explain some but not the bulk of the difference across disciplines, it is natural to ask: What are the economics-specific factors that can narrow this gap?

Our more extensive working paper examines the underlying factors in more detail, first by exploring the race-related topics that have been studied in economics and how those topics differ from other disciplines. This analysis helps shed light on under-researched areas that may provide important contributions on the causes and consequences of racial inequalities. Second, we examine in more detail the incentives researchers have to produce race-related research by looking at publication outcomes and citations. Third, we ask how this interacts with the selection of individuals from minorities into economics. It is through understanding these three dimensions – production, incentives, and selection – that we might begin to identify the economics-specific interventions that may remedy the current situation.

DATA APPENDIX

Data Sources. The main dataset of publications is from *JSTOR*'s *DFR* service (`jstor.org/dfr`). We downloaded publication-level data using the *JSTOR* categorizations by subject: economics, sociology, and political science. The list of journals by subject is available at `jstor.org/subjects`.

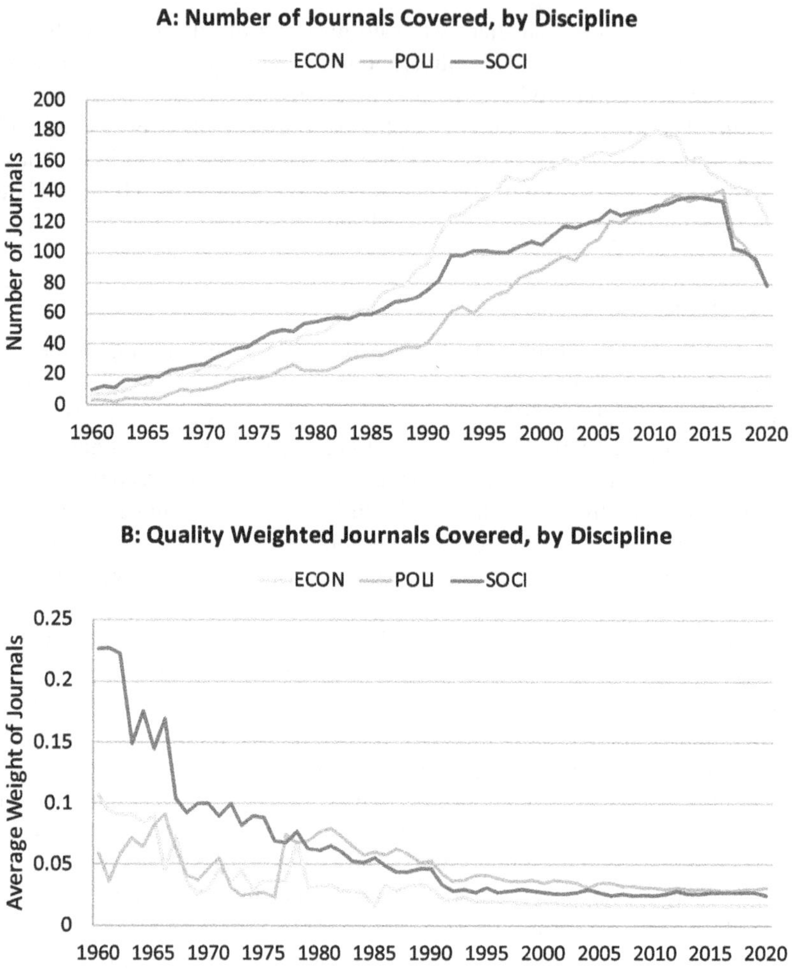

Figure A9.1 Journal coverage.

Notes: Panel A shows the number of journals observed in our corpus of publications each year for economics, political science, and sociology. Panel B plots the average journal weight across years and disciplines, derived from Angrist et al. (2020).

We use *JSTOR*'s discipline definition for each journal, except when Angrist et al. (2020) specify an alternative classification. For example, *JSTOR* lists the *Journal of Legal Studies* in law as well as economics, while the Angrist et al. (2020) weights specify it only as a journal in economics. When a journal is deemed to belong to multiple disciplines, we split the number of publications in that journal equally across disciplines.

Our second data source is *Web of Science* (*WoS*). We use the search API service offered by Clarivate. To download data, we started with the lists of

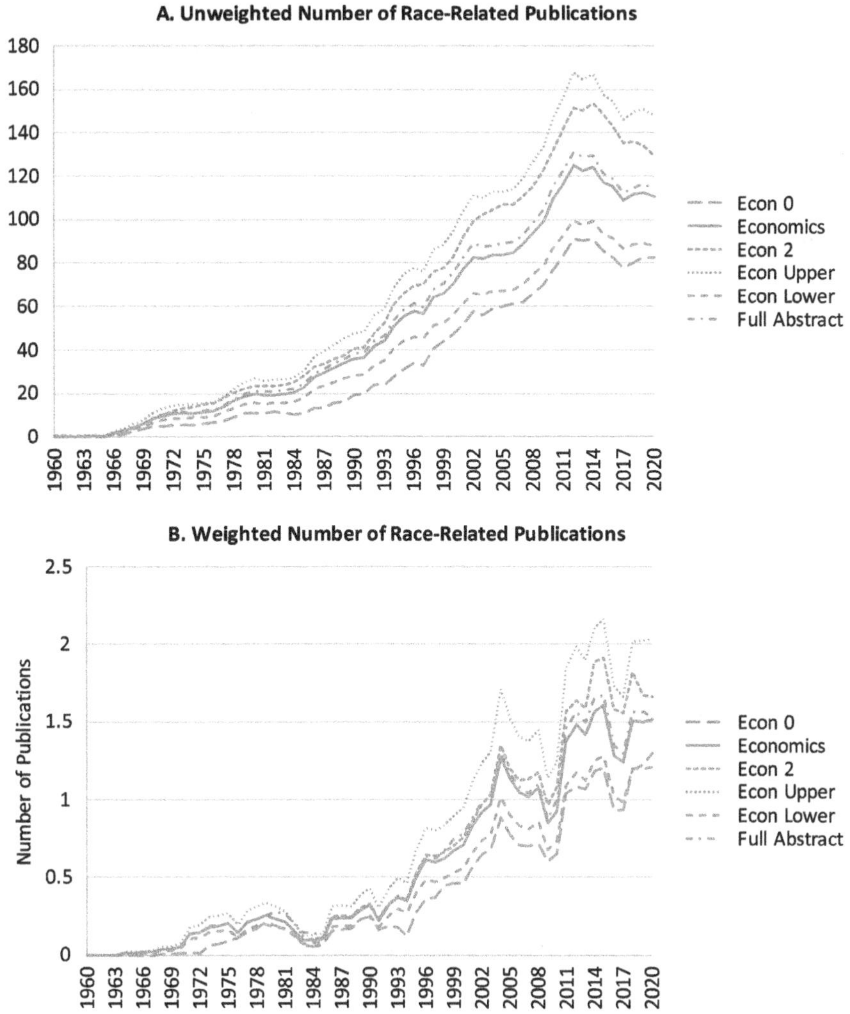

Figure A9.2 Bounds on number of race-related publications in the social sciences.

Notes: We create upper and lower bounds according to the number of false positives and false negatives of our algorithm on all the articles from Top 5 economics journals. The thick dotted lines are lower/upper bounds while the thin dotted lines are results from the varying definitions of groups covered in algorithms. In Panel A, series Econ 0, Economics, and Econ 2 show how the number of articles we count as being race-related vary as we vary the number of group keywords included in the algorithm. The three series include groups in Band 0, 1, and 2 progressively. See Table A9.1 for the definitions of different bands. Series Econ Upper/Lower in Panel A show the bounds constructed using the frequencies of false positives and false negatives. Series Full Abstracts in Panel A relaxes the restriction that the group keywords must appear before the last sentence of an abstract. Panel B reports a journal-weighted version of Panel A using the journal quality weights from Angrist et al. (2020). All series shown here are 5-year moving averages.

journals from *JSTOR* and Angrist et al. (2020). We searched for these journals in the *WoS* "source" field. We then exported the resulting JSON data and extracted publication date, title, and abstract.

The third source for publications is *Scopus*, another API-based service hosted by Elsevier. Some recent articles, especially in the top-five economics journals, are available in *Scopus* but not the other databases.

For each source we retain the same fields for each publication: subject(s), journal, publication date, title, and full text of the abstract.

Corpus Coverage. We start with the set of journals covered by *JSTOR* and use *WoS* and *Scopus* to fill in missing publications. Most missingness occurs over the post-2009 period. Articles in *WoS* but not in *JSTOR* were detected based on normalized publication title and publication date. We insert publications from *Scopus* when we cannot find another publication in the same journal and same year with the same title. For example, some prominent economics journals, such as *Journal of Public Economics* and *Review of Black Political Economy*, are not included in *JSTOR* but are available on *WoS*.

A number of journals are excluded because they do not report abstracts. For example, *American Economic Review Papers & Proceedings* never have abstracts. Other journals are excluded for those years in which abstracts are not included. For example, prior to 1994, the *Economic Journal* did not report abstracts.

The earliest article in *JSTOR* is from 1887, but coverage remains patchy until the mid-1900s. Hence our working sample starts in 1960. *WoS* includes abstracts starting in the 1990s, and these are consistently provided until around 2018. *JSTOR* abstracts drop off around 2015. Many of these missing abstracts are found through *Scopus*.

As a result of these data issues, we have a slight rise in publication numbers in the 1990s, caused by the availability of *WoS* filling in missing data from *JSTOR* – this can be seen in Panel A of Figure A9.1. The drop-off after 2015 is from *JSTOR* dropping publications, and these being only imperfectly filled using *WoS* and *Scopus*.

Identifying Race-Related Publications. We performed string matching on the titles and abstracts for each publication. Our algorithm selects a publication as being race-related if: (i) at least one group keyword is in the title; or (ii) at least one group keyword and at least one issue keyword are mentioned in the title or abstract. For rule (ii) we drop the last sentence of the abstract to avoid false positives from research that only mentions race parenthetically, say because it is part of some robustness check rather than the primary focus of study.

Each race/ethnicity keyword is divided into one of six groups: Non-Specific, African-American, Latinx, Native American, Asian, White, and Religious. Each race-related issue keyword is divided into one of five groups: discrimination, inequality, diversity, identity, and historical. The regular expressions for each pattern, as well as the division into categories, are listed in Tables A9.1 and A9.2, respectively.

Table A9.1 *Race/ethnicity group keywords with regular expression patterns*

	Non-Specific – Band 0	
rac[a-zA-Z]{0,3}	non-white[a-zA-Z]{0,1}	advantaged-group[a-zA-Z]{0,1}
person[a-zA-Z]{0,1} of color[a-zA-Z]{0,1}	colored[a-zA-Z]{0,1}	advantaged group[a-zA-Z]{0,1}
ethnic[a-zA-Z]{0,4}	caste[a-zA-Z]{0,1}	dominant group[a-zA-Z]{0,1}
underrepresented minorit[a-zA-Z]{0,3}	disadvantaged minor[a-zA-Z]{0,5}	dominant-group[a-zA-Z]{0,1}
non-western[a-zA-Z]{0,1}	people of color[a-zA-Z]{0,1}	people-of-color[a-zA-Z]{0,1}
	Main Ethnic Groups – Band 1	
African-American	Latinx	Native American
african-american[a-zA-Z]{0,1}	hispanic[a-zA-Z]{0,1}	native-american[a-zA-Z]{0,1}
african american[a-zA-Z]{0,1}	latino[a-zA-Z]{0,1}	american-indian[a-zA-Z]{0,1}
black[a-zA-Z]{0,1}	mexican-american[a-zA-Z]{0,1}	native american[a-zA-Z]{0,1}
negro[a-zA-Z]{0,2}	hispanic-american[a-zA-Z]{0,1}	american indian[a-zA-Z]{0,1}
black-american[a-zA-Z]{0,1}	latino-american[a-zA-Z]{0,1}	native[a-zA-Z]{0,1}
black american[a-zA-Z]{0,1}	mexican american[a-zA-Z]{0,1}	
	hispanic american[a-zA-Z]{0,1}	
	latino american[a-zA-Z]{0,1}	
	Less Prominent Ethnic and Religious Groups – Band 2	
Asian	White	Religious
south asian[a-zA-Z]{0,1}	white[a-zA-Z]{0,1}	jew[a-zA-Z]{0,3}
japanese-american[a-zA-Z]{0,1}	caucasian[a-zA-Z]{0,1}	hebrew[a-zA-Z]{0,1}
chinese-american[a-zA-Z]{0,1}		yiddish
korean-american[a-zA-Z]{0,1}		arab
vietnamese-american[a-zA-Z]{0,1}		muslim[a-zA-Z]
indian american[a-zA-Z]{0,1}		islam[a-zA-Z]
indian-american[a-zA-Z]{0,1}		
japanese american[a-zA-Z]{0,1}		
chinese american[a-zA-Z]{0,1}		
orientals		

Note: [a-zA-Z]{0,k} indicates that we allow any 0 to k lower or characters to be matched.

Table A9.2 *Race-related issue keywords with regular expression patterns*

Discrimination	Inequality	Diversity	Identity	Historical
discriminat[a-zA-Z]{0,4}	rac[a-zA-Z]{0,3} disparit[a-zA-Z]{0,3}	desegregat[a-zA-Z]{0,3}	rac[a-zA-Z]{0,3} identit[a-zA-Z]{0,3}	reconstruction[a-zA-Z]{0,1}
prejudi[a-zA-Z]{0,3}	rac[a-zA-Z]{0,3} gap[a-zA-Z]{0,1}	segregat[a-zA-Z]{0,3}	identity	jim crow
rac[a-zA-Z]{0,3} bias[a-zA-Z]{0,3}	rac[a-zA-Z]{0,3} differen[a-zA-Z]{0,4}	rac[a-zA-Z]{0,3} integration[a-zA-Z]{0,1}	identities	lynch[a-zA-Z]{0,3}
rac[a-zA-Z]{0,3} stereotyp[a-zA-Z]{0,3}	rac[a-zA-Z]{0,3} inequalit[a-zA-Z]{0,3}	ethnic integration[a-zA-Z]{0,1}	acting white	whitecapping
statistical discrimination [a-zA-Z]{0,1}	ethnic disparit[a-zA-Z]{0,3}	rac[a-zA-Z]{0,3} composition[a-zA-Z]{0,1}		emancipat[a-zA-Z]{0,3}
animus	ethnic gap[a-zA-Z]{0,1}	ethnic composition[a-zA-Z]{0,1}		slave[a-zA-Z]{0,2}
animosit[a-zA-Z]{0,3}	ethnic differen[a-zA-Z]{0,4}	tipping point		eugenics
rac[a-zA-Z]{0,3} profiling	ethnic inequalit[a-zA-Z]{0,3}	apartheid		postbellum
anti-discrimination	disadvantage	representation		southern farm
antidiscrimination	disadvantaged	ethnic fragmentation[a-zA-Z]{0,1}		the great migration
ethnic bias[a-zA-Z]{0,3}	gap[a-zA-Z]{0,1}	ethnic-fragmentation[a-zA-Z]{0,1}		tuskegee
ethnic stereotyp[a-zA-Z]{0,3}	black youth[a-zA-Z]{0,1}	social fragmentation[a-zA-Z]{0,1}		civil rights
rac[a-zA-Z]{0,3} interact[a-zA-Z]{0,4}	black-white	social-fragmentation[a-zA-Z]{0,1}		race riot[a-zA-Z]{0,3}

ethnic interact[a-zA-Z]{0,4}	negro-white	racial fragmentation[a-zA-Z]{0,1}	race relation[a-zA-Z]{0,1}
antisemitism	stratification	racial-fragmentation[a-zA-Z]{0,1}	social activis[a-zA-Z]{0,1}
anti-semitic	inequality	ethnic diversity	social-activis[a-zA-Z]{0,1}
anti-black		ethnic-diversity	political disenfranchisement
attitude[a-zA-Z]{0,1}		social diversity	black vot[a-zA-Z]{0,3}
hatred		social-diversity	
group bias		racial diversity	
ethnic division[a-zA-Z]{0,1}		racial-diversity	
ethnic-division[a-zA-Z]{0,1}		racial heterogene[a-zA-Z]{0,5}	
social division[a-zA-Z]{0,1}		ethnic heterogene[a-zA-Z]{0,5}	
social-division[a-zA-Z]{0,1}		affirmative action[a-zA-Z]{0,1}	
racial division[a-zA-Z]{0,1}		affirmative-action[a-zA-Z]{0,1}	
racial-division[a-zA-Z]{0,1}		underrepresent[a-zA-Z]{0,3}	
ethnic exclusion[a-zA-Z]{0,1}			
ethnic-exclusion[a-zA-Z]{0,1}			

(continued)

Table A9.2 *(cont.)*

Discrimination	Inequality	Diversity	Identity	Historical
social exclusion[a-zA-Z]{0,1}				
social-exclusion[a-zA-Z]{0,1}				
racial exclusion[a-zA-Z]{0,1}				
racial-exclusion[a-zA-Z]{0,1}				
apartheid				
systemic racism				
institutional racism				
structural discrimination				
institutional discrimination				
implicit bias[a-zA-Z]{0,2}				
intergroup				
inter-group				
out-group				
outgroup				
in-group				
ingroup				
exploitation				
oppress[a-zA-Z]{0,3}				

Note: [a-zA-Z]{0,k} indicates that we allow any 0 to k lower or characters to be matched.

REFERENCES

Advani, A., E. Ash, D. Cai, and I. Rasul (2020). *The Study of Race in Economics, and Other Social Sciences*. Social Science Prediction Platform. https://socialscienceprediction.org/s/dybafd.

Advani, A., E. Ash, D. Cai, and I. Rasul (2021). *On the Study of Race and Ethnicity in Economics: Production, Incentives and Selection*. Mimeo, University College London.

Angrist, J., P. Azoulay, G. Ellison, R. Hill, and S. F. Lu (2020). "Inside job or deep impact? Using extramural citations to assess economic scholarship," *Journal of Economic Literature* 58: 3–52.

Charles, K. (2021). *Transcript of Remarks from, "What Can Economics Do For Racial Justice?" Panel*. Econometric Society World Congress Monograph.

Cook, L. D. (2021). *Transcript of Remarks from, "What Can Economics Do For Racial Justice?" Panel*. Econometric Society World Congress Monograph.

Cook, L. D., and T. Logan (2020). *Racial Inequality, Economists for Inclusive Prosperity*. Research Brief.

Derenoncourt, E., and C. Montialoux (2021). "Minimum wages and racial inequality," *Quarterly Journal of Economics* 136: 169–228.

Heckman, J. J., and S. Moktan (2020). "Publishing and promotion in economics: The tyranny of the top five," *Journal of Economic Literature* 58: 419–470.

Kleven, H. (2018). *Language Trends in Public Economics*. Mimeo, Princeton University.

Koffi, M. and L. Wantchekon (2021). *Racial Justice from Within? Diversity and Inclusion in Economics*. Econometric Society World Congress Monograph.

CHAPTER 10

Racial Justice from Within? Diversity and Inclusion in Economics

Marlène Koffi and Leonard Wantchekon

This chapter investigates the determinants of racial disparities in economics, using data on NBER membership. The data originates from the publication records and measures of the academic impact of research associates and faculty research fellows of the political economy and development economics groups, as well as a group of "eligible" but not selected African economists. The preliminary evidence points to some degree of discrimination as an explanation for the under-representation of African economists in NBER (DEV and POL). We find that the median of our group of "eligible" African economists may be at least as qualified as 50% of those who become faculty research fellows up to three years after their PhD. We also find that nearly 70% of NBER members are alumni of six graduate programs. This high degree of institutional concentration might make racial disparities at NBER worse, given that minority scholars in general, and Africans in particular, are vastly under-represented at those six schools. We conclude with suggestions that would make the Bureau more racially diverse and inclusive.

10.1 INTRODUCTION

A number of recent studies have documented racial diversity issues in the economics profession. According to the *American Economic Association Report on Minorities*, Blacks represent around 3% of economics faculty members and PhD graduates. The patterns become even more striking when we look at representation of Africans. For instance, less than 12 of the 144 papers about Africa published in top-five economics journals during the past 20 years have African co-authors (Panin, 2020; Porteous, 2020). Other studies indicate that only 11% of impact evaluation studies by the World Bank and only 7% of publications on African development in the *Journal of Development Economics* have African co-authors (Mendiratta, 2011). This extends to presence on editorial boards; the ten economics journals with most publications on international development have only 3% of editorial board members who are affiliated to

We would like to thank Gabriel Grajeda, Gray Collins, Gabriel Mekbib, and Khalimath Oyekan for excellent research assistance. We would also like to thank Yashna Gungadurdoss, Sarah Pollnow, Julio Solis Arce, Kristia Wantchekon, and the audience of the Session on Racial Inequalities at the World Congress of the Econometric Society (2020) for comments and suggestions. The usual caveat applies.

African universities (Chelwa, 2021). Examining these questions begs the question of whether this paucity of representation is driven by discrimination or differences in academic productivity.

In order to provide credible evidence on discrimination in the academy, we need to show that equally productive individuals are treated differently in hiring and promotion in the profession. To this end, we create a novel dataset on publication records and academic impact of research affiliates and research fellows from political economy and development economics groups in the National Bureau of Economic Research (NBER) and a group of "eligible" African economists.

Reflecting the pattern of overall lack of diversity in economics, NBER groups on political economy (POL) and development economics (DEV) only have 3% of African scholars as members. We use the data to argue that this lack of representation could be driven at least to some extent by discrimination, as defined in Bertrand and Mullainathan (2004). We find that PhD graduates or affiliates from a top program (Harvard, MIT, Princeton, Yale, Berkeley, or LSE) represent more than 70% of NBER membership. We also find that around the 60th percentile of NBER members entering up to two years after their PhD have the typical "African" profile (to be defined below) and exhibit some tail effects where three African non-members would be in the 80th–90th percentile of some recruiting cohorts.

We draw in part from insights by Bertrand and Mullainathan (2004). They sent fictitious resumes to job calls and manipulated the perception of race by using typically Black and White first names. They found that White-sounding names receive around 50% more callbacks for interview. We aim to provide similar insights using coarse matched data, as in Sarsons (2017) on medical references and other recent studies on discrimination.

A recent paper by Card et al. (2020) analyzes the gender gap in the selection of Fellows of the Econometric Society. In this chapter, we narrowly focus on NBER DEV and POL over 30 years as opposed to ES with data over 80 years. However, given the pivotal role that NBER could play in the career trajectory of young economists, our results and the recommendations that they generate may have some immediate impact on the professional development of economists from minority groups.

The remainder of the chapter is organized as follows: Section 10.2 describes the data collection; Section 10.3 presents results from the comparison of the productivity profile between NBER members and Africans in our sample; Section 10.4 concludes with some policy implications.

10.2 DATA DESCRIPTION

10.2.1 Background

The NBER is one of the most prestigious organizations in economics. As of December 2020, it has more than 1550 affiliated members, including 32 winners of the Nobel Prize.

The selection of members is a highly competitive process. Applicants are first screened based on their primary affiliations, which must be a North American university. They are subsequently nominated and then elected. Applicants who do not yet have tenure are selected as Faculty Research Fellows, while applicants with tenure are considered for appointment as Research Associates.

The NBER is structured around 20 research programs. Conferences, seminars, and symposia are regularly organized to allow researchers to share and discuss cutting-edge research topics. The NBER also grants research funds to support researchers and provides them with a platform for publishing their work, in particular with the NBER working papers series.[1]

10.2.2 Data Collection Protocol

We restrict our study to two fields of economics: political economy and development economics. As the first step of the analysis, this restriction is justified because several Africans, particularly emerging African economists, specialize in one or both of these fields. Given this chapter's purpose, which is to highlight the potential of minorities, this restriction is reasonable.

Further, we separate our data into two categories: NBER members and African economists. For each of the authors listed, we have collected their CV. This allows us to extract their academic information (e.g., years active, employment status) and career trajectories.

To build the NBER members' database, we began with the list of NBER members specializing in political economy (POL) and/or development economics (DEV) available on the NBER website. In addition to the authors' names, we extracted their appointment date at the NBER, status at NBER (FRF – Faculty Research Fellow or RA – Research Associate), years spent as FRF (if available), RA promotion year, and total years of NBER membership. It is important to note that the status retrieved from the website is the current status of members. Since only the current designation of FRF or RA is reflected on the NBER's site, we examined archives/snapshots of that site over time to find the change in designation using Wayback Machine. Although a precise date/month was not available, we could thus pinpoint the year of promotion.[2]

We then supplemented this information with the authors' demographic characteristics such as nationality, gender, and ethnicity. The nationality and ethnicity variables held our attention the most because they allowed us to break

[1] According to the NBER website, the POL program aims "to examine the interactions among political institutions, participants in the political system, such as voters and elected officials, and economic outcomes broadly defined." The DEV program aims to "stud[y] the forces that contribute to economic development, particularly in less developed nations. It explores the role of decisions by households, firms, and governments, the effects of development aid policies, and the consequences of rising incomes in emerging economies."

[2] However, the Wayback Machine does not track before 2010. For authors who were promoted from FRF to RA after 2010, we searched the web for their names along with "research associate" and "research faculty fellow" to find their year of promotion wherever possible.

down members by race and origin (with a finer subdivision between Africans and Afro-Americans, for example).

We also collected variables related to the authors' academic backgrounds and professional status. These include the institutions where they earned their undergraduate degree and their PhD, their current affiliation, their past affiliations, their status within the affiliation (Assistant, Associate, Full Professor). Finally, we extracted bibliometric information and author citations by year on Google Scholar using a web scraping procedure. The data collection took place from June to September 2020. We restricted our collection to peer-reviewed publications and excluded from our count any proceedings, books, comments, and so on. The collection protocol is presented in more detail in the appendices.[3]

Similarly, we built a database of African economists in POL and DEV. This database is primarily based on the research area and is formed by taking a list of emerging Africans who have studied in the North American educational system. Except for variables related to NBER membership, we collect all the same variables for Africans.

10.2.3 Descriptive Statistics

10.2.3.1 Demographic Characteristics

There are 229 economists in POL and DEV considered in the database. Among them, 209 are affiliated to the NBER, and 20 are African economists not affiliated to the NBER.

Figure 10.1 shows the racial and ethnic distribution of the NBER members. Nearly 64% of our sampled economists are White, and 21% are defined as "Asian." The remaining 15% includes Latinos or Hispanics, White Africans, African Americans, and Black Africans. In total, about 3% of the members are Africans (Blacks or not), and 1.5% are Blacks. The database, therefore, contains three Black economists out of 209 members.[4]

10.2.3.2 Institutional Concentration

We further analyze the distribution by PhD-granting institutions and by current affiliations. The distribution of PhD-granting institutions is quite concentrated. About 70% of members obtained their PhD from one of six institutions: Harvard, MIT, University of California Berkeley (UC Berkeley), Yale, Princeton, or London School of Economics and Political Science (LSE). In

[3] We have also collected additional variables such as the name of the author's thesis advisor(s) and the organizations of which the author is a member (e.g., Econometric Society, CEPR, etc.). When the names of the thesis advisors were not available on the CV, we used RePEc Genealogy to trace the author's academic lineage. However, at this stage, the number of observations does not enable us to fully exploit the richness of the collected database.

[4] The sample also includes 59 women, or about 30% of the members. The unconditional gender distribution is quite in line with the gender distribution in the profession. See CSWEP report 2019.

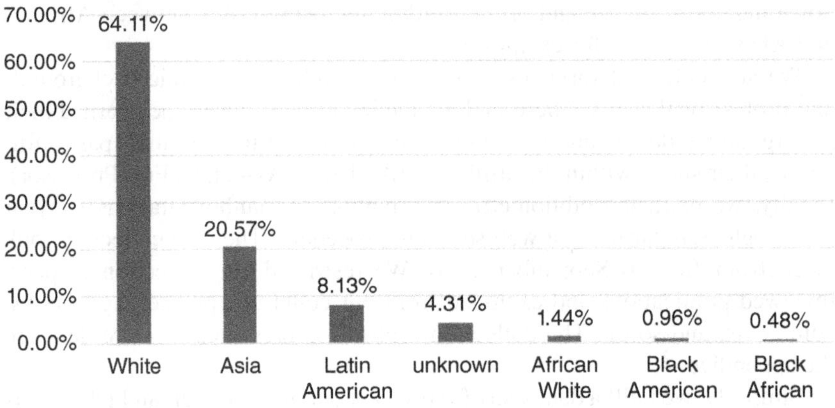

Figure 10.1 Institutional distribution of the NBER members.
The figure shows the distribution of race and ethnicity for the 209 NBER members in POL and DEV.

total, we identify 37 individual PhD-granting institutions (70% of which are North American institutions) for the 209 NBER members. On the other hand, the distribution of institutional affiliations is less concentrated than that of PhD institutions. The six dominant PhD-granting institutions constitute just over 35% of the institutions with which authors are currently affiliated. A total of 44 affiliations are represented, and only three are located in Europe. The fact that NBER members are affiliated mostly with top-ranked institutions is less surprising than the extreme concentration of PhD-granting institutions. Clearly, the institution where an economist earned his or her PhD may be a key determinant to becoming a NBER member (at least for political economy and development), even more important than the economist's current affiliation.

Given this institutional concentration, it could be assumed that one of the reasons for the under-representation of minorities, and Africans in particular, is that these individuals are less likely to be affiliated with these institutions. However, the sample of Africans in our study is a strong testament to the contrary. Indeed, more than 80% of the African economists we examine obtained their PhD or are affiliated with the aforementioned institutions, including some in the top six (Harvard, LSE, Princeton, UC Berkeley).[5] In addition, all hold positions in North American universities. Five are full professors; five are associate professors; ten are assistant professors (two of them moved to international organizations after starting an academic career).

10.2.3.3 Rewarding "Potential" vs. "Accomplishment"?

The majority of NBER members (63%) become members between zero and five years after receiving their PhD; 22% are recruited within a single year of defending their PhD thesis and 15% are recruited after the second year. In all,

[5] By aforementioned, we mean the 44 universities or 37 PhD programs the current NBER members are affiliated with.

almost half of the members (45%) are awarded membership within three years of receiving their PhD.

It is clear that a substantial fraction of NBER members were elected at the earliest stages of their career. This early-stage selection is more common at the NBER than it is at other elite organizations in economics, such as the Econometric Society, the American Academy of Arts and Sciences (AAAS), the National Academy of Sciences (NAS), the American Economic Association (AEA), and the Alfred P. Sloan Foundation.

As a result, the selection committee may give more weight to the candidate's potential than the candidate's actual accomplishment. However, any assessment of "potential" likely encompasses some error term or even some degree of subjectivity. The best prediction one can make of an individual's future in academia is the individual's current productivity. As we will see in the next section, Africans do not lag behind other economists in terms of their research productivity early in their careers.

10.3 PRODUCTIVITY PROFILE OF NBER MEMBERS AND AFRICANS

In this section, we compare the productivity profile of authors who are members of the NBER and African authors who are not NBER members. We focus on NBER members who enter with FRF status. To do this, we first use the total number of publications and the number of publications in the top-five journals. The top-five journals list includes the traditional list of top journals in economics: *American Economic Review*, *Quarterly Journal of Economics*, *Journal of Political Economy*, *Review of Economic Studies*, and *Econometrica*.

10.3.1 General Comparison of Productivity Profile of NBER Members Before NBER vs. Africans

Table 10.1 shows the results of such a comparison. Consider the individuals who became NBER members within five years of receiving their PhD. 50% of those who became members within one or two years of receiving their PhD had zero or one publication at the time of appointment. For those who joined three years after receiving their PhD, the median number of publications at the time of appointment is two. This median rises to three for those appointed in the fourth year and four for those appointed in the fifth year after receiving their PhD. Looking to the publication activity of the African economists in our dataset, we see little difference. 50% of the African economists in our sample had their work published within a year of obtaining their PhD. The median number of publications increases to two for individuals two years after their PhD, still at two three and four years after their PhD, and it rises again to three publications for individuals five years after their PhD.

We can also compare the NBER members and African economists with respect to number of works published in the top-five journals, and we will

Table 10.1 *Comparison of productivity profile: NBER vs. Africans*

Time after PhD before membership	Publications (median)		Top 5 (median)	
	NBER	African	NBER	African
1	1	1	0	0
2	1	2	0	0
3	2	2	1	0
4	3	2	1	0
5	4	3	1	0

The table shows NBER members' productivity profile compared to a subset of African economists in POL and DEV. For the total number of publications and the total number of top-five, the values displayed are the median of each cohort. For example, reading the first line, among the members entering zero to one years after their PhD, 50% have less than one publication, while one year after their PhD, 50% of the Africans also have one publication. The sample of NBER members entering within five years as Faculty Research Affiliates includes 112 scholars. The sample of Africans includes 20 scholars.

again find little discrepancy in accomplishment in the early stage. Over 80% of NBER members who entered within a year of receiving their PhD did not have any work published in a top-five journal at the time of their appointment. The median increased to one for those becoming members three years after their PhD and remains at one for up to five years after their PhD.

Overall, more than half of the current NBER members who were recruited up to two years after their PhD present a median "African" profile: less than one publication and zero top-five publications. In other words, if we used current members' publishing histories to construct a criterion for NBER membership, at least ten other Africans should become members.

10.3.2 African Productivity Distribution's Tail

The overall distribution of Africans can hide huge heterogeneities.[6] Indeed, if we look at the African sample's tail, we can find an African economist with one top-five publication within a single year of receiving his PhD. Therefore, he would fall in the 95th percentile of the distribution of number of top-five publications for NBER members recruited one year after their PhD. Another African economist in our sample has one top-five publication and six total publications within five years of receiving his PhD. Therefore, he is part of the 80th percentile of top-five publications and the 75th percentile overall publication distribution of members recruiting five years after their PhD. Another one has two top-five publications over five years. Therefore, he is part of the 99th percentile of top-five publications distribution of members recruiting five years after their PhD. However, none of the three are members of the NBER.

[6] We acknowledge that the general distribution of NBER members can also hide heterogeneities as well. But as we are interested in shedding light on the potentialities of minorities, we analyze in a particular way the tail of the minority distribution.

10.3.3 Divergence of Productivity Distribution

The difference in research productivity between NBER members and the non-member African economists in our sample emerges after the former are admitted as NBER members, and it continues to deepen after that.

To analyze this, consider the economists who entered the NBER within three years of receiving their PhD and who had at that time no top-five publications and at most one other publication (i.e., a median African profile one year after the PhD). Figures 10.2 and 10.3 show us the total number of publications

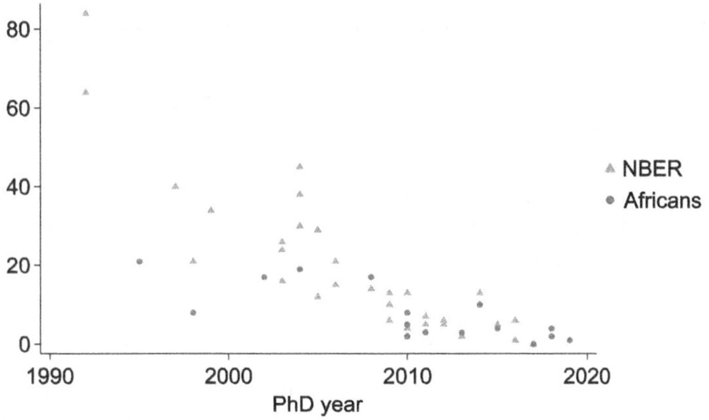

Figure 10.2 Comparison of total publications by PhD year after membership. The figure shows the number of publications after entering NBER by PhD granting year for NBER members with a median African profile one year after PhD (one publication and zero top five). Those are compared to the overall publications of Africans in the sample.

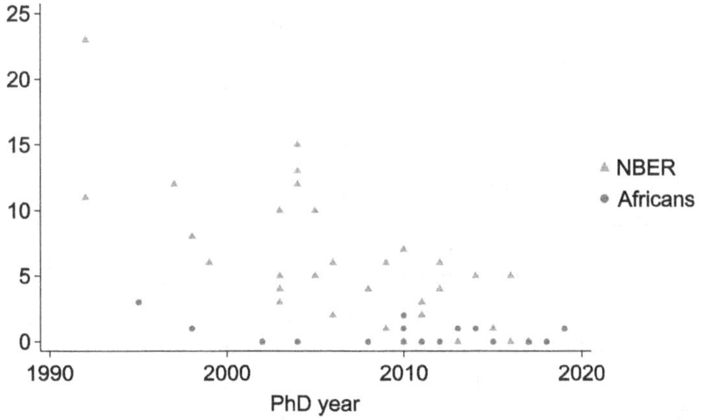

Figure 10.3 Comparison of top-five publications by PhD year after membership.
The figure shows the number of publications after entering NBER by PhD granting year for NBER members with a median African profile one year after PhD (one publication and zero top five). Those are compared to the overall publications of Africans in the sample.

and the top-five counts of these individuals after becoming members. The distribution of Africans is below that of NBER members. In particular, 50% of the members have at least 14 publications, and six publications in top-five journals. For the most recent generation of academics (those who received their PhD after 2010), the median is five total publications, around three of which are top-five publications. Meanwhile, the median number of top-five publications for African economists in the same time horizon is still zero. However, even these two curves depict profiles of Africans who, even though not members of the NBER, display publication levels just as important as certain members several years after the latter become so.

The differences observed can be explained by several factors. Indeed, it is possible that the potential-based selection process actually produced the desired results either through the correct assessment of candidates or through self-fulfilling prophecies. It is also possible that the NBER offers opportunities that promote a certain emergence in the profession, increasing the research productivity of its members. In any case, this descriptive analysis highlights a complex phenomenon hitherto ignored. We present in the following section some thoughts on the subject.

10.4 POLICY DISCUSSIONS AND CONCLUSION

This chapter provides preliminary evidence suggesting that the under-representation of African economists on the NBER (DEV and POL) might, at least in part, be driven by discrimination. We identify research productivity (number of publications some given years after receiving a PhD) as an objective measure of early-career merit and use this criterion to compare current NBER members with a sample of African scholars in the same field. We find that 70% of the members come from six PhD programs, with nearly half selected within three years after earning their PhD. In addition, more than half of the current NBER members who were recruited up to two years after their PhD present a median profile of African scholars in our sample. However, later in their career they become more productive than our median African scholar. This is likely due to the network benefits and enhanced institutional access afforded by membership in the NBER.

The approach we utilize could be applied to other subgroups; for example, the institutional concentration we see at the PhD-granting institution may exclude some productive PhD graduates from slightly lower-ranked institutions. This may have implications for inclusion and diversity in the profession, in light of the fact that minority students are more severely under-represented in the graduate programs that produce the vast majority of NBER members (AEA-CSMGEP reports, various years, job market candidate data).

Two main policy implications emerge from the current findings. First, it is critical to effectively address the diversity issue by expanding the eligible candidate pool, particularly to lower-ranked graduate programs. We would also suggest that the NBER release transparent and more specific eligibility requirements for their selection (e.g., at least one publication in a field journal). Furthermore, eligibility for election as Faculty Research Fellows should be at least three years after graduation. This would provide more opportunities for an expanded pool of early-career economists to signal or realize their academic potential and to increase their chances of being selected, in addition to providing a more objective basis for comparison between candidates.

Finally, we acknowledge that further empirical exercises are needed to provide more robust evidence for discrimination. To that end, our companion paper (Koffi and Wantchekon, 2020) uses more comprehensive data and advanced econometric methodology to extend the analysis to other subfields, and identify the "NBER effect" on professional development of young economists.

APPENDIX DATA COLLECTION PROTOCOL

Variable	Source	Notes
Name	NBER name	
Nationality	CV/General search	
Gender	Observed	
Ethnicity	Observed	"Unknown" when ambiguous
NBER affiliation	NBER	
Appointment Date	NBER	
Years spent as FRF	CV/Wayback Machine/General search	Since that designation is reflected in the NBER site, we looked at archives/snapshots of that site over time to find the change in designation using Wayback Machine. Although a precise date/month is not available, we can pinpoint the year of promotion. I.e., in this example the designation changed between Aug. 29, 2011 and Oct. 27, 2011. However, it doesn't track before 2010 and for those authors we've been trying searching their names along with "research associate" and "research faculty fellow" and specifying the year. However, for authors who were appointed in the 80s and 90s, it has been difficult to find that information.
RA promotion year	Same method as "Years spent as FRF"	

(cont.)

Variable	Source	Notes
Total years of NBER membership	NBER	
Number of publications prior to membership	CV	Counting "refereed/peer reviewed journals." Not including "forthcoming," "working papers," book chapters, and "American Economic Review Papers and Proceedings" towards the total number of publications *Not top 5 but include in number of publications *Don't count book chapters (would double count) *Impact factor the journal publication
Number of citations prior to membership year	Google Scholar	Counted this as prior to the year of membership (e.g., if someone was inducted in 2010, I would add up their citations from 2009, 2008, etc.) Web of Science as an alternative to Google Scholar (when Google Scholar profile is unavailable) but note different ways of citations
Number of top 5 publications prior to membership	CV	American Economic Review (AER) Econometrica (ECMA) Journal of Political Economy (JPE) Quarterly Journal of Economics (QJE) Review of Economic Studies (ReStud)
Number of publications between FRF and RA promotion	CV	
Number of citations between FRF and RA promotion	Google Scholar	Counted this as prior to the year of membership (e.g., if someone was inducted in 2010, I would add up their citations from 2009, 2008, etc.)
Number of top 5 publications between FRF and RA promotion	CV	
Number of journal publications total	CV	
Number of top 5 publications total	CV	
Number of citations total	Google Scholar	
Summary of main publications	Google Scholar/CV/ Personal website	Google Scholar's categorization of interest areas; however, when not available using terms from personal websites/CV

(cont.)

Variable	Source	Notes
PhD received year	CV	
Name of advisor	https://genealogy.repec.org/list.html#V	Subsequent searches can include: "author name dissertation [graduating year]" to find acknowledgements
Institutional Affiliation	CV	
Undergraduate institution	CV	
PhD institution	CV	
Membership affiliations	CV/Personal website	American Academy of Arts and Sciences (AAAS) American Economic Association (AEA) American Finance Association (AFA) American Law and Economics Association (ALEA) American Philosophical Society (APS) Becker Friedman Institute (BFI) British Academy (BA) Bureau for Research and Economic Development (BREAD) Center for Competitive Advantage in the Global Economy at Warwick (CAGE) Center for Development Economics and Policy (CDEP) Center for Economic and Policy Research (CEPR) Center for Effective Global Action (CEGA) Center for Global Development (CGD) Cowles Foundation for Research in Economics (Cowles) Econometric Society (ES) Economic Research on Identity, Norms and Narratives (ERINN) Institute of Fiscal Studies (IFS) International Growth Center (IGC) Institute for Labor Studies (IZA) JPAL (Abdul Latif Jameel Poverty Action Lab) National Academy of Medicine (NAM) National Academy of Sciences (NAS) National Institute of Health (NIH) National Science Foundation (NSF) Society of Labor Economists (SLE) Yale Research on Innovation and Scale (YRISE)

REFERENCES

Bertrand, M., and S. Mullainathan (2004). "Are Emily and Greg more employable than Lakisha and Jamal? A field experiment on labor market discrimination," *American Economic Review*, 94(4), 991–1013.

Card, D., S. DellaVigna, P. Funk, and N. Iriberri (2020). "Gender neutrality in economics: The role of editors and referees." Working Paper, University of California Berkeley.

Chelwa, G. (2021). "Does economics have an 'African problem'?," *Economy and Society*, 50(1), 78–99.

Committee on the Status of Minority Groups in the Economics Profession (CSMGEP) Reports, various years. https://www.aeaweb.org/about-aea/committees/csmgep/annual-reports.

Koffi, M., and L. Wantchekon (2020). "Racial diversity and inclusion in economics." Working Paper, Princeton University.

Mendiratta, V. (2011). *Report on Impact Evaluation in Sub-Saharan Africa* (No. DT/2011/13).

Panin, A. (2020). "Economics experiments in Africa: How many and by whom?," *Codesria Bulletin*, 4, 23–28.

Porteous, O. (2020). "Deserts and oases: Evidence from 27 thousand economics journal articles on Africa." Working Paper, Middlebury College.

Sarsons, H. (2017). "Interpreting signals in the labor market: Evidence from medical referrals." Working Paper, University of Chicago.

CHAPTER 11

Lightly Edited Comments of Remarks Given at 2020 Econometric Society Session of Racial Equity

Kerwin Charles

Eliana, thank you so much for the introduction, and thanks to you and the panel for introducing me and including me in this discussion. I will make only a few comments.

My comments will touch on the three areas in which our profession can work to achieve racial equity in economics. I'm going to speak first about *access* or *presence*; I mean by this what each of us can do to increase diverse racial representation in our profession. Second, I'll discuss research and publishing success – the most important outcomes for academic economists. Having helped increase the number of persons from under-represented racial groups entering economics, what can the profession do to help ensure that these economists thrive as scholars? Finally, how can we, as practicing economists, help advance racial inequality in the broader society? We play multiple roles while discharging our duties as professional economists – teacher, scholar, and colleague. My comments about what we can do to collectively address the disparities and inequities that perturb us highlight actions we can take in these different capacities.

Let me begin with the issue of *access*. How might greater racial diversity among practicing economists be achieved, and what is our collective role in achieving that increased representation? It seems to me that we have two problems in this arena. On the one hand, there is what one might call an "intake" problem: the relative paucity of persons of color entering, or seeking to enter, the profession of economics in the first place. What can practicing economists do to affect that intake? Here, it seems to me the role we play as teachers and mentors is especially salient. Imagine, for example, that one is teaching an undergraduate course. One of our obligations as instructors, in my view, is to identify persons with the requisite talent to pursue graduate training in our field successfully. This challenge of spotting talent – a kind of "identification problem" – is a crucial aspect by which we can affect representation in our role of instructor.

Identifying talent is not the only way we increase representation in our role as teachers. It is also necessary to inspire said talent, and that inspiration comes, in part, from how and what we teach. What examples do we cite to make a point? Thoughtful consideration of the illustrations and examples we use while teaching might enkindle a desire to more deeply understand economics in a talented undergraduate African American or Latina, who previously doubted the relevance of material she is learning to her community or concerns of especial interest to someone of her background. I remember how the examples chosen by my instructors convinced me that this thing called economics was an exciting and useful thing, with both profound relevance and analytical force, for the questions that interested me.

Of course, there is no guarantee that the student, whose talent a committed instructor has identified, and whose desire to learn more has been stimulated by good teaching, will decide to devote her life to the challenging course of pursuing graduate training and a career in economics beyond that. This talented student has options. She can go to law school, or business school, or undertake any number of rewarding paths. What can the instructor do to nudge her to consider devoting her life to economics? I submit that some amount of *persuasion* is helpful. If possible, the professor – the teacher – concerned about representation should get to know this student, discuss ideas with her, provide some reassurance. In short, whenever possible, a professional economist, concerned about increasing diversity and representation, should in the role of instructor engage in active persuasion to get a student like the one described to seriously consider making our profession her career. This active persuasion is all the more important for students of color since the relatively low representation of such persons in our field means that she will not be otherwise receiving that knowledgeable encouragement.

Our role as instructors matters not only for intake but also for the opposite end of the PhD training pipeline; our collective decisions can affect the premature exit from PhD training of students of color. Many of us have had this experience of seeing a grad student of color, whom we'd gotten to know and admire, perhaps through their work for us as a research assistant, leave the program. The specific stumbling block varies from case to case – sometimes, it is the Macro prelim. Other times, it is the second half of Metrics; in yet other instances, it is the inability to produce a good second-year research paper.

I am discussing here a PhD student who has been through our core, whom we've taught or spoken with or observed in a seminar – someone whose talent we can see, and about whose ultimate success in economics we feel reasonably confident. Now, because of whatever the relevant hurdle is in her case, she has to leave the program. "You've got to go," we have to say. Do we have to say? I am not convinced about that. If we observe that we are losing people we'd prefer to keep because of the barriers that we ourselves have erected, it is incumbent upon us, and well within our power, to re-examine those barriers. Notice I am not arguing here for an irresponsible relaxation of standards or rules that, after all, serve an essential gatekeeping function. However, I believe that it behooves us to consistently reassess our rules, especially when they appear to pose a disproportionately insurmountable obstacle for persons from under-represented groups.

Consider now the next stage of the career. The person is now an economist: they have been identified and inspired; successfully navigated the difficulties of graduate school; received useful counsel during the crafting and writing of the dissertation; and all the rest. PhD in hand, they enter the profession. He is, let's say, an African American academic economist. Having been vital in the role of instructor, what can a practicing economist do, in the other roles he plays, to ensure the young scholar's professional success? This is my second topic.

Increasingly it seems to me, and this is especially true in empirical economics, the slice of our world that I know best, publishing success increasingly requires access to secure or hard-to-get data. One needs connections to data-granting authorities, engagement with teams of senior researchers scattered around the country and internationally, and presence in various sorts of clubs. I don't use the word "club" here pejoratively. Nor do I have in mind aggregations of distinction such as, say, "The Econometrics Society." I mean instead that a young scholar, plying her trade somewhere in her first or second year, needs to get her work seen, needs to understand what people in her area are working on, needs to know what editors believe to be interesting, needs to know why this thing is a dead-end and a settled matter, and so forth. In the absence of connections, if I may use that word, she has no way of gathering this information.

We can affect her presence in things like the National Bureau of Economic Research (NBER), Allied Social Science Associations (ASSA), and Bureau for Research and Economic Analysis of Development (BREAD). Membership in, or even engagement with, these clubs matters. It probably matters disproportionately for faculty of color because historically under-represented groups have no ready mechanisms for otherwise acquiring the benefits that access to these clubs provides. Positive steps must be taken by those of us who can address this kind of exclusion. It's not a willful, deliberate exclusion but it matters for various determinants of professional success: data, connection to new research partners, exposure to new questions, critical feedback on early work, and the like.

Through our work as scholars, there is another way that we can affect this young scholar's research success. Many of the questions of greatest interest to this young researcher are things about which she may have important intuitions and insights, but which don't fit neatly into the workhorse frameworks used by economists. Let's take the idea of systemic racism, an idea around which there is much current conversation by scholars from many different fields. She would like to work in this area. As research scholars, we can provide the intellectual theoretical underpinnings for this idea. All of us have responsibility here as a field to define, to clarify, to describe equilibrium constructs and to, for example, produce testable predictions and implications that can be taken to data, or theoretically extended, by new scholars entering the field.

Our field provides at least one powerful example, concerning race, of this beneficial aspect of our research efforts. Few economists, before Becker's dissertation, wrote papers in economics about market racial discrimination. Becker's theory of discrimination gave us all a way of capturing a phenomenon, whose existence economists in the 1930s, 1940s, and 1950s certainly knew of even if they lacked formal language and formal framework to precisely describe or produce convincing tests. Becker's framing – distinguishing between the negative sentiment that some people hold towards others of different races (what he called animus) and racial differences in market realizations; long- versus short-run time frames and employer versus customer considerations; equilibrium sorting; the marginal discriminator; and the like – gave us the lens and the tools in economics to investigate and rigorously analyze something whose existence I think we never doubted. Arrow and others' writings about statistical discrimination serve much the same function.

The rich literature on market discrimination, to which Black scholars in economics have devoted disproportionate attention, may not have existed if those giants of our field from an earlier era had not rolled up their sleeves and tackled these questions.

There is a need for this kind of effort today. What, precisely, are microaggressions, and how do we integrate them into economics models? We hear of (and some of us personally experience) this phenomenon, so we suspect that racial outcomes might be affected in crucial ways by this force. But, given our tools and the standards of evidence and reasoning on which our field appropriately insists, what precise relationships or patterns in the data should economists seeking to understand this idea be studying?

For the many of us eager to see research progress on these and similar issues, there is a strong hope that innovations on the theoretical and empirical innovations will soon appear to enable us to use the formidable tools of economics to tackle these important topics in convincing and novel ways.

In closing, I will say a few words about how, as professional economists, we can affect policy concerning racial equity. I hear the term "statistical discrimination" bandied about by non-economists, irresponsibly and inaccurately, in policy debates. We can weigh in on those debates. Let me write an op-ed, one of us might say, clarifying what the term means and what it does not. Policing is obviously on everyone's mind; there is debate, disagreement, and controversy in economics about the role and effectiveness of policing. I want to hear economists talk about that. That conversation should not be left to one economist or two but to us acting severally. Other examples will come to your mind, but the point is if we seek to address and effect change, we have to each be involved under all of the hats we wear: scholar, teacher, colleague, public commentator. If we do those things and we do them vigorously and in earnest, we can help achieve racial equity in economics.

CHAPTER 12

Lightly Edited Comments of Remarks Given at 2020 Econometric Society Session of Racial Equity

Lisa Cook

What can economics do for racial justice? I think, like Kerwin, we can do a lot.

We were asked to address these two questions that Eliana posed at the beginning. And I would like to address each one in turn – the first one with respect to research, and the second one, both with respect to research and the profession.

Is research currently done in economics helpful to reduce racial inequalities in our society? I would say, "No." Our profession has not been as helpful as it could have been with respect to reducing racial inequality, which has its roots in systemic racism in our society. We have spent decades and millions of pages of journals asking two related questions. One, does racial discrimination exist? If so, is it due to statistical discrimination, which we interpret as being based on probabilities? And it is considered okay. Actually, it is neither okay nor excusable. Or racial animus or intent? We have done a lot to establish that racial discrimination exists. However, we, as economists, do not answer the question of what to do about it. Other social science disciplines, like political science or sociology, do.

Moreover, the race variable is doing way too much work in economics. That is, we put a lot of emphasis on the race variable when we include it in regressions, and we really do not interpret it. We just take the negative coefficient on it as a given, an immutable thing, value-free and unencumbered with meaning. Given the wide variety of outcomes for which the race variable is negative and significant, it seems that systemic racism is a reasonable interpretation of it.

You have probably heard the story of my paper recently. It is a paper on violence and economic growth. The story of it suggests that the economics profession is or has been unwilling to imagine the full range of research questions related to racial inequality, for example in patenting and innovation. I remember when I undertook this research, I was posed with the question, "Why would I ever study African Americans as a reference group in innovation?" This economist was essentially saying, "African Americans do not invent anything. So why even study them?" The implication was that we did not see it in the data or were unaware of it, and therefore it was not worth studying. I would think the opposite. If we do not see it, we need to ask why we do not see it. I think that is an equally compelling question.

I will address the second question that Eliana mentioned. What can we do to improve, and what are some practical suggestions? I have sets of suggestions for both research and the profession.

For context, I currently serve on the Executive Committee of the American Economic Association (AEA). I was elected to serve last year. And I also serve as the director of the AEA Summer Program. I will say a bit more about that in just a moment. First, we have to acknowledge that systemic racism exists, not just racial disparities. We like to talk about racial disparities, but it's more than racial disparities. What's at the root of those disparities? They are everywhere, which suggests that there is a system in place that drives these disparities. It is systemic or structural racism. I think in the current environment, we have been challenged to think about these disparities as being structural, and not just from one sector or the other.

We need to acknowledge that systemic racism exists both in research and in the profession. If we needed any empirical validation of this claim, the AEA Climate Study published a year ago provided it. For example, it shows that Black women report being discriminated against more than any other group in economics. They report taking more steps than any other group in economics to avoid racist and sexist behavior, and they disproportionately report being discriminated against with respect to promotion and pay.

Second, after we acknowledge that this racism exists, we should take active steps to combat it. Kerwin already gave some examples. I would pose a series of questions as well. Are we recommending only our friends and classmates for editor positions at journals or to be referees at journals? Are we inviting only people we know to give or be discussants on papers or organize and chair sessions at conferences? Are we nominating only our close friends and colleagues and others in our inner circle for prizes and awards? Are we using examples in our courses and textbooks that include or are only relevant for White men? Are we standing by and saying nothing when something racist is being said to or about a colleague in a faculty meeting or to students in classes when they are the sole member of a minority group? Are we asking the Black people in the profession to do disproportionate service and not reward and pay them for it? Are we not hiring, promoting, and tenuring Black women because of the narrow conception of "fit"? All of these things hinder the free flow of ideas, lessen broad participation in economics, and make economic research less vibrant and relevant. I would suggest that all economists take a look at the AEA Code of Conduct that was adopted and has been posted on the AEA website and pledge to abide by it, whether in AEA-specific or other professional settings. There are lots of resources on the AEA website, such as best practices as well. But at least we should start with the Code of Conduct as something to guide our actions, especially with respect to what not to do.

Third, we should open our imagination, and be more curious about economic behavior. Regardless of the quarters from which that economic behavior is derived, we need to be fundamentally more curious about our peers and their lived experiences, as well as those outside our circles of friends, family, and colleagues. I find lots of research on Black people that is not informed by the lived experiences of Black people. I believe that my paper on violence and economic activity was not published very readily because referees were likely asking whether anything related to Black people (a minority population within the United States) could be generalizable and of general interest. I hear the same kind of question posed about fundamental economic research that is derived from data on Native Americans. We can learn something about human economic behavior from any and all groups of human beings. Another concrete step is to improve the pipeline and mentoring activities. For example, these opportunities exist in the AEA Summer Program and in grassroots activities, like the Sadie Collective and the Research in Color Foundation. We should seek to enhance mentoring at every stage in the economics profession, especially given the exponential growth in pre-doc (or post-bac) programs, and generally improve the workplace environment for economists, regardless of whether they are in academia, government, industry, or elsewhere. To be clear, it is not just the pipeline. This should include reporting and prosecuting racial and gender harassment and misconduct and addressing racial and gender discrimination in any corner of the profession where it exists.

To conclude, I am hopeful about the future. And I am hopeful that we will study racial and ethnic identity as we study gender. I believe that we have constructed algorithms to specifically identify gender, and, therefore, to study gender. And I think we can do the same with race in many, though not all, cases.

I would echo the words of Kerwin to finish. Everyone has to take responsibility and get involved. It is on all of us. Thank you.

PART VI

TOPICS IN MICROECONOMIC THEORY

CHAPTER 13

Analogy-Based Expectation Equilibrium and Related Concepts: Theory, Applications, and Beyond

Philippe Jehiel

A unified definition of analogy-based expectation equilibrium (ABEE) for strategic environments involving multiple stages and private information is presented. Various alternative interpretations of the concept are proposed, as well as a discussion of how to use ABEE in practice. A variety of applications, including two new ones related to speculative trading and personnel economics, are reviewed. A discussion of a number of alternative equilibrium concepts follows, emphasizing the links and differences with ABEE. Finally, a discussion of possible next steps in particular related to the endogenization of analogy partitions is proposed.

13.1 INTRODUCTION

Standard solution concepts in game theory (and economic theory) typically assume that players (or economic agents) hold rational expectations about the consequences of their actions and about the behaviors of others. While it seems implausible that economic agents would be able to reach this state of knowledge by pure introspection,[1] an appealing approach to the rational expectation assumption relies on learning: as evidence is accumulated, economic agents would gradually correct their mistakes, and eventually behave as the standard concepts assume.

This chapter was prepared for the (virtual) World Congress of the Econometric Society, Milan, 2020. I wish to thank Kai Barron, Milo Bianchi, David Ettinger, Antonio Guarino, Steffen Huck, Frédéric Koessler, Konrad Mierendorff, Dov Samet, Larry Samuelson, Juni Singh, and Giacomo Weber for fruitful collaborations on related topics, as well as Ken Binmore, Olivier Compte, Ignacio Esponda, Drew Fudenberg, Simon Gleyze, Laure Goursat, Johannes Hörner, Ariel Rubinstein, Rani Spiegler, and seminar participants at various webinars for useful conversations or comments. This project has received funding from the European Research Council (ERC) under the European Union's Horizon 2020 research and innovation program (Grant Agreement No. 742816).

[1] Even putting plausibility aside, the pure introspective approach to the rational expectation assumption raises conceptual difficulties, as discussed in Binmore (1987).

Yet, in complex environments, expectations concern so many different situations that it is unlikely that economic agents would be able to collect enough evidence to correct every conceivable mistake.[2] I would argue that in such environments, economic agents (similarly as statisticians or analysts) are more likely to form their view of the world based on aggregate statistics that summarize coarsely the behaviors of others.[3] It is then of importance to understand how economic agents forming their expectations based on such aggregate statistics would interact in strategic settings, and how the induced behaviors differ from those predicted in the rational case.

In the past years, I have developed a solution concept, the analogy-based expectation equilibrium (ABEE), aimed at modeling how economic agents exposed to statistics that aggregate (behavioral) data across different situations would behave in steady state. In essentially all applications of ABEE so far, how data are aggregated for players is taken exogenously. That is, one characteristic of a player is how behavioral data are bundled for him, as summarized by his analogy partition. The analogy partition together with the utility function and the private information provides a complete description of the characteristics of the player. Interactions are next described as usual, making it precise who moves when and what the available actions are.

I have considered various strategic environments, covering normal-form games played in parallel as well as extensive-form games of complete information (Jehiel, 2005), static games of incomplete information (Jehiel and Koessler, 2008), and also some classes of multi-stage games with asymmetric information (Ettinger and Jehiel, 2010). Below, I consider all these settings at once, assuming that the private information is defined at the start of the interaction and that the past actions of players are publicly observable within the game. In such settings, the analogy partition of a player is a collection of subsets of contingencies referred to as analogy classes where a contingency specifies the player j under consideration, the profile of players' types τ, and the history h of past actions.[4] When two contingencies $(j, \tau h)$ and $(j', \tau' h')$

[2] Strictly speaking, a given economic environment is never encountered twice in exactly the same conditions, thereby making the pooling of some evidence/data coming from different sources somehow necessary. Savage (1954) makes the related observation that states as envisioned by decision-makers must be simplifications of the objective states viewed as complete descriptions of the world (which are necessarily unique). This leads him to adopt a subjective formulation of the state space that he does not relate to the objective states. One distinctive feature of the approach developed below consists in linking the subjective representation to objective characteristics.

[3] Such statistics would be obtained from the pooling of behavioral data corresponding to past play in different situations, and they may either be passed by third parties to new inexperienced players or else correspond to simplified processing of the raw data about past play constructed by the players themselves to facilitate learning. See further discussion below.

[4] As the word "partition" indicates, different analogy classes have an empty intersection and their union is the set of all contingencies.

belong to the same analogy class, I require that the action space of player j at h is the same as the action space of player j' at h' so that there is a well-defined action space in each analogy class (this is to make the pooling of the behavior of j at τh and j' at $\tau' h'$ operational in a simple way).[5] In an ABEE, every player i is assumed to have learned, in each of his analogy classes α_i, the aggregate behavior, referred to as the analogy-based expectation $\beta(\alpha_i)$. Given his private information and his utility, player i plays a best response to the belief that player j in contingency $(j, \tau h)$ behaves according to $\beta(\alpha_i)$, where α_i is the analogy class to which $(j, \tau h)$ is assigned. While I discuss several motivations for this notion of best response, my favorite one is based on simplicity: in ABEE, players consider the simplest view of the world that is consistent with their (partial) knowledge, as given by β. That is, player i assumes that the behavior in every contingency $(j, \tau h)$ of any of his analogy classes α_i matches the aggregate behavior $\beta(\alpha_i)$ in α_i he is informed about, and he best responds to this view of the world.

In steady state, I also require for each player i and each possible analogy class α_i, that $\beta(\alpha_i)$ correctly represents the aggregate behavior in the analogy class.[6] The correctness of the analogy-based expectations is viewed as the outcome of a collective learning process in which, before playing the game, an individual subject assigned to the role of player i receives feedback concerning past behaviors in the various analogy classes α_i corresponding to his type. He chooses his strategy as a best response to the induced belief about others' behaviors as constructed from the empirical distributions, thereby generating new behavioral data. When a steady state is reached, the play must be that of an ABEE.

In the rest of the chapter, I present more precisely the ABEE concept, develop further the interpretations of it, and discuss applications with a focus on two new ones related to speculative trading and personnel economics, respectively, and I highlight how the ABEE approach can explain puzzles (such as the use of absolute auctions or the emergence of bubbles) or new phenomena (such as deception) that would be hard to capture in the standard rationality benchmark. I also provide some guidance on how to choose analogy partitions in the various applications. In particular, I distinguish three different motivations for the choice of analogy partitions. In the first one, the feedback received by players is viewed as being exogenously coarse, thereby viewing the choice of analogy partitions as being dictated by the kind of coarse statistics about past play that is passed to new players. In the second one, the analogy partitions are viewed as representing what players find more salient in the various contingencies, and this can be used to formalize various psychological biases such as cor-

[5] A possible elaboration of this would view the player as subjectively identifying actions across different contingencies. I will briefly discuss this later on.

[6] To cover analogy classes that would not be reached in equilibrium, I consider trembling-hand perturbations in the vein of Selten (1975). I note that such a refinement is not used in most applications of ABEE.

relation neglect, selection neglect, or the fundamental attribution error, among others. In the third one, the analogy partitions are viewed as simplifying learning devices used by players to interpret more effectively the raw data available to them.[7] After the exposition of ABEE and its applications, I describe how ABEE relate to a number of other concepts including the Bayes Nash equilibrium with subjective prior, the self-confirming equilibrium, the cursed equilibrium, the Bayesian network equilibrium (BNE), the Berk–Nash equilibrium, and other equilibrium approaches with some bounded rationality element. Finally, I suggest what I regard as possible next steps for the ABEE research agenda, including possible routes to endogenize the analogy partitions.

13.2 THE ANALOGY-BASED EXPECTATION EQUILIBRIUM

13.2.1 Strategic Setup

I consider multi-stage games with observed (past) actions and possibly incomplete information. This allows me to cover simultaneously the setups studied in Jehiel (2005), Jehiel and Koessler (2008), and Ettinger and Jehiel (2010).[8] Each player $i \in I = \{1, ..., n\}$ can be one of finitely many types $\tau_i \in T_i$. Player i knows his own type τ_i but not the types τ_j of the other players $j \neq i$. Nature initially selects the profile of types $\tau = (\tau_i)_{i=1}^n$ according to a probability distribution $p(\tau)$, which is commonly known to all players (see below for a discussion of applications in which $p(\cdot)$ is not known to the players).

The game involves finitely many stages. Nature as well as the players may be called to play at various stages of the game. The sequence of possible moves is the same whatever the profile of types τ.

A history refers at the various stages of the game to the string of earlier actions chosen by the various players (as well as nature if applicable), but it does not include the initial selection of types τ. It will be denoted h, and the set of h will be denoted H. A complete history that includes the initial choice by nature of τ as well as h will be denoted τh. The set of τh will be denoted TH.

Player i plays at the same subset H_i of histories H whatever his type τ_i. The action space of player i at history $h \in H_i$ is common to all types τ_i, and it is denoted $A_i(h)$. Observe that h may belong to H_i for several i, thereby allowing me to cover the case of simultaneous moves. The set of terminal histories z is denoted Z, and each player is endowed with a von Neumann–Morgenstern utility function u_i defined over lotteries over Z that may vary with $\tau = (\tau_i, \tau_{-i})$.

7 That categorizations are viewed as facilitating learning has, of course, many precedents (see, in particular, Anderson, 1991).

8 I am considering games of perfect recall and perfect monitoring. Allowing for imperfect recall and/or imperfect monitoring raises no conceptual difficulties but requires heavier notation (see Jehiel, 2021 for an illustration of ABEE in a context with imperfect recall and Jehiel and Samuelson, 2023 for an illustration of ABEE in repeated games with imperfect monitoring).

Specifically, $u_i(z;\tau_i,\tau_{-i})$ denotes player i's payoff if the terminal node z is reached and the profile of types is $\tau=(\tau_i,\tau_{-i})$.[9]

Notion of Type. The non-standard aspect of the strategic environment lies in the definition of types τ_i. A type τ_i of player i consists of two components $\tau_i=(\theta_i,c_i)$, where $\theta_i\in\Theta_i$ is the standard type of player i that in particular can affect players' preferences (payoff-irrelevant signals – such as signals about θ_{-i} – can be part of θ_i as well) and $c_i\in C_i$ specifies the aggregate statistics (about the behaviors of the various players) player i has access to. I will refer to c_i as the cognitive type or analogy partition of player i.

As seems natural to assume, the cognitive types of players do not affect players' preferences over the various terminal nodes. That is, for each terminal node $z\in Z$, it holds that $u_i(z;\tau_i,\tau_{-i})=u_i(z;\tau_i',\tau_{-i}')$ whenever $\tau_i=(\theta_i,c_i)$ and $\tau_i'=(\theta_i,c_i')$ have the same standard type θ_i, and $\tau_{-i}=(\theta_{-i},c_{-i})$ and $\tau_{-i}'=(\theta_{-i},c_{-i}')$ have the same standard type θ_{-i}.[10]

Cognitive Type. The cognitive type or analogy partition c_i is defined as follows. It is a partition of the set of contingencies described as

$$\left\{(j,\tau h)\text{ with } j\in I,\ \tau\in T,\text{ and } h\in H_j\right\}.$$

A typical element of partition c_i will be denoted α_i and referred to as an analogy class of player i. I impose that if $(j,\tau h)$ and $(j',\tau' h')$ belong to the same analogy class α_i, the action space of player j at h is the same as the action space of player j' at h'. That is, $A_j(h)=A_{j'}(h')$. One can then speak of the common action space $A(\alpha_i)$ in the analogy class α_i.

The idea behind the cognitive type c_i of player i is that this player would only be informed about the aggregate distribution of behavior in each of the analogy classes α_i in c_i, and he would not be informed of more detailed aspects of others' strategies. In order to speak of aggregate behavior, one needs to be able to identify actions across different contingencies $(j,\tau h)$ in α_i, and the common action space requirement is a simple way to make this operational.

Observe that, unlike in Jehiel (2005), I am allowing player i to also include player i's own contingencies in his analogy partitions (as $(j,\tau h)\in\alpha_i$ with $j=i$ is permitted). This should not be confused with the fact that within the interaction I am assuming player i has perfect recall (he remembers his past actions as well as his strategy). Allowing player i to include contingencies of the form $(i,\tau h)$ in an analogy class α_i will allow me to capture applications in which the feedback received by player i about past play aggregates the (past)

[9] When intermediate payoffs are obtained in the course of the interaction, one should think of $u_i(z;\tau_i,\tau_{-i})$ as aggregating all these intermediate payoffs possibly through the standard exponential discounting formula or any other formula that sounds appropriate.

[10] An alternative, commonly used representation of the standard type θ_i involves an underlying state space Ω endowed with some probability distribution, and θ_i is the information set of player i informing this player in which subset of Ω the true state $\omega\in\Omega$ lies. With this representation, the underlying utility would depend on ω (possibly with some aspects of ω being payoff-irrelevant).

behaviors of subjects in the roles of players i and $j \neq i$ in various contingencies (see the learning interpretation below and the anonymous analogy partition for an illustration).

13.2.2 Solution Concept

Analogy-Based Expectations. An analogy-based expectation for player i with analogy partition c_i specifies for each analogy class α_i of c_i, a probability distribution over the action space $A(\alpha_i)$. I will let $\beta(\alpha_i) \in \Delta A(\alpha_i)$ refer to this distribution, and $\beta_{c_i} = (\beta(\alpha_i))_{\alpha_i \in c_i}$ refer to the analogy-based expectation of player i with analogy partition c_i. I will also let $\beta^i = (\beta_{c_i})_{c_i \in C_i}$ refer to the profile of analogy-based expectations for all possible cognitive types of player i, and $\beta = (\beta^i)_{i \in I}$ refer to a profile of β^i for all players $i \in I$.

Strategy. A (behavioral) strategy of player i is denoted σ^i. Following standard approaches, it is a mapping that assigns for every type τ_i of player i and every history $h \in H_i$ at which player i must move, a probability distribution over $A_i(h)$. I let $\sigma_{\tau_i}(h) \in \Delta A_i(h)$ refer to this distribution, and refer to $\sigma_{\tau_i} = (\sigma_{\tau_i}(h))_{h \in H_i}$ as the strategy of type τ_i. A strategy of player i can then be viewed as $\sigma^i = (\sigma_{\tau_i})_{\tau_i \in T_i}$. The set of σ^i will be denoted Σ^i, $\sigma = (\sigma^i)_{i \in I}$ will denote the strategy profile, and Σ the set of σ.

Best-Response. Knowing the aggregate behavior $\beta(\alpha_i)$ in α_i (and no more detailed information within α_i), it seems natural that player i would expect player j at τh with $h \in H_j$ to behave according to $\beta(\alpha_i)$ whenever $(j, \tau h) \in \alpha_i$. Formally, this leads player i with cognitive type c_i to adopt the following representation of the strategy of player j. For every $j \neq i$ and every $\tau h \in TH$ with $h \in H_j$:

$$\widehat{\sigma}_j[c_i;\beta](\tau h) = \beta(\alpha_i) \text{ whenever } (j, \tau h) \in \alpha_i,$$

for each analogy class α_i of c_i.[11]

In multi-stage games of incomplete information, one classic difficulty is that some histories may not be reached, making the inference about the types of other players at such histories and the ensuing continuation best-response calculation non-trivially defined. I adopt the approach of (extensive-form) trembling hand proposed by Selten (1975) to get around this difficulty.[12] Specifically, in a first step, I assume for every player i with type τ_i that every action $a_i \in A_i(h)$ of player i at every history $h \in H_i$ must be played with a probability no smaller than $\varepsilon(a_i, h, \tau_i)$, assumed to be strictly positive.[13] I refer to the corresponding best response as an ε-perturbed best

[11] Observe that I consider only players $j \neq i$ because player i need not form a theory about himself (he remembers his strategy (perfect recall) and he does not interact with other subjects in the role of player i).

[12] I should add that the trembling-hand refinement is not needed in most applications of ABEE, to the extent that in most applications all analogy classes are reached in equilibrium.

[13] As in Selten (1975), I assume there is no correlation across the trembles at different nodes.

response where $\varepsilon = (\varepsilon(a_i,h,\tau_i))_{a_i,h,\tau_i}$. In a second step I consider sequences of $\varepsilon = (\varepsilon(a_i,h,\tau_i))_{a_i,h,\tau_i}$ such that all $\varepsilon(a_i,h,\tau_i)$ converge to 0.

Formally, an ε-perturbed best response is defined as follows:

Definition 13.1 *σ^i is an ε-perturbed best response to β^i if and only if for every $\tau_i = (\theta_i, c_i)$, σ_{τ_i} is a best response to $\widehat{\sigma}_{-i}[c_i;\beta]$ where the optimization must respect the lower bounds imposed by ε.*

In Definition 13.1, I have not made explicit whether the optimization is made at an ex-ante stage or at each history where player i must move. Given that all histories are reached whenever all $\varepsilon(a_j,h,\tau_j)$ are strictly positive, and that I am considering games of perfect recall, these two notions of best response are equivalent here.[14]

Consistency. A key equilibrium requirement is the consistency of analogy-based expectations. Specifically, I require that, for every possible analogy class α_i, the analogy-based expectations $\beta(\alpha_i)$ should correctly represent the aggregate behavior in α_i, as implied by the strategy profile σ (and how nature selects types). To define this formally, I let $P^\sigma(\tau h)$ denote the probability that the full history τh is reached when nature selects τ according to $p(\cdot)$ and players behave according to σ. When strategies are fully mixed (i.e., all actions are played with strictly positive probability at every history), $P^\sigma(\tau h) > 0$ for all τh, allowing me to unambiguously define consistency as follows:

Definition 13.2 *Assume that σ is totally mixed. The profile of analogy-based expectations β is consistent with σ if and only if for all possible analogy classes α_i of any player i, it holds that*

$$\beta(\alpha_i) = \frac{\sum_{(j,\tau h)\in\alpha_i} P^\sigma(\tau h)\sigma_{\tau_j}(h)}{\sum_{(j,\tau h)\in\alpha_i} P^\sigma(\tau h)}. \tag{13.1}$$

To understand the consistency condition (13.1), think of a third party (e.g., a statistician) who would collect information from many different plays about the frequencies of actions played in α_i. Assume also that players keep playing according to σ in all interactions. Such a third party would end up having frequencies that should be a weighted average of the frequencies observed in the various $(j,\tau h) \in \alpha_i$. That is, it should be a weighted average of $\sigma_{\tau_j}(h)$ for the various $(j,\tau h) \in \alpha_i$. Moreover, the weight attached to a specific contingency $(j,\tau h)$ in α_i should be proportional to the frequency of visit of this specific $(j,\tau h)$ as such a frequency indicates how often the behavior in contingency $(j,\tau h)$ will contribute to the observed aggregate frequency profile. The weighting of $\sigma_{\tau_j}(h)$ by $P^\sigma(\tau h)$ is the mathematical formulation of this

[14] A possible alternative definition of best response would view player i at different nodes as different players, and each such player could form a belief about the other players in the role of player i using the subjective representation derived from β. In contexts in which a given subject assigned to the role of player i is viewed as choosing an entire plan of actions, the chosen definition is more appropriate.

(given that the frequency of $(j, \tau h)$ in α_i should be proportional to $P^{\sigma}(\tau h)$). A consequence of this is that if one contingency $(j, \tau h)$ in α_i is much more likely to be visited than another contingency $(j', \tau' h')$ in α_i, then $\sigma_{\tau_j}(h)$ will contribute much more than $\sigma_{\tau_{j'}}(h')$ to $\beta(\alpha_i)$, and player i will be induced to believe the behavior of $\tau_{j'}$ at h' is in fact influenced a lot by the behavior of τ_j at h. This extrapolation feature from more frequent contingencies to less frequent contingencies is a key aspect of the analogical expectation formation.

Analogy-Based Expectation Equilibrium. Putting together the best-response and consistency requirements yields the following definitions:

Definition 13.3 *A strategy profile σ is an ε-perturbed analogy-based expectation equilibrium if there exists a profile of $\beta = (\beta^i)_{i \in I}$ such that for every player $i \in I$:*

1. *σ^i is an ε-perturbed best response to β^i; and*
2. *β is consistent with σ.*

Definition 13.4 *A strategy profile σ is an analogy-based expectation equilibrium if there exists a sequence of strategy profiles σ_ε such that for every ε, σ_ε is an ε-perturbed analogy-based expectation equilibrium, and σ_ε converges to σ as ε converges to* 0.

13.2.3 Preliminary Properties and Learning Interpretation

13.2.3.1 Link to Trembling-Hand Equilibrium

In the special case in which every player i can only have one cognitive type that puts every $(j, \tau h)$ in a singleton analogy class, it is readily verified that consistency implies that players should have correct expectations, and thus analogy-based expectation equilibria coincide with trembling-hand equilibria.[15]

Proposition 13.1 *When every player uses the finest analogy partition, analogy-based expectation equilibria coincide with extensive-form trembling-hand equilibria.*

13.2.3.2 Existence

Allowing for arbitrary cognitive types, the existence of analogy-based expectation equilibria is guaranteed in finite environments required to have finitely many types, finitely many actions, and finitely many stages.

Proposition 13.2 *Whatever the environment assumed to be finite, there always exists an analogy-based expectation equilibrium.*

[15] It is the extensive-form version of the trembling-hand equilibrium, since trembles were introduced separately at each node.

Proof. The strategy of proof is very similar to that for the existence of trembling-hand equilibria or sequential equilibria (see Kreps and Wilson, 1982) in finite environments. For fixed ε, the existence of an ε-perturbed analogy-based expectation equilibrium σ_ε is obtained using Kakutani's fixed-point theorem (the consistency mapping is continuous in the admissible range of strategy profiles and the ε-perturbed best-response correspondence is upper-hemicontinuous, thereby allowing for the use of Kakutani's fixed-point theorem). Then the compactness of the strategy space in finite environments ensures the existence of accumulation points of such σ_ε when ε goes to 0, and any such accumulation point is an analogy-based expectation equilibrium. ♦

13.2.3.3 Learning Interpretation

I think of ABEE as the outcome of a learning process. Specifically, think of the game as described above as being played by infinitely many different teams of subjects in the role of the various players. Each subject would just play once (similarly as in the recurring game environments considered by Jackson and Kalai, 1997).[16] When a new subject in the role of player i comes in, think of his cognitive type c_i as informing him of the aggregate behavior from past play in each of the analogy classes α_i in c_i. That is, when in a previous play the history τh was reached and j played a_j, this action is added to the α_i dataset where $(j, \tau h) \in \alpha_i$. A player with cognitive type c_i is informed of the frequencies of actions in the various analogy classes α_i of c_i. Such a player then best responds to the frequencies in the various α_i as in Definition 13.1, that is, assuming that the strategy of j at τh matches the aggregate frequency in $\alpha_i(j, \tau h)$ where $\alpha_i(j, \tau h)$ is the analogy class in c_i to which $(j, \tau h)$ belongs. He may also tremble with some small probability and play any action when called to play. His behavior generates new data that are used by future generations.[17]

Such procedures generate dynamic systems that are parameterized by the initial play as well as the shape of the trembles and possibly whether and to what extent more remote observations are thrown away from the datasets. A key motivation for the approach is given by the following observation:[18]

16 I could consider that subjects play several times but importantly I have in mind that the aggregate statistics as opposed to the own experience would be the main driver for the choice of strategy.

17 The learning dynamics just described has some similarities with the fictitious play dynamics first proposed by Brown (1951) in the context of normal-form games with the following essential differences. First, I am considering more complex games here and the frequencies are aggregated over different $(j, \tau h)$, which is the key distinctive feature of the present approach as opposed to the more traditional approach in (fictitious-play) learning. Second, I am considering populations of different teams who would just play once whereas the classic fictitious-play dynamics considers that the same players keep playing again and again.

18 See also Gonçalves (2022) for a more Bayesian formulation of a learning model in which players sample in an optimal fashion to form their expectations about the play of other players. He establishes that his steady-state concept coincides with ABEE in the simpler context of

Proposition 13.3 *The analogy-based expectation equilibria are the steady states of such dynamic systems.*

The result follows because once the play has settled down on a steady state, the long-run frequencies observed in each analogy class have to give rise to consistent analogy-based expectations as given by condition (13.1) of Definition 13.2, and players have to best respond to the induced analogy-based expectations (when not trembling), thereby fulfilling the conditions characterizing the analogy-based expectation equilibrium.[19] A complementary study not covered in this chapter but discussed at the end as a possible direction for future research is when we should expect such dynamic systems to converge to a steady state.

13.2.4 Preliminary Discussion

13.2.4.1 Interpretations of the Coarse Analogy Partitions

I suggest here several possible interpretations of the coarse analogy partitions that I divide into three broad families. In the first one, following the learning interpretation just provided, a player may receive feedback for each of his analogy classes without having any control on the type of feedback he receives. This would fit with situations in which, depending on his environment (cultural or otherwise), an agent is exposed to (possibly agent-specific) aggregate statistics. With this interpretation, it is natural to view the analogy partition of a player as part of the description of the environment in the same way as his information partition. I will refer to this as the **exogenously coarse feedback interpretation**.

The second family differs from the first one in that the coarseness of the analogy partition of a player is viewed as a subjective characteristic of this player. Specifically, some aspects of the data describing how players previously behaved in the various contingencies may be more salient than others, and what appears as more salient may be agent-specific. The clustering into analogy classes may then formalize what features players with different types find more salient when collecting data from past interactions (in this interpretation, a player with cognitive type c_i would only recognize from a past contingency $(j, \tau h)$ the analogy class $\alpha_i(j, \tau h)$ to which it belongs and $\alpha_i(j, \tau h)$ can then be interpreted as the salient part of contingency $(j, \tau h)$ perceived by such a player). I will refer to this as the **salience-based interpretation**, and it will be used to model various biases as identified by psychologists.[20]

Bayesian games with well-chosen feedback structure and uniform prior when the sampling costs tend to 0.

[19] The steady-state formulation is reminiscent of the self-confirming equilibrium, which will be discussed later on.

[20] In more specific contexts, Bordalo et al. (2012) and Kőszegi and Szeidl (2013) propose to structure salience on the basis of the degree of difference of the states as measured by some

Finally, in the third family, players can have access to all the characteristics of the raw data describing the observed past behaviors in the various contingencies, but players are viewed as simplifying what they try to learn so as to facilitate learning. The fewer the analogy classes, the less a player has to learn about his environment, and presumably the less demanding is the requirement that analogy-based expectations are consistent. I will refer to this as the **simplified learning interpretation**. While I find such a view appealing in light of some basic insights drawn from statistics (in particular in relation to the bias–variance trade-off), articulating a full-fledged theory formalizing it will require further understanding of how players envision this simplification exercise. I will touch upon this toward the end of the chapter.

13.2.4.2 Simplicity of the Subjective Representations Given the Feedback

An important aspect of ABEE is that in the face of the aggregate statistics $\beta(\alpha_i)$ in the various analogy classes α_i of c_i, player i best responds assuming that τ_j in τh behaves according to $\beta(\alpha_i(j,\tau h))$, where $\alpha_i(j,\tau h)$ is the analogy class in c_i to which $(j,\tau h)$ belongs.

The main argument for this assumption is simplicity. When one only knows the aggregate behavior $\beta(\alpha_i)$ in α_i, the simplest theory compatible with this is that in every contingency $(j,\tau h)$ in α_i, the corresponding behavior of player j at τh matches the aggregate behavior $\beta(\alpha_i)$. To make the link to simplicity formal, I can make use of the complexity theory as envisioned in the automaton literature that relates the complexity of a strategy to the number of states its algorithmic (or automaton) representation requires (see Neyman, 1985 or Rubinstein, 1986). Indeed, in the ABEE modeling, player i needs just one state to describe the strategy in α_i, whereas any alternative theory compatible with $\beta(\alpha_i)$ would require more states. In addition, checking whether the considered subjective theory is compatible with β is trivial for the subjective theory considered in ABEE, but it would necessitate non-trivial calculations for any alternative theory, thereby providing another complexity-based argument in favor of the ABEE modeling.

There are alternative possible rationales that would work in some cases. One of them is related to the principle of insufficient reason. This principle has been formalized in the statistical physics literature by proposing a selection device based on the maximum entropy criterion (see Jaynes, 1957). When the choice of theory (here subjective strategies attributed to others) does not affect the perceived probability of reaching the various elements in α_i, entropy would be maximized by requiring that behaviors are uniformly the same across the various contingencies $(j,\tau h)$ in α_i, as in the ABEE modeling.

distance (absolute or relative). Such features can be used to put structure on the analogy partitions in such contexts. More generally, Gärdenfors (2000) discusses more extensively how to think of categorization in relation to similarity (see also Rubinstein, 1988 for a related view in the context of choices over lotteries).

However, in extensive-form games and for general analogy partitions, maximizing the entropy may result in quite complex computations, thereby making this rationale less compelling as a general principle.[21]

13.2.4.3 What Players Need to Know in an ABEE

In many (if not most) game theory applications, it is argued that the structure of the game – preferences, information structure, and game tree – is common knowledge among players. While the common knowledge assumption is not required even for classic notions of equilibrium when one thinks of equilibria as the outcome of learning processes,[22] it is of interest to address explicitly what players need to know about their strategic environments in the presence of types with coarse analogy partitions. In particular, do subjects need to know the distribution of analogy partitions of other players as well as other aspects of the strategic environment?

Given the interpretation of the consistency condition in terms of learning, I would argue that players need to know very little about their environment. In particular, a given player i with cognitive type c_i need not have any knowledge about the implication of the cognitive types of others, nor does he need to know the preferences or the implication of the private information for others. Player i need only know his own preference structure u_i, the game tree, as well as the distribution of the type profiles τ. He should also know the aggregate behavior in each of his analogy classes α_i in c_i. But, importantly, as already

[21] To give a concrete illustration of this, assume a player must decide at node N_1 whether to Pass or Take, and if he Passes (thereby reaching node N_2), this player must again decide whether to Pass or Take. Assume the two nodes N_1 and N_2 of this player form a single analogy class for other players, and let $p \in (\frac{1}{2}, 1)$ denote the aggregate probability of Pass in this analogy class. Letting p_i be the conjectured probability of Pass at node N_i, consistency of (p_1, p_2) with p boils down to

$$p = \frac{p_1 + p_1 p_2}{1 + p_1},$$

which given that $p > \frac{1}{2}$ requires

$$p_2 = \frac{p - (1-p)p_1}{p_1} \qquad (13.2)$$

is strictly positive.

The resulting probability of reaching Take after node N_1 is $1 - p_1$, Take after node N_2 is $p_1(1-p_2)$, and Pass after node N_2 is $p_1 p_2$.

The resulting entropy viewed as a function of p_1 after replacing p_2 by expression (13.2), $Ent(p_1)$, has a derivative (w.r.t. p_1) equal to

$$-p \ln p - (1-p)\ln(1-p) > 0$$

at $p_1 = p$. Thus, $Ent(p_1)$ is not maximized at $p_1 = p$, where $p_1 = p$ would correspond to the belief in the ABEE. In order to maximize the entropy, p_1 should be set above p so as to better equalize the probabilities that all three alternatives are reached.

[22] Such a claim is illustrated, for example, by Kalai and Lehrer (1993). In their learning model, one gets convergence to Nash equilibrium while players need not know anything about the preference of others.

highlighted, I regard the latter knowledge as the result of learning coming from the processing of behavioral data observed in previous interactions. As a result, this knowledge does not require any understanding (or knowledge) about how other players reason.

It should be mentioned that, in the above setting, the knowledge of u_i as well as of the distribution $p(\cdot)$ of types is required so as to allow player i to compute the best response as specified in Definition 13.1. Viewing Nature as a player (as I do in some applications) would allow player i to not know $p(\cdot)$, and player i would then form a subjective perception about $p(\cdot)$ in the same way as he currently forms a subjective perception about σ_{-i} (using a coarse analogy partition). Such uses of ABEE will be discussed later on.

13.2.4.4 Is there a Universal Type Space?

The notion of type in ABEE is non-standard given the cognitive dimension c_i. From a theory viewpoint, one may be interested in exploring whether one can define a notion of universal type space that would include the cognitive dimension in the same way as is done for classic Bayesian games (see Harsanyi, 1967–1968 and Mertens and Zamir, 1985). It turns out that one cannot in general define a universal type space (at least if one sticks to the representation of types as proposed above). The reason for this makes use of the classic result of Cantor who has established the impossibility of constructing bijections between the set of subsets of a set and the set itself. Indeed, given that a cognitive type can be viewed as specifying partitions of the cognitive types of others (as well as other elements such as the regular type θ and the node h), it is readily verified using Cantor's theorem that it is not possible to define a universal type space. This is different from the usual approach to types in Bayesian games in that an information type in the classic case is a partition not over the type space of others but over an appropriately defined state space so that one can avoid the self-referential aspect of the partitioning in the classic case but not in the present context.[23]

I should add that I do not regard this theoretical observation as problematic from an applied viewpoint. Every strategic environment corresponds to a given set of types and the cognitive types correspond to different ways of pooling data from past observations. The relevant set of types is then dictated by the application one has in mind. To give a concrete illustration of this, in many applications, it would seem natural that the cognitive type of a player is never observed even ex post, in which case analogy partitions can be reduced to partitions of $(j, \theta h)$, where θ refers to the profile of regular types. In this case,

[23] Heifetz and Samet (1988) offer a related, even if a bit different, perspective on a related issue. They show that one cannot define a universal knowledge space (unlike for probablistic belief spaces as considered by Harsanyi); they attribute this impossibility to a lack of continuity in the knowledge operator. A formal investigation in the line of Heifetz and Samet for the present context should be the subject of further research.

the self-referential problem related to Cantor's theorem would disappear and the set of all types can be defined unambiguously.[24]

13.2.4.5 Similarity in Actions

In the above framework, I have assumed that when two contingencies $(j, \tau h)$ and $(j', \tau' h')$ belong to the same analogy class α_i of player i, the action space of player j at h should be the same as the action space of player j' at h', that is, $A_j(h) = A_{j'}(h')$. I motivated this as a way to introduce in an operational way the notion of aggregate distribution of actions in the analogy class α_i. This view of common objective action space seems particularly legitimate when considering the exogenously coarse feedback interpretation of the approach in which the labels of actions would typically be chosen by the third parties in charge of passing the aggregate statistics.[25] However, with the other proposed interpretations of analogy partitions, one could envision more general situations in which players could subjectively consider various identifications of actions across different contingencies. This would lead to enriching the cognitive type of player i so as to include a specification for this player of which action of j at h is identified with which action of j' at h'.[26]

13.2.4.6 Link to Nash Equilibrium

A question of theoretical interest is whether the ABEE is a novel concept or whether, after an appropriate modification of the game, it can be viewed as a familiar equilibrium such as the Nash equilibrium. To shed light on this question, I consider the following simple setup. There are two possible stage games G_1 and G_2 chosen with equal probability by Nature. These games are symmetric, involve two players $i = 1, 2$ and two actions a and b, with player 1's payoff as shown in the following tables (where player 2's payoffs can be inferred by symmetry):

G_1	a	b
a	x	z
b	y	t

G_2	a	b
a	t	y
b	z	x

[24] Even if c_i is not observed in applications, sometimes some aspects of θ_i can be correlated with c_i. In such applications, analogy partitions of $(j, \theta h)$ can have an effect similar to those obtained when a partition of $(j, \tau h)$ is considered.

[25] Even with this interpretation, one could envision situations in which the action spaces in different contingencies of α_i are not the same and yet player i is informed of the aggregate distribution of behaviors in α_i. In this case, I would suggest that, for $(j, \tau h) \in \alpha_i$, player i expects player j at τh to behave according to the aggregate distribution $\beta(\alpha_i)$ conditional on the action of j being in $A_j(h)$.

[26] It would then lead to the weaker requirement that the cardinality of the action spaces across different contingencies is the same, except if one is willing to consider the possibility that different actions in the same contingency are considered as similar to one another by the player, as in the work of Arad and Rubinstein (2019), in which case no restriction would be imposed on the cardinality.

Assume that players observe the stage game they are in, and that they use the coarsest analogy partition (putting the two games together for each of the players). Playing a in game G_1 and b in game G_2 is a symmetric ABEE whenever $x+z \geq y+t$. This follows because for the analogy-based expectation β to be consistent with this strategy profile, it should be that β assigns equal probability to a and b (remember that both games are equally likely), and a (resp. b) is the best response to such β in G_1 (resp. G_2) whenever $x+z \geq y+t$.

Observe that this ABEE is not a Nash equilibrium whenever $y > x$.[27] It is not either the Nash equilibrium of the game in which players would not be informed whether the stage game is G_1 or G_2, as with such an information structure, players would have to behave in the same way in G_1 and G_2, which is not so in the ABEE just constructed.[28,29]

Of course, if one allows oneself to change the payoffs x, y, z, t to alternative values x', y', z', t', one can view the ABEE with payoffs x, y, z, t as a Nash equilibrium with payoffs x', y', z', t', for example by letting $x' = 1$ and $y' = z' = t' = 0$. But this is a tautological statement as any behavior can be rationalized in such a way.[30]

A more interesting inquiry is when there are several ABEE, whether a single change of payoffs and information structure is enough to identify the set of all Nash equilibria in the modified setting with the set of all ABEE in the original setting. The answer to this question is negative, as illustrated in the above class of symmetric setup with coarse analogy partition when $x > t > y = z = 0$. In this case, the symmetric pure ABEE is such that either a is played in both games, or b is played in both games, or a is played in game G_1 and b is played in game G_2. But note that b in game G_1 and a in game G_2 is not an ABEE, the

27 In game G_1, players choose a and not b, which is the best response to a in this game because they (wrongly) expect their opponent to be playing according to β, thereby leading them to (subjectively) find a optimal.

28 In general, the ABEE cannot be related either to the Bayes Nash equilibrium in which players have subjective prior information about their opponent (here whether or not they know the stage game). I do not develop this here, as the Bayes Nash equilibrium with subjective prior will be discussed later.

29 A somewhat dual investigation one could consider is whether the cognitive types c_i alone could capture the various forms of asymmetric information as usually modeled by θ_i (I thank Jannes Hörner for suggesting this question). The answer is negative, thereby illustrating that the two dimensions in the type play a different role. To illustrate this, consider the same two-game scenario and assume that players do not know the game G_1 or G_2 they are in. It is readily verified (exploiting symmetry) that the mixed strategy which assigns equal probability to a and b in each game and for each player would be a Bayes Nash equilibrium. Given that such play would be the same across all contingencies, consistency would imply that players must have the correct expectation about their opponent's behavior no matter how analogy partitions are defined. Yet, if players know the game they are in, they would strictly prefer a in game G_1 whenever $x+z > y+t$ with such a correct expectation, thereby establishing that the proposed strategy profile cannot be an ABEE under complete information no matter how the cognitive types are defined.

30 For a solution concept like ABEE that preserves symmetry (G_2 is obtained from G_1 by exchanging the roles of a and b), it is enough to simply consider changes of x, y, z, t to x', y', z', t' that themselves preserve symmetry.

reason being that if it were so, the analogy-based expectation β would have by consistency to assign equal probability to a and b, and the best response to this would be a and not b in game G_1 (given that $x > t$). Now, consider a modified setting in which the payoffs can be changed (I will refer to G_1' and G_2' as the corresponding stage games) and the players may or may not be informed of the stage game. Clearly, given that in at least one ABEE the behaviors are not the same in G_1 and G_2, players need to know in which game they are. But then, no matter how x', y', z', t' are chosen, it would not be possible to rule out the behaviors b in G_1' and a in G_2' as a Nash equilibrium when the other three combinations would be Nash equilibria.[31]

13.2.4.7 Consistency in Extensive-Form Games

A key aspect of ABEE lies in the consistency condition, as defined in (13.1). In particular, the endogenous weighting arising in extensive-form games can give rise to new theoretical properties that would not arise had the weighting been exogenously fixed. To illustrate this, consider the following simple two-player, two-stage game with complete information. Player 1 moves first and chooses an action L or R. After observing player 1's action (L or R), player 2 chooses an action l or r. Assume that it is strictly optimal for player 2 to choose r after L and to choose l after R. Assume that $(2, L)$ and $(2, R)$ form a single analogy class α for player 1. The interaction is depicted in Figure 13.1.

In the standard rationality case, L or R would be perceived by player 1 to be optimal in the subgame perfect Nash equilibrium (SPNE). Under the conditions shown below, the coarse analogy partition of player 1 forces him to randomize in ABEE.

Claim. If $u_1(Rl) < u_1(Ll)$ and $u_1(Lr) < u_1(Rr)$ there is no ABEE employing pure strategy: player 1 must be mixing in ABEE.

[31] The modifications just considered assume that the payoffs $\widetilde{u}^j$ in stage game G_j can only depend on the actions a^j chosen in that game. If one instead allows for the possibility that the payoff of a player in game G_j depends also on the actions in game G_{-j}, more can be done. Specifically, consider the normal-form game with four players denoted (i, j) with $i = 1,2$ and $j = 1,2$ in which the payoff of player (i, j) is

$$\widetilde{u}_i^j(a_i^j, a_{-i}^j, a_{-i}^{-j}) = p_j u_i^j(a_i^j, a_{-i}^j) + p_{-j} u_i^j(a_i^j, a_{-i}^{-j}),$$

where a_i^j denotes the action of player (i, j) identified with the action of player i in game G_j in the original setting. If p_j is the probability of G_j and $u_i^j(a_i, a_{-i})$ is the utility of player i in game G_j when the actions are (a_i, a_{-i}) in the original setting, it is readily verified that the Nash equilibria of the modified normal-form game coincide with the ABEE of the original setting. The reason why such a transformation can be done in a way that works for all ABEE is that in the case of static games as considered in Jehiel and Koessler (2008), the probabilities of the various elements of an analogy partition can be determined independently of the equilibrium. Such a transformation would not in general work in multi-stage settings in which such probabilities would be endogenously determined by the equilibrium (as reflected by the terms $P^\sigma(\tau h)$ in the consistency condition (13.1)).

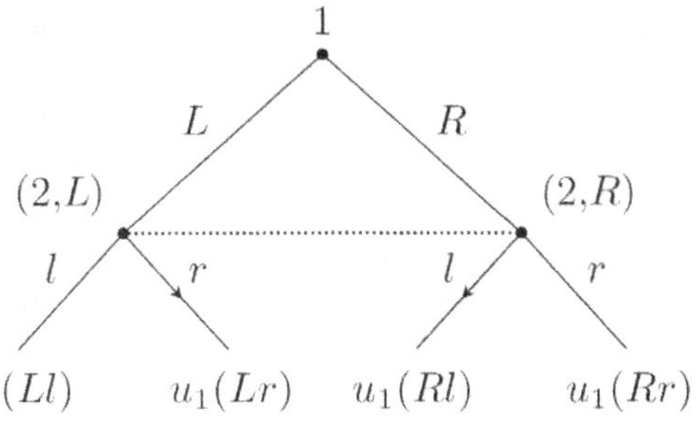

Figure 13.1 Extensive form.

Proof. Assume in ABEE, player 1 always chooses L. Consistency implies that $\beta(\alpha) = r$, but then player 1's best response to β is R, since $u_1(Lr) < u_1(Rr)$. So player 1 cannot be choosing L with probability 1 in ABEE. Similarly, if player 1 were to always choose R, then $\beta(\alpha) = l$ by consistency, which would lead player 1 to choose L by the best-response application. This shows that there is no ABEE in pure strategy. The ABEE (which exists by Proposition 13.2) must be in mixed strategy. ♦

Observe that if the weighting in the consistency formula had been fixed independently of the strategy of player 1 (e.g., say putting equal weight on the behavior of player 2 after both L and R), then (at least) one of the two actions L or R would have been perceived by player 1 to be optimal, and having player 1 play this action with probability 1 would have been part of an equilibrium. It is the endogeneity of the weighting that forces player 1 in ABEE to be randomizing.[32] To go further in understanding the shape of the randomization in this setting, consider the following payoff matrix that indicates the payoffs of players 1 and 2 for each action profile:

	l	r
L	$(x,0)$	$(z,1)$
R	$(y,1)$	$(t,0)$

with $x > y$ and $t > z$ so that the conditions of the claim are satisfied.

It is readily verified that there is a unique ABEE in which action L is played with probability $\frac{x-y}{t-z+x-y}$ and action R is played with probability $\frac{t-z}{t-z+x-y}$ so that the aggregate distribution of behavior of player 2 is $\beta = \frac{x-y}{t-z+x-y} r \oplus \frac{t-z}{t-z+x-y} l$ – a lottery assigning probability $\frac{x-y}{t-z+x-y}$ to r (which is observed when player 1 chooses L) and probability $\frac{t-z}{t-z+x-y}$ to l (which is observed when player 1

[32] More generally, and beyond the simple environment of Figure 13.1, the weighting of the contingencies in the analogy-based expectation cannot be viewed as exogenous, as soon as some strategic decision is to be made prior to a contingency in the analogy class.

chooses R). Note that the mixing of player 1 in the ABEE is chosen so that the induced aggregate behavior of player 2 as given by the consistency condition makes player 1 feel he is indifferent between choosing L or R. As a result, in the ABEE, player 1 chooses more often action L when x and z are increased, which stands in contrast with what comes out in the Nash equilibrium of the normal-form game in which player 1 would choose L and R with equal probability 0.5 irrespective of x, y, z, and t (the insensitivity of the strategy to one's own payoffs is sometimes regarded as a counterintuitive prediction of the Nash equilibrium in mixed strategies).

From another perspective, if we have in mind that subjects observe fully the profile of past plays in similar interactions, in the proposed ABEE, the observation would result in the (L, r) profile with frequency $\frac{x-y}{t-z+x-y}$ and in the (R, l) profile with frequency $\frac{t-z}{t-z+x-y}$. The proposed ABEE setting would then model subjects in the role of player 1 who are subject to correlation neglect, missing the correlation between the actions of players 1 and 2 and trying only to construct the marginal distribution of behaviors of subjects assigned to the role of player 2 from the data they observe. I will discuss further the use of the ABEE setting to model correlation neglect as well as other psychological biases.

13.2.4.8 ABEE in the Lab

While this chapter almost exclusively emphasizes the theoretical properties as well as the various applications of ABEE, I regard the experimental validation of the approach as a necessary step. The experimental validation is still in its infancy, and my hope is that more tests will appear in the future. In Huck et al. (2011), we have provided the simplest experimental test of ABEE. Subjects either in the role of Column player or in the role of Row player were faced with two possible stage games that they played overall the same proportion of time. The feedback that subjects in a given role (Column or Row) received concerned the past play of subjects assigned to the other role, and it could either be coarse in the sense that the behaviors over the two stage games were aggregated or fine in the sense that this feedback was cleanly distinguished according to the game. There were additional treatments in which the feedback consisted of raw data of past play with no statistical treatments. The results in the basic treatments were quite in line with the ABEE predictions and illustrative of the exogenously coarse feedback interpretation of the concept. The treatments with raw data illustrated that when data are made difficult to process, in some instances, subjects focus on simplified statistics such as those resulting from aggregating data from different situations (as in ABEE) in line with the interpretation in terms of simplifying learning device.

This study is encouraging that the ABEE may be useful to describe the behavior of agents exposed to coarse (or hard to process) feedback. But what this study is not addressing (because it would require richer environments) is when subjects are exposed to raw data and there are several possible ways of aggregating data, what bundling device subjects use and when (see, however,

Grimm and Mengel, 2012 for some hints related to that). It is also not touching on the effect of having multiple stages and private information.[33]

13.2.5 On the Use of Analogy Partitions

Clearly, several possible analogy partitions can be considered. This is somehow similar to the observation that different information partitions can be considered in the classic Bayesian setting. As for the modeling of information, I would say the application and context one has in mind should inform the modeler what kinds of analogy partitions are more relevant. I suggest some hints below.

13.2.5.1 Some Classes of Analogy Partitions

With the exogenously coarse feedback interpretation in mind, some analogy partitions emerge more prominently depending on what seems more natural to assume about what is observed or not from past similar interactions. In particular, the following analogy partitions seem natural in a number of applications.

Anonymous Analogy Partition. Consider situations in which all players play at the same time and share the same action space. Sometimes, when observing past behaviors from previous interactions, it is not known whether player i or j was behind the action. This is particularly relevant when the feedback one obtains about past play is anonymous. In such a case, it would seem natural to consider anonymous analogy partitions in which, for any h and τ, all permutations of $(i, \tau h)$ with respect to the set of players would belong to the same analogy class. I have considered such an analogy partition in the context of asymmetric first-price auctions (Jehiel, 2011).

History-Independent Analogy Partition. Consider multi-stage interactions with complete information in which the action space of players is the same at all stages. Sometimes, when being told the actions from past interactions, it is not known after which history (sequence of actions) the actions were chosen. In such cases, it is natural to consider history-independent analogy partitions defined so that, for each player, all histories at which the player must move are bundled into one analogy class. The personnel economics application discussed later on will illustrate this.

Payoff-Relevant Analogy Partition. In a number of contexts, it is difficult to have access to what previous agents engaged in similar interactions knew at the time they made their decisions. In such cases, it is natural to consider the payoff-relevant analogy partition defined so that all $(j, \tau h)$ corresponding

[33] I have been involved in a few other experiments in relation to ABEE, which include Ettinger and Jehiel (2021) as a test of the theory of deception developed in Ettinger and Jehiel (2010), and Barron et al. (2024) as a test of Jehiel (2018) (see also Jehiel and Singh, 2021 for a test of valuation equilibrium, which is closely related to ABEE, as explained below).

to the same payoff-relevant information but possibly different information at the time of the interaction are bundled into the same analogy class. I have considered such an analogy partition in the context of social learning (Guarino and Jehiel, 2013) and of auction mechanisms (Jehiel and Mierendorff, 2024).

In situations in which a natural distance $d(\cdot,\cdot)$ can be defined on the (standard) state space Θ, it is not uncommon that behaviors observed in nearby states would be pooled together when constructing aggregate summary statistics, thereby leading to the following family of analogy partitions.

Neighborhood Analogy Partition. Consider a set of representative elements θ^k in Θ, and assign every θ in Θ to the closest category k defined such that $d(\theta,\theta^k) = \min_r d(\theta,\theta^r)$. A neighborhood analogy partition for player i is such that $(j,\tau h)$ and $(j,\tau' h)$ belong to the same analogy class whenever θ and θ' as appearing in τ and τ' belong to the same category k. This is related to the clustering idea familiar in machine learning, and I will consider this idea again toward the end of the chapter.

A different idea of bundling by closeness is for each θ to consider a neighborhood of θ, call it $N(\theta)$, in Θ, and view player i as expecting the behavior in θ to match the aggregate behavior in $N(\theta)$ (this can be related to the k-nearest-neighbors algorithm familiar in machine learning, and Steiner and Stewart, 2008 can be viewed as considering such a bundling device in the context of coordination games).[34] I would argue that this latter form of bundling by closeness is better suited to model situations in which the player himself being informed of the state θ would decide how to bundle the data whereas the neighborhood analogy partition as previously defined describes better situations in which the aggregate statistics are made available by third parties without knowing which state will be drawn.

13.2.5.2 Link to Cognitive Biases

While the above examples of analogy partitions were motivated by the kind of information about past interactions that is passed to newcomers, analogy partitions can also be used to formalize a number of biases as identified by psychologists. Some examples follow. They can be viewed as illustrations of the salience-based interpretation of the analogy partitions.

Extrapolation Bias. ABEE can directly be linked to the idea of extrapolation. For example, if players are engaged in two different types of interactions, say A and B, involving the same action space in both, one captures the idea that

[34] While this would not lead to a partitioning of Θ given that the same state can belong to several such neighborhoods (mathematically, $N(\theta) \cap N(\theta')$ need not be empty when $\theta \neq \theta'$), it should be mentioned that, if one considers that player i in state θ is not the same player as player i in state θ', one can represent such situations using the (analogy) partitioning formulation. This simply requires endowing player i in state θ with an analogy partition in which one analogy class bundles the decision nodes of all players j in states $\theta' \in N(\theta)$ (the other analogy classes for this player are irrelevant, since player i's utility depends only on what happens in the realized state θ).

behaviors observed in either interaction are extrapolated to both interactions by putting the two interactions in the same analogy class. If one interaction is more frequent than the other, the behavior in that interaction has more weight on the overall expectation, as follows from the consistency requirement. I have considered such a use of ABEE in environments with bargaining and ultimatum interactions, as explained later.

Correlation Neglect. Another common bias of interest in behavioral economics is related to correlation neglect (see Ellis and Piccione, 2017 for some recent study of correlation misperception or Levy and Razin, 2019 for a recent survey on the implications of correlation neglect in political economy; see also the cursed equilibrium of Eyster and Rabin, 2005 to be discussed later for a model of correlation neglect in strategic environments). To illustrate it, consider the following simple setting. Two variables, say b and c, are correlated and distributed according to $f(b,c)$. Agents may fail to appreciate the correlation and reason as if these variables were independently distributed. A natural way to model this is to consider that (b,c) would be perceived to be distributed according to the product distribution $\widetilde{f}(b,c) = f_b(b)f_c(c)$, where $f_x(x)$ denotes the marginal distribution of $x = b$ or c, as derived from the joint distribution $f(b,c)$.

Such misspecifications can easily be accommodated in the framework of the analogy-based expectation equilibrium. For simplicity, assume that b and c are variables chosen by nature even though in general one or both variables could be decisions made by some players. Consider the following extensive-form game in which Nature is decomposed into three different players referred to as Nature, N_b, and N_c. At the root of the interaction, Nature chooses ω defined to be (b,c) and drawn according to $f(.,.)$ (assumed not to be known by the decision-maker; see the above comments on the possibility that players would not know the prior distribution of types). Then N_b and N_c move simultaneously. N_b chooses $b = b(\omega)$ and N_c chooses $c = c(\omega)$, where $b(\omega)$ and $c(\omega)$ denote the first and second coordinate of ω, respectively. Other player(s) may then proceed in their interaction based on how (b,c) as chosen by N_b and N_c is distributed.

If a player puts all contingencies (N_b, ω) into one analogy class α_b and all contingencies (N_c, ω) into another analogy class α_c, the perceived distribution of (b,c) will be given by $f_b(b)f_c(c)$ in equilibrium (as follows from the application of consistency), thereby showing how correlation neglect can be captured using the analogy-based expectation equilibrium framework.

Fundamental Attribution Error. The fundamental attribution error (FAE), as coined by Ross (1977), is "the tendency to believe that what people do reflects who they are," or more generally, the tendency to pay insufficient attention to the context in which actions are performed to form beliefs about the kind of person one is facing. In Ettinger and Jehiel (2010), we have proposed to model FAE using the ABEE framework. In an environment with several groups x of agents and several groups $g \in G$ of interactions, if all (g,x) with $g \in G$ and the same x are bundled into one analogy class α_x to assess the behavior of agents in group x, one precisely implements the idea that agents reason based on the aggregate attitude of agents in group x and make inferences based on this aggregate knowledge. In other words, this type of ABEE modeling captures the bias consisting in thinking that what people do is only determined by their group x and not by the situation g they are in, which seems very much in line with how social psychologists informally refer to the FAE.

Selection Neglect. Selection bias has been recognized in statistics and econometrics as an important source of mistakes in estimation exercises. When the selected sample that one observes is not representative because, say, it is determined by endogenous decisions made by agents, a good analyst should be cautious when extrapolating from observed data (e.g., see Heckman, 1979 for an influential analysis on how to correct for selection bias).[35] One mistake or bias suggested by psychologists is that not only bad analysts but also (some or even many) human beings may be victims of selection neglect (e.g., see Koehler and Mercer, 2009).

Selection neglect can be accommodated in the analogy-based expectation equilibrium framework. For concreteness, think of a decision-maker who has to choose between $a = 1$ (spending one more year at school) and $a = 0$ (dropping out of school). For the sake of illustration, let $\theta = (b, c)$ denote a state characterizing the decision problem where the cost c but not the benefit b attached to $a = 1$ is observed by the decision-maker. In a standard description of the interaction, nature chooses θ according to distribution $f(\cdot)$, then the agent observes c and chooses $a = 0$ or 1 with payoff consequences given by $u(a;\theta) = b - c$ if $a = 1$ and $u(a;\theta) = 0$ if $a = 0$.

A rational agent would choose $a = 1$ whenever $E(b \mid c) > c$. By contrast, a selection neglect agent would assess the distribution of b by extrapolating from the distribution of b observed from other agents who chose $a = 1$. To model this mistaken behavior with ABEE, consider the following alternative formulation of the interaction now described as a two-player game. After Nature chooses θ and the agent chooses $a = 1$, player N_b chooses $b = b(\theta)$, where $b(\theta)$ denotes the first coordinate of θ. By putting all the $(N_b, (\theta,\ a = 1))$ contingencies in a single analogy class so as to assess the distribution of b as chosen by N_b, the agent will in equilibrium form an expectation about b identical to that of a selection neglect agent. That is, only those c for which $a = 1$ is chosen will contribute to the expectation formation, and the agent will choose $a = 1$ whenever $E(b \mid a = 1) > c$. Interestingly, even though we are in a decision problem, there is an equilibrium construction to the extent that $E(b \mid a = 1)$ determines the instances c such that $a = 1$ is found to be the optimal decision, and the decision

[35] A classic example is related to the estimation of returns to schooling. If one extrapolates from those who attend extra years of schooling to estimate the benefit of these extra years, one ignores that those attending these extra years are generally not random subjects but subjects who thought these extra years would be beneficial, thereby leading to systematic biases in the estimations.

strategy in turn affects $E(b \mid a = 1)$.[36] Jehiel (2018) provides an illustration of such a selection-neglect construction in investment decision contexts.

Other Biases. Other biases can be modeled using the analogy-based expectation equilibrium. For example, the bias consisting of attributing to others one's own information can be modeled by considering the private information analogy partition in which $(j, \tau h)$ and $(j, \tau' h)$ are assigned to the same analogy class by player i whenever $\tau_i = \tau_i'$. Indeed, if player i believes that other players share his own information (and have no other information), it is then natural to assume that player i will bundle the behavior data of player j according to player i's own information (since player j's behavior could then only depend on i's information), hence the private information analogy partition. Note that in static environments, this corresponds to the fully cursed equilibrium of Eyster and Rabin (2005) that I will discuss later on.[37] One may also capture the idea that player i would believe he has superior information by endowing player i with an analogy partition that would be coarser than player i's information partition (as given by τ_i).

In other contexts, player i may believe that player j's strategy depends only on some characteristics of the history, for example what is payoff-relevant or the recent history, thereby leading player i to bundle $(j, \tau h)$ according to such characteristics. When the retained characteristic is the payoff-relevance criterion, this may seem related to the Markov perfect equilibrium (MPE). Yet, a key difference is that in the ABEE modeling, unlike the MPE modeling, the premise that the strategy of j depends only on what is payoff-relevant need not be correct. In a similar vein, the literature on sunspot equilibria assumes that some payoff-irrelevant aspects (the sunspots) affect behaviors, but, like for MPE, this assumption is correct in equilibrium, making the sunspot equilibrium closely related to the (publicly) correlated equilibrium rather than the analogy-based expectation equilibrium. Two early illustrations of that kind of ABEE modeling not collapsing with standard approaches are worth mentioning. One of them is the moonspot equilibrium discussed by Azariadis and Guesnerie (1982) toward the end of their paper, in which some economic agents think some variables depend on moonspots when in reality they depend on other characteristics. The other one is a multi-stage monopoly problem studied by Piccione and Rubinstein (2003) who consider consumers who only recognize patterns of prices of some fixed length l.[38]

36 The dependence of the bias on how c affects the decision a makes this bias distinct from correlation neglect as usually considered, even if at some general level one can view selection neglect as a special form of correlation neglect (in which the variable b would be viewed as independent of a and c).

37 See also Madarasz (2012) for an alternative modeling of this bias that he refers to as information projection.

38 While Piccione and Rubinstein's setup can be captured in the ABEE setting by assuming that histories h are categorized according to their last l action profiles, it should be mentioned that the resulting ABEE equilibrium can also be viewed as an equilibrium with imperfect recall of the multi-self sort analyzed by the same authors in an earlier publication (Piccione and Rubinstein, 1997).

13.3 ILLUSTRATIONS

To show possible applications of the analogy-based expectation equilibrium, I start with two illustrations specifically developed for this chapter. The first one can be viewed as a stylized study of how traders basing their strategy on coarse statistics may be led to trade in contexts in which the no-trade theorem would normally apply. It is an elaboration of the betting game example discussed in Jehiel and Koessler (2008). The second one considers a personnel economics application in which the coarse statistics the employer has access to leads sophisticated employees to engage in deceptive tactics in probation periods in an attempt to obtain more discretion in the subsequent phase of the labor relationship. It is an elaboration of the monitoring example discussed in Ettinger and Jehiel (2005) (which is the working paper version of Ettinger and Jehiel, 2010). While the former application is concerned with a static Bayesian environment, the latter considers a multi-stage environment with multiple types, thereby providing illustrations of ABEE in strategically diverse environments. I end the section with a quick presentation of other ABEE applications, as appearing in the literature. A reader willing to see a discussion of the connection of ABEE to other approaches should jump to Section 13.4.

13.3.1 On Speculative Betting

13.3.1.1 Strategic Betting Environment

Two players $i = 1,2$ are engaged in betting games involving four possible scenarios referred to as $k = e,b,c,d$. Players 1 and 2 decide simultaneously to bet or not bet, $a_i \in \{B,D\}$ for $i = 1,2$. If either player chooses D, the bet is not implemented and each player gets 0. If both players choose B, the bet is implemented and the payoffs of the players depend on the scenario k as well as the realization of some random variable $x = (x^k)_{k=e,b,c,d}$. Specifically, in scenario k with x realization, $u_1(B,B;k,x) = x_1(k) = x^k$ and $u_2(B,B;k,x) = x_2(k) = -x^k$.

Players are informed of the realized x but not of the scenario k. About k, player $i = 1,2$ can either receive the signal that k lies in $\{e,b\}$ or $\{c,d\}$ – this information structure will be referred to as $\overline{I}$ – or that k lies in $\{e,c\}$ or $\{b,d\}$ – this information structure will be referred to as $\underline{I}$. A profile of information structures (I_1,I_2) for the two players will be referred to as I.

I will be assuming that each scenario k can arise with the same probability $1/4$, that the information structure of each player is equally likely to be $\overline{I}$ or $\underline{I}$, and that the probability that the two players have the same information structure (i.e., $I_1 = I_2$) is $\gamma \in \left[\frac{1}{2},1\right]$, where $\gamma = 1/2$ corresponds to the case of independence and $\gamma = 1$ corresponds to the case of perfect correlation in the draws of the information structures of the two players. Moreover, each x_k for $k = e,b,c,d$ is drawn independently of each other from the same distribution, assumed to be symmetric around 0 with no mass on 0.

In any Bayes Nash equilibrium of this game, no bet can possibly be implemented in equilibrium. This follows because the interaction is zero-sum and every player can guarantee an ex-ante 0 payoff by always choosing D no matter what the private information is. The formal analysis of such games appears in Sebenius and Geanakoplos (1983). It can be seen as an illustration of the so-called no-trade theorem (see Milgrom and Stockey, 1982 for a general formulation of it).

Consider now the following cognitive environment. Each player $i = 1,2$ can have only one cognitive type c_i, so that I can identify a state ω with (x,k,I).[39] Moreover, the analogy partition considered by player $i = 1,2$ consists of partitioning the set of $(i, \omega = (x,k,I))$ according to whether $x_i(k) > 0$ or $x_i(k) < 0$.[40]

Such an analogy partition can be interpreted as considering that players are informed (for past similar plays) about the aggregate probability of bet whenever it was in the ex-post interest of the player to bet (this corresponds to the class including (i,ω) when $x_i(k) > 0$) – call this aggregate probability β^+ – and the aggregate probability of bet whenever it was not in the ex-post interest of the player to bet (this corresponds to the class including (i,ω) when $x_i(k) < 0$) – call this β^-. Or to use the language of statistics, this can be interpreted as players receiving feedback from past play on the proportion of betting errors of types 1 and 2 (with the notion of errors defined at an ex-post stage when full information on ω is available). Having in mind that such two-type-error statistics are somehow salient when describing the behaviors of previous players, such an analogy partition sounds natural to consider in this application.

13.3.1.2 Analysis

Given β^+ and β^- assumed to be strictly positive, the strategy choice of players is straightforward. To fix the ideas, consider player 1, and assume that he receives the signal that k is in $\{e,b\}$ as well as observing x. If $x^e > 0$ and $x^b > 0$, clearly player 1 will choose B. Similarly, if $x^e < 0$ and $x^b < 0$, player 1 will choose D. The non-trivial case is when $x^e = x^+ > 0$ and $x^b = x^- < 0$ (or vice versa). In this case, best response to $\beta = (\beta^+, \beta^-)$ requires that player 1 chooses B whenever

$$\beta^- x^+ + \beta^+ x^- > 0 \tag{13.3}$$

and D otherwise.[41] This is because in scenario e, player 2 would be getting $-x^+ < 0$ in case the bet is implemented and thus player 1 perceives player 2 to be betting with probability β^- in such a case. Similarly, in scenario b, player 1 perceives player 2 to be betting with probability β^+. Since the two scenarios e and b are equally likely, playing B is perceived to yield $(\beta^- x^+ + \beta^+ x^-)/(\beta^- + \beta^+)$ in expectation to player 1, hence the choice of strategy.

[39] As usual, one can link the ω formulation to the type θ formulation used in Section 13.2 by identifying θ_i with (x, I_i).

[40] Contingencies $(i, \omega = (x,k,I))$ with $x_i(k) = 0$ are irrelevant given that the distributions of x^k have no mass on 0.

[41] I am implicitly assuming that in case of indifference, the player chooses D.

Despite the simplicity of the betting decision criterion (13.3), it implicitly hides some non-trivial inference process. While a fully naive player would bet whenever $x^+ + x^- > 0$ given that the two scenarios are a priori equally likely, here player 1 infers from his knowledge of β^+ and β^- that if player 2 chooses to bet, the odds that the scenario is e rather than b is shifted from 1 to $\frac{\beta^-}{\beta^+}$, hence leading to criterion (13.3).

A key question of interest then is how β^+ compares to β^- in equilibrium, and whether and when the bet is implemented. In general, β^+ and β^- are determined by the consistency conditions, which are influenced by the chosen distribution of x_k. For example, assume that each x_k is drawn from a distribution that is either the uniform distribution on $[-1,1]$ with probability $1-\mu$ or the distribution putting equal mass $1/2$ on ε and $-\varepsilon$ (with ε being arbitrarily small) with probability μ. Solving for the fixed point in (β^+,β^-) that results from the consistency conditions for the two analogy-based expectations yields[42]

$$\beta^- = -1/4 + (1-\mu^2)/8 + \left(1/2 - ((1-\mu^2)/4)^2 + \mu(1-\mu)\right)^{1/2}/2,$$
$$\beta^+ = 1/2 + \beta^-.$$

When $\mu = 0$ or 1, $\beta^- = 0$ and $\beta^+ = 1/2$ so that there is no bet that is implemented in equilibrium. But when $0 < \mu < 1$, we have $0 < \beta^- < 1/2 < \beta^+ < 1$, and thus some bets are implemented in an ABEE. For example, when $\mu = 1/2$, one gets $\beta^- \approx 0.14$ and $\beta^+ \approx 0.64$, so that a non-trivial bet is implemented when player 1 has information structure $\overline{I}$, player 2 has information structure $\underline{I}$, scenario $k = b$ occurs, $x^e = x^+$, $x^b = x^-$, $x^c < 0$, or $|x^c/x^b| < \beta^-/\beta^+$.

Moving away from the special distributions just considered, one can show that $\beta^+ \geq \beta^-$ quite generally, for any distribution, and for any ABEE.[43] This observation implies that when both players have the same information, that is, when the information structure of both players is the same, $I_1 = I_2$, no bet is implemented in the ABEE, as necessarily one of the two players would find D optimal.[44] Observe also that the consistency conditions remain the same independently of the correlation γ in the information held by the two players, so that keeping all other parameters fixed, the share of bets that are implemented

42 The consistency conditions can be written as

$$\beta^+ = \frac{3}{2}\mu(1-\mu) + \frac{\mu^2}{2} + \frac{(1-\mu)^2}{2}\left(1 + \frac{\beta^-}{2\beta^+}\right),$$
$$\beta^- = \frac{\mu(1-\mu)}{2} + \frac{(1-\mu)^2}{2}\frac{\beta^-}{2\beta^+},$$

from which the expressions of β^- and β^+ can be derived.

43 This is because, if $\beta^+ < \beta^-$, (13.3) would imply that there is betting when $x^+ \geq x^-$ and, given the independence of distributions, this would imply by the consistency condition that $\beta^+ \geq \beta^-$, thereby leading to a contradiction.

44 To see this, suppose both players are informed that $k \in \{b,e\}$. If x^k for $k = b,e$ have the same sign, the player who would receive negative payoff from the bet must choose D so that the bet is not implemented. When the signs of x^b and x^e are different, the fact that one of the players chooses not to bet is an immediate consequence of the observation that $\beta^+ > \beta^-$.

in an ABEE decreases as the correlation γ of the two players' information structures increases. Such qualitative properties match the intuitive idea that in order to induce some speculative trade (here some betting activity), a necessary feature is that agents should observe different pieces of information. Observe that this same conclusion need not hold in environments with subjective priors (the formal definition of which will be reiterated later on), as sometimes proposed to get around the no-trade theorem.[45]

Turning to the specific distribution of x^k as considered above, and considering the magnitude of β^- as a measure of the betting activity, one can see that β^- is minimized when $\mu = 0$ or 1, and maximized for an interior value of μ. Interpreting the values ε and $-\varepsilon$ as insignificant ones, the possibility of insignificant $x^k = -\varepsilon$ when associated with $x^{k'} > 0$ in an information structure in which k and k' are not distinguished leads to an increase of β^-, which in turn allows for some betting activity. While very stylized, this illustrative example is suggestive that the possibility of insignificant payoffs may in some cases have important overall economic consequences (here in terms of betting activity) through the indirect effect of modifying the overall expectations of agents (as a result of the analogical derivation of the expectation).

13.3.2 On Manipulative Behavior in Probation Periods: A Personnel Economics Application

13.3.2.1 Strategic Environment

Consider an interaction between an employer or principal (referred to as P) and an employee or agent (referred to as A) consisting of two phases 1 and 2. Phase 1 is the probation phase in which P (the principal) watches the behavior of A (the agent) when there is no contractual arrangement between them. At the end of phase 1, the principal decides on the contractual arrangement, which consists in either giving the agent discretion (action D for delegation) – this will be the same as the no contractual arrangement prevailing in phase 1 – or exerting tight monitoring (action C for control). Phase 1 lasts n_1 periods and phase 2 lasts n_2 periods. I have in mind that $n_2 > n_1$. Some of the analysis will be presented for the case in which n_1 and n_2/n_1 tend to ∞.

In each period of both phases, the agent has to decide on a (productive) effort level $e \in [0,1]$, where $1-e$ can be thought of as the non-productive effort. When there is no contractual arrangement as in phase 1 or when the principal has chosen D in phase 2, the stage game payoffs in each period are

$$u_P(e) = \pi \cdot e,$$
$$u_A(e) = w + b_{PB} \cdot (1-e) + b \cdot e$$

45 Indeed, when the signs of the relevant x^k are not the same, if each player thinks the state which is favorable to him is sufficiently more likely, betting can occur in a Bayes Nash equilibrium with such subjective priors. See Liang (2020) for a recent study of learning allowing for speculative trade along such lines in complex enough environments.

for P and A, respectively. In these expressions, w can be interpreted as the per period wage received by the agent, e as the productive effort of the agent, $1-e$ as the non-productive effort, $b \cdot e$ as the bonus received by the agent in proportion of his productive effort, $b_{PB} \cdot (1-e)$ as the private benefit received by the agent in proportion of his non-productive effort, and πe as the payoff (assumed to be proportional to the productive effort of the agent) obtained by the principal. I will be assuming that $b_{PB} > b$.

When contract C prevails (in phase 2), the stage game payoffs of the principal and the agent are respectively

$$u_P(e;C) = \pi - c,$$
$$u_A(e;C) = w + b \cdot e,$$

where c can be interpreted as the cost of control incurred by the principal. In the C regime, whatever productive effort e the agent (initially) chooses, control leads him to execute the task (as resulting from productive effort $e = 1$) while losing the private benefit attached to the non-productive effort with a bonus proportional to his initial productive effort. In the C regime, the principal safely guarantees π irrespective of e, but this comes at the cost of control c.

Both the principal and the agent are aggregating strings of stage game payoffs according to the standard exponential discounting formula. I will consider two types of agents: the patient ones who have a discount factor close to 1 and the impatient ones who have a discount factor close to 0 (and accordingly, only care about their current stage game payoff). The ex-ante probability that the agent is patient is $\mu_0 \in (0,1)$. The principal, on the other hand, will be assumed to be patient with a discount factor close to 1. In line with the general class of games considered above, I assume that whether the agent is patient or impatient is not observed by the principal, and that the profile of effort decisions in phase 1 is observed by the principal at the end of the probation phase.

If the principal and the agent were rational, the analysis would be as follows. Given that $b_{PB} > b$, the only way for the principal to incentivize the agent to exert productive effort is to have the C contract. It follows that at the end of phase 1, the principal would choose C no matter what happens in phase 1. As a consequence, the agent irrespective of whether he is patient or not would choose $e = 0$ in all periods of phase 1 (since he would see no impact on his phase 1 behavior on the C/D choice of contractual arrangement). Moreover, in all periods of phase 2, the agent would choose $e = 1$ (resp. $e = 0$) if C (resp. D) is chosen by the principal.

I will now consider a different cognitive environment in which the principal forms his expectations based on the aggregate effort attitudes of each type of agent, not distinguishing those as a function of history. Or in the ABEE language, I will assume that the principal uses two analogy classes that distinguish behaviors of the agent according to whether he is patient or not but not according to the history of play (including which contractual arrangement

C or D is chosen by the principal at the end of phase 1). I will further assume that the agent, whether patient or not, is rational.[46]

13.3.2.2 Analysis

The statistics on which the principal bases her reasoning are β^p, the aggregate effort distribution of patient agents, and β^i, the aggregate effort distribution of impatient agents. Note that I have in mind that these statistics concerning other similar interactions have been passed to the principal, not that the principal constructs herself these statistics from her own past experience. Such coarse statistics in turn lead the principal to reason as if she were facing an adverse selection problem in which there are two types of agents with different effort attitudes (as reflected by β^p and β^i). The effort choices observed in phase 1 (the probation phase) are then used by the principal to update the likelihood that the agent is either one of the two types, which is used to determine which of contract C or D looks subjectively best to the principal. From the perspective of the agent, the behavior of the principal dictates the best-effort choice to make in phase 1. The nature of the interaction looks then like a signaling game (on the agent's side) with some screening taking place at the end of the probation phase (on the principal's side). Importantly, the misperception of the principal is a consequence of the coarse statistics she has access to, which do not allow her to understand the causal effect of the choice of contract on the effort attitude of the agent.

To analyze this environment, observe first that the behavior of impatient agents is straightforward. It is $e = 0$ in all periods of phase 1, and $e = 1$ (resp. $e = 0$) in all periods of phase 2 if the principal chooses contract C (resp. D). Concerning patient agents, their behavior is the same as that of impatient agents in phase 2 for each possible contract C or D, but their behavior in phase 1 has to be determined.

Clearly, patient agents would prefer having the D contract rather than the C contract at the end of phase 1, since such a D contract would allow them in the subsequent periods to obtain $w + b_{PB}$ rather than $w + b$, the stage game payoff they obtain when the contract C is chosen (remember that $b_{PB} > b$).

I will construct an ABEE in which a patient agent chooses his effort decisions $e = 0$ or 1 in the probation phase so as to obtain the D contract at the end of phase 1, and the principal chooses contract C after observing the historical effort record of an impatient agent in the probation phase.[47] Under

[46] Impatient but rational agents can equivalently be viewed as patient but coarse agents (who would use a single analogy class to assess the C/D decision of the principal so that they would not see the effect of their phase 1 behavior on the principal's choice and accordingly behave as if they were myopic).

[47] There is another ABEE in which both types of agents behave in the same way and the coarse principal randomizes between contracts C and D so that the induced aggregate effort behavior of agents makes the contracts C and D equally attractive to the principal. Such an equilibrium would be the only ABEE if there were only impatient agents. I note, however, that in the two-type case, such an ABEE is not robust to the introduction of behavioral types who would

such circumstances, consistency would imply that β^i is a distribution assigning probability $\beta^i(1) = \frac{n_2}{n_1+n_2}$ on effort $e = 1$ and probability $\beta^i(0) = \frac{n_1}{n_1+n_2}$ on effort $e = 0$ (given that for impatient agents, contract C would be chosen on-the-path, thereby leading to the frequency $\frac{n_2}{n_1+n_2}$ of observed effort $e = 1$ for such agents). Concerning β^p, it would be a distribution on $e \in \{0, 1\}$ with a probability mass on 0 at least equal to $\frac{n_2}{n_1+n_2}$ given that in phase 2, a patient agent would always be choosing $e = 0$ (after the choice of D contract made by the principal).

Focusing on the case in which n_2 is large compared to n_1, impatient agents are thus perceived to be choosing $e = 1$ with a large probability (close to 1) while patient agents are perceived to be playing $e = 0$ with a large probability (close to 1). If the principal thought she was facing an impatient agent for sure by the end of phase 1, she would choose contract D, expecting to get next $\pi\frac{n_2}{n_1+n_2}$ in each period, rather than contract C that would only give $\pi - c$ to the principal in each period.

Assuming n_1 is large enough, if a patient agent were to always choose $e = 1$ in phase 1, he would convince the principal by the end of the probation period that he is almost surely an impatient agent, thereby ensuring that the principal chooses contract D. A patient agent will not need to exert effort $e = 1$ in all periods of phase 1 though. Given that he myopically likes $e = 0$ better than $e = 1$ (in phase 1), he will choose the minimum number of periods in which he chooses $e = 1$ so as to persuade the principal to pick the D contract. Call this minimum number n_1^*.[48] Consistency would then imply that β^p assigns probability $\beta^p(1) = \frac{n_1^*}{n_1+n_2}$ to effort $e = 1$ and the complementary probability to effort $e = 0$.[49] The above considerations ensure that

always choose $e = 1$ in phase 2 (as then patient agents would have an incentive in phase 1 to build a reputation for being this behavioral type in an attempt to obtain the D contract for sure).

48 Given discounting, the patient agent will choose $e = 0$ in the first $n_1 - n_1^*$ periods and $e = 1$ in the last n_1^* periods of the probation phase.

49 To complete the characterization of the equilibrium value of n_1^*, let μ^* be the threshold belief about the agent being patient such that any lower belief would lead the principal to choose contract D. Given the aggregate effort attitudes of the two types of agents (as defined by β^p and β^i), the threshold belief μ^* is defined by the indifference condition

$$\pi(\mu^*\beta^p(1) + (1-\mu^*)\beta^i(1)) = \pi - c.$$

Given that $\beta^p(1) = \frac{n_1^*}{n_1+n_2}$ and $\beta^i(1) = \frac{n_2}{n_1+n_2}$ would be close to 0 and 1, respectively, as $\frac{n_2}{n_1}$ grows large, it is readily verified that μ^* would get close to $\frac{c}{\pi}$ in this limit.
The equilibrium number n_1^* will be the minimum integer k such that

$$\frac{\mu_0}{1-\mu_0}\frac{(\beta^p(1))^k(1-\beta^p(1))^{n_1-k}}{(\beta^i(1))^k(1-\beta^i(1))^{n_1-k}} < \frac{\mu^*}{1-\mu^*},$$

where the left-hand side of the inequality is simply the posterior likelihood that the agent is patient relative to being impatient after observing k periods with $e = 1$ and $n_1 - k$ periods with $e = 0$ in phase 1. The definition of n_1^* ensures that the patient agent makes the minimum number of effort $e = 1$ decisions so as to trigger the choice D of contract. Assuming n_2/n_1 and n_1 are large, $\beta^p(1) \simeq 0$, $\beta^i(1) \simeq 1$, and it is readily verified that n_1^* should be close to $n_1/2$ irrespective of μ_0.

for n_1, n_2/n_1 sufficiently large, one can construct an ABEE with the desired properties.

13.3.2.3 Comment

An interesting feature of the proposed ABEE concerns the mistaken belief of the principal about which type of agent she is facing at the end of phase 1. When she faces an impatient agent, she observes n_1 periods with $e = 0$, which makes the principal very confident she is facing a patient agent (who is perceived to be exerting effort $e = 0$ with very high probability as n_1 and n_2/n_1 tend to infinity). By contrast, when she faces a patient agent, her belief at the end of phase 1 is that she is facing an impatient agent (viewed as overall exerting effort $e = 1$ with large probability) with enough probability (so that contract D looks best to her). Moreover, it is precisely by behaving in a way other than that of an impatient agent in phase 1 that a patient agent manages to increase the belief in the principal's mind that he is an impatient agent overall exerting effort $e = 1$ with a large enough probability. These features illustrate how belief manipulation in ABEE differs from that in traditional reputation/signaling models in which the belief (in others' minds) about being another type necessarily decreases over time in expectation (it is a submartingale). It is an illustration of how ABEE can account for deception and manipulation in a way that is not feasible in the traditional paradigm with full rationality.

13.3.2.4 Discussion

This simple personnel economics model can be enriched in many directions. I now consider several possible variants and indicate their likely effects while leaving the detailed analysis for future research.

I first consider adding a share of rational principals that can be viewed as experienced principals, while still assuming that coarse principals – viewed as novice principals – know only the aggregate effort behavior of patient and impatient agents (across all periods and all possible matches, i.e., whether an agent is matched with a rational or a coarse principal). Clearly, rational principals would choose contract C at the end of the probation period no matter what the observed behaviors are in phase 1, as this is the only way to incentivize the agent to exert effort and choose $e = 1$ in phase 2. When the share of rational principals is not too large, one can support an ABEE very similar to the one shown above in the absence of rational principals. As before, in this ABEE, rational patient agents adjust their phase 1 behavior so as to obtain contract D at the end of the probation period when they face a coarse principal. The effect of the rational principals is to increase the aggregate probability that $e = 1$ for patient agents as represented by $\beta^p(1)$ given that when patient agents face rational principals, patient agents choose $e = 1$ (and not $e = 0$) in phase 2. This increase of $\beta^p(1)$ in turn forces patient agents to choose $e = 1$ more often in phase 1 in an attempt to persuade coarse principals that it is preferable to go for the D contract.[50] Thus, the presence of rational principals induces two costs for patient agents. On the one hand, they make the manipulation less effective as there is a chance for patient agents that they face rational principals. On the other hand, they make the manipulation more costly for patient agents as more effort periods are now required in phase 1 to persuade coarse principals to choose the D contract. It should also be mentioned that coarse principals benefit from the presence of rational principals as these induce more effort from patient agents in phase 1. When the share of rational principals is too large, such an ABEE cannot be sustained anymore, and patient agents turn to behaving like impatient agents. Interestingly, when the share of rational principals becomes very large, coarse principals would then believe that all agents exert $e = 1$ with a large probability and accordingly would go for contract D at the end of phase 1. In this case, the presence of rational principals would be detrimental to coarse principals. These various effects illustrate the potential positive or negative externalities that rational principals can exert on coarse principals as well as on patient and impatient agents.

Another possible variant is to allow the principal at least in some cases to fire the agent at the end of phase 1, in which case the principal would hire a new agent drawn from the pool of agents (and decide with this freshly drawn agent whether to choose the D or C contract). Suppose the firing option is only available with some probability z assumed to be not too big (maybe because firing costs are large in a majority of cases). One can construct an ABEE similar to the one shown in the main analysis. Patient agents will seek to obtain the D contract by an appropriate behavior in phase 1. Firing whenever available will only be used for impatient agents as these would be observed to have consistently chosen $e = 0$ in phase 1. Moreover, if the share of patient agents is large, the principal would choose the C contract in case of new hire in phase 2, since such agents would be viewed as exerting little effort and these are more numerous. This in turn would increase $\beta^p(1)$, the aggregate probability that patient agents choose the $e = 1$ effort (while $\beta^i(1)$ would remain close to 1 as n_1, n_2/n_1 tend to infinity), and this would overall induce the patient agents to choose more often $e = 1$ in the probation phase (so as to obtain the D contract). If, on the other hand, the proportion of impatient agents is large, the principal would choose the D contract in case of new hire. This would lower the value of $\beta^i(1)$ (while not affecting much the value $\beta^p(1)$, which would be close to 0 as n_1, n_2/n_1 tend to infinity), and this would lead patient agents to choose $e = 1$ less often in the probation phase.

There are, of course, many extra variants that could be considered, including the possibility that the principal changes the contract in the course of phase 2 (as a response to unexpected effort observations made then) or that agents may differ in characteristics other than the impatience, making the screening at the

[50] More precisely, as n_1 and $n_2/n_1 \to \infty$, rational agents would choose $e = 1$ a proportion $\frac{1+\beta^p(1)}{2}$ of the time in phase 1 (where the $e = 0$ choices would all appear at the start of phase 1 due to discounting).

end of phase 1 potentially valuable even for rational principals. I hope the above discussion will trigger further work in such directions.

13.3.3 Other Applications

In this section, I review the various applications of ABEE I am aware of (with an obvious bias toward my own work). They are grouped by themes.

13.3.3.1 Bargaining and Ultimatum

In Jehiel (2005), I have considered two possible applications of ABEE to bargaining. First, I have considered setups consisting of both bargaining and ultimatum interactions where the former differs from the latter in that after an offer is rejected, a counter-offer can be made. I have considered the case in which to assess the rejection rate of offers, both interactions are bundled into one analogy class, thereby formalizing the idea that acceptance/rejection observations made in bargaining would be extrapolated to ultimatum and vice versa. The first finding is that the standard prediction in which a balanced offer is made in bargaining and an imbalanced one is made in ultimatum both being accepted with probability 1 does not emerge as an ABEE. Indeed, if it were so, the belief would be that offers, whether balanced or imbalanced, are accepted in all interactions due to the observation that both balanced and imbalanced offers would be made in equilibrium (although not in the same interaction), and they would always be accepted. Such a belief would lead the proposer to make an imbalanced offer also in bargaining, as this would be perceived to be more advantageous, and such an offer would in turn be rejected, invalidating the construction of the putative ABEE. The ABEE must take a different form. If bargaining is much more common than ultimatum, one can establish that in an ABEE, a balanced offer would have to be made in both interactions, as an imbalanced offer would be considered to be rejected with high probability due to the analogy with what happens in bargaining.[51] Thus, the analogy between bargaining and ultimatum may explain why not so imbalanced offers are made in ultimatum as observed experimentally, without any reference to fairness considerations as usually assumed.

Second, focusing on single bargaining interactions (say of the ultimatum type in which the rejection of the responder would lead to positive even if welfare-inferior payoffs), I have considered the possibility that the proposer would assess the rejection rate of his offers, not for every offer separately but only according to whether the offer is generous or not (say above or below an exogenously given threshold). In such a cognitive environment, the proposer could in ABEE make offers above what would make the responder indiffer-

[51] This approach is distinct from the one pursued in Samuelson (2001), who follows the automaton approach by assuming that a player suffers an extra cost when using a strategy that is not the same across different interactions.

ent between accepting and rejecting (as the traditional analysis would imply). The key to understanding this insight is that, following the logic of the best response in ABEE, if the proposer decides to make an offer in an analogy class, he would go for the least generous offers among those given that he would predict the same rejection probability for all such offers. The ensuing analysis of ABEE is then very similar to that obtained when the action space of the proposer is assumed to contain only these discrete offers, thereby providing the desired result.

13.3.3.2 Cooperation in Finite-Horizon Interactions and Bubbles

In the finitely repeated prisoner's dilemma, the SPNE predicts that there should be universal defection at all histories. Similarly, in the centipede game (Rosenthal, 1982), players should Take at all nodes in the SPNE. This follows from the logic of backward induction. In the last period, such behaviors correspond to a dominant strategy. Anticipating such behaviors in all subsequent periods of the game implies that the same behaviors should apply in the current period no matter what the history is. The same logic would lead to the conclusion that there can be no bubbles in finite economies (see Tirole, 1982). Such predictions are, however, not observed in lab experiments (e.g., see Embrey et al., 2018; Selten and Stoecker, 1986; Smith et al., 1988).

In Jehiel (2005), I have considered the ABEE in the centipede game assuming that players put all the nodes of their opponent in a single analogy class. Such an analogy partition can be viewed as modeling a scenario in which players would only be informed of the aggregate Pass rate in past similar interactions or alternatively as modeling a possible bias in which players would wrongly consider the strategy of their opponent to be history-independent. A key observation is that some Pass behavior can arise in an ABEE, and the predictions are that either Take occurs early in the game (as in the SPNE) or very late (and more so as there are more periods) but not in the middle of the game.[52,53] In Bianchi and Jehiel (2010), the same logic has been extended to provide some possible rationale to the emergence of bubbles in finite economies.[54] More recently, using the ABEE tool, Antler (2019) has enriched the basic insight of cooperation in the centipede game to provide a rationale for pyramid scams.

[52] To see this, observe that if Take were to occur in a pure-strategy ABEE in the middle of the game, one of the players would only be Passing on the path and thus the expectation of the other player as defined by consistency would be that this player Passes always, leading him to prefer Passing in the middle of the game rather than Taking.

[53] The observation that the Take phase is shorter as there are more periods is in line with some recent experimental findings derived in the centipede game (Krockow et al., 2018); see also Danz et al. (2016) for an experiment playing on the feedback and Garcia-Pola et al. (2020) for another recent experiment.

[54] See Moinas and Pouget (2013) for an experimental setting related to bubbles.

13.3.3.3 *Reputation and Deception*

In Ettinger and Jehiel (2010), we have used ABEE to model the FAE and develop a theory of deception. We have applied it to study a stylized bargaining problem in which the seller of a house, by acknowledging small deficiencies with the heating system, would be able to persuade the potential buyer that he is more likely to be honest, making the next (more significant) claim that there is another buyer in line more credible. In Jehiel and Samuelson (2012), the same theme has been pursued to revisit the classic theory of reputation (Fudenberg and Levine, 1989) in which a long-run player faces a sequence of short-run players always playing the same stage game, and the long-run player may either be rational or mechanical (in which case he always behaves in the same way). The departure from the classic reputation model is that the short-run players are assumed to only know the aggregate behavior of the rational type over all histories and time periods. That is, the short-run players aggregate for each type of long-run players the behavior across all histories into one analogy class. The obtained ABEE differs from the classic analysis in a number of respects. In particular, while traditional models emphasize that reputation motives arise when there is a value to commitment, the analysis with ABEE suggests that reputation building may be at work even when there is no value to commitment (as in zero-sum games) in an attempt to manipulate the belief of boundedly rational agents. The personnel economics application developed above is another illustration of deception and reputation building with analogical reasoning.

13.3.3.4 *Social Learning*

In the classic social learning model (Banerjee, 1992; Bikhchandani et al., 1992), agents make binary decisions (A or B) in sequence on the basis of a binary signal that is informative about whether A or B is better as well as the observation of previous agents' decisions. When all signals are equally informative, long-run inefficiencies and herding may occur, as the information publicly conveyed by past choices may be superior to the private information. Smith and Sørensen (2000) have modified the basic setup to allow individual agents to receive private information of different precisions. When the precision can be unbounded, they have shown that in the long run, there are no inefficiencies. The key driving force behind this asymptotic efficiency result is that when an agent breaks a long series of equal decisions (a local herd), the next agents infer that the deviating agent must have had very precise information going against the crowd, and they are happy to follow him when their own information is not very precise. Smith and Sørensen (2000) refer to this as the overturning principle.

In Guarino and Jehiel (2013), we have considered such social learning environments, assuming that agents make their inferences based on the payoff-relevant analogy partition. That is, agents would have learnt from past similar social learning games, the proportion of time option A was chosen when it was the better alternative, and similarly the proportion of time option B was chosen when it was the better alternative, but not the precise distribution of actions as a function of the history.[55] The ABEE prediction in this case is that even if the precision of signals can be unbounded, there must be inefficiencies in the long run.[56] The logic of the overturning principle does not apply in the ABEE because agents do not make proper inferences from the timing of the decisions. In Guarino and Jehiel (2013), we have also considered the setting of Lee (1993), in which actions vary in the continuum, and obtain there with the same payoff-relevant analogy partition that in the long run there would be no inefficiencies, despite the excessive weight attached to early signals.[57]

13.3.3.5 Auctions

I have developed three insights using ABEE in auction environments. First, in private value environments with independent distributions of valuations across bidders, I have considered asymmetric first-price auctions with bidder-anonymous feedback partition (see Jehiel, 2011). I note that such an analogy partition can be motivated by the common practice of auction sites to disclose past bids but not bidders' characteristics. In the case of two bidders, I have shown that ABEE results in an efficient allocation and that the revenue is larger than that generated by the second-price auction.[58] Such an insight reveals that by making the feedback about past bids anonymous, it is possible to do better than the second-price auction from a revenue perspective without sacrificing welfare efficiency. Such an insight sharply contrasts with a traditional insight obtained with full rationality, suggesting a necessary trade-off between efficiency and revenue (as follows from the celebrated allocation equivalence result holding when the distributions of valuations are independent across bidders, as assumed here).

[55] I would argue such (coarse) statistics describe the most salient aspects of past decisions, and as such they are more likely to be accessible in real-life applications than the history-dependent ones (which require access to very detailed information).

[56] To get a sense of the result, observe that if there were no inefficiencies in the long run, past observations in the sequence would be almost perfectly informative of the state, implying that agents (except in the first period) would not make use of their information. But such behaviors would lead to long-run inefficiencies, as in the classic social learning model, leading to a contradiction.

[57] Our insight in Lee's model is to be contrasted with that obtained by Eyster and Rabin (2010), who consider a model that mixes elements of cursedness (see below) with elements of subjective priors (in their model, subjects subjectively believe that their predecessors are more cursed than they really are). See also Bohren (2016) and Bohren and Hauser (2019) for further modeling of this.

[58] Efficiency immediately follows from the bidder-anonymous feedback partition, as such an analogy partition implies that a bid is a sole function of the valuation and not of the identity of the bidder. That revenue is increased in the case of two bidders follows from the observation that it makes every bidder feel he is competing with a bidder of average strength, which in turn leads a strong bidder to bid more agressively than if he knew he were competing with a weak bidder.

Second, Jehiel and Lamy (2015) have considered competing auction environments in private value environments. When buyers form their expectation about others' participation in the various auctions in a coarse way, that is, not seeing the link between the reserve price and the participation decisions, competition between (rational) sellers leads them to set zero reserve price (or absolute auctions) even if their value for keeping the good is strictly positive. This follows from a logic similar to that in Bertrand competition, and differs sharply from the traditional insight in competing auction environments, which would predict that the reserve price should be set at the value of the seller (e.g., see McAfee, 1993). Jehiel and Lamy (2015) also provide a rationale for the use of secret reserve price auctions when some share of buyers aggregate the reserve price choices across situations where they are kept secret and situations where they are publicly disclosed (thereby breaking the logic of the unraveling argument that prevails in the standard rationality case and that makes secret reserve price auction hard to rationalize). To the extent that absolute auctions and secret reserve prices are often used, the ABEE methodology provides a rationale for such auction formats that was missing with the standard rationality approach.

Third, Jehiel and Mierendorff (2024) consider private value auctions with correlation in which, at the time of the auction, bidders receive noisy signals about their ex-post value. It then seems plausible that when looking at past auctions, such signals would not be accessible and only the bids and the ex-post values would. This suggests that at least some bidders would use the ex-post payoff-relevant analogy partition (relating the distribution of others' bids to their own ex-post values). In the case of correlation, such coarse analogy partitions lead bidders to reason as in interdependent value models, and when there are both coarse and rational bidders, inefficiencies then arise in the second-price auctions as well as in every auction-like mechanism.

13.3.3.6 Strategic Communication

Several insights mixing ABEE with strategic communication setups have been developed. First, in cheap talk environments à la Crawford and Sobel (1982), Jehiel and Koessler (2008) have considered a setup in which to interpret the communication strategy of the sender; the receiver partitions the state space into two intervals. In some cases, the resulting ABEE induces more communication than in the standard rationality case.

Second, Ettinger and Jehiel (2021) have considered a repeated expert/agent relationship à la Sobel (1985), in which one of the periods has more weight and the expert may either be rational or else be committed to always telling the truth (about a state that the expert is informed about and that changes in every period). When the rational expert and the agent have opposite preferences, and the agent reasons coarsely based on the aggregate behavior of the two types of experts across all periods, the ABEE is such that the rational expert should tell the truth up to the key period, and lie at the key period (a behavior we refer to as a deceptive tactic) so as to take advantage of the inflated belief of the coarse agent that the expert must be a truth-teller. This prediction differs from that in the sequential equilibrium (analyzed by Sobel) in which the sender should be mixing and the deceptive tactic should not be more rewarding than any other chosen tactic (due to the indifference implied by the equilibrium mixing).[59]

Third, I have considered cheap talk environments in which a lying sender would not remember his past lies, and I have modeled the expectation of a forgetful liar by requiring that such a sender would conjecture he previously sent messages according to the aggregate distribution of lies (i.e., aggregating all states where there is a lie in a single analogy class to form his expectation; see Jehiel, 2021).[60] While in one-shot communication protocols, such an asymmetric memory between liars and truth-tellers would make no difference relative to the standard analysis, in situations in which the sender is asked several times to report what he knows, it can be shown that the only possible ABEE requires that there is almost perfect elicitation of what the sender knows in the limit when the grid of possible states gets finer and finer. I note that a similar insight would not hold if liars were assumed to know how the distribution of lies depends on the state (i.e., removing the aggregation idea), and I use the obtained insights to suggest a novel rationale to practices commonly used in criminal investigations that consist in asking suspects similar questions several times.[61]

13.3.3.7 Mechanism Design

In Jehiel (2011), I have considered mechanism design environments in which, in addition to the usual auction rule instruments, the designer can decide to disclose the feedback about past bids in a more or less disaggregated way. For example, the designer can employ different auction formats in various proportions and disclose past bids as aggregated over different formats, or she can disclose feedback in an anonymous way, as discussed above in the context of asymmetric first-price auctions. In other words, through her choice of feedback policy, the designer is viewed as choosing the analogy partitions used by the bidders. A key insight is that the designer can always achieve a revenue that is strictly larger than in Myerson's (1981) optimal auction by an appropriate choice of auction formats and an appropriate choice of feedback

[59] The main object of Ettinger and Jehiel (2021) concerns an experiment. In the experimental data, while we do not see all senders employing the deceptive tactic, we observe that it is chosen with a probability much above that predicted by the sequential equilibrium and that it is more rewarding on average than the other chosen strategies. We interpret the heterogeneity of the data by assuming that a share of the subjects is coarse while the rest is rational.

[60] To model such imperfect memory with ABEE reasoning, I model the sender at two different times, as different players sharing the same objective. This is similar in spirit to the multi-self modeling in Piccione and Rubinstein (1997).

[61] There are other uses of ABEE in strategic communication applications. These include applications to signaling (Bilancini and Boncinelli, 2018; Hagenbach and Koessler, 2017; Mullainathan et al., 2008) as well as the modeling of coarse language on the sender's side in Hagenbach and Koessler (2020) or on the receiver's side in Eliaz et al. (2020), who develop a model in which the sender can choose the analogy partition of the receiver as in Jehiel (2011).

policy.[62] This suggests a new role for the choice of feedback about past auctions that is typically not discussed in traditional mechanism design.

From a different perspective, in Jehiel (2019) I have suggested revisiting mechanism design questions assuming that at least some share of agents would rely on the payoff-relevant analogy partition, so as to reflect the constraint that it is generally hard to have access to the beliefs of agents at the time they submitted their report in the mechanism. The idea that beliefs may be hard to access is also at the heart of the motivation for the robust mechanism design literature (Bergemann and Morris, 2005). This has led a number of authors to consider stronger notions of implementation, such as ex-post implementation, which would work well irrespective of the beliefs of agents. Unfortunately, as shown in Jehiel et al. (2006), this is a very strong notion of implementation, so strong that in rich enough (i.e., multidimensional) environments it is hopeless to rely on it. An alternative could be to rely on an ABEE setting in which some share of agents would rely on the payoff-relevant analogy partition. Jehiel and Mierendorff (2024) can be viewed as an illustration of this, where the notion of payoff-relevance is understood there at the ex-post stage.

13.3.3.8 Investment and Selection Neglect

As already noted, ABEE can be used to model selection neglect. I have considered such a use of ABEE in the context of investment decisions (see Jehiel, 2018). In that application, every investor observes a noisy signal about his project and he has to decide whether or not to implement it. Investors know the cost but not the potential benefit associated with the project. To form his expectation about the mapping between the signal and the distribution of benefits, the investor considers those projects that have been implemented by others and for which he obtains the same signal. He extrapolates as if the obtained sample were representative. Accordingly, in the risk-neutral case, he invests when the average benefit in the sample exceeds the cost. When the signals obtained by various investors about the same project are always the same, such a heuristic does not result in mistakes. But when the signals may vary across investors (say because each economic agent adds an idiosyncratic error of his own when generating information on projects), such a selection neglect results in bias. When the signal and benefit satisfy a monotone likelihood ratio property, the mistake results in an overoptimism bias with excessive investment in equilibrium. Moreover, the bias obtained in ABEE for those selection neglect investors is largest when the informativeness of signals is intermediate or when there are more rational investors around. Compared to models of overconfidence with subjective priors (see discussion below), the ABEE

[62] To make the study of the optimal design interesting, one needs to place some constraints on the mechanisms, such as those resulting from the ability of the buyers to reject the deal ex post. This is because, otherwise, the seller would be able to make an infinite amount of money with risk-neutral buyers, by (mis)leading buyers into having incorrect views on the distribution of some variables (as a result of their analogical reasoning) and then using betting devices related to these variables.

approach allows for an endogenous analysis of the effects of the underlying signal technology and/or of the share of sophisticated agents on the magnitude of the overoptimism bias. Such predictions have been confirmed in an experimental setting in Barron et al. (2024).

There have been other models related to selection neglect (see, in particular, Esponda, 2008 and Esponda and Vespa, 2014). I will come back to the concept introduced in Esponda (2008) later.

13.3.3.9 Some Further Applications

There have been a number of other applications of ABEE in different subfields. First, Jehiel and Koessler (2008) have revisited the email game studied by Rubinstein (1989) with the payoff-relevant analogy partition to establish that more equilibrium outcomes could then be supported. Second, there have been a number of finance applications in which traders hold different theories as parameterized by how they categorize Markovian states into different analogy partitions (see Eyster and Piccione, 2013 in a setup à la Harrison and Kreps, 1978 or Mailath and Samuelson, 2020 for a study of whether traders with different theories or analogy partitions can disagree in the long run; see also Piccione and Rubinstein, 2003). Third, there have been some applications to contractual relationships (see the working paper version of Jehiel, 2015, in which coarse analogy partitions are considered in moral hazard in team interactions, and Schumacher and Thysen, 2020 for a study of optimal contracts with boundedly rational agents with a model that employs the Bayesian network machinery of Spiegler, 2016). Fourth, there have been some public economics applications in which agents may not see properly the effect of the change of some policy instruments (e.g., taxes) on other variables of interest (e.g., public goods) (see Dal Bó et al., 2018 for an experimental study). Finally, Antler and Bachi (2020) consider a matching application of ABEE in a dynamic setting in which agents eventually remain unmatched due to their coarse analogy partitions used to assess the probability of acceptance of the other side of the market.

13.4 RELATED APPROACHES

In this section, I discuss how ABEE relates to other equilibrium concepts. I start the discussion with two classic concepts, the Bayes Nash equilibrium with subjective prior and the self-confirming equilibrium. I then discuss three approaches closely related to ABEE before opening the discussion to other equilibrium approaches to bounded rationality in games.

13.4.1 Pre-existing Approaches

Two important notions of equilibrium that depart from the standard Nash equilibrium with objective prior have been proposed early in the literature. These are the Nash equilibrium with subjective priors proposed by Harsanyi

(1967–1968) and the self-confirming equilibrium that has appeared in various forms (see, in particular, Battigalli, 1987; Dekel et al., 2004; Fudenberg and Levine, 1993).[63] I will now describe these equilibrium notions in the context of two-player static Bayesian games, and discuss how they relate to ABEE.

13.4.1.1 Nash Equilibrium with Subjective Priors

Consider the following two-player strategic situation. Player i's utility is $u_i(a_i, a_{-i}; \theta_i, \theta_{-i})$, where $-i$ refers to the player other than i, $a_j \in A_j$ refers to j's action, and $\theta_j \in \Theta_j$ refers to j's type for $j = i, -i$. A Bayesian game also specifies a distribution $p(\theta_i, \theta_{-i})$ over types, which I will interpret as an objective distribution (as chosen by Nature). When this distribution is commonly known, a Bayes Nash equilibrium σ requires that if player i with type θ_i chooses a_i^* with positive probability, or in mathematical symbols if $\sigma_{\theta_i}[a_i^*] > 0$, then

$$a_i^* \in \arg\max_{a_i} \sum_{a_{-i}, \theta_{-i}} p(\theta_{-i} \mid \theta_i) \sigma_{\theta_{-i}}[a_{-i}] u(a_i, a_{-i}; \theta_i, \theta_{-i}).$$

That is, σ_{θ_i} should be a best response to the correct view about how type θ_{-i} is distributed given θ_i (as reflected by the conditional distribution $p(\cdot \mid \theta_i)$) and the correct view about the probability with which player $-i$ with type θ_{-i} chooses the various actions a_{-i} (as given by $\sigma_{\theta_{-i}}[a_{-i}]$).

Harsanyi (1967–1968) proposed a solution concept in which player i would be allowed to have his own subjective view about how θ_{-i} is distributed as a function of θ_i. Let $\widehat{p}^i(\cdot \mid \theta_i)$ denote this subjective distribution. The corresponding solution concept, called Bayes Nash equilibrium with subjective prior, requires that player i best responds to such a subjective perception about how types are distributed, together with the correct perception about how the opponent behaves as a function of his type. Formally:

Definition 13.5 *A Bayes Nash equilibrium with subjective priors $\widehat{p} = (\widehat{p}^i)_{i=1,2}$ is a strategy profile σ such that, for every θ_i, if $\sigma_{\theta_i}[a_i^*] > 0$ then*

$$a_i^* \in \arg\max_{a_i} \sum_{a_{-i}, \theta_{-i}} \widehat{p}^i(\theta_{-i} \mid \theta_i) \sigma_{\theta_{-i}}[a_{-i}] u(a_i, a_{-i}; \theta_i, \theta_{-i}).$$

While appealing in some respects, this solution concept is problematic in others. First, it suggests an asymmetric treatment in the expectation formation about the strategy of Nature (in charge of choosing the distribution of types) and the strategy of the opponent (in charge of choosing the distributions of actions as a function of the type). While arbitrary subjective beliefs are allowed for the former, correct beliefs are required for the latter. Presumably, the idea behind this concept is to allow for subjective beliefs about the strategy of Nature in the tradition of Savage (1954), while sticking to the disciplining device imposed by the correct expectation assumption in Nash equilibrium.

[63] The works of Kalai and Lehrer (1993) and Kurz (1994) can also be related to the self-confirming equilibrium.

However, it is somewhat unclear how to interpret such a concept from a learning perspective. If there are enough data to assess properly how the opponent behaves as a function of his type, it is then likely that there are also enough data to assess properly the strategy of Nature.[64] But then, one should consider Bayes Nash equilibria with common objective priors and not with subjective priors. A related concern is raised in Dekel et al. (2004).

This is to be contrasted with the ABEE concept. In ABEE, players have a subjective belief about the play of other players (possibly including Nature; see some of the above applications in which Nature is treated as a player), and these subjective beliefs are structured through the consistency requirement by the equilibrium play together with how players bundle contingencies into analogy classes. This in turn explains why ABEE can be interpreted as a limiting outcome of a learning process with coarse feedback (see Section 13.2.3 above for a sketch of a learning model supporting this view), while such a rationale is not readily available for the Bayes Nash equilibrium with subjective priors.

Another concern about the Bayes Nash equilibrium with subjective prior is that it is silent on how players choose their subjective priors. Without guidance on this, the approach is not very predictive, as many different behaviors can be rationalized by varying the subjective priors.[65] Of course, one may use some of the insights derived experimentally in behavioral studies to suggest which kinds of subjective priors would be more relevant. For example, biases such as overconfidence may be modeled by requiring that players think their private information is more precise (about the state of the economy) than it really is. A number of influential models in behavioral finance rely on such modeling (e.g., see Scheinkman and Xiong, 2003). Observe that this view of overconfidence should be contrasted with the overoptimism derived in the investment decision problem considered in Jehiel (2018), in which the overoptimism is endogenously shaped by the objective statistical structure relating the variables of interest and the presumption that decision-makers extrapolate from the

[64] Think of a situation in which (a, θ) would be observed after the play of a game so as to allow us to assess correctly how a_{-i} is distributed for each θ_{-i}. Such a dataset would also allow us to assess correctly how θ_{-i} is distributed for each θ_i, making the subjective view difficult to motivate. And even if player i cannot recover how (θ_i, θ_{-i}) is distributed, I would say the choice of subjective prior $\widehat{p}_i$ is somehow arbitrary, as it is not guided by any objective information available to i.

[65] A related concern can be raised about ABEE, as one considers the span of behaviors that can be rationalized when varying the choices of analogy partitions. I see several possible responses to such a concern in the ABEE context. First, when the analogy partitions are viewed as resulting from the objective feedback subjects are exposed to, these can be considered as part of the description of the interaction in the same way as information partitions are (and there is no reason to worry about which predictions would arise with other analogy partitions). Second, assuming it is not known which aggregate feedback players are exposed to, studying which insights are robust to various analogy partitions seems less demanding than studying which insights are robust to various subjective priors, at least when the number of contingencies is not too large. While not much has been done in relation to robustness in the ABEE setting, I certainly regard the robustness question as a valid research question worthy of extra work. See also the final part of the chapter for further elaborations on the choice of analogy partitions.

sole observations of past implemented projects (as captured by appropriately defining analogy partitions; see the above discussion of selection neglect).

13.4.1.2 Self-confirming Equilibrium with General Feedback Structure

I describe a formulation of self-confirming equilibrium somewhat similar to that in Dekel et al. (2004), which I adapt to capture that I have in mind that a given subject in the role of a player would not play repeatedly. The strategic situation is still that of a static Bayesian game with two players i and $-i$ with an objective distribution of types as given by $p(\cdot,\cdot)$. Such a game is played many times by pairs of subjects $(i,-i)$ randomly matched from the population of players i and $-i$. After a game is played, some signals y_i and y_{-i} are made available to subjects in the population of players i and $-i$, respectively. Formally, if the played action profile is $a=(a_i,a_{-i})$ and the profile of types is $\theta=(\theta_i,\theta_{-i})$, subjects in the population of player i receive a signal y_i assumed to take finitely many values in Y_i, where y_i is drawn from a distribution $\widetilde{y}_i(a;\theta)$ that may depend on $(a;\theta)$. Such a signal y_i may include information on i's obtained payoff (as almost always assumed in the self-confirming literature where the same player i is viewed as playing many times) or any other element that would be informative of some characteristics of $(a_i,a_{-i},\theta_i,\theta_{-i})$.

A self-confirming equilibrium aims at capturing situations in which player i could hold subjective theories both about how Nature chooses types and how players behave as a function of their type where the subjective theories of player i are required to give rise to a distribution of y_i that matches the observed frequencies. Formally:

Definition 13.6 *A strategy profile σ is a self-confirming equilibrium (given $\widetilde{y}_i$, $\widetilde{y}_{-i}$) if, for every player i, there exist $\widehat{p}^i$, $\widehat{\sigma}^i=(\widehat{\sigma}^i_{\theta_{-i}},\widehat{\sigma}^i_{\theta_i})$ such that*

1. *If $\sigma_{\theta_i}[a_i^*]>0$ then $a_i^*\in\arg\max_{a_i}\sum_{a_{=i},\theta_{=i}}\widehat{p}^i(\theta_{-i}\mid\theta_i)\widehat{\sigma}^i_{\theta_{-i}}[a_{-i}]$ $u(a_i,a_{-i};\theta_i,\theta_{-i})$ and*
2. *For every $\bar{y}_i\in Y_i$, $\Pr_{p,\sigma}(y_i=\bar{y}_i)=\Pr_{\widehat{p}^i,\,\widehat{\sigma}^i}(y_i=\bar{y}_i)$.*

A self-confirming equilibrium can be viewed as a steady state of a dynamic process in which subjects in the role of player i would observe signals y_i from previous interactions, and form their subjective theories based on these observations. While the first condition in Definition 13.6 ensures that player i chooses a best response to his subjective theories, the second condition ensures that the subjective theories of player i induce the same distribution of signals y_i as the distribution that is truly observed, which is generated by the true p and the true σ (which player i is assumed not to know). Another way to think of the second condition is that if it were not satisfied, the data observed by subjects in the population of player i would allow them to conclude that their subjective theories cannot be true. It is called self-confirming equilibrium in recognition of the property that the observed data do not refute (or less accurately confirm) the subjective theories.

I suggest several comments in relation to Definition 13.6. First, a Bayes Nash equilibrium (with objective prior p) is always a self-confirming equilibrium, no matter what the signal specification $\tilde{y} = (\tilde{y}_i, \tilde{y}_{-i})$ is.[66,67] Of course, for many signal specifications $\tilde{y}_i$, it is unclear how player i would be able to have the correct theory (think of the case in which $\tilde{y}_i$ would be totally uninformative). But the definition of self-confirming equilibrium makes no restriction on the subjective theories, as long as they are not refuted by the observations. Since the correct theories are obviously not refuted, it follows that a Bayes Nash equilibrium is always a self-confirming equilibrium (even when there is no clear way/procedure for the players to guess the correct theories from the feedback they receive). In contexts in which the full description of the game is common knowledge to the players, it is possible to refine the subjective theories to only allow those that can be justified by some rational behavior. This leads to the rationalizable self-confirming equilibria as defined in Rubinstein and Wolinsky (1994).[68] For reasons similar to those just expressed, note that all Bayes Nash equilibria (with objective prior p) are always rationalizable self-confirming equilibria whatever the signal specification $\tilde{y}$.

A second comment is that I have allowed, in Definition 13.6, player i to form subjective theories about the play of other subjects in the population assigned to the role of player i. While this subjective theory plays no role in the first (best-response) condition, it may in the second, as the behavior of other subjects in the role of player i may affect the distribution of observed signals. This is somewhat unusual in the literature on self-confirming equilibrium, in which it is generally assumed that the same subject would be in the role of player i, but I would argue it is natural once one has in mind situations in which different subjects would play the role of player i.[69]

A third comment is that Definition 13.6 assumes that all subjects in the role of player i have the same subjective theories. This is referred to as the unitary case in the self-confirming equilibrium literature (see Fudenberg and Levine, 1998) and can be generalized to allow different subjects in the role of player i to entertain heterogeneous subjective theories, all assumed to satisfy the second (consistency) condition.

It should be mentioned here that the analogy-based expectation equilibrium in Bayesian games, as considered in Jehiel and Koessler (2008), can be related

66 This follows because if $\widehat{p}^i = p$ and $\widehat{\sigma}^i = \sigma$, the second condition is trivially satisfied. And replacing $\widehat{p}^i$ by p on the one hand and $\widehat{\sigma}^i$ by σ on the other in the first condition directly implies the condition for a Bayes Nash equilibrium.

67 This has led game theorists to characterize the conditions on y that would ensure that the set of self-confirming equilibria coincides with the set of Bayes Nash equilibria. For example, if $\widetilde{y}_i(a;\theta)$ completely identifies $(a;\theta)$, all self-confirming equilibria are Bayes Nash equilibria. This is also so in private value settings, if $\widetilde{y}_i(a;\theta)$ identifies (a_{-i}, θ_i) so that i can properly learn the distribution of a_{-i} conditional on his type θ_i.

68 See Dekel et al. (1999) for a related concept in extensive-form games when players observe the equilibrium path.

69 A similar view (with players forming conjectures about players assigned to the same role) appears in Fudenberg and Kamada (2018).

to the self-confirming equilibrium for a particular class of signal structure y. Indeed, considering a Bayesian game with analogy partitions defined over the state space of Θ, one can view an ABEE in such a setting as a self-confirming equilibrium in which, after a play $(a;\theta)$, a subject in the population of players i receives the signal $y_i(a;\theta) = (a_{-i}, \alpha_i(\theta))$, where $\alpha_i(\theta)$ denotes the analogy class of player i to which θ belongs. This is so because the signals y_i allow subjects in the role of player i to recover the aggregate distribution of player $-i$'s action in each analogy class α_i (corresponding to $\beta(\alpha_i)$ in the ABEE setting), and obviously the subjective theory that views the distribution of behavior of $-i$ at θ as coinciding with $\beta(\alpha_i(\theta))$ automatically satisfies the second requirement in the definition of a self-confirming equilibrium.

From this perspective, a key distinctive feature of the ABEE is that the subjective theory used in ABEE is not any theory compatible with the feedback, but a special one derived from the feedback in a trivial way (very similar to the identity mapping), thereby making the mapping from the signal specification y_i to the subjective theory more transparent than in the self-confirming equilibrium. An implication of this is that the ABEE corresponds to a refinement of self-confirming equilibrium, and it is no longer the case that a Nash equilibrium is necessarily an ABEE (a conclusion that cannot be obtained with the self-confirming equilibrium). As already highlighted, the selection principle in ABEE can be related to the central theme of simplicity in bounded rationality: the subjective theory considered by player i is the simplest one that is compatible with the observed feedback y_i (see discussion above). While the feedback considered for ABEE allows for a natural simplicity-based selection of the subjective theories, an open question is whether a similar approach can be proposed for other signal specifications in an insightful way.

More recently, Battigalli et al. (2015) have proposed extending the self-confirming equilibrium to allow players to exhibit ambiguity aversion over the various possible subjective theories compatible with the feedback y (see also Lehrer, 2012). While their most general approach always includes the traditional self-confirming equilibria as possible outcomes, one idea discussed in their paper is the maxmin self-confirming equilibrium in which the worst-case criterion is applied to the entire set of all subjective theories compatible with the feedback. The maxmin self-confirming equilibrium so defined is a refinement of the self-confirming equilibrium. Such a refinement can be viewed as an alternative to ABEE. I see, however, several issues with the general use of this refinement in applications. First, given that in the proposed maxmin approach all compatible theories are considered, the maxmin criterion should be regarded as modeling an extreme form of ambiguity aversion, and there is no reason in general to believe that all agents would have such an extreme attitude toward ambiguity (in decision contexts, this has led Klibanoff et al., 2005 to consider smoother versions of ambiguity aversion, which is the main modeling approach in Battigalli et al., 2015). Second, even accepting this extreme form of ambiguity aversion, the mere determination of the set of all subjective theories that would be compatible with the observed feedback may be quite challenging (not to mention the complexity of determining the maxmin computed on the basis of this set). Given this, it is unclear to me whether such a selection can capture the behavior of real (boundedly rational) economic agents.[70]

13.4.2 Closely Related Approaches

In this part, I discuss the cursed equilibrium introduced by Eyster and Rabin (2005) contemporaneously to the ABEE concept, as well as the BNE and the Berk–Nash equilibrium introduced later by Spiegler (2016) and Esponda and Pouzo (2016), respectively. These concepts are closely related to the ABEE, as I will explain.

13.4.2.1 Cursed Equilibrium

Consider Bayesian games as defined in the previous subsection. Given a strategy profile σ and a type θ_i of player i, define $\overline{\sigma}_{-i}^{\theta_i}$ as the type-independent strategy of player $-i$ satisfying

$$\overline{\sigma}_{-i}^{\theta_i}[a_{-i}] = \sum_{\theta_{-i}} p(\theta_{-i} \mid \theta_i)\sigma_{\theta_{-i}}[a_{-i}].$$

It is the strategy of player $-i$ aggregated over the realizations of θ_{-i} conditional on the realization θ_i of i's type.

The partially cursed equilibrium of Eyster and Rabin assumes that player i with type θ_i best responds to the belief that player $-i$ plays a strategy that is a convex combination between $\overline{\sigma}_{-i}^{\theta_i}$ and the true strategy σ_{-i}. Formally, for each χ, σ_{-i}, θ_i, define $\sigma_{\theta_{-i}}^{\chi,\,\theta_i}$ such that

$$\sigma_{\theta_{-i}}^{\chi,\,\theta_i}[a_{-i}] = \chi\overline{\sigma}_{-i}^{\theta_i}[a_{-i}] + (1-\chi)\sigma_{\theta_{-i}}[a_{-i}].$$

Definition 13.7 *A χ-cursed equilibrium is a strategy profile σ such that for every player i and every type θ_i, if $\sigma_i[a_i^*] > 0$ then*

$$a_i^* \in \arg\max_{a_i} \sum_{a_{-i},\theta_{-i}} p(\theta_{-i} \mid \theta_i)\sigma_{\theta_{-i}}^{\chi,\,\theta_i}[a_{-i}]u(a_i, a_{-i}; \theta_i, \theta_{-i}).$$

Several comments are in order. First, when $\chi = 0$, a cursed equilibrium coincides with a Bayes Nash equilibrium. Second, when $\chi = 1$, the cursed equilibrium referred to as a fully cursed equilibrium by Eyster and Rabin coincides with an ABEE in which the analogy partition of player i coincides with his private information. This can be seen as the aggregate distribution of a_{-i}

[70] Of course, only empirical/experimental studies can address this question in a fully satisfactory manner. As a possible partial exploration of this, note that in the context of the centipede game, providing feedback on the aggregate pass rate as in Danz et al. (2016), the maxmin self-confirming equilibrium would coincide with the Nash equilibrium. Experimental data suggest otherwise (they are more in line with the ABEE; see Danz et al., 2016).

over all states $\theta = (\theta_i, \theta_{-i})$ with the same player i's type θ_i precisely coinciding with $\overline{\sigma}_{-i}^{\theta_i}$, and thus the best-response requirement in the fully cursed equilibrium is exactly the same as that for an ABEE with private information analogy partitions in this class of Bayesian games.

Considering interior values of χ allows Eyster and Rabin to go smoothly from the case of full sophistication as arising in a Bayes Nash equilibrium (with $\chi = 0$) to a case of full naivete (with $\chi = 1$), viewed here as the failure to appreciate the link of others' strategy to their private information (which matters for interdependent value contexts for which this concept was introduced). Such a modeling of partial sophistication differs from that in ABEE, in which the degree of sophistication is parameterized by the coarseness of the analogy partition. An advantage of Eyster and Rabin's approach compared to ABEE is that it is more parsimonious (even if by its focus on Bayesian games with interdependent values, it is also more limited in scope).[71] But this advantage comes at a cost, as Eyster and Rabin do not provide a rationale for how player i with type θ_i would be led to have a belief about player $-i$'s strategy as given by $\sigma_{\theta_{-i}}^{\chi,\,\theta_i}$ when χ lies in the interior of $[0,1]$. Clearly, if player i needs to know separately $\sigma_{\theta_{-i}}$ and $\overline{\sigma}_{-i}^{\theta_i}$ to determine $\sigma_{\theta_{-i}}^{\chi,\,\theta_i}$, this is not satisfactory, as the separate knowledge of $\sigma_{\theta_{-i}}$ should allow player i to determine the best response to the actual behavior of player $-i$. But then we are left to find an alternative argument as to how player i would have a belief given by $\sigma_{\theta_{-i}}^{\chi,\,\theta_i}$ when there is no knowledge of $\sigma_{\theta_{-i}}$. One possible idea in the vein of the self-confirming equilibrium would be to assume that player i observes from past interactions the aggregate behavior of player $-i$ for each possible θ_i as in the motivation for the private information analogy partition. The χ-cursed equilibrium is a self-confirming equilibrium with this signal structure. However, while $\sigma_{\theta_{-i}}^{\chi,\,\theta_i}$ is a possible subjective theory that would give rise to what player i observes from past interactions, I would argue it is unclear how player i would get at such a subjective theory (given that i has no knowledge of $\sigma_{\theta_{-i}}$, and only $\overline{\sigma}_{-i}^{\theta_i}$ is accessible from the data coming from past interactions). In my view, a satisfactory rationale for the partially cursed equilibrium is missing.[72] Some

71 I would like to add that in my view parsimony alone is not a good criterion to select a theory or model (see also Spiegler, 2019 who expresses a similar view). An analogy with the classic treatment of information in games may be instructive. In the spirit of the partially cursed equilibrium, one might have modeled partial information by requiring that a player plays a convex combination between what is optimal to do for him when he is fully informed of the state and what is optimal for him when he is totally uninformed. This is not how partial information is modeled though, and a partitional approach is generally adopted instead. I would say this is so because the partitional approach but not the convex combination approach can receive a natural interpretation in this case.

72 Miettinen (2009) suggests an interesting way to view a partially cursed equilibrium as an ABEE of a different Bayesian game in which the state space would be enlarged. However, the construction does not relate to a natural feedback structure, making such a construction more of theoretical than practical interest.

readers may wonder whether it is not possible to interpret the χ-cursed equilibrium as an ABEE in which a share χ of players would use the private information analogy partition and a share $1-\chi$ of players would use the finest analogy partition.[73] However, such an interpretation is incorrect, as in a χ-cursed equilibrium, player i with type θ_i always holds the same belief, which is $\sigma_{\theta_{-i}}^{\chi,\theta_i}$, whereas in the ABEE proposed alternative, a fraction χ would hold the belief $\overline{\sigma}_{-i}^{\theta_i}$ and a fraction $1-\chi$ would hold the belief $\sigma_{\theta_{-i}}$ (resulting in general in different best responses).

13.4.2.2 Bayesian Network Equilibrium

The BNE introduced by Spiegler (2016) can be described as follows. Inspired by the work on causal networks of Pearl (2009), Spiegler proposes endowing decision-makers (or more generally players) with subjective causality binary relations that specify which variable is caused by which other variables. Formally, such a causality network is represented by a direct acyclic graph (DAG) relating the various variables of interest, $x_0, x_1, \ldots, x_K$. When $i \rightarrow j$ in the DAG, it means that the decision-maker thinks that (the distribution of) x_j is influenced by the realization of x_i, thereby formalizing the intuitive idea that x_i is a cause of x_j.[74] From a game-theoretic viewpoint, one of the most interesting aspects in Spiegler's (2016) approach is the equilibrium nature of the concept, which is due to the endogenous character of one variable, the action a of the decision-maker.

To present formally the concept, let $x = (x_0, x_1, \ldots, x_K)$ be the variables of interest, where $x_0 = a$ denotes the action to be chosen by the decision-maker. Given the DAG considered by the decision-maker, one can define for each i the set of j such that there is a link $j \rightarrow i$. Call this set $R(i) \subset K = \{0, 1, \ldots, K\}$. The variables x_k, $k \in R(i)$ and only those are viewed by the decision-maker as causing x_i.

To simplify the presentation, I will be assuming that the decision-maker receives no private information before making his choice of action. Importantly, I will also be assuming that 0 (corresponding to the decision-maker's action) is the ancestor of the subjective DAG considered by the decision-maker. I would argue this can be viewed as deriving from logical implications, as the

Spiegler (2020) suggests a different interpretation of the partially cursed equilibrium in which players would be exposed to two sets of statistics, one corresponding to the private information analogy partition and the other corresponding to the fine analogy partition, and players would mix the two theories using a convex combination of the corresponding expectations. I will investigate at the end how a player exposed to different coarse statistics corresponding to different analogy partitions could behave. While the mixture corresponding to the partially cursed equilibrium is a possibility, I suggest several others as well. Moreover, it is unclear why the two coarse statistics needed for the partially cursed equilibrium should naturally be assumed to be available to players in applications, making this rationale a bit weak for applied purposes.

73 If this were so, we would have a rationale for the χ-cursed equilibrium similar to that for ABEE with heterogeneous analogy partitions.

74 Moreover, as indicated in the term DAG, there is no cycle in the graph, that is, one cannot have $x_1 \rightarrow x_2 \cdots \rightarrow x_n \rightarrow x_1$ for any subset of variables $(x_1, \ldots, x_n)$.

decision-maker's choice of action can hardly be thought of as being influenced by variables he does not observe. The true joint distribution of x will be given by $p(x)$ taking the form $p(x) = p(a)p(x_{-0} \mid a)$, where $x_{-0} = (x_1, \ldots, x_K)$. The key object in a BNE is the subjective perception of how variables are distributed given the subjective DAG considered by the decision-maker. It is given by the factorization formula

$$p^{DAG}(x) = \prod_{i \in K} p(x_i \mid x_{R(i)}), \tag{13.4}$$

where $x_{R(i)}$ denotes the profile of x_k for $k \in R(i)$. The interpretation of this formula is that from the observed data generated by p, the decision-maker can construct the conditional distributions $p(x_i \mid x_{R(i)})$, and given that the decision-maker thinks there are no other dependences beyond those described by DAG, p^{DAG} is viewed as (subjectively) describing the data-generating process. The decision-maker then chooses a so as to maximize

$$\sum_x p^{DAG}(x_{-0} \mid a)u(a, x_{-0}), \tag{13.5}$$

where u is the von Neuman–Morgenstern utility as usually defined. In order to ensure that $p^{DAG}(x_{-0} \mid a)$ is well defined from p^{DAG} for all a, Spiegler considers a trembling-hand formulation in which all actions should be played with probability no smaller than ε. Formally:

Definition 13.8 *A fully mixed strategy $p(a)$ is a personal ε-perturbed equilibrium if, whenever $p(a) > \varepsilon$, a maximizes (13.5). A Bayesian network equilibrium is the limit of a personal ε-perturbed equilibrium as ε tends to* 0.

I will now explain how a BNE can be viewed as an ABEE of an appropriately defined extensive-form game with appropriately defined analogy partition. I would like to suggest that the link to ABEE should come as no surprise given that the conditional probabilities $p(x_i \mid x_{R(i)})$ can precisely be viewed as the aggregate frequencies of x_i in the pool of data in which $x_{R(i)}$ is kept the same. That is, viewing Nature in charge of choosing x_i as a player, say player i, the causality idea behind $R(i)$ means that the decision-maker considers the strategy of i to be the same whenever $x_{R(i)}$ is kept constant. The ABEE is well suited to model such (partial) independences. It requires though defining a multi-stage game in which x_i is viewed as being chosen by player i, as just explained, where player i is viewed as moving after player j if $j \in R(i)$. It also requires that another player, viewed as irrelevant from the viewpoint of the objective of the decision-maker, call it Nature, chooses x right after the choice a of the decision-maker according to $p(\cdot \mid a)$, as objectively defined.[75] Player i down the tree is then required to choose an x_i that matches the initial choice

[75] Observe that it is the same decomposition of Nature into several players as the one considered above to model correlation neglect.

made by Nature.[76] While the game tree so constructed is subjective, I would argue it is naturally derived from the DAG to the extent that a causality link $i \to j$ directly suggests that the causing variable x_i must be decided before the consequence x_j.

More precisely, consider a multi-player extensive-form game with one different player for each variable x_k, $k \in K$. Call the player in charge of x_k with $k \neq 0$, player k. The decision-maker is player 0, and he chooses $x_0 = a$ at the root of the extensive-form game. Then Nature, also viewed as a player, decides how $\omega = (x_k)_{k \in K}$ is distributed as a function of a according to the objective conditional distribution $p(\omega \mid a)$. The extensive-form game specifies that each player k plays in sequence in an order that respects the order in the DAG. That is, all players in $R(i)$ must move before i.[77] Player k chooses x_k and his strategy is exogenously specified to be $x_k = x_k(\omega)$, where $x_k(\omega)$ is the kth element in ω as chosen by Nature after the action a of the decision-maker. The objective of the decision-maker is $u(a;x)$, where a is his action, $x = (x_k)_{k \in K \setminus \{0\}}$ is the profile of actions chosen by players $k \in K \setminus \{0\}$, and u is the von Neuman–Morgenstern utility function defined above.

Regarding the analogy partition of the decision-maker, consider the following. Decision nodes of different players belong to different analogy classes. For every player $i \neq 0$, assume that all his nodes corresponding to the same $x_{R(i)}$ define one analogy class.[78,79] By varying $i \neq 0$ and $x_{R(i)}$, one obtains an analogy partition.

It is readily verified that the ABEE of the strategic setting just defined is the Bayesian network equilibria, as defined in Spiegler (2016). This is so because condition (13.4) is equivalent to the consistency condition in ABEE, and the ensuing maximization of (13.5) corresponds to the best response in ABEE.

This construction allows me to view BNE as a special case of ABEE.[80] As such, the various applications of BNE can also be viewed as applications of ABEE.[81] Importantly, the construction requires that the DAG considered by the decision-maker is such that $R(0)$ is empty, as the decision-maker is

[76] I need such a decomposition (between Nature choosing x_{-0} right after a and then player i choosing x_i later on) to allow for the true generating process not to share the factorization structure imposed by the subjective DAG.

[77] Observe that one can always find such an order due to the absence of cycles in a DAG. There may sometimes be multiple extensive-form games that are compatible with the order in the DAG (e.g., think of the case where the DAG is empty, in which case any order is possible), but any of those would lead to the same set of equilibrium outcomes.

[78] Observe that this is well defined because the extensive-form game is such that players in $R(i)$ play before i.

[79] For Nature, the player moving second, note that the partitioning of its nodes is irrelevant (given that $u(a;x)$ does not depend on ω).

[80] In fact, within the extensive-form game just defined, analogy partitions not corresponding to BNE can be considered, for example putting together nodes of different players i and j. This suggests that the ABEE formulation allows for forms of bounded rationality not covered by BNE.

[81] I would like to stress that the motivation of analogy partitions through causality is new to Spiegler (2016) and does not appear in earlier work on ABEE (maybe with the slight exception of the monitoring game in Ettinger and Jehiel, 2005, in which some causality interpretation –

assumed here not to have any private information.[82] If this were not the case, or more generally if the decision-maker were allowed to think his action is caused by variables he does not observe (as allowed but not considered in applications by Spiegler, 2016–2020), then it would not be possible to make this construction (because the causality network would require that i plays before the decision-maker when $i \to 0$ in the proposed construction, and the maximization of (13.5) implicitly requires that the decision-maker thinks his choice of a affects x_i through the term $p^{DAG}(x_{-0} \mid a)$, which would not be so in the corresponding ABEE). As argued above, I think that the requirement that $R(0)$ is empty when the decision-maker has no private information is natural, and dropping it would in my view require a more severe form of bounded rationality (involving some extra form of logical inconsistency on the part of the decision-maker).

It should be mentioned that when Spiegler (2016, 2017, 2019, 2020) discusses ABEE in relation to BNE, he refers to the ABEE formulation in static Bayesian games as developed by Jehiel and Koessler (2008). In such contexts, when applied to decision problems, ABEE cannot capture the equilibrium nature of the strategy $p(a)$ of the decision-maker in BNE. Yet, as just discussed, the equilibrium nature of $p(a)$ is captured by ABEE when applied to the extensive-form game, as defined above and allowed for in Jehiel (2005).

13.4.2.3 Berk–Nash Equilibrium

Esponda and Pouzo (2016) present a general solution concept in games aimed at capturing limiting outcomes of learning processes in which players would have misspecified theories to represent their environment. Their solution concept is parameterized by the game, what is observed by the various players at the end of each game, as well as the set of subjective theories each player considers. Their solution concept combines ideas from statistics (in particular as developed by Berk, 1966), with equilibrium ideas (as in the Nash equilibrium), hence the term Berk–Nash equilibrium.

To present succinctly the key ingredients of the concept, consider a class of normal-form games with two players $i = 1,2$ in which player i chooses $a_i \in A_i$, player i observes $y_i \in Y_i$ after the game is played, and the stage game payoff of player i is $u_i(a, y_i)$, where $a = (a_i, a_{-i})$ is the action profile chosen by the players. The true distribution of y_i given a is governed by some objective distribution $p(y_i \mid a)$, which is not known to player i. Instead, player i is endowed with a set Φ_i of subjective theories ϕ_i, where $\phi_i \in \Phi_i$ specifies a distribution $\phi_i[a_i]$ over (a_{-i}, y_i) for each $a_i \in A_i$. I will be assuming that A_i, Y_i, Φ_i are all finite sets.[83] I do not specify the prior of player i over Φ_i, as this is not needed

moral hazard vs. adverse selection – is mentioned). As illustrated by the many insightful applications of BNE, bringing a new motivation broadens the scope of applications.

[82] More generally, $R(0)$ should contain at most those i such that the decision-maker observes x_i when there is private information.

[83] Esponda and Pouzo (2016) consider the case when Φ_i have infinitely many elements so as to capture the case of parametric estimations.

to define the Berk–Nash equilibrium. Importantly, Φ_i may be misspecified in the sense of not including the ϕ_i such that for every a_i, $\phi_i[a_i]$ would be the true distribution over (a_{-i}, y_i) as generated by p and the strategy σ_{-i} of player $-i$.

The general principle behind a Berk–Nash equilibrium is as follows. Assume players keep playing according to σ. Together with p this induces, for each $a_i \in A_i$, a true distribution of y_i after action a_i of player i. Denote the corresponding probability of y_i by $p_{a_i,\sigma}[y_i]$. Viewing player i as trying to learn which $\phi_i \in \Phi_i$ to consider would lead him to only keep those ϕ_i which minimize[84]

$$KL_i(\phi_i, \sigma) = \sum_{a_i} \sigma_i[a_i] \sum_{y_i} p_{a_i,\sigma}[y_i] \ln \frac{p_{a_i,\sigma}[y_i]}{\phi_i[a_i][y_i]},$$

where $\phi_i[a_i][y_i]$ denotes the probability that signal y_i arises when i plays a_i according to the distribution $\phi_i[a_i]$.

KL_i is the expected (with respect to a_i) Kullback–Leibler divergence from ϕ_i to $p_{\cdot,\sigma}$. The work of Berk (1966) ensures that if the true process is governed by $p_{\cdot,\sigma}$, only subjective theories in $\arg\min_{\phi_i \in \Phi_i} KL_i(\phi_i, \sigma)$ can be in the support of the long-run belief μ_i of player i, as these are the theories which have the largest likelihood in Φ_i given the long-run observations of a_i and y_i.

The other requirement in a Berk–Nash equilibrium is the familiar best-response idea: σ_i should be a best response to player i's belief about (a_{-i}, y_i) after each possible a_i, where such a belief can be inferred from the probability μ_i assigned by player i to the various ϕ_i in Φ_i. Putting together these two conditions yields[85]

Definition 13.9 *A strategy profile σ is a Berk–Nash equilibrium if, for every player i, there exists a belief μ_i over Φ_i such that*

1. *$\mu_i[\phi_i^*] > 0$ implies that $\phi_i^* \in \arg\min_{\phi_i \in \Phi_i} KL_i(\phi_i, \sigma)$ and*
2. *$\sigma_i[a_i^*] > 0$ implies that*
   $a_i^* \in \arg\max_{a_i} \sum_{\phi_i} \mu_i[\phi_i] E_{a_{-i},y_i}(u(a_i, a_{-i}, y_i) \mid a_i, \phi_i)$.

Under some extra assumptions, the existence of a Berk–Nash equilibrium is guaranteed (see Esponda and Pouzo, 2016). Recent research shows that not all Berk–Nash equilibria can emerge as the limiting outcome of learning processes (see Fudenberg et al., 2020), but I will abstract in my discussion from the resulting refinements.

How does the Berk–Nash equilibrium relate to ABEE? A first observation is that it is possible to interpret the ABEE as a limiting outcome of a learning environment in which each player i would (subjectively) believe that, for

[84] This is assuming that i knows σ_i, which fits applications in which the same player i keeps playing. Otherwise, ϕ_i could also specify a theory about how other players in the role of player i behave (see the above comments surrounding the definition of self-confirming equilibrium).

[85] I give here the definition without trembling. As for many other approaches, it is possible to refine the concept by imposing some (vanishing) trembles that allow player i to have observations for all actions and not only those in the support of σ_i.

every analogy class α_i in the analogy partition of player i, the behavior is the same for all elements belonging to α_i. Indeed, with such misspecifications, the observations of the behaviors of j at τh for the various $(j, \tau h) \in \alpha_i$ would lead, in the long run, player i to adopt the view (using the notation introduced for ABEE) that player j behaves according to $\widehat{\sigma}_{-i}[c_i;\beta]$, where β should be consistent with σ (as such a subjective view would be what minimizes the Kullback–Leibler divergence from the admissible subjective theories of player i to the true long-run data-generating process).

Note that with this interpretation, the signal y_i observed by player i at the end of a game should include a record of the actions observed in the various analogy classes, but it may include more information as well given that, in the Berk–Nash equilibrium approach, the belief $\widehat{\sigma}_{-i}[c_i;\beta]$ is a result of the misspecified prior rather than the coarseness of the observation y_i.[86] This is different in spirit from how I interpreted ABEE above, when I viewed the belief $\widehat{\sigma}_{-i}[c_i;\beta]$ as a consequence of the coarseness of y_i (together with some simplicity considerations) and not as a consequence of an initial misspecification of the prior (see the above learning interpretation of ABEE and the discussion surrounding the self-confirming equilibrium).

More generally, Esponda and Pouzo (2016) take the subjective theories Φ_i of the various players i as a primitive that is unrelated to the underlying objective characteristics of the game (as represented by the utility, information, and feedback y associated with each player). To make good use of their approach, it would be required in my view to have a better understanding of how the subjective theories considered by the players may be shaped by the objective characteristics of the environment.[87,88] To some extent, the ABEE provides an illustration of how the feedback structure y may shape the subjective priors for a special class of y. An open question concerns the possibility of going beyond the class of y allowed for in ABEE.

13.4.3 Other Approaches

I now discuss various equilibrium approaches with some bounded rationality element. I also include a discussion of case-based reasoning and learning classifier systems that share some common motivations with ABEE, even if not taking the form of equilibrium approaches.

86 In particular, even if player i observes finely the behavior of the various players at every node and for every type, the same Berk–Nash equilibrium would arise.

87 This is particularly relevant if one has in mind that it is not possible to have access (in the field) to the set of subjective theories of the players, since allowing for any possible such sets would make the predictive power of the approach less strong.

88 Such a concern may be related to a concern I expressed above in relation to Bayes Nash equilibria with subjective priors when I questioned how subjective priors should be chosen. To some extent, Heidhues et al. (2018) suggest a possible way to make practical use of the Berk–Nash equilibrium: motivate a mistaken misspecification with some behavioral findings (in their case, overconfidence in one's own ability) and look for the Berk–Nash equilibria with this misspecification alone.

13.4.3.1 Valuation Equilibrium

Jehiel and Samet (2007) define a solution concept for extensive-form games of complete information, the valuation equilibrium, that can be viewed as the limiting outcome of a learning process in the tradition of reinforcement learning models in which, instead of reinforcing strategies, players reinforce clusters of moves referred to as similarity classes. The valuation equilibrium (VE) can be viewed as the reinforcement learning counterpart of ABEE.

To give a quick description of the concept, consider an extensive-form game of complete information with players $i = 1, \ldots, n$ (and possibly Nature), where Z is the set of terminal nodes, N is the set of non-terminal nodes, A is the set of arcs (n, m) in the tree, N_i is the set of nodes where player i must move, $M_i(n) = \{m \mid (n,m) \in A\}$ is the set of moves of player i at node $n \in N_i$, and $u_i : Z \to \Re$ is the von Neuman–Morgenstern payoff function defined over terminal nodes.

The key novel parameter of the strategic setting in VE is, for each i, the similarity partition Λ_i of player i, which is a partition of $M_i = \bigcup_{n \in N_i} M_i(n)$, the set of all moves that player i may choose in the game. For any $m \in M_i$, I let $\lambda(m)$ denote the similarity class in Λ_i to which m belongs, and $Z(\lambda)$ the set of terminal nodes which are descendant of at least one $m \in \lambda$.

A valuation $v_i : \Lambda_i \to \Re$ of player i is a mapping from M to $\Re$, where $v_i(\lambda)$ refers to player i's valuation of the similarity class $\lambda \in \Lambda_i$. A strategy σ_i for player i specifies, for each $n \in N_i$, a distribution $\sigma_i(n)$ over $\Delta M_i(n)$. For any strategy profile σ, and $z \in Z$, I let $P^{\sigma}(z)$ denote the probability that z is reached given σ.

A VE requires that at every node $n \in N_i$, player i chooses a move belonging to a reachable similarity class with maximum valuation and that valuations are consistent with the strategy profile. I give here the definition without trembles, and like other previously defined concepts, it can be refined by adding trembling-hand perturbations (see Jehiel and Samet, 2007 for details).

Definition 13.10 *A valuation equilibrium is a strategy profile σ such that*

1. *For all $n \in N_i$, Supp $\sigma_i(n) \subseteq \arg\max_{m \in M_i(n)} v_i(\lambda(m))$ and*
2. *For all $\lambda \in \Lambda_i$ such that $P^{\sigma}(Z(\lambda)) > 0$,*
   $v_i(\lambda) = \sum_{z \in Z(\lambda)} P^{\sigma}(z) u_i(z) / P^{\sigma}(Z(\lambda))$.

The interpretation of a VE is as follows. For given valuations, the criterion used in part 1 of Definition 13.10 requires (for player i) identifying the value of a move with the valuation attached to the similarity class to which the move belongs. I would say this is a fairly natural criterion, very much in line with how players would choose a move in a game like checkers or chess, based on some coarse evaluation of the board position (such as the number of pieces ahead or a weighted version of it). Concerning part 2 of Definition 13.10, this is a consistency requirement similar to that introduced for ABEE. It can be thought of as follows. Assume the play has stabilized to some strategy profile σ. A statistician in charge of assessing the value for player i of the similarity class $\lambda \in \Lambda_i$ can, for each play, check whether a move in λ was chosen and in such a case add the obtained player i's payoff in a box labeled λ. By considering the long-run average payoffs put in box λ, the statistician will end up with the valuation $v_i(\lambda)$ as expressed in part 2 of Definition 13.10 whenever $P^{\sigma}(Z(\lambda)) > 0$.

The learning environment as just described is one in which players do not form beliefs about others' strategy, and instead try to assess the values to them of different courses of behaviors based on the performance they obtain in relation to these. While this feature is shared by models of reinforcement learning, a specificity here is that what players try to assess does not correspond to strategies as usually considered but to similarity classes. From another perspective, the idea of valuation as defined over similarity classes (and not strategies) should be thought of as a familiar object from the viewpoint of game-playing programs (see Samuel, 1959 for first developing such programs in checkers) in which nodes (or board positions) are typically assessed according to some simplifying device. From that perspective, the novel feature here is the derivation of the valuations of similarity classes from the strategy profile through the consistency mapping as expressed in part 2 of Definition 13.10.

In Jehiel and Samet (2007), we prove the existence of the VE in general finite environments, we establish the link of the trembling-hand version of the VE to the subgame perfect Nash equilibrium when players use the finest similarity partition (see Jehiel and Samet, 2005 for the convergence analysis of the corresponding learning model), and we illustrate through various examples how, for a number of similarity partitions, the VE offers predictions that differ from those obtained with the Nash equilibrium when varying the information structure.

How does the VE relate to ABEE? The VE was conceived as the reinforcement learning counterpart of ABEE. The focus on one's own performance in the VE as opposed to others' behavior in ABEE has led to a different notion of coarseness in the two approaches, which is parameterized by the similarity partition in the VE and the analogy partition in ABEE. Beyond that general (and somewhat informal) connection, I note that in some simple situations, the VE can be viewed as an ABEE of an appropriately defined setting. This is in particular so when Nature first decides which decision problem x arises according to some probability distribution $p(\cdot)$, and then in each problem x the same decision-maker has several alternatives $a \in A(x)$ resulting in terminal node z with payoff $u(z) = f(x,a)$.[89] In this case, the VE for any partitioning of the moves a at the various x can be captured as an ABEE of an appropriately defined setting. To see this, add a player after each (x,a) in charge of choosing the payoff $f(x,a)$, and consider the analogy partition such that if move a at x and move a' at x' were originally in the same similarity class, then the nodes xa and $x'a'$ at which the newly introduced player must choose the decision-maker's payoff are in the same analogy class. It is readily verified that the VE

[89] Such situations cover examples 1 and 2 in Jehiel and Samet (2007) (that are used, among other things, to illustrate the difference of VE with sequential equilibrium) as well as the experimental setting studied in Jehiel and Singh (2021).

of the original setting is isomorphic to the ABEE in the modified two-player game. A similar construction would not work for more general extensive-form games such as the stopping games discussed in Jehiel and Samet (2007), in which the same player must make several decisions in sequence.

13.4.3.2 Sampling Equilibrium

Osborne and Rubinstein (1998) have introduced a notion of equilibrium for static games, that will be referred to as $S(k)$ or sampling equilibrium, in which players base their choice of strategy on the average performance obtained for each possible action in samples of size k.[90] By considering heuristics based on performances (as opposed to theories about the other players), their approach can be related to the tradition of reinforcement learning, and their steady-state formulation of the $S(k)$ equilibrium can be interpreted as a limiting outcome of such a learning model.

But a distinctive feature of their approach is that each individual player is viewed as basing his strategy on observations of finite samples (and the steady state is reached only at the population level). In deterministic situations (requiring both that strategies are deterministic and that the payoffs attached to the various action profiles are deterministic), the heuristic based on finite samples would lead to no mistakes. Also, if the sample sizes were infinite, there would be no mistakes either, even in non-deterministic environments, as a consequence of the law of large numbers. Mistakes arise for finite sample sizes and non-deterministic environments.

To give an illustration of their concept, consider a symmetric 2×2 game with actions $\{x,y\}$ whose payoffs for player 1 are indicated for each action profile in the following table:

	x	y
x	a	c
y	b	d

Assume that all a,b,c,d are distinct and that $b > a$ and $c > d$ so that there is no symmetric pure Nash equilibrium. Consider a symmetric $S(1)$ equilibrium in which players make their choice of actions on the basis of a (payoff) sample of size 1 for each action. Formally, it specifies a probability p that x is played. There are four possible sample profiles of size 1 (for actions x and y) where each sample profile gives rise to a specific choice of action.[91] Steady state

[90] See Osborne and Rubinstein (2003) for a belief-learning counterpart of the $S(k)$ equilibrium which they refer to as sampling equilibrium and Spiegler (2006a, 2006b), Bianchi and Jehiel (2015, 2020), and Salant and Cherry (2020) for various applications and/or extensions.

[91] With probability p^2, x is perceived to give a and y is perceived to give b, leading to a choice of y given that $b > a$. With probability $(1-p)^2$, x is perceived to give c and y is perceived to give d, leading to a choice of x given that $c > d$. With probability $p(1-p)$, x is perceived to give a and y is perceived to give d, leading to a choice of x whenever $a > d$ and y otherwise. With probability $(1-p)p$, x is perceived to give c and y is perceived to give b, leading to a choice of x whenever $c > b$ and y otherwise.

requires that the resulting probability that action x is chosen coincides with p. For example, when $c > b > d > a$, the symmetric $S(1)$ equilibrium satisfies

$$p = 1 - p + p(1 - p)$$

or $p = \frac{-1+\sqrt{5}}{2}$, which typically differs from the mixed Nash equilibrium probability.

The sampling equilibrium can be viewed as formalizing the bias that agents tend to extrapolate from small samples to form their expectations (here about how good the various available actions are).

The mistake in ABEE can also be related to a form of (erroneous) extrapolation, to the extent that players wrongly believe that the aggregate observation in an analogy class applies equally to all elements of the analogy class. While the extrapolation in the sampling equilibrium can be viewed as identifying the individual (sampled) observation with the behavior in the general case, in ABEE it can be viewed as identifying the aggregate observation with the behaviors in the individual cases. Also, in ABEE, the observation is not based on small samples, unlike in the sampling equilibrium. Clearly, one could combine the ABEE approach with the idea that in each analogy class, players observe finite samples and extrapolate from those, as in the sampling equilibrium.

It may be worth highlighting that in both the sampling equilibrium and ABEE, the heuristic used by the agents can be viewed as being exclusively based on what these agents are assumed to have learnt about their environment: the aggregate distribution of behaviors in each analogy class in ABEE, and the finite sample for each action in $S(k)$. While in ABEE the heuristic can be phrased as requiring that agents assume the general aggregate knowledge in a group of contingencies applies separately to each contingency in the group, the heuristic in $S(k)$ can be phrased as requiring that the average payoff obtained in the sample is viewed as representative of how good the action is. This direct explicit mapping from the feedback to the subjective theories held by agents distinguishes ABEE and the sampling equilibrium from the Berk–Nash equilibrium but also from the self-confirming equilibrium in which such a mapping is not made explicit (see the above discussion of self-confirming equilibrium).[92]

13.4.3.3 Limited Foresight Equilibrium

In the context of repeated alternate move games, Jehiel (1995) has introduced the concept of limited foresight equilibrium in which players are assumed to make forecasts only within a limited horizon. Here, the sophistication of a

[92] The VE and the limited foresight equilibrium to be described next also share this property. Regarding the BNE, if one interprets it as resulting from the subjective causality relations considered by the decision-maker, the BNE does not share this property, but Spiegler (2017) offers another interpretation (with missing data) that would allow us to include the BNE as well. Of course, one could also use the ABEE interpretation of the BNE and its associated feedback structure to do this as well.

player is parameterized by how far ahead the player makes predictions. Given the stationarity of the environment considered in Jehiel (1995), players are assumed to consider the discounted sum of payoffs within their horizon of forecast as their criterion, and, in equilibrium, forecasts are assumed to be correct. Jehiel (2001) looked at repeated simultaneous-move games, and considered stochastic criteria as an alternative modeling of how players assess the payoffs in the periods lying beyond the horizon of forecast.

To give a flavor of the concept, consider a two-player setting in which in every period t, the stage game payoff of player i is $u_i(a^t)$, where $a^t = (a_1^t, a_2^t) \in A = A_1 \times A_2$ is the action profile at t, and players discount future payoffs with a common discount factor δ. In alternate-move games, player 1 can change his action a_1 in every odd period, player 2 can change his action in every even period, and actions remain the same until they are changed. In standard repeated games, players can change their action in every period.

Player i is assumed to have a forecast horizon n_i. Player i decides his period-t action a_i^t at history h on the basis of his forecast $f_i(a_i \mid h)$ about what will happen within his horizon of forecast if he plays a_i. In general, $f_i(a_i \mid h)$ is a distribution over action profiles from the current period t till period $t + n_i$ and player i's forecast includes player i's own actions in all future periods within the horizon of forecast.[93] I let $v_i(a_i \mid f_i, h)$ be the criterion used by player i to compare the various actions a_i based on the forecasting rule f_i and the history h. In Jehiel (1995), I considered the deterministic criterion consisting of the discounted sum of payoffs within the horizon of forecast. In Jehiel (2001), I considered a stochastic version of this allowing the unpredicted time periods to contribute in a noisy fashion to the criterion. For the sake of simplicity, I will have in mind the deterministic criterion in what follows.

As usual, a strategy σ_i for player i specifies for every history h (where i must move) a probability distribution over the action space A_i assumed to be finite. I let $\sigma_i^h[a_i]$ denote the corresponding probability that a_i is played, and $\sigma = (\sigma_1, \sigma_2)$ denote a strategy profile. I also let $q(a_i \mid h, \sigma)$ denote the distribution over paths from h onwards generated by σ when player i plays a_i at h, and $[q(a_i \mid h, \sigma)]_{n_i}$ denote the marginal of $q(a_i \mid h, \sigma)$ over the next n_i periods after h. A limited foresight equilibrium is defined as follows:

Definition 13.11 *A strategy profile σ is a (n_1, n_2)-limited foresight equilibrium if for $i = 1, 2$ there exists a forecasting rule f_i such that for all h, a_i, a_i^*:*

1. *If $\sigma_i^h[a_i^*] > 0$ then $a_i^* \in \arg\max_{a_i} v_i(a_i \mid f_i, h)$ and*
2. *$f_i(a_i \mid h) = [q(a_i \mid h, \sigma)]_{n_i}$.*

93 An alternative would be to limit the forecast to the reaction function of player $-i$, and allow player i to choose an optimal plan within the horizon of forecast. Given the rolling nature of the horizon of forecast, this alternative modeling would lead to time inconsistencies, which I find undesirable. Besides, I would argue that, in a number of contexts, the real object of choice at a given time period is the current action and not the plan of action, leading me to prefer the formulation of the forecast as a function of the current action (see Jehiel, 1995 and Rubinstein, 1998 for further discussion of this).

While condition 1 ensures that the strategy is related to the forecasting rule, as dictated by the criterion v_i, condition 2 imposes that the limited forecasts are correct on and off the equilibrium path. In Jehiel (1995), I consider repeated alternate-move games and further impose that the strategy of player i depends at most on the last N_i periods in addition to the calendar time. I show that limited foresight equilibria in pure strategies always exist, that they are cyclical, and that strategies can only depend on the last action in addition to the calendar time. I also note that players may sometimes be better off with shorter horizons of forecast. In Jehiel (1998), I consider a learning model and establish the convergence of it to a limited foresight equilibrium, thereby providing a learning justification to the correctness of the forecasts assumed in the limited foresight equilibrium.[94] In Jehiel (2001), I consider repeated simultaneous-move games with noisy criteria, provide a general method to construct all limited foresight equilibria (this requires elaborations on the standard dynamic programming techniques), and observe that limited foresight may make cooperation easier to sustain than universal defection in repeated prisoner's dilemmas.[95]

The limited foresight equilibrium, like the other solution concepts discussed so far, leads (sometimes) players to make suboptimal decisions, given that the criterion v_i in the limited foresight equilibrium need not always coincide with the rational criterion. Obviously, the mistakes in the limited foresight equilibrium are different from those in ABEE, but a common feature is that the criterion used by the players is related in a simple way to the object the players are supposed to learn (the analogy-based expectations in ABEE and the limited forecasts in the limited foresight equilibrium). It may be worth mentioning that the desiderata to have a simple formulation of the criterion v_i based solely on the forecasting rule f_i has led me to restrict the study of limited foresight equilibria to repeated games or repeated alternate-move games for which, due to the stationarity of the environment, it was somehow natural to view the payoff obtained within the horizon of foresight as representative of the overall payoff. Moving away from such stationary environments, the limited foresight equilibrium would require defining a criterion to assess the frontier nodes at the boundary of the forecast horizon. Such criteria are commonly used in game-playing programs, and the methodology developed for the valuation equilibrium (see above) could be combined with the methodology of the limited foresight equilibrium to cover such extensions. Of course, one could also relax the assumption that the forecasts are fully correct within the horizon of forecast, for example using the methodology of the analogy-based expectation equilibrium. The first unpublished version of ABEE allowed for such a combination (see Jehiel, 1999).

94 See Mengel (2014) for another learning model with limited foresight in finite-horizon interactions.

95 Rampal (2017) or Ke (2019) develop alternative approaches to limited foresight which are based on introspection rather than learning.

13.4.3.4 Behavioral Equilibrium

In the context of adverse selection models of the "market for lemons" type, Esponda (2008) defines a solution concept that mixes the idea that the buyer fails to appreciate the link between the information of the seller and his behavior, as in the fully cursed equilibrium or the ABEE with coarse analogy partition, with the idea that the buyer forms his belief about the distribution of the quality of the good based on the payoff observation when there is a transaction. The naive behavioral equilibrium assumes that the buyer views the qualities observed when there is a transaction as representative of the overall quality distribution, and adjusts his behavior optimally given this conjecture.

To give a concrete illustration of the concept, let me use the leading example in Esponda (2008).[96] The seller S is privately informed of the quality q of his good, where q is assumed to be uniformly distributed on $[0,1]$. The values of the good to the seller and the buyer B are $v_s(q) = q$ and $v_b(q) = q + b$ (with $0 < b < \frac{1}{2}$), respectively. The seller and buyer simultaneously quote a price p_s, for the seller, and p_b, for the buyer. There is a transaction whenever $p_b > p_s$, and the transaction price is p_b so that quoting price $p_s = v_s(q)$ is a weakly dominant strategy for the seller.

The price p^{NBE} quoted by the buyer in a naive behavioral equilibrium satisfies

$$p^{NBE} = \arg\max_{p_b}[E(q+b \mid q < p^{NBE}) - p_b]\Pr(q < p_b),$$

where the term $E(q+b \mid q < p^{NBE})$ represents the experienced value of the good for the buyer when there is a transaction (i.e., when $q < p^{NBE}$) and $\Pr(q < p_b)$ represents the probability of getting the good when quoting p_b that is correctly computed on the basis of the observed distribution of p_s. Solving for p^{NBE} yields $p^{NBE} = \frac{2b}{3}$, which is less than b (the Nash equilibrium price p_b) and a fortiori (when $b < \frac{1}{2}$) less than $\frac{2b+1}{4} = \arg\max_{p_b}[E(q+b) - p_b]\Pr(q < p_b)$, the fully cursed equilibrium price p_b. Unlike in the fully cursed equilibrium, the buyer is not mistaken about the equilibrium value of the good when he buys it (since the term $E(q+b \mid q < p^{NBE})$ correctly represents this value), and the mistake comes from the buyer's failure to appreciate that when he changes his quoted price p_b, this affects the average quality of the transacted goods. This failure leads to less trade than in the rational case (as downward – resp. upward – deviations are perceived as weakly more – resp. less – profitable than they really are).[97]

How does the naive behavioral equilibrium relate to ABEE? A priori, in the naive behavioral equilibrium, coarse agents mix two kinds of feedback, one

[96] The naive behavioral equilibrium as defined more generally in Esponda (2008) need not always exist, thereby justifying the focus on the lemon setup where it is well defined (see Esponda, 2008 for further elaborations on this).

[97] If one observes more trade than the rational approach predicts, one cannot rely on the naive behavioral equilibrium to explain it (see Fudenberg and Peysakhovich, 2016 for an experiment on this).

on the distribution of others' actions and the other on their own payoff, which does not seem compatible with the machinery of ABEE (this mixture is also responsible for the inexistence of naive behavioral equilibrium in some cases). Yet, in the context of the adverse selection problem just outlined, it is possible by a suitable choice of extensive-form game and analogy partitions to view the NBE as an ABEE.

To see this, consider the following extensive-form game. The seller's type is q as usually defined. Then players S and B simultaneously choose p_s and p_b, as described above. When there is a transaction, that is, $p_b > p_s$, another player called N_q chooses the quality or equivalently the value to the buyer specified to be $v_b^n = v_b(q) = q + b$, where q is the type of the seller. And the utility of the buyer is defined to be $v_b^n - p_b$ when there is a transaction and 0 otherwise. When all the decision nodes of player N_q form a single analogy class, and all the decision nodes of the seller form another analogy class, it is readily verified that the ABEE so obtained coincides with the naive behavioral equilibrium as previously defined. From a broader perspective, the ABEE in its extensive-form variant allows the modeler to capture effects of the selection bias type as arising in the naive behavioral equilibrium or the investment problem studied in Jehiel (2018).

The equilibrium approaches to be described next are somehow less closely related to ABEE. I include a discussion of them in an attempt to offer a broader perspective on how complexity/bounded rationality issues have been approached in the literature, while each time indicating the difference of perspective with ABEE.

13.4.3.5 Equilibrium with Strategy Restrictions

When the strategic environment is too complex, it sounds plausible that players would only consider a restricted set of strategies, and choose the best strategy within this restricted set. It is then natural to consider the Nash equilibria of the game appropriately modified to account for the restrictions in the strategy sets.

Formally, consider a strategic environment with players $i = 1, 2$. Denote by Σ_i the set of all possible strategies of player i, and by σ_i a representative strategy in Σ_i. Let $u_i(\sigma_i, \sigma_{-i})$ denote the expected utility obtained by player i when player i plays according to σ_i and player $-i$ plays according to σ_{-i}. Observe that such a formalism may accommodate applications in which player i would engage in several different interactions, in which case a strategy would allow the player to adjust his behavior to the interaction, or interactions with private information, in which case a strategy would allow the player to adjust his behavior to his private information, or multi-stage interactions (with private information), in which case the strategy would allow the player to vary his behavior as a function of history (and the private information). In this reduced-form presentation, a strategy can be thought of as a complete (possibly contingent) plan of actions to be chosen at an ex-ante stage before the plan is executed.

Restrictions in strategy sets can be modeled by assuming that player i only considers strategies σ_i in the subset $\Sigma_i^s \subseteq \Sigma_i$. An equilibrium with such strategy restrictions is a strategy profile $\sigma^s = (\sigma_i^s, \sigma_{-i}^s) \in \Sigma^s$ such that for each i, $\sigma_i^s \in \arg\max_{\sigma_i \in \Sigma_i^s} u_i(\sigma_i, \sigma_{-i}^s)$. That is, it is a Nash equilibrium of the normal-form game defined by the utility functions u_i, u_{-i} and the action spaces Σ_i^s, Σ_{-i}^s for players i and $-i$, respectively. As such, it is not a novel solution concept,[98] and the challenge is to propose reasonable choices of Σ_i^s and Σ_{-i}^s in each application as well as to understand how such strategy restrictions affect the equilibrium analysis. Equilibrium with strategy restrictions is the route followed by Compte and Postlewaite (2018) to revisit a number of classic economic applications.

The potential appeal of the approach from a bounded rationality perspective is that players have fewer aspects to learn than in the usual Nash equilibrium case. Indeed, assuming the behavior of player $-i$ does not change (as should be the case in steady state), it is enough for each player i to find out the optimal strategy in the restricted set Σ_i^s as opposed to the entire strategy set Σ_i (thus suggesting an easier maximization/learning process). I made a related comment for ABEE when I noted that, in ABEE, player i only has to learn the aggregate behavior in each analogy class, which is easier than having to learn the behavior in every contingency separately. But the underlying learning environments are different in the two cases. While ABEE finds its motivation in (coarse) belief-based learning models in which learning occurs at the population level (see the above learning motivation for ABEE), the equilibrium with strategy restrictions is better viewed as the outcome of a reinforcement learning model in which the same players would be playing many times and these would seek to learn the performance of the various strategies in their consideration set.[99]

A critical aspect in the equilibrium with strategy restrictions concerns the choice of the restricted strategy sets Σ_i^s. Compte and Postlewaite (2018) consider a variety of illustrations, many of which amount to reducing the strategy sets to one-dimensional families of strategies that they think of as plausible restrictions for their applications. Despite these many illustrations, I think it is fair to say that Compte and Postlewaite do not provide a general recipe for

[98] Existence of a Nash equilibrium with strategy restrictions is not guaranteed in general and it typically requires some conditions on the sets Σ_i^s (in particular, related to convexity).

[99] There has been a long debate in the learning literature whether belief-based or reinforcement learning models explain better observed behaviors (e.g., see in particular Camerer and Ho, 1999). I would suggest the answer to this question depends on the environment one has in mind. If the same player keeps playing again and again, and if he has easy access to his performance, then reinforcement learning models sound plausible. On the other hand, if players do not play themselves many times but are instead exposed to some statistics describing past play (as for the motivation of ABEE), reinforcement learning models seem inappropriate. I would add that even if the same player keeps playing again and again, his performance may be observed with a lag and in a noisy fashion, making it less natural that players would rely on reinforcement learning models in such contexts.

how to choose such strategy restrictions, making in my view the use of their approach not straightforward.[100]

It should also be mentioned that the equilibrium with strategy restrictions has precedents in the literature. For example, in the context of multi-stage games, Neyman (1985) considers restricting the players to use strategies that can be described by automata using at most n states. With a similar machinery but a different context in which players would be exposed to different interactions, one may consider that players categorize the interactions into a finite number of categories while imposing that the behavior is the same within the same category (using an approach similar to that of Rubinstein, 1986,[101] Samuelson, 2001 and Mengel, 2012 develop such models; see also the rule of thumb theme developed by Rosenthal, 1993 and the rule rationality theme developed by Aumann, 2008 for related ideas).

13.4.3.6 Equilibria with Imperfect Optimization

Another approach to the complexity of finding best responses is to allow for mistakes in the best responses. One such approach is the ε-equilibrium in which a player is only required to choose a strategy that induces an expected payoff no more than ε away from the maximum achievable payoff (see Radner, 1980, who uses this concept to explain cooperation in finite-horizon interactions). The ε-equilibrium can be related to the satisficing idea of Simon (1956) according to which a decision-maker is viewed as being satisfied with his strategy, as long as it delivers an expected payoff no less than his aspiration level.[102] In the ε-equilibrium, the aspiration level of a player is set ε below the maximum payoff this player can achieve in equilibrium. While it is not clear why the aspiration level would be set in this way, it should be noted that if it were set above the maximum achievable payoff, the considered strategy profile would not be in equilibrium (given that the player would then not be satisfied with his strategy). The ε-equilibrium can be viewed as offering a simple way to capture satisficing behaviors in steady-state environments (even if, with this interpretation, there is no reason to assume that ε is small, as usually considered in the literature).

[100] As already mentioned I believe that, in the ABEE context, the choice of analogy partitions is less subject to a similar critique whenever the analogy partitions are viewed as representing exogenously coarse feedback. See also the next section for elaborations on the choice of analogy partitions when these are viewed as learning-facilitating devices.

[101] Rubinstein (1986) considers a setup in which players care about the complexity of their strategy in addition to their payoff, as usually defined where the complexity is measured by the number of states that the automaton representation of the strategy requires. It should be mentioned though that the lexicographic criterion considered by Rubinstein (1986) does not allow us to view his concept as an equilibrium with exogenous strategy restrictions. Rubinstein's concept can be viewed as a Nash equilibrium in which one would have to modify players' utility to include players' concern about the simplicity of their strategy.

[102] See Gigerenzer (2001) for more recent developments of the satisficing approach, this time applied to heuristics that can be viewed as focal strategies on which players focus their attention (similarly as in the restricted strategy set approach discussed above).

Another approach to imperfect optimization consists in allowing players to stochastically choose each of their various available actions while requiring that those actions involving larger payoff losses would be chosen with lower probabilities. This is the idea behind the quantal response equilibrium (QRE) developed by McKelvey and Palfrey (1995). The most popular parameterization of QRE follows the logit specification. In a normal-formal game with finite action space A_i and utility function $u_i(a_i, a_{-i})$ for player i, σ is a QRE with noise parameters $\lambda = (\lambda_i, \lambda_{-i})$ if the probability that a_i^* is chosen satisfies

$$\sigma_i[a_i^*] = \frac{\exp \lambda_i V_i(a_i^*; \sigma_{-i})}{\sum_{a_i} \exp \lambda_i V_i(a_i; \sigma_{-i})},$$

where $V_i(a_i; \sigma_{-i}) = \sum_{a_{-i}} \sigma_{-i}[a_{-i}] u_i(a_i, a_{-i})$ is the expected utility of player i when he plays a_i and player $-i$ follows σ_{-i}. When $\lambda_i = 0$, player i randomizes uniformly across all actions, and when $\lambda_i = \infty$, player i plays an exact best response to his environment. When all players i use $\lambda_i = \infty$, the QRE is a Nash equilibrium. Intermediate values of λ_i accommodate situations in which player i is responsive to payoff differences but in a smooth way.

QRE can be viewed as formulating, in a game-theoretic context, familiar ideas from the discrete choice literature (McFadden, 1973). From that perspective, the criterion used by players may be thought of as a reduced-form representation where the true preference of player i attached to action a_i would be the sum of $V_i(a_i; \sigma_{-i})$ and some idiosyncratic term. As shown by McFadden, when the idiosyncratic term is independent across actions and follows an extreme value distribution, one obtains the logit formulation. Viewing the QRE in this way makes this concept in fact coincide with the Bayes Nash equilibrium of the game in which the idiosyncratic terms would be private information to the player. Some researchers interpret QRE differently, viewing the noisy criterion as a manifestation of mistakes (see, in particular, Chen et al., 1997). But this interpretation requires that players would be able to adjust the magnitude of the mistake to the payoff loss, and it is not clear through which mechanism boundedly rational agents could achieve this.

The ε-equilibrium as well as the QRE are clearly touching on aspects of bounded rationality that differ from those considered in ABEE to the extent that they do not challenge the rational expectation assumption.[103] In my view, the QRE methodology is quite useful to analyze experimental data which are

[103] See, however, an alternative to QRE proposed by Friedman and Mezzetti (2005) and more recently by Friedman (2022), who consider putting (white) noise in the belief about σ_{-i} rather than in the criterion (see also the M-equilibrium introduced by Goeree and Louis, 2021, which combines both noisy best responses and partially erroneous beliefs). Note that, except for the sampling heuristic discussed above, these papers (in particular, Friedman, 2022) do not provide explicit heuristic mechanisms through which the distribution of noisy beliefs would be centered around the correct distribution.

inevitably noisy. As such, it can naturally be combined with other approaches including ABEE, as illustrated in Huck et al. (2011).[104]

13.4.3.7 Mean-Field Equilibrium

When there are many players, such as in trading environments or in complex network environments, it is somehow natural for players to summarize the state of the economy by some moments of the distribution of plays where such moments, as well as possibly individual characteristics, are viewed as determining the individual preferences. This is the approach pursued in mean-field game theory (see Lasry and Lions, 2006), where it is assumed that individual players take the moments and their dynamics as given, optimize against these, and the evolution of the moments is endogenized by aggregating the individual behaviors, as in rational expectation models.

The ABEE shares with mean-field game theory the idea that players base their strategy on a simplified representation of their environment. But a crucial difference is that while in mean-field game theory the aim is to study rational agents and the simplification is viewed as a legitimate approximation of Nash equilibrium when there are many players, the aim of ABEE is to propose a framework to describe different forms of bounded rationality (as obtained by varying the analogy partitions) and study their implications for equilibrium predictions.

To give an illustration of the difference, consider a game with many players, each having to make a binary decision $a \in \{0, 1\}$ (e.g., a technology adoption in a network). In the tradition of mean-field game theory, one could consider anonymous environments,[105] and assume that players care about the adoption rate of their neighbors as well as their number. One could then assume that players make their choice of technology assuming every neighbor follows the aggregate adoption rate, and that the number of neighbors is drawn from a distribution that respects the degree distribution as observed in the true network. The resulting equilibrium would approximate the Bayes Nash equilibrium of a setup with many players in which individuals would make no observation about the network, assumed to be formed stochastically in agreement with the degree distribution.

One could instead assume that players observe very well the specific network they are in, or at least the number of neighbors their neighbors and themselves have, but to form their expectation about the adoption rate of their neighbors, they rely on the aggregate adoption rate in the network. Now, the adoption rate of a player may depend on the number of his neighbors, since this number is observed, but players' expectations about their neighbors' adoption rates would generally be incorrect, since every player would assume his neighbors all behave according to the aggregate adoption rate when in reality

[104] Haile et al. (2008) challenge the predictive power of QRE if one allows for arbitrary distributions of the noise terms. Similar considerations can be developed when combining QRE with other approaches.

[105] Anonymous environments are also the subject of the large games studied by Kalai (2004).

their adoption rate would be influenced by their degree. That kind of environment is well captured by ABEE assuming, for the given network, that players use the coarsest analogy partition that puts together all players in the network in the same analogy class. In some sense, it is suggestive of how the mean-field game theory agenda could be extended to cover situations in which the mean-field approach would allow us to approximate ABEE rather than Nash equilibria.

***

I have so far discussed equilibrium approaches. I end this section with a discussion of two non-equilibrium approaches initially introduced in artificial intelligence (AI) and psychology that rely on learning procedures that share some common motivation with ABEE and/or related concepts. These are case-based reasoning and learning classifier systems.

13.4.3.8 Case-Based Reasoning

Case-based reasoning, as introduced by Schank (1982) in AI, is, in broad terms, the process of solving new problems based on the solutions of similar past problems. It requires memorizing past cases, identifying which past cases are similar to the problem of interest, and possibly adapting the solutions that worked well in past similar cases to the current problem. Relatedly, but with a simpler focus on decision theory as conceived by economists, Gilboa and Schmeidler (1995) have developed a theory in which, in order to evaluate an action a^* in a new problem p, the decision-maker would look at past cases M consisting of triples (q,a,r), where q denotes a problem previously encountered, a denotes the chosen action in q, and r denotes the outcome, and he would assess a^* in p according to the criterion

$$U_{p,M}(a^*) = \sum_{(q,a^*,r)\in M} s(p,q)u(r), \tag{13.6}$$

where $s(p,q)$ is the similarity between problems p and q and $u(r)$ is the utility derived from the outcome r. That is, the decision-maker assesses a^* in problem p according to the weighted sum of utilities he derived in the various past problems q when a^* was chosen, where the weight given to past problem q is defined by the similarity $s(p,q)$ between q and p.

Case-based reasoning shares with the learning approach I used to motivate ABEE the idea that observations made in past, possibly different situations would be used to make assessments and decisions in the current situation of interest. In both case-based decision theory and ABEE, whether and to which degree other situations are used is given exogenously by the analogy partition in ABEE and the similarity function in CBDT.[106] But there are important differences both in terms of the pursued methodology and in terms of

[106] I note that the case-based reasoning of Schank suggests the additional desiderata that only analogies that help achieve better outcomes should be considered and that past solutions that worked well in previous problems may need to be adapted to the current problem for efficiency

objectives. First, ABEE is concerned with strategic environments and past cases are used to assess frequencies of opponents' actions over different analogy classes. As such, it builds on belief-based learning models, whereas case-based reasoning is closer to the reinforcement learning tradition in which past cases are used to assess how good the various possible options are. From that perspective, CBR shares more with VE than ABEE. Second, ABEE is concerned with a steady state in which lots of data have been accumulated, whereas CBR and CBDT are concerned with the resolution of new problems. This has led to an equilibrium formulation in ABEE in which the beliefs are related to the strategies and the analogy partitions through a consistency requirement (similar to the Nash equilibrium) when there is no such endogeneity in CBDT. Third, ABEE can be viewed as relying on a frequentist approach in which subjects are exposed to frequencies of actions in the various analogy classes, whereas such a frequentist interpretation is less readily available for CBDT.[107] I would argue that the frequentist approach makes it easier to interpret ABEE as resulting from subjects being exposed to coarse statistics (possibly as given by society), whereas such an interpretation would be less natural in CBDT (in CBDT, M is what the decision-maker remembers from the past and s is the subjective similarity function that he considers). Finally, and in relation to Schank's view, I note that the main objective of ABEE consists in describing better the actual behaviors of economic agents, which contrasts with the AI objective of finding good solutions to new problems. This has led me to use ABEE as a tool to explore whether observed puzzles could receive reasonable explanations and to not worry whether subjects could be performing suboptimally.

13.4.3.9 Learning Classifier Systems

Learning classifier systems (LCS), as introduced by Holland (1975), consider complex decision problems in which the system may evolve from state to state depending on the chosen actions and in each state the agent may consider various rules of thumb or classifiers to make his choice of action. LCS allow for new generations of classifiers, but for now I will assume that the classifiers are exogenously given (I will come back to the generation of new classifiers in the next section). At every step t of the learning process, different strengths or indices are attached to the various classifiers. When, at some state s, the agent is required to choose the available classifier with maximum (current) strength, call it C. Then some instantaneous payoff observation u_t is made and the system moves to another state s'. The strength of the classifier C is then adjusted from $v_t(C)$ to $v_{t+1}(C)$ according to some rule in the spirit of dynamic

purposes. I would interpret the latter idea of adaptation in relation to the idea that the notion of analogy should be extended to actions.

[107] CBDT can accommodate the frequentist approach by imposing that the similarity is either 0 or 1 and by normalizing expression (13.6) by the number of similar cases in which action a^* was chosen. While this is discussed by Gilboa and Schmeidler, it is not considered as the main model of CBDT, which allows for general similarity functions.

programming. For example, in contexts with standard exponential discounting, a typical updating rule would require that $v_{t+1}(C)$ is a convex combination between $v_t(C)$ and $u_t + \delta v_t(C')$, where δ is the discount factor and C' is the classifier that would be chosen at s' on the basis of the profile of the time t strengths (as given by $v_t(\cdot)$).

The main objective of such learning systems, as viewed by machine learning researchers, is to find out (or at least approximate) optimal solutions. The Q-learning algorithm defined for Markovian processes in which the classifiers consist of the set of all possible actions at every state (similar to standard reinforcement learning models) leads asymptotically to the optimal solution when the adjustments of the classifier strengths are slow enough (see Watkins and Dayan, 1992). But for other contexts and more limited sets of classifiers, such convergence results need not hold.

The main objective of researchers dealing with bounded rationality in economics is different and can be related to whether an approach like LCS can give rise to predictions different from the ones arising with rational expectations. To my knowledge, there have not been many such uses of LCS in economics, with the notable exceptions of Marimon et al. (1990) and Lettau and Uhlig (1999) in macroeconomics. For the purpose of the present chapter, let me now abstract away from convergence issues, and assume, for a given set of classifiers, that the classifier strengths have converged. In such a limiting situation, the strengths of the classifiers would satisfy a consistency requirement that relates those strengths to the true underlying process, including the effective choices of classifiers at each state. Moreover, at every state, the agent would choose a classifier with maximal (current) strength. The obtained limiting outcome is somehow related to the VE introduced above if one identifies a similarity class and its valuation in VE with a classifier and its strength in LCS. But there are some differences between the two. First, the similarity class in VE is viewed as dictated by the kind of feedback (about past problems) provided to subjects, whereas the classifiers are viewed as (available) local models. Second, I allowed for multiple players in VE, which is not so in LCS. Third, consistency in LCS would not be defined as I considered it for VE. In VE, I assumed that the total payoff obtained in the game could directly be related to the similarity class (thereby leading to consistency, as shown in Definition 13.10). In LCS, consistency would relate the strengths of the various classifiers through the dynamic programming formula. While an exact and general formulation of consistency for LCS is to be developed, I note that the two approaches to consistency in VE and LCS would correspond to environments that differ whether total payoffs can be observed quickly (for VE) or not (for LCS).

13.5 WHAT'S NEXT?

In this section, I indicate what I regard as possible next steps of the ABEE research agenda. Of course, this list is in no way exhaustive, as there are surely many other relevant directions for future research.

13.5.1 How to Choose Analogy Partitions

I have indicated three different ways of interpreting the analogy partitions in Section 13.2.4. When analogy partitions are viewed as the result of exogenous feedback limitations, there is no reason to seek further endogenization except if these limitations can be influenced by some economic agents. In Section 13.5.1.1, I suggest such a perspective. When analogy partitions are viewed as a way to formalize psychological biases, I would say the input of psychologists is probably the most useful to better understand what aspects of contingencies agents find most salient. Finally, when analogy partitions are viewed as a device to simplify learning, I would say more is needed to understand how the choice of analogy partitions may facilitate learning. In Section 13.5.1.2, I suggest some reduced-form approaches to this.

13.5.1.1 Analogy Partitions as Influenced by Third Parties

When analogy partitions are viewed as resulting from the exogenously coarse feedback players have access to, sometimes some economic agents can have control on this. If one thinks societies can exert such control, then a natural question is how the feedback should be chosen to maximize welfare or some other measure of efficiency. This can be viewed as being related to the debate on transparency (an attempt to impose increasing criteria of transparency to economic actors such as banks, firms, etc.), but note that transparency in most of the economics literature is generally thought of in relation to the information transmission within the interaction of interest rather than feedback related to data concerning previous interactions as in the ABEE framework. If, on the other hand, one thinks of economic agents possibly with non-benevolent interest who can exert such control, it may suggest a new role for regulation, as there is no reason that the best choice of analogy partitions from a private interest viewpoint would coincide with what society likes best (the study of manipulative auction design in Jehiel, 2011 can be viewed as providing an illustration of this).

Moving one step further, one could also envision situations in which different agents would propose different aggregate statistics to players. A question then arises as to how players faced with competing aggregate statistics would behave. I will discuss possible ways to cope with this in the next subsection. Once this is settled, one would still have to understand the equilibrium behavior of competing economic agents offering such aggregate statistics.

13.5.1.2 Analogy Partitions as Chosen by Individuals

In this part, I assume that players exert some control on the choice of analogy partition that they consider.

Analogy Partitions, Statistics, and Machine Learning. When viewing the motivation for analogy partitions as simplifying devices to interpret rich datasets, an obvious branch of literature that sounds relevant is machine learning.

One fundamental idea in statistics and machine learning is the so called bias-variance trade-off.[108] If contingencies are categorized too finely, the obtained statistics in each category are not reliable enough, and if they are categorized too coarsely, the statistics may be less relevant for adjusting the best-response. One possible reduced-form approach to this in the ABEE setting would be to require that analogy classes be reached with a probability no smaller than some positive threshold where this threshold would be viewed as a primitive of the model. I have considered in the end part of Jehiel (2005) a related idea where I imposed in extensive form games that off-the-path contingencies should be bundled with some on-the-path contingencies. Going beyond this, when one can define a natural distance between contingencies, the bias-variance trade-off suggests that players would bundle contingencies according to how close they are as in the neighborhood analogy partitions mentioned in Section 13.2.5.1 with the extra constraint that each analogy class should be reached with a sufficiently high probability.[109]

Another classic tool in machine learning is the so called K-means clustering, which addresses the question of how to best cluster n points into K categories so as to minimize the sum of the square distance between each original point and the representative element of the cluster to which the point is assigned. This method has been extended to cover other notions of closeness such as the Kullback-Leibler divergence when points are distributions (see, in particular, Banerjee et al., 2005). In Jehiel and Weber (2024), we use the clustering idea to propose an endogenization of the analogy partitions in contexts involving n different stage games. In doing so, we identify a cluster in machine learning with an analogy class in ABEE. Like in the K-means clustering, we postulate that players rely on K analogy classes, and the choice of analogy partition should satisfy the property that the distribution of opponent's behavior in a game γ is closest to the average distribution in the analogy class $\alpha(\gamma)$ to which γ is assigned than any other average distribution as appearing in the other analogy classes α' considered by the player. We refer to this property as a stability idea, as it ensures that a player checking whether a given game γ is well assigned given the considered analogy partition would stick to his original analogy partition. Compared to the classic clustering idea, there is an extra endogeneity which is related to the ABEE formulation. Each grouping or clustering affects the distribution of points, unlike in the classic machine learning exercise in which the points are exogenously given. This endogeneity in turn makes the existence of pure stable ABEE problematic for some situations, in which case one has to extend the definition to allow for mixed stable

[108] In non-strategic contexts, Fryer and Jackson (2008) have used this trade-off to model discrimination. Mohlin (2014) has developed a model to best solve this trade-off in simple non-strategic settings. In relation to this trade-off, Olea et al. (2019) have suggested that models with fewer explanatory variables may subjectively be considered as more reliable in the face of small datasets.

[109] Jehiel and Mohlin (2024), which was completed after the first version of this chapter was written, develops such an approach.

ABEE. We have applied the approach to the study of symmetric two-player games with one-dimensional action spaces, and derived qualitatively different insights according to whether players' actions are strategic substitute or complements (see Jehiel and Weber, 2024 for elaboration on the interpretation and more applications).

One may also mention the machine learning ideas developed in genetic algorithm (see Holland, 1975) to generate new rules of thumb or classifiers from old ones as a possible route to induce new choices of analogy partitions. One possible idea I see in relation to this is that if the variance of behavior observed in a given analogy class is too large, the player could somehow split the analogy partition into several pieces, and if the aggregate behaviors observed in two analogy classes are close enough to each other, the player could decide to merge them. There are clearly other ideas that could be considered in relation to this.[110] Obviously, more work is needed to understand this better.

Optimization Approaches. As an alternative to machine learning, one could adopt more rational approaches to the choice of analogy partitions. One such approach is that of a two-stage procedure. First, players choose their analogy partitions, then players play the corresponding ABEE. A question arises as to how players assess the effect of their choice of analogy partitions in the first stage, and how ABEE is defined in the second stage when a player considers arbitrary (including off-the-equilibrium-path) analogy partitions. One option that I discuss at the end of Jehiel (2005) is that the ABEE played in the second stage corresponds to the choices of analogy partitions in the first stage (whether on or off the equilibrium path) and that the criterion for the first stage choice is the true expected payoff (it also corresponds to the approach in Heller and Winter, 2020, who use this methodology to endogenize general families of biased beliefs in normal-form games).[111] Several concerns can be raised about this approach. First, I find the commitment feature resulting from the assumption that the ABEE is the one corresponding to the individual choice of analogy partitions problematic in a number of applications, as the aggregate feedback in the ABEE is more naturally interpreted as coming from many different players (not just oneself).[112] Second, it is not clear how players would have the correct understanding about how their choices of analogy partitions

[110] In particular, the LCS literature suggests ideas in the spirit of Axelrod's tournament (see Axelrod, 1984).

[111] I used this approach to obtain that in some cases, players would not adopt the finest analogy partition even if possible because it would give them some commitment power to choose a coarser analogy partition that turns out to be favorable in some interactions. This is similar to observations made in Dekel et al. (2007).

[112] One can drop this commitment aspect but if one places no restrictions on the analogy partitions, then it becomes weakly dominant to choose the finest analogy partition. Of course, it may be more reasonable to put constraints on the analogy partitions that players can consider, but then the equilibrium choice of analogy partitions will heavily hinge on these constraints and it should then be the subject of further analysis to understand which categorizations emerge.

translate into true payoffs.[113] One could invoke some evolutionary or imitation process to give some rationale to this. The study of this is left for future research.

A somewhat different route is related to the rational inattention approach. One interpretation of the coarse feedback is that the agent does not pay full attention to every detail in the feedback (assumed to take the form of exhaustive and unprocessed raw data about past behaviors and other aspects of the interaction) and focus on some aspects of it.[114] In the tradition of rational inattention models (à la Sims, 2003), one could attach a cost to processing more finely the information conveyed by the feedback, and one could assume that players choose their analogy partitions optimally, taking into account the processing cost associated with the chosen analogy partition. I personally find the rational inattention approach to the choice of analogy partitions very demanding in terms of the level of rationality imposed on the players. It may be that the rational inattention approach can be viewed as a reduced form for a cognitively less demanding process, but a full-fledged argument supporting this view is still to be developed.[115]

Choosing Among Competing Analogy Partitions. In many instances, one may not have the full freedom to choose from the entire set of all analogy partitions, and one may only be exposed to the feedback corresponding to just a few analogy partitions, for example as provided by different experts or different statistical institutes. One possibility for the agent is to try to combine the information conveyed by the various types of feedback. Such a combination could take the form of attaching different weights (or probabilities) to the various analogy partitions, and assessing strategies according to the perceived expected utility that results from this. Alternatively, the agent may only consider the most likely analogy partition, and optimize only the corresponding subjective utility. Note that in multi-stage settings, this selected

[113] This is somehow related to the infinite regress problem discussed in Mongin and Walliser (1988), Lipman (1991), and Conlinsk (1996).

[114] The salience perspective suggested above is related to this but with a psychological rather than a rational viewpoint.

[115] The sparsemax model developed by Gabaix (2014) in the spirit of LASSO suggests a simplified version of the rational inattention model in which utilities are approximated by their second-order Taylor expansion in models with continuous variables. While the simplification alleviates some of my concerns related to the rational inattention approach, it is unclear to me whether the proposed Taylor approximation can be viewed as capturing a behaviorally sensible heuristic.

From another perspective, Gagnon-Bartsch et al. (2020) develop an approach that they refer to as channeled attention, which can be viewed as similar to the rational inattention approach except that it is based on a possibly misspecified prior belief of the agent. Such an approach can explain why agents would pay limited attention to the data and as a result be unable to detect the possible misspecifications of their prior. In my view, as with models of subjective priors or models with misspecifications (e.g., the Berk–Nash equilibrium), one would need to have a better understanding of how the misspecifications are formed in applications to make good use of such an approach.

analogy partition may change as more observations are made in the interaction.[116] As yet another alternative, agents could choose the analogy partition that subjectively promises the highest expected payoffs (where the computation for a given analogy partition adopts the subjective representation attached to this analogy partition). This is similar in spirit to the optimal expectation framework of Brunnermeier and Parker (2005), with the constraint that beliefs should correspond to those generated by the available analogy partitions.[117] In my view, more work, including on the experimental side, is needed to better understand how agents make use of different sources of feedback.

13.5.2 Learning to Play ABEE

An important question not addressed so far is when learning dynamics of the type suggested after the definition of ABEE would converge to a steady state (and if so which one).[118] This is a similar question to that pursued in the theory of learning in games (e.g., see the textbooks of Fudenberg and Levine, 1998; Weibull, 1997; Young, 2004), with a focus on ABEE rather than the Nash equilibrium. In the standard case, dominance solvable games are known to induce nice learning convergence. The setup in Huck et al. (2011) suggests a similar notion for ABEE. In the example considered there, if one iteratively eliminates those strategies that are strongly dominated against all possible beliefs that are consistent in the ABEE sense for some remaining strategy profile, one eventually pins down a single strategy profile. This very property guarantees in turn the convergence of most learning models to ABEE, similar to the standard case. More work should be done to develop convergence results in other classes of games.[119]

I end this subsection with two classic observations made in the context of learning in games, and I discuss how they could affect ABEE. First, some of the learning literature has suggested that the correlated equilibrium rather than the Nash equilibrium should be the right benchmark in the classic learning scenario with a single normal-form game (e.g., see Hart, 2005; Hart and Mas-Colell, 2003). It should be stressed that such conclusions concern learning dynamics in which players learn as they keep playing against the same opponents (and the common history can then play the role of a coordinating device used to correlate the strategies of the players). In learning dynamics

[116] Mullainathan et al. (2008) adopt the maximum likelihood approach to study a model of persuasion with coarse reasoning of the ABEE type. See also Schwartzstein (2014).

[117] Using the Bayesian network machinery, Eliaz and Spiegler (2020) develop such an approach to analyze a model of competing narratives.

[118] If these do not converge, then dynamic studies of the type considered in agent-based models may be more appropriate to describe long-run behaviors.

[119] Another class of games for which belief-based learning models of the fictitious play type are known to have good convergence properties is the class of 2×2 games (see Miyasawa, 1961). Li Calzi (1995) provides a similar result for families of 2×2 games in which players would use the coarsest analogy partition.

in which a given subject assigned to the role of a player plays just once as considered to motivate the ABEE, there is no common history on which players can coordinate their choice of strategy, and learning operates only at the level of the population. In this case, the ABEE formulation seems to be the appropriate long-run notion (exactly as the Nash equilibrium would be in the standard case). Of course, one could well consider scenarios in which there is correlation between the types of the various players in the matching process, but this is covered in the ABEE formulation to the extent that any joint distribution of types (concerning both the regular and the cognitive dimension of the type) is allowed.

Second, a key insight from the literature on learning in multi-stage games is that unless the trembles are viewed as arising exogenously, it may not be obvious to justify the correctness of beliefs off-the-path, as assumed in traditional concepts such as sequential equilibrium (see Fudenberg and Kreps, 1995). The same comment applies to ABEE, but it should be noted that the coarser the analogy partition, the less likely it is that an analogy class would be unreached in equilibrium. Such an observation can be used to restrict attention to analogy partitions and ABEE such that all analogy classes of all analogy partitions are reached with positive probability in the ABEE (see also the above discussion on the bias–variance trade-off).

13.5.3 Mixing ABEE with Other Forms of Reasoning

A popular approach to interpret experimental data in early rounds of multi-player interactions is the so-called level-k approach (Nagel, 1995; Stahl and Wilson, 1995; see also Crawford and Iriberri, 2007 for an application to Bayesian games). When the payoff and information structures of the opponent are known to subjects (as is often the case in lab experiments), one can iterate the best-response mapping up to some level k, assuming the level-0 behavior of the opponent corresponds to some focal strategy such as the uniform randomization over the possible actions. A level-k player is best responding to the belief that the opponent behaves according to the level-$k-1$ strategy. The cognitive hierarchy model (Camerer et al., 2004) proposes a related approach in which at level k, instead of best responding to level $k-1$, the player best responds to the behavior generated by a distribution (assumed to be Poisson) over lower levels.

These models aim to capture early rounds of interactions, and as such they do not propose equilibrium concepts in which the beliefs are related to the actual behaviors. This is a priori very different from the environments envisioned in ABEE, in which beliefs are coarse but tightly related to the actual behaviors (as a result of some possibly collective underlying learning process). Despite this fundamental difference, I can think of possible ways to combine the two approaches. Specifically, I would imagine an ABEE treatment to the determination of level-0 behavior, having in mind that the focal (level-0) behavior in these models is derived from some coarse statistics about aggregate behaviors as in ABEE. From this perspective, the level-0 behavior would be determined in an equilibrium fashion, aggregating past behaviors in the various analogy classes (as in ABEE), where the behaviors would be generated by the assumed distribution of level-k agents in the population. Clearly, more work is needed to see if such a combination can bring new insights, be fruitful, and in which contexts. One limitation I see is that such an approach requires a knowledge of the payoff and information structures of the opponent (to be able to iterate the best response), and in many field (or real-life) contexts, I would imagine such a knowledge is not directly available and has to be inferred from accessible observations (e.g., past behaviors).

More generally and beyond the level-k formulation, one could combine the ABEE approach with the so-called theory of mind as developed in philosophy and psychology, in which subjects are viewed as putting themselves in the shoes of others before making their choice of strategy. For every player i, endowing other players $-i$ with beliefs formed in the ABEE sense, given the analogy partition of player i, would look like a natural approach to me.

In a number of situations, especially if one plays several times, one may receive feedback on one's own performance as well as feedback on others' behaviors. A question then arises as to how to combine reasoning based on feedback about others' behaviors (as in ABEE) with reasoning based on performance (as in VE or sampling equilibrium). Alternatively, these different modes of reasoning can be regarded as competing ones, and a player may engage into selecting among these theories, possibly using the methods described above to model the choice between competing analogy partitions. Obviously, more work is required to make progress on these questions.

13.6 CONCLUSION

There are obviously many ways to approach the modeling of bounded rationality in games. In this chapter, while I have discussed (sometimes succinctly) a number of these approaches, I have focused on the analogy-based expectation equilibrium. In ABEE, players are viewed as forming their expectations based on aggregate statistics describing behavioral data in their various analogy classes, and the corresponding equilibrium is viewed as a steady state of a learning process in which agents would form their expectations in this way.[120] The ABEE framework is flexible enough to accommodate many different types of mistaken expectations, as results from the possibility of varying the analogy partitions. In my view, an appealing aspect of ABEE is the plausibility of the deliberation process attributed to the players, which depends only on the aggregate statistics players are assumed to have access to. More generally, and beyond ABEE, I would argue that it is desirable to impose that the deliberation

[120] In a broad sense, viewing bounded rationality through a statistical lens agrees with the general theme pursued by Sargent (1993) in macroeconomics, with an emphasis on the data-pooling idea (here) rather than dynamic programming (in Sargent).

process of players does not depend on aspects of the environments players are not assumed to know or have learned about. Obviously, more work can and should be done to further understand how players' analogy partitions are formed, especially when these are viewed as learning-facilitating devices. This should involve theoretical, experimental, and also empirical research effort. In particular, on the empirical side, I would imagine econometricians seeking to estimate the distribution of analogy partitions in the same way as they estimate the distribution of private information in the standard case, assuming now that the play is governed by ABEE rather than the Nash equilibrium. I hope I will have persuaded the reader that there is more to be done in terms of broadening the scope of applications of ABEE, developing the theory, and developing empirical and experimental methods suited for ABEE.

REFERENCES

Anderson, J. R. (1991). "The adaptive nature of human categorization," *Psychological Review*, 98(3), 409–429.

Antler, Y. (2019). "Multilevel marketing: Pyramid-shaped schemes or exploitative scams?" Mimeo.

Antler, Y., and B. Bachi (2020). "Searching forever after." Mimeo.

Arad, A., and A. Rubinstein (2019). "Multidimensional reasoning in games: Framework, equilibrium, and applications," *American Economic Journal: Microeconomics*, 11(3), 285–318.

Aumann, R. (2008). "Rule-rationality versus act-rationality." Discussion Paper Series dp497, The Federmann Center for the Study of Rationality, The Hebrew University, Jerusalem.

Axelrod, R. (1984). *The Evolution of Cooperation*. New York: Basic Books.

Azariadis, C., and R. Guesnerie (1982). "Prophéties cré atrices et persistance des théories," *Revue économique*, 33(5), 787–806.

Banerjee, A. (1992). "A simple model of herd behavior," *Quarterly Journal of Economics*, 107, 797–817.

Banerjee, A., S. Merugu, I. S. Dhillon, and J. Ghosh (2005). "Clustering with Bregman divergences," *Journal of Machine Learning Research*, 6(58), 1705–1749.

Barron, K., S. Huck, and P. Jehiel (2024). "Everyday econometricians: Selection neglect and overoptimism when learning from others," *American Economic Journal: Microeconomics*, 16(3), 182–198.

Battigalli, P. (1987). "Comportamento razionale ed equilibrio nei giochi e nelle situazioni sociali." Unpublished.

Battigalli, P., S. Cerreia-Vioglio, F. Maccheroni, and M. Marinacci (2015). "Self-confirming equilibrium and model uncertainty," *American Economic Review*, 105(2), 646–677.

Bergemann, D., and S. Morris (2005). "Robust mechanism design," *Econometrica*, 73, 17711813.

Berk, R. (1966). "Limiting behavior of posterior distributions when the model is incorrect," *Annals of Mathematical Statistics*, 37, 51–58.

Bianchi, M., and P. Jehiel (2010). "Bubbles and crashes with partially sophisticated investors." Mimeo. Available at https://philippe-jehiel.enpc.fr/wp-content/uploads/sites/2/2018/03/bubbles.pdf.

Bianchi, M., and P. Jehiel (2015). "Financial reporting and market efficiency with extrapolative investors," *Journal of Economic Theory*, 157, 842–878.

Bianchi, M., and P. Jehiel (2020). "Bundlers' dilemmas in financial markets with sampling investors," *Theoretical Economics*, 15(2), 545–582.

Bikhchandani, S., D. Hirshleifer, and I. Welch (1992). "A theory of fads, fashion, custom, and cultural change as informational cascades," *Journal of Political Economy*, 110, 992–1026.

Bilancini, E., and L. Boncinelli (2018). "Signaling to analogical reasoners who can costly acquire information," *Games and Economic Behavior*, 110, 50–57.

Binmore, K. (1987). "Modeling rational players: Part 1," *Economics and Philosophy*, 3(2), 179–214.

Bohren, A. (2016). "Informational herding with model misspecification," *Journal of Economic Theory*, 163, 222–247.

Bohren, A., and D. Hauser (2018). "Social learning with model misspecification: A framework and a characterization." PIER Working Paper, 18-017.

Bordalo, P., N. Gennaioli, and A. Shleifer (2012). "Salience theory of choice under risk," *Quarterly Journal of Economics*, 127(3), 1243–1285.

Brown, G. W. (1951). "Iterative solutions of games by fictitious play." In T. C. Koopmans (ed.), *Activity Analysis of Production and Allocation*. New York: Wiley.

Brunnermeier, M. K., and J. A. Parker (2005). "Optimal expectations," *American Economic Review*, 95(4), 1092–1118.

Camerer, C., and T. H. Ho (1999). "Experience-weighted attraction learning in normal form games," *Econometrica*, 67(4), 827–874.

Camerer, C. F., T. H. Ho, and J. K. Chong (2004). "A cognitive hierarchy model of games," *Quarterly Journal of Economics*, 119(3), 861–898.

Chen, H.-C., J. Friedman, and J.-F. Thisse (1997). "Boundedly rational Nash equilibrium: A probabilistic choice approach," *Games and Economic Behavior*, 18, 32–54.

Compte, O., and A. Postlewaite (2018). "Ignorance and uncertainty," Econometric Society Monograph.

Conlinsk, J. (1996). "Why bounded rationality?" *Journal of Economic Literature*, 34(2), 669–700.

Crawford, V., and J. Sobel (1982). "Strategic information transmission," *Econometrica*, 50, 1431–1451.

Crawford, V. P., and N. Iriberri (2007). "Level-*k* auctions: Can a nonequilibrium model of strategic thinking explain the winner's curse and overbidding in private-value auctions?" *Econometrica*, 75(6), 1721–1770.

Dal Bó, E., P. Dal Bó, and E. Eyster (2018). "The demand for bad policy when voters underappreciate equilibrium effects," *Review of Economic Studies*, 85(2), 964–998.

Danz, D., S. Huck, and P. Jehiel (2016). "Public statistics and private experience: Varying feedback information in a take-or-pass game," *German Economic Review*, 17(3), 359–377 (special issue in honor of Reinhard Selten).

Dekel, E., J. C. Ely, and O. Yilankaya (2007). "Evolution of preferences," *Review of Economic Studies*, 74(3), 685–704.

Dekel, E., D. Fudenberg, and D. K. Levine (1999). "Payoff information and self-confirming equilibrium," *Journal of Economic Theory*, 89, 165–185.

Dekel, E., D. Fudenberg, and D. K. Levine (2004). "Learning to play Bayesian games," *Games and Economic Behavior*, 46, 282–303.

Eliaz, K., and Spiegler, R. (2020). "A model of competing narratives," *American Economic Review*, 110(12), 3786–3816.

Eliaz, K., R. Spiegler, and H. C. Thysen (2020). "Strategic interpretations." Mimeo.

Ellis, A., and M. Piccione (2017). "Correlation misperception in choice," *American Economic Review*, 107(4), 1264–1292.

Embrey, M., G. R. Fréchette, and S. Yuksel (2018). "Cooperation in the finitely repeated prisoner's dilemma," *Quarterly Journal of Economics*, 133(1), 509–551.

Esponda, I. (2008). "Behavioral equilibrium in economies with adverse selection," *American Economic Review*, 98, 1269–1291.

Esponda, I., and D. Pouzo (2016). "Berk–Nash equilibrium: A framework for modeling agents with misspecified models," *Econometrica*, 84(3), 1093–1130.

Esponda, I., and E. Vespa (2018). "Endogenous sample selection: A laboratory study," *Quantitative Economics*, 9(1), 183–216.

Ettinger, D., and P. Jehiel (2005). "Towards a theory of deception." PSE Working Paper.

Ettinger, D., and P. Jehiel (2010). "A theory of deception," *American Economic Journal: Microeconomics*, 2(1), 1–20.

Ettinger, D., and P. Jehiel (2021). "An experiment on deception, reputation, and trust," *Experimental Economics*, 24, 821–853.

Eyster, E., and M. Piccione (2013). "An approach to asset pricing under incomplete and diverse perceptions," *Econometrica*, 81(4), 1483–1506.

Eyster, E., and M. Rabin (2005). "Cursed equilibrium," *Econometrica*, 73(5), 1623–1672.

Eyster, E., and M. Rabin (2010). "Naïve herding in rich-information settings," *American Economic Journal: Microeconomics*, 2(4), 221–243.

Friedman, E. (2022). "Stochastic equilibria: Noise in actions or beliefs?," *American Economic Journal: Microeconomics*, 14(1), 94–142.

Friedman, J., and C. Mezzetti (2005). "Random belief equilibrium in normal form games," *Games and Economic Behavior*, 51(2), 296–323.

Fryer, R., and M. Jackson (2008). "A categorical model of cognition and biased decision-making," *Contributions in Theoretical Economics*, 8(1), 0000102202193517041357.

Fudenberg, D., and Y. Kamada (2018). "Rationalizable partition-confirmed equilibrium with heterogeneous beliefs," *Games and Economic Behavior*, 109, 364–381.

Fudenberg, D., and D. M. Kreps (1995). "Learning in extensive games I: Self-confirming and Nash equilibrium," *Games and Economic Behavior*, 8, 20–55.

Fudenberg, D., G. Lanzani, and P. Strack (2020). "Limits points of endogenous misspecified learning." Mimeo.

Fudenberg, D., and D. K. Levine (1989). "Reputation and equilibrium selection in games with a patient player," *Econometrica*, 57(4), 759–778.

Fudenberg, D., and D. K. Levine (1993). "Self-confirming equilibrium," *Econometrica*, 61, 523–545.

Fudenberg, D., and D. K. Levine (1998). *Learning in Games*. Cambridge, MA: MIT Press.

Fudenberg, D., and A. Peysakhovich (2016). "Recency, records, and recaps: Learning and nonequilibrium behavior in a simple decision problem," *ACM Transactions on Economics and Computation*, 4(4), 1–18.

Gabaix, X. (2014). "A sparsity-based model of bounded rationality," *Quarterly Journal of Economics*, 129(4), 1661–1710.

Gagnon-Bartsch, T., M. Rabin, and J. Schwartzstein (2020). "Channeled attention and stable errors." Mimeo.

Garcia-Pola, B., J. Kovarik, and I. Nagore (2020). "Non-equilibrium play in centipede games," *Games and Economic Behavior*, 120, 391–433.

Gärdenfors, P. (2000). *Conceptual Spaces: The Geometry of Thought*. Cambridge, MA: MIT Press.

Gigerenzer, G. (2001). "The adaptive toolbox." In G. Gigerenzer and R. Selten (eds.), *Bounded Rationality: The Adaptive Toolbox*. Cambridge, MA: MIT Press, pp. 37–50.

Gilboa, I., and D. Schmeidler (1995). "Case-based decision theory," *Quarterly Journal of Economics*, 110, 605–639.

Goeree, J., and P. Louis (2021). "M equilibrium: A theory of beliefs and choices in games," *American Economic Review*, 111(12), 4002–4045.

Gonçalves, D. (2022). "Sequential Sampling Equilibrium." Mimeo.

Grimm, V., and F. Mengel (2012). "An experiment on learning in a multiple games environment," *Journal of Economic Theory*, 147(6), 2220–2259.

Guarino, A., and P. Jehiel (2013). "Social learning with coarse inference," *American Economic Journal: Microeconomics*, 5(1), 147–174.

Hagenbach, J., and F. Koessler (2017). "The Streisand effect: Signaling and partial sophistication," *Journal of Economic Behavior and Organization*, 143, 1–8.

Hagenbach, J., and F. Koessler (2020). "Cheap talk with coarse understanding," *Games and Economic Behavior*, 124, 105–121.

Haile, P. A., A. Hortaçsu, and G. Kosenok (2008). "On the empirical content of quantal response equilibrium," *American Economic Review*, 98, 180–200.

Harrison, J. M., and D. M. Kreps (1978). "Speculative investor behavior in a stock market with heterogeneous expectations," *Quarterly Journal of Economics*, 92(2), 323–336.

Harsanyi, J. C. (1967–1968). "Games with incomplete information played by Bayesian players. Parts I, II, III," *Management Science*, 14 (3, 5, 7).

Hart, S. (2005). "Adaptive heuristics," *Econometrica*, 73(5), 1401–1430.

Hart, S., and A. Mas-Colell (2003). "Uncoupled dynamics do not lead to Nash equilibrium," *American Economic Review*, 93(5), 1830–1836.

Heckman, J. (1979). "Sample selection bias as a specification error," *Econometrica*, 47(1), 153–161.

Heidhues, P., B. Köszegi, and P. Strack (2018). "Unrealistic expectations and misguided learning," *Econometrica*, 86(4), 1159–1214.

Heifetz, A., and D. Samet (1988). "Knowledge spaces and arbitrarily high rank," *Games and Economic Behavior*, 22, 260–273.

Heller, Y., and E. Winter (2020). "Biased-belief equilibrium," *American Economic Journal: Microeconomics*, 12(2), 1–40.

Holland, J. (1975). *Adaptation in Natural and Artificial Systems: An Introductory Analysis with Applications to Biology, Control, and Artificial Intelligence*. Cambridge, MA: MIT Press.

Huck, S., P. Jehiel, and T. Rutter (2011). "Learning spillover and analogy-based expectations: A multi-game experiment," *Games and Economic Behavior*, 71(2), 351–365.

Jackson, M., and E. Kalai (1997). "Social learning in recurring games," *Games and Economic Behavior*, 21(1–2), 102–134.

Jaynes, E. T. (1957). "Information theory and statistical mechanics," *Physical Review, Series II*, 106(4), 620–630.

Jehiel, P. (1995). "Limited horizon forecast in repeated alternate games," *Journal of Economic Theory*, 67, 497–519.

Jehiel, P. (1998). "Learning to play limited forecast equilibria," *Games and Economic Behavior*, 22, 274–298.

Jehiel, P. (1999). "Predicting by analogy and limited foresight in games." CiteSeer.

Jehiel, P. (2001). "Limited foresight may force cooperation," *Review of Economic Studies*, 68, 369–391.

Jehiel, P. (2005). "Analogy-based expectation equilibrium," *Journal of Economic Theory*, 123, 81–104.

Jehiel, P. (2011). "Manipulative auction design," *Theoretical Economics*, 6(2), 185–217.

Jehiel, P. (2015). "On transparency in organizations," *Review of Economic Studies*, 82(2), 736–761.

Jehiel, P. (2018). "Investment strategy and selection bias: An equilibrium perspective on overoptimism," *American Economic Review*, 108(6), 1582–1597.

Jehiel, P. (2019). "Robust mechanism design: An analogy-based expectation equilibrium perspective." In J. F. Laslier, H. Moulin, M. Sanver, and W. Zwicker (eds.), *The Future of Economic Design*. Cham: Springer, pp. 321–325.

Jehiel, P. (2021). "Communication with forgetful liars," *Theoretical Economics*, 16(2), 605–638.

Jehiel, P., and F. Koessler (2008). "Revisiting Bayesian games with analogy-based expectations," *Games and Economic Behavior*, 62, 533–557.

Jehiel, P., and L. Lamy (2015). "On absolute auctions and secret reserve prices," *Rand Journal of Economics*, 46(2), 241–270.

Jehiel, P., M. Meyer-ter-Vehn, B. Moldovanu, and W. R. Zame (2006). "The limits of ex-post implementation," *Econometrica*, 74, 585–610.

Jehiel, P., and K. Mierendorff (2024). "Auction design with data-driven misspecifications: Inefficiency in private value auctions with correlation," *Theoretical Economics*, 19, 1543–1579.

Jehiel, P., and E. Mohlin (2024). "Categorization in games: A bias-variance perspective." Mimeo.

Jehiel, P., and D. Samet (2005). "Learning to play games in extensive form by valuation," *Journal of Economic Theory*, 124, 129–148.

Jehiel, P., and D. Samet (2007). "Valuation equilibrium," *Theoretical Economics*, 2, 163–185.

Jehiel, P., and L. Samuelson (2012). "Reputation with analogical reasoning," *Quarterly Journal of Economics*, 127, 1927–1969.

Jehiel, P., and L. Samuelson (2023). "The analogical foundations of cooperation," *Journal of Economic Theory*, 208, 105609.

Jehiel, P., and J. Singh (2021). "Multi-state choices with aggregate feedback on unfamiliar alternatives," *Games and Economic Behavior*, 130, 1–24.

Jehiel, P., and G. Weber (2024). "Endogenous clustering and analogy-based expectation equilibrium." Mimeo.

Kalai, E. (2004). "Large robust games," *Econometrica*, 72(6), 1631–1665.

Kalai, E., and E. Lehrer (1993). "Rational learning leads to Nash equilibrium," *Econometrica*, 61(5), 1019–1045.

Ke, S. (2019). "Boundedly rational backward induction," *Theoretical Economics*, 14(1), 103–134.

Klibanoff, P., M. Marinacci, and S. Mukerji (2005). "A smooth model of decision making under ambiguity," *Econometrica*, 73(6), 1849–1892.

Koehler, J. J., and M. Mercer (2009). "Selection neglect in mutual fund advertisements," *Management Science*, 55(7), 1107–1121.

Kőszegi, B., and A. Szeidl (2013). "A model of focusing in economic choice," *Quarterly Journal of Economics*, 128(1), 53–104.

Kreps, D., and R. Wilson (1982). "Sequential equilibria," *Econometrica*, 50, 863–894.

Krockow, E. M., B. D. Pulford, and A. M. Colman (2018). "Far but finite horizons promote cooperation in the Centipede game," *Journal of Economic Psychology*, 67, 191–199.

Kurz, M. (1994). "On rational belief equilibria," *Economic Theory*, 4, 859–876.

Lasry, J-M., and P-L. Lions (2006). "Jeux à champ moyen. II. Horizon fini et contrôle optimal" [Mean field games. II. Finite horizon and optimal control]. *Comptes Rendus Mathematique*, 343(10), 679–684.

Lee, I. H. (1993). "On the convergence of informational cascades," *Journal of Economic Theory*, 61, 395–411.

Lehrer, E. (2012). "Partially specified probabilities: Decisions and games," *American Economic Journal: Microeconomics*, 4(1), 70–100.

Lettau, M., and H. Uhlig (1999). "Rules of thumb versus dynamic programming," *American Economic Review*, 89(1), 148–174.

Levy, G., and R. Razin (2019). "Echo chambers and their effects on economic and political outcomes," *Annual Review of Economics*, 11, 303–328.

Liang, A. (2020). "Games of incomplete information played by statisticians." Mimeo.

Li Calzi, M. (1995). "Fictitious play by cases," *Games and Economic Behavior*, 11, 64–89.

Lipman, B. L. (1991). "How to decide how to decide how to ...: Modeling limited rationality," *Econometrica*, 59(4), 1105–1125.

Madarasz, K. (2012). "Information projection: Model and applications," *Review of Economic Studies*, 79(3), 961–985.

Mailath, G., and L. Samuelson (2020). "Learning under diverse world views: Model based inference," *American Economic Review*, 110(5), 1464–1501.

Marimon, R., E. McGrattan, and T. J. Sargent (1990). "Money as a medium of exchange in an economy with artificially intelligent agents," *Journal of Economic Dynamics and Control*, 14(2), 329–373.

McAfee, R. P. (1993). "Mechanism design by competing sellers," *Econometrica*, 61(6), 1281–1312.

McFadden, D. (1973). "Conditional logit analysis of qualitative choice behavior." In P. Zarembka (ed.), *Frontiers in Econometrics*. New York: Academic Press, pp. 105–142.

McKelvey, R., and T. Palfrey (1995). "Quantal response equilibrium for normal form games," *Games and Economic Behavior*, 10, 6–38.

Mengel, F. (2012). "Learning across games," *Games and Economic Behavior*, 74(2), 601–619.

Mengel, F. (2014). "Learning by (limited) forward looking players," *Journal of Economic Behavior and Organization*, 108, 59–77.

Mertens, J.-F., and S. Zamir (1985). "Formulation of Bayesian analysis for games with incomplete information," *International Journal of Game Theory*, 14, 1–29.

Miettinen, T. (2009). "The partially cursed and the analogy-based expectation equilibrium," *Economics Letters*, 105(2), 162–164.

Milgrom, P., and N. Stockey (1982). "Information, trade and common knowledge," *Journal of Economic Theory*, 26, 17–27.

Miyasawa, K. (1961). "On the convergence of the learning process in a 2 × 2 non-zero-sum game," Economic Research Program, Princeton University, Research Memo 33.

Mohlin, E. (2014). "Optimal categorization," *Journal of Economic Theory*, 152, 356–381.

Moinas, S., and S. Pouget (2013). "The bubble game: An experimental study of speculation," *Econometrica*, 81, 1507–1539.

Mongin, P., and B. Walliser (1988). "Infinite regressions in the optimizing theory of decision." In B. R. Munier (ed.), *Risk, Decision and Rationality*. Dordrecht: Reidel, pp. 435–457.

Mullainathan, S., J. Schwartzstein, and A. Shleifer (2008). "Coarse thinking and persuasion," *Quarterly Journal of Economics*, 123, 577–619.

Myerson, R. B. (1981). "Optimal auction design," *Mathematics of Operations Research*, 6(1), 58–73.

Nagel, R. (1995). "Unraveling in guessing games: An experimental study," *American Economic Review*, 85, 1313–1326.

Neyman, A. (1985). "Bounded complexity justifies cooperation in the finitely repeated prisoners' dilemma," *Economics Letters*, 19(3), 227–229.

Olea, J. L., P. Ortoleva, M. M. Pai, and A. Prat (2019). "Competing models." Mimeo.

Osborne, M., and A. Rubinstein (1998). "Games with procedurally rational players," *American Economic Review*, 88, 834–847.

Osborne, M. J., and A. Rubinstein (2003). "Sampling equilibrium, with an application to strategic voting," *Games and Economic Behavior*, 45(2), 434–441.

Pearl, J. (2009). *Causality: Models, Reasoning and Inference*. Cambridge: Cambridge University Press.

Piccione, M., and A. Rubinstein (1997). "On the interpretation of decision problems with imperfect recall," *Games and Economic Behavior*, 20, 3–24.

Piccione, M., and A. Rubinstein (2003). "Modeling the economic interaction of agents with diverse abilities to recognize equilibrium patterns," *Journal of the European Economic Association*, 1, 212–233.

Radner, R. (1980). "Collusive behavior in non-cooperative epsilon equilibria of oligopolies with long but finite lives," *Journal of Economic Theory*, 22, 121–157.

Rampal, J. (2017). *Limited Foresight Equilibrium*. Technical Report.

Rosenthal, R. (1982). "Games of perfect information, predatory pricing and the chain-store paradox," *Journal of Economic Theory*, 25, 83–96.

Rosenthal, R. (1993). "Rules of thumb in games," *Journal of Economic Behavior and Organization*, 22, 1–13.

Ross, L. (1977). "The intuitive psychologist and his shortcomings." In L. Berkowitz (ed.), *Advances in Experimental Social Psychology*, vol. 10. New York: Academic Press, pp. 173–220.

Rubinstein, A. (1986). "Finite automata play the repeated prisoner's dilemma," *Journal of Economic Theory*, 39(1), 83–96.

Rubinstein, A. (1988). "Similarity and decision-making under risk (is there a utility theory resolution to the Allais paradox?)," *Journal of Economic Theory*, 46, 145–153.

Rubinstein, A. (1989). "The electronic mail game: Strategic behavior under 'almost common knowledge'," *American Economic Review*, 79, 385–391.

Rubinstein, A. (1998). *Modeling Bounded Rationality*. Cambridge, MA: MIT Press.

Rubinstein, A., and A. Wolinsky (1994). "Rationalizable conjectural equilibrium: Between Nash and rationalizability," *Games and Economic Behavior*, 6, 299–311.
Salant, Y., and J. Cherry (2020). "Statistical inference in games," *Econometrica*, 88(4), 1725–1752.
Samuel, A. L. (1959). "Some studies in machine learning using the game of checkers," *IBM Journal of Research and Development*, 3, 210–229.
Samuelson, L. (2001). "Analogies, adaptation, and anomalies," *Journal of Economic Theory*, 97, 320–366.
Sargent, T. J. (1993). *Bounded Rationality in Macroeconomics*. Oxford: Clarendon Press.
Savage, L. J. (1954). *The Foundation of Statistics*. New York: Wiley.
Schank, R. (1982). *Dynamic Memory: A Theory of Learning in Computers and People*. New York: Cambridge University Press.
Scheinkman, J. A., and W. Xiong (2003). "Overconfidence and speculative bubbles," *Journal of Political Economy*, 111(6), 1183–1219.
Schumacher, H., and H. Thysen (2018). "Equilibrium contracts and boundedly rational expectations." Mimeo.
Schwartzstein, J. (2014). "Selective attention and learning," *Journal of European Economic Association*, 12(6), 1423–1452.
Sebenius, J. K., and J. Geanakoplos (1983). "Don't bet on it: Contingent agreements with asymmetric information," *Journal of the American Statistical Association*, 78, 424–426.
Selten, R. (1975). "A reexamination of the perfectness concept for equilibrium points in extensive games," *International Journal of Game Theory*, 4(1), 25–55.
Selten, R., and R. Stoecker (1986). "End behavior in sequences of finite prisoner's dilemma supergames," *Journal of Economic Behavior and Organization*, 7, 47–70.
Simon, H. A. (1956). "Rational choice and the structure of the environment," *Psychological Review*, 63(2), 129–138.
Sims, C. (2003). "Implications of rational inattention," *Journal of Monetary Economics*, 50(3), 665–690.
Smith, L., and P. Sørensen (2000). "Pathological outcomes of observational learning," *Econometrica*, 68, 371–398.
Smith, V. L., G. L. Suchanek, and A. W. Williams (1988). "Bubbles, crashes, and endogenous expectations in experimental spot asset markets," *Econometrica*, 56(5), 1119–1151.
Sobel, J. (1985). "A theory of credibility," *Review of Economic Studies*, 52, 557–573.
Spiegler, R. (2006a). "Competition over agents with boundedly rational expectations," *Theoretical Economics*, 1(2), 207–231.
Spiegler, R. (2006b). "The market for quacks," *Review of Economic Studies*, 73(4), 1113–1131.
Spiegler, R. (2016). "Bayesian networks and boundedly rational expectations," *Quarterly Journal of Economics*, 131, 1243–1290.
Spiegler, R. (2017). "Data monkeys: A procedural model of extrapolation from partial statistics," *Review of Economic Studies*, 84, 1818–1841.
Spiegler, R. (2019). "Behavioral economics and the atheoretical style," *American Economic Journal: Microeconomics*, 11, 173–194.
Spiegler, R. (2020). "Behavioral implications of causal misperceptions," *Annual Review of Economics*, 12, 81–106.

Stahl, D., and P. Wilson (1995). "On player's modals of other players: Theory and experimental evidence," *Games and Economic Behavior*, 10, 218–254.

Steiner, J., and C. Stewart (2008). "Contagion through learning," *Theoretical Economics*, 3(4), 431–445.

Tirole, J. (1982). "On the possibility of speculation under rational expectations," *Econometrica*, 50(5), 1163–1182.

Watkins, C., and P. Dayan (1992). "Q-learning," *Machine Learning*, 8, 279–292.

Weibull, J. W. (1997). *Evolutionary Game Theory*. Cambridge, MA: MIT Press.

Young, H. P. (2004). "Strategic learning and its limits." Arne Ryde Memorial Lectures.

CHAPTER 14

Cooperation in Large Societies

Alexander Wolitzky

I survey models of cooperation in large populations. Topics include repeated games with public monitoring, random-matching games, games on networks, infinite-population games, and models of legal or coercive enforcement. I emphasize how the scope of cooperation depends on the structure of social interactions, the information available to agents, and the feasibility of different types of rewards and punishments.

14.1 INTRODUCTION

Economists and other social scientists have long recognized that trust, cooperation, and reciprocity are critical determinants of societal outcomes. But what determines society's prospects for supporting cooperative behavior? Following seminal contributions by scholars such as Olson (1965), Williamson (1985), North (1990), Ostrom (1990), and Greif (1993), this question has been studied from a variety of perspectives, including (and often combining) game theory, historical and anthropological research, empirical economic analysis, and lab and field experiments. This chapter surveys the game theory literature in this area, focusing on repeated games and related models of long-run interaction.

I begin in Section 14.2 by discussing three empirical cases where societal cooperation is supported by long-run incentives: the provision of schools and wells in rural Western Kenya (Miguel and Gugerty, 2005), informal lending and borrowing in Peruvian shantytowns (Karlan et al., 2009), and large-scale decentralized exchange on eBay (Resnick and Zeckhauser, 2002; Tadelis, 2016). These cases illustrate some real-world situations that repeated-game models can shed light on – although the models I will focus on are not specifically tailored to these settings. They also highlight the wide range of conceptual issues that our models seek to understand, such as the structure of social interactions, the role of information, and the potential sanctions that are available to the community.

The bulk of this chapter surveys the repeated-game literature on cooperation in large societies. Traditional repeated-game models are typically motivated

For helpful comments, I thank Daron Acemoglu, Anne Carlstein, Dan Clark, Drew Fudenberg, Bob Gibbons, Matt Jackson, George Mailath, Eric Maskin, Stephen Morris, Eitan Sapiro-Gheiler, and Takuo Sugaya.

by situations with a small number of relatively sophisticated players and "centralized" interactions and information, such as collusion in Cournot oligopoly (Green and Porter, 1984) or relational contracting (Bull, 1987; Levin, 2003; MacLeod and Malcomson, 1989). As we will see, the usual assumptions and results in this literature must be substantially modified to account for settings with a large number of diverse participants and "decentralized" interactions and information, like those discussed in Section 14.2. Nonetheless, it is useful to start by briefly reviewing the standard repeated-game model, as well as some recent results for the large-population case – where, for example, players may have long time horizons or high discount factors, but the discount factor may not be high "in comparison to the population size." As I show in Section 14.3, results in this case are quite different from standard folk theorems.

Section 14.4 covers the simplest and most canonical model of "decentralized" repeated games: games with uniform random matching. I offer a somewhat revisionist account of these games. Classic results in this area suggest that communities can sometimes rely on the threat of collective sanctions to sustain cooperation despite very limited monitoring. In contrast, I will argue that in a slightly richer and more realistic model that allows for a small amount of incomplete information, community enforcement instead requires personalized sanctions that rely on extensive information and communication.

Interactions in large groups are typically not only decentralized, but also non-random. Models with interaction structures other than uniform random matching are surveyed in Section 14.5, under the heading of "repeated games on networks." Some of these models literally assume a fixed network structure of interactions or information flows, while others allow more flexible forms of non-random matching (the latter case is, however, relatively understudied). Here it is interesting to consider how standard results from fixed-partner repeated games or random-matching games change when network structure is introduced. In addition, one can also ask new, network-specific questions, such as how network position determines which players take more cooperative actions.

In settings like E-commerce or modern credit and insurance markets, the population size is effectively infinite. There are essentially two ways to support cooperation in infinite populations: individual pairs or finite subsets of players can interact repeatedly (as in, e.g., long-term employment relationships), or players can have access to some centralized source of information about their current partner (as in, e.g., online ratings systems). I consider such models in Section 14.6. A theme here is that the scope for cooperation often depends on the type of information that players have access to – for example, information about one's partner's past actions only, as opposed to richer information about the context of these actions, or about the partner's "social standing."

Finally, Section 14.7 discusses a few models that go beyond the standard repeated-game framework by introducing some kind of "institution" that can help support cooperation, either by providing some new type of information or by introducing new sanctioning instruments. These models aim to interpolate between repeated-game models of informal enforcement and more traditional economic models, which implicitly assume that agreements are enforced by a powerful legal system. While it is still in its infancy, this approach may someday yield a more unified view of enforcement across different institutional settings.

The questions of how large societies support cooperation – and how researchers can productively model this behavior – are inherently interdisciplinary. This survey focuses on work by economists, but there are also related strands of research in other fields. The most active of these is probably the literature on "indirect reciprocity" in evolutionary biology (Alexander, 1987; Nowak and Sigmund, 1998; see Sigmund, 2010 for a survey). The models considered in this literature are essentially repeated games; however, this literature tends to focus on comparing the performance of a few pre-specified strategies (*Always Cooperate*, *Always Defect*, *Tit-for-Tat*, etc.) and the resulting evolutionary dynamics, rather than analyzing the set of equilibria when players can choose any strategy. Evolutionary dynamics in this type of model have also been studied by physicists (Szabó and Fath, 2007). Models of large-group cooperation also play a role in sociology (Coleman, 1990; Granovetter, 1985), political science (Axelrod, 1984; Fearon and Laitin, 1996; Keohane, 1984), anthropology (Boyd and Richerson, 1992; Henrich, 2004), law (Ellickson, 1994), and computer science (Friedman and Resnick, 2001).

14.2 CASE STUDIES

I begin by reviewing some real-world examples of informal (repeated game) enforcement of public goods provision and bilateral exchange in large groups. These cases serve to (i) illustrate some applications we can bear in mind when considering the subsequent models, (ii) show how repeated-game-type modeling can help guide empirical work in this area, and (iii) raise several theoretical issues that have not yet received much formal attention.

14.2.1 Public Goods in Rural Kenya

Why do some groups provide high levels of public goods, while others do not? An important empirical finding is that ethnically diverse groups generally provide fewer public goods (Alesina et al., 1999; Easterly and Levine, 1997). This association is intriguing – Banerjee et al. (2005) call it "one of the most powerful hypotheses in political economy" – but the underlying mechanism is controversial. Early explanations focused on commonalities of preferences or altruism among co-ethnics (Alesina and La Ferrara, 2000; Luttmer, 2001; Vigdor, 2004). However, some subsequent evidence favors an alternative interpretation based on repeated-game effects: it may be easier to apply sanctions for failing to contribute to public goods within ethnic groups rather than across groups, which leads to higher equilibrium contributions within groups.

Miguel and Gugerty (2005) argue for the importance of this social sanctioning mechanism in the context of public goods provision in rural Western Kenya. They find that ethnic diversity predicts not only lower primary school funding, worse school facilities, and worse maintenance of water wells, but also fewer social sanctions and less verbal pressure directed at non-contributors, as recorded in the minutes of school committee meetings. For example, school committees in more ethnically diverse areas were less likely to exhort parents who were behind on their school fees to pay promptly, or to recommend that the village chief visit these parents to encourage payment. The authors' explanation for these findings is that "social sanctions and coordination are possible within groups due to the dense networks of information and mutual reciprocity that exist in groups but are not possible across groups."[1] However, their formal model simply assumes that sanctions are possible within groups but not across groups, rather than deriving this property as an implication of differences in network structure, information, or the existence of cooperative equilibria in a larger dynamic game. As we will see, explicitly modeling these features not only provides a foundation for the authors' assumption, but also leads to new, more detailed predictions, for example about how an individual's contributions may vary with her position in the social network.

Further evidence that causality runs from ethnic diversity to (lack of) social sanctions, and thence to (lack of) public goods, comes from lab experiments run in Kampala, Uganda by Habyarimana et al. (2007). These authors find that subjects in a dictator game are equally generous toward co-ethnics and other participants when the recipient cannot observe the offerer's identity, but are substantially more generous toward co-ethnics when the offerer's identity is observable. The interpretation of the difference between the two treatments is that the non-anonymous treatment proxies for real-world situations where future punishment is possible (following Hoffman et al., 1996), so the results indicate that greater generosity toward co-ethnics is due to fear of punishment. Consistent with this interpretation, the authors obtain similar results in a prisoner's dilemma experiment where the possibility of punishment by a third party is explicitly introduced. In contrast, little support is found for mechanisms based on common preferences or altruism within groups.[2]

1 Besley et al. (1993) previously emphasized the importance of social sanctions in supporting collective action in their study of rotating savings and credit associations (Roscas).

2 Additional experimental evidence consistent with Habyarimana et al.'s results comes from Glaeser et al. (2000), who find that Harvard undergraduates with more mutual friends exhibit more trusting and trustworthy behavior; and from Leider et al. (2009) and Ligon and Schechter (2012), who use anonymous and non-anonymous variants of dictator games to distinguish between altruistic and repeated-game motives for giving in different contexts.

14.2.2 Lending and Borrowing in Peru

Repeated game effects also play a role in informal contract enforcement, as in the large literature on risk sharing without commitment (e.g., Coate and Ravallion, 1993; Fafchamps and Lund, 2003; Foster and Rosenzweig, 2001; Ligon et al., 2002; Udry, 1994). An example of such an analysis, which combines theory and empirics, is Karlan et al.'s (2009) study of "socially collateralized" lending and borrowing.[3] I will review Karlan et al.'s model in Section 14.5, but the key implication is that the maximum amount that individual i can credibly promise to repay to individual j – and hence the maximum amount that j is willing to lend to i – equals the "maximum flow" from i to j in a weighted social network, where the weight on the link between two individuals is the (exogenously given) value of maintaining their bilateral relationship beyond the current interaction. The interpretation is that players along a path from i to j can "vouch" that i will repay j, and that these relationships are lost if i fails to repay. The model is thus a reduced-form repeated game, where it is assumed that any deviation in a relationship causes the relationship to be permanently destroyed. This model makes strong predictions about the scope of lending and borrowing between any two agents. For example, since a path from i to j affects the maximum flow between these agents only through the weakest link in the path (i.e., the least valuable bilateral relationship), the model implies that the predictive value of adding a new path between i and j for lending and borrowing between them likewise depends only on its weakest link.

The authors test the model using survey data they collected from two shantytown communities with several hundred residents in Lima, Peru. Respondents were asked to name up to ten individuals with whom they spend the most time in an average week, as well as the set of friends from whom they borrowed money in the previous twelve months. The authors use the amount of time a pair of individuals spent together to proxy for the value of their relationship, and study how the resulting weighted social network predicts lending and borrowing. They find evidence in favor of some subtle predictions of the theory, such as a prediction that direct and indirect links matter roughly equally for borrowing, and a prediction that the importance of a path in the social network is largely determined by its weakest link. This is a nice example of how detailed, repeated-game-type modeling can inform empirical work on cooperation in large groups.

14.2.3 Reputation Systems in Online Platform Markets

Informal enforcement is not confined to local communities like Kenyan villages or Peruvian shantytowns. In large online marketplaces like eBay or

[3] Other papers emphasizing the role of repeated-game effects in supporting informal credit arrangements in developing economies include Karlan (2007), Feigenberg et al. (2013), Giné and Karlan (2014), and De Quidt et al. (2016).

Airbnb, buyers and sellers can be separated by thousands of miles and often interact only once. These markets also feature a wide scope for opportunistic behavior, as when an eBay seller delivers a substandard product, or an Airbnb guest trashes an apartment. Such opportunism cannot be effectively constrained by the legal system, which involves itself in these transactions only in the most egregious cases of misbehavior. Instead, online marketplaces use centralized ratings systems to facilitate informal contractual enforcement: if individual i cheats individual j, j can give i a bad rating, which is observed by i's future potential partners and may discourage them from trading with i. A large literature (surveyed by Cabral, 2013 and Tadelis, 2016) documents the practical effectiveness of these ratings systems. Note that, as in the other case studies discussed in this section, the enforcement of cooperative behavior here is "multilateral," in that punishments are ultimately delivered by third parties. Just as a villager who fails to repay a loan may lose valuable relationships with individuals other than the lender, so an eBay seller who receives a bad rating may lose business from many potential buyers.

To successfully facilitate trade, online ratings systems must contend with several challenges, which interact with standard repeated-game considerations in interesting ways. For instance, an individual is usually free to quit a platform and then rejoin under a different name. This availability of "cheap pseudonyms" implies that an established agent's continuation payoff can never fall below that of a new entrant. Friedman and Resnick (2001) show that, if there is a positive chance of random "mistakes" in the players' interactions, this constraint imposes an upper bound on payoffs in the prisoner's dilemma with random matching, which applies for any discount factor. Payoffs close to this bound can be attained with simple "dues-paying" strategies, where new entrants trade with established agents on unfavorable terms (e.g., new entrants always cooperate in the prisoner's dilemma, while established agents who match with new entrants sometimes defect), which discourages entrants from cheating and then re-entering under a pseudonym.

Another important challenge for ratings systems is eliciting honest feedback. When a given pair of agents interact only once, why do they rate each other accurately, or even bother leaving a rating at all? A particular difficulty is that, if agents on both sides of the market rate each other, an agent who has been cheated may hesitate to give her partner a bad rating, for fear that the partner will retaliate by rating her badly in return. Bolton et al. (2013) find strong evidence of retaliatory behavior by sellers in eBay transactions in 2006 and 2007: ratings were highly correlated between the two parties to a transaction, and sellers disproportionately rated buyers shortly after buyers rated them, especially in instances where both parties left negative feedback. In 2008, eBay switched to a one-sided reputation system where only sellers are rated, likely in response to concerns about retaliatory rating (Tadelis, 2016).

14.3 REPEATED GAMES WITH MANY PLAYERS

Repeated-game models are economists' main tool for understanding long-run cooperative relationships of the kind discussed in the previous section. Repeated games have been well studied for many decades, and in principle can allow any number of players, N. However, some important assumptions and results that seem natural when N is small become unrealistic when N is large. For example:

1. Much research on repeated games concerns the limit case where players are very patient: that is, where the discount factor δ converges to 1. If we want to model cooperation among a large number of patient players, it is more natural to vary N and δ simultaneously, so that $\delta \to 1$ but $(1-\delta)N$ may or may not converge to 0.
2. Classical repeated games often assume that players condition their behavior only on publicly available information. But information in large societies is typically decentralized. For example, each player may accurately observe her current trading partner's behavior, while knowing little about other agents' behavior.
3. Classical repeated games usually assume that all players are rational and play equilibrium strategies. But in large societies the possibility that at least a few players may be irrational cannot be ignored.

While I will eventually consider models that relax all of these assumptions, it is useful to start by quickly reviewing the classical repeated-game model and some standard results, with a focus on the large-N case. This is done in Sections 14.3.1–14.3.3.[4] Section 14.3.4 then considers the implications of varying N and δ simultaneously in the classical model, which leads to quite different results. Subsequent sections introduce decentralized information (i.e., private monitoring) and irrational player types.

14.3.1 The Standard Repeated-Game Model

This section introduces the standard repeated-game model and the accompanying notation. Readers familiar with repeated games may wish to skim or skip it.

A (finite) *stage game* $G = (I, A, u)$ consists of a finite set of players $I = \{1, \dots, N\}$, together with a finite set of actions A_i and a payoff function $u_i : A \to \mathbb{R}$ for each player $i \in I$. Here, $A = \times_{i \in I} A_i$, and $u : A \to \mathbb{R}^N$ is given by $u(a) = (u_i(a))_{i=1}^N$ for each $a \in A$.[5] Payoff functions extend linearly to mixed actions:

[4] See Mailath and Samuelson (2006) for a thorough textbook treatment of this material.

[5] In general, given a collection of sets $(X_i)_{i=1}^N$ with generic elements $x_i \in X_i$, their product is denoted $X = \times_{i \in I} X_i$ with generic element $x \in X$. I also write $X_{-i} = \times_{j \in I \setminus \{i\}} X_j$ with generic element $x_{-i} \in X_{-i}$.

given a mixed-action profile $\alpha \in \times_{i\in I}\Delta A_i$, we have $u(\alpha) = \sum_{a\in A} \Pr(a|\alpha)\, u(a)$. The *feasible payoff set* is

$$V = \text{conv}\left\{v \in \mathbb{R}^N : v = u(a) \text{ for some } a \in A\right\},$$

where conv denotes convex hull. Player i's (mixed-action) *minmax payoff* is

$$\underline{v}_i = \min_{\alpha_{-i}\in\times_{j\in I\setminus\{i\}}\Delta A_j} \max_{a_i\in A_i} u_i(a_i, \alpha_{-i}).$$

A payoff vector v is *individually rational* if $v_i \geq \underline{v}_i$ for all i. Thus, the set of feasible and individually rational payoff vectors is

$$V^* = \left\{v \in V : v_i \geq \underline{v}_i \text{ for all } i \in I\right\}.$$

For example, in the *prisoner's dilemma* (PD) stage game, given by

	C	D
C	$1,1$	$-\ell, 1+g$
D	$1+g, -\ell$	$0,0$

with $g, \ell > 0$ and $g < 1 + \ell$, each player's minmax payoff is 0, so $V^* = \text{conv}\left\{(0,0), \left(0, \frac{1+g+\ell}{1+\ell}\right), \left(\frac{1+g+\ell}{1+\ell}, 0\right), (1,1)\right\}$. I will return to this stage game repeatedly.

In a (discounted) repeated game, the stage game is played repeatedly in periods $t = 1, 2, \ldots$, players get some information before taking actions in each period, and players maximize discounted expected payoffs. Formally, a *repeated game* $\Gamma = (G, \delta, Y, p)$ consists of a stage game G, a discount factor $\delta \in (0,1)$ (assumed, for simplicity, to be common among the players), and a *monitoring structure* (Y, p), which summarizes the players' information. Here, $Y = \times_{i=1}^N Y_i$, where Y_i is the set of possible *signal realizations* for player i, and at the end of each period t a signal $y_t \in Y$ is drawn according to the probability distribution $p(\cdot|a_t) \in \Delta Y$, where $a_t \in A$ is the period-t action profile. Note that this notation implicitly assumes that the monitoring structure remains the same in every period, and that the distribution of signals depends only on current-period actions. Special monitoring structures include *perfect monitoring*, where $Y_i = A$ for all $i \in I$ and $p(y|a) = \mathbf{1}\{y_i = a \forall i \in I\}$ (where $\mathbf{1}\{\cdot\}$ is the indicator function), and *public monitoring*, where $Y_i = Y_j$ for all $i, j \in I$ and $p(y|a) > 0$ implies $y_i = y_j$ for all $i, j \in I$. The general, non-public case is called *private monitoring*.[6]

A *history* $h_i^t \in H_i^t$ for player i at the beginning of period t takes the form $h_i^t = (a_i^t, y_i^t)$, where $a_i^t = (a_{i,0}, \ldots, a_{i,t-1})$ and $y_i^t = (y_{i,0}, \ldots, y_{i,t-1})$, with $a_i^0 = y_i^0 = \emptyset$. Letting $H_i = \bigcup_{t=1}^{\infty} H_i^t$, a (behavior) *strategy* $\sigma_i \in \Sigma_i$ for player i is a mapping $\sigma_i : H_i \to \Delta A_i$. That is, players can condition their play on their own past actions

[6] It is sometimes assumed that in every period the players can also observe the outcome of a *public randomizing device*: for example, a uniform $[0,1]$ random variable, independent of actions and signals. None of the results surveyed here require this assumption, although allowing public randomization simplifies some proofs.

and observations. Player i's discounted expected payoff under strategy profile i (measured in per-period terms) is $U_i(\sigma) = (1-\delta)\sum_{t=1}^{\infty} \delta^{t-1}\mathbb{E}^{\sigma}[u_i(a_t)]$, where $\mathbb{E}^{\sigma}[\cdot]$ denotes expectation under the probability distribution over histories induced by strategy profile σ.[7] As usual, a *Nash equilibrium* is a strategy profile σ where $U_i(\sigma) \geq U_i(\sigma_i', \sigma_{-i})$ for all $i \in I, \sigma_i' \in \Sigma_i$. A *subgame perfect equilibrium* of a repeated game with perfect monitoring is a strategy profile where the prescribed continuation play at any history forms a Nash equilibrium. Further refinements of Nash equilibrium, such as perfect public equilibrium and sequential equilibrium, are defined below as needed.

14.3.2 The Folk Theorem with Perfect Monitoring

Perhaps the best-known result on repeated games is the "folk theorem," which says that if players are patient, monitoring is perfect, and V^* has non-empty interior (as a subset of $\mathbb{R}^N$), then every payoff vector in intV^* is attainable in subgame perfect equilibrium. This is a classical formalization of the idea that the "shadow of the future" can incentivize cooperation when it weighs heavily and when behavior is well observed.[8] The folk theorem is an important benchmark result that we will return to repeatedly under different sets of assumptions. Of course, it may be possible to support some cooperative behavior in equilibrium, even if the full conclusion of the folk theorem fails, and we will also see some settings where this occurs.

Theorem 14.1 (Perfect Monitoring Folk Theorem) *Assume that* int$V^* \neq \emptyset$. *For any $v \in$ intV^*, there exists $\bar{\delta} < 1$ such that, for every $\delta > \bar{\delta}$, there is a subgame perfect equilibrium of the repeated game with discount factor δ that gives payoff vector v.*

Proving the perfect monitoring folk theorem at this level of generality is not trivial, but a simple case that suffices for our purposes arises when $v = u(a)$ for some pure action profile $a \in A$ and v strictly Pareto-dominates a static Nash equilibrium payoff vector, v^{NE}. In this case (which was addressed by Friedman, 1971), the theorem is proved by considering "Nash-reversion" strategies that prescribe action profile a so long as a has always been taken so far, and that otherwise prescribe a static equilibrium that gives payoff vector v^{NE}. If we denote player i's maximum static deviation gain at action profile a by $d_i = \max_{a_i' \in A_i} u_i(a_i', a_{-i}) - v$, it is easy to see that these strategies form a subgame perfect equilibrium whenever

$$d_i \leq \frac{\delta}{1-\delta}\left(v_i - v_i^{NE}\right) \qquad \text{for all } i \in I.$$

[7] Formally, this can be defined recursively starting from $t = 1$.

[8] Early versions of the perfect monitoring folk theorem were developed by several authors, including Friedman (1971), Aumann and Shapley (1976), and Rubinstein (1979). The version reproduced here is due to Fudenberg and Maskin (1986); see also Abreu et al. (1994) and proposition 3.8.1 of Mailath and Samuelson (2006).

Observe that, so long as the deviation gain is bounded from above and the desired payoff vector v is bounded away from v^{NE}, the discount factor δ does not need to be excessively close to 1 for Nash reversion strategies to form an equilibrium. Moreover, the required discount factor is independent of N. There is thus no obvious reason why it is more difficult to support cooperation in larger groups under perfect monitoring.[9] However, the perfect monitoring assumption – which is already a strong assumption when N is small – seems even more extreme when N is large. For example, it is hard to imagine that all actions are observed by everyone in the community in any of the settings discussed in Section 14.2. For this reason, most models of cooperation in large groups assume some form of imperfect monitoring.

14.3.3 The Folk Theorem with Imperfect Public Monitoring

The simplest form of imperfect monitoring is *public monitoring*, where all players observe the same signal. Fudenberg et al. (1994) show that the folk theorem extends to imperfect public monitoring, if the monitoring structure satisfies appropriate statistical conditions.[10] To give one of their sufficient conditions, let Y_0 denote the set of possible public signal realizations, and for any mixed action profile $\alpha \in \times_{i \in I} \Delta A_i$ and any pair of players i and j, define the $|A_i| \times |Y_0|$ matrix $R_i(\alpha_{-i})$ with elements $[R_i(\alpha_{-i})]_{a_i,y} = p(y|a_i, \alpha_{-i})$, and define the $(|A_i| + |A_j|) \times |Y_0|$ matrix $R_{ij}(\alpha)$ given by stacking the matrices $R_i(\alpha_{-i})$ and $R_j(\alpha_{-j})$. Say that action profile α has *pairwise full rank for players i and j* if $\text{rank} R_{ij}(\alpha) = |A_i| + |A_j| - 1$.[11] Intuitively, this condition says that any deviation from α by player i or player j is statistically identifiable, and that moreover deviations by player i and player j are statistically distinguishable from each other. Fudenberg et al. show that, to establish the folk theorem for payoffs that Pareto-dominate a static Nash equilibrium, it suffices to assume that all Pareto-efficient pure action profiles have pairwise full rank for all pairs of players.[12] Their result concerns *perfect public equilibria*, which are profiles

[9] This statement of course assumes that the players play an equilibrium, and furthermore coordinate on the desired equilibrium. One might wonder if the problem of coordinating on a desired equilibrium – what Bowles and Gintis (2013) call the "missing choreographer" problem – is more difficult in larger groups. The literature on large-population coordination games following Kandori et al. (1993) and Young (1993) bears on this type of question in static games. I am not aware of such work in repeated games.

[10] Related ideas appear in Matsushima (1989), Fudenberg and Levine (1994), and Kandori and Matsushima (1998). Mertens and Parthasarathy (1987) and Abreu et al. (1990) develop important results on the structure of the equilibrium payoff set in repeated games with imperfect public monitoring.

[11] Note that $|A_i| + |A_j| - 1$ is the maximum possible rank of the matrix $R_{ij}(\alpha)$, because $\alpha_i R_i(\alpha_{-i}) = [p(y|\alpha)]_y = \alpha_j R_j(\alpha_{-j})$.

[12] They also show that a minmax-threat folk theorem holds if, in addition, every pure action profile a has *individual full rank*, which means that the matrix $R_i(a_{-i})$ has full row rank for every player i.

of strategies that depend only on the history of public signals y^t, and that form a Nash equilibrium conditional on any such history.

Theorem 14.2 (Imperfect Public Monitoring Folk Theorem) *Assume that* int$V \neq \emptyset$ *and that all Pareto-efficient pure action profiles have pairwise full rank for all pairs of players. For any* $v \in$ int$V$ *that Pareto-dominates a static Nash equilibrium, there exists* $\bar{\delta} < 1$ *such that, for every* $\delta > \bar{\delta}$, *there is a perfect public equilibrium of the repeated game with discount factor* δ *that gives payoff vector* v.

This important result influenced research on problems such as collusion among oligopolists (Athey and Bagwell, 2001) and relational contracts in organizations (Levin, 2003). Two issues should be borne in mind regarding its implications for cooperation in larger groups. The first is that, as I have already noted, monitoring in large groups is often far from public, as is the case when interactions are decentralized and players observe only their current partners' behavior. I discuss models of this type in Sections 14.4–14.6.

The second issue is that, even under public monitoring, Theorem 14.2 does not address how the value of the discount factor δ and the "precision" of the monitoring structure (Y, p) that are required to provide incentives vary with the population size N. In particular, note that Theorem 14.2 makes no reference to the signals' statistical informativeness. Intuitively, even if $p(y|a) \approx 1/|Y_0|$ for all y – so that signals are almost completely uninformative – strong incentives can still be provided on the basis of these signals when δ is sufficiently large, because large changes in continuation payoffs can offset noisy signals. Of course, the less informative are the signals, the higher δ must be.[13] For example, if the number of possible signal realizations $|Y_0|$ is held fixed as N grows, the informativeness of the signals for distinguishing between deviations by different players necessarily decreases: while pairwise full rank may hold for any N, as N grows large the full row rank submatrices of the matrix $R_{ij}(\alpha)$ must become close to singular for some pairs of players (i, j). A corresponding increase in δ is then required to preserve incentives.

This discussion indicates that the scope for cooperation in large-population repeated games with imperfect public monitoring depends on a three-way interaction among N, δ, and "monitoring precision." This interaction is the subject of the next subsection (where some results will also apply under private monitoring).

14.3.4 Anti-Folk Theorems with Many Players

A series of papers by Green (1980), Sabourian (1990), Levine and Pesendorfer (1995), Fudenberg et al. (1998), Al-Najjar and Smorodinsky (2000, 2001), and Pai et al. (2016) provide conditions under which, as the population size

[13] Kandori (1992a) formalizes this point.

$N \to \infty$ for a fixed discount factor δ, players behave approximately myopically in every repeated game equilibrium. These negative results concerning the prospects for cooperation ("anti-folk theorems") establish continuity at the infinite population limit, where players act myopically.

The key feature of these models is that, in a large population, most players' individual actions have only a small effect on the signal distribution, and hence on other players' behavior. This condition is directly assumed in Green and Sabourian's models. Subsequent models (e.g., Fudenberg et al., 1998; Al-Najjar and Smorodinsky, 2000, 2001) instead derive this feature from an assumption that signals are generated through *individual noise*: each player's action a_i stochastically determines an *individual outcome* x_i (independently across players), and the distribution of the signal profile y depends on the action profile a only through the profile of individual-level outcomes $x = (x_i)_{i=1}^N$. For example, when there are two individual outcomes for each player, and each individual outcome occurs with probability at least $\varepsilon > 0$ due to noise, Al-Najjar and Smorodinsky (2000) show that the average probability that a player is pivotal for the realization of a binary signal $y \in \{0,1\}$ is maximized when each player "votes" yea and nay with probability ε each (and abstains with probability $1-2\varepsilon$), and the signal takes value 1 iff the yea votes exceed the nays. This scheme yields a pivot probability of order $1/\sqrt{\varepsilon(1-\varepsilon)N}$, the reciprocal of the standard deviation of the number of yea votes. Since the impact on a player's continuation payoff in the event that her action is pivotal is of order at most $1/(1-\delta)$, it follows that non-trivial incentives cannot be provided if $N \to \infty$ while δ and the number of possible signal realizations $|Y|$ are held fixed, or more generally if $(1-\delta)\sqrt{N} \to \infty$ while $|Y|$ is fixed.[14]

Sugaya and Wolitzky (2024) study the three-way interaction among N, δ, and $|Y|$ in more detail, under the same ε-individual noise assumption as in Fudenberg et al. and Al-Najjar and Smorodinsky. Let $K = \log_2 |Y|$, so the signal can be viewed as a K-dimensional binary random variable. Their main result implies that if $(1-\delta)N/K \to \infty$ along any sequence of games where N, δ, and K vary simultaneously (subject to a uniform upper bound on stage-game payoffs $|u_i|$ and a uniform lower bound on individual noise ε), then only vanishingly weak incentives can be provided in any Nash equilibrium. To state this result formally, for any player i and any distribution over action profiles $\alpha \in \Delta A$, denote player i's maximum expected deviation gain at action distribution α by

$$d_i(\alpha) = \max_{\tilde{a}_i : A_i \to A_i} \sum_r \alpha(r)\left(u_i(\tilde{a}_i(r_i), r_{-i}) - u_i(r)\right).$$

In addition, for any number $\eta > 0$, say that a payoff vector $v \in \mathbb{R}^N$ is *consistent with η-myopic play* if there exists an action distribution $\alpha \in \Delta A$ such that $u(\alpha) = v$ and $\sum_i d_i(\alpha)/N \leq \eta$: that is, if the per-player average deviation gain at α is less than η.

[14] Fudenberg et al. (1998) derive a similar result.

Theorem 14.3 (Limits of Individual Incentives) *Fix any upper bound on stage-game payoffs and any lower bound on individual noise. For any $\eta > 0$, there exists $k > 0$ such that, for any repeated game satisfying these bounds as well as the condition that $(1-\delta)N/K > k$, any Nash equilibrium payoff vector in this repeated game is consistent with η-myopic play.*

Under the stronger hypothesis that $(1-\delta)\sqrt{N/K} \to \infty$, the theorem's conclusion follows from probability results which imply that the average "influence" of N independent binary random variables on a K-dimensional binary random variable is of order at most $\sqrt{K/N}$, and that therefore the maximum per-player incentive that can be provided on the basis of such a random variable is of order at most $\sqrt{K/N}/(1-\delta)$. The hypothesis can be weakened to $(1-\delta)N/K \to \infty$ by combining this type of probability result with recursive methods developed in Sugaya and Wolitzky (2023a).

Theorem 14.3 can be further generalized to apply for any monitoring structure where the *mutual information* between signals and actions is bounded by K, which is a weaker condition on the monitoring structure than the requirement that $\log_2 |Y| = K$. Conversely, a folk theorem holds for some sequence of monitoring structures satisfying $(1-\delta)N\log(N)/K \to 0$: for example, it suffices to perfectly monitor the actions of K randomly selected players in every period.[15] These results imply that the scope for cooperation in many-player repeated games is determined by the ratio of the discount rate $(1-\delta)$ and the number of "bits of information per player," K/N (up to the $\log(N)$ gap between the necessary and sufficient conditions for cooperation). Thus, a high degree of patience and/or a large amount of information are required to incentivize cooperation in large groups.

How restrictive is the condition that discounting is low relative to per-player information? The answer depends on the type of game under consideration. The condition is restrictive in situations where a large population of players are monitored by a fixed "aggregate signal" that does not scale with the population size. For example, this case arises when the signal is the market price facing Cournot competitors, the level of pollution in a common water source, or the output of team production. On the other hand, the condition is much less restrictive in situations where players are monitored "separately," in a manner that scales with the population size. For example, this situation arises in the random-matching games studied in Section 14.4, where each player observes her partner's action, as well as in games where a centralized rating system records a signal of each player's action, as in the models studied in Section 14.6. In sum, in public-monitoring models such as those of Fudenberg et al. (1998), Al-Najjar and Smorodinsky (2000, 2001), and Sugaya and Wolitzky (2023a), the obstacle to supporting cooperation is that societal information is

[15] The basic logic is that if a player is monitored with probability K/N, she can then be provided with an incentive of "size" $K/(N(1-\delta))$. The extra $\log(N)$ term provides some slack that is used in the equilibrium construction.

insufficiently precise; meanwhile in the community enforcement models covered in Sections 14.4 and 14.6, the obstacle is instead that societal information is *disaggregated*.

While the condition in Theorem 14.3 may already be restrictive, matters are far worse if we restrict attention to *strongly symmetric equilibria*, where all players have the same continuation payoff at every history, so that rewards and punishments are provided only "collectively."[16] Collective incentives have the well-known shortcoming that they encourage free-riding in large populations. In the repeated-game context, the following result (also due to Sugaya and Wolitzky, 2024) formalizes this intuition by showing that incentives can be provided in strongly symmetric equilibria only if $\delta \to 1$ almost as fast as $\exp N \to \infty$, which is an extremely restrictive condition.

Theorem 14.4 (Limits of Collective Incentives) *Fix any upper bound on stage-game payoffs and any lower bound on individual noise. For any $\eta > 0$ and $\rho > 0$, there exists $k > 0$ such that, for any repeated game satisfying these bounds as well as the condition that $(1-\delta)\exp\left(N^{1-\rho}\right) > k$, any strongly symmetric equilibrium payoff vector in this repeated game is consistent with η-myopic play.*

To understand this result, suppose we wish to enforce a symmetric pure action profile a at which the maximum static deviation gain equals η. Once we restrict ourselves to strongly symmetric equilibria, it is without further loss to restrict attention to "tail tests," where continuation values take one (low) value whenever the number n of players who take action a falls below a cutoff n^*, and another (high) value whenever $n \geq n^*$. Under ε individual noise, the number n follows a binomial distribution with mean $(1-\varepsilon)N$ and standard deviation $\sqrt{\varepsilon(1-\varepsilon)N}$. Thus, the probability that each player is pivotal for passing the tail test is maximized by setting $n^* \approx (1-\varepsilon)N$, which yields a pivot probability of order $1/\sqrt{\varepsilon(1-\varepsilon)N}$, as in Fudenberg et al. (1998) or Al-Najjar and Smorodinsky (2000, 2001). Now, to enforce action profile a, the static deviation gain η must be less than the product of the pivot probability (a term of order $1/\sqrt{N}$) and the maximum difference between any two continuation payoffs (a term of order $1/(1-\delta)$). Hence, if η is to remain bounded away from 0 as $N \to \infty$ and $\delta \to 1$, the product $(1-\delta)\sqrt{N}$ cannot explode.

The more restrictive condition of Theorem 14.4 – that $(1-\delta)\exp\left(N^{1-\rho}\right)$ cannot explode for any $\rho > 0$ – follows because if $n^* \approx (1-\varepsilon)N$, then the tail test is failed with probability bounded away from 0 in every period, which leads to the destruction of all continuation value when $\delta \to 1$. To prevent this value destruction while still providing incentives, the *statistical score* of the tail test – that is, the ratio $\Pr(n = n^*)/\Pr(n \leq n^*)$ – must increase linearly with

[16] Strongly symmetric equilibria are defined only in symmetric games. However, the same results hold for a class of "linear equilibria" in general games, where all players' continuation payoffs are required to lie on a line.

the variance of n, and hence with N.[17] Since the distribution of n is approximately normal when N is large, and the density of the normal distribution decreases exponentially with the score,[18] it follows that $\Pr(n = n^*)$ – the pivot probability – must decrease exponentially with N. Theorem 14.4 now follows because the product of the pivot probability and $1/(1-\delta)$ cannot explode if η is to remain bounded away from 0.[19]

To summarize, in large-population repeated games with imperfect monitoring, collective incentives cannot be provided unless δ is extremely high, and even individual incentives can be provided only if δ is high and/or signals are informative. While this is a rather negative result for settings where a large population of players is monitored by a fixed aggregate signal, sufficiently informative monitoring structures arise naturally in "decentralized" settings such as random-matching games or games on networks. These settings are the subject of the following two sections.

14.4 REPEATED GAMES WITH RANDOM MATCHING

First introduced by Rosenthal (1979), repeated games with random matching are a canonical model of cooperation in decentralized groups. There are several versions of the model, which can all be formally nested as special cases of the general repeated-game model presented in Section 14.3.1. In this section, I consider games with *uniform random matching*, meaning that in each period the population of N players (here assumed to be even) breaks into pairs to play a two-player stage game $\tilde{G} = (\tilde{A}, \tilde{u})$, where each player's partner is selected uniformly at random from among the other $N-1$ players.

Matching is *anonymous* if players choose actions without observing their current partner's identity, so that A (the action set in each period of the N-player repeated game) is the same as $\tilde{A}$ (the action set in the two-player stage game). Matching is *non-anonymous* if players observe their current partner's identity before choosing actions, in which case $A = \tilde{A}^{(N-1)}$, the set of mappings from the partner's identity to the stage-game action. Either way, I assume that each player perfectly observes her current partner's action at the end of each period, but learns nothing about the actions taken in other matches.[20] The model thus abstracts from monitoring imperfections within each match but completely rules out public signals, in stark contrast to the public monitoring structures considered in Section 14.3.

[17] Sannikov and Skrzypacz's (2007) result that collusion in Cournot duopoly is impossible with frequent actions and Brownian noise depends on a similar observation; see also Fudenberg and Levine (2007, 2009).

[18] Because $\phi(z)/\Phi(z)$ is of order $|z|$, where ϕ and Φ are the standard normal pdf and cdf.

[19] Conversely, tail tests can support a Nash-threat folk theorem if there exists $\rho > 0$ such that $(1-\delta)\exp(N^{1+\rho}) \to 0$.

[20] Monitoring structures of this type, where each action is observed either perfectly or not at all, are sometimes called *semi-standard monitoring* (Lehrer, 1990), *partial monitoring* (Ben-Porath and Kahneman, 1996), or *network monitoring* (Wolitzky, 2013).

14.4.1 Anonymous Matching

Because players receive so little information under anonymous random matching, a natural first question is whether non-myopic play can be supported at all. Early results by Kandori (1992b), Ellison (1994), and Harrington (1995) show that cooperation can be supported in the PD by relying on a form of collective punishment called *contagion strategies*. Contagion strategies are simply grim trigger strategies adapted to anonymous random-matching games: each player starts by playing C (cooperate), but switches to D (defect) whenever she observes a single play of D. Note that each player i is incentivized to play C on path (i.e., when she has observed only C so far) because playing D causes her current partner j to switch to D in the next period, which subsequently causes j's future partners to switch to D, and so on until the contagion of playing D spreads throughout the population, eventually reducing i's payoff. We obtain the following result of Kandori's.

Theorem 14.5 (Anonymous Cooperation in Nash Equilibrium) *In the repeated PD with anonymous random matching, there exists $\bar{\delta} < 1$ such that, for every $\delta > \bar{\delta}$, there is a Nash equilibrium where all players take C in every period along the equilibrium path.*

This result depends on an implicit order of limits between N and δ. For any N, contagion spreads throughout the population in finite time with high probability, so deviating from C to D is unprofitable whenever δ is sufficiently high (and hence contagion strategies form a Nash equilibrium, since C is prescribed at every on-path history). However, the amount of time that it takes for contagion to spread goes to infinity as $N \to \infty$, so for any $\delta < 1$, deviating from C to D is profitable when N is sufficiently high. Nevertheless, the joint condition on N and δ required for contagion strategies to form a Nash equilibrium is actually quite permissive. Since the diffusion of contagion is well approximated by a logistic curve, the number of "infected" players increases exponentially until a substantial fraction of the population is infected, so it can be shown that contagion strategies form a Nash equilibrium whenever $(1-\delta)\log N \to 0$.[21]

Another apparent limitation of Theorem 14.5 is that it applies only to Nash equilibrium. A more natural solution concept in this model is sequential equilibrium (Kreps and Wilson, 1982), which requires sequential rationality with respect to beliefs that arise as the limit of conditional probabilities derived from completely mixed strategies. The simplest version of contagion strategies – where switching from C to D is permanent – may be inconsistent with sequential equilibrium, because a patient player who observes D in period 1 (say) may benefit from playing C for several periods to slow the spread of

[21] That contagion spreads approximately logistically in an N-player random-matching model can be shown by arguments akin to those in Frieze and Grimmett (1985), who consider a similar process whereby a "rumor" spreads through a finite population in discrete time.

contagion.[22] However, Ellison (1994) shows that contagion strategies can be modified to form a sequential equilibrium.[23] The key observation is that, under contagion strategies, switching to D is more attractive when a greater number of other players have already switched to D. Hence, if the severity of the punishment incurred by starting contagion is reduced to the point where a player is indifferent to starting contagion on path (i.e., when only C has been observed), then spreading contagion is always optimal off path (i.e., once D has been observed). Ellison describes two ways of reducing the severity of contagion: occasionally restarting cooperation according to a public randomizing device, and conditioning play on calendar time in such a way that a given occurrence of contagion only periodically affects play (a technique now known as "threading"). While the realism of such strategies is debatable, they suffice to establish the following important result.

Theorem 14.6 (Anonymous Cooperation in Sequential Equilibrium) *In the repeated PD with anonymous random matching, there exists $\bar{\delta} < 1$ such that, for every $\delta > \bar{\delta}$, there is a sequential equilibrium where all players take C in every period along the equilibrium path.*

While suitably modified contagion strategies can be used to support cooperation as a sequential equilibrium in the repeated PD, it is not straightforward to extend these strategies to support non-myopic behavior in other games (or to support outcomes in the PD other than mutual cooperation, such as profiles where some players cooperate while others defect). For example, consider the *product choice game*, where player 1 produces a high or low-quality product, player 2 buys or does not buy, and payoffs are given by

	B	$\neg B$
H	$1,1$	$-\ell,0$
L	$1+g,-c$	$0,0$

with $g,\ell,c > 0$. This is an asymmetric game, so let us suppose that there are separate, equal-sized populations of player 1s and player 2s, where every period each player 1 meets a random player 2. Suppose we try to support the outcome (H,B) with the threat of contagion to the Pareto-inferior Nash equilibrium $(L,\neg B)$: that is, each player 1 takes H so long as (H,B) is observed, and otherwise switches to L; and each player 2 takes B so long as (H,B) is observed, and otherwise switches to $\neg B$. These strategies form a Nash equilibrium whenever δ is sufficiently high, but modifying them to form a sequential

22 If such a player believes that not only her period-1 partner but also all of the other $N-2$ players in the population deviated to D in period 1, then playing D from period 2 on as prescribed by contagion strategies is sequentially rational. Since seeing one's partner take D in period 1 is off path, this belief is consistent with Bayes' rule, and hence with (weak) perfect Bayesian equilibrium. However, it is not consistent with the belief that the opponents "tremble" independently, and hence is not consistent with sequential equilibrium.

23 Kandori (1992b) showed that standard contagion strategies already form a sequential equilibrium for some parameters.

equilibrium is challenging. To see the problem, suppose that some player 2 sees his partner deviate to L in period 1. By Kreps–Wilson consistency, this player 2 must believe no one other than his period 1 partner deviated in period 1, and that therefore (in a large population) his period 2 partner is very likely to play H. But then player 2 should play B rather than $\neg B$ in period 2, since this yields a higher expected stage-game payoff, as well as slowing contagion. In general, the problem is that since the "punishment" profile $(L, \neg B)$ is not in dominant strategies (in contrast to the punishment profile (D, D) in the PD), players who observe deviations do not want to switch to the punishment profile unless they believe that sufficiently many other players have already switched, and this belief may not be consistent under contagion strategies.

Deb and González-Díaz (2019) use a clever and intricate argument to extend contagion strategies to establish a partial folk theorem (in sequential equilibrium, for symmetric payoffs that Pareto-dominate a static Nash equilibrium) for a class of stage games that includes the product choice game. The key idea is to specify that deviations from the desired action profile (e.g., (H, B) in the product choice game) during a long "trust-building" phase at the beginning of the game do not spark contagion until after the end of the trust-building phase. Due to the existence of the trust-building phase, once players are supposed to switch to the punishment profile, they are free to believe that the earliest deviation actually occurred a long time ago, and that consequently many other players have already switched (or will switch at the same time). This belief then rationalizes the prescribed switch.[24]

The strategies considered by Kandori, Ellison, and Deb and González-Díaz all rely on collective punishment: if a single player deviates, the entire community is eventually punished. While such strategies seem natural in anonymous games, individualized incentives can also be provided even under anonymity. For example, suppose that some particular player – say player 1 – is prescribed to take D in each of T consecutive periods in the repeated PD, while the other $N-1$ players are prescribed to take C during this T-period block. This behavior is potentially enforceable, because if some player other than player 1 deviates to taking D during the block, then there will be two players taking D rather than one, which is statistically detectable by the other players. Asymmetric behavior of this type features in a construction by Deb et al. (2020), which establishes the full folk theorem for anonymous random-matching games. The construction is rather complicated, and it resembles equilibria used to establish the folk theorem for general private monitoring structures (in particular, the "block belief-free" strategies introduced by Matsushima, 2004 and Hörner and Olszewski, 2006) more than it does contagion strategies.[25] In the following statement of their theorem, V^* refers to a set of feasible and individually

[24] Deb (2020) proves a more general folk theorem when matched players can communicate by cheap talk.

[25] Sugaya (2022) extends block belief-free strategies to prove a general folk theorem for repeated games with private monitoring under standard full-support and statistical identifiability conditions. These conditions are robustly violated in random-matching games.

rational payoffs in the N-player stage game induced by anonymous random matching. For example, if the underlying two-player stage game is the PD, then the payoff vector that results when player 1 takes D while everyone else takes C is feasible (and also individually rational, if N is large), while the payoff vector that results when player 1 takes D while everyone else takes C iff they match with player 1 is infeasible, as it cannot be attained under anonymity.

Theorem 14.7 (Anonymous Folk Theorem) *Assume that* $\text{int}V^* \neq \emptyset$. *For any* $v \in \text{int}V^*$, *there exists* $\bar{\delta} < 1$ *such that, for every* $\delta > \bar{\delta}$, *there is a sequential equilibrium of the anonymous random-matching repeated game with discount factor* δ *that gives payoff vector* v.

The positive results reported in Theorems 14.5–14.7 may strike the reader as being "too good to be true." Even if we are willing to assume that players can coordinate on the most efficient sequential equilibrium, however complicated, is it really possible that large, decentralized groups can support cooperation when players are completely anonymous and have no information beyond their own personal experiences? If not, what explains the discrepancy between the model's prediction that cooperation is possible despite minimal information, and our intuition that this prediction is likely too optimistic?

One possible explanation is that the models considered in this subsection do not allow "noise": actions are implemented without error, and within-match monitoring is perfect. At first glance, contagion strategies seem extremely non-robust to noise, since a single error would spark contagion.[26] However, Ellison shows that the modified contagion strategies used to prove Theorem 14.6 are robust to introducing sufficiently small noise. To see the intuition, note that under the modified contagion strategies that make players indifferent to starting contagion on path, the expected number of periods before cooperation "restarts" following an episode of contagion converges to a finite number as $\delta \to 1$. Hence, contagion is rarely triggered when noise is small, and the payoff loss when it is triggered is finite. Consequently, in the iterated limit where first $\delta \to 1$ and then $\varepsilon \to 0$, Ellison's contagion strategies support mutual cooperation in almost every period of the repeated game.

While this result provides some reassurance that Theorems 14.5–14.7 are not entirely non-robust, it still faces some limitations (as Ellison himself observed). First, the result is sensitive to the order of limits between N and ε: it applies when $\varepsilon \to 0$ for fixed N, but not if we instead consider a sequence where $N\varepsilon$ (the expected number of "errors" in the population each period) remains fixed, much less when $N \to \infty$ for fixed ε. Second, it applies only when noise takes the form of implementation or monitoring errors that are independent across periods. A different type of "noise" that is likely realistic in large populations arises when a small fraction of players may be irrational,

[26] Fearon and Laitin (1996) take this observation as a starting point for considering when relations between ethnic groups lead to contagion-like "spirals," rather than being contained through "within-group policing."

and thus deviate from equilibrium play in a manner that is correlated across periods. As we will see, introducing a small amount of this kind of incomplete information is quite devastating for contagion strategies, as well as for any other strategies that might attempt to provide non-myopic incentives in anonymous repeated games.

14.4.2 Incomplete Information and Non-Anonymous Matching

Following a suggestion in Ellison (1994), Sugaya and Wolitzky (2020) investigate the effect of introducing a slight probability of irrationality in anonymous repeated games.[27] They derive an anti-folk theorem for a large class of symmetric, anonymous games, which specializes as follows to the repeated PD with anonymous random-matching and independent player types. (Note that the theorem's negative conclusion holds for all Nash equilibria, and thus does not depend on equilibrium refinements.)

Theorem 14.8 (Anonymous Anti-Folk Theorem with Irrational Types) *Consider the repeated PD with anonymous random matching where each player is committed to the strategy "play D in every period" with probability* ε*, independently across players. For any* $\eta > 0$*, there exists* $\bar{N}$ *such that, for any population size* $N > \bar{N}$ *and any discount factor* δ*, in every Nash equilibrium the population average payoff is less than* $u(D,D) + \eta$*.*

That is, if each player is committed to the strategy *Always D* with some fixed independent probability $\varepsilon > 0$ (which may be arbitrarily small), equilibrium population payoffs are always close to the mutual defection payoff $u(D,D)$ whenever N is sufficiently large (even if δ is arbitrarily high, so that for instance $(1-\delta)N$ can be arbitrarily small). The proof is rather simple. Note that, if a rational (non-committed) player deviates by playing *Always D* and the realized number of committed players is some number n, then the population distribution of actions will be the same as it would have been if this player had not deviated and the realized number of committed players had instead been $n+1$. When players' types are independent and N is large, the probability that there are n or $n+1$ committed players is similar, so a deviation by a single rational player to *Always D* has only a small impact on the population action distribution. Since a rational player must prefer following her equilibrium strategy to deviating to *Always D*, it follows that *Always D* cannot perform much better than the rational-player equilibrium strategy against the equilibrium population action distribution. But, since D is strictly dominant in the stage game, this implies that the rational-player equilibrium strategy must itself almost always take D. Finally, if committed players always take D and

[27] A stage game is *anonymous* if each player's payoff depends only on her own action and the number of other players taking each action (and not their identities). Anonymous random matching games are an important special case.

rational players almost always take D, population payoffs must be close to $u(D,D)$.[28]

Theorem 14.8 brings discouraging news about the prospects for cooperation under anonymity. However, anonymous matching may be viewed as a theoretical benchmark rather than a realistic model of large-group cooperation: in most real-world settings, it seems likely that players can usually recognize and remember their partners. It is thus natural to ask whether the presence of irrational types of the sort considered in Theorem 14.8 still obstructs cooperation under non-anonymous matching.[29]

This question is addressed by Sugaya and Wolitzky (2021). A first observation is that the stark negative conclusion of Theorem 14.8 does not fully extend to non-anonymous matching: if players are sufficiently patient, they can simply treat the N-player random-matching game as a collection of two-player games and play grim trigger in each of them, and these strategies support cooperation among rational players when ε is sufficiently small. More specifically, these "bilateral trigger strategies" form an equilibrium if $(1-\delta)N$ is small, which corresponds to situations where each *pair* of players meet frequently.[30] To understand whether multilateral, community-based enforcement of cooperation is effective, it therefore makes more sense to consider the case where δ is close to 1 but $(1-\delta)N$ is large, so that each player interacts with other players frequently but meets each particular partner only infrequently. Somewhat unexpectedly, the result here parallels the negative conclusion of Theorem 14.8.

Theorem 14.9 (Non-Anonymous Anti-Folk Theorem with Irrational Types) *Consider the repeated PD with non-anonymous random matching where each player is committed to the strategy "play D in every period" with probability ε, independently across players. For any $\eta > 0$, there exists $k > 0$ such that, if the population size N and the discount factor δ satisfy $(1-\delta)N > k$, then in every Nash equilibrium the population average payoff is less than $u(D,D)+\eta$.*

28 This argument is related to Mailath and Postlewaite's (1990) theorem on the impossibility of large-population public good provision. An intuition for their theorem is that a player will not reveal that she values a public good unless her reported value has either a large impact on the probability of provision or a small impact on her expected payment. Since the former is impossible when N is large, payments must be insensitive to values, and hence the public good cannot be provided unless every possible type is willing to pay a $1/N$ share of the cost.

29 Sugaya and Wolitzky (2023b) extend the analysis of the 2020 paper to stage games which are symmetric but not anonymous. The negative result of the 2020 paper extends for symmetric, non-anonymous games under a certain "population dominance" condition. However, this condition is violated in the repeated PD with non-anonymous random matching.

30 To see why $(1-\delta)N$ is an inverse measure of the meeting rate for each pair of players, fix the real-time discount rate r and suppose matching occurs every Δ unit of real time, so $\delta = e^{-r\Delta}$, which is close to $1-r\Delta$ when Δ is small. Then, on average, each pair of players interact $1/(\Delta(N-1)) \approx r/((1-\delta)N)$ times per unit of real time.

A rough intuition for this result can be given as follows. In light of Theorem 14.8, collective incentives – strategies where players do not condition their play on their opponent's identity – are ineffective in the presence of irrational types. So the only hope for supporting cooperation lies with individualized incentives – strategies that somehow monitor all N players' actions. In the repeated PD with non-anonymous matching, in every period, each player observes one bit of information concerning the profile of her opponents' actions: the current opponent's action, C or D. However, it can be shown that monitoring N players' actions with non-vanishing precision as $N \to \infty$ requires $O(N)$ bits of information,[31] and so it takes $O(N)$ periods of play to accumulate enough information to monitor everyone's actions. But if $(1-\delta)N$ is large, rewards or punishments delivered $O(N)$ periods in the future are insufficient to motivate cooperation, so defection prevails in every equilibrium.

As this intuition suggests, Theorem 14.9 continues to hold if players observe any additional K-dimensional signal each period – such as the most recent action of each of K randomly chosen players, or K signals about the average level of cooperation is the population – for any number K fixed independently of N.[32] While this is a stark negative result, there do exist realistic mechanisms by which players can obtain enough information to support cooperation. For instance, suppose that matched partners can communicate freely via cheap talk before taking actions, so that (for example) each player can tell her partner her opinion of the "standing" of each of the other $N-2$ players in the population. This form of "gossip" provides a number of bits of information that grows linearly with N, and indeed Sugaya and Wolitzky (2021) show that allowing such gossip supports a folk theorem under permissive conditions.[33] One reason why this is interesting is that gossip seems to help support cooperation in reality through a roughly similar mechanism as in the theory.[34]

Overall, Theorems 14.8 and 14.9 suggest that the view of large-group cooperation under minimal information expressed in Theorems 14.5–14.7 is probably too optimistic. In reality, cooperation in large societies likely requires substantially richer information than these minimalist, first-generation community enforcement models allowed. Fortunately, sufficient information can

31 This observation extends the pivot probability bounds of Fudenberg et al. (1998) and Al-Najjar and Smorodinsky (2000), which were discussed in Section 14.3.4.

32 A subtlety here is that signals that arrive at the end of period t are assumed to be independent of the period $t+1$ match realizations. For example, the signal where each player observes only her *next* partner's most recent action is excluded. That kind of signal can sometimes support cooperation even in infinite populations, and is thus considered in Section 14.6.

33 The required sufficient condition is $(1-\delta)\log N \to 0$. This condition is also almost necessary for non-myopic incentives to be provided in any model where information is exchanged through pairwise meetings, as if $(1-\delta)^{1+\rho}\log N \to \infty$ for any $\rho > 0$ then with high probability a player never meets anyone who met anyone who... met her within a payoff-relevant time frame.

34 Pertinent discussions of the role of gossip include Gluckman (1963), Noon and Delbridge (1993), Ellickson (1994), Baumeister et al. (2004), Dunbar (2004), Sommerfeld et al. (2007), and Feinberg et al. (2014).

sometimes be obtained in practice, depending on the communication opportunities and other "informational institutions" available to the group. I will return to this theme in Section 14.6, which focuses on the question of what kind of information players need to support cooperation in infinite populations.

14.5 REPEATED GAMES ON NETWORKS

I now turn to models with interaction structures that are richer than uniform random matching. This section focuses on "repeated games on networks," meaning that a network determines the payoff or information structure.[35] Some models in this literature assume that the network is fixed over time, while others allow it to be redrawn in every period of the repeated game – note that the latter assumption allows random pairwise matching as a special case. Important new issues here include how the network structure determines the scope for cooperation, and how an individual's network position determines her behavior.

14.5.1 Multilateral Punishment and Contagion in Networks

A key question in any model of community enforcement of cooperation is how social interactions facilitate multilateral punishment: that is, punishment by third parties. The canonical example of multilateral punishment in random-matching games is the contagion strategy, discussed in Section 14.4.1. For games played on a fixed network (which, depending on the specifics of the model, determines the payoff and/or monitoring structure of the game), multilateral punishment arises when a player's misbehavior toward one player in the network eventually leads to an adverse reaction by other players. In the typical case where a player's payoff is determined only by the actions of her network neighbors, this means that misbehavior toward one neighbor eventually causes a negative response by other neighbors.

While not explicitly concerned with networks per se, Bernheim and Whinston's (1990) early paper on "multimarket contact" is an important starting point for understanding multilateral punishment on networks. The paper asks whether it is easier for oligopolists to collude when they interact in many markets rather than just one, and models this by considering a population of players who play m PD stage games simultaneously (of course, the m games can be formally viewed as one big stage game). They first establish an "irrelevance theorem": if (i) the m stage games are identical, (ii) payoffs are additive across the stage games, and (iii) actions in all stage games are perfectly observed (so the repeated game has perfect monitoring), then the equilibrium condition for cooperation to be supportable in the repeated game is independent of the number of stage games, m. The intuition is simply that a player's most profitable deviation involves defecting in all m games simultaneously, while the harshest

[35] Repeated games on networks are also surveyed by Nava (2016).

punishment for any deviation is permanent mutual defection in all m games. So, both the deviation gain and the harshest punishment are proportional to m, and hence the equilibrium condition is independent of m.

By the same logic as in Bernheim and Whinston's irrelevance theorem, if N players on a network simultaneously play identical two-player PDs with each of their neighbors under perfect (network-wide) monitoring with additive payoffs, the condition for cooperation to be supportable in the overall repeated game is the same as the condition for cooperation to be supportable in a single two-player PD. Consequently, if network structure is to affect the possibility of cooperation, at least one of the conditions of the irrelevance theorem must be violated. As Bernheim and Whinston note, the irrelevance theorem breaks down if the stage games are not identical, monitoring is imperfect, or payoffs are not additive across the stage games. Many papers on repeated games on networks can be organized according to which of these violations they involve.

If the stage games are not identical, any slack in the equilibrium conditions in one game can be used to relax those in the other games. For example, suppose that two PDs are played every period, but the games differ in the value of the parameter g in the PD payoff matrix from Section 14.3.1. Suppose that the value of this parameter is g_1 in the first game and g_2 in the second, where

$$g_1 < \frac{\delta}{1-\delta}, \quad g_2 > \frac{\delta}{1-\delta}, \quad \text{and} \quad g_1 + g_2 < \frac{2\delta}{1-\delta}.$$

If these games are played separately, then cooperation is supportable in the first game but not the second, while if the games are played together, then cooperation can be supported in both of them by specifying that a deviation in either game leads to punishment in both. This and related points are developed further in the network context by Spagnolo (1999), Mihm et al. (2009), Lippert and Spagnolo (2011), and Mihm and Toth (2020).

Imperfect monitoring arises naturally in games on networks, for example in the much-studied case where players observe only their neighbors' actions (so the network determines the monitoring structure, perhaps in addition to the payoff structure). An important special case of imperfect monitoring arises when m stage games are played asynchronously, as in this case we can consider a player's "action" to be a mapping from the stage game to be played in the current period to her action in that game, so that the player's realized action is an imperfect signal of this mapping. Indeed, multilateral interaction clearly helps support cooperation with asynchronous stage games, because when the games are played one-by-one, the maximum deviation gain is independent of m, while the harshest punishment is still increasing in m, as a deviation in one game can eventually lead to punishments in other games. Note that the extent to which multilateral interaction facilitates cooperation depends on how quickly information about a deviation in one stage game spreads to the other stage games. This information spreads instantaneously under perfect monitoring, but more generally it spreads through the network according to a contagion-type process.

Understanding how the percolation of information through a network affects the scope for cooperation is the subject of papers by Wolitzky (2013) and Ali and Miller (2013). In the former paper, in every period each player i chooses a "cooperation level" $a_i \in \mathbb{R}_+$, and payoffs are given by

$$u_i(a) = \left(\sum_{j \neq i} f_{ij}(a_j) \right) - a_i,$$

where f_{ij} is an increasing, concave, and bounded function that measures the benefit that i receives from j's cooperation. The stage game is thus a continuous-action version of the PD. At the end of every period, each player observes some other players' actions perfectly, while observing nothing about the remaining players' actions, where the network of "who observes whom" is drawn i.i.d. across periods and is itself publicly observed.[36] For example, if players randomly match in pairs and observe only their partner's action, we recover the standard PD with anonymous random matching studied by Kandori and Ellison (albeit with continuous actions, and assuming that the realized matching process is observable). On the other hand, if each player observes the actions of the same set of opponents in every period, we have a repeated game with a fixed (directed) monitoring network.

Define player i's "average cooperation level" under a strategy profile σ by $(1-\delta)\sum_{t=1}^{\infty} \delta^{t-1}\mathbb{E}^{\sigma}[a_{i,t}]$. Note that, since the functions f_{ij} are concave, if there happens to exist a stationary strategy profile that maximizes each player's average cooperation level, Jensen's inequality implies that this profile must also maximize utilitarian social welfare, so long as each player i's average cooperation level is below the "first-best" level defined by $\sum_{j \neq i} f'_{ji}(a_i^{FB}) = 1$. The paper's main result is that such a strategy profile does exist, and it is given by contagion strategies. To state this result, fix a period T, and for any two players $i, j \in I$ and any number t, let π_{jit} denote the probability that, by the beginning of period $T+t$, player j has observed a player who has observed a player who... observed player i's period-T action.[37] For example, if the monitoring network is fixed across periods, then $\pi_{jit} = 1$ if the distance from j to i is at most t, and otherwise $\pi_{jit} = 0$.

36 In particular, player i does not observe her own payoff $u_i(a)$. This assumption is unproblematic in several cases. First, since $u_i(a)$ is additively separable in the opponents' actions, it can be interpreted as player i's expected payoff at action profile a, where player i's realized payoff depends only on actions that she observes (e.g., on the actions of her current-period partners). Second, the infinitely repeated game can be interpreted as a game of uncertain finite duration, where δ is the probability that the game continues for another period, and all payoffs are received at the end of the game.

37 This probability does not depend on T, by the assumption that the monitoring network is i.i.d. across periods.

Theorem 14.10 (Maximal Cooperation with Network Monitoring) *There exists a component-wise maximal action profile $a^* \in \mathbb{R}^N$ that satisfies*

$$a_i^* = (1-\delta)\sum_{t=1}^{\infty}\delta^t \sum_{j \neq i} \pi_{jit} f_{ij}\left(a_j^*\right) \quad \text{for all } i \in I. \tag{14.1}$$

In every Nash equilibrium, each player i's average cooperation level is at most a_i^*. Moreover, the following contagion strategy profile gives a perfect Bayesian equilibrium where each player i's average cooperation level equals a_i^*: in every period, each player i takes action a_i^* so long as she has never observed another player $j \neq i$ taking any action $a_j \neq a_j^*$; otherwise, she takes action 0.

Since the functions f_{ij} are increasing and actions can be bounded from above by individual rationality, the existence of a maximal vector a^* satisfying equation (14.1) follows from Tarski's fixed-point theorem. That the contagion strategies described in the theorem form a Nash equilibrium is true almost by construction: the left-hand side of equation (14.1) is player i's per-period cost of taking a_i^* in every period rather than deviating to the myopically dominant action 0, while the right-hand side is her expected, discounted lost benefits from others' foregone cooperation if she deviates. Moreover, equation (14.1) implies that each player i is indifferent between action a_i^* and action 0 at every on-path history, and hence she strictly prefers action 0 at every off-path history, by a similar argument as in Ellison (1994): consequently, the strategy profile is also sequentially rational.[38] Finally, Tarski's theorem also implies that cooperation levels above a^* cannot be supported in any Nash equilibrium where players use stationary strategies (i.e., where each player's actions are constant on path). The most subtle part of Theorem 14.10 is therefore the claim that such cooperation levels also cannot be supported by non-stationary strategies.[39]

Equation (14.1) is useful for characterizing which network structures support higher levels of cooperation, as well as which players in a fixed network have greater maximum cooperation levels than others. For example, suppose that the functions f_{ij} are all identical (so each agent benefits equally from every other agent's effort), and say that player i is *recursively more central* than player j if i has more distance-t neighbors than j does (for each t), i's distance-t neighbors have more distance-t' neighbors than j's distance-t neighbors do (for each t and t'), and so on. In this case, it is not hard to see that equation (14.1) implies $a_i^* \geq a_j^*$, for any δ and f. That is, recursively more central

[38] The feature that "maximal" Nash equilibria are always sequentially rational in a continuous-action PD also arises by Ali and Miller (2013). In contrast, Haag and Lagunoff (2006) consider a repeated local-interaction model with binary actions, where off-path incentives are non-trivial.

[39] This last claim is also the only part of the theorem that uses the assumption that the monitoring network – "who observes whom" – is itself observable. The proof involves averaging incentives across a player's information sets and applying monotone methods.

players in a network take higher actions in all equilibria that support maximal cooperation.[40]

Ali and Miller (2013) consider a related model, where instead of taking a single cooperative action each period that benefits every opponent, players interact with their neighbors asynchronously in continuous time and take actions that benefit only the current partner. They show that symmetric contagion strategies on a clique graph of degree d maximize utilitarian welfare among all stationary Nash equilibria on all graphs when each player has at most d neighbors. The intuition is that cliques maximize a quantity that Ali and Miller term *viscosity*, which is similar to the right-hand side of equation (14.1), and likewise captures a player's future payoff loss when she deviates from equilibrium play. Other versions of the point that cooperative incentives are strengthened when information percolates through the network faster – and that some types of networks support faster percolation than others, and hence support stronger incentives – have been made by Raub and Weesie (1990), Klein (1992), Ahn and Suominen (2001), Dixit (2003a,b), Vega-Redondo (2006), Bloch et al. (2008), Lippert and Spagnolo (2011), Fainmesser (2012), Balmaceda and Escobar (2017), Larson (2017), and Fainmesser and Goldberg (2018). For example, Lippert and Spagnolo consider a model where cheap talk communication can potentially spread information more quickly than can contagion via actions, and show that this feature can rationalize "forgiving" strategies where contagion is temporary, because players who observe a deviation under permanent contagion strategies have no incentive to tell others about the deviation, whereas such communication can be incentivized under temporary contagion strategies. Similarly, Ali and Miller (2016, 2022) show that strategies where deviators are "ostracized" only temporarily can induce truthful communication about each player's standing, while "permanent ostracism" strategies cannot.[41]

The papers considered in this section so far study how the threat of multilateral punishment can enforce cooperation when the discount factor δ is too low for bilateral punishment to do so. A related literature derives folk theorems in network games where bilateral incentives are insufficient even when δ is close to 1. For example, this situation arises when payoffs are not additively separable across bilateral interactions (while monitoring is nonetheless determined by a network). A key obstacle to establishing the folk theorem in this setting is that decentralized information about each player's action must be aggregated across the network, but individual players may sometimes benefit from misrepresenting or concealing information. Thus, a typical sufficient condition for the folk theorem is that the network is *2-connected* – meaning that the network remains connected when any single player is removed – as this

[40] Recursive centrality is similar to the "ordinal centralities" studied by Sadler (2020). Sadler shows that if i is ordinally more central than j, then i takes a higher action than j in the maximal equilibrium of any game with strategic complements.

[41] Bowen et al. (2013) and Barron and Guo (2021) discuss other mechanisms by which the need to induce honest communication constrains community enforcement.

condition ensures that a single player cannot prevent the rest of the community from aggregating information.[42] Papers on this topic include Ben-Porath and Kahneman (1996), Renault and Tomala (1998), Tomala (2011), Laclau (2012, 2014), Kinateder (2013), and Cho (2014). Nava and Piccione (2014) establish a folk theorem for binary-action local interaction games, using strategies that are independent of players' beliefs about the global network structure. Wolitzky (2015) asks the related question of when the equilibrium payoff set in a network game is the same when players observe only their neighbors' actions or everyone's actions. The answer again hinges on 2-connectedness when players communicate with their neighbors through cheap talk, while a positive answer is given for any network if players can exchange a form of hard evidence akin to fiat money.

14.5.2 Robustness and Renegotiation in Networks

As we discussed in the context of random-matching games in Section 14.4.1, an important concern regarding contagion strategies is their possible non-robustness to various types of noise. The basic point that the simplest version of contagion strategies are not robust – so that some type of error tolerance or forgiveness is necessary in the presence of noise – applies whether interactions are organized by random matching or a network. Other considerations are specific to the network context, such as a possible desire for the repercussions of a single deviation not to spread too far in the network, or a concern that a subnetwork of players might jointly deviate by splitting off from the rest of the group.[43]

Jackson et al. (2012) consider an asynchronous PD-type game on a network, where in each period a random player i gets an opportunity to do a favor for a random neighbor of hers, j. The arrival of favor opportunities, as well as whether the favor was done, are publicly observed. The authors assume that if i ever declines to do a favor for j, then i and j never do favors for each other in the future: equivalently, the link between them is permanently severed. The main case of interest is when this bilateral punishment is insufficient to motivate favors, and instead a player provides a favor iff she loses at least $m \geq 2$ links if she declines to provide it. Clearly, the strongest incentives to do favors are provided by multilateral punishment strategies, where a player loses all her links if she ever fails to do a favor. Under these strategies, a favor-exchange network is sustainable if each player has at least m links.

42 The earliest reference to this type of condition in the repeated-games literature that I am aware of is Fudenberg and Levine (1991).

43 Another issue is that – whether the interaction structure is given by random matching or a network – robustness concerns differ in binary-action games (like those of Kandori and Ellison) and continuous-action games (like those of Wolitzky and Ali and Miller). In binary-action games, on-path incentive constraints are often slack when δ is high, so softening punishments by introducing some error tolerance can be costless. In continuous-action games, on-path incentive constraints bind in the maximal equilibrium, so softening punishments reduces the maximal incentive-compatible level of cooperation. There is thus a tradeoff between robustness and incentives in continuous-action games.

However, the authors argue that these strategies are not renegotiation-proof: while it is assumed that i and j can never repair their link if i declines to do a favor for j, this presumption does not extend to links between i and her other neighbors. This reasoning leads the authors to introduce a recursive definition of renegotiation-proof networks, where a network is renegotiation-proof if, whenever a player i fails to do a favor for a neighbor j (and hence the ij link is deleted), i ends up with at least m fewer links in the largest renegotiation-proof network that is a subnetwork of the original network without the ij link. Many networks are renegotiation-proof in this sense, but the authors then additionally impose a form of "robustness against contagion," which says that if a link ij is deleted and the largest renegotiation-proof subnetwork forms, players other than mutual neighbors of i and j cannot lose any links. It turns out that robustness against contagion and renegotiation-proofness jointly implies that the network must take a particular form that the authors call a "social quilt," which is a union of m-player cliques.[44] Finally, one implication of this structure is that each ij link is "supported" – meaning that i and j have at least one mutual neighbor, k – and the authors verify that most links are supported in survey data on social networks in a sample of Indian villages.

Karlan et al. (2009) and Ambrus et al. (2014) consider a different type of renegotiation in models of informal lending and risk-sharing, respectively. In Karlan et al.'s model (which was briefly discussed in Section 14.2.2), an agent i needs a loan from another agent j. If i gets the loan, she can then obtain some gain g by strategically defaulting; however, doing so may cause her to lose her relationship with j, as well as possibly her relationships with some third parties. These losses are costly because each relationship is assumed to have some value, which is given exogenously but can be interpreted as a reduced form for some continuation play.

Without renegotiation, the harshest possible punishment would specify that i loses all of her relationships if she defaults on the loan. However, the authors assume that i can organize a coalitional deviation by offering to pay third parties to maintain some of their relationships. For example, if the set of players is $\{i, j, k\}$ and the relationship values satisfy $0 = v_{ij} + v_{jk} < g < v_{ij} + v_{ik}$, then the threat to destroy the valuable ik relationship (in addition to the ij relationship) if i fails to repay j is deemed non-credible, because if i fails to repay j while paying k an amount v_{jk} (which compensates k for the potential loss of his relationship with j), then i nets a profit of $g - v_{ij} - v_{jk} > 0$. Extending this logic, the authors show that the maximum amount that i will repay to j when only renegotiation-proof punishments are allowed is equal to the maximum flow from i to j in the weighted network where the weight on each link equals

[44] Jackson et al.'s approach depends on assuming that some punishments – in particular, deleting link ij when i fails to do a favor for j – cannot be renegotiated. Ali et al. (2017) consider a related model without this assumption and show that the resulting notion of renegotiation-proofness is much less restrictive. Notions of renegotiation for general repeated games (where all punishments can be renegotiated) were previously developed by Farrell and Maskin (1989), among others.

the corresponding relationship value. This result follows from the max-flow min-cut theorem (Ford and Fulkerson, 1956), because coalitional deviations correspond to network "cuts" that separate i and j, where the amount i must pay third parties to go along with the deviation equals the value of the cut (i.e., the total value of all severed relationships), and the max-flow min-cut theorem says that the value of the least expensive cut that separates i and j equals the maximum flow from i to j. As discussed in Section 14.2.2, the authors find some empirical support for the model's predictions.

Ambrus et al. (2014) consider a similar model, where now many agents may be called upon simultaneously to make bilateral transfers (which are similar to the repayments in Karlan et al.) as part of a risk-sharing arrangement. Such an arrangement is coalition-proof if no set of agents $S \subset N$ is called upon to jointly transfer to the remaining agents $S^c = N \backslash S$ an amount of money that exceeds the total value of all relationships between agents in S and agents in S^c. In the special case where all relationships are equally valuable, this observation has interesting implications about the geometry of networks that support a high degree of risk-sharing. For example, if society tries to support perfect risk-sharing, the most tempting deviation for coalition S arises when everyone in S has the maximum possible income (say 1) and everyone else has the minimum possible income (say 0). In this case, the total on-path consumption of agents in S is given by $|S|^2 / N$ (which equals the size of coalition S, $|S|$, multiplied by per-capita consumption under perfect risk-sharing, $|S| / N$), while the maximum total consumption of these agents if they deviate equals $|S|$. Therefore, the coalition S will share risk as prescribed iff the difference $|S| - |S|^2 / N = |S| (1 - |S| / N)$ is less than the per-relationship value v multiplied by the size of the *perimeter* of S, denoted $c(S)$, which is the number of links between S and S^c. This condition reduces to $a(S) v \geq 1 - |S| / N$, where $a(S) = c(S) / |S|$ is the *perimeter-to-area ratio* of the set S. This condition implies in particular that perfect risk-sharing is sustainable only if the perimeter-to-area ratio of every set of agents consisting of less than half the community is at least $1/2$, which is a restrictive condition. For example, if agents are arranged on a two-dimensional grid and S is rectangle, then $c(S)$ is of order $\sqrt{|S|}$, so $a(S)$ is of order $1/\sqrt{|S|}$, which is much less than $1/2$ when $|S|$ is large. However, the paper goes on to characterize conditions for partial risk-sharing (i.e., relaxing the assumption that risk is shared perfectly even after extreme shocks like the one where everyone in S has income 1 and everyone else has income 0), and shows that these conditions are satisfied in "plane-like" networks of the kind often encountered in actual village economies.[45]

[45] A related kind of coalitional deviation arises in some models of repeated games where players choose their partners. Such models are considered by Jackson and Watts (2010) in the context of general finitely repeated games, and by Xing (2020) in the context of repeated risk-sharing games. These models are also related to the endogenous matching games discussed in Section 14.6.1. Relatedly, Bendor et al. (2022) analyze how frequently to "re-shuffle" players across parallel repeated games.

14.6 REPEATED GAMES IN INFINITE POPULATIONS

In order to understand, say, informal contract enforcement on an online platform like eBay, or the cooperative norms that prevail in large modern societies more broadly, we must consider situations where the population size is effectively infinite. If matching in an infinite population is uniformly random, then strategies based only on players' personal experiences – such as contagion strategies – are ineffective, because it is very unlikely that an individual meets someone who met someone who... met her within a payoff-relevant time frame.[46] There are thus two broad ways in which cooperation can be supported in an infinite population: matching can be non-random (as when pairs of players can form long-term relationships), or players can have access to some additional information about their current partner's history (e.g., a user's rating on an online platform, or a consumer's credit rating). I consider the former type of model in Section 14.6.1 and the latter type in Section 14.6.2.

14.6.1 Endogenous Matching

Many economic relationships are naturally modeled as long-term partnerships that can be ended voluntarily by either party, where separation triggers a search process for both parties that eventually leads to rematching with new partners. The canonical example is the employment relationship between a worker and a firm, but business and romantic partnerships also fit the model well. Such voluntarily severable relationships are a hybrid of standard, fixed-partner repeated games, and random-matching games of the kind discussed in Section 14.4. As compared to fixed-partner games, the ability to separate and rematch poses a new obstacle to cooperation, as it can allow a deviating agent to escape punishment. As compared to random-matching games, the ability to stick with one's current partner helps support cooperation, as it can allow an agent who behaves well to enjoy future rewards.

The seminal voluntary separation model is Shapiro and Stiglitz's (1984) work on unemployment as a worker-disciplining device. In their model, employees who are caught shirking are fired and return to the pool of unemployed workers, where it takes time to match with a new firm. To incentivize workers to exert effort, firms pay "efficiency wages" that exceed the present value of unemployment. Shapiro and Stiglitz's key observation – that incentive provision depends on matched agents' continuation payoffs strictly exceeding unmatched agents' – is fundamental in voluntary separation models.

To see how these models work, suppose there is a continuum of identical agents, and consider the frictionless benchmark case where each agent is always matched with a partner. In each period $t = 1, 2, \ldots$, fraction $1 - \gamma$ of agents die and are replaced by newborns who immediately form matches, and

[46] By some reasoning laid out in Section 14.4.1, the same argument applies when N is finite but larger than $\exp(1/(1-\delta))$. So there is no discontinuity between large finite populations and infinite ones.

each matched pair of players play the PD stage game from Section 14.3.1. Note that the survival probability γ replaces the discount factor δ: the per-period expected lifetime payoff of a player whose expected payoff in her tth period of life is u_t equals $(1-\gamma)\sum_{t=1}^{\infty}\gamma^{t-1}u_t$. Assume, for simplicity, that matched partners always die at the same time. At the end of every period t, each player can sever her match, which sends both partners back to the pool, whereupon they immediately rematch with random unmatched agents at the beginning of period $t+1$. Assume that players are anonymous, so when a player forms a match she does not know if her partner is a new agent or an old agent whose match has just broken up.[47] Players perfectly observe behavior in their own matches, but get no information about behavior in other matches.

In this model, there is no Nash equilibrium where players cooperate in every period. For, if there were, players would take C in the first period of every new match; but then a deviant who in every period takes D and then separates from her current partner and rematches would obtain a payoff of $1+g$ in every period, which exceeds the mutual cooperation payoff of 1. This observation just restates the point that incentive provision depends on matched agents' continuation payoffs strictly exceeding unmatched agents'.

While cooperation cannot be supported in every period, it can be supported in most periods if γ is sufficiently high.[48]

Theorem 14.11 (Cooperation with Voluntary Separation) *For any $T \in \mathbb{N}$ such that*

$$\gamma^{T+1} \leq \gamma-(1-\gamma)g, \tag{14.2}$$

there exists a sequential equilibrium where each player's per-period expected payoff equals γ^{T+1}. In particular, for any $\varepsilon > 0$, there exists $\bar{\gamma} < 1$ such that, for every $\gamma > \bar{\gamma}$, there is a sequential equilibrium of the voluntary separation game with survival probability γ where each player's per-period expected payoff exceeds $1-\varepsilon$.

This result follows from considering *T-period trust-building strategies*, where newly matched partners play D for the first T periods of their relationship and then switch to playing C forever, with any deviation punished by immediate break-up. This strategy profile – which I will denote by σ^T – gives each player an expected payoff of γ^{T+1}, since on path $u_t = 0$ for the first T periods of a player's life and $u_t = 1$ thereafter. To see when strategy σ^T forms an equilibrium, note that there is nothing to be gained by deviating from D

[47] The difference between the voluntary separation models covered in the current section and models where players have the option of exiting and re-entering under a pseudonym (as in Friedman and Resnick, 2001) is that in the latter case, the partner of a player who exits can carry his reputation over to his next match – his record is not wiped clean just because his partner's is. Thus, while the two models are similar, there are more equilibria in "cheap pseudonym" models than in standard voluntary separation models.

[48] This type of result seems to have been first noted by Datta (1993) and Kranton (1996a).

to C during the first T periods of a relationship, or by breaking up a relationship prematurely (since continuation payoffs increase over the course of each relationship). So, the only tempting deviation is playing D rather than C in a relationship that has already lasted more than T periods. A player who deviates in this way gets a current-period payoff of $1+g$ and then rematches, for a total continuation payoff of $(1-\gamma)(1+g)+\gamma^{T+1}(1)$. Therefore, σ^T is an equilibrium iff this deviation payoff is less than the equilibrium continuation payoff of a player whose relationship has already lasted more than T periods, which equals 1. This inequality reduces to equation (14.2). Finally, the right-hand side of equation (14.2) converges to 1 as $\gamma \to 1$, so T can be chosen as a function of γ so that $\sigma^{T(\gamma)}$ is an equilibrium yielding payoffs that converge to 1 as $\gamma \to 1$. This last step reflects the fact that, when $\gamma \approx 1$, approximately g periods of trust building are required to deter deviations, and waiting g periods before starting to cooperate is almost costless when $\gamma \approx 1$.

The essential feature of trust-building strategies is that newly matched players do not immediately start cooperating. This feature is reflected in many real-world social and economic relationships, presumably for much the same reason as in the model: if strangers are trusted as thoroughly as long-term partners, the ability to repeatedly exploit new partners destroys cooperation. This and related points are discussed by Carmichael and MacLeod (1997), who also note that other mechanisms besides delay can serve to build trust, such as ceremonial gift exchanges at the start of relationships that amount to a form of "money-burning." The exchange of wedding rings is a standard example.[49]

While trust-building strategies are approximately efficient when the survival probability γ is high, they can generally be improved upon for a given value of γ. Eeckhout (2006) shows that one way to do this is through "endogenous segregation," where a payoff-irrelevant trait like skin color determines the time at which cooperation commences in each relationship. In his model, skin color serves as a correlating device, the availability of which is shown to yield a strict Pareto improvement for generic values of the parameters (g, ℓ, γ). To see the basic idea, suppose that γ is low enough that one-period trust-building strategies (i.e., σ^1) form an equilibrium, and that moreover so do strategies where new partners mix between C and D with some probabilities in the first period of their relationship (before taking C with probability 1 beginning in the second period). Such independent mixing between C and D typically entails some inefficiency as compared to the case where the players can jointly mix between (C,C) and (D,D), which becomes possible if a correlating device is available. Fujiwara-Greve and Okuno-Fujiwara (2009) show that it is also possible to improve on the T-period trust-building strategy σ^T without exogenously introducing correlating devices, by instead considering equilibria where players mix between σ^T and σ^{T-1}.

49 The relationship-building role of gift exchanges has also been intensively studied by anthropologists, dating back to the foundational works of Malinowski (1922) and Mauss (1925).

It is also interesting to consider the effects of introducing adverse player types in voluntary separation models, such as a fraction of players who are committed to always playing D (like the commitment types in Section 14.4.2). Ghosh and Ray (1996) show that the presence of such types can sometimes *help* support cooperation. This is because the presence of adverse types in the matching pool discourages players from exploiting and then separating from their current partners. For example, in this model σ^0 (i.e., immediate cooperation in each relationship) is an equilibrium iff the population share of adverse types is intermediate. Indeed, if the share of adverse types is close to 0, then rational player payoffs under σ^0 are close to 1, while a deviator who always takes D gets a payoff close to $1+g$. If the share of adverse types is close to 1, then rational player payoffs under σ^0 are close to $-\ell$, while a deviator who always takes D gets a payoff close to 0. However, it is not hard to show that σ^0 is sometimes an equilibrium for an intermediate share of adverse types.[50]

14.6.2 Uniform Matching and Record-Keeping

The applications just discussed notwithstanding, there are also many economic relationships which are necessarily short-term: for instance, a consumer is typically interested in transacting at most once with any one eBay seller or Airbnb host. In an effectively infinite population with short-term relationships, incentives can be provided only if players have access to some information about their current partners' histories. We will see that the richness of this information is a key determinant of the scope for cooperation. In particular, if players receive information about their partners' past actions but not about the context of these actions – such as, for example, what actions their partners' past partners took toward them – then whether non-myopic play can be supported may depend on the details of the stage game. In contrast, the folk theorem holds quite generally when this type of contextualizing information is available.

To state these results precisely, we must first specify a model of repeated games with random matching in an infinite population, given an underlying symmetric, two-player stage game (A,u). There are two main ways of doing this. The first adapts the fixed finite-population models discussed in Section 14.4.1 to a fixed infinite population, and in particular assumes that all players start the game at the same time, share a common notion of calendar time, and are infinitely lived with discount factor δ. This approach is taken by Okuno-Fujiwara and Postlewaite (1995) and Takahashi (2010). The second approach modifies the models with entry and exit covered in Section 14.6.1 by replacing

[50] Conversely, features of the environment that improve payoffs for the pool of anonymous, unmatched players can undermine cooperation by making separation more attractive. Kranton (1996b) argues that the development of market exchange can play such a role (see also Baker et al., 1994). Gagnon and Goyal (2017) analyze a related model where long-run relationships are governed by a network, and Banerjee et al. (2021) develop an empirical application to credit markets in rural India.

voluntary separation with uniform random matching, and thus considers steady states in a model where each player has a geometric lifespan with survival probability γ. This approach is taken by Clark et al. (2020). As we will see, many results in these two classes of models are similar, although there are also some differences.

In either model, one assumes that each player carries a *record* r that summarizes some information about her history, and that when two players meet, each observes the other's record but no further information.[51] At the end of each period, a player's record is updated according to an exogenous rule that typically depends on at most the current partner's record and both players' actions. If the updating rule depends only on a player's own action, the record is called *first-order*. A leading example of first-order records arises when a player's record consists of the entire history of her own actions, so that players perfectly observe their partners' past play but get no further information – this is the case considered by Takahashi (2010). If the updating rule additionally depends on the partner's action – as for example in the case where a player's record consists of the entire history of the (*own action, opponent's action*) outcomes of her past matches – the record is called *second-order*. In the general case where the updating rule can also depend directly on the partner's record – as in certain models of "social standing" (Sigmund, 2010) – records are called *interdependent*.

Second-order records turn out to be rich enough to support a general folk theorem. Let A_0 denote each player's stage-game action set, and let $\underline{v}^P = \min_{a_j \in A_0} \max_{a_i \in A_0} u(a_i, a_j)$ denote the pure-strategy minmax payoff.

Theorem 14.12 (Folk Theorem with Second-Order Records) *There exists a second-order record system such that the following holds: for any action a_0 satisfying $u(a_0, a_0) > \underline{v}^P$, there exists $\bar{\delta} < 1$ such that, for every $\delta > \bar{\delta}$, there is a sequential equilibrium of the repeated game with discount factor δ where all players take a_0 in every period along the equilibrium path.*

This result combines ideas from Okuno-Fujiwara and Postlewaite and Clark et al.[52] It applies equally for fixed-population games and games with geometric player lifespans (with γ in place of δ). To prove it, fix a minmaxing action $a^- \in \operatorname{argmin}_{a_j \in A_0} \max_{a_i \in A_0} u(a_i, a_j)$ and a best response $a^+ \neq a_0$ to a^-, and let (α, α) be a symmetric stage-game Nash equilibrium.[53] Suppose that each player's record is *Good* if the outcome of each of her past matches is either

[51] The term *record* is from Clark et al. Okuno-Fujiwara and Postlewaite call the same object a *status level*; Kandori (1992b) calls it a player's *state*; and the evolutionary biology literature surveyed by Sigmund (2010) often calls it a player's *standing*.

[52] Sugden (1986) and Kandori (1992b) established related results.

[53] Such (a^-, a^+) always exist unless a_0 is the unique best response to every minmaxing action. In this case, Theorem 14.12 remains true, but the proof requires a more complicated construction. See theorem 2(i) of Clark et al. for the details.

(a_0, a_0) or (a^-, a^+), and is *Bad* otherwise: note that, by definition, such records are second-order. Finally, suppose that when two players meet, both take a^0 if both of their records are *Good*; both take α if both of their records are *Bad*; otherwise the *Good*-record player takes a^- and the *Bad*-record player takes a^+. To see that these strategies form an equilibrium when δ is sufficiently high, note that the *Bad* record is absorbing and that *Bad*-record players always take myopic best responses. Since $a^+ \neq a_0$, a *Good*-record player who meets a *Good*-record opponent (and thus anticipates that the opponent will play a_0) must play a_0 to maintain her *Good* record; similarly, a *Good*-record player who meets a *Bad*-record opponent must play a^- to maintain her record. Note that in equilibrium all players' records are *Good*, so a *Good*-record player's continuation payoff is $u(a_0, a_0)$, while that of a *Bad*-record player is $\underline{v}^P$. Therefore, when δ is sufficiently high, it is optimal for *Good*-record players to play a_0 against *Good*-record opponents and to play a^- against *Bad*-record opponents, as prescribed.

This argument invites the question of whether Theorem 14.12 is robust to introducing noise – for example, constraining players to take each action with at least ε probability – which would guarantee that a positive share of players has every possible record. Clark et al. show that the result is indeed robust, in that there exists a sequence of equilibrium steady states that converges to the steady state where all players have *Good* records in the double limit where $(\gamma, \varepsilon) \to (1, 0)$. Moreover, the corresponding equilibria are strict, which ensures robustness to various further perturbations of the model.

Theorem 14.12 shows that a relatively small amount of contextualizing information is enough to support cooperation in large populations: it suffices to observe summary statistics of one's partner's past *outcomes*, meaning both their own actions and what actions were taken toward them. However, in some settings, contextualizing information is entirely absent, such as when a platform user's rating depends only on the quality of the products she has sold, so that only first-order records are available. In this case, whether cooperation is supportable for high δ turns out to depend on the details of the stage game.

To see the idea, consider again the PD stage game introduced in Section 14.3.1, and suppose that records are first-order, so that a player's continuation payoff at the beginning of period $t+1$ depends only on her own period-t record and action. If a player is supposed to take C rather than D against an opponent whom she expects to take C, her continuation payoff must be *at least* g utils higher when she takes C rather than D (because she would gain g in the current period by taking D). On the other hand, if she is supposed to take D against an opponent whom she expects to take D, her continuation payoff must be *at most* ℓ utils higher when she takes C rather than D (because she would lose ℓ in the current period by taking C). In particular, if $g > \ell$ – so that the game is *strictly submodular*, meaning that C is relatively more attractive when the opponent takes D – then it is impossible to motivate a player to take C against opponents who take C while taking D against opponents who take D. Moreover, in the absence of such "reciprocating" behavior, it can be shown that cooperation cannot be supported in any strict equilibrium.[54]

Theorem 14.13 (Anti-Folk Theorem with First-Order Records) *For any first-order record system and any discount factor δ, if the stage game is the submodular PD then the unique strict equilibrium in the repeated game is* Always Defect.

By contrast, in the strictly supermodular PD (where $g < \ell$) with a fixed population of infinitely lived players, Takahashi shows that there exists a strict equilibrium where players cooperate in every period along the equilibrium path. This result follows by using Ellison's "threading" technique to tune the effective discount factor so that the difference in a player's continuation payoff when she takes C rather than D lies in between g and ℓ. However, if one introduces noise in the model, then eventually play in such an equilibrium converges to mutual defection in every period, so these equilibria do not seem very robust. Consistent with this intuition, Clark et al. establish necessary and sufficient conditions for mutual cooperation to be supported in a robust equilibrium steady state with geometric player lifespans and noise when $(\gamma, \varepsilon) \to (1,0)$, and find that these conditions are strictly more restrictive than $g < \ell$.[55]

While Theorem 14.13 shows that cooperation with first-order records in the PD is delicate, cooperation becomes much more robust if the game is augmented with an "exit option," which yields some payoff between 0 and 1 for both players whenever either player takes it. Intuitively, the problem with first-order records in the PD is that they cannot distinguish between "justified" defections that are taken to punish an opponent with a bad record, and "unjustified" defections that are taken to exploit an opponent with a good record. If punishments are instead delivered by "exiting," this distinction does not need to be drawn, because a player who expects her opponent to cooperate is not tempted to exit. Clark et al. formalize this point by deriving a folk theorem with first-order records for games where such "unprofitable punishments" are available.[56]

[54] This result was established for fixed-population games by Takahashi, and for games with geometric player lifespans by Clark et al. Heller and Mohlin (2018) derive the same result in a model with infinitely lived players and doubly infinite time. Takahashi shows that cooperation can be supported in a non-strict, belief-free equilibria when $g \geq l$; however, Heller and Mohlin exhibit a sense in which these equilibria are non-robust. Dilmé (2016) establishes related results, focusing on the case where $g = l$.

[55] Heller and Mohlin (2018) derive related conditions for the existence of cooperative equilibria in their doubly infinite time model. Their equilibria are not strict but do satisfy a stability condition.

[56] This result resonates with a debate in evolutionary biology as to whether the inability to distinguish warranted punishments from unwarranted deviations is a significant impediment to supporting cooperation. Fehr and Gächter (2002) and Boyd et al. (2003) argue for the importance of costly punishments, while Baumard (2010) and Guala (2012) suggest that human cooperation is supported by the threat of simply avoiding deviators (an example of an "unprofitable punishment"), rather than actively punishing them.

The models discussed so far involve normal-form stage games. Bhaskar and Thomas (2019) consider a sequential-move stage game, where a lender decides whether to extend a loan, and then a borrower decides whether to repay. They show that cooperative equilibria unravel when records are of any bounded length T (under a "purifiability" refinement), because lenders cannot be prevented from lending to borrowers who last defaulted exactly T periods ago, which effectively reduces records to length $T - 1$, and so on. However, cooperation is restored if lenders learn only whether or not the borrower defaulted at some point in the last T periods. This result provides a rationalization for coarse credit reports.[57]

Finally, a number of important papers analyze how specific institutional mechanisms provide enough information for large groups to cooperate in particular contexts. In addition to the work on online ratings systems and credit ratings already discussed, these include Milgrom et al. (1990) on private judges in medieval trade fairs, Kiyotaki and Wright (1993) on fiat money, Greif et al. (1994) and Clay (1997) on merchant coalitions in medieval Europe and nineteenth-century California, respectively, Kandori and Obayashi (2014) on Japanese labor unions, and Abadi and Brunnermeier (2019), Biais et al. (2019), and Budish (2025) on blockchains.

14.7 INSTITUTIONALIZED ENFORCEMENT

In all of the models I have considered so far, cooperative behavior is enforced informally through repeated-game effects. In contrast, traditional economic models implicitly assume the existence of an all-powerful legal system that perfectly enforces any agreement that agents may make. In reality, incentives derive from both informal, relational sources and formal, institutionalized ones. A number of recent papers have tried to understand how these different sources of incentives interact. For example, what types of behaviors are, or should be, enforced only informally, and when instead does the legal system or another institution with coercive power involve itself in regulating behavior? Are formal and informal incentives "complements" or "substitutes"? Given that judges, police officers, and armed goons are presumably all rational agents in their own right, should we even distinguish between formal and informal enforcement at all, rather than viewing all of society as being constantly engaged in a single "game of life" (Binmore, 1994)? No standard modeling approach for addressing these questions has yet emerged, but I will nonetheless try to give a snapshot of the state of the literature.

I will distinguish between two general perspectives on how institutionalized enforcement relates to standard repeated-game enforcement of the kind discussed in earlier sections. The first is that institutionalized enforcement is that subset of repeated-game enforcement which is carried out by special

[57] Other studies of credit reporting as an information system in a repeated game include Klein (1992) and Padilla and Pagano (2000).

agents whom we call "judges," "police," or "goons," where these agents differ from "regular agents" in that they have access to special types of punishing actions, such as imprisonment or corporal punishment. This perspective of "institutional enforcement as special sanctions" is taken by Ramey and Watson (2002), Dixit (2003a,b, 2004), Sánchez-Pagés and Straub (2010), Aldashev et al. (2012), Andreoni and Gee (2012), Masten and Prüfer (2014), Acemoglu and Jackson (2016), Levine and Modica (2016), Aldashev and Zanarone (2017), and Acemoglu and Wolitzky (2020, 2021). The second perspective is that institutionalized enforcement refers to a special type of payoff-irrelevant signal or message that serves to coordinate the players in the game, such as a legal ruling or royal decree. This perspective of "institutional enforcement as special communication" (which is related to the analysis of information systems in Section 14.6.2) is taken by Myerson (2004), Benabou and Tirole (2011), Hadfield and Weingast (2012), McAdams (2015), Mailath et al. (2017), Basu (2018), and Jackson and Xing (2024). A thorough survey of this literature would require its own chapter, so I will just discuss a couple of articles from each of these two lines of research that are especially closely related to standard repeated-game models of community enforcement.[58]

Acemoglu and Wolitzky (2020) add agents specialized in coercive enforcement to a standard community enforcement model, so the population consists of N "regular agents" and M "enforcers," where for simplicity I here take $M = 1$. Every period, each regular agent i chooses a "cooperation level" $a_i \in \mathbb{R}_+$, which provides a benefit of $f(a_i)$ to every other agent (both the other regular agents and the enforcer) at a cost of a_i to agent i, where f is an increasing, concave, and bounded function.[59] At the end of every period, after observing each regular agent's chosen cooperation level, the enforcer chooses a "punishment level" $b_i \in \mathbb{R}_+$ for each regular agent i, which inflicts a disutility of $g(b_i)$ upon agent i at a cost of b_i to the enforcer, where g is another increasing and concave function (which may or may not be bounded). Thus, just as regular agents must be incentivized to operate their "production technology" f, so the enforcer must be incentivized to operate his "punishment technology" g. The game is repeated under perfect monitoring, and all agents (both regular agents and the enforcer) share a common discount factor δ.

The paper asks what subgame perfect equilibrium maximizes cooperation among regular agents.[60] Since monitoring is assumed to be perfect, an obvious candidate is grim trigger strategies, where regular agents take some prescribed action a^* so long as no regular agent has yet deviated, and otherwise take the

[58] There are also other perspectives on institutional enforcement besides these two. For example, a third perspective, emphasized by North et al. (2009), is that laws are distinguished by being "impersonal": that is, by treating agents differently based only on their societal positions, rather than their personal identities.

[59] The modeling of regular agents here is thus as in Wolitzky (2013), which I discussed in Section 14.5.1.

[60] This equilibrium also maximizes utilitarian social welfare if the maximum cooperation level is below the first-best level.

myopically optimal action 0. These strategies always form an optimal equilibrium without an enforcer, but they are *never* optimal when an enforcer is present (though they remain *an* equilibrium, since everyone can always ignore the enforcer). The reason is that grim-trigger strategies give the enforcer no incentives to operate the punishment technology: under these strategies, cooperation completely breaks down after any deviation, so the enforcer has no incentive to exert "punishment effort" himself.

Instead, consider "repentance strategies," where if some regular agent i deviates in period t, she is supposed to be punished by the enforcer at the end of period t, and then is supposed to cooperate in period $t+1$ while all other regular agents exert 0 effort. Then (assuming that the enforcer punishes agent i at the end of period t and agent i exerts effort in period $t+1$), all regular agents resume cooperation at the original on-path level a^* in period $t+2$. It is not hard to see that in the absence of an enforcer, repentance strategies support the same maximum cooperation level as grim-trigger strategies.[61] Hence, since repentance strategies provide some incentive to the enforcer, they support a strictly higher cooperation level in the game with an enforcer. Indeed, the optimal equilibrium with an enforcer can be shown to take a form similar to repentance strategies, with the difference that if the punishment technology is sufficiently effective, the optimal equilibrium may involve no reduction in effort by regular agents following a deviation by another regular agent. In this case, the threat of reduced effort by regular agents is used exclusively to motivate the enforcer; and, conversely, regular agents are motivated solely by the threat of being punished by the enforcer. A sufficient condition for such "enforcer punishment strategies" to be optimal is that $g'(b) \geq 1$ for all $b \in \mathbb{R}_+$.

Acemoglu and Wolitzky (2021) extend this model to develop a theory of the emergence of legal equality. Suppose that the coercive punishment technology is now in the hands of a "state," and that there are two types of productive agents: "regular agents" and "elites." The difference between these two types of agents is that elites are partially immune to coercive punishment: while the state can inflict a punishment of g on a regular agent, it can only inflict a punishment of ρg on an elite, where $\rho \in [0,1]$ is a parameter that measures the extent to which elites are "above the law." The paper asks what level of ρ is collectively preferred by elites. Intuitively, a higher value of ρ (corresponding to greater legal equality) commits elites to exerting more effort, which is myopically costly but has the benefit of increasing continuation values for both regular agents and elites, which in turn increases the maximum incentive-compatible effort level of regular agents. A key comparative static is that the elite-preferred level of ρ is decreasing in g: that is, the greater is the "coercive capacity" of the state, the less inclined are elites to move toward legal equality.

[61] Intuitively, under repentance strategies, the deviator "burns her own utility" instead of facing future punishment. The observation that optimal equilibria are stationary when unbounded money-burning is available is similar to results that arise in repeated games with transferable utility (Levin, 2003; Goldlücke and Kranz, 2012).

The logic of this result is that, since there are diminishing returns to effort (i.e., f is concave), trading off greater own effort for greater normal-agent effort by increasing ρ is less attractive for elites when the threat of coercive punishment already induces a higher level of normal-agent effort.

Turning from enforcement-based theories to informational ones, Hadfield and Weingast (2012) articulate a view of legal decisions as mechanisms for coordinating multilateral punishment. In their model, a seller interacts repeatedly with each of two buyers. The seller has occasional opportunities to short-change each buyer, and can be deterred from doing so by the threat of a coordinated boycott, where both buyers break off trade; however, the threat of a unilateral boycott is assumed to be insufficient to deter opportunism by the seller. Each buyer receives a private signal of whether she was short-changed in the current period, so it is possible for each buyer to threaten to boycott the seller when she is short-changed. But, since it is assumed that the buyers cannot communicate with each other, a buyer cannot threaten to boycott the seller when the *other* buyer is short-changed, and hence seller opportunism cannot be deterred.[62] To this model, Hadfield and Weingast add a "classification institution," where each buyer reports her signal to the institution at the end of each period, and the institution then issues a public "ruling" regarding the seller's behavior. The authors show that, if the institution's rulings are sufficiently accurate, they can form the basis for coordinated boycotts, and can thereby deter seller opportunism.

Jackson and Xing (2024) develop another model where legal decisions coordinate multilateral punishment, with the novel feature that these punishments can be carried out only within an individual's own community. In the model, each individual needs a task to be completed in every period. A binding societal convention dictates which tasks are to be completed within the community, and which are to be completed in the market. Due to gains from specialization, tasks can always be completed more efficiently in the market. However, agents are assumed to interact in the market anonymously, whereas their identities are observed within their community. This implies that an agent who fails to complete another community member's task can be completely ostracized within her community, while an agent who fails to complete a market task can only be forced to pay a fine (which is assumed to be capped at a certain level). There is thus a familiar tradeoff between more-efficient market exchange and better-monitored and enforced community exchange. The model adds to this standard situation the assumption that if an agent shirks a market

[62] This situation is similar to the models of multilateral enforcement on networks that we encountered in Section 14.5.1. View the seller as the center node in a three-node line, and suppose that simultaneous PDs are played on each link, and that the peripheral nodes cannot directly communicate with each other. Then cooperation by the seller can be supported iff it can be supported in each bilateral relationship independently. This result is formalized by proposition 1 in Wolitzky (2015).

task, then not only is she fined, but with some probability the information that she shirked in the market spreads to her community, in which case she may also be ostracized by her community. Due to this effect, allocating more tasks to the community effectively makes market exchange more enforceable, as it increases the penalty for shirking in market exchange (i.e., the fine plus the product of the probability of ostracism and the loss from being excluded from community tasks). Together with the assumption that market exchange is more efficient, this effect implies that it is typically optimal to allocate some tasks to the market and others to the community. The model thus uncovers a novel complementarity between community and market exchange.

14.8 CONCLUSION

Our theoretical understanding of large-group cooperation has already come a long way. A generation ago, economists were just beginning to understand the importance of informal contractual enforcement and collective action, as well as the role of information and repeated interaction in supporting these behaviors. We now have a much more sophisticated understanding of, for example, the interaction among group size, patience, and information; the distinct roles of collective and individual sanctions; the significance of whether behavior is monitored through centralized, public signals or decentralized, private ones; the role of social structures such as networks and voluntarily separable relationships; and the importance of various types of informational and coercive institutions.

Nonetheless, in reviewing this literature I am mostly struck by how much we still have to learn. In almost every area I have touched on, only a couple of papers have been written (or at most a small handful), and there are many wide-open questions with prima facie relevance to important applied questions. For example, while we are beginning to appreciate the significance of various model features, such as whether signals are public or private, whether noise is modeled as independent shocks or the presence of adverse types, or whether matching is random or network-like, we seem to know extremely little about how these different features interact with each other. Since theory research in this area aspires to influence more applied thinking on social cooperation as well as empirical work (which are, of course, proceeding apace), constructing more unified models that take these interactions into account seems to be a relatively urgent task.

Finally, I have said very little about other areas of economic theory that bear on social cooperation, such as behavioral economics (e.g., Sobel, 2005), organizational economics (Baker et al., 2002; Kreps, 1990), and political economy (Acemoglu and Robinson, 2012; Myerson, 2008; North et al., 2009). Synthesizing some of the core models in these areas – such as models of social preferences, corporate culture, and organizational or political hierarchies – with those considered in this survey is another promising direction for future research.

REFERENCES

Abadi, J., and M. Brunnermeier (2019). "Blockchain economics." NBER Working Paper No. 25407.

Abreu, D., P. K. Dutta, and L. Smith (1994). "The folk theorem for repeated games: A NEU condition," *Econometrica*, 62(4), 939–948.

Abreu, D., D. Pearce, and E. Stacchetti (1990). "Toward a theory of discounted repeated games with imperfect monitoring," *Econometrica*, 58(5), 1041–1063.

Acemoglu, D., and M. O. Jackson (2017). "Social norms and the enforcement of laws," *Journal of the European Economic Association*, 15(2), 245–295.

Acemoglu, D., and J. A. Robinson (2012). *Why Nations Fail: The Origins of Power, Prosperity, and Poverty*. New York: Crown Currency.

Acemoglu, D., and A. Wolitzky (2020). "Sustaining cooperation: Community enforcement versus specialized enforcement," *Journal of the European Economic Association*, 18(2), 1078–1122.

Acemoglu, D., and A. Wolitzky (2021). "A theory of equality before the law," *Economic Journal*, 131, 1429–1465.

Ahn, I., and M. Suominen (2001). "Word-of-mouth communication and community enforcement," *International Economic Review*, 42(2), 399–415.

Aldashev, G., I. Chaara, J. P. Platteau, and Z. Wahhaj (2012). "Using the law to change the custom," *Journal of Development Economics*, 97(2), 182–200.

Aldashev, G., and G. Zanarone (2017). "Endogenous enforcement institutions," *Journal of Development Economics*, 128, 49–64.

Alesina, A., R. Baqir, and W. Easterly (1999). "Public goods and ethnic divisions," *Quarterly Journal of Economics*, 114(4), 1243–1284.

Alesina, A., and E. La Ferrara (2000). "Participation in heterogeneous communities," *Quarterly Journal of Economics*, 115(3), 847–904.

Alexander, R. D. (1987). *The Biology of Moral Systems*. Livingston, NJ: Transaction Publishers.

Ali, S. N., and D. A. Miller (2013). "Enforcing cooperation in networked societies." Working Paper.

Ali, S. N., and D. A. Miller (2016). "Ostracism and forgiveness," *American Economic Review*, 106(8), 2329–2348.

Ali, S. N., and D. A. Miller (2022). "Communication and cooperation in markets," *American Economic Journal: Microeconomics*, 14(4), 200–217.

Ali, S. N., D. A. Miller, and D. Yang (2017). "Renegotiation-proof multilateral enforcement." Working Paper.

Al-Najjar, N. I., and R. Smorodinsky (2000). "Pivotal players and the characterization of influence," *Journal of Economic Theory*, 92(2), 318–342.

Al-Najjar, N. I., and R. Smorodinsky (2001). "Large nonanonymous repeated games," *Games and Economic Behavior*, 37(1), 26–39.

Ambrus, A., M. Möbius, and A. Szeidl (2014). "Consumption risk-sharing in social networks," *American Economic Review*, 104(1), 149–182.

Andreoni, J., and L. K. Gee (2012). "Gun for hire: Delegated enforcement and peer punishment in public goods provision," *Journal of Public Economics*, 96(11–12), 1036–1046.

Aumann, R. J., and L. S. Shapley (1976). "Long-term competition—a game-theoretic analysis." Mimeo.

Athey, S., and K. Bagwell (2001). "Optimal collusion with private information," *RAND Journal of Economics*, 32(3), 428–465.

Axelrod, R. (1984). *The Evolution of Cooperation*. New York: Basic Books.

Baker, G., R. Gibbons, and K. J. Murphy (1994). "Subjective performance measures in optimal incentive contracts," *Quarterly Journal of Economics*, 109(4), 1125–1156.

Baker, G., R. Gibbons, and K. J. Murphy (2002). "Relational contracts and the theory of the firm," *Quarterly Journal of Economics*, 117(1), 39–84.

Balmaceda, F., and J. F. Escobar (2017). "Trust in cohesive communities," *Journal of Economic Theory*, 170, 289–318.

Banerjee, A. V., A. G. Chandrasekhar, E. Duo, and M. O. Jackson (2021). "Changes in social network structure in response to exposure to formal credit markets." Available at SSRN: 3245656.

Banerjee, A., L. Iyer, and R. Somanathan (2005). "History, social divisions, and public goods in rural India," *Journal of the European Economic Association*, 3(2–3), 639–647.

Barron, D., and Y. Guo (2021). "The use and misuse of coordinated punishments," *Quarterly Journal of Economics*, 136(1), 471–504.

Basu, K. (2018). *The Republic of Beliefs: A New Approach to Law and Economics*. Princeton, NJ: Princeton University Press.

Baumard, N. (2010). "Has punishment played a role in the evolution of cooperation? A critical review," *Mind & Society*, 9(2), 171–192.

Baumeister, R. F., L. Zhang, and K. D. Vohs (2004). "Gossip as cultural learning," *Review of General Psychology*, 8(2), 111–121.

Bendor, J., L. Bolte, N. Immorlica, and M. O. Jackson (2022). "Interactions across multiple games: Cooperation, corruption, and organizational design." Working Paper.

Ben-Porath, E., and M. Kahneman (1996). "Communication in repeated games with private monitoring," *Journal of Economic Theory*, 70, 281–298.

Benabou, R., and J. Tirole (2011). "Laws and norms." NBER Working Paper No. 17579.

Bernheim, B. D., and M. D. Whinston (1990). "Multimarket contact and collusive behavior," *The RAND Journal of Economics*, 21(1), 1–26.

Besley, T., S. Coate, and G. Loury (1993). "The economics of rotating savings and credit associations," *The American Economic Review*, 83(4), 792–810.

Bhaskar, V., and C. Thomas (2019). "Community enforcement of trust with bounded memory," *Review of Economic Studies*, 86(3), 1010–1032.

Biais, B., C. Bisiere, M. Bouvard, and C. Casamatta (2019). "The blockchain folk theorem," *Review of Financial Studies*, 32(5), 1662–1715.

Binmore, K. G. (1994). *Game Theory and the Social Contract*. Cambridge, MA: MIT Press.

Bloch, F., G. Genicot, and D. Ray (2008). "Informal insurance in social networks," *Journal of Economic Theory*, 143, 36–58.

Bolton, G., B. Greiner, and A. Ockenfels (2013). "Engineering trust: Reciprocity in the production of reputation information," *Management Science*, 59(2), 265–285.

Bowen, T. R., D. M. Kreps, and A. Skrzypacz (2013). "Rules with discretion and local information," *Quarterly Journal of Economics*, 128(3), 1273–1320.

Bowles, S., and H. Gintis (2013). *A Cooperative Species: Human Reciprocity and its Evolution*. Princeton, NJ: Princeton University Press.

Boyd, R., H. Gintis, S. Bowles, and P. J. Richerson (2003). "The evolution of altruistic punishment," *Proceedings of the National Academy of Sciences*, 100(6), 3531–3535.

Boyd, R., and P. J. Richerson (1992). "Punishment allows the evolution of cooperation (or anything else) in sizable groups," *Ethology and Sociobiology*, 13(3), 171–195.

Budish, E. (2025). "Trust at scale: The economic limits of cryptocurrencies and blockchains," *Quarterly Journal of Economics*, 140(1), 1–62.

Bull, C. (1987). "The existence of self-enforcing implicit contracts," *Quarterly Journal of Economics*, 102(1), 147–159.

Cabral, L. (2012). "Reputation on the Internet." In M. Peitz and J. Waldfogel (eds.), *The Oxford Handbook of the Digital Economy*. Oxford: Oxford University Press, pp. 343–354.

Carmichael, H. L., and W. B. MacLeod (1997). "Gift giving and the evolution of cooperation," *International Economic Review*, 38(3), 485–509.

Cho, M. (2014). "Cooperation in the repeated prisoner's dilemma game with local interaction and local communication," *International Journal of Economic Theory*, 10(3), 235–262.

Clark, D., D. Fudenberg, and A. Wolitzky (2021). "Record-keeping and cooperation in large societies," *Review of Economic Studies*, 88, 2179–2209.

Clay, K. (1997). "Trade without law: Private-order institutions in Mexican California," *The Journal of Law, Economics, and Organization*, 13(1), 202–231.

Coate, S., and M. Ravallion (1993). "Reciprocity without commitment: Characterization and performance of informal insurance arrangements," *Journal of Development Economics*, 40(1), 1–24.

Coleman, J. (1990). *Foundations of Social Theory*. Cambridge, MA: Harvard University Press.

Datta, S. (1996). "Building trust." Working Paper No. 1996/305. Suntory and Toyota International Centres for Economics and Related Disciplines, LSE.

Deb, J. (2020). "Cooperation and community responsibility," *Journal of Political Economy*, 128(5), 1976–2009.

Deb, J., and J. González-Díaz (2019). "Enforcing social norms: Trust-building and community enforcement," *Theoretical Economics*, 14(4), 1387–1433.

Deb, J., T. Sugaya, and A. Wolitzky (2020). "The folk theorem in repeated games with anonymous random matching," *Econometrica*, 88(3), 917–964.

De Quidt, J., T. Fetzer, and M. Ghatak (2016). "Group lending without joint liability," *Journal of Development Economics*, 121, 217–236.

Dilmé, F. (2016). "Helping behavior in large societies," *International Economic Review*, 57(4), 1261–1278.

Dixit, A. (2003a). "Trade expansion and contract enforcement," *Journal of Political Economy*, 111(6), 1293–1317.

Dixit, A. (2003b). "On modes of economic governance," *Econometrica*, 71(2), 449–481.

Dixit, A. K. (2004). *Lawlessness and Economics: Alternative Modes of Governance*. Princeton, NJ: Princeton University Press.

Dunbar, R. (2004). "Gossip in evolutionary perspective," *Review of General Psychology*, 8(2), 100–110.

Easterly, W., and R. Levine (1997). "Africa's growth tragedy: Policies and ethnic divisions," *Quarterly Journal of Economics*, 112(4), 1203–1250.

Eeckhout, J. (2006). "Minorities and endogenous segregation," *Review of Economic Studies*, 73(1), 31–53.

Ellickson, R. C. (1994). *Order Without Law: How Neighbors Settle Disputes*. Cambridge, MA: Harvard University Press.

Ellison, G. (1994). "Cooperation in the prisoner's dilemma with anonymous random matching," *Review of Economic Studies*, 61(3), 567–588.

Fafchamps, M., and S. Lund (2003). "Risk-sharing networks in rural Philippines," *Journal of Development Economics*, 71(2), 261–287.

Fainmesser, I. P. (2012). "Community structure and market outcomes: A repeated games-in-networks approach," *American Economic Journal: Microeconomics*, 4(1), 32–69.

Fainmesser, I. P., and D. A. Goldberg (2018). "Cooperation in partly observable networked markets," *Games and Economic Behavior*, 107, 220–237.

Farrell, J., and E. Maskin (1989). "Renegotiation in repeated games," *Games and Economic Behavior*, 1(4), 327–360.

Fearon, J. D., and D. D. Laitin (1996). "Explaining interethnic cooperation," *American Political Science Review*, 90(4), 715–735.

Fehr, E., and S. Gächter (2002). "Altruistic punishment in humans," *Nature*, 415(6868), 137–140.

Feigenberg, B., E. Field, and R. Pande (2013). "The economic returns to social interaction: Experimental evidence from microfinance," *Review of Economic Studies*, 80(4), 1459–1483.

Feinberg, M., R. Willer, and M. Schultz (2014). "Gossip and ostracism promote cooperation in groups," *Psychological Science*, 25(3), 656–664.

Ford, L. R., and D. R. Fulkerson (1956). "Maximal flow through a network," *Canadian Journal of Mathematics*, 8, 399–404.

Foster, A. D., and M. R. Rosenzweig (2001). "Imperfect commitment, altruism, and the family: Evidence from transfer behavior in low-income rural areas," *Review of Economics and Statistics*, 83(3), 389–407.

Friedman, E. J., and P. Resnick (2001). "The social cost of cheap pseudonyms," *Journal of Economics and Management Strategy*, 10(2), 173–199.

Friedman, J. W. (1971). "A non-cooperative equilibrium for supergames," *Review of Economic Studies*, 38(1), 1–12.

Frieze, A. M., and G. R. Grimmett (1985). "The shortest-path problem for graphs with random arc-lengths," *Discrete Applied Mathematics*, 10(1), 57–77.

Fudenberg, D., and D. K. Levine (1991). "An approximate folk theorem with imperfect private information," *Journal of Economic Theory*, 54(1), 26–47.

Fudenberg, D., and D. K. Levine (1994). "Efficiency and observability with long-run and short-run players," *Journal of Economic Theory*, 62(1), 103–135.

Fudenberg, D., and D. K. Levine (2007). "Continuous time limits of repeated games with imperfect public monitoring," *Review of Economic Dynamics*, 10(2), 173–192.

Fudenberg, D., and D. K. Levine (2009). "Repeated games with frequent signals," *Quarterly Journal of Economics*, 124(1), 233–265.

Fudenberg, D., D. Levine, and E. Maskin (1994). "The folk theorem with imperfect public information," *Econometrica*, 62(5), 997–1039.

Fudenberg, D., D. Levine, and W. Pesendorfer (1998). "When are nonanonymous players negligible?," *Journal of Economic Theory*, 79(1), 46–71.

Fudenberg, D., and E. Maskin (1986). "The folk theorem in repeated games with discounting or with incomplete information," *Econometrica*, 54(3), 533–554.

Fujiwara-Greve, T., and M. Okuno-Fujiwara (2009). "Voluntarily separable repeated prisoner's dilemma," *Review of Economic Studies*, 76(3), 993–1021.

Gagnon, J., and S. Goyal (2017). "Networks, markets, and inequality," *American Economic Review*, 107(1), 1–30.

Ghosh, P., and D. Ray (1996). "Cooperation in community interaction without information flows," *Review of Economic Studies*, 63(3), 491–519.

Giné, X., and D. Karlan (2014). "Group versus individual liability: Short and long term evidence from Philippine microcredit lending groups," *Journal of Development Economics*, 107, 65–83.

Glaeser, E. L., D. I. Laibson, J. A. Scheinkman, and C. L. Soutteret (2000). "Measuring trust," *Quarterly Journal of Economics*, 115(3), 811–846.

Gluckman, M. (1963). "Papers in honor of Melville J. Herskovits: Gossip and scandal," *Current Anthropology*, 4(3), 307–316.

Goldlücke, S., and S. Kranz (2012). "Infinitely repeated games with public monitoring and monetary transfers," *Journal of Economic Theory*, 147(3), 1191–1221.

Granovetter, M. (1985). "Economic action and social structure: The problem of embeddedness," *American Journal of Sociology*, 91(3), 481–510.

Green, E. J. (1980). "Noncooperative price taking in large dynamic markets," *Journal of Economic Theory*, 22(2), 155–182.

Green, E. J., and R. H. Porter (1984). "Noncooperative collusion under imperfect price information," *Econometrica*, 52(1), 87–100.

Greif, A. (1993). "Contract enforceability and economic institutions in early trade: The Maghribi Traders' Coalition," *American Economic Review*, 83(3), 525–548.

Greif, A., P. Milgrom, and B. Weingast (1994). "Coordination, commitment, and enforcement: The case of the merchant guild," *Journal of Political Economy*, 102, 745–776.

Guala, F. (2012). "Reciprocity: Weak or strong? What punishment experiments do (and do not) demonstrate," *Behavioral and Brain Sciences*, 35, 1–59.

Haag, M., and R. Lagunoff (2006). "Social norms, local interaction, and neighborhood planning," *International Economic Review*, 47(1), 265–296.

Habyarimana, J., M. Humphreys, D. N. Prosser, and J. M. Weinstein (2007). "Why does ethnic diversity undermine public goods provision?," *American Political Science Review*, 101(4), 709–725.

Hadfield, G. K., and B. R. Weingast (2012). "What is law? A coordination model of the characteristics of legal order," *Journal of Legal Analysis*, 4(2), 471–514.

Harrington Jr., J. E. (1995). "Cooperation in a one-shot prisoners' dilemma," *Games and Economic Behavior*, 8(2), 364–377.

Heller, Y., and E. Mohlin (2018). "Observations on cooperation," *Review of Economic Studies*, 85(4), 2253–2282.

Henrich, J. (2004). "Cultural group selection, coevolutionary processes and large-scale cooperation," *Journal of Economic Behavior and Organization*, 53(1), 3–35.

Hoffman, E., K. McCabe, and V. L. Smith (1996). "Social distance and other-regarding behavior in dictator games," *The American Economic Review*, 86(3), 653–660.

Hörner, J., and W. Olszewski (2006). "The folk theorem for games with private almost-perfect monitoring," *Econometrica*, 74(6), 1499–1544.

Jackson, M. O., T. Rodriguez-Barraquer, and X. Tan (2012). "Social capital and social quilts: Network patterns of favor exchange," *American Economic Review*, 102(5), 1857–1897.

Jackson, M. O., and A. Watts (2010). "Social games: Matching and the play of finitely repeated games," *Games and Economic Behavior*, 70(1), 170–191.

Jackson, M. O., and Y. Xing (2024). "The incentive complementarity between formal and informal enforcement," *Journal of the European Economic Association*, 22(5), 2294–2328.

Kandori, M. (1992a). "The use of information in repeated games with imperfect monitoring," *Review of Economic Studies*, 59(3), 581–593.

Kandori, M. (1992b). "Social norms and community enforcement," *Review of Economic Studies*, 59(1), 63–80.

Kandori, M., G. J. Mailath, and R. Rob (1993). "Learning, mutation, and long run equilibria in games," *Econometrica*, 61(1), 29–56.

Kandori, M., and H. Matsushima (1998). "Private observation, communication and collusion," *Econometrica*, 66(3), 627–652.

Kandori, M., and S. Obayashi (2014). "Labor union members play an OLG repeated game," *Proceedings of the National Academy of Sciences*, 111(Suppl. 3), 10802–10809.

Karlan, D. S. (2007). "Social connections and group banking," *The Economic Journal*, 117(517), F52–F84.

Karlan, D., M. Möbius, T. Rosenblat, and A. Szeidl (2009). "Trust and social collateral," *Quarterly Journal of Economics*, 124, 1307–1361.

Keohane, R. (1984). *After Hegemony*. Princeton, NJ: Princeton University Press.

Kinateder, M. (2013). "Delayed perfect monitoring in repeated games," *International Journal of Game Theory*, 42(1), 283–294.

Kiyotaki, N., and R. Wright (1989). "On money as a medium of exchange," *Journal of Political Economy*, 97(4), 927–954.

Klein, D. B. (1992). "Promise keeping in the great society: A model of credit information sharing," *Economics & Politics*, 4(2), 117–136.

Kranton, R. E. (1996a). "The formation of cooperative relationships," *The Journal of Law, Economics, and Organization*, 12(1), 214–233.

Kranton, R. E. (1996b). "Reciprocal exchange: A self-sustaining system," *The American Economic Review*, 86(4), 830–851.

Kreps, D. M. (1990). "Corporate culture and economic theory." In J. E. Alt and K. A. Shepsle (eds.), *Perspectives on Positive Political Economy*, pp. 90–142. Cambridge: Cambridge University Press.

Kreps, D. M., and R. Wilson (1982). "Sequential equilibria," *Econometrica*, 50(4), 863–894.

Laclau, M. (2012). "A folk theorem for repeated games played on a network," *Games and Economic Behavior*, 76(2), 711–737.

Laclau, M. (2014). "Communication in repeated network games with imperfect monitoring," *Games and Economic Behavior*, 87, 136–160.

Larson, J. M. (2017). "Networks and interethnic cooperation," *The Journal of Politics*, 79(2), 546–559.

Leider, S., M. M. Möbius, T. Rosenblat, and Q. A. Do (2009). "Directed altruism and enforced reciprocity in social networks," *Quarterly Journal of Economics*, 124(4), 1815–1851.

Lehrer, E. (1990). "Nash equilibria of n-player repeated games with semi-standard information," *International Journal of Game Theory*, 19(2), 191–217.

Levin, J. (2003). "Relational incentive contracts," *American Economic Review*, 93(3), 835–857.

Levine, D. K., and S. Modica (2016). "Peer discipline and incentives within groups," *Journal of Economic Behavior & Organization*, 123, 19–30.

Levine, D. K., and W. Pesendorfer (1995). "When are agents negligible?," *American Economic Review*, 85, 1160–1170.

Ligon, E., and L. Schechter (2012). "Motives for sharing in social networks," *Journal of Development Economics*, 99(1), 13–26.
Ligon, E., J. P. Thomas, and T. Worrall (2002). "Informal insurance arrangements with limited commitment: Theory and evidence from village economies," *Review of Economic Studies*, 69(1), 209–244.
Lippert, S., and G. Spagnolo (2011). "Networks of relations and word-of-mouth communication," *Games and Economic Behavior*, 72(1), 202–217.
Luttmer, E. F. P. (2001). "Group loyalty and the taste for redistribution," *Journal of Political Economy*, 109(3), 500–528.
MacLeod, W. B., and J. M. Malcomson (1989). "Implicit contracts, incentive compatibility, and involuntary unemployment," *Econometrica*, 57(2), 447–480.
Mailath, G. J., and A. Postlewaite (1990). "Asymmetric information bargaining problems with many agents," *Review of Economic Studies*, 57(3), 351–367.
Mailath, G. J., S. Morris, and A. Postlewaite (2017). "Laws and authority," *Research in Economics*, 71(1), 32–42.
Mailath, G. J., and L. Samuelson (2006). *Repeated Games and Reputations: Long-Run Relationships*. Oxford: Oxford University Press.
Malinowski, B. (1922). *Argonauts of the Western Pacific: An Account of Native Enterprise and Adventure in the Archipelagoes of Melanesian New Guinea*. London: Routledge & Kegan Paul.
Masten, S. E., and J. Prüfer (2014). "On the evolution of collective enforcement institutions: Communities and courts," *The Journal of Legal Studies*, 43(2), 359–400.
Matsushima, H. (1989). "Efficiency in repeated games with imperfect monitoring," *Journal of Economic Theory*, 48(2), 428–442.
Matsushima, H. (2004). "Repeated games with private monitoring: Two players," *Econometrica*, 72(3), 823–852.
Mauss, M. (1925). *The Gift: The Form and Reason for Exchange in Archaic Societies*. London: Routledge.
McAdams, R. H. (2015). *The Expressive Powers of Law*. Cambridge, MA: Harvard University Press.
Mertens, J-F., and T. Parthasarathy (1987). "Equilibria for discounted stochastic games." Université catholique de Louvain, Center for Operations Research and Econometrics (CORE) No. 1987050.
Miguel, E., and M. K. Gugerty (2005). "Ethnic diversity, social sanctions, and public goods in Kenya," *Journal of Public Economics*, 89, 2325–2368.
Mihm, M., and R. Toth (2020). "Cooperative networks with robust private monitoring," *Journal of Economic Theory*, 185, 104974.
Mihm, M., R. Toth, and C. Lang (2009). "What goes around comes around: A theory of indirect reciprocity in networks." CAE Working Paper No. 09-07.
Milgrom, P. R., D. C. North, and B. R. Weingast (1990). "The role of institutions in the revival of trade: The law merchant, private judges, and the champagne fairs," *Economics and Politics*, 2, 1–23.
Myerson, R. B. (2004). "Justice, institutions, and multiple equilibria," *Chicago Journal of International Law*, 5(1), 9.
Myerson, R. B. (2008). "The autocrat's credibility problem and foundations of the constitutional state," *American Political Science Review*, 102(1), 125–139.
Nava, F. (2016). "Repeated games and networks." In Y. Bramoullé, A. Galeotti, and B. Rogers (eds.), *The Oxford Handbook of the Economics of Networks*. Oxford: Oxford University Press.

Nava, F., and M. Piccione (2014). "Efficiency in repeated games with local interaction and uncertain local monitoring," *Theoretical Economics*, 9(1), 279–312.

Noon, M., and R. Delbridge (1993). "News from behind my hand: Gossip in organizations," *Organization Studies*, 14(1), 23–36.

North, D. C. (1990). *Institutions, Institutional Change, and Economic Performance*. Cambridge: Cambridge University Press.

North, D. C., J. J. Wallis, and B. R. Weingast (2009). *Violence and Social Orders: A Conceptual Framework for Interpreting Recorded Human History*. Cambridge: Cambridge University Press.

Nowak, M. A., and K. Sigmund (1998). "Evolution of indirect reciprocity by image scoring," *Nature*, 393(6685), 573–577.

Okuno-Fujiwara, M., and A. Postlewaite (1995). "Social norms and random matching games," *Games and Economic Behavior*, 9(1), 79–109.

Olson, M. (1965). *The Logic of Collective Action: Public Goods and the Theory of Groups*. Cambridge, MA: Harvard University Press.

Ostrom, E. (1990). *Governing the Commons: The Evolution of Institutions for Collective Action.* Cambridge: Cambridge University Press.

Padilla, A. J., and M. Pagano (2000). "Sharing default information as a borrower discipline device," *European Economic Review*, 44(10), 1951–1980.

Pai, M. M., A. Roth, and J. Ullman (2016). "An antifolk theorem for large repeated games," *ACM Transactions on Economics and Computation*, 5(2), 1–20.

Ramey, G., and J. Watson (2002). "Contractual intermediaries," *Journal of Law, Economics, and Organization*, 18(2), 362–384.

Raub, W., and J. Weesie (1990). "Reputation and efficiency in social interactions: An example of network effects," *American Journal of Sociology*, 96(3), 626–654.

Renault, J., and T. Tomala (1998). "Repeated proximity games," *International Journal of Game Theory*, 27, 539–559.

Resnick, P., and R. Zeckhauser (2002). "Trust among strangers in Internet transactions: Empirical analysis of eBay's reputation system," *The Economics of the Internet and E-commerce*, 11(2), 23–25.

Rosenthal, R. W. (1979). "Sequences of games with varying opponents," *Econometrica*, 47(6), 1353–1366.

Rubinstein, A. (1979). "Equilibrium in supergames with the overtaking criterion," *Journal of Economic Theory*, 21(1), 1–9.

Sabourian, H. (1990). "Anonymous repeated games with a large number of players and random outcomes," *Journal of Economic Theory*, 51(1), 92–110.

Sadler, E. (2022). "Ordinal centrality," *Journal of Political Economy*, 130(4), 926–955.

Sanchez-Pages, S., and S. Straub (2010). "The emergence of institutions," *The B.E. Journal of Economic Analysis & Policy*, 10(1), 1–38.

Sannikov, Y., and A. Skrzypacz (2007). "Impossibility of collusion under imperfect monitoring with flexible production," *American Economic Review*, 97(5), 1794–1823.

Shapiro, C., and J. E. Stiglitz (1984). "Equilibrium unemployment as a worker discipline device," *American Economic Review*, 74(3), 433–444.

Sigmund, K. (2010). *The Calculus of Selfishness*. Princeton, NJ: Princeton University Press.

Sobel, J. (2005). "Interdependent preferences and reciprocity," *Journal of Economic Literature*, 43(2), 392–436.

Sommerfeld, R. D., H-J. Krambeck, D. Semmann, and M. Milinski (2007). "Gossip as an alternative for direct observation in games of indirect reciprocity," *Proceedings of the National Academy of Sciences*, 104(44), 17435–17440.
Spagnolo, G. (1999). "Social relations and cooperation in organizations," *Journal of Economic Behavior & Organization*, 38(1), 1–25.
Sugaya, T. (2022). "Folk theorem in repeated games with private monitoring," *Review of Economic Studies*, 89(4), 2201–2256.
Sugaya, T., and A. Wolitzky (2020). "A few bad apples spoil the barrel: An anti-folk theorem for anonymous repeated games with incomplete information," *American Economic Review*, 110, 3817–3835.
Sugaya, T., and A. Wolitzky (2021). "Communication and community enforcement," *Journal of Political Economy*, 129, 2595–2628.
Sugaya, T., and A. Wolitzky (2023a). "Monitoring versus discounting in repeated games," *Econometrica*, 91(5), 1727–1761.
Sugaya, T., and A. Wolitzky (2023b). "Bad apples in symmetric repeated games," *Theoretical Economics*, 18(4), 1345–1373.
Sugaya, T., and A. Wolitzky (2024). "Moral hazard and repeated games with many agents." Working Paper.
Sugden, R. (1986). *The Economics of Rights, Co-operation and Welfare*. Basingstoke: Palgrave Macmillan.
Szabó, G., and G. Fath (2007). "Evolutionary games on graphs," *Physics Reports*, 446(4–6), 97–216.
Tadelis, S. (2016). "Reputation and feedback systems in online platform markets," *Annual Review of Economics*, 8, 321–340.
Takahashi, S. (2010). "Community enforcement when players observe partners' past play," *Journal of Economic Theory*, 145(1), 42–62.
Tomala, T. (2011). "Fault reporting in partially known networks and folk theorems," *Operations Research*, 59(3), 754–763.
Udry, C. (1994). "Risk and insurance in a rural credit market: An empirical investigation in northern Nigeria," *Review of Economic Studies*, 61(3), 495–526.
Vega-Redondo, F. (2006). "Building up social capital in a changing world," *Journal of Economic Dynamics and Control*, 30(11), 2305–2338.
Vigdor, J. L. (2004). "Community composition and collective action: Analyzing initial mail response to the 2000 census," *Review of Economics and Statistics*, 86(1), 303–312.
Williamson, O. (1985). *The Economic Institutions of Capitalism*. New York: Free Press.
Wolitzky, A. (2013). "Cooperation with network monitoring," *Review of Economic Studies*, 80(1), 395–427.
Wolitzky, A. (2015). "Communication with tokens in repeated games on networks," *Theoretical Economics*, 10(1), 67–101.
Xing, Y. (2020). "Who shares risk with whom and how? Endogenous matching and informal risk sharing." Working Paper.
Young, H. P. (1993). "The evolution of conventions," *Econometrica*, 61(1), 57–84.

Index

Other titles in the series (*continued from page iii*)

- R. Blundell, W. Newey, & T. Persson (eds.), *Advances in Economics and Econometrics: Theory and Applications, Ninth World Congress, Vols. I, II, & III*, 2006
- J. Roemer, *Democracy, Education, and Equality*, 2006
- C. Blackorby, W. Bossert, & D. Donaldson, *Population Issues in Social Choice Theory, Welfare Economics and Ethics*, 2005
- R. Koenker, *Quantile Regression*, 2005
- C. Hsiao, *Analysis of Panel Data, 2nd ed.*, 2003
- M. Dewatripont, L. P. Hausen, & S. J. Turnovsky (eds.), *Advances in Economics and Econometrics: Theory and Applications, Eighth World Congress, Vols. I, II, & III*, 2003
- E. Ghysels, N. Swanson, & M. Watson (eds.), *Essays in Econometrics: Collected Papers of Clive W. J. Granger, Vols. I & II*, 2001
- S. Strøm (ed.), *Econometrics and Economic Theory in the 20th Century: The Ragnar Frisch Centennial Symposium*, 1999
- A. C. Cameron & P. K. Trivedi, *Regression Analysis of Count-Data*, 1998
- D. Jacobs, E. Kalai, & M. Kamien (eds.), *Frontiers of Research in Economic Theory: The Nancy L. Schwartz Memorial Lectures*, 1998
- D. M. Kreps & K. F. Wallis (eds.), *Advances in Economics and Econometrics: Theory and Applications, Seventh World Congress, Vols. I, II, & III*, 1997
- R. Guesnerie, *A Contribution to the Pure Theory of Taxation*, 1995
- C. Sims (ed.), *Advances in Econometrics, Sixth World Congress, Vols. I & II*, 1994
- H. White, *Inference, Estimation and Specification Analysis*, 1994
- J.-J. Laffont (ed.), *Advances in Economic Theory, Sixth World Congress, Vols. I & II*, 1992
- W. Härdle, *Applied Nonparametric Regression Analysis*, 1990
- A. Roth & M. Sotomayor, *Two-Sided Matching*, 1990
- T. Lancaster, *The Econometric Analysis of Transition Data*, 1990
- L. G. Godfrey, *Misspecification Tests in Econometrics*, 1989
- H. Moulin, *Axioms of Cooperative Decision-Making*, 1988
- T. Bewley (ed.), *Advances in Economic Theory, Fifth World Congress, Vols. I, II, & III*, 1987
- C. Hsiao, *Analysis of Panel Data*, 1986
- J. Heckman & B. Singer, *Longitudinal Analysis of Labor Market Data*, 1985
- A. Mas-Colell, *The Theory of General Economic Equilibrium: A Differentiable Approach*, 1985
- R. J. Bowden & D. A. Turkington, *Instrumental Variables*, 1985
- B. Peleg, *Game Theoretic Analysis of Voting in Committees*, 1984
- F. M. Fisher, *Disequilibrium Foundations of Equilibrium Economics*, 1983
- J.-M. Grandmont, *Money and Value*, 1983
- G. Debreu, *Mathematical Economics*, 1983
- G. S. Maddala, *Limited Dependent and Qualitative Variables in Econometrics*, 1983
- W. Hildenbrand (ed.), *Advances in Economic Theory*, 1983
- W. Hildenbrand (ed.), *Advances in Econometrics*, 1983

Printed by Integrated Books International,
United States of America